CUBAN FIRE

Cuban Fire

THE STORY OF SALSA AND LATIN JAZZ

Isabelle Leymarie

continuum
LONDON • NEW YORK

To the memory of Odilio Urfé, Machito, Charlie Palmieri, and Chico O' Farrill, dear friends and irreplaceable musicians and human beings

Continuum
The Tower Building, 11 York Road, London, SE1 7NX
370 Lexington Avenue, New York, NY 10017–6503

English edition first published 2002 by Continuum by arrangement with Bayou Press Ltd

Originally published in French as *Cuban Fire: musiques populaires d'expression cubaine*

British Library Cataloguing-in-Publication Data
A catalogue record for this book is available from the British Library.

ISBN 0–8264–5586–7 (hardback)

Library of Congress Cataloging-in-Publication Data
Leymarie, Isabelle
[Cuban Fire. English]
Cuban Fire : the story of salsa and Latin jazz / Isabelle Leymarie.
    p. cm.
Translation of: Cuban fire: musiques populaires d'expression cubaine.
Includes bibliographical references, discography, and index.
ISBN 0-8264-5586-7
1. Popular music — Cuba — History and criticism. 2. Folk music — Cuba — History and criticism. I. Title.

ML3486.C8 L38 2002
781.64'09729—dc21   2001047160

Designed and typeset by Ben Cracknell Studios
Printed and bound in Great Britain by Biddles Ltd, Guildford and King's Lynn

contents

Introduction   1

    Acknowledgments   6

I The roots

  1 From African liturgies to Creole rhythms   9

    Sacred music   9

    Traditional secular music   18

    The *clave*   37

    Rhythm instruments   39

II The 1920s and 1930s: *son*, rumba, and *conga*

  2 Havana and Cuba   44

    Emergence of the Havana *son*   50

    The rise of *charangas*, the bolero, and the *guajira*   68

    The beginnings of jazz   78

  3 The United States and Puerto Rico   83

    The awakening of the Barrio   85

    Music in Puerto Rico   98

III The 1940s and 1950s: the golden age of Cuban music

  4 Havana and Cuba   108

    From *nuevo ritmo* to cha-cha: the great *charangas*   111

    Updating the *son*   121

    Big bands, combos, and *descargas*   130

    Singers in Cuba   142

  5 The United States and Puerto Rico   157

    ¡Qué rico el mambo!   158

    The Afro-Cubans   165

Tito Puente, Tito Rodríguez, and other Latin bands   174
Singers in the U.S. and Puerto Rico   186
Chano Pozo and his disciples   189
Expansion of Latin jazz   199

IV The 1960s: the *pachanga*, the boogaloo, and Latin soul

6 Havana and Cuba   208
The explosion of rhythms   210

7 The United States and Puerto Rico   216
The *pachanga* and the boogaloo era   216
Emergence of *charangas*   228
Revival of the *bomba* and the *plena*   232
Latin jazz and Latin soul   238

V From the 1970s until today: advent of the *songo*

8 Havana and Cuba   244
Traditional music   245
The *songo* and *charangas*   247
The *son*   250
The *nueva timba*   253
The *Buena Vista Social Club* phenomenon   256
Latin jazz   258
Other bands   265
Vocalists   265

9 The United States and Puerto Rico   267
Instrumental salsa   267
The salsa vocalists   289
Salsa in Puerto Rico, California, and Florida   297
The *merengue*   306
New horizons for Latin jazz   315
Latin rock and Latin disco   326

10 The rest of the world   329
Influence of Cuban and Puerto Rican music abroad   329

VI Conclusion   341

Glossary   343
Interviews   348
Discography   360
Bibliography   365
Index   370

introduction

"Undeniably, the fact that a Cuban writer should declare that for centuries Cuban dance music has had as important an impact on the Old World as on the New, cannot be attributed merely to an excess of patriotism," exclaimed the great essayist and folklorist Fernando Ortíz. And as Alejo Carpentier added: "Cuba possesses authentic national music whose value is international . . . Throughout its history, the island of Cuba has elaborated musical folklore of an astonishing vitality, receiving, blending and transforming a wide variety of contributions that gave rise to highly distinctive musical genres."

Sensuous and happy, Cuban music is indeed among the richest and most enchanting in the world. In the course of the twentieth century, the "Green Caiman" (thus called by the poet Nicolás Guillén on account of its elongated shape and lush vegetation) gave birth to an impressive number of new musical forms, from the *son* to the *songo*, which have had a marked influence on classical music, jazz, and pop; today, with its offshoots in salsa and Latin jazz, Cuban music has established a tremendous international presence. Many classical composers, among them Ravel, Debussy, Milhaud, Varèse, and Gershwin, have borrowed themes, rhythms and percussion instruments from Cuban music. "Cuban rhythms represent something truly admirable and in a certain way unique in the music of the world," marveled Manuel de Falla, and Aaron Copland, author of a *Danzón cubano*, allowed that "a real Cuba rhumba orchestra . . . can also teach us a thing or two about the hectic use of polyrhythms." Many writers, from Robert Desnos to Julio Cortázar, have also been bewitched by its rhythms and drums, and whole generations have swayed to the sounds of its *rumbas*, *mambos*, or *cha-chas*, more versatile and easygoing than many Anglo-Saxon dances, and hummed *The Peanut Vendor*, *Que rico vacilón*, or *Guantanamera*. The *conga*, the *bongo*, the *timbales*, the *güiro* and the *claves*, drums, and other percussion instruments now currently used in popular music and sometimes in symphony orchestras also come from the land of rum and tobacco.

Despite its tumultuous history and current problems, Cuba, a place where multiple cultures converge and intermingle, has remained a musical Eden: one cannot visit it without enjoying the exuberant hustle and bustle of its streets, its unabashed sensuality, its heady tunes, rising from balconies or courtyards, the singsong lilt of its speech, and the swinging walk of its inhabitants. Even in its darkest moments, this generous and fertile country has always retained its passion for festivity and enjoyment.

Though often toned down or trivialized to pander to foreign audiences, Cuban musical genres have played a major role in shaping the aesthetics of twentieth-century music, and, in the United States in particular, they have to no small degree become absorbed into the mainstream. At a time of increased mechanization and uniformity, Cuban music and its offshoots, with their extraordinary expressiveness, have generally managed to preserve their vigor and authenticity, a fact that once prompted *conguero* Ray Barretto to declare that *salsa* was "the last bastion of honest music" (although his avowed preference is now for the more harmonically stimulating Latin jazz).

Cuba – long a highly cosmopolitan island – owes its stunning musicality in great part to its rich ethnic mix, and to the cultural connections it maintained for many years with both Europe and the Americas. The evolution of its popular music, however, has not been limited to the island: major chapters have been written in the United States and throughout the Spanish-speaking Caribbean (in Puerto Rico, Colombia, Venezuela, the Dominican Republic, Mexico, and Panama).

Cuban rhythms first began to spread to neighboring islands and continental Latin America towards the middle of the nineteenth century, but it was only in the early 1920s, when American companies started intensively recording local bands, that these rhythms truly began gaining currency abroad. The growing Latin scene in New York coincided with the first important migrations of Puerto Ricans and Cubans to the city. Alberto Socarrás, Augusto Coen, Rafael Hernández, Mario Bauzá and scores of other Cuban, Puerto Rican, and Dominican musicians settled there, turning New York into the major Latin music center outside Havana and San Juan. Hispanics, relegated to a marginal status in the Big Apple, often moved into black neighborhoods, and new musical genres sprang up from the interaction between Latin and Afro-American strains.

Cross-fertilization between Afro-American and Caribbean music had already occurred in and around New Orleans at the dawn of the twentieth century. In places like the old Congo Square, blacks rattled jawbones and plucked the same rumba boxes as their brothers in Santiago or Matanzas, and names like Augusto Centeño, the three Tíos (Lorenzo Sr., his son Lorenzo Jr., and his brother "Papa" (Luis) Tío, of Cuban origin), Alcide "Yellow" Núñez, the cornettists Ray López or Manuel Pérez (Pérez, born in Havana in 1863, also led his own ensembles) cropped up in the first jazz bands. In the 1850s the Creole composer Louis Moreau Gottschalk, who had spent time in Cuba, Puerto Rico, and other Caribbean islands, introduced the *habanera* and other "tropical" rhythms in New Orleans. These gave rise to the so-called "tango bass" or "Spanish bass," which crept in around the start of the twentieth century, as we shall see later, in rags and other genres.

Cuban music and bebop came together in the 1940s – a "marriage of love," according to the singer "Machito" (Frank Grillo), giving rise to "cubop," later called "Latin jazz" as its scope broadened and it incorporated other kinds of Latin American rhythms. While continuing to support themselves primarily by performing dance music, Machito, Noro Morales, Tito Puente, Ray Barretto in New York, Armando Peraza and Willie Bobo on the West Coast, Bebo Valdés and Cachao in Havana, among others, gradually shaped this new genre. But just as bebop took jazz fans away from the dance floors, so cubop became music to listen to, thereby alienating some of its audience, yet also confounding the stereotyped view of Cuban music as being facile and unsophisticated. Latin jazz became – though by no means necessarily – a music for initiated listeners, while most Latin audiences called for the highly charged salsa or *merengue*. Salsa, merengue, and the Cuban *nueva timba* have remained treats for the feet, and as such truly music of the people. But of course, one finds salsa which is complex and challenging, just as one can hear Latin jazz which is accessible and easy to dance to. The boundaries often blur.

This book tells the story of Cuban music in its homeland and in the United States, but it also includes Puerto Rico – Cuba's musical sister – and the Dominican merengue, currently merging with salsa and Latin jazz. It concludes with an overview of the international influence of Cuban music in its different forms of expression. To each decade there correspond roughly one or two major rhythms: in the 1920s the *son*; in the 1930s the rumba and the *conga*; in the late 1940s and early 1950s the mambo, followed by the cha-cha, and in Cuba the *batanga*; in the 1960s the *pachanga*, the *mozambique*, and other rhythms, while in New York the pachanga was followed by the *boogaloo*; in the 1970s salsa, and later the *songo*, a Cuban creation currently enjoying wide popularity in the United States; more recently the *nueva timba*, also hailing from Cuba, and Latin rap, born Stateside but popular today throughout Latin America. *Baladas*, folk, and political songs – which are not directly relevant to the development of Cuban dance music, salsa, and Latin jazz – have been deliberately left out of this book. They warrant another specialized study.

The word "salsa" ("sauce"), today overworked and erroneously used, in Europe in particular, to designate just about any type of Latin American music, has long fanned the flames of controversy. Cubans were at first wont to argue that the term was only a commercial moniker and that salsa capitalized on their own music. It consisted of nothing but Cuban genres of the 1940s and 1950s, they claimed. Cuban percussionist Armando Sánchez, for one, dismissed it as "*son* disguised with trombones," and Cubans from the island denounced it as "imperialist." In recent years, though, as dollar-hungry Cuba eagerly reopened its doors to tourism, and foreigners discovered its treasure trove of music, Cuba finally accepted the term. (Singer Issac Delgado, for one, refers to himself as a *salsero* – rather than as a more traditional *sonero*.)

Although of Cuban origin, salsa was actually first heard in New York around the mid- to late 1960s, and given its particular sound and identity mainly by Puerto Ricans. The word "salsa," however, had already appeared in the 1920s, for example, in Ignacio Piñeiro's *Échale salsita* ("Put a little sauce on it"), praising the delicious sausages sold in the town of Madruga by a Congo street-vendor named Rubén Armenteros. Some twenty years later, *La Ruñidera*, composed by "Mulatón" (Alejandro Rodríguez) and popularized by Machito, included the line: *"Fui a bailar a La Ruñidera, la salsa me gustó"* ("I went to dance at La Ruñidera and liked the sauce"). In the 1940s singer Cheo Marquetti led a band called Los Salseros, and the Septeto Típico entitled one of its albums *Salsa y sabor*. In addition, Cuban bandleaders had used the expression *"salsa!"* to egg on musicians, as with the *"olé"* at bullfights. The word *salsa* also suggests spiciness – in music and people: *"Tiene salsa,"* a man can say of a spirited woman.

According to the Venezuelan salsa chronicler César Miguel Rondón, the word "salsa" was introduced in the United States in the mid-1960s by the Puerto Rican pianist Richie Ray who, when in Caracas, heard the radio show entitled "La hora del sabor, la salsa y el *bembé*" hosted by the DJ "Phidias" (Danilo) Escalona. In New York, the Cuban violinist Pupi Legaretta then started to use it to refer to Cuban music. Soon it caught the ear of New York DJ Izzy Sanabria, and record producers Jerry Masucci and Johnny Pacheco, of the fledgling Fania label, who found it colorful and easy to remember. In a matter of years, "salsa" became a household name.

Besides salsa, culinary metaphors abound in Latin music. The word *"sabor"* ("flavor," "taste," but also "feeling"), for instance, crops up in countless song and record titles: Rolando Laserie's *Sabor*, Orquesta Sensación's *Tiene sabor* or Walfredo de los Reyes's *Sabor cubano*, to name only a few. Salsa, with its gastronomic and erotic undertones, eloquently conveys the zestfulness of Caribbean cultures and their concern with gustatory and other sensory pleasures. Women – who both cook and inspire desire – are one of Latin music's favorite topics, although, in true *machismo* spirit, they are sometimes presented as insatiable gluttons, as in Machito's *Dale jamón a la jeva*, which says "give ham to the woman, she loves to eat," or Patato Valdés and Totico Arango's *Quimbombó con salsa*:

¡Como le gusta el quimbombó!	How this *mulata* loves okra!
¡Como se pone esta mulata	How she changes
cuando le quitan la razón!	When she loses her senses!
Ella menea la cuchara	She stirs with her spoon
y ella se come el quimbombó.	And eats up the okra.

Guillermo Rodríguez Fife's emblematic *guaracha Bilongo* (a Bantu word meaning "spell"), imitating the black Cuban speech, tells of a man bewitched by the culinary talents of his *negra*[1] Tomasa:

Estoy tan enamorado	I'm so in love
de la negra Tomasa	with black Tomasa
que cuando sale de casa	that when she leaves home
que triste me pongo . . .	I get all sad . . .
Na' ma' que me gusta la comida	I only like the food she cooks
qu'ella cocina	I only like the coffee she prepares.
na' ma' que me gusta la café, qu'ella	
me cuela.	

Interestingly, on another level, *Bilongo*'s refrain, reflecting Cuba's ecumenism, happily conjoins a Congo word, *kikiribu*, and a Mandinka reference:

Kikiribú Mandinga	The Mandingo died,
kiriribú Mandinga	the Mandingo died,
¡ay, ay, ay! . . .	alas, alas, alas! . . .

The fervently celebrated trinity food–love–African religion – life's essential means of sustenance (food being physical, love emotional, and religion spiritual nourishment) – constitutes the foundation of Cuban music. And as the jazzman "cooks," the *salsero* "*guisa*" or "*cocina*." Africanisms also survive in Caribbean cuisine: in the Bantu-sounding *mondongo* or *mofongo*; and in a famed merengue, a *sancocho prieto* (a kind of stew) reminds a man of the skin color of the woman he loves.

Dozens of definitions have been proposed for salsa. We find Celia Cruz's the most eloquent and poetical: "a little animal that gets into your eyes and ears, and when it reaches your heart, it bursts out and you can't avoid it." Both virile and witty, "salsa" could be broadly described as urban Cuban-derived music from the Spanish Caribbean. It is not a rhythm *sui generis* (though under the influence of the Nuyorican dancer Eddie Torres and others, salsa, as a dance, at least, has now become increasingly codified) but a compendium of rhythms and dances, among them *boleros*, mambos, *sones*, *guarachas*, and merengues, with the occasional additions of *bombas*, *plenas*, *cumbias*, and other Caribbean variations. In New York, salsa has grown streetwise and nervy, but without losing its tropical flavor, and as it spread to other Latin American countries, in each of those lands it has adopted local characteristics while keeping its core identity.

Like salsa, Latin jazz stems from Cuban music, but in recent years it has branched out in many directions, becoming a true *lingua franca* for Latin American and Caribbean musicians. Harmonically sophisticated, exuberant, open, and generally preferring the euphoria of tropical azure to the poignancy of the blues, it has injected new blood into jazz. If, after the free jazz excesses of the 1970s and the fusion mush of the 1980s, jazz has often espoused a neo-classicism, Latin jazz keeps on resolutely forging ahead, charting new territories.

The history of popular Cuban music, salsa, and Latin jazz is a colorful saga of jubilation and tribulations, of ritzy cabarets and dives, of shady deals and heart-breaking *mulatas*. While countless books have been written on Afro-American music, few until recently have told the stories of musical giants such as Arsenio Rodríguez, Chano Pozo, or Machito. In part due to prejudice and ignorance of Latin cultures, and because Latin music – considered frivolous – had often been packaged for entertainment and diluted for mass consumption, the easygoing atmosphere in which it tended to be performed, the musicians' flashy outfits and irreverent nicknames ("Patato"; "Chocolate") have sometimes evoked contemptuous amusement from non-Latins. In addition, artists such as Danilo Pérez or Steve Turre have complained that jazz critics tend to take their "straight" jazz more seriously than their Latin explorations, however considerable they may be. The gaudy covers of many Latin albums (now often collectors' items, however!), the dearth of credits and liner notes, and the often raw and suggestive or at best superficial lyrics may have deterred some listeners. But things are changing: Cuban music, salsa, and Latin jazz have now proved their staying power, marketability, and universal appeal.

Afro-Cuban, Latin, *típica* or tropical music, salsa or Latin jazz, the often restrictive labels given by producers for marketing purposes or by musicologists obsessed with terminology are not what is crucial. In the last resort, what matters most for musicians, dancers, and listeners is inspiration, heart, feeling. And "*¡a gozar!*", Latin music's irresistible injunction to enjoy oneself, remains a universal rallying cry.

Acknowledgments

All my heartfelt thanks to Leonardo Acosta, Azuquita, Toni Basanta, Joe Cuba, Cristóbal Díaz Ayala, Jean-Paul Dumontier, Guillermo and Rosanna Fellové, Héctor Herrera, Óscar López, Lupe O'Farrill, Laude Menéndez, William Navarrete, Orlando Poleo, Ralph Mercado Management (and Omar Pardillo Jr.), Ñico Rojas, Mongo Santamaría, and Celso Valdés. ¡Mucho aché!

the roots

CHART OF THE MAJOR LATIN RHYTHMS

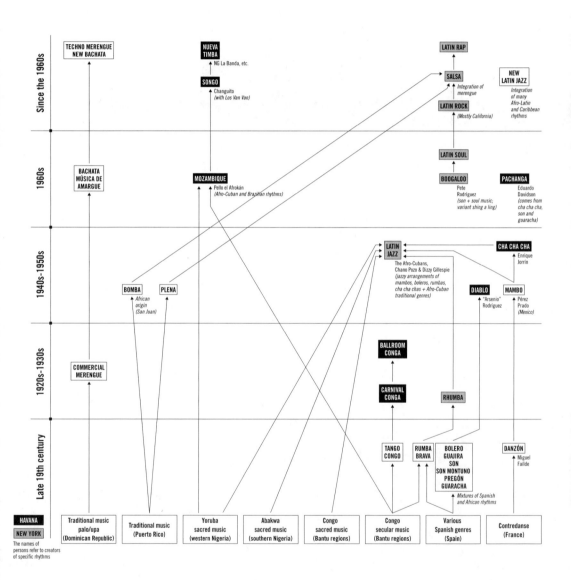

	Since the 1960s	1960s	1940s-1950s	1920s-1930s	Late 19th century

TECHNO MERENGUE / NEW BACHATA

NUEVA TIMBA
▲ NG La Banda, etc.

SONGO
▲ Changuito
(with Los Van Van)

LATIN RAP

SALSA
↑ Integration of merengue

NEW LATIN JAZZ
Integration of many Afro-Latin and Caribbean rhythms

LATIN ROCK
(Mostly California)

BACHATA MÚSICA DE AMARGUE

MOZAMBIQUE
▲ Pello el Afrokán
(Afro-Cuban and Brazilian rhythms)

LATIN SOUL

BOOGALOO
Pete Rodríguez
(son + soul music; variant shing a ling)

PACHANGA
Eduardo Davidson
(comes from cha cha cha, son and guaracha)

LATIN JAZZ
The Afro-Cubans, Chano Pozo & Dizzy Gillespie
(jazzy arrangements of mambos, boleros, rumbas, cha cha chas + Afro-Cuban traditional genres)

CHA CHA CHA
▲ Enrique Jorrín

BOMBA
▲ African origin (San Juan)

PLENA

DIABLO
▲ "Arsenio" Rodríguez

MAMBO
▲ Pérez Prado (Mexico)

BALLROOM CONGA

COMMERCIAL MERENGUE

CARNIVAL CONGA

RHUMBA

TANGO CONGO

RUMBA BRAVA

BOLERO GUAJIRA SON SON MONTUNO PREGÓN GUARACHA
▲ Mixtures of Spanish and African rhythms

DANZÓN
▲ Miguel Faílde

HAVANA
NEW YORK
The names of persons refer to creators of specific rhythms

Traditional music palo/upa (Dominican Republic)

Traditional music (Puerto Rico)

Yoruba sacred music (western Nigeria)

Abakwa sacred music (southern Nigeria)

Congo sacred music (Bantu regions)

Congo secular music (Bantu regions)

Various Spanish genres (Spain)

Contredanse (France)

from African liturgies
to Creole rhythms

Sacred music

Con los santos no se juega	One does not play with the gods.
Dame un baño	Give me a bath
Tienes que hacerte una limpieza	You have to purify yourself
Con el rompe saragüey	With the *rompe saragüey*.[1]

Sandunga, a Spanish word meaning "elegance" or "grace," best expresses the hybrid quality of Cuban music. For, as Cuban musicologist Fernando Ortiz wittily put it, "*sandunga* is the mixture of *sa*," the white salt of Andalusia, and *ndungu*, the black pepper of Africa (with, I would add, a more liberal dose of the latter). For over three hundred years, *jotas, soleares, malagueñas, tanguillos gaditanos, romances, villancicos*, minuets, contredanses, rigadoons, mixed with the various religious and secular African dances, gave rise to rhythms that constitute the essence of popular Cuban music. Like jazz, which feeds on both the sacred exultation of gospel and the raunchiness of the blues, popular Cuban music oscillates between sacred Abakwa, Yoruba, and Congo chants and *guarachas, boleros*, and *rumbas* – more erotic but no less sublime. Similarly, Spanish thrown together with Yoruba, Fon, Ibibio, or Bantu expressions spawned linguistic hybrids which continue to give Cuban songs a distinctive flavor.

Virtually nothing remains of the music of the Taino and Siboney Indians who inhabited Cuba at the time of the Spanish conquest. Versions of the *güiro*,

[1] A plant dedicated to Changó and used in some Afro-Cuban rituals.

a serrated gourd scraped with a stick, and the *maracas* – whose origin is often traced back to the Indians – also existed in Africa, and the indigenous influence on popular Cuban music is only attested to by nostalgic songs such as *Siboney* or *Anacanoa*, evocative of Indian lore.

Music of Spanish origin tended to prevail among the *guajiros* (peasants of the interior), but African rhythms colored popular Cuban music more strongly. "*Quien no tiene de Dinka² tiene de Mandinga*" ("He who does not have Dinka stock at least has Mandinka in him"), or again, "*Quien no tiene de Congo³ tiene de Carabalí*,"⁴ claim two Cuban proverbs, implying that however one tries to present oneself, an African heritage is inescapable. Slavery was officially abolished in 1880, but it persisted illegally for about another ten years, reinforcing the black presence in Cuba.

On the island, popular music has long been dominated by people of African descent. Musicologist Odilio Urfé mentions that in 1831 there were three times as many black musicians in the country as there were white. It was in that year that José Antonio Saco published his *Memorias sobre la vagancia en Cuba*, in which he made precisely this observation, lamenting the fact that the arts were "in the hands of colored people." Blacks added syncopations to European tunes, transformed triple times into more swinging duple ones, and favoured *hemiolas*. The *clave* – a two-bar pattern of African origin – became the foundation of popular Cuban music, giving it a smooth, round, and propulsive feel. To the untrained ear, the instruments in a Cuban band never seem to fully enunciate the beats. They create a rich mesh of sound, with rhythms interlocking in subtle and precise ways.

The slave trade, linked to the plantation economy, began at the outset of the sixteenth century, and the Africans brought with them their languages, religious beliefs, and music. In Cuba, with astounding resourcefulness, they reproduced as best they could the instruments they had left behind, using whatever materials were available to them; they took up European ones (mandolin, guitar, tuba, ophicleide, etc.), brought boxes, crates, jawbones, spoons, frying pans, hoes, and other objects and tools into their bands, and invented an impressive collection of new instruments. Among them were the *tres* – a kind of guitar with three double strings – the *conga*, the *timbales*, and the *bongo*. A small double drum with a large "female" and a small "male" head, the bongo embodies the African principle of sexual complementarity and it constitutes, as Fernando Ortiz acutely suggested, a Creole transposition of the African cult of twins. In the rural regions of Oriente, the bongo, used as a signal drum and called *bongó del monte* (bongo of the mountain), indicates to the guests the place where a festivity is about to take place.

Cuba is par excellence the land of music, dance, and also of African gods, ubiquitous, each one with his or her own personality, worshiped with trance-inducing songs and drums. For Hispanic musicians and singers, the Afro-Cuban rituals, preserved to various degrees on the island, constitute the *fundamento*. Gilberto Valdés, Machito, Miguelito Valdés and countless other musicians were

2 An ethnic group from the Sudan.

3 Generic name given, in Cuba, to persons of Bantu origin.

4 A person hailing from the Calabar coast, in southern Nigeria.

nurtured on this *fundamento,* so deeply rooted in the Cuban soil. Tunes such as Mongo Santamaría's *Afro Blue*:

or *Ubane*

were inspired by Lucumí (Yoruba), Abakwa, or Congo liturgies. Chano Pozo, Santamaría, and later Julio Collazo played an essential role in introducing these liturgies and *toques* into the United States, where they now attract a growing number of adepts.

From the seventeenth century, free blacks in urban centers, resisting the colonial authorities who were hell-bent on preventing former slaves uniting, organized themselves into *cabildos* (literally "town councils") which represented different ethnic groups. These *cabildos,* banished to the outskirts of the cities so that the drums would not bother the whites, functioned as mutual aid, religious, and recreational societies and contributed to the preservation of African cultural traits. Among them were the Cabildo Lucumí, placed under the aegis of Santa Barbara, the Mandinga Lucumí, Arará Dajomé, Arará Magino, and Nación Congo Real, to name only a few. At various times *cabildos* were outlawed and blacks forbidden to dance and play their drums in public. In 1909, president José Miguel Gómez, somewhat more liberal than some of his predecessors, despite his nickname "Tiburón" (shark), allowed *comparsas* (groups of dancers and musicians from the *cabildos*) to perform for carnivals. But anti-black sentiment flared up once again, reaching

Santería dance.
Photo: Jean-Paul Dumontier

a climax during the presidency of Mario García Menocal (1913–21), a former police officer and lackey of the United States. However, drums were merely hidden away, and rituals continued covertly, even attracting whites and Orientals. Despite the repeated persecutions, solidarity networks, secretly woven in black communities, provided fertile ground for the growth and blossoming of a lively music. Works by Eliseo Grenet and Amadeo Roldán, and such popular songs as *La cumbancha* or Benny Moré's *Los componedores* derive from old *cabildo* tunes.

Yoruba music

The Yorubas (also called Lucumís in Cuba) played a crucial part in the cultural history of the island. Despite the *cabildos'* efforts to maintain their own cultural traditions, ethnic groups blended together in the urban swirl. Catholicism provided a cover for the worship of African deities, and the merging of Yoruba and Christian elements gave rise to a synchretic cult called *santería* (from the Spanish *santo* – "saint") or *regla de ocha*. Yoruba deities (*orishas*), each with his or her own personality and attributes, found counterparts in Catholic saints: for example, Yemayá, goddess of the sea, corresponds to the Virgin of Regla (Regla being a small town outside Havana), Ochosí to Saint Norbert, and Changó, god of thunder, to Saint Barbara. Each *orisha* has its own chants and rhythms, and the Yoruba liturgy, sometimes enriched by other contributions, is of haunting beauty and complexity.

Eladde Osún (invocation to the *orisha* Ochún). From Graciela Chao Carbonero, *Bailes yorubas de Cuba*, p. 33.

Second *batá toque* for the *orisha* Elegguá. From Fernando Ortiz, *La africanía de la música folklórica de Cuba*, p. 383.

The *orishas* are invoked with *batá*, which originate from Nigeria and consist of a set of three hourglass-shaped drums held on the musician's lap. They each have two skins, with erotic names and different sounds: the *enú* ("mouth") and the *chachá*, or *culata* ("rump"). The *batá* belong to Changó, and consecrated drums can only be played by initiated and morally irreproachable men. The imposing *iyá* ("mother", in Yoruba), adorned with a red ribbon – red being the color of Changó – and a ring of small bells (*chaworó*), takes the lead; the medium-sized *itótele* and the small *okónkolo* (or *omelé*) respond in a complex polyphony. The metallic vibration of the *chaworó*, appreciated for its sound, also protects from evil influences.

The *toques*, considered as *caminos* (roads) leading to the *orishas*, include many rhythm changes introduced by *viros* (breaks), and as each of the numerous *orishas* has his or her own *toques*, achieving mastery of the repertoire takes several years. The *olubatá* (drummers) who accompany the singers must also have a thorough knowledge of the chants in order to know exactly when to come in.

Masters such as Andrés "El Sublime" and Emilio Silvestre in the nineteenth century and, later, José del Carmen de la Trinidad Torregrosa y Hernández, Pablo Roche ("Okilapka"),[5] Agüedo Morales, and Jesús Pérez, former director of the percussion ensemble of the Conjunto Folklórico Nacional, kept the *batá* tradition alive in Cuba.

5 Literally "strong arm" in Yoruba. (He was also designated by the Spanish nickname "Brazo fuerte," also meaning "strong arm.")

The sacred *batá* contain an object (*añá*) inside them symbolizing the presence of the gods. The drums "speak," that is, they enunciate sentences reproducing the tones of the Yoruba language, to invoke the deities. Once a new instrument has been built, before being used, it must "receive its voice" from an older drum in a special ritual. Offerings of animal blood are regularly made to the drums to maintain their vital force (*aché*); and, in order to perform at ceremonies, musicians must undergo a purification process and, among other requirements, abstain from sexual intercourse before touching their instrument.

The *aché*, transmitted to human beings, is an essential concept of Yoruba culture. The benevolent greeting "¡aché!" unites members of the Yoruba diaspora, and it appears in such popular songs as Celina y Reutilio's *Flores para tu altar*, evoking the *orisha* Ochún:

Aché, o mío Yemayá	Hail, o my Yemaya
oñí pa' Ochún.	honey for Ochún.[6]

Other types of *batá*, built with slight structural differences and without a secret object inside: the *ilú*, *aberikula*, or *judíos* ("Jewish") *batá*, are reserved for secular music.

In 1936, composer Gilberto Valdés used *batá* drums in a symphonic work, and recorded *Tambó*, the first recording in which these drums were featured. Around the same time, Fernando Ortiz borrowed them to illustrate his ethnomusicology lectures. In the United States the *batá* were, until the early 1970s, confined to the realm of *santería*. Only somewhat inauthentic recordings could be bought, available in *botánicas*, shops selling *santería* paraphernalia. Also, in the mid-1930s, in Cuba, the group Irakere popularized the *batá* in jazz (although Bebo Valdés, Obdulio Morales, Chico O'Farrill, and other Cuban musicians had already shown interest in these drums). However, traditionalists cringed at the desecration of the drums and at the fact that they were being made commercially (sometimes out of fiberglass instead of the traditional wood). *Batá* incorporating the *iyá*, the *itótele*, and the *omelé* into a single unit are now being used by some percussionists, among them the Venezuelan Gustavo Ovalle. Other Yoruba ritual instruments, such as clapperless bells (*agogós*) and *shekeres* (also called *güiros*), big gourd rattles covered with a bead-strewn

6 Cited by Jorge and Isabel Castellanos in *Cultura Afrocubana*, No. 4, p. 370.

Venezuelan percussionist Orlando Poleo playing one of the *batá* drums. Orlando Poleo Collection

mesh which are shaken or struck with the palm of the hand, have been used in a secular context and adopted in popular music.

In the *bembés*, semi-secular festivities, the gods are invoked "without touching them," according to the expression of the percussionist and *babalawo* (*santería* priest) "Puntilla" (Orlando Ríos), that is, without directly soliciting them, and specific rhythms are played using *bembé* drums plus güiros, *agogós*, and a hoe beaten with a stick.

Abakwa music

The Abakwa (also called Carabalí or, disparagingly, *ñáñigos* in Cuba) come from the coast of Calabar, in south-eastern Nigeria, and they include people descended from Ibo, Ibibio, Ejagham, and other ethnic groups. In the nineteenth century, in Havana, Matanzas, and Cardenas, they formed secret societies which recruited the bulk of their members among stevedores and other dock workers. These *ñáñigos* held a particular fascination with their mysterious rituals, which they long refused to divulge. Their lodges (*potencias*) only admitted true and tried men who had proved their courage and virility at initiation rituals (*plantes*) featuring music and dancing. Admitted to these ceremonies when he came to perform in Cuba in 1958, Nat "King" Cole was completely entranced. But at the turn of the century, *potencias* also became a means of gaining position and power. Lydia Cabrera mentions that in Regla, Guanabacoa, Pogolotti, or Marianao, in and around Havana, the Abakwa "obtained influence in certain towns and marched to the sound of drums on the eve of elections." In the late nineteenth century, *ñáñigos* were thought to perform human sacrifices, and initiates were said to go out, after ceremonies, and kill the first passer-by as a test of bravery to gain admission into their fraternity. Some *potencias* attracted thugs, conjuring up in the Cuban mind a terrifying vision of Abakwa lore. But such violence subsided in the twentieth century, and members of *potencias* were in fact required to abide by a stringent code of honor.

After the Revolution, *plantes* almost vanished on the island. The Uriabón Efí brotherhood in the Simpson district of Matanzas was, some years ago, one of the last Abakwa strongholds in Cuba. Nowadays, however, there has been, in and around Havana and especially Matanzas, a strong resurgence of Abakwa culture, especially among young Blacks, who are fascinated by its mystique and feel empowered by its secrets.

On certain occasions *íremes*, also called *diablitos* ("little devils"), characters in African dress enforcing respect for ancestral customs, danced in the streets, perpetuating a tradition still extant in southern Nigeria and northern Cameroon. Upon leaving their sanctuaries, once the ceremonies were over, dancers and musicians marched in the streets to the *efó* and then the faster *efí* rhythms, corresponding to the Efor and Efik ethnic groups of the Cross River estuary.

During the preparation of the ritual objects before the ceremonies, a chant based on a particular *clave*,[7] the *wemba clave*, was intoned:

Example of *wemba clave*

Sacred drums such as the *sese eribó*, with its emblematic plumes, were not played and were kept hidden from public view. The voice of the *ekwé* – a friction drum producing a kind of grunt recalling that of the Brazilian *cuica* – evoked the roar of the totemic leopard. Other drums, with membranes maintained by strings and wedges, included the *bonkoenchemiyá*, *biankomé*, *obí-apá*, and *kuchí-yeremá*. A clapperless bell, bells, and percussive sticks complemented the instrumentation. Abakwa drummers used a friction technique called *fragaya*. It produced a whine that sounds like the *glissé* done by sliding a finger on the skin of a bongo, and when *bongoceros* in dance bands started using *glissés*, fights erupted between them and Abakwa sect members, who claimed they had stolen the *fragaya* from them.

Abakwa music now has to some extent found its way into Cuban popular music and jazz, and several numbers evoke Abakwa culture. Among them Ignacio Piñeiro's *Los cantares del abacuá*, recorded by the María Teresa Vera-Rafael Zequeira duo, Afrocuba's *En lloro mi ñankwe*, Tata Güines's *rumba Ecué ecué*, and *El abakúa*, recorded by Richie Ray and containing a traditional invocation.

Congo music

Bantu people, known as Congos in Cuba, became assimilated faster into white society than other African groups, thereby losing some of their religious traditions. However, with their rhythms, instruments, and colorful vocabulary, they considerably enriched Cuban popular music. As we shall see later, the rumba, for instance, stems in great part from ritual Congo dances.

The Congos had several sects roughly corresponding to different ethnic groups: the *regla mayombe*, the *palo monte*, the *regla kimbiasa* (or *kimbisa*) and its traditional enemy the *regla biyumba*. *Lube lube*, a tune played by the Puerto Rican band La Sonora Ponceña, takes its title from a *regla biyumba* chant alluding to the Lube – a Bantu ethnic group:

7 See p. 37.

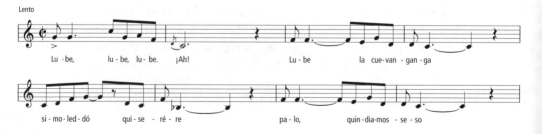

Lu - be,   lu - be, lu - be.   ¡Ah!

Lube Lube (Biyumba chant) – Transcribed by Argeliers León in: Argeliers León, *Música folklórica cubana*, p. 43.

Many Cuban musical terms, among them "conga,""bongo," and "mambo," are Congo. "Conga" is said to come from a Bantu word signifying both "song" and "tumult." "Mambo" means "prayer," "conversation with the gods,"and "sacred dance" (in Haiti it also designates a voodoo priestess), and "Mamba" is the Congo goddess of water. In Congo parlance, *güiri mambo* means "listen to what I have to tell you."

Besides the long cylindrical *bocú* drums played at the Santiago carnivals, the main traditional Congo instruments are cylindrical *ngoma* drums, which are complemented by a *guataca* (hoe) struck with a metallic stick and maintaining a steady beat; *yuka* and the large *makuta* (two traditional Congo dances) drums; small bells worn by drummers on their wrists (*nkembi*) which, like the *chaworó* of the *iyá* drum, protect both men and drums from evil influences and provide a type of rattling sound. The *tingo talango* (or *tumbandera*) – a musical bow recalling the Brazilian *birimbau* – and the *kinfuiti* friction drum have virtually disappeared, although the *tingo talango* is evoked in a popular number of the same name written by Julio Cueva.

Congo songs abound with satire, piques, and nonsensical elements (*disparates*). These also crop up in such profane songs as Justi Barreto's *A Nueva York*, in which a man talks to his dog, or in the *columbia rumba Iyá mi ilé Oyá* by Los Muñequitos de Matanzas, in which a man discerns all kinds of fantastic things in pumpkin seeds, among them "*un sacerdote, un pastor con mucha oveja, y en una esquina una vieja empinando un papalote*" ("a priest, a pastor with many ewes, and, in a corner, an old woman flying a kite"). Some Congo invocations have also absorbed the Arabic salute *salaamu aleikum*, transformed in Cuba into *salamaleco*, and which has cropped up in some popular songs.

Music of Dahomeyan origin

The Araras,[8] most of whom came from the Fon people of Dahomey, are generally found in the region of Matanzas and Jovellanos. Their culture has been greatly diluted, although attempts are now being made to revive it, and their religion has absorbed Yoruba elements: like Changó, Hebioso is the god of the drums and of thunder, and Asoyí and Sakuatí are often likened to the *orishá* Babalú Ayé, as in sacred Arara chants such as Celina and Reutilio's song *Asoyí, Asoyí*. Three drums with their skins held by pegs, the drum-bodies beaten with sticks (*junga*), plus metallic rattles (*cheré*) and a clapperless bell (*ogán*) usually provide the accompaniment.

8 The word perhaps derives from the ancient Dahomeyan city of Ardra, from which slaves were sent to the Americas.

Haitians of similar cultural origin who settled in Cuba in the late eighteenth century and were called *negros franceses* (French blacks) formed in the province of Oriente hierarchized, recreational societies, the *tumbas francesas*, headed by a male or female president.[9] They still meet regularly to dance to the sound of drums, sing songs in French patois mixed with Spanish words, and share food and drinks. The soloist intones the verses, to which a choir of *tumberas* – women clad in traditional costume recalling those of the French Antilles – responds. The dances are led by the *mayor* or the *mayora de plaza*, who whistles to indicate the different moves.

The instruments consist of three large painted drums, each with a skin held by wooden pegs: the *premier*, which improvises, the *bulá*, and the *segón*; and a double-skinned *tambora* used for the *masón* dance. A wooden cylinder beaten with sticks (*catá*) maintains a steady pulse while the singers or the *mayor de plaza* shake metallic rattles (*chachás*).

Around Camagüey and in Oriente, a few communities of Haitian origin practice *vodú* (voodoo) with musical instruments similar to the ones found in Haiti.

Traditional secular music

Carnival rhythms

Despite repression, from the seventeenth century until the end of the nineteenth century, *cabildos* were allowed to participate in the Corpus Christi and Epiphany processions, and they spilled out into the streets in a staggering orgy of colors and sounds. They availed themselves of these opportunities to vent their frustrations with satirical songs, a tradition which lived on in the carnivals. The march was followed by the *saludo*, where the procession stopped to salute the town officials; the quadrilles – a specialty of the *tumbas francesas*; and finally, the *tango congo*, performed by the Congo *comparsas* (carnival groups of singers, musicians, and dancers). The *tumbas francesas* also did a fast dance called *cocoyé*, singing their famous refrain "*abre que ahí viene el cocoyé*" ("open, here comes the cocoyé") and sang patois songs such as *Tabatié moin tombé* ("My Snuffbox Fell").[10]

The *cocoyé* is based on a rhythmic unit called *cinquillo*. Said to have been brought to Cuba by the *negros franceses*, the *cinquillo* is also found, however, in other Afro-Latin dances such as the Puerto Rican *bomba*. According to Fernando Ortiz, the composer Raimundo Valenzuela considered the *cinquillo* a secret which must be closely guarded lest foreign musicians steal it. It nevertheless spread abroad, and it evolved from the following motif:

9 From a drum called "tumba."

10 Later sung by Benny Moré under the title *Se me cayó el tabaco*.

to a pattern called *tumbao*, played with several variations, in dance bands, by the bass and the conga:

Example of bass *tumbao*

The *tango congo* inspired the songs *Siboney* and *Mama Inés*; two tunes from Gonzalo Roig's *zarzuela Cecilia Valdés*; and *Tumba la caña* (1912), included by Cuban composer Jorge Anckermann (1877–1941) in his operetta *La casita criolla* and adopted by the famed Havana *comparsa El alacrán*:

Siembra la caña, anda ligero.	Sow the sugarcane, hurry up.
Mira que ya	Look,
Viene el mayoral[11]	The overseer is coming,
Sonando el cuero!	Cracking his whip!

Toward the late nineteenth century, *comparsas* such as Los Negros Rumberos, and Los Negros Catedráticos (the latter taking their name from stock vaudeville characters ridiculing blacks with intellectual pretensions) performed at the Tacón theater in Havana. Led by a director who supervised the music and organized the choreography, *comparsas* represented various districts of Havana, Santiago, or other cities, inviting comparison with the samba schools of Rio de Janeiro. During carnival, they vied with each other with extravagant costumes and floats, singing their theme songs.

Progressively, the *tango congo* evolved into the carnival *conga* lines (true "walking ballets," as Alejo Carpentier called them), with hundreds of dancers swaying in rhythm behind each other. In 1915 the *comparsa* Los Turcos de Regla (which used a "Turkish" bass drum) brought the conga dance and musical genre from Matanzas to the capital, where they then took on a political character. During electoral campaigns, the candidates of the liberal and conservative parties paraded with *conga* bands in the streets of Havana. *La Chambelona* ("The Lollipop"), a song brought from Camajuaní to Havana by Rigoberto Leyva, livened up the electoral campaigns of José Miguel Gómez and, in 1924, of Gerardo Machado, then vice-president of the Electric Bond and Share Company. The street bands that played for the Liberal Party were subsequently given the name *chambelonas*, while those that supported the Conservative Party were named *congas*. "Some candidate had had the ineffable idea of enthroning the spirit of the colonial conga in their propaganda celebrations," wrote Carpentier in *Ecué-Yamba-O*. "Thus when the meeting was important and the brass band of the opposite stand started to play before its scheduled time, the speaker, flabbergasted, would see his audience transformed into a sea of rumba dancers, while his words were drowned out by a noisy offensive of Aé, aé, aé la chambelona! The electors would walk down the

11 Another ironic nickname given to President Mario García Menocal.

main street to the beat of a *comparsa* and, buttoning up their shirts, come back to listen to another speech."[12] *Conga* songs also alluded to current events: under Gómez, a *conga* evoked the reinstatement of the lottery, and in 1924 another one, ridiculing Mario García Menocal, contributed to his defeat.

Today, *comparsas* perform at carnivals or to pay homage to certain personalities, and a host of percussionists, Chano Pozo, Mongo Santamaría, and Daniel Ponce among them, started out playing with these hell-fire ensembles. At the exhilarating Santiago carnival, bands consisting of trombones, *cornetas chinas*,[13] whistles, *bombos*, *galletas*, *bocús*, and other drums as well as spoons and frying pans wind down the streets in a deafening din towards the harbor. Desi Arnaz, whose father had been mayor of Santiago, described those revelries in his autobiography: "Thousands of people in the streets form a conga line and they go all over the town, singing and dancing for three days and nights to the beat of African conga drums. They also use frying pans, nailed to boards, bottom side up, which they beat with hard sticks, making a sharp *ding-ding-ding-ding it-ding it-ding-ding* sound, keeping tempo with the conga drum going *boom-boom-boom-BOOM*. It's a simple beat. You can hear this sound approaching from ten blocks away and it keeps getting louder and louder and more exciting."[14]

Comparsa melody (played on the trumpet or the cornet)

In Havana, *comparsa* members carry picturesque *faroles* (tall, sometimes beribonned, sticks bearing torches) that create an eerie sight.

12 Alejo Carpentier, 1933, p. 87.

13 Oboes introduced by the Chinese who were brought to Cuba in the late nineteenth century, after the abolition of slavery, in order to lay railroad tracks and perform other tasks.

14 In: *A Book*, p. 59.

The *guaracha*

In the eighteenth century, a lively dance appeared in the taverns of the Havana harbor, the *guaracha*. This "dance of the lowly rabble," as Estebán Pichardo called it in his 1875 dictionary of cubanisms, proliferated. The *guaracha* was also sung. One such example, the famous *Guabina* dating from the beginning of the nineteenth century, in which the fish (*guabina*) – sacred emblem of the Abakwa – takes on a sexual character, incensed the newspaper *Regañón de La Habana*, which dismissed it as "obscene trash."

Piano

La mu - la - ta Ce - les - ti - na   le ha

co - gi - do mie - do al mar.   La mu - la - ta Ce - les - ti - na   le ha   co - gi - do mie - do al   mar

La Guabina

But the *guaracha* triumphed despite bourgeois prudishness, taking root in the capital, and songs such as the boastful *guaracha, Negro José Caliente* ("The Hot Black Man José"), written in 1836, became huge successes:

Los hombres me tienen miedo	Men are afraid of me
Y las mujeres amor.	And women love me.
Probar al momento puedo	Anytime and to anyone
A cualquiera mi valor.	I can prove my worth.

By the 1850s, *guarachas*, with their flighty uptempo rhythm, racy lyrics, lascivious choreography, and broad humor, became a staple of the *teatro bufo*, of Spanish and Neapolitan origin, and Cuba's answer to vaudeville. And works such as Enrique Guerrero's *La prieta santa* or *La pluma de tu sombrero* were popular throughout the country.

The *guaracha*, generally consisting of a four- to eight-bar introduction, two or three repeated parts on which the singer improvised, and a refrain, was first sung with guitar accompaniment. Beginning in the 1930s, it was adopted by virtually all dance bands. Ñico Saquito, Julio Gutiérrez, Arsenio Rodríguez (*Yo nací del África*), José Curbelo (*Que no que no*), Félix Cárdenas (*El rey del mambo*), the Venezuelan Simón Díaz (*Caballo viejo*), produced spicy *guarachas* that, like the *son*, chronicled the daily goings-on; and in the 1950s, Celia Cruz was crowned "Guarachera de Cuba." Today the *guaracha* no longer has a particular structure, and the word generally refers to a medium-tempo topical piece.

The *danzón*

The *danzón*, which surfaced at the end of the nineteenth century, is the matrix from which the mambo and the cha-cha evolved. It continues to inspire musicians: Chucho Valdés, Irakere, Gonzalo Rubalcaba, El Conjunto Libre, Cachao López, Arturo Sandoval, Omar Sosa, and many others.

Derived from an English country dance, the *contredanse*, after delighting the French court, was brought to Cuba in the late eighteenth century by French planters from Santo Domingo fleeing the revolt of their slaves. There it was transformed into the creolized *contradanza*. The first example of this form, *San Pascual Bailón*, was published in 1830. The choreography was formal and elaborate, in the European manner. In 1830, French refugees fleeing from oppression by Spanish garrisons in South America settled in Cuba, their presence awakening new interest in French dances. Moral censors protested against this surge of Gallic libertinage but were unable to check the progress of the *contradanza*. This musical form then gradually acquired black elements, as, for example, in Antonio Boza's *La Francesita*, which included fragments of Haitian songs from Oriente, and *La mano abajo*. By the end of the nineteenth century, the *contradanza* had become a favorite genre for Cuban composers. It was played by bands made up of fife, cornet, clarinet, three violins, and bass, plus güiro and timbales which lent it a distinct creole flavor.

In Matanzas, around the same time, people began to tire of the choreographic stiffness of the *contradanza*. They started to dance together and improvise at will, and this new dance acquired the name of *danzón*. In 1877 Miguel Faílde Pérez (1851–1922), a young cornet player from the small town of Guamacaro, composed four graceful *danzones*: *El delirio*, *La ingratitud*, *Las quejas*, and *Las Alturas de Simpson*, named after a Matanzas neighborhood famed for its *rumbas* and *cabildos*:

Las Alturas de Simpson – Miguel Faílde

"Lola María" (María Dolores Ximena y Cruz), a writer from Matanzas, marveled at Faílde's skills: "He played with so much fervor and virtuosity that his eyes seemed to fall out of their orbits." The band, whose members were all in their early twenties, included Faílde's brothers Eduardo on clarinet and Cándido on trombone. As earlier in the case of the *guaracha*, the bourgeoisie branded the *danzón* as a "lascivious, devilish black dance," but *Las Alturas de Simpson* achieved enormous popularity and the *danzón* prevailed.

In 1880, the pianist Antonio Torroella ("Papaíto") and the trombonist Raimundo Valenzuela brought the *danzón* to Havana. A talented composer and music teacher, Valenzuela had worked with Juan de Dios Alfonso's famed outfit, La Flor de Cuba. In the 1870s he formed a *típica* including saxophones – then a novelty in Cuban popular music – bassoons and cornet. His arrangements allowed the brass – especially the cornet, played by his brother Pablo – to improvise. In 1882, he added to his *danzón El combate* a coda on which he performed fiery trombone solos. This coda foreshadowed the transformations which the *danzón* would undergo in the late 1930s. After Valenzuela's death, in 1905, Pablo took over the leadership of the band.

In 1879, Faílde and Valenzuela provided the music at various Havana dances. Everyone raved, and high society finally fell in love with the *danzón*, which acquired four sixteen-bar sections: the *paseo*, repeated after each of the other sections to enable dancers to rest and chat; the clarinet *trío* (allegretto), the violin *trío* (andante), which later disappeared, and the brass *trío* (allegro). *Danzón* bands, called *típicas*, employed such brass instruments as tubas, ophicleides, valve trombones, and cornets.

A spate of *danzones* were published in the 1880s, among them the hit *Los Chinos* and those by Rafael Landa, Félix Valdés, and flautist "Tata" (Octavio) Alfonso (*Las perlas de tu juramento*). Alfonso, Valenzuela, clarinettist Enrique Peña, pianist Enrique Guerrero, and cornettist Félix Cruz drew on black themes in their compositions (*Negra tú no va a queré, El demonio de la negra, El negro bueno, El congo libre, El lucumí, La africana, Yeyé olube, El Náñigo*, inspired by an Abakwa chant), and blacks generally took delight in fast and highly rhythmical *danzones*.

El negro bueno – Raimundo Valenzuela

Around 1902 the *danzón* was further simplified, into two 32-bar sections: the first in 2/4 time, and the second in 6/8 (as in *El Náñigo*). By then, *típicas* consisted of two clarinets and two violins, weaving their delicate arabesques around the melody, plus trombone, ophicleide, cornet, bass, timbales, and güiro.

Between 1910 and 1930 the outstanding clarinettist José Urfé (1879–1957), co-founder of Peña's *típica*, wrote an impressive number of *danzones*, including *Se mató Goyito*, *El dios chino*, *Maldición*, *Mira que eres bonita*, and especially *El bombín de Barreto*, inspired by a bowler hat worn by his friend, violinist Julián Barreto, and *Fefita*. In *El bombín de Barreto*, which began with a Chinese melody, reflecting the presence of Asian immigrants in Cuba, he, like Valenzuela, developed the final section (*montuno*), allowing musicians and dancers to improvise on it. *Fefita* (1925), which premiered in a Güines club "for colored persons," has become a classic of Cuban music. Like Valenzuela before him, Urfé included a *son* motif in the coda. This new coda, called *otra* (other), became a fixture of the *danzón*. Subsequently, *danzón* composers also borrowed ideas from jazz, classical works, rumbas, *pregones* (street-vendors' ditties) and other types of music. Numerous *danzones* had topical titles; for example, at the turn of the century, *El dengue*, which alluded to an epidemic, or *El teléfono de larga distancia*, which celebrated the advent of the long-distance telephone in Cuba. "Over a period of forty years, there wasn't a single event," Carpentier noted, "that wasn't commented upon or celebrated by means of a danzón."

Several *típicas* dominated the Cuban music scene, among them those led by the ophicleide player Felipe González (with clarinettists Remigio and Abelinito, bassist Safora and cornettist Millán), by Domingo Corbacho, and by the Pinar del Río trombonist and trumpeter Jacobo González Rubalcaba (grandfather of pianist Gonzalo Rubalcaba and composer of the fetching *danzón El cadete constitucional*, written in 1936). Chencho Cruz and the Santiago bandleader Enrique Bueno also offered interesting *danzones*. In 1909 the American firm Edison recorded *danzones* by Pablo Valenzuela, Enrique Peña, Felipe Valdés, and others; five years later, the first *danzón* rolls for pianola appeared.

The *típicas* survived until the early 1930s, with Felipe González and Pablo Zerquera leading the last of them.

The *rumba brava*

The authentic *rumba* (called *rumba brava*) – a complex and gripping ritual including drumming, singing, declamation and dancing – thrives in back alleys and courtyards, where African blood courses strongly in the veins of the inhabitants. Early *rumbas* were organized as entertainment by slaves working in plantations and sugar mills, and they employed as percussion instruments whatever objects were available – often agricultural tools. Later, in Havana and

Matanzas, dockworkers played *rumbas* on packing crates loaded or unloaded from the ships, and bakers from the Havana district of Carraguao on flour crates. Today the *rumba* flame keeps burning with the same fervor, and every *barrio* of the capital, particularly Los Pocitos, in Marianao, boasts of playing the best *rumba*.

Rumba singers have had a profound effect upon vocalists such as Machito, Cheo Marquetti, Miguelito Valdés, and Benny Moré; and composers such as Jorge Anckermann, creator of the *zarzuela La gran rumba* (1894), Carlos Borbolla, who produced eighteen *rumbas*, and Alejandro García Caturla, creator of *La rumba* (1933), have also drawn from this genre. In 1935, the American composer Harl McDonald used *rumba* themes in the third movement of his *Rumba Symphony* (1935), claiming that "they seem to be a part of the pulse of our times."

The word *rumba* evokes a mood, an atmosphere of noise and celebration. *Ir de rumba* ("to go to the rumba") means to go on a festive spree. The sensuous *mulata de la rumba*, a rumba dancer and singer and fun-loving creature, is one of the major Cuban archetypes. A bottle of rum, a group of friends, a few makeshift instruments, and a *rumba* springs up anywhere, like the samba in Rio.

The *rumba*, with its intricate cross-rhythms, started to take shape in the eighteenth century in Matanzas. Lola María, the writer so thrilled by Miguel Faílde, described a black dance of the mid-nineteenth century which would appear to have been a rumba. At the turn of the twentieth century, mutual-aid societies often made up of *rumberos* (called *coros de clave* or *bandos*), among them Los Congos de Angunga, La Violencia, Los Colombianos, and the famed Bando Azul, competed with each other in Matanzas. Some of the most dazzling *rumberos*: "Candunga la China" (Margarita Zequeira), Quirino Yin, Estanislao Luna, "Malanga" (José Rosario Oviedo) hailed from Las Alturas de Simpson, and from Unión de Reyes, on the outskirts of the city.

The enigmatic "Malanga" became a legend in Cuba. Born on October 5, 1885, to an unknown father and a black woman named Funciana Oviedo, he indulged a penchant for women, parties, and *aguardiente*, the sugarcane spirit that burns the guts and stirs the soul. On *cajones*, which were crates used as conga drums, he challenged his peers, such stalwarts as Mulence, Papá Montero, José Calazán Drake, and Joseíto Drake. When he died at the age of thirty-six or thirty-seven, as mysteriously as he had lived, he still looked like a child. Rumors circulated that Mulence or another *rumbero*, perhaps by the name of Chenche, had murdered him by putting crushed glass into his drink. The *rumba Llora timbero* ("Cry, Drummer"), composed in his memory, described Unión de Reyes as mourning his passing. Papá Montero, known as "the scoundrel of rumba," also entered Cuban folklore and inspired a well-known poem:

Señores, señores	Gentlemen, gentlemen,
Los familiares del difunto[15]	The family of the deceased
Me han confiado	Have asked me
Para que despida el duelo	To take care of the funeral
Del que en vida fue	Of him who, when alive,
Papá Montero.	Was Papá Montero.
¡A llorar a Papá Montero!	Let's mourn Papá Montero!
¡Zumba!	Zumba!
Canalla rumbero.	Rumba rascal!

During the 1920s and 1930s in the heyday of the *rumba, rumberos* calling themselves *los invasores* ("the invaders") crashed parties in the barracks of the sugarcane plantations and gave impromptu *rumbas* which went on all night. In Havana "Roncona" (Benito González), a powerful baritone and superb improviser of lyrics, percussionist "Manano," the great dancer "Descoyuntado" (Disjointed), "Calabaza," "Tanganito," Magnesia, "Dionisio," "Alambre," "El Niño," "Flor de Amor" (Agustín Pina), and others "invaded" *solares*[16] such as Atarés, in Los Sitios, or El África, in Cayo Hueso. In New York, "Machito" (Frank Grillo) fondly recalled their exciting parties. His father, who ran a food store, used to give them pork, beans, beer, and other treats, and the young Machito was allowed to join his *rumbero* friends on their sprees.

15 *Cadáver* ("corpse") in some versions.

16 Tenements with common lavatories and kitchens, sometimes with balconies overlooking a common courtyard.

Rumba brava in Cuba. Panart Records

Like the *son*, the *rumba* expresses a vast range of emotions, from unrequited love to political discontent. *Los Caramelos*, for example, a well-known *rumba* penned by "Tío Tom" (Gonzalo Asencio Hernández), satirized the racial situation in Cuba:

A la fiesta de los caramelos	To the toffees' (whites') party
No pueden ir los bombones.	The chocolates (blacks) cannot go.

Born in 1919 in Cayo Hueso, Hernández – a prolific composer – also wrote *Consuélate como yo*, whose refrain: *Si tú me lo das, por qué me lo quitas* ("If you give it to me, why do you take it back?") has become a staple of *rumbas*, and *Changó va vení* (also sung as *Changó ta' vení*):

Changó va vení	Chango is about to come
Con el machete en la mano	With a machete in his hand
Tierra va tembla'	The earth is going to tremble
Sarabanda malongo	Sarabanda malongo
Mundo acaba'	The world is coming to an end.
....	....
Abran paso pa' lo de arriba	Make room for those from above
Que vienen bailando el mambo	Who come dancing the mambo,
Sarabanda Changó va' vení.	Sarabanda Chango is about to come.

Having roots in both the Congo and Andalusia, the rumba has also incorporated West African genres. And it has been carried back to Spain, where gypsy guitarists now play what they call *rumbas flamencas*. Through its Congo lineage, the *rumba* is descended from the *makuta*, a fertility dance characterized by pelvic thrusts (as in other Bantu dances of the Caribbean and Latin America), the bellicose *makúa*, and from the more recent *yuka*, a profane dance still done by Congo groups in the province of Pinar del Río and in Sagua la Grande, in the Santa Clara region. Because of moral censorship by whites, however, pelvic movements were frequently moderated, replaced by the suggestive swaying of hips, a symbolic handkerchief, a foot or hand gesture laden with meaning. In Placetas, in the former province of Las Villas, in the center of Cuba, there existed a Congo pugilistic dance, the *maní*, similar to the Brazilian *capoeira*, the Trinidadian *kalinda* and the Antillean *laghia* and used by slaves to settle their differences. Though it has died out, its competitive acrobatics and atmosphere of bravado, also widespread in other black cultural manifestations, have survived in the rumba, as drummers, dancers, and singers try to outdo each other. In *Ecué-Yamba-O*, Carpentier eloquently renders the tensions and the flashy nature of the *rumba*: "He was gravitating upon himself, his feet almost motionless, sketching circular salutes like a tired top. Suddenly his body stopped and a shudder went down his limbs to his ankles. He looked like a mummy, rigid except for the feet, which were moved by an electric vibration. Then his soles started to slide on the ground, trembling dizzyingly like a hornet's wings."

Carleton Beals, an American writer who traveled to Cuba in the 1930s, also gave an account of a rumba: "A swift writhe of the hips, and he picks up a kerchief in his teeth; then on taut hands and feet, with even faster roll and twist of the body, now face downward, now face skyward, the movements chime in with a steady lalalalalalaleeee longing . . . 'Maria de la Ooo . . . I'm going to bathe'."[17]

The first *rumbas*, called *rumbas de tiempo España* (*rumbas* of the Spanish era), were often mimetic. *Mama 'buela* evoked a child scolded by his grandmother because he refused to go to school, the *papalote* imitated someone flying a kite; and in *Lala no sabe hacer na'*, the male dancer indicated to his female partner the household chores she had to accomplish. In Havana, the bakers of the Carraguao district created the *tahona*, perhaps derived from an old *cabildo* tune, and played on flour crates serving as drums. The show-business type of rumba performed in theaters and cabarets incorporates various styles. In Santiago, especially during the carnival, one often sees *rumbas de chancletas*, in which dancers create rhythms by clacking their sandals on the floor.

The rumba is antiphonal, with a lead singer, and a chorus taking up the refrain in unison. Lyrics may contain African words, and accents obey the dictate of rhythm. Traditional verses such as the one below, often sung by Machito, may be used at the beginning of a rumba:

¿Qué le gusta a la negra prieta?	What does the black woman like?
El ñame con manteca.	Yam with lard.

The *guaguancó*

Of the three prevalent forms of rumba – the *guaguancó*, the *yambú*, and the *columbia* – the *guaguancó* has had the greatest impact on popular Cuban music, often serving as a vehicle for Latin jazz. The theme of the *guaguancó* is sexual possession, symbolized by pelvic contact (*vacunao*). According to an ancient Congo tradition, the *guaguancó* is danced in a circle (*oya*), which is the sacred form of the universe. The man tries to achieve the *vacunao*; and while coyly flirting with him, the woman tries to avoid this contact by abruptly stepping away from him, by hip movements (*botaos*), by folding her skirt in front of her genitals or covering them with her hands – unless she symbolically decides to yield to the man's advances.

The *guaguancó* is played on three barrel-shaped congas: the *quinto*, which guides the dancers and improvises (unlike in the African tradition, where this role usually devolves to the bass drum), the *segundo* (also known as *tres golpes* or as *tres dos*), and the *tumbadora*, or bass drum, which maintains the basic beat. A complementary rhythm is beaten with sticks on the side of a drum (*cáscara*),

17 (1933:49). María de la O was, like María de la Regla, a famous mulatto dancer from Santiago. *María de la O* is also the title of a *guaguancó*.

or on a stool, a table, or a wooden board (where it then becomes known as *guagua*).

Machito once suggested to me that the word *guaguancó* came from the Cuban expression *"ir de guaguancó"* (from *guagua*, bus), which means to ride a bus without paying, although the etymology remains obscure. The *guaguancó*, first seen in Havana, is also said to have been created by members of an Abakwa *cabildo* or, according to other versions, by prisoners of the Castillo del Príncipe. *Guaguancó* also evokes the *guaguas*, pieces of sugarcane beaten with a pair of fine sticks, which the Congos used instead of drums.

Before the advent of the *guaguancó* proper (in the late nineteenth to early twentieth centuries), groups of singers, dancers and musicians sometimes including fifty or more persons, the *coros de clave* and *coros de guaguancó*, would perform in the streets of Havana: Los Roncos, from the Pueblo Nuevo neighborhood, for instance, vied with El Paso Franco or Los Jesuitas. They played claves, string instruments, and *violas* – stringless vihuelas used as percussion – and the *coros de clave* sang songs with a 6/8 time signature called *claves*. In 1893 a *danzón* named *Guaguancó* became popular in Havana, but *Guaguancó coro miyaré* is considered the first real *guaguancó* rumba. And the memory of such founding fathers of the *guaguancó* as dancers Cha Chá, Saldiguera, El Niño, Machaco still lives on.

The structure of the *guaguancó* consists of an opening statement, a refrain, and finally the dance. In salsa bands, the piano, the guitar or the *tres*[18] sometimes play a type of contrapuntal pattern referred to as *montuno de guaguancó*:[19]

Guaguancó montuno

The *yambú*

The *yambú* surfaced in 1850 with the song *El yambú*. An urban *rumba*, it describes the courtship of old people. The rhythm is slow, almost suspended, the dancing devoid of pelvic thrusts *"en el yambú no se vacuna"* ("in the yambú, there is no *vacunao*"), one sings in this *rumba*. The dancers are elderly, or dance as if they were. The woman, who has the more interesting role, can pretend to perform domestic chores, washing the floor on her knees, for example, but with enticing, sometimes lascivious, movements of the rump. The man can seize a handkerchief lying on the ground with his teeth to show his partner he is still virile and physically capable.

The *yambú* opens with a *lamento* or *llorao* (lamentation) or a *diana* (call) punctuated by ritual invocations: *"bélé bélé belé," "a la la la," "a na na na," "o yo yo yo," "lo li lo la la,"* or *"que bueno, que bueno aé."* It then proceeds with the verse

18 See p. 42.

19 From *monte*: mountain, a word also symbolizing the rural regions of the interior of Cuba.

(*canto*), consisting of a short melody in a major mode with improvisation by the lead singer. The refrain (*capetillo*), sung in unison by the choir, and then the dance follow. A well-known *yambú*, *Ave María Morena*, exalts the beauty of a black woman:

Ave María morena	Hail Black Mary
Cuanto tienes	How much you have,
Cuanto vales.	How much you're worth.

The *yambú* is normally played on *cajones*, wooden crates that stood in for drums in former times when the latter were outlawed. *Cajoncitos de velas* (candle boxes) served as high-pitched congas, while *cajones de bacalao* (codfish crates), chosen for the sonorous quality of their wood, stood in for *tumbadores* (low-pitched congas). Barrels, olive kegs, drawers, chairs, stools, frying pans and other objects can add their own rhythms. In the *rumba de cajones*, a *cajón* can be beaten with spoons, to produce a high-pitched sound. Carleton Beals described some of the instruments used in the rumba: "The drumheads are warm. Now the performers are beating on them. The bongo, later discarded for a small packing case covered over with a special wood, is held tightly between the knees. The two players hammer the end with two sticks; for some of the dances, two spoons, or a spoon on a frying pan. Another shakes a hollowed-out gourd."[20] Today *cajones* are sometimes combined with congas, more specifically *segundos* (also called *tres golpes* or *tres dos*), which maintain the basic beat.

The *columbia*

A convulsive, strenuous and competitive men's dance, the *columbia* appeared in the rural areas of Unión de Reyes, Sabanilla, and Alacranes, near Matanzas. The name is said to derive from that of a residence called Columbia, located in the small town of Chucho de Mena, not far from the railroad tracks leading to the various sugar mills. Celestino Domecq, Angel Timbor, José Dreke, Gonzalo Dreke, and Andrea Baró (the first woman to challenge male prerogative and dance the *columbia*) were the pioneers (*decanos*: "doyens") of this genre. Lyrics consist of short phrases peppered with africanisms (sometimes elements of Congo, Lucumí or Abakwa chants) or traditional interjections : "*a co a co,*" "*cocori o co,*" "*agua yu seré,*" and wails (*lloraos*), answered by the chorus.

As in certain parts of Africa, dancers gesture for permission to salute the drums. Before starting to dance they prostrate themselves in front of them – a custom deriving from sacred Congo dances. The choreography is precise, characterized by an upright torso, with trembling of the spine and sometimes disjointed leg and shoulder movements. Dancers, striving for virtuosity, may balance bottles or glasses filled with water on their head or, in rural areas, wield knives or machetes. In the old *mañunga*, dancers have to move around a bottle

20 Op. cit., p. 28.

without knocking it over. Each participant tries to outdo his rivals in terms of dexterity and rhythmic imagination. The high-pitched *quinto* improvises and accents the dancer's steps. As with *yuka* drums, the player can wear small bells on his wrists. And agricultural tools beaten with sticks add their voices to the concert.

Example of *columbia tumbao*

The *son* and its variations

The *son* embodies the very soul of Cuba. "Without heart there's no *son*," says the singer Ibrahím Ferrer. It is the backbone of salsa, and it has also inspired composers, among them Amadeo Roldán, whose beautiful *Motivos de son* is considered a masterpiece of Cuban classical music.

The musicologist Alberto Muguercia has enumerated some of the old meanings of the word *son*. In nineteenth-century Santiago, the word characterized a black style of dancing rather than a specific dance. It was also applied, at the start of the twentieth century, to small bands playing dance music; around 1920, *son*, in the tobacco region of Vueltabajo, in the western part of Cuba, was synonymous with festivity.

Alejo Carpentier claimed that the sixteenth-century *Son de la Ma' Teodora* was the first *son* ever known in Cuba:

¿Dónde está la Ma' Teodora?	Where is Mother Teodora?
Rajando la leña está.	She's cutting wood.
¿Con su palo y su bandora?	With her drum[21] and her bandora?
Rajando la leña está.	She's cutting wood.
¿Dónde está que no la veo?	Where is she? I can't see her.
Rajando la leña está.	She's cutting wood.

According to legend, "Ma'Teodora" (Teodora Ginés) was a free black woman hailing from Santiago de los Caballeros, Santo Domingo, where she and her sister Micaela had been tobacco pickers. The two women then moved to Santiago de Cuba. There, with Micaela and Sevillian violinist Pascual de Ochoa, Teodora formed a trio that performed for both secular and religious occasions. The women played *bandoras*, mandolins of Spanish origin. Fifes sometimes completed the band. Eventually, Micaela and Ochoa settled in Havana, where they formed another successful group with Portuguese clarinettist Jacomo Viceira and the Malagueño Pedro Almanza on violin. They also utilized castanets and güiro. Teodora stayed in Santiago from 1586 to 1592 and set up an ensemble which included fifes, a güiro, and a tambourine.

Controversy has surrounded the seminal *Son de la Ma' Teodora*. Muguercia has pointed out that the transcription reproduced by Carpentier is included in Laureano Fuentes's book *Las artes en Santiago de Cuba*, published in 1893, and in Bachiller y Morales's *Cuba Primitiva*. Fuentes obtained his information on *Ma' Teodora* from a description of Havana written by Don José María de la Torre in 1598. Furthermore, a similar version of this *son* allegedly exists in Colombia, and the melody is said to resemble that of a *romance* from Extremadura. As Carpentier showed, however, the syncopated melody and the responsorial form indicate black influences, thus making *Son de la Ma' Teodora* a Creole song, and not just a Spanish one.

The *son* surfaced in the late nineteenth century in various small towns of Oriente, emerging from the fusion of various songs, including *pregones* (street-vendor ditties). Musicians first played it on rudimentary instruments: *marímbula* – a wooden box with a hole in the middle and plucked metallic tongues recalling the African *mbira*; *botija* – a jug with a lateral hole through which one blew, and which played the role of the bass;[22] *tres*,[23] sometimes made out of codfish crates and usually strummed in a percussive way.

Then appeared the *bungas*,[24] small rural groups first consisting of guitar or *tres* and singers or – later – bongo, *marímbula*, güiro, maracas, *tres* and *botija*, or *tres*, timbales, accordion, or harmonica. They were followed by *estudiantinas*, named after the *tunas* of Spanish students. These bands, which mostly performed *sones* and *danzones*, included two *tres* (first and second), two guitars, trumpet, timbales, cowbell, güiro, jug or bass, and three singers (first, second, and falsetto). Among these *estudiantinas* were Secre, led by Aurelio Speck, and those run by "Cocuyo" (José) Hechevarría, Kiko Salas, and trumpeter Pepe Macías. *Soneros*

21 *Palo* also means a stick but more precisely, it designates a Congo drum from Santo Domingo.

22 The jug was also used by Black musicians in the South of the United States.

23 According to the singer, guitarist, and composer Sindo Garay, the *tres* was invented in Baracoa.

24 From the name of clay pots used to carry oil.

(*son* singers) often improvised lyrics, a tradition still alive today in salsa. The Puerto Rican singer Ismael Rivera once explained that the *sonero* "is like a poet of the people. He has to make up a story from a chorus that is given to him, without departing from the theme. He must know the vernacular, because he has to inject things from our daily life. He has to come from a humble background in order to touch people. He has to use the words that one uses on street corners."[25]

According to the *tresista* "Pillo" Ortega, the first *sonero* was the mulatto "Nené" Manfugas, in the nineteenth century. Manfugas played a home-made *tres*, and at the Santiago carnivals, he liked to taunt his rivals with the following song:

Cantador que se dilata	A singer who lags behind
Conmigo no forma coro.	Doesn't get to sing with me.
Si tiene diente de oro	If he has a gold tooth
Se lo pongo de lata.	I turn it into tin.

The *tresistas* Benjamín Castellanos (celebrated in a *son* later performed with slight changes by Benny Moré), Pablo Armiñán, Juan Limonta, "El Diablo Wilson" (Herminio García Wilson), and Augusto Puente Guillot livened up parties, and the evenings of the "*son* societies," founded in Oriente around 1905. Their repertoire included *changüís*, *bachatas*, or *nengones* – rural forms of *son* later perpetuated or revived by Santiago musicians Mosquedo, Masó, Mongo Tomé, and Elio Revé.

The *changüí*, which originated in the middle of the nineteenth century on farms and in sugar refineries around Guantánamo, was played at parties. Originally the name *changüí* was given to the bands performing this music, and to the festivities themselves. In some houses, called *casas de changüí*, *changüís* sometimes lasted a whole week. Danced with small steps, the *changüí* ends with a sometimes accelerated break (*cierre*). Highly syncopated and responsorial, it has its own *clave*. The instrumentation consists of *guayo* (a metallic güiro which progressively replaced the old cassava graters), *marímbula*, two singers (one playing maracas and the other a *guayo*), *tres*, and bongo (a bongo slightly different from the one prevailing in popular music and usually played with the female head on the left). Today the traditional *changüí* is kept alive by the excellent group Changüí de Guantánamo. Other variations of the rural Oriente *son* include the *bachata*, the *kiribá*, and the *nengón*, with the *kiribá* and the *nengón* particularly in evidence in and around Baracoa.

In January 1909, in order to avert conspiracies in the military (known as José M. Gómez's Permanent Army), President Gómez swapped the companies stationed in Havana and Oriente. Some of the soldiers were musicians and the relocation of the companies brought the *son* to Havana, and the *guaguancó* to Oriente. Three soldiers in particular, *tresista* Sergio Danger, guitarist Emiliano di

25 In: Ramón Luis Brenes: "A puerta cerrada con Ismael Rivera," p. 60.

Full, and *bongocero* Mario Mena, are said to have introduced the *son* to Havana in May of the same year. More likely, however, the *son* spread there gradually and started to take root.

Most of the early *son* musicians played by ear. As with the old Southern blues, the *son* was ill defined at first, but it progressively acquired a more precise structure. It was characterized by a rhythmical figure called *anticipación*, played on the offbeat, and an octosyllabic verse sung by two male singers or a female soloist, the *clarina*. The refrain generally consisted of a repeated phrase. In salsa, it is carried by the *coro* (chorus) on the section called the *montuno*. In the *son* bands known as *septetos*, which appeared in the mid- to late 1920s, the melody, usually given to the trumpet, was followed by a break, and then by the refrain. Today, the *son* generally consists of a theme followed by *montunos* sections which allow for improvisation. In salsa, breaks or riffs (called *mambos*), played in unison by the rhythm instruments, separate the various sections, and the theme is stated by the vocalist or by a horn. As with the rumba, pronunciation is subservient to rhythm, and syllables may be dramatically shortened or dragged out. Finally, over the years, the greatly accommodating *son* has often been married to other musical genres, including, more recently, rap.

Full of bawdiness, satire, puns, and double-entendre, the *son* extols the beauties of nature, the motherland, and women, and, like the *calypso* and the Puerto Rican *plena*, it is a savory chronicle of daily life.

The *son montuno* – a slower variety of *son*, derives from the *guajira*, a form of Spanish origin sung by *guajiros* to the accompaniment of guitars, bongos and güiros. The *son montuno* and the *guajira* are often romantic, bucolic or patriotic. Solos, based on a simple chord progression (I-IV-V), generate interesting rhythmic tensions that make up for the lack of harmonic sophistication.

The *sucu sucu*, devised in the 1920s in the Isle of Pines (renamed Isla de la Juventud, Island of Youth, by Fidel Castro), absorbed musical forms from the Cayman and other English Caribbean islands, brought there by agricultural workers. It somewhat recalls the *changüí*, and, according to Cuban musicologist María Teresa Linares, a *son* from San Luis entitled *Muchacha no seas boba*. The word "sucu-sucu" refers both to a dance (itself derived from another dance, the *contunto*) and to a kind of festive music. The instrumentation consists of accordion or harmonica (sometimes violin), guitar or *tres*, timbales or bongo, and güiro or machete, used as a scraper; or, sometimes, of marímbula, guitar or *tres*, bongo, claves, and maracas. The *sucu sucu* tradition has been perpetuated by "El Boy" Rives, and by La Tumbita Criolla, led by El Boy's son "Mongo" (Ramón).

The *bolero*

The *bolero* is Latin America's favorite romantic song form, and there is hardly a Cuban or a salsa album, no matter how upbeat the band, that does not include a bolero. Derived from an old ternary Spanish dance, it appeared in Oriente around 1810, soon becoming the hallmark of *trovadores*,[26] singers accompanying themselves on the guitar. In Cuba, under the influence of black musicians, the guitar is often strummed in a syncopated way called *rayado*. Towards the end of the nineteenth century, *Tristeza* ("Sadness"), written in 1885 by singer and guitarist Pepe Sánchez (1856–1916), served as a template for other boleros. A self-taught musician and a tailor by trade, Sánchez is considered the father of the *trova*, and he trained Emiliano Blez and other *trovadores*. He played for social functions in and around Santiago, sang jingles for the soft drink Paloma Real and wrote a vast number of songs, among them *La Cubana* and *Cuba mi patria querida*. Juan Logas, Marcelino Latamblé, Eulalio Limonta, Oscar Hernández, and the legendary "El Diablo" Wilson also contributed to the rise of the bolero. Patricio Ballagas, born in Camagüey, changed its time signature from 2/4 to 4/4 and wrote boleros meant to be performed by two vocalists (a tenor, carrying the melody, and a baritone, harmonizing) singing different sets of lyrics. *La timidez*, dedicated to "the pretty and sculptural Señorita Blanca Rosa Soler y Miró," is among the most outstanding of his works.

Under the influence of jazz, the syncopated figure originally played by the bass was simplified. In the 1930s, *afros*[27] were also used to support boleros, and verses became based on eight- or twelve-syllable lines. With their beautiful harmonies, boleros are Cuba's answer to jazz ballads, and they have frequently been orchestrated for big bands. The Cuban bolero tends to be played at a medium tempo, while the Puerto Rican or Mexican bolero is generally slower. Although some commercial boleros have degenerated into cloying mush, the real bolero, with its strongly marked beat, remains both poignant and powerful, fraught with dramatic tension.

The *zapateo*, the *punto*, and the *tonada*

In the countryside, the *guajiros*, engaged in subsistence farming, often organize parties (called *guateques* or *bachatas*) in order to break the monotony of their work. In older times, they performed the *zapateo*, a dance of Andalusian origin featuring leaps, and in which the toe and then heel of the shoe struck the ground. It has a triple meter, and it was accompanied by a *bandurria* (a kind of lute), a *tiple* (a small guitar), and a güiro.

Tonadas, and *puntos* – songs of Canarian or Andalusian origin expressing peasants' problems and concerns – mainly survive in the west and in the center of Cuba – the *punto*, in particular, is still performed in Antonio de los Baños, near Havana. These genres are also accompanied by stringed instruments, but despite their Spanish origin, they, too, as most other Cuban popular genres, have absorbed African influences. The *punto fijo*, with often patriotic topics, has a fixed meter; the *punto libre* allows free improvisation,

26 From the French *trouvère* or *troubadour*.

27 This medium-tempo genre based on the following rhythmic figure:

became popular around the same time.

and there are many regional variants, among them the *punto espirituano*, from Sancti Spíritus. Celina González, with her proud *Yo soy el punto cubano*, introduced the *punto* into the popular repertoire, and the *zapateo* has occasionally inspired Cuban jazzmen. Overall, however, these genres have had little impact on dance music and Latin jazz, but as in Puerto Rico, these rural song forms nevertheless give rise to exciting *controversias* – duels between two *decimistas* (improvisers of *décimas* – ten-line verses[28]), who often exchange humorous jibes.

Also of rural origin, the *criolla* had themes similar to those of the *son montuno* of the *guajira*. Generally bucolic, and with a 6/8 time signature, it was popularized before the First World War by the flautist and bandleader Luis Casa Romero (1882–1950) with his tune *Carmela*, and flourished in the first half of the twentieth century.

The *claves* and the *piquetes*

The *coros de clave* have already been mentioned in the section about the *guaguancó*. Inspired by the Catalan choirs founded by Anselmo Clavé (hence their name), these *coros* included a lead singer, the *clarina*; a *decimista*, who improvised verses; a *tonista*, who ensured that the choir was in tune; and a *censor*, who checked on the suitability and literary qualities of the lyrics.

In Cuba and in Puerto Rico, there also existed *piquetes*, small groups of carollers singing during religious festivities in exchange for food and other small gifts; in addition, in Cuba *piquetes* was the name given to bands playing in circuses.

The *pregón*

Pregones, too, have inspired Cuban songwriters and composers (*El manisero, El botellero, El mondonguero, Frutas del caney, Mango mangüé*). In the first half of the century, street vendors advertised their wares with inventive and often beautiful tunes, but unfortunately, these *pregones* have all but disappeared in Cuba. Ñico Saquito's risqué *Atésame el bastidor* (straighten up my bed frame) constitutes a striking example of the use of this genre in popular music:

28 Among the different types of verse forms of Spanish origin the *espinela*, the *octavilla* and the *redondilla*.

Aquí va el atesador	Here comes the straightener
atesando bastidores	straightening bed frames
oiga bien mi pregón . . .	listen carefully to my song . . .
Que por veinte kilo	For twenty cents
te lo pongo duro	I get it hard
te lo pongo tieso	I get it straight,
como quiera que tú quieras	as you want it,
te lo pongo.	so I get it.
Te levantas estropeadita	You get up all sore
porque quieres caserita . . .	because you want to, young woman.
Ateso, ateso bastidor	I straighten up, I straighten up bed
atésalo bien durito	frames.
que dé inspiración dormir	Make it real hard,
porque cuando está blandito	so that it encourages me to sleep,
qué manera de sufrir . . .!	because when it is limp,
	what a suffering it is . . .!

In salsa, the word *pregón* has often become synonymous with "song" (as in Héctor Lavoe's *Escucha mi pregón*, for instance), and the verb *pregonar* with "singing."

The organs from Oriente

One finds in Cuba many other forms of traditional music, among them street organs, of French origin, played in places like Manzanillo, Holguin or Palma Soriano, accompanied by timbales, güiro, conga, and hoe beaten with a stick.

The clave

Popular Cuban music and its offshoots are based on the *clave*. This deceptively simple two-bar pattern of African origin can in fact prove disconcerting, bewildering even, to non-Latinos or even to musicians grounded in the jazz mainstream. According to Patato Valdés: "The *clave* can neither be given nor be bought. One is born with it, it is a question of feeling." There exist several variations of the *clave*, according to the type of rhythm played. The most common, in the *son* and in salsa, is the so-called "2/3" one:

There is also a "3/2" *clave*:

$$\frac{4}{4} \| \quad \| $$

a *guaguancó clave*:

$$\frac{4}{4} \| \quad \| $$

a 12/8 *columbia clave*:

$$\frac{12}{8} \| \quad \| $$

or a Yoruba *clave*:

$$\frac{12}{8} \| \quad \| $$

The *clave*, of which there are still other examples in use, remains steady throughout a musical piece. It is maintained by two claves – wooden sticks struck together: one "male" (*macho* – the one which strikes), the other "female" (*hembra*), held in the cupped left hand. The Venezuelan bandleader Edmundo Ros stated that "for the layman, the claves can appear as the simplest of all Latin-American instruments. However, the one who plays it is, undoubtedly, the most important member of the band. The perfection of the performance depends on him: his timing must be perfect and he must produce a crisp, clear and penetrating sound, heard above the rest of the outfit." As Tito Puente exclaimed: "It's amazing what those two little sticks can do!"

If *claves* are not used, the *clave* is internalized by the musicians and remains implicit. If it is not respected, the rhythm becomes turned around (one says *fuera de clave*), and the overall equilibrium of the band, contingent upon the subtle overlapping of all the instruments – each with a clearly defined role – is destroyed. While jazz allows for a great deal of rhythmic freedom, Cuban music is more exacting.

Example of the rhythm section accompaniment

The *clave* also works well with many jazz or popular tunes, and in Latin jazz, many American standards are played with an underlying *clave*.

Rhythm instruments

The timbales

Timbales (called *pailas* in Cuba) derive from the old military timpani used by the Cuban army. In the late nineteenth century, soldiers from the black batallions that fought in the independence war against Spain (*batallones de pardos y morenos*) used to play them with a particular swing, and these drums were adopted by *típicas* and then by *charangas*. Considerably smaller today, *timbales* consist of two snare drums mounted on a metallic stand, with the addition of two cowbells (*cencerros*) of different sizes and a woodblock.[29] For the *bolero*, sticks generally strike the metallic side of the drums. For other musical genres, the right-hand stick strikes the cowbell and a *timbal*, while the left hand without a stick accents the second beat with an open sound and the fourth with a muffled sound. The *timbales* play an accompanying rhythm called *cáscara* (literally "shell"):

Example of cáscara

Some sections of the *danzón* are introduced by a riff called *abanico* (literally "fan"), consisting of a rim shot followed by a roll or another rim shot. In the 1950s, *timbaleros* also used *baqueteos*, two-bar patterns consisting of a succession of regular strikes on the various parts of the instrument.

The *conga*

The *conga* (known as *tumbadora* or *timba* in Cuba) evolved from the Congo *ngoma* drums, and surfaced in Havana during the colonial era. Since the advent of Chano Pozo, some percussionists have been using up to five or six drums, each one producing a different pitch. While in former times their tension was adjusted near the heat of a flame, today congas are tuned with metallic keys, generally a second, a fourth, or a fifth apart. They are held between the legs, or mounted on a stand for a more powerful sound and, when several drums are used, for greater freedom of movement. Various tones can be produced: a closed one, an open one, a slap played on the rim of the conga, a sound obtained with the palm of the hand on the center of the skin, muffled ones obtained with the elbow, *glissés* performed by sliding a finger on the skin, and more sonorous ones, achieved by striking the body of the instrument with sticks or mallets. The Cuban virtuoso Tata Güines, who

29 Its Spanish name, *caja china* (Chinese box) testifies to the geographical origin of this instrument.

Shekere

Bongos

Claves

Cowbell and
Woodblock

Conga

Guïro

Maracas

Timbales

Cuban percussion instruments

draws a huge variety of tonal colors from his congas, also uses his nails. In salsa, the conga plays a basic rhythm (*tumbao*), one of which could be rendered onomatopoeically as: *kutún-pá*. With each of several congas tuned differently, highly musical *tumbaos* can be produced. The melody of the *tumbao* (one uses the word *repique* when the improvisations are more complex) varies according to the musical genres. Thus it becomes in the *guaguancó*, for example:

Guaguancó tumbao

The *bongo*

"The antidote of Wall Street," as Alejo Carpentier humorously describes it, the *bongo* also evolved in Oriente. It consists of two small, rather high-pitched drums joined by a wooden slat. Like the conga, the bongo is made of wood or fiberglass and, today, the drums are also tuned with metallic keys, a fourth or a fifth apart. Held between the knees or sometimes also mounted on a metallic stand, the bongo is played with the tip of the fingers. It provides a basic beat, the *martillo*, phonetically *tiqui-tiqui-toqui-tiqui*, but in the *changüí*, the accompaniment is more on the offbeats. One can also play tremolos (*redobles*), and apply a variety of conga techniques, including the *glissé*.

Other percussion

Among other widely used percussion instruments are the güiro or *guayo* (a serrated gourd or scraper played with a stick), or, for the merengue the *güira*, a larger metallic instrument scraped with a metallic comb; the cowbell (*cencerro*), a clapperless metallic bell usually played by the *bongocero* on the *montuno* sections; and the maracas, seed-filled gourds with handles, mostly used for the cha-cha, the bolero, and the *changüí*.

Example of basic maraca pattern

Maraqueros can improvise complex rhythms. The right hand leads and marks the accents, although some *maraqueros* – Champito Rivera among them, in the 1920s – have been ambidextrous. "Machito" (Frank Grillo) also had a very active left hand when playing maracas.

The bass

The double bass (or baby bass or electric bass, current in salsa and Cuban dance music) maintains a syncopated accompaniment also known as *tumbao*:

Today, in Latin jazz, some bass players alternate for greater variety between walking lines and *tumbaos*.

The piano, the guitar, the vibes, the *tres*, and the *cuatro*

During solos in particular, the piano, the guitar, the vibraphone, the *tres*, and the *cuatro* (a Puerto Rican instrument with five double strings, played with a pick) maintain contrapuntal patterns called *montunos* (or *guajeos*).

The *tres* and the *cuatro* are usually reserved, respectively, for the *son* and for Puerto Rican *jíbara* (country) music, although they have also cropped up in popular music and Latin jazz.

Today, Latin jazz pianists and guitarists often employ a mixture of chords, jazz lines, and *montunos* in their comping.

The vibes, popularized in U.S. Latin music by Tito Puente, Cal Tjader, Joe Cuba, and Pete Terrace among others, are more widespread in Latin jazz than in salsa, although the late Louie Ramírez, for one, was a brillant salsa vibist.

the 1920s and 1930s: son, rumba, and conga

CHAPTER TWO

Havana and Cuba

The Cuban republic, inaugurated on May 20, 1902, under President Tomás Estrada Palma, began in a euphoric atmosphere despite the United States' control over Cuba. The upper classes gave splendid costumed balls, brass bands played in the gardens of the Vedado, singers performed in the Palatino park while the Alhambra, the Martí, the Politeama, and other theaters attracted enthusiastic crowds. "Havana is rotten and has no shame," noted Irene Wright, an American traveler dismayed by the over-abundance of entertainment in the capital.

From the 1920s on, with the development of radio and the growing interest of the American record industry in Cuban music, the *son*, the *guaracha*, the *rumba*, and other rhythms spread abroad and began to attract international notice.

In the 1920s and 1930s, Cuba went through politically turbulent yet culturally fascinating times. Around 1909, Estrada Palma, and then his successors, Miguel Gómez, Mario García Menocal, and Alfredo Zayas had unsuccessfully strived to eradicate black culture from the island (Zayas, in particular, had outlawed the *rumba brava*). Menocal's rival, general Gerardo Machado y Morales – a former cattle thief and butcher who seized power on May 20, 1925 – was even more ruthless. During his second mandate, from 1928 to 1933, he prohibited carnival *comparsas* and forbade the playing of *son* in public. Bongos, deemed too "African," were banned, although *timbales*, which looked more "European," were tolerated.

His righteous and overzealous minister Rogelio Zayas Bazán censored films, tried to close down dance schools, and even fined men who complimented women in the street! In 1929, following Machado's example, the mayor of Santiago also forbade congas and bongos – a painful reminder, for black Cubans, of the days of slavery. One *son* group, however, the Sexteto Habanero, enjoyed Machado's favors. They, exceptionally, had permission to use a bongo, and were even invited to perform at the presidential palace.

Machado suborned the army and stole public funds. Corruption increased, the political climate worsened and, in equal measure, so did the musicians' lot. Strikes broke out and the leaders of workers' movements were arrested. The great zarzuela singer Esther Borja was blacklisted. Composer Eliseo Grenet, whose *Lamento cubano* (*"Oh, Cuba hermosa, primorosa, quien diría que tu cielo azul nublara el llanto"* – "Oh, beautiful, ravishing Cuba, who would have thought sorrow would darken your blue sky") was considered subversive, and percussionist Armando Sánchez left the country in 1932; and Ñico Saquito's *La columbina* and *Al vaivén de mi carreta* were also banned because of their note of social protest. Grenet and Sánchez returned to Cuba the following year, after the dictator, ousted, fled to Nassau. The country's situation had worsened in 1929 with the Wall Street Crash, which led to the collapse of the price of sugar on the international market. Various sugar mills closed down, thus accelerating the rural exodus, and Americans acquired roughly one-fifth of the country's land at very low prices. Scores of impoverished peasants, many of them black, flocked to Havana and its suburbs looking for work.

Although considered by the Constitution as full-fledged citizens, blacks were denied access to political life, to the major entertainment centers, certain private schools, and even, in some parts of the island, choice areas in public parks as well as certain streets. As with their counterparts in the United States, sports and music were practically their only opportunities to acquire a decent income, social advancement, and recognition. In Havana, the majority of the black population lived far from the glitter of the tourist areas, in squalid and congested districts such as Los Sitios, Pogolotti, Cayo Hueso, La Loma de Belén, Jesús Peregrino, Buena Vista, El Cerro, and Jesús María, by the docks. And most musicians had to do small jobs on the side in order to survive. "Music was very poorly paid," pianist Pepecito Reyes remembers. "We had to play from 9 p.m. to 3 a.m. and only earned about one peso. And the cable car cost us twelve centavos. We also had to pay a nickel to the union. Luckily, food was cheap in those days."[1]

The increase of North American tourism, partly favored by Prohibition, and the U.S. takeover of the Cuban economy exacerbated racism, and discrimination began to occur in previously integrated bands. The Hotel Nacional refused to admit Josephine Baker during her visit to the island. The Seville turned down boxing champion Joe Louis in 1933, but this time, however, its action caused an uproar.

1 Personal communication.

The major hotels and clubs favored foreign musicians, considered more prestigious than the local ones, or, if hiring Cubans, preferred them light-skinned. In 1926, despite the abundance of local talent, it was an Italian band led by pianist Tomaso Aquino that played at the swank Havana Country Club, churning out some bland "continental music." The bourgeoisie, disdaining Cuban rhythms, feverishly adopted the tango, the black bottom, the two-step, the fox-trot, and the charleston, endowed in their eyes with superior virtues. But, claimed a caricature of that era, published in the weekly *La política cómica* and ridiculing these dances – most of them North American: "*¡Eso es pegar brincos sin ton ni son, cuanto más sabroso es nuestro danzón!*" ("Those are just meaningless leaps, how much more exciting our *danzón* is!").

As in Harlem, black musicians had to enter through the back door of clubs and hotels, and were forbidden to socialize with patrons. Sometimes there was even a line traced on the floor to separate black and white dancers. Racism divided the *academias de baile* (hostess clubs where men had to buy a ticket for each dance) and *sociedades* – social clubs attracting top bands and dancers. Whites favored the Habana Sport or the Sport Antillano, blacks the Club Atenas, La Fantástica, on Galiano Street, Los Aguilas, Los Tulipanes, the Unión Fraternal, on Revillagigedo Street, or El Antilla. Discrimination also split the black community: in Guantánamo and Baracoa, for instance, mulattoes used to socialize in their own clubs, different from the ones frequented by blacks. Certain societies of *Negros finos* ("Refined blacks") turned their backs on their less distinguished brothers, and, denying their African origins, gave their associations European names: "Club Atenas" (Athens Club),[2] "Jóvenes del vals" ("The young ones of the waltz"). Music was fraught with painful incidents: when the young Miguel Matamoros first came to Havana, he was barred from the Lafayette hotel and the Habana Yacht Club on account of his skin color; and pianist Anselmo Sacasas, who was white, remembered the following anecdote: one day when he worked with the *charanga*[3] led by black flautist Luis Carrillo, they played in a house whose owner – also black – organized a clandestine lottery. The man first refused to admit Sacasas for fear the latter would reveal to outsiders the existence of the lottery. He finally relented, however, after hearing how well he played.

An Independent Colored Party had been founded in 1907. Five years later, black upheavals and strikes erupted at the crucial time of the harvest. Gradually, an Afro-Cubanism movement emerged, which coincided with the growing enthusiasm for black art forms in Europe and the United States with, in particular, the publication of articles, Fernando Ortiz's lectures and essays, Nicolás Guillén's poetry, Victor Manuel's paintings, and countless musical works.

Alejo Carpentier has invoked the rallying cry of the Afro-Cuban musicians of that era: "*¡Abajo la lira, viva el bongó!*" ("Down with the lyre, long live the bongo!") Various classically trained instrumentalists[4] turned to popular music, and some composers displayed an authentic passion for black traditions, writing

2 The Club Atenas refused to admit cleaning women among its members!

3 See p. 68.

4 Among them Alberto Socarrás, Ernesto Azpiazu, Mario Bauzá, René Touzet.

songs which sometimes became hits. Amadeo Roldán (1900–1939) made a living playing violin in cabarets and restaurants; Alejandro García Caturla (1906–1940) was a *danzón* and jazz pianist, as well as a saxophonist, clarinettist, percussionist, and singer. In addition to traveling with his Cuban Boys, Ernesto Lecuona (1895–1963), whose pianistic skills elicited Ravel's admiration, also wrote in a popular vein the *congas Panamá* and *Para Vigo me voy* (originally known as *Say sí sí*), the bolero *Por un beso de tu boca*, the *pregón Siboney* and the *zarzuela María la O*, supervised the music of the film *Under Cuban Skies*, and sought inspiration from Abakwa music in his *Danza de los Ñáñigos*:

Ernesto Lecuona.
Óscar López Collection

One of Ernesto Lecuona's relatives, Margarita Lecuona, wrote two standards of the Cuban repertoire: *Tabú*, boldly alluding to the fact that looking at white women was then taboo for black men, and *Babalú Ayé*, and she foreshadowed the *filin*[5] movement that would gain prominence in the 1950s. Eliseo Grenet (1893–1950) conducted in 1926 the band of Arquímedes Pous's variety company, composed with Lecuona, the following year, the operetta *Niña Rita*, and penned the *danzón-son La mora*, the lullaby *Drume negrita*, and the score of the film *Maracas y bongó*. He brought the *conga* dance to New York and Europe, popularized the *sucu-sucu* in 1936 (with his racy song *Felipe Blanco*), and in the 1940s composed the hits *Papá Montero*, *El tamalero*, *Espabílate*, *Negro bembón* (The Thick-lipped Black), and *Mama Inés*. Emilio Grenet set to music several poems by Nicolás Guillén: *Yambambo*, *Quirino con su tres*, the poignant *Sóngoro cosongo* (1931), telling the story of a jilted lover seeing his woman pass by on the street, and whose sonorous African-flavored refrain is an incitement to dance:

Sóngoro cosongo	Sóngoro cosongo
De mamey	Like mamey,
Sóngoro la negra	Sóngoro the black woman
Baila bien.	Dances well.

and *Bito Manué no sabe inglé* – which satirizes a black man who does not know how to speak English:

Con tanto inglé que tú sabía	All dat English you used to know,
Bito Manué	Lil' Manuel,
Con tanto inglé, no sabe ahora	All dat English,
Desi yé.	Now can't even say yes.[6]

Gonzalo Roig (1890–1970) wrote the bolero *Quiéreme mucho* (1911), and the enormously popular *zarzuela Cecilia Valdés* (1932), brilliantly sung by Rita Montaner. Gilberto Valdés (1905–1971) composed *El bembé*, the beautiful *Ogguere*, and *La conga viene ya*. In 1941 he conducted Cuba's Symphony Orchestra, lent to him for the occasion by Gonzalo Roig with, as featured soloists, *batá* drummers Pablo Roche, "El Calvo" (Pedrito Díaz), and "El Niño," and vocalist Oscar López, who gave the first performance of Valdés's *pregón El comprador de botellas* ("The bottle buyer"). Better known as *El botellero*, the song evokes street-vendors who bought bottles from people and sold them back to manufacturers for a few coins:

5 See p. 154.

6 Translation by Langston Hughes and Ben Frederic Carruthers.

Botellero que ya me voy	Bottle buyer I'm leaving.
Aquí me ven cambiando	Here they see me exchanging
Los pirulís por botella	Bottles for lollipops
A la puerta de un colegio	At the entrance of a high school
Del barrio de Cayo Hueso.	Of the Cayo Hueso district.

Flautist, clarinettist, violinist, bassist, and pianist, Rodrigo Prats (1883–1946) also conducted Arquímedes Pous's orchestra. Prats, who held a degree in pharmacy, taught composition and led various ensembles, including show bands. He wrote the bolero *Ausencia*, the *criolla Una rosa de Francia* (1924), which became a major success of the *filin* era, as well as arrangements for José Fajardo and other musicians. He is also known for his operetta *Amalia Batista* (1936), evoking an irresistible Congo woman:

Amalia Batista	Amalia Batista
Amalia Mayombe	Amalia Mayombe
¿Qué tiene esa negra	What does this black woman have
Que amarra a los hombres?	That captivates men?

In the late 1930s, after Machado's fall, Cuban cinema also turned to black music, with such films as *Tin tan o el origen de la rumba* ("Tin Tan or the Origin of the Rumba"), released in 1937.

The Americanization of Cuba had further insidious effects on music. The competition fostered by record companies bred antagonism between artists, and commercial pressure led to exploitation and musical compromise. But neither the political and economic difficulties nor the grim racial situation could dampen Cuba's love for music. Singers and instrumentalists gravitated to Havana from all over the island. Dancing remained a favorite diversion. Masked balls were organized in many clubs and hotels and the greatest dancers flocked to the *academias de baile* and the gardens of the beer halls La Tropical and La Polar, which offered non-stop music for hours on end. Major nightspots catering for tourists, such as Chez Sloppy Joe's, Jugg's Waterfront Cabaret, the Tropical Gardens, the Moulin Rouge, and the Alhambra, tended to feature show-biz acts, but they also hired Cuban relief bands that gave foreigners a taste of local rhythms.

From 1913 to 1915, the American record companies Victor and then Columbia had swamped Santo Domingo with records of Cuban *zarzuelas*, *danzas* and *danzones*. In the early 1920s they increased their Cuban output, hoping to market it in the United States and the rest of Latin America, and they spread the *danzón*, the *son*, the *guaracha*, and the bolero abroad, labeling almost everything "rumba."

The excitement generated by Cuban music was in great part due to the explosion onto the Havana scene of the *son*. Jazz also penetrated the island. It gradually merged with local music, laying the foundations of the Latin jazz styles that would later crystalize in New York and in Havana.

Emergence of the Havana son

Ésta es la canción del bongó　　　Here is the bongo song
El que más fino sea　　　　　　　May the finest of you all
Responde, si llamo yo.　　　　　Answer, if I call.

Nicolás Guillén

Trovadores and estudiantinas

Several musicians from Oriente, attracted by the dazzling cultural atmosphere of Havana, its bustling nightlife and work opportunities, settled in the capital during the 1910s and 1920s. Among them were *trovadores* Floro y Miguel (Floro Zorrilla and Miguel Zaballa), the Enrizo brothers (Nené and Sungo), "El Galleguito" (José Parapar), Higinio Rodríguez, "Nano" (Romín) León, Justo Vásquez, "Pancho Majagua y Tata Villegas" (Francisco Salvo Salazar and Carlos de Villegas), "Teofilito" (Rafael Gómez) and his Pensamiento trio, the El Blanco y el Negro duet (with the guitarist and *tresista* "Santiago" Smood – a former American soldier established in Cuba, and the pianist "El Gallego" Menéndez), the Patricio Ballagas-Oscar Hernández duet, and the one set up by José Castillo and Manuel Luna, composer of the famed *La cleptómana*, with its beautiful lyrics by Agustín Acosta:

Era una cleptómana de bellas fruslerías,
robada por un goce de estética emoción.
Linda fascinadora de cuyas fechorías
jamás supo el severo juzgado de instrucción.

She was a kleptomaniac of beautiful trinkets,
driven by the pleasures of aesthetic emotion.
Pretty bewitcher whose misdeeds
the severe examining judge never found out about.

Other *estudiantinas* such as La Estrella Italiana, La Estudiantina Oriental, La Arrolladora, led by *tresista* "Guayabito" (Narciso Sánchez), Los Apaches, La Creme de Vie, and Los Guajiros also worked in Havana.

Trovadores sought to recreate the atmosphere of Oriente in *peñas*, musical gatherings held in theaters and in cafes, that fostered creativity. They often performed such rural forms of *son* as the *son reginero*,[7] typical of the town of Manzanillo. Some of these artists were greatly instrumental in establishing the *son* and the bolero in Havana. Many, however, leading carefree lives and often exploited by record companies, survived in dire poverty: Miguel Companioni,

7 Based on a verse form called *regina*.

for instance, never received any royalties for his hit *Mujer perjura* (1918), recorded by María Teresa Vera.

A few *trovadores* and composers of *sones*

Born in Sancti Spíritus, in the former province of Las Villas, Miguel Companioni Gómez (1884–1965) became blind as a child. He worked in a bakery store, sold pharmaceutical products, and around 1902 decided to dedicate himself fully to music. He studied guitar, piano, flute, violin, and bass, and composed poetical and slightly precious songs: *Por qué latió mi corazón, A lé lé, Juana, La fe, La lira rota*:

> *Tú rompiste el encanto de mi vida bohemia,*
> *Silenciaste mi lira, destrozaste mi amor.*
> *Y mi ruta poblaste de tormentos y sombras*
> *Y mi fe en las mujeres, tu perfidia mató.*
> *No me pidas ahora nuevos cantos de amores,*
> *Tú rompiste mi lira, ya no puedo cantar.*
> *Aquel amor inmenso que en mi vida mataste,*
> *A vivir como entonces nunca más volverá.*

>> You destroyed the charm of my bohemian life,
>> You silenced my lyre, crushed my love.
>> You filled my path with torments and shadows
>> And your perfidy destroyed my faith in women.
>> You broke my lyre, I can't sing any more.
>> That immense love which you killed in my life
>> Will never live again as it once did.

A prolific songwriter (*Redención, Naturaleza,* the *pregón Se va el dulcerito*), Rosendo Ruiz (1885–1983) was born in Santiago into a poor family. He studied the guitar with Pepe Sánchez, played locally with his friend Manuel Rubio, and among other songs wrote the *danzón Venganza de amor*, the *bambuco*[8] *Entre mares y arena* (1911), and *Dos lindas rosas* (1913). In Havana, where he continued to work as a tailor as he had done in Oriente, he met pianist Antonio María Romeu, who helped him publish *Entre mares y arenas*. Although Ruiz greatly admired Garay, the older *trovador*, resenting Ruiz's success, penned *Perfidia* (distinct from Alberto Domínguez's song of the same name) with him in mind. Ruiz then composed *Gela, Confesión, De mi Cubita es el mango*, which became an international hit, and *Junto a un cañaveral*, immortalized by Abelardo Barroso. He also led the Trío Habana (with José Hernández and Enrique Betancourt), the Cuarteto Cuba, and in 1934 the Trío Azul, in which composer Guillermo Rodríguez Fife sang. He died destitute in Havana.

8 An Afro-Colombian genre.

With his handsome and sensitive face, Manuel Corona wrote many refined and lyrical songs such as *Mercedes, Nubes de ensueño, La Alfonsa* (for which he devised four different versions, sung simultaneously by him, Patricio Ballagas, Rafael Zequeira, and María Teresa Vera). He also specialized in musical rejoinders: *La Habanera*, for instance, was an answer to Garay's *La Bayamesa, Gele amada* to Ruiz's *Gele hermosa, Animada* to Patricio Ballagas's *Timidez, Tú y yo* to Oscar Hernández's *Ella y yo*. Born in Caibarién in 1880 in a humble family, he moved to Havana at the age of fifteen, where he worked as a cigar-maker. In 1900 he wrote the bolero *Doble inconsciencia*. Two years later he went to Santiago, where he befriended the *trovadores* Manuel Delgado, Pepe Sánchez, and Pepe Banderas. In 1916 he composed the *guaracha-rumba El servicio obligatorio*, criticizing the compulsory military draft imposed by Menocal's government, and evoking the rooster (*gallo*), an archetype of the Cuban male:

Hay quien dice acongojado	Some say with anxiety
Mi pobrecita mujer	If I am drafted against my will
Si me llevan obligado	My poor little woman
Se quedará sin comer.	Will go without food.
Uno que se siente gallo	One who feels like the rooster
De una gallina sin par	Of a hen without equal,
Dice que le parta un rayo	Wishes lightning would strike him
Si lo mandan a pelear.	If they should send him to fight.

Two years later he created the superb bolero *Longina*:

En el lenguaje misterioso de tus ojos	In the mysterious language of
hay un tema que destaca	your eyes,
sensibilidad.	a theme stands out:
En las sensuales líneas de tu cuerpo	sensitivity.
hermoso,	In the sensuous lines of your
las curvas que se admiran	beautiful body
despiertan ilusión.	the curves one admires
	awaken desire.

Towards the end of his life, suffering from tuberculosis, he spent time in a sanatorium and then returned to sing in the cafés of Havana. He died in Marianao in 1950, like Ruiz, penniless and forgotten.

Born in Palmira, in the former province of Las Villas, and raised in Cienfuegos, Eusebio Delfín (1893–1965) was a banker by trade. An excellent guitarist and smooth singer, he accompanied himself with great finesse, in a style generally less percussive than that of his peers from Oriente, featuring many arpeggios. In 1923, with composer Eduardo Sánchez de Fuentes, he organized a Cuban song festival at the Teatro Nacional, in Havana; he led a *conjunto* and facilitated the guitar's acceptance in the capital. He is mostly known for *La guinda roja* (1924), *Aquella boca*, and *¿Y tú que has hecho?* (also known as *En el tronco de un árbol*, "In a Tree Trunk"), songs for which he wrote only the music.

¿Y tú que has hecho? – Eusebio Delfín

Born in Santiago, Ñico Saquito (Benito Antonio Fernández Ortiz, 1902–1982) sought inspiration from proverbs, jokes, or events of daily life for his *sones* and *guarachas*: *Cuidadito compay gallo*, *Cosas del compay Antón*, *Que lío compay Andrés*, *Menéame la cuna*, *Ramón*, about the disagreements of married life, *Estoy hecho tierra*, *La negra Leonó*, *Yo no escondo mi abuela* ("I don't hide my grandmother"), and the humorous *El peluquero*:

Dios bendiga al peluquero,	God bless the hairdresser,
al peluquero que disfraza a mi	the hairdresser who disguises
mujer.	my wife.

He worked as a foundryman, mechanic, groom, street-vendor, and sugarcane cutter while singing with his guitar, writing songs (he penned numbers for the famed Carabalí Izuama *comparsa*) and playing baseball. During the 1930s, he formed various groups, was lead singer of Manolo Castillo's Cuarteto Castillo, and wrote such hits as *Al vaivén de mi carreta* and *María Cristina*. In 1936 he moved to Havana, where his career picked up. He performed on the radio with singer Alberto Aroche, guitarists José Antonio Piñares and Senén Suárez, and trumpeter "El Guajiro." He also toured Latin America, playing in Venezuela with Los Guaracheros de Oriente. After living there for several years, he returned to Havana in 1960, singing at La Bodeguita del Medio.

Little is known about the life of Bienvenido Julián Gutiérrez (1900–1966). Born in Havana, he was self-taught. He did not play a musical instrument himself and composed by ear for various vocal groups, among them Los Roncos. His modern-sounding *sones* – *Inolvidable, Convergencia, Que extraño es eso, Ta' caliente, Los tres Juanes, El huerfanito* – possess great charm and originality.

Also from Havana, Oscar Hernández (1891–1967) formed trios with Manuel Corona and Juan Carbonell, but he mostly composed, writing highly romantic songs such as *La rosa roja, En el sendero de mi vida*, and *Para adorarte*.

Sextetos and *Septetos*

At the turn of the century, Isaac Scull, Carlos Godínez, Vasarnilla, and other musicians from Havana having learned to play the *tres* in Oriente, then brought this instrument back to the capital. In the 1930s, the music of the *trovadores* became marginal, but the *son* continued to rise. It almost displaced the *danzón*, and was performed by various groupings of musicians.

If the rustic *guajira* and the delicate *danzón* still smacked of Europe, the bawdier *son* was more "African," and many of its exponents practiced *santería* or *palo* (Congo cults) or belonged to Abakwa *potencias*. As with jazz in New Orleans, the *son* first thrived in the rough-and-tumble atmosphere of the black neighborhoods of Havana: in the dives, courtyards, and tenements of Los Pocitos, Jesús María, Pogolotti, Cayo Hueso, Belén, and in the rowdy cabarets of Marianao beach: La Gloria, El Pompilio, Panchín. In Marianao, which flautist José Fajardo called "the school of popular music," rhythms sprang forth day and night, and heated jam-sessions pitted against each other such stellar percussionists as José Manuel Carriera Incharte ("El Chino"), Santos Ramírez, and *timbalero* "El Chori" (Silvano Shueg Hechevarría), who later led the Rumba Palace band.

Despite Machado's crackdown, the music industry furthered the success of the *son*, which finally achieved acceptance among the more affluent classes. Records of the 1920s give but a poor idea of the bands' exuberance. As on early jazz discs, the sound tends to be blurred and at times the percussion is either barely audible or drowns out the other instruments. And songs, limited to about three minutes so they could fit on the record, do not always show the complete development of the music, although its pervasive charm still comes through.

By the early 1930s, Havana was gripped by a *son* fever. In its bustling streets, dancers showed off fancy steps and *son* bands from different neighborhoods competed before juries which evaluated their literary and musical merits. As with the calypso on the island of Trinidad, *son* contests sometimes degenerated into fights to which the police had to be summoned, lest they escalated into full-scale riots. In *Ecué Yamba-O*, Carpentier evoked the jail sentence given to musicians from the Sexteto Boloña – all members of an Abakwa sect – for disturbing the public peace. On Sundays, crowds flocked to the Jardines Tropicales, a park where several bands took turns and played for hours. The *son* also flourished in the *academias de baile*; the famed Alhambra theater featured *son* and *rumba* dancers "Pepe" (José Benito) Serra, "Garabateo," Evaristo Bemba, Juan Olimpo Lastre, and, some fifteen years later, Carmen Curbelo and the team of René and Estela (René Rivero Guillén and Ramona Ajón); and Yolanda and Pablito danced at the Rumba Palace.

Sextetos followed in the wake of *bungas* and *estudiantinas*. They comprised two singers (the first one singing tenor and accompanying himself with *claves*, the second singing baritone and playing maracas), *tres* or guitar, bongo, güiro, and bass. In 1927, the addition of trumpet, borrowed from jazz, turned these groups into *septetos*. Trumpeters "Florecita" (Óscar Velazco) and José Interián elaborated on their horns a sober and lyrical way of playing known as "*septeto* style," and *bongoceros* Óscar Sotolongo, Santos Ramírez, "El Chino," "Montoto" and his son "Manana" (Agustín Gutiérrez) laid the foundation of the modern bongo style. The *son* grew increasingly complex and syncopated. If, around that time, jazz was more harmonically sophisticated than popular Cuban music, rhythmically the *son* had the edge. The Cuban phrasing, based on the *clave*, is quite different from the jazz one: the lines are more compact, the spacing broader; and, in the 1920s, bongos provided more interesting syncopations than the still rudimentary trap drums of New Orleans jazz, with their steady rhythms. The trumpet wailed above the bongo, producing notes that seemed to float behind the beat, and then the *coro* answered. With this simple but efficient scheme, the *son* finally won the hearts of all Cubans and became one of their most enduring musical symbols.

During Machado's second mandate, the *son* continued to grow covertly. *Soneros* hid in rough neighborhoods like Los Pocitos, where the police never dared to set foot. Certain *sones* such as Miguel Matamoros's *La mujer de Antonio* (1929) expressed in thinly veiled allusions the social and political discontent then brewing everywhere on the island:

Mala lengua	Bad mouth,
No sigas hablando mal de	Stop criticizing Machado
Machado	Since he has set up a market
Que te ha puesto ya un mercado	And he fills up your belly.
Y te llena la barriga.	

Protests also cropped up in other songs such as the *guaracha La bomba lacrimógena*, deploring the use of tear-gas bombs by the police.

One of the first *son* groups to record was the Agrupación Boloña. Founded in Havana in 1915 by *bongocero*, guitarist, and *marimbulero* (*marímbula*-player) Alfredo Boloña, it turned into a *sexteto* in 1923. Author of *Güaguina yirabó* and other lively songs, Boloña (1890–1964) first joined Gerardo Martínez's Trío Oriental – which included guitarist Guillermo Castillo and *tresista* Carlos Godínez (all three were also members of Los Apaches) – as *bongocero*, thus turning the trio into a *cuarteto*. Martínez left the group in 1910, which subsequently recorded under the name of Orquesta Habanera de Godínez. The same year, Boloña also worked with a band which included Manuel Corona (on guitar), Graciano Gómez, Manuel Valdés, and singer Hortensia Valerón. When Boloña founded his own Agrupación, he took Valerón with him and recruited *maraquero* Victoriano López, *bongocero* Joaquín Velázquez and *tresista* Manuel Menocal.

The ensemble later became a *sexteto* and, with the arrival of trumpeter José Interián, a *septeto*, and it performed in New York and in Venezuela. As musicians easily shifted their allegiances according to work opportunities, Boloña's personnel often fluctuated. At various times, trumpeter Félix Chappotín and his brother, *bongocero* and bassist Vicente, Mongo Santamaría, the composer and daring *tresista* Eliseo Silveira, and singers Mario Rosales, Frank Grillo (the future "Machito" of the Afro-Cubans), and Abelardo Barroso also worked with the group.

In the United States in October 1926, with "El Chino" on bongo, Tabito on bass, and Abelardo Barroso and José Vega on vocals, Boloña cut several sides which established their fame. Among them were *Échale candela*, *Aurora en Pekín*, the hit *Juana Calavera* (about a noted prostitute), *Carolina mulata*, and *A la cuata co y co*, an evocation of *santería* that contained Yoruba words:

Me tengo que hacer un ebbo	I must make a sacrifice
con coco, maíz y jutía,	with coconut, corn and an
y un gallo pa' Yemayá.	agouti,
Refrain:	and a rooster for Yemayá.
A la cuata co y co	*Refrain:*
Oya sile oya deo	Half-and-half
a la cuata co y co.	Oya sile oya deo[9]
	half-and-half.

9 An invocation to Oya, an *orisha* of *santería*.

10 The group has included some of the best *son* singers and musicians, among them Rafael Hernández ("El Pitcher"), Eliseo Silveira, Félix Chappotín, José Interián, Manuel Corona, "Chocolate" (Alfredo) Armenteros, "Cheo" (José) Jiménez, Panchito Riset, Miguelito García, "El Chino," Mario Carballo, and *tresista* Juan Irene.

In 1935 Vega and another vocalist, "Tata" Gutiérrez, left the band in order to form the Septeto Bolero, and the Septeto Boloña disintegrated.

In these early days of the *son*, one of the leading ensembles was the Sexteto Habanero. Many musicians regarded it as a model, and Nicolás Guillén once said that this *sexteto*, along with the Trío Matamoros, strongly influenced his poetry. Set up in 1920, also with members of Los Apaches, it outlived Boloña's Agrupación. It is still active today (although with a different line-up), and Cubans fondly remember its old songs: *A la Loma de Belén, Espabílate, A mí que me importa Usted, Mama Inés* (evoking the Havana neighborhood of Jesús María), *Alza los pies, Congo*, or *Criolla carabalí*. Probably influenced by the *bongocero* Agustín Gutiérrez, who belonged to an Abakwa brotherhood, *Criolla carabalí*, sung in the old efik language, alluded to the Efí Abarakó *potencia*.[10]

Guillermo Castillo played with Godínez for the 1920 Havana carnival, and shortly thereafter, he organized the Sexteto Habanero, which comprised Godínez,

Antonio Bacallao (*botija*), "El Chino" or Óscar Sotolongo[11] (bongo), Gerardo Martínez (lead singer, *claves*), and Felipe Neri Cabrera (vocals, maracas). Cabrera wrote for the group the lilting *Bururú barará*, recalling the rural *son* of Oriente with its abrupt call-and-response:

Bururá barará	Bururá barará
¿Cómo ta' Migué?	How is Miguel?
Bururá barará	Bururá barará
Bámono con él.	Let's go with him.

Soon the group's *botija* was replaced by a more melodic *marímbula*, and then by a bass, even more versatile and modern-sounding.

One day in 1924 Abelardo Barroso, who then worked as a taxi-driver, happened to have members of the Sexteto Habanero in his cab, and as he was driving, he started to sing to himself. Impressed by his talent, they took him into the band and, with him, the group then recorded *A pie*, *La camaronera*, and other numbers.

Gifted with superb intonation and a spectacular voice which earned him the nickname "Caruso," Barroso (1905–1972) was one of Cuba's finest all-round vocalists, and he influenced a host of singers, Benny Moré among them. The son of a cigar-roller who loved music, he grew up in a home often visited by Manuel Corona, "El Galleguito," Higinio Rodríguez, Arquímedes Pous, and other musicians. He also earned his living as a boxer, skater, and baseball-player, and he readily acknowledged his musical good fortune: "I moved up in life thanks to music. Early in my career, I could never have guessed that I would one day sing in front of the King of Spain!"

11 One of the first *bongoceros* in Havana – he played bongo there as early as 1913 – Sotolongo later led the Septeto Típico Habanero.

Óscar López and Abelardo Barroso. Óscar López Collection

In early 1926, Habanero recorded in the Victor studios in New Jersey (*No me maltrates nena, Guantánamo, Nieve de mi vida*). During this trip, Agustín Gutiérrez introduced the bongo into the United States. Upon their return to Cuba, Castillo adapted as a *son* the *danzón Tres lindas cubanas* by pianist Antonio María Romeu. Derived from a popular tune from the city of Cárdenas, *Tres lindas cubanas* celebrated the various regions of Cuba:

<table>
<tr><td>

Tres, tres, lindas cubanas,
Pinar del Río, La Habana
Matanzas y Santa Clara.
Cuando me voy a Camagüey,
Oriente me llama.

</td><td>

Three, three, pretty Cuban
  girls,
Pinar del Rio, Havana,
Matanzas and Santa Clara.
When I go to Camagüey,
Oriente calls me.

</td></tr>
</table>

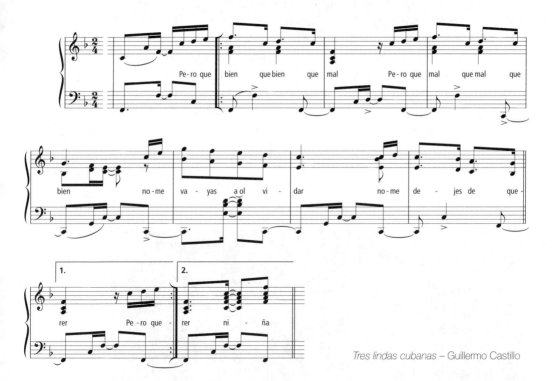

Tres lindas cubanas – Guillermo Castillo

On May 23 of the following year, the song earned the band first prize in a national *son* contest, a distinction which brought them instant fame. Four months later, Habanero recorded it, along with *Caballeros silencio, Un meneíto suave, A la Loma de Belén*, and other numbers. In 1928, trumpeter Enrique Hernández (later followed by Félix Chappotín) joined the band, and among other recordings they issued were *Mama Inés, No juegues con los santos, Bongó del habanero*, and Miguel Matamoros's poetical *Olvido*:

Aunque quieras olvidarme, ha de ser imposible
Porque eterno recuerdo siempre tendrás de mí,
Mis caricias serán el fantasma terrible
De lo mucho que sufro, de lo mucho que sufro alejado de tí.

Although you want to forget me, it is impossible
Because you will always remember me,
My caresses will be the terrible reminder
Of how much I suffer, of how much I suffer away from you.

In the beginning, the *son*, considered vulgar, had been rejected by black social clubs, which thought they would disgrace themselves in the eyes of whites if they featured it. And so ironically, after a tour of Oriente, it was at the posh Habana Yacht Club, Miramar Yacht Club, and Vedado Tennis Club that the predominantly black Septeto Habanero played, breaking down racial barriers and carving an important niche for themselves in Havana's competitive music scene. Singer Rafael Ortiz recalled their historic engagement at the Miramar Yacht Club: "When the grand ladies saw those six black guys tuning their instruments they had a fit, but when the Sextet broke into a montuno it went straight to their feet and not a couple was left seated."[12]

In 1926, joining in the race for Cuban music, Columbia signed up the Sexteto Occidente. Led by the two strong personalities María Teresa Vera and Ignacio Piñeiro, Occidente also became one of the most influential *son* groups of the late 1920s. A young and pretty *mulata*, Vera (1895–1965) was one of the first Cuban female musicians to achieve international recognition. Unlike most *trovadores* she came from Pinar del Rio, the beautiful tobacco region in the western part of the island. When Vera was a child, her mother moved to Havana, working as a maid for a wealthy family. Vera studied guitar with José Díaz, Patricio Ballagas, and Manuel Corona, who became one of her closest friends and wrote two of her favorite songs: *Longina* and *Santa Cecilia*. As a singer and composer, Vera was self-taught. She penned several tunes, among them *Esta noche tocó perder, Noche criolla,* and especially *Veinte años,* her major success. At the age of sixteen she made her debut at the Politeama theater in Havana, in a tribute to Arquímedes Pous, dubbed the following year "most popular *negrito* of Cuban music" by the magazine *Teatro Alegre.* A few years later, she recorded her first song: *Gela,* with Rosendo Ruiz, and then formed a duo with Rafael Zequeira, with whom she also recorded. In 1926, two years after Zequeira's death, she formed yet another duo, with Miguelito García, and then the Sexteto Occidente.[13]

Piñeiro and singer Miguelito García made the most substantial contributions to Occidente's repertoire. Steeped since childhood in Afro-Cuban culture, Piñeiro was an inspired and prolific composer and a natural poet (*Mi yambú,* the guaguancó *Como voy a sufrir,* the guajiras *Alma guajira, Canto a la vueltabajera,* and *Rin rin lea,* the risqué *son Entre tinieblas,* the poignant *Sobre una tumba una rumba*).

12 In: Olga Fernández, *Strings and Hide,* p. 102.

13 The band's line-up also varied. At different times it included *bongoceros* Manuel Reynoso and Ramón Castro, *tresistas* Julio Viáñez, Eliseo Silveira and "Mulatón" (Alejandro Rodríguez), guitarists Eutimio Constantín and Nené Enrizo, clarinettist Alberto Iznaga, and vocalists Frank Grillo, Miguel Sabaya, Panchito Solares, Miguelito García, Abelardo Barroso, "Carusito" (Florencio Hernández Cuesta), Bienvenido Granda, Vicentico Valdés, and Sungo Enrizo.

SONES CUBANOS

Septeto Naciona

Canta la vueltabajera

Esas no son cubanas

Lejana campiña

Bardo

Castigador

de Ignacio Piñeir

Ignacio Piñeiro. Seeco Records

Born in Jesús María, Piñeiro (1888–1969) befriended Cuba's greatest *soneros* and *rumberos* (Tomás Pérez Sanguily, Eliás Aroguí, Tomás Eriza) as well as members of Abakwa *potencias*. After working as blacksmith, cooper, stevedore, cigar-maker, and bricklayer, he sang, at the turn of the century, with various *coros de clave* and *coros de guaguancó*, among them El Timbre de Oro and Los Roncos, eventually becoming their musical director. He wrote for them ¿*Dónde estabas anoche?*, *El Eden de Los Roncos*, *Cuando tu desengaño veas*, and *Mañana te espero, niña*, and briefly belonged to Renascimento.

In New York, Occidente recorded several songs by García and by Piñeiro, among them *El globero*, *Esas no son cubanas*, *Ninfa del valle*, and *Perro flaco*, which became classics. Sessions followed, under other names, for other record labels. But back in Havana, Vera, jealous of Piñeiro's success, had a falling-out with him, whereupon he left to join the Sexteto Nacional. In 1937 Vera formed a duo with Lorenzo Hierrezuelo (who subsequently founded Los Compadres). She later sang on Radio Cadena Suaritos, and performed well into her later years. When she died, the great Barbarito Diez sang *Veinte años* as a tribute, before her coffin.

Within Nacional there were no personality clashes. Piñeiro could give free rein to his imagination and, under his leadership, it became the most exciting *septeto* in Cuba and a training ground for many musicians. An offshoot of a group formed by "Vaquero" Collazo, it was originally run by singers Juan Ignacio de la Cruz and Alberto Villalón, until Piñeiro assumed the leadership. In addition to Piñeiro (bass), Nacional included de la Cruz (tenor voice, claves), Bienvenido León (baritone voice, claves), Villalón (guitar, *coro*), "El Chino" (bongo), and Francisco González Solares (*tres*, first voice of the *coro*). With his splendid voice and sunny personality, León – lured away from Nano León's *cuarteto* – was one of the group's major assets.

Riding on the success of its first recordings, the *sexteto* made a highly acclaimed debut at the Habana Sport, in 1927. In 1927 and 1928 they recorded in New York with Abelardo Barroso, and Piñeiro helped Barroso develop his *soneo* (improvisations). Two years later, Lázaro Herrera ("El Pecoso"), former trumpeter of Felipe Valdés's *típica*, Agustín Gutiérrez,[14] and singer Alfredo Valdés joined the band, which then became a *septeto*, and a dancer by the name of Tomasa occasionally livened up performances. Valdés, who came from a family of musicians (his brothers were Marcelino and Vicentico Valdés), brought to the group his exceptional mastery of Afro-Cuban rhythms.

After a new string of recordings, among them the *rumba Como voy a sufrir*, with a guitar accompaniment reminiscent of *rumbas flamencas*, and the *son montuno Entre preciosos palmares*, Nacional travelled to the Sevilla Fair. They had just recruited "Cheo" Jiménez – a former singer of the Sexteto Facenda – but Jiménez died of pneumonia in the New York harbor, on board the boat about to take them to Spain. The band nevertheless fulfilled its engagement, and Piñeiro's *Suavecito* won over Spain as it had Cuba. The refrain, with its racy allusions ("slow and easy is how I like it best"), contrasted with the lyrical praise of the *son* expressed in one of the stanzas:

> *El son es lo más sublime* There is nothing more sublime
> *Para el alma divertir*   than the *son*
> *Se debería de morir*   To gladden the soul.
> *Quien por bueno no lo estime.* Whoever does not appreciate it
>   Ought to die.

Suavecito was later covered by countless artists, among them Antonio Machín, whose rendition included stirring vocal improvisations.

14 Later replaced by Miguel Angel Portillo.

In 1930 the Septeto Nacional took on another first-rate vocalist, "Rapindey" (Marcelino Guerra). Three years later, they performed at the Chicago World's Fair, along with another Cuban group, La Clave Oriental, and *rumba* dancers who aroused the enthusiasm of the American public. There Piñeiro introduced his famous *son-pregón Échale salsita*:

Alfredo Valdés. SAR Records. At first a member of "Nano" (Romín) León's *cuarteto*, Valdés, with his wonderful gift for harmonizing, was considered one of the best second voices singing *sones*.

Salí de casa una noche aventurera
Buscando ambiente de placer y de ventura
¡Ay mi Dios, cuando gocé!
En un sopor la noche pasé.
Paseaba alegre nuestros lares luminosos
Y llegué al bacanal.
En Catalina me encontré con lo no pensado,
La voz de aquél que pregonaba así:
"Échale salsita, échale salsita."

I left home on an adventurous night,
Looking for an atmosphere of pleasure and joy.
O God, how much fun I had!
I spent the night in a state of stupor.
I was happily passing by our well-lit houses
And I arrived at the party.
In Catalina I suddenly heard
An unexpected voice which sang:
"Put a little sauce on it, put a little sauce on it."

Échale salsita impressed Gershwin, who had traveled to Cuba the previous year. Piñeiro had shown him his song, and Gershwin used its opening motif in his *Cuban Overture*:

Échale salsita – Ignacio Piñeiro

Upon its return from the United States, Nacional performed at the prestigious Miramar Yacht Club and appeared in the movies *La veguerita, El frutero,* and *Sucedió en La Habana.* Shortly thereafter, Piñeiro left the band. Lázaro Herrera took over its leadership, but between 1937 and 1954 Nacional gave no performances.

A small group from Santiago, the intense and rhythmical Trío Matamoros, vied with the best Havana ensembles. Founded by the singer and *tresista* Miguel Matamoros, it had a lasting influence throughout Latin America as well as in Africa, where it contributed to the birth of the Zairean and Congolese rumba.

Matamoros was an outstanding composer, and with their witty lyrics and catchy melodies, the songs of the trio: *Luz que no alumbra, Olvido, Él que siembra su maíz,* expressed the quintessence of Oriente. *Son de la loma,* in particular, became a worldwide hit, almost equaling the popularity of *Guantanamera.*

The tune occurred to Matamoros as sometime in 1922 he and his cousin Alfonso del Río were singing under the windows of a Santiago sanatorium: one of the windows opened and a woman and her daughter started listening to them. The girl then asked where the musicians came from and expressed her desire to meet them:

Mamá yo quiero saber	Mother I want to know
De dónde son los cantantes	Where these singers come from,
Que los encuentro muy galantes	For I find them very gallant
Y los quiero conocer,	And would like to meet them,
Con sus trovas fascinantes	With their fascinating songs
Que me las quiero aprender.	Which I want to learn.
Refrain:	*Refrain:*
¿De dónde serán?	Where are they from?
¿Serán de La Habana?	Maybe from Havana
¿Serán de Santiago? Tierra soberana.	Maybe from Santiago, noble land.
Son de la loma y cantan en el llano.	They come from the hill and sing in the plain,
Ya verás, tú veras.	You will see, you will see.

Son de la loma – Miguel Matamoros

The verb *son*, meaning "they are," also evokes the musical genre (the *son*) of this song, and according to Matamoros, the word *loma* (hill) refers to Santiago and *llano* (plain) to Havana.

Matamoros's copious output deals with the most diverse topics. Another of his songs, *Hojas para baño*, for instance, advising a woman to give her husband a bath with ritual plants in order to increase his sexual power, evokes *santería*; *Lágrimas negras*, a woman (in fact a neighbor of Matamoros abandoned by her husband) wishing happiness to the man who left her; and *El paralítico*, a Spanish doctor who, in Havana in the late 1920s, recommended totally ineffective treatments for paralysis, with the famous refrain exhorting: "*Suelta la muleta y el bastón/y podrás bailar el son*" ("Drop your crutch and your cane and you will be able to dance the *son*").

Born in the exuberant Santiago *barrio* of Los Hoyos, famous for its *comparsa*, Matamoros (1894–1971), while still a child, began to play harmonica for rich cigar- and rum-manufacturers. At seven he wrote his first song, the bolero *El consejo*. The following year, his parents gave him a guitar and he soon became known in local circles for his musical abilities. He also built his own *tres* which, since he was left-handed, he played backwards. His father died when Matamoros was still young and, in order to support himself, he held a variety of small jobs, among them house-painter and telephone repairman. He took a few *tres* lessons with Augusto Puente Guillot and his reputation grew. At fifteen, he was already gigging around town, and three years later he gave his first public recital, at the Heredia theater. He also formed a duo with a friend, Trino Martinelli, and around 1919 he teamed up with *bongocero* Juan Corona. Two years later he left for Havana but, disheartened by the racial incidents he experienced, he returned to Santiago.

Trío Matamoros. Tumbao Records

There, in 1924, he formed a duo with Rafael Cueto,[15] with whom he had performed at the Albizú theater in Havana. The following year, he recruited the fine baritone singer Siro Rodríguez – a blacksmith by trade – and founded the Trío Oriental. Cueto fired up the group with his propulsive guitar *tumbaos*, Rodríguez harmonized and played claves, and everyone contributed songs, Cueto *Pico y pala*, Rodríguez *Tu boca*, and the spirited *guaracha-son La China en la rumba*:

A una fiesta que yo fui	A party to which I went
escasearon las mujeres	Lacked women
y ahora verán Ustedes	And now you will see
como yo me resolví.	How I resolved this.
A la China mandé a buscar,	I had China come by,
A la reina de la rumba.	The queen of rumba.
A esta China sí le zumba	This China gets one all excited
Por su manera de bailar.	With the way she dances.
Y si viene la China	If China comes
Me pongo a bailar.	I will start dancing.
Si se va,	And if she leaves,
Yo también.	I'll leave too.
Oye el son como resuena	Hear how the *son* sounds
Camina, China, tú eres muy buena.	Go ahead, China, you are so great!
Pero mira, mira el son como resuena,	See, see how the *son* sounds,
Camina, China, tú eres buena.	Go ahead, China, you are so great!

In 1926, the trio left for Havana, where Eusebio Delfín encouraged them to stay in the capital. Matamoros took a job as a chauffeur, continuing all the while to write songs. Among them the bolero *La droga milagrosa* ("The miraculous drug"), and especially the *son montuno El que siembra su maíz*, inspired by a corn-peddler from Santiago who used to yell "*¡huye! ¡huye!*" ("run away! run away!") to advertise his *piñoles* (a sweet paste made with roasted and ground corn). "*El que siembra su maíz/Que se coma su piñol*" ("Let whoever sows his corn/Eat his piñol"), the refrain announces.

And then, with no apparent connection, the allusive verse admonishes:

Muchacha, dice tu abuela,	Hey girl, says your grandmother,
No te metas en la cocina	Don't go into the kitchen
Porque tiene gasolina	Because there is gasoline
No hay de jugar con candela.	And one mustn't play with fire.

Jumping from one subject to the other, the following stanza lambasts women's fickleness – another obsessional theme of Latin music – and introduces the archetype of the rooster:

15 A former baseball champion, apprentice to a tailor, mechanic, and customs officer, Cueto played guitar and cornet.

La mujer en el amor (sí señor)	In love the woman (yes sir)
Se parece a la gallina (como no)	Is like a hen (and how)
Que cuando se muere el gallo	When the rooster dies
(sí señor)	(yes sir)
A cualquier pollo se arrima (como no).	She grabs any old cock (and how).

With its "*sí señor*" and "*como no*" – a typically Cuban idiomatic formula coming like a leitmotiv at the end of each verse – this *montuno* section, with its antiphonal form, recalls the rhythm of the *changüí*.

In 1928 Matamoros signed a contract with the Victor label and the trio went to record in the United States (*Promesa, Lágrimas negras, Olvido, El que siembra su maíz*). There Matamoros was informed that a Trío Oriental already existed, led by guitarist Roberto de Moya, and he renamed his group Trío Matamoros. They then performed at Havana's Campoamor theater, whereupon Matamoros's boss wrote to him: "An artist of your quality deserves a better fate and it would be unfair of me to keep employing you as a chauffeur." Thus dismissed, Matamoros dedicated himself fully to music and wrote another hit, *La mujer de Antonio*. The trio toured to Mexico and then returned to Havana for a series of recording sessions, one of them with Antonio María Romeu. Their already busy schedule picked up in the 1930s with countless recordings, some with humorous titles (*Nudism in Cuba, The Cocaine Addict, Kill, God Forgives You, The Miracle Drug*), an appearance in the Paramount movie *Mosáicos Internacionales*, and performances in Santo Domingo, Puerto Rico, Europe (along with Orquesta Siboney), Panama, Venezuela, Colombia, and New York. For some sessions, "Pepe" (José) Macías or José Quintero (trumpets), Manuel Povedo or Agustín Gutiérrez (bongo), Paquito Portela or Cristóbal Mendive (bass), Manuel "Mozo" Borgellá (tres), Ramón Dorca (piano), and other musicians would be added to the trio.

In the early 1930s, female bands had become a new gimmick in the United States. The vogue also spread to Cuba, with Ensueño, created in 1931 by Guillermina Foyo; the Sexteto Casiguaya; Orbe, led by Esther Lines and then Carmita Franco; Conchita Fernández's Sexteto Caracusey; and, especially, Orquesta Anacaona, still active today.

Formed in Havana in 1931 by singer Elia Oreli, Anacaona consisted of the Castro sisters of Chinese descent: "Cuchito" (Concepción), the eldest (musical director, tenor saxophone, alto clarinet), "Bolito" (Olga, alto saxophone, clarinet, flute, maracas), Caridad (bass), Alicia (saxophone, clarinet, bass), Ondina (first trumpet), Xiomara (second trumpet), Ada (trumpet, violin, *tres*), the outstanding "Millito" (Argimira, drums, bongo, timbales), plus Elsa Rigual, sister of composer Pedro Rigual, Delia Valdés or Hortencia Palacio (piano), Anita Permuí de Valdés, wife of Alfredo Valdés (guitar), Xiomara Junco (violin), and possibly a woman named Rita (bass).

The Anacaona Orchestra. Óscar López Collection

Their friends Ignacio Piñeiro and Lázaro Herrera gave them useful advice and the band made their debut in 1932 at the Dora Café, on the elegant Prado Avenue, astounding audiences with their professionalism. In 1933 Oreli was replaced by Machito's sister, the winsome Graciela Pérez, then seventeen years old.

First specialized in the *son*, Anacaona progressively opened up to jazz and the Castro sisters also performed and recorded as an independent *septeto* (*Después que sufres, Amor inviolado*). In 1936 the orchestra toured Latin America. Two years later, under flautist Alberto Socarrás's musical direction, they played at the Havana Madrid, in New York, on the same bill as Enrique Madriguera, Nilo Menéndez, and Marcelino Valdés, to an appreciative audience of musicians, and then in Paris: at the Moulin Rouge, at Les Ambassadeurs, and Chez Florence, alternating there with Django Reinhardt. "We used to lock ourselves up in our room to smoke and do all kinds of silly things," Graciela remembered. The band became the toast of the town but at the onset of the Second World War were forced to return to Cuba, and Graciela went on to join Machito's orchestra in New York.

In the late 1930s, *son* bands acquired two new instruments: the conga – heretofore regarded as a mere carnival drum – and the piano, introduced by Estrellas Cubanas, La Sonora Matancera, and singer Fernando Collazo's Septeto Cuba. Towards the end of the following decade, Arsenio Rodríguez used a conga, a piano, and three trumpets in his ensemble, setting a pattern for bands which then became known as *conjuntos*. *Conjuntos*, along with *charangas*, are still the most common types of groupings in salsa.

Countless other *son* outfits competed in Cuba's restless music scene. Among them the aforementioned Septeto Cuba, founded in 1930 and consisting of Enrique García (first voice, claves), Óscar Pelegrín (*tres*), José Interián (trumpet), Alfredo Rivero (bass), Heredio López (second voice, maracas), and Marino González (bongo) (pianist Armando Valdés later joined the band); the *septeto* Jóvenes del Cayo, founded in 1924 by singers Domingo Vargas and Miguelito Valdés; the Grupo Típico Oriental; *tresista* Isaac Oviedo's Septeto Matancero, which included Graciano Gómez (guitar and flute), Julio Govín, Barbarito Diez, Hermano Bien (bongo), and Óscar "Florecita"Velazco (trumpet); the Sexteto Gloria Cubana (with pianist María Teresa Ovando); the Quinteto Típico, co-led by Oviedo and the ubiquitous Graciano Gómez; the Sexteto Liborio; Óscar Sotolongo's Septeto Típico Cubano; Botón de Rosa; Terry 1927; Gloria Matancera, founded in 1929 by singer Juan Manuel Díaz ; *bolerista* Mario Ruiz's Conjunto Kubanacán; Abelardo Barroso's Sexteto Agabamar, formed with musicians who also played with the Septeto Nacional (Alfredo Valdés, Eliseo Silveira, Manolo Reynoso, Sungo and Nené Enrizo, Agustín Gutiérrez, Machito, and later Cheo Marquetti on vocals and bass); the Sexteto Munamar, founded by stevedores from the harbor of Regla; the Sexteto Universo, also set up by Barroso; guitarist Raul Díaz's Conjunto Apollo; Estrellas Habaneras; Ignacio Carrillo's Sexteto Típico; the Sexteto Unión de Redención (originally called Líderes de Redención); Rafael Ortiz's Sexteto Cienfuegos, in which Marcelino Guerra sang; the Sexteto Facenda; the group led by the Enrizo brothers; and, in Cienfuegos, Los Naranjos, founded in 1926 and initially consisting of timbales, two *marímbulas*, two *tres*, jawbone, claves, güiro, and vocals. It added a bongo the following year, removed other instruments, and in 1930 introduced a trumpet and swapped its *marímbula* for a bass.

The rise of charangas, *the bolero, and the* guajira

The *charangas*

In the early 1920s, *típicas* had been Cuba's favorite type of band. Flautist "Tata" Alfonso, who injected elements of *rumba brava* into his *danzones*, led one of the best ones, and several of his musicians – pianist Jesús López, güiro player Abelardo Valdés and *timbalero* Ulpiano Díaz – later rose to fame. Cornettists Pablo Valenzuela, Pablo Zerquera, and Domingo Corbacho, flautist "Tata" (Juan Francisco) Pereira, saxophonist Aniceto Díaz, ophicleide virtuoso Félix González (with Aniceto Díaz on güiro), and clarinettists José Belén Puig and José Urfé were, however, serious rivals. Tata Pereira followed a rather unusual musical path: he started out playing music in the Saint Theresa convent, in Matanzas, and later set up the marching band of the Havana police! In 1920 a *típica*,

Orquesta Alemán, performed in Tampa, Florida, which had a sizeable community of Cuban tobacco workers.

In 1924, the pianist and composer Moisés Simons (previously called Simón) organized a *danzón* concert at the Payret theater in Havana, but *típicas* fizzled out shortly thereafter. Their cumbersome brass instruments were too loud for small clubs, and they were superseded by the smaller and more flexible *charangas* "*a la francesa*" – so called because both the *danzón* they played and the flute they used were of French origin. The instrumentation consisted of piano – introduced into *charangas* by Antonio Torroella – wooden flute with keys, violins, bass, timbales, and güiro (eventually replaced by maracas). The trilling French flute sounded wonderful, but it had to soar high above the percussion, greatly taxing the flautists' stamina, and later, it was often supplanted by the metallic flute, more versatile and physically easier to play.

As early as 1911, the pianist Antonio María Romeu (1876–1955) had formed one of the very first *charangas*. Known as "*El mago de las teclas*" ("The wizard of the keyboard"), he had begun his career as a teenager and in 1899 joined Leopoldo Cervantes's *típica*, which already resembled a *charanga* with its violin, flute, bass, timbales, and güiro line-up. It would become a true *charanga* a few years later, with the acquisition of a piano. Romeu took on two of Cervantes's best musicians: the marvelous bassist Rafael Calazán and *timbalero* Remigio Valdés. In addition, Romeu played on the radio – alone or accompanied by simply a güiro – and at the famed La Diana café, a favorite hangout for musicians, where his brother Horacio, also a pianist, held sway. Romeu wrote countless *danzones*: *Ojos triunfadores* – said to have influenced Darius Milhaud in his *Saudades do Brasil* – *Huyéndole a un ratón*, *Jibacoa*, *Que linda eres tú*, the delightful *Flauta mágica* (in collaboration with Alfredo Brito), inspired by flautist "Panchito" (Francisco) Delabart, in which Brito played brillant solos, and *Marcheta*.

In 1926 Romeu gave the first performance of his *danzón Tres lindas cubanas* at the Sociedad Unión Fraternal. Shortly thereafter, Romeu recorded it with a long piano solo. This historic solo was left practically unchanged by other bands on subsequent recordings of it. Popularized by the Sexteto Habanero, *Tres lindas Cubanas* became a classic. In 1928 Romeu obtained a gold medal at the Sevilla Fair for his compositions and the following year he recorded various numbers with Miguel Matamoros (among them *Quince* and *Bolichán*), in one of the tresista's rare sessions with *charanga* musicians. And in 1931 he produced the humorous *Los chamacos*, subtitled *Fumando marihuana* ("Smoking Marihuana").

The flautist "El Moro" (Miguel Vázquez) was another imaginative improviser, and he too brought in the habit of soloing at length, backed by the rhythm section, on the coda of *danzones*, inspiring other flautists to do likewise. *Típicas* and *charangas* were purely instrumental ensembles until Romeu hired the singer Fernando Collazo for his *charanga*. A cigar-roller by trade, the handsome Collazo appeared in the 1932 "Maracas y bongó" – Cuba's first talkie – with his Sexteto Cuba, wooing women with his dark eyes and winsome smile. In 1935 he also

Fernando Collazo.
Óscar López Collection

recorded in New York with Armando Valdespí. Collazo greatly contributed to Romeu's fame, but on October 16, 1939, at the age of thirty-seven, Collazo committed suicide in Havana, in mysterious circumstances, his early death driving his female admirers to distraction.

Shortly before Collazo's death, the young "Barbarito" (Idilio Bárbaro) Diez had replaced him in the Sexteto Matancero, with which Collazo had also sung, and was recruited by Romeu (and then Filiberto Hernández) to handle the vocals. Following in Collazo's foosteps was daunting enough, but Diez easily rose to the task, and his clear diction and thorough elegance soon attracted notice.

When Diez (born in 1909 in Bolondrón, near Matanzas) was four, his father took up a job at a sugar mill, the Central Manatí. While in his teens, Diez started performing locally with a guitarist, but his father placed him as an apprentice to a tailor and then in a garage. However, desperately wanting to make music, Diez escaped to Havana. There, at the cafés Los Recuerdos and Vista Alegre, frequented by *trovadores*, he met Romeu, Sindo Garay, Graciano Gómez, and Isaac Oviedo. Author of the bolero *En falso* and of the beautiful *Lección de piano*, which Diez would later record, Gómez formed a *cuarteto* in 1912, followed by the Conjunto Matancero, and then, with Oviedo, the Quinteto Típico. Gómez persuaded Diez to complete his *quinteto* (which was in fact a *cuarteto*), and, diminutives being in fashion at the time, he renamed Diez "Barbarito."[16]

16 The friendship between Diez, Oviedo, and Gómez would last many years: they later performed as a trio (which audiences dubbed Los Gracianos); in the 1940s, along with singer Rolando Scott, they joined the *cuarteto* Selecto.

Diez was an excellent *trovador*, but it is mostly his sensitive and graceful *danzones* and his boleros, sung with Romeu or under his own name (*La rosa roja, Idilio, Ojos malvados*), which touched audiences. Like many other bandleaders, Romeu noticed that vocalists stole the show, and he ended up keeping them for his radio engagements.

In 1934, the pianist "Cheo" (José) Belén Puig, whose father, clarinettist José Belén Puig, had run a major *típica*, founded another excellent *charanga*. He surrounded himself with flautist "El Cojo" (José Antonio Díaz), bassist Julio Safora, and vocalist Pablo Quevedo, who would be for him what Fernando Collazo had been for Romeu. Born in Matanzas in 1907, Quevedo had worked as a baker and, like Collazo, as a cigar-maker. In 1928 he had formed a duo in Havana with Panchito Carbó, and then sang with the *típica* Los Caciques and on the radio. Like Collazo, Quevedo had enormous success with women, and like him, he met with an untimely end, dying three years before him, at the age of twenty-nine. He was then followed in Puig's band by a stream of top-notch singers: Alberto Aroche, Alfredo Valdés, Vicentico Valdés, Óscar Valdés, and Paulina Alvarez. Puig later hired pianist Odilio Urfé and then, giving up his band, he joined Joseíto Valdés's *típica*.

Founded in 1930 by the pianist Armando Valdés Torres, the buoyant Orquesta Gris also achieved an appreciable measure of fame. Valdés Torres had honed his skills with Calixto Allende's band, the Septeto Cuba, and bassist Estanislao Serviá's Orquesta Habana. He, in turn, recruited Collazo, as well as three outstanding musicians: flautist Antonio Arcaño, güiro-player Óscar Pelegrín, and *timbalero* Rafael Blanco. In 1936, Arcaño left Valdés Torres to form his famed Maravillas, taking Pelegrín with him, and "El Rubio" (Aurelio Herrera) replaced Arcaño.

The fine band led by flautist Belisario López recorded prolifically and performed in the United States. It made its debut in 1928 in Havana at the *academia de baile* Rialto, on the same bill as the Sexteto Occidente, and it included at different times flautist Alfredo Brito, violinist Feliciano Facenda, güiro-player José de la Merced, pianists Raúl Valdespí and Facundo Rivero, and singers Rigoberto Díaz and Joseíto Nuñez.

Other *charangas* also rose to prominence: the one led by Rafael Morales; Orquesta Ideal, founded in 1936 by flautist Joseíto Valdés; the Charanga Típica, with its virtuoso *maraquero* "Palito"; pianist "Neno" (Luis) González's Orquesta Típica Cubana;[17] and the groups directed by pianists Ernesto Muñoz, Odilio Urfé, Obdulio Morales, Frank Emilio, Calixto Allende,[18] Tomás Cormán, Ricardo Reverón, Silvio Contreras, Enrodo Silva, Pedro López, Estanislao Serviá; violinist Virgilio Diago; and flautists Pastor Gómez (with his great pianist "Pepito" Piedra), Juan Pablo Miranda, Aurelio Herrera, "El Cojo," and Luis Carrillo.

Several *charangas* were also run by women: Edén Habanero, and those of Irene Herrera Laferté, "Paulina" (Raimunda de Paula Peña) Álvarez, and María Cervantes. Álvarez (1912–1965) had joined in 1931, as vocalist, the flautist Edelmiro Pérez's Orquesta Elegante, in which Obdulio Morales played piano. In 1934 she

17 It has included at different times flautists "El Cojo" and Belisario López, and singers Alberto Aroche, Paulina Álvarez, and Orlando Contreras.

18 He later settled in Brazil, where he created a society band.

also worked with Neno González, forming her own band seven years later. Known as "the *danzonete*[19] empress," she sang with great feeling, accompanying herself with *claves*, and she was an early influence on Celia Cruz. She wrote several songs, among them *No vale la pena*, *Flores negras*, and *Alma de mujer*. Cervantes (born in Havana in 1885), author of *Lejos de tí*, *Los lunares*, and other pieces, was the daughter of composer Ignacio Cervantes. She played highly romantic music and sang with a clear soprano voice (*Tus manos blancos*).

In the 1920s and 1930s *danzones* such as Pablo Zerquera's *Habana Park*, Juan Pablo O'Farrill's *Virgen de Regla*, Antonio Sánchez's syncopated *Bella Unión*, Armando Romeu's *Cuba mía*, or Silvio Contreras's *Masacre* also won over Cuba.

The *danzonete*

By the late 1920s, the increasing success of the *son* affected *charangas*. In 1929, trying to find a compromise between the *danzón*, and the *son*, Aniceto Díaz, a *charanga* musician from Matanzas, invented a hybrid which he called the "*danzonete*." The composer of popular *danzones*, among them *La pulga* (1910), *La princesa del dollar* (1911), *La niña de los besos* (1912), and *El teléfono de larga distancia* (1919), Díaz (1887–1964) had started out by working as a tailor. After studying bass tuba with his uncle Justo Cuellar (a member of Matanzas's brass band) and ophicleide with Eduardo Betancourt, who played with Miguel Faílde's *típica*, he replaced Betancourt in this band in 1902. He then took up flute, saxophone, and piano, joined Ramoncito Prendes's *charanga*, and, in 1914, formed his own ensemble, in which he played flute and his son, Aniceto Jr., the güiro.[20] Díaz recounted the birth of the *danzonete*: "One day, in a social club in Alacranes, near Matanzas, the crowd acclaimed a *sexteto* featured on the same bill and ignored my band. Noticing that the *son* had overshadowed the *danzón*, I decided to combine both of them."

He then wrote and dedicated to composer Gonzalo Roig the *danzonete Rompiendo la rutina*, which included a sung part, and added a trumpet to jazz up his band. During a rehearsal, one of the musicians invited Díaz's sister to dance, creating steps which anticipated those of the mambo. Sung by Arturo Aguilo, *Rompiendo la rutina* premiered on June 8, 1929 at Matanzas's elegant Sociedad Casino Español. This *danzonete* had a 2/4 time signature and consisted of four parts: an introduction, a lyrical *trío* based on a *danzón* rhythm, an engaging refrain based on a *son* rhythm (*estribillo*), and a short coda.

19 See below.

Trío:	Trío:
Allá en Matanzas se ha creado	There in Matanzas
Un nuevo baile de salón	A new ballroom dance has been created
Con un compás bien marcado	With a well-marked rhythm
Y una nueva armonización.	And a new harmonization.
Para las fiestas del gran mundo	For the parties of the high society
De la elegancia y distinción,	Of elegance and distinction

Será el bailable preferido	It will be the favorite dance
Por su dulce inspiración.	For its sweet inspiration.
Refrain:	Refrain:
Danzonete	*Danzonete*
Prueba y vete	Try it and come
Yo quiero bailar contigo	I want to dance with you
Al paso del danzonete.	To the rhythm of the *danzonete*.

Rompiendo la rutina became an instant hit. Díaz subsequently recorded it and continued to write *danzonetes*: *Son igual que el cocodrilo, Delia, Engreída y majadera, Pidiendo de nuevo, Zona franca*. Eliseo Grenet with *Hatuey* (recorded in New York by Oscar Calvet) and other musicians also turned to writing *danzonetes* – with often bawdy lyrics. Bandleader "Calabaza" (Gerardo Pérez), with his singer "Machito" (Francisco Pérez), introduced this genre in Havana, at the *academia de baile* Sport Antillano. Many musicians (and practically all the singers, among them Celia Cruz but most notably Paulina Álvarez) adopted the *danzonete*, whose vogue lasted until the late 1930s; in 1931, Abelardo Barroso even hosted a radio program devoted exclusively to this musical genre. The *sonsonete* – a kind of extended *son*, invented as an answer to the *danzonete* – never really caught on.

20 It also included Domingo Becerra on timbales, José Claro Fumero on trombone, Enrique Mira and Juan de Armas on violin, René Oliva on trumpet, and Pedro Díaz on bass.

Rompiendo la rutina – Aniceto Díaz

The bolero

The highly poetical bolero, with its beautiful harmonies and melodies, also inspired many composers of the popular repertoire, among them María Cervantes, Miguel Compañoni, Ñico Saquito, Rosendo Ruiz, Manuel Corona, Alberto Villalón, and Sindo Garay.

A cousin of Miguel Matamoros, "Sindo" Garay (Antonio Gumersindo Garay y García), who lived to the age of 101, was a revered figure of the *trova*. Born in Santiago in 1867, he grew up in the intense musical atmosphere of the town. His father played drums with the municipal brass band, and the young Sindo took a few guitar lessons with Pepe Sánchez, although he was chiefly self-taught. He wrote *Voy a partir, ingrata,* and the bolero *Quiéreme, trigueña,* inspired by his music teacher, with whom he was in love, and supported himself by working as a harness-maker and a circus acrobat while singing in a duo with Emiliano Blez. In 1906 he moved to Havana, organizing memorable musical evenings with fellow *trovadores* in his small apartment, and then to Puerto Plata, Santo Domingo, where he married and had five sons, all given Amerindian names. In 1928 he performed with his son Guarionex, Rita Montaner, Paco Lara, and a *timbalero* by the name of Rafael, first in Paris and then in Mexico.

Garay created subtle and haunting melodies with impressionistic overtones. Among them *Germania,* inspired by Wagner's music, the diaphanous *Perla marina, El huracán y la palma,* and *Mujer bayamesa,* better known as *La bayamesa,* evoking the war of independence against Spain.

La tarde – Sindo Garay

Another of his songs decried the 1898 U.S. invasion of Guantánamo. And in yet another patriotic outburst, he paid tribute to poet José Martí (*Martí*), and evoked the slaughter of the Indians by the Spaniards:

> *Así murieron los indios por su adoración*
> *Jamás supieron los traidores su maldad.*

> Thus the Indians died for their faith.
> The traitors never knew of their wickedness.

He continued to perform until late in life, and at his funeral, in the Oriente town of Bayamo, all the *trovadores* who attended the ceremony sang *La bayamesa* to honor him.

After studying the guitar with his sister América and with Pepe Sánchez in his native Santiago, Alberto Villalón Morales (1882–1995) composed in 1906 the music for the revue *El triunfo del bolero*. The following year he moved to Havana, where, along with Sindo Garay, he was instrumental in popularizing the bolero. He recorded for the Edison label and, in 1923, performed on the radio. He wrote *Perfidia*, *La ninfa*, the macabre *Boda negra*, inspired by verses by the Colombian poet Julio Flórez about a man unearthing his deceased beloved from her tomb and finally lying in bed next to her (*y para siempre se quedó dormido, al esqueleto rígido abrazado* – "and forever he lay asleep, holding the rigid skeleton in his arms"), and humorous *sones-rumbas* (*El diablo es mi mujer* – "The devil is my wife," *La neurasténica*).

Beginning in the 1930s, Mexican *boleristas* Los Hermanos Martínez Gil and the melodramatic Trío Tarácuri captivated Cuba. But it was increasingly soloists who came to the fore, and the legendary Agustín Lara (1901–1970) had the greatest impact, when he performed there. Self-taught ("I was born with a soul to create music and with the ability to express it, although nobody taught me how to do it," he boldly proclaimed), he had listened, during his formative years, to Sindo Garay, Septeto Habanero, and started out playing piano in Mexico's speakeasies. A jealous mistress slashed his face, and his moving boleros reflected his sentimental woes. Along with Armando Manzanero, José Sabre Marroquín, and other compatriots, he also influenced the *filin* movement. Vicentico Valdés, Panchito Riset, Roberto Ledesma, and Olga Guillot later disseminated the Cuban bolero outside the island, and Mexico continued to cultivate this romantic genre with unabashed emotionalism.

The *guajira*

Like *tonadas* and other rural Cuban forms, the *guajira*, related to the *son montuno*, is traditionally sung with a guitar or other stringed instrument and, like the *son*, it often extols the beauty of nature or deals with rural life. With its medium tempo and simple harmonies, it quickly spread throughout Cuba and then abroad via records and the radio, and often became part of the repertoire of trios such as the Trío Godínez, the Trío Azul, the Trío Toronto, and later Los Guaracheros de Oriente.

The quintessential *guajira*, emblematic of Cuba, is undoubtedly *Guajira guantanamera* ("The country girl from Guantánamo"), written by Joseíto Fernández in 1928, after a melody by the Guantánamo *tresista* "El Diablo" Wilson. Some have claimed it derives from a Spanish folk tune. Others have compared its beginning to the old Spanish *Romance de Gerineldo*. But whatever the exact origin of the tune, Fernández was the one who gave it shape and popularized it. He also wrote boleros, the *guaracha Elige tú que canto yo* – Benny Moré's battle cry – and the *guaguancó De tumbao*.

A simple and charming man, who first worked as a shoemaker, Fernández (1908–1979), far from being a *guajiro*, was a dyed-in-the wool Habanero, born in the district of Los Sitios. In the 1920s he sang in the capital with Juventud Habanera, Los Dioses del Amor, and Amate y Jiguani. In the 1930s, he performed on the radio with Raimundo Pía y Rivero's group, and then founded a *danzón* band. He improvised lyrics on *Guantanamera*, which he recorded in 1941 as *Mi biografía*. The number – for which Pepecito Reyes, then Fernández's pianist, wrote the introduction and the coda – was used as a theme song for a Radio CMQ show. Fernández used it as a vehicle to recount daily events, varying the lyrics each time he performed it, and it caught the listeners' attention. Alfredo Valdés later covered it in New York. Several different sets of lyrics were adapted to this melody (including risqué ones later recorded by Graciela Pérez in New York). But the real success story of the tune began in the 1950s, when composer Julián Orbón set José Martí's *Versos Sencillos* to it:

Yo soy un hombre sincero	I am a sincere man
De donde crece la palma.	From the land where palm trees grow.
Y antes de morir quiero	And before I die I want to
Echar mis versos del alma.	Express the verses from my soul.
Refrain:	*Refrain*:
Guantanamera	Guantanamera,
Guajira guantanamera	Country girl from Guantánamo.
Guantanamera	Guantanamera,
Guajira guantanamera.	Country girl from Guantánamo.

In the United States, it then came to the ears of the Sandpipers and then of Pete Seeger, who performed it in 1963 at Carnegie Hall as an anti-Vietnam war anthem and, two years later, recorded it, turning it into a worldwide hit.

Three great singers also put the *guajira* on the map: Cheo Marquetti, Guillermo Portabales, and later Celina González. Leader of the Sexteto Hatuey and of Los Salseros, "Cheo" (José) Marquetti (1909–1967) also sang with the Orquesta Cuba, the Septeto Nacional, Cheo Belén Puig, Ernesto Muñoz, and the *sextetos* Facenda and Habanero, and he often vied with Abelardo Barroso.

Guajira Guantanamera –
Joseíto Fernández

Joseíto Fernández

"He was one of the best improvisers of Cuba. He sang the *son* wonderfully and was unrivaled for the *guaguancó*,"Mongo Santamaría once told me.[21] Marquetti created a livelier type of *guajira*, called *guajira-son*, while Guillermo Portabales popularized a rather sophisticated type of guajira known as *guajira de salón*.

A guitarist and singer with a clear and vibrant voice, Guillermo "Portabales" (Quesada del Castillo) was born in 1911 in Rodas, in the former province of Las Villas, and he grew up in Cienfuegos. His mother died when he was six years old, and when he was eleven he started work as an apprentice in a printing shop. In 1928 he began to sing on the radio, with a wide repertoire, but with his listeners requesting mostly *guajiras*, he thereafter specialized in that genre in order to please them. In 1936 he performed in Puerto Rico, achieving success with Ñico Saquito's *Adiós compay gallo*. He then toured Latin America, going back to Cuba in 1940 and also giving concerts in the United States. In 1953 he settled in Puerto Rico and recorded prolifically, in particular, in 1956, with Noro Morales. He died in 1970, at the age of fifty-nine, run over by a car. His major hit, *El carretero*, a song about a cart driver that imitated the rhythm of a horse walking on a country road, achieved worldwide popularity.

The beginnings of jazz

On January 30, 1917, a white group from New Orleans, the Original Dixieland Jazz Band, whose style emulated the city's black and creole bands, cut one of the first jazz recordings, at the Columbia studios in New York.

In the late nineteenth century, the Crescent City – a true Caribbean metropolis with its tropical climate, variegated population, and Creole heritage – throbbed with Latin rhythms, brought there by immigrants from various countries including, as the Cuban musicologist Leonardo Acosta pointed out, black Cubans who moved there after the abolition of slavery.[22]

At the dawn of the twentieth century, a sizeable number of Hispanic musicians worked in the town's clubs and speakeasies. Under their influence Latin syncopations crept into works such as Jesse "Old Man" Picket's *The Dream* (1870), Neil Moret's *Cubanola*, Robert Hampton's *Agitation Rag*, Artie Matthews's *Pastime Rag No. 5*, or rags by Scott Joplin or Louis Chauvin, while *Tiger Rag* carried echoes from the 1880s Mexican hit *Sobre las olas* (Over the waves). William Christopher Handy, self-proclaimed "inventor of the blues," had traveled to Cuba in 1910 with the U.S. Army, when *típicas* were in full swing. He brought a few Latin rhythms back to Louisiana and incorporated a *habanera* in his *St. Louis Blues*, written four years later.

Latin elements also found their way into the music of Jelly Roll Morton (*Mamanita* and *La Paloma* among them), "Professor Longhair" (Henry Byrd),[23] and other African-American musicians. Morton used to speak about the "Spanish" or "Latin tinge" in jazz and he once told Alan Lomax, "In fact if you

21 Here and throughout this book, such references to personal communications will not be footnoted.

22 In: *El jazz cubano: una historia de casi un siglo*, p. 4.

23 Among other Latin tunes, Professor Longhair drew inspiration from *Son de la loma*.

can't manage to put tinges of Spanish in your tunes, you will never be able to get the right seasoning, I call it, for jazz." The Argentinian tango also absorbed *cinquillos* through Cuban sailors who brought the habanera to the Rio de la Plata. (Tango orchestras that included a piano, a double bass, and violins would come to be called *típicas*, like the Cuban *danzón* groups with similar instrumentation.) Cuban music and jazz, sharing African and European roots, were indeed destined to meet, and their union still endures.

Acosta also notes that black soldiers from the U.S. Army that intervened in Cuba in the independence war against Spain had, at the outset of the twentieth century, sown the seeds of what would become jazz.[24] Jazz itself, which would become a symbol of the roaring twenties and of a resolutely modernist aesthetics, reached Cuba during the First World War. Such American clubs as the Inferno, the Black Cat, and the Jockey Club (which featured, among its acts, a band led by the American Ted Naddy) opened in Havana and contributed to the dissemination of American music on the island. Acosta mentions that as early as about 1910, jam-sessions took place frequented by the guitar- and banjo-player Hugo Siam (who would later become Don Azpiazu's bassist), the *tres*- and trombone-player Pucho Jiménez, the bassist José Dolores Betancourt, the drummer César Arjona, and the pianist "El Americano" (Bienvenido Hernández Delgado); there were also the proto-jazz-bands of pianist Pedro Stacholy (1914), of violinists Max Dolin and Jimmy Holmes, and one led by Froilán Maya (later founder of Los Diplomáticos de Maya), as well as the quartet comprised of Hernández Delgado, Lolo Betancourt (trombone), Pucho Jiménez (tuba), and Hugo García (bass and guitar.)[25]

The trumpet and the cornet, key instruments of New Orleans jazz – would play a major role in *son* bands. Around 1909, W. C. Handy had introduced a saxophone into his dance band. This instrument, invented in 1840 by the Belgian Adolphe Sax, was still rather rare in popular music, although Mexican musicians had been playing it for several years in Louisiana. In 1912, Antonio María Romeu added a tenor saxophone to his *típica*. Following suit, Germán Lebatard, who worked at the Almendares hotel in Havana, Luis López Viana, who played at the Sevilla hotel, and Antonio María Romeu's nephew Armando also acquired this new instrument (Romeu bought his from a musician in Ted Naddy's group). And in 1924, "Don" (Justo Ángel) Azpiazu recruited the saxophonists Alfredo and Julio Brito into his Havana Casino Orchestra.[26]

In 1922 the flautist, clarinettist, pianist, violinist, bassist, and composer Jaime Prats organized his Cuban Jazz Band, and three years later, the *tresista* "Caney" (Fernando Storch) formed his Krazy Cats, comprising three saxophones, a trumpet, a piano, a bass, and a banjo, although they offered fox-trots, waltzes, and Cuban tunes rather than real jazz. Only in the next decade would the saxophone really take hold in Cuba.

The island also welcomed the trap drum, and Alberto Jiménez Rebollar became one of Cuba's first fully-fledged jazz drummers. In the 1970s this

24 Acosta, *op. cit.*

25 *Op. cit.* and personal communication.

26 Also a guitarist, vibist, and then drummer, Julio Brito composed film scores and various songs, among them the boleros *Mira que eres linda* and *Ilusión china*.

instrument, widespread in the big bands of the 1940s and 1950s, would also find its way into *conjuntos* and *charangas*, at first shocking some conservative souls, who considered its intrusion iconoclastic. Aniceto Díaz used a banjo for American tunes, but soon losing its exotic appeal, this rather tart-sounding instrument was supplanted by the warmer-sounding guitar. *Son* groups, however, continued to prefer the more pungent and idiomatic *tres*, closely linked to the music's origins.

As Havana became a tourist Mecca, show bands proliferated. One of the earliest ones had been Arturo Guerra's, founded in 1920. Pianist and bandleader Moisés Simón entertained rich patrons at the Havana Casino (later known as the Casino Nacional), the Jockey Club, the Plaza hotels, and other night spots. Born in Havana in 1889, Simón studied classical music with his father and other teachers. After working as an organist and choirmaster in several churches, he turned to popular music, composing *Marta, Palmira, Colibrí*, and, especially, the famed *Chivo que rompe tambó* and *El manisero*. After directing the orchestra of the Martí theater, he led his own band for nine years, playing at the Havana Casino, and at the Jockey Club. With his revue "Cubanola," he traveled to Paris in the early 1930s. During the Second World War he changed his name from Simón to Simons. He also spent two years in a concentration camp, and he died in Madrid in 1945.

The classically trained flautist Alberto Socarrás, who had worked with Simons, ran a band which alternated at the posh Montmartre Club with Eliseo Grenet's ensemble. Socarrás would later sow the seeds of Latin jazz in New York. "With our arrangements peppered with jazz riffs and classical touches, we sometimes overshadowed Grenet, although he was far more famous than us," he remembered. Born in 1908 in Manzanillo, a town in Oriente known for its organ-grinders and celebrated in a humorous *son* proclaiming: "*En Manzanillo se baila el son, en calzoncillo y en camisón*" ("In Manzanillo one dances the *son*, wearing underpants and a nightshirt"),[27] Socarrás had started out by playing with the family band led by his mother Dolores Eustacia, a renowned guitarist and composer, and in Arquímedes Pous's "Género Bufo" variety show, before joining the Havana Philharmonic Orchestra.

Don Azpiazu played at the Seville hotel, at the Havana Casino and other swank venues where, with his vocalists Miguelito García, Óscar López, and Antonio Machín, he succeeded in imposing a Cuban repertoire (*El manisero, La Bayamesa*).

During the 1920s, various amusement parks – the Havana Park, the Palisades Park, located in front of the Maceo Park, the Luna Park – hired American-type ensembles, among them the Orquesta Hermanos Avilés. A former *típica* founded in 1882 in Holguín (in the center of the island) by Miguel Avilés Lozano and fourteen of his children, the group – Cuba's oldest still extant – switched to a big-band format with the advent of jazz.

In 1926, Teddy Henríquez formed a jazz quartet. In the late 1920s, Pedro Carbó combined jazz and Cuban rhythms in his ensemble, and Armando Romeu, Mario

27 After the Revolution, this last verse was bowdlerized and changed into the prudish and bland "*en camiseta* y en pantalón" ("with a short-sleeved shirt and trousers").

Bauzá, trumpeter René Oliva, pianists Célido Curbelo and Rod Rodríguez, and others like them fell in love with the swing and stimulating harmonies of jazz.

Big bands copied the ground-breaking formula created by Don Redman for Fletcher Henderson, with the reeds playing legato lines and the brass staccato ones, but they performed a predominantly Cuban repertoire. Among them were Los Diplómaticos de Pego, and various sibling outfits such as Los Hermanos Curbelo, Los Hermanos Lebatard (with brothers Germán, Gonzalo, Luis, and Julio), Los Hermanos Morales, Los Hermanos Castro, and Los Hermanos Palau. Started by saxophonist Manuel Castro and his brothers Antonio (trombone), Andrés (trumpet), and Juan (piano), Los Hermanos Castro performed in Latin America and in New York and played on the sound-track of the Warner Brothers film *Havana Cocktail*. They also backed Olga Guillot, and continued working until the 1960s. First called Los Califates, Los Hermanos Palau, founded in 1920 by the brothers Manolo (piano, leader), Rafael (bass), and Felipe and Luis (trumpets), included at various times trumpeter Julio Cueva, Eliseo Grenet (on piano), and singers Rita Montaner and "Cascarita" (Orlando Guerra).

In the 1930s, under the sway of American music, combos utilizing drums rather than timbales almost threatened *son* bands. Duke Ellington startled the world with his expressionist jungle style,[28] replete with dissonances, noises, and animal cries, rendered by mutes, plungers, and wa-was. Echoes of this jungle style would later crop up in Mario Bauzá's *Tanga*. Two new groups marked by jazz also surfaced in 1933: that of saxophonist and flautist Armando Romeu, and the more commercially oriented Lecuona Cuban Boys.

In the early 1930s, Ernesto Lecuona had recruited musicians from the Hermanos Lebatard to assemble a show band. In 1933, stricken by pneumonia

28 So called because at the Cotton Club the orchestra performed in front of a jungle backdrop.

Lecuona Cuban Boys. Harlequin Records

while performing in Madrid, he was forced to return to Cuba. The talented Cuban pianist and composer Armando Oréfiche, then only 22 years old, also happened to be in Spain. Author of the beautiful *Bolero árabe*, of *Cubana soy*, of the afro *Mesié Julián*, immortalized by Bola de Nieve, and of many other pieces, he would greatly contribute to the dissemination of Cuban music abroad. He took over the band, which would soon be comprised of trumpets, trombones, saxophones, a clarinet, a flute, a guitar, a piano, a bass, timbales, claves, maracas, a bongo, and three vocalists: Fernando Torres, the Italian Alberto Rabagliati-Vinata, and the dapper Agustín Bruguera, winner in 1927 of the Hollywood contest to select the "successor to Rudolph Valentino." Despite slightly stiff-sounding pieces (*Panamá, Tabú, Puchunguita*), the Lecuona Cuban Boys were a hit in Europe, and paved the way for other Latin ensembles. They even blazed new trails in Egypt with their original arrangements. In 1939, however, as the Second World War loomed, Oréfiche headed back to Cuba. The band would later criss-cross Latin America, go to Europe again, and then North Africa. In 1945, Oréfiche renamed the band the Habana Cuban Boys.

Jazz also spread to the various regions of Cuba: the Jazz Band of Cienfuegos, the combo led in Caibarién by Alejandro García Caturla, and the one run in Sagua la Grande by Pedro Stacholy achieved a certain celebrity, and several arrangers, among them Roberto Sánchez Ferrer and Rafael Somavilla, devoted themselves wholeheartedly to this new genre.

the United States and Puerto Rico

Now we are here to let you know
The Puerto Ricans have landed
Live on the scene, If you know what I mean
As we get busy with our Spanglish routine.

Latin Empire (Nuyorican rap group)

On March 2, 1917, with the Jones-Shafroth Act, the U.S. Congress granted Puerto Ricans American citizenship. In the same year, James Weldon Johnson became the first black execcutive secretary of the NAACP (National Association for the Advancement of Colored People); however, for the underprivileged ethnic minorities, the struggle was just beginning.

Many Puerto Ricans left their primarily agricultural island and moved to New York in search of better economic opportunities, only to contend with new difficulties and face formidable challenges. They grew from 554 in 1910 to 7364 ten years later. In 1928 the San Felipe hurricane that devastated Puerto Rico sped up the migration process, swelling their ranks to 45,000 by 1930. They first settled near the Brooklyn Navy Yard, where their ships docked, and then fanned out to other areas: Brownsville, Bedford-Stuyvesant, East New York, Washington Heights, and East Harlem, a former Jewish and then Italian neighborhood soon nicknamed "El Barrio." Unskilled laborers for the most part, they toiled in factories, kitchens, and workshops for minimal wages and lived in crowded and squalid tenements. They also started fighting for their civil rights, for increased participation in the political arena, and for better economic conditions; and, while trying to adapt to their new homeland, they struggled to protect their language and their culture in the face of an often hostile or at best indifferent environment. Life in the U.S. would always consist, for them, of a traumatic conflict between the desire to assimilate and the affirmation of their cultural identity.

By the turn of the century, New York Puerto Rican workers had founded a Free Federation which included a band, of which we know almost nothing. In the 1920s, organizing themselves more actively, they created another union, the Alianza Obrera Puertorriqueña.

In 1929, the Crash brought America's speculative frenzy to an abrupt halt. Three years later, there were twelve million unemployed, with Blacks and Puerto Ricans among the hardest hit. In 1933, Roosevelt launched his New Deal policy and the economy gradually recovered. The swing era expressed this newfound optimism: big bands proliferated, record sales boomed, and the radio, the movies, and juke-boxes, conveying this heady *joie de vivre*, favored sentimental and often silly tunes such as the smash *Life Is Just a Bowl of Cherries*.

In Harlem, dancers at the Savoy Ballroom enjoyed the thrill of the jitterbug, while jazzmen challenged each other in cutting contests. Duke Ellington displayed his sophisticated palette, with sounds already quite remote from the jovial exuberance of New Orleans jazz. The Barrio, located a few blocks away from black Harlem, became the heart of New York's Latin music. With its bustling market, La Marqueta, its restaurants, theaters, *bodegas* (grocery stores), *cuchifritos* (colorful fried-food stores selling blood pudding, stuffed potatoes, grilled pork rind, plaintains, and tropical fruit juices), social clubs, and Spanish-language newspapers, it symbolized for Hispanics the American dream, as Harlem had done for Southern Blacks a few years earlier.

In New York, Puerto Ricans clung to their music as a means of resisting cultural alienation in an individualistic, competitive, and puritanical society which often oppressed and aggrieved them. During moments of nostalgia, they relished *Borinquen tiene bandera* ("Puerto Rico has a flag"), *Vuelvo a mi Borinquen* ("I'm going back to my Puerto Rico"), or tunes evoking the mythical *jibarito* (peasant – equivalent of the Cuban *guajiro*), crystalizing their hopes, their concerns, and their frustrations and reminding them of their friendly and warm island. With his peasant attire, country singer "Ramito" (Florencio Morales Ramos), who stayed in New York in the mid-1920s, epitomized this romanticized *jibarito*.

A few Cuban, Puerto Rican, and Dominican musicians had already performed in New York before the arrival of the first significant wave of Puerto Rican migrants: in 1902, the Cuban *trovador* Tata Villegas had sung with the Sexteto Manhattan and appeared at Carnegie Hall; in 1907 Alberto Villalón had recorded for the Edison label; Miguel Companioni had given recitals in 1911; the Puerto Rican singer "Canario" had cut several sides in 1917; the following year María Teresa Vera had performed at the old Apollo Theater, in Harlem, which regularly organized Latin shows. In the 1910s, specialized stores sold cylinders of Puerto Rican music and in social clubs, small Latin bands such as Augusto Cara and His Floridians played a hodgepodge of tangos, paso dobles, fox-trots, and other rhythms.

In the early 1920s the Cuban dance team of Pérez y Ramona appeared in various New York theaters; singers Floro y Miguel, Floro himself as Floro Zorrilla, and María Teresa Vera recorded for the Columbia and Victor labels; four years later, Vera returned to New York with Manuel Corona and again, in 1926, with the Sexteto Occidente, and in 1923, the Cuban *danzón* pianist Enrique Bryon cut a few sides. In the space of a few months, flautist and saxophonist Alfredo Brito led Paul Whiteman's orchestra, and various Latin musicians also collaborated with jazz and other American dance bands: these included saxophonists Carmelo Jejo and Ramón Hernández and Puerto Rican bassist and tuba-player Rafael Escudero with the Savoy Bearcats; Escudero also with Wilbur Sweatman, in the black musical *Shuffle Along*, with Fletcher Henderson, and McKinney's Cotton Pickers; clarinettist "Moncho" (Ramón) Usera with Noble Sissle; the Puerto Rican trombonist Fernando Arbello with Earle Howard, Wilbur de Paris, and June Clark; alto saxophonist José Barreto and tuba-player John de León with Bill Brown and His Brownies. Alberto Socarrás, Augusto Coen, Rafael Escudero, and Moncho Usera played, too, in ensembles accompanying black musicals; and the Panamanian pianist Luis Russell led his Saratoga Club Orchestra.

Musicians who did not read or only knew traditional styles were mostly confined to low-paid jobs in the *barrios*. Versatility was the key to survival : many Hispanic musicians worked with American groups and with different kinds of "ethnic" ensembles, and most Latin groups played an eclectic repertoire. In the history of Latin jazz, except in New Orleans, it was generally Latin musicians who first adapted to jazz, rather than the reverse.

The awakening of the Barrio

With the arrival of a growing number of Cubans and Puerto Ricans, scores of Latin clubs opened in Manhattan, among them the Park Plaza, in the Barrio (with the Park Palace, lower down in the same building), the Yumuri Club, the Cuban Casino, the Havana Madrid, El Chico, the Bongo Club, and the Flamenco; and the Waldorf Astoria featured such Latin acts as Dominican singer Eduardo Brito. But East Harlem was the hub of Latin music. There the Cuban Frank Martin ran El Toreador, his compatriot Julio Mella running El Mella, located a few blocks further uptown. In 1927, the Puerto Rican guitarist and composer Rafael Hernández and his sister Victoria – a piano teacher – opened the city's first Latin store, the Almacenes Hernández, which became a focal point of the Barrio. Their countryman Gabriel Oller, a relative of the Puerto Rican impressionist painter Francisco Oller, founded a music store, Tatay's Music Center, and in 1934 started the Dynasonics record label, specializing in Cuban and Puerto Rican artists. As Hispanics progressively

Rafael Font, one of the early orchestra leaders in the Barrio.
The Justo A. Martí Photographic Collection, Centro de Estudios
Puertorriqueños, Hunter College, CUNY

displaced other ethnic groups, the American theaters[1] of the Barrio turned into Latin venues. The Teatro Hispano, located at the corner of Fifth Avenue and 116th street, and the Campoamor, inspired by its Havana namesake, all featured Latin shows.

One of the early Cuban bands working in town was Antobal's Cubans, run by Don Azpiazu's brother. But though Cuban music was predominant well into the 1950s, an increasing number of Puerto Ricans started to make significant musical statements. Among them was the cornettist Augusto Coen, who led the Golden Casino Orchestra. His ensemble included a trumpet, a trombone, three saxophones, and a rhythm section, and Puerto Rican singer "Davilita" (Pedro Ortiz Dávila) fronted it.

Born in 1895 in Ponce, on the southern coast of Puerto Rico, Coen had first played professional baseball and then enlisted as a musician in the U.S. Army during the First World War. In 1929 he moved to New York, working at the Audubon Theater in Harlem and then, briefly, with Duke Ellington and Fletcher Henderson, as well as in bands accompanying the black Broadway shows *Rhapsody in Black* and *Blackbirds of 1928*. After many years in New York, he returned to Puerto Rico, where he remained until his death in 1970.

In 1934 he founded Augusto Coen y Sus Boricuas,[2] hiring such musicians as Noro Morales, "Moncho" Usera, saxophonist José "Pin" Madera, and Cuban clarinettist and arranger Alberto Iznaga. At first, Coen leaned more towards Cuba, but in his compositions he eventually turned to the folk music of his native island, ushering in the Puerto Rican sound that was to coalesce in the 1950s.

Another Puerto Rican, percussionist "Federico" (Arsenio) Pagani, later known as "the godfather of Latin music," founded in the late 1930s Los Happy Boys. Pagani had come to New York from San Juan in 1925, and had studied music with Noro Morales and worked as Augusto Coen's bandboy. Los Happy Boys included Vicente Chappotín (trumpeter Félix Chappotín's brother) on bass, Decupuy on trumpet, Osvaldo Nieto, Alfredo González, and "Agugue" (D. López) on saxophone, Rafael de Tomás on piano, and Carlos Montesino – New York's first *timbalero* – about whom Xavier Cugat said that "if he had been white, he would have had a prodigious success." For commercial reasons, promoters often organized battles of the bands. In the theaters and clubs of the Barrio, Alberto Socarrás often vied with Augusto Coen, the Happy Boys were pitted against the band of the Cuban Alberto Iznaga, and Montesino against Escollíes – his Cuban counterpart. However, apart from these artificial conflicts, musicians from different Latin countries usually worked harmoniously side by side in the same groups, finding fertile ground for artistic expression in both jazz and Latin music.

1 Among them the Golden Casino, the Park Plaza, located at the corner of 110th Street and Fifth Avenue (an intersection celebrated in a tune by Puerto Rican pianist Noro Morales) and just below, in the same building, the Park Palace, the San José (ex-Photoplay Theater), and the Mount Morris Theater.

2 From Borinquen, Amerindian name of Puerto Rico.

Augusto Coen and his Golden Casino Orchestra. Empire Photographers, The Postcards Collection, Centro de Estudios Puertorriqueños, Hunter College, CUNY

The Cuban *tresista* "Caney" (Fernando Storch) livened up the nights of El Toreador with his Cuarteto Borinquen and then his *sexteto* Los Ecos de Cuba. Leaving his Crazy Cats in Havana, he had gone to the United States in 1927 to try out his luck there. After working at the Ford plant in Detroit, he moved to New York in 1930. And, like many of his Latin and black American colleagues, he also played for rent parties to supplement his income.

Storch surrounded himself with the Puerto Rican trumpeter Quique García, pianists Frank Valdés and then Rafael Audinot, and in 1933 Puerto Rican singer Johnny López (with Elio Osacar on bass).He first recorded in 1936, and two years later cut a few sides for Decca with Cuban vocalists Alfredo Valdés and Panchito Riset. Riset's specialty being boleros, López recommended Machito for faster tunes. Machito recorded duos with López and then with Manolo Suárez (a former Riverside Orchestra member) and also with Valdés. He performed the *son Juramento en las tinieblas*, *Pare cochero*, the *pregones El zapatero* and *El carbonero*, and under a pseudonym, so as to hide his Cuban origin, *joropos*.[3] The Cuarteto Caney's fame then grew with Audinot's *Rumba Rhapsody* and with two Cuban numbers: *Mis cincos hijos* and *Un brujo de Guanabacoa*. Daniel Sánchez, Tito Rodríguez (under his real name, Pablo Rodríguez), Payo Flores, and Polito Galíndez also sang with this group.

Known as *El rey del pregón borincano* (The king of Puerto Rican song), the congenial "Johnny" Rodríguez (Juan de Capadocia Rodríguez Lozada) – Tito Rodríguez's elder brother – sang at the Campoamor and worked with Noro Morales and with Armando Valdespí (recording with him). He had founded several ensembles in Puerto Rico, among them the *cuarteto* Estrellas Boricuas, with Ralph Sánchez, Rafael Muñoz, and Mario Dumont, a trio with the singers and guitarists Pedro Juan Sabat and Millito Cruz, and another trio with Pellín Boria and Claudio Ferrer, and had appeared in 1934 in the film *Romance tropical*, backed by the Rafael Muñoz orchestra.

3 A Venezuelan rhythm.

The RCA Victor label, increasingly interested in Latin music, added a few Puerto Rican artists to its roster, among them Francisco Quiñones, Canario, the Quinteto Borinquen, the Borinquen Orchestra, Rafael Hernández's Trío Borinquen and Orquesta Grillón, followed by Los Borinqueños, the Sexteto Puerto Rico, with which Juan Irene Pérez played *tres* in the late 1930s, the Sexteto Borinquen, and Roberto Roqués's group. These bands, often influenced by the *jíbaro* tradition, used guitars and a güiro – an instrument which had pretty much fallen into disuse in Cuba with the decline of *típicas*. Other Puerto Rican groups: the Trío Criollo, Heriberto Torres's trio, and Los Jardineros – an ensemble with frequent changes of personnel – livened up dances and parties with *jíbaro* music, Cuban tunes, and fox-trots.

The composer José La Calle and then Enrique Madriguera, both directors of the Latin music department of Columbia records, signed up such artists as Rita Montaner, Nilo Menéndez, and Rafael Hernández. And in New York, Armando Valdespí recorded sensuous boleros (*Alma de mujer, Beso loco*).

Sola y triste – Armando Valdespí

In 1930, the *tresista* "Mulatón," Don Azpiazu, his vocalist Antonio Machín, and the clarinettist, saxophonist, and trumpeter Mario Bauzá sailed together from Havana to New York. Each of them would shape the course of Latin music in their new country.

Mulatón popularized the *tres* in the United States, and at El Mella led a *cuarteto* which included two of his former colleagues from the Sexteto Occidente:

Vicente Chappotín and "Machito" (Frank Grillo), as well as a *bongocero* by the name of Evaristo. Then with Machito, Vicente Chappotín, Iznaga (violin), El Prajo (guitar), and Negret (vocals), Mulatón formed the Sexteto Estrellas Habaneras, which performed at the Campoamor and at the Cadillac Hotel in Detroit. In 1936, along with Agustín Gutiérrez, he accompanied Cuban dancers René and Estela during their stay in the Big Apple.

Most of these groups enjoyed considerable recognition in the Hispanic community, but, as the stride pianist Willie "The Lion" Smith noted in his autobiography, *Music on My Mind*, "back then a Cuban or Spanish band couldn't get to first base." However, Azpiazu did accomplish that feat. In April 1930, he and his Havana Casino orchestra performed at Keith's Palace Theater, on Broadway, and as part of the show, Machín sang Moisés Simons's *El manisero*. A rhythmic *son-pregón*, it had been hastily scribbled for singer Rita Montaner on a café table. Some argued that it derived from a dance by Gottschalk, itself inspired by a Cuban folk song. But whatever its origin, it was to become one of Latin music's most monumental and enduring hits:

Maní, maní,	Peanut, peanut,
Si te quieres por el pico divertir	If you want a snack
Cómete un cucuruchito de maní.	Eat a handful of peanuts.
…	…
Maní, maní, manisero se va	Peanut, peanut, the peanut vendor is leaving.
Caserita no te acuestes a dormir	Young girl, don't go to bed
Sin comerte un cucurucho de maní,	Without eating a paper cone of peanuts.
Cuando la calle sola está,	When the street is empty,
Casera de mi corazón,	Sweetheart,
El manisero entona su pregón	The peanut vendor sings his song,
Y si la niña escucha este cantar,	And if the girl listens to this tune,
Llamará de su balcón.	She will call him from her balcony.
Refrain:	*Refrain:*
Ya se va el manisero	The peanut vendor is leaving.
Ya se va.	He's leaving.

El Manisero – Moisés Simons

Two years earlier, in Havana, Simons had included *El manisero* in his revue "Cubanola," and Rita Montaner had recorded it and sung it in Paris, backed by pianist Rafael Betancourt. The tune was subsequently translated into English as *The Peanut Vendor*. Azpiazu brought it to the studios in May of 1930 with an arrangement by Alfredo Brito and a trumpet solo by "Chino" (Remberto) Lara – supposedly Latin music's first trumpet solo ever to be recorded. Unsure of its commercial potential, RCA Victor waited six months before releasing the record, finally marketing the tune as a "rumba." It triumphed in the United States, stunning the music industry, and then throughout the world, generating hundreds of covers, from Louis Armstrong to Maurice Chevalier and Paquito D'Rivera, with a particularly original version by Bola de Nieve and even a parody by Xavier Cugat, *The Coconut Pudding Vendor*.

With the bass systematically accenting the third, fourth, and first beats, the rumba suffered from a certain degree of stiffness, yet it invaded dance halls and even inspired a few jazzmen: in 1939 Willie "The Lion" Smith, for one, recorded *Baba Rhumba* and *Rosa Rhumba*, and even Billie Holiday went rumba with *I Get A Kick Out Of You*. The whole of America soon became intoxicated with Cuban music, and as Latin music's popularity soared, Latin bands began to fan out from the Barrio. In 1935, swayed by the Cuban craze, Louis Armstrong used claves on his vocal rendition of La *cucaracha*, featuring Luis Russell on piano.

Riding high on his success, Azpiazu recorded prolifically (with, in particular, American singers Chick Bullock and Bob Burke, probably imposed by his producers), and his music was heard in the movies *Swing High* and *Cuban Love Song*. In 1932 he played in Europe with trumpeter Julio Cueva, saxophonist Francisco González, and singers "Chiquito" (José Pereira Socarrás) and his uncle "Chepín" (José Socarrás). In Paris he recorded Cuban and Puerto Rican tunes (*Chivo que rompe tambó, El panquelero, La mulata rumbera, Lamento borinqueño*, also presented as a rumba). He then toured the United States for a year, but his star gradually faded. In New York, Chiquito Socarrás performed in the major Latin clubs, appeared in the movie *Midnight*, starring Claudette Colbert (and composed a conga for the soundtrack), and recorded under his own name, with arrangements by Fernando Mulens.

Pedro Vía (Azpiazu's other trumpet player) and singer and guitarist Daniel Sánchez, who had arrived from Cuba with Azpiazu and Machín, also settled in the Big Apple. There Vía founded a group which performed for a while in the Barrio. Machín fared better than Vía: in 1934, he set up a *cuarteto* with Daniel Sánchez (second voice, guitar), and sometimes Davilita, Cándido Vicenty (*tres*, guitar), or Mulatón (*tres*), and the Puerto Rican Plácido Acevedo or Favelo on trumpet. He produced abundant material and, with Remberto Lara on trumpet, performed both Cuban and Puerto Rican material. Among his first records were *Nació in Oriente, Yo soy candela, Mulata rumbera, A Baracoa me voy, Desvelo de amor*, and *Blancas azucenas*. (For *Mulata rumbera*, Lara was unavailable, and was replaced by Mario Bauzá on trumpet. And though it is generally said that Bauzá taught himself to play the trumpet a few weeks prior to the session by listening to Louis Armstrong, Phil Napoleon, and Red Nichols, he had in fact learned this instrument in Havana in 1928 with Lázaro Herrera.)

Like Azpiazu, Machín too sparked the Cuban music momentum abroad. Born in 1900 in Sagua la Grande, in 1926 he formed a duo in Havana with Miguel Zaballa, sang with *tresista* Enrique Peláez, and then with Manuel Luna's Trío Luna. He performed on the radio accompanied by pianist Jesús López (the first time a *sonero* was backed by a pianist) and recorded with Antonio María Romeu's *charanga* (*Tata Cuñengue, Aquellos ojos verdes, Se va el dulcerito*). He traveled to London in the mid-1930s with the show of dancer Delita, then started a band in Paris and finally settled in Spain, where he became a celebrity of sorts until his death in Madrid, in 1977.

A former Havana Philharmonic Orchestra member and sideman of Vicente Sigler and Augusto Coen, Cuban violinist, clarinettist, and saxophonist Alberto Iznaga founded the Orquesta Siboney in 1939; its repertoire ranged from Puerto Rican *danzas* to paso dobles and Bauzá wrote some of the arrangements. Composed of himself (clarinet), Machito (vocals), Frank Ayala (piano), Rafael Pesante (bass), José Budet (violin, clarinet, tenor saxophone), Alvaro Félix and René Edreira (trumpets), and Antonio Escollíes (timbales, bongo), this band, which was run as a cooperative, performed mostly in Latin venues. Machito left the band the following year in order to organize his Afro-Cubans, taking Escollíes with him, and Iznaga renamed his ensemble Orquesta de Alberto Iznaga.

Easy to grasp, the conga – a simplistic form of the conga line done at the Cuban carnivals – also captured the fancy of the Americans, who indulged in it with wild abandon. It made its U.S. debut at the Coconut Grove of the Ambassador Hotel, in Los Angeles, and then at the Rainbow Room of the Waldorf Astoria. Desi Arnaz and Eliseo Grenet both claim the honor of having introduced it abroad. Both did indeed perform outside Cuba in 1936 (Grenet in New York, where he hired Panchito Riset). Rhythmically easier than the rumba, the conga was danced in imitation of the carnival conga *trenes* (trains) or *colas* (lines), holding the person in front by the waist or the shoulders and kicking on the fourth beat.

Uno, dos y tres – Rafael Ortíz

"Desi" (Desiderio) Arnaz (1917–1986) is chiefly known as an actor and for the TV show *I Love Lucy*, in which he starred with his wife Lucille Ball and which featured Cuban pianist Marco Rizo as musical director. With its endearing skits about a Latin macho, the program entertained audiences for many years. The son of the mayor of Santiago de Cuba, as a youngster Arnaz took part in the town's ebullient carnivals. He started out in 1936 in Miami as a vocalist with the Siboney Septet (a local group distinct from Siboney bands led by Julio Brito, Isolina Carrillo, and Alberto Iznaga), and then toured with Xavier Cugat, whose show featured such celebrities as Johnny Weissmuller, Eleanor Holm, and Buster Crabbe. In 1938 he formed an ensemble that played at La Conga, in Miami. The following year he appeared at La Conga on Broadway, and also played the part of "Manolito" in the Rodgers and Hart musical *Too Many Girls*. One of Arnaz's claims to fame was his wild *Babalú Ayé* act, borrowed from Miguelito Valdés. He used and abused it so much that Charlie Barnet complained in his autobiography: "He used to bring his guitar and on the slightest pretext, he would whip it out and play and sing *Babalú*. Maybe he knew other tunes but that was the only one he ever did."

Johnny Rodríguez recorded *La conga del año nuevo*, Alberto Iznaga and pianist Anselmo Sacasas *Va la conga*. Rafael Ortiz's *Uno, dos y tres* contributed to the success of Xavier Cugat, who covered it under the explicit title *One, Two, Three, Kick!*; Cab Calloway offered *The Congo Conga, Chili con conga*, and *Goin' Conga*. The conga took Hollywood and Broadway by storm (The musical *Too Many Girls* featured a conga). And then done to death, the conga faded out.

A few Dominicans also obtained contracts with American record companies or performed in the United States. Among them the Santo Domingo Serenaders, comprising a mixture of Dominican, Cuban, and Panamanian musicians, Mario Bauzá's cousin, trumpeter René Edreira, the Dueto Quisqueya,[4] the Grupo Dominicano, consisting of Enrique García (first guitar), Bienvenido Troncoso (second voice, guitar), "Chita" (Luis María) Jiménez (*requinto*,[5] maracas, güiro, claves), and Eduardo Brito (first voice, conga, *tambora*[6]). The Grupo Dominicano recorded *La mulatona* and *Oye mi vidita*, in 1928; Nilo Menéndez brought out Julio Alberto Hernández's merengue *Santiago*; and with his Conjunto Típico Cibaneño, Angel Viloria cut *Vete lejos*. But in those days the merengue – Santo Domingo's national rhythm – generated little interest in the United States. Its time would not come until the 1950s. RCA Victor also flirted with Colombia and Venezuela, and added a few numbers from these countries to its catalogue as "novelty music."

Besides Azpiazu, other Latin artists, among them pianists Nilo Menéndez and Noro Morales and flautist Alberto Socarrás, managed to rise above the ranks, thanks to their talent and adaptability.

Described by Desi Arnaz as "brilliant," the Matanzas-born Menéndez (1906–1987) led a band that accompanied a Cuban show at the Harlem Opera House. One of his most famous compositions was the bolero *Aquellos ojos verdes* (1929), inspired by a female friend, with lyrics by Adolfo Utrera. It alternates between duple and triple meter, and the melody has impressionistic tinges. Recorded by Jimmy Dorsey and other musicians under the title of *Green Eyes*, it became an international hit:

Fueron tus ojos los que me dieron	It was your eyes that gave me
El tema dulce de mi canción.	The sweet topic of my song.
Tus ojos verdes, claros, serenos,	Your green, limpid, serene eyes,
Ojos que han sido mi inspiración.	Eyes that were my inspiration.

4 Quisqueya is the Indian name for Santo Domingo.

5 Kind of small guitar.

6 A double-skinned drum typically used in merengue.

Fue - ron tus o - jos los que me die - ron

el te - ma dul - ce de mi can - ción, __

Aquellos ojos verdes –
Nilo Menéndez

The very active Menéndez went on to form the Stork Club Orchestra – with which the Puerto Rican vocalist "Maso" (Tomaso) Rodríguez occasionally sang, and which recorded numbers with occasional jazz inflections – wrote several film scores, played with Cugat at the Waldorf Astoria, and with Ernesto Lecuona.

Alberto Socarrás also helped Cuban music to establish itself in the United States. In 1928 he settled in Harlem – a lively district at the height of its Renaissance. The neighborhood, teeming with dance halls and clubs, attracted the most creative African-American artists, and its stupendous dancers inspired the Mexican painter Miguel Covarrubias. Combining Cuban rhythms, classical music, and jazz, Socarrás paved the way for Latin jazz. Dizzy Gillespie, who played with him in the late 1930s, said he learned his first rudiments of Cuban music from him, and noted in his autobiography: "He had the most perfect vibrato of any flautist I've ever heard. Man, he sounds like a bird with his flute." And Mongo Santamaría considers Socarrás a "genius."

Towards the late 1920s, Fletcher Henderson and Duke Ellington revolutionized jazz, "learning," as Nathan Irvin Huggins wrote, "to give orchestral form to a music of improvisation and virtuosity." The blues became urbanized and stride piano virtuosos like James P. Johnson imposed their dazzling pyrotechnics. With their advanced harmonies and incisive left hand, Fats Waller, who reigned in New York, and Earl Hines, who accompanied Jimmy Noone in Chicago, heralded the modern piano styles. In the midst of this intense cultural atmosphere, Socarrás struck up friendships with Ethel Waters, and with Bessie Smith, whose *Poor Man's Blues*, recorded in 1928 for Columbia in its "race" series, expressed the frustration of many Blacks, whose suffering would only increase with the recession:

> *Mister rich man, open up your heart and mind (bis)*
> *Give the poor man a chance, help stop these hard hard times.*
> *While you're livin' in your mansion,*
> *You don't know what hard times means.*[7]

Shortly after his arrival in the Big Apple, Socarrás joined Vicente Sigler's band. American musicians were astonished by the versatility of the young Cuban, who proved capable of handling all kinds of musical assignments, and soon the unknown flautist, saxophonist, and clarinettist from Manzanillo was gigging with the Trinidadian vocalist Sam Manning, pianist and composer J. C. Johnson, trumpeter "Jock" Bennett, Lizzie Miles, King Oliver, and other bands. In February 1929, he played on recording sessions led by Clarence Williams, the New Orleans pianist who had organized the historic engagements with Louis Armstrong and Sidney Bechet. He was featured on clarinet on *Candy Lips*, on flute on *Have You Ever Felt That Way* (believed to be the first jazz flute solo ever recorded – even before Wayman Carver's), and on saxophone on other numbers; and he performed with Nilo Menéndez at the Harlem Opera House.

Black musicals such as *Shuffle Along* were the rage on Broadway, and had revealed some distinctive musical voices. Along with Coen, Socarrás also worked in *Blackbirds of 1928*, starring Ethel Waters, Florence Mills, Adelaide Hall, and Josephine Baker, and he probably played in its famed Plantation Orchestra. Cab Calloway, who saw *Blackbirds* at the Cotton Club, described it as "a marvelous variety show." In 1929 *Blackbirds* played at the Moulin Rouge in Paris where it met with wild acclaim.

Back in New York, Socarrás formed a big band which accompanied shows at the Cubanacán and the Mount Morris Theater, and in which Coen and, later, Noro Morales and José Curbelo played (Morales for only a month, in 1935). A promotional brochure described it as having a mixture of "classical textures in the melodic instruments" and "savage intensity in the Afro-Cuban section," and a photograph taken around that time shows its drummer with a lovely painted drum-set surmounted with several woodblocks. In 1937, continuing to alternate between Latin music and jazz, Socarrás played, along with Cab Calloway and Duke Ellington, in the Cotton Club Parade. The following year, along with Panamanian pianist Nicolás Rodríguez, he worked with Benny Carter, and traveled to Paris with the Orquesta Anacaona as musical director. He then joined the bands of Erskine Hawkins and of Sam Wooding, and put together a new ensemble, the Afro-Cuban Rumbas, which included Nicolás Rodríguez (piano), Harold Blanchard (alto saxophone), Cecil Scott (tenor saxophone), and Gus Aiken (trumpet). It performed at the Campoamor, the Apollo Theater and in

7 In: *Bessie Smith, Empress of the Blues*, Schirmer Books. Copyright Empress Music Inc. 1975, New York.

various previously segregated U.S. clubs; and recommended by W. C. Handy, Socarrás gave a recital at Carnegie Hall.

The Savoy Ballroom also attracted Latin dancers, and whenever the Sultans – then the house band – were on tour, Socarrás replaced them. Dizzy Gillespie occasionally blew his horn with the Sultans, and he and Socarrás probably met at the Savoy in 1938. Dizzy eventually worked with Socarrás, who offered this comment about the young and upcoming trumpeter: "We played Cuban music first, like bolero and things like that, and he phrased his solos marvelously. Then we played rhumbas, fast numbers, and his style was very Cuban. To him it was easy as American music was to me."[8]

An outstanding pianist (and occasional singer), "Noro" (Norberto Osvaldo) Morales also shone brightly on the Latin music scene. An ingratiating Buddha-like man, a high-liver and womanizer, he was, like Louis Armstrong or Fats Waller, a beloved entertainer whose antics sometimes overshadowed, for the untrained ear, his true musical qualities. His sober and rhythmic playing, subtle phrasing, and lilting lines appealed to both Latins and Americans. He was also a peerless accompanist and one of the few Puerto Rican artists capable of rivaling his Cuban counterparts in popularity, and to this day he remains a source of inspiration for many Latin pianists.

Born in Puerta de Tierra, Puerto Rico in 1911 into a musical family (his father played violin and bass and all his siblings also mastered musical instruments), he studied trombone, bass, and piano and first accompanied silent films. In 1924 his family moved to Venezuela, invited by President Juan Gómez to serve as his official orchestra. His father died shortly thereafter and Noro assumed the leadership of the band. He returned to Puerto Rico, where he joined several ensembles, and finally settled in New York in 1935 along with brothers José, saxophonist, "Esy" (Ismael), flautist, and Humberto, *timbalero*. There he worked at the Toreador and other East Harlem clubs, with Alberto Socarrás, Augusto Coen, the Septeto Caney, Chiquito Socarrás, and other bands. In 1937 he founded Los Hermanos Morales, renamed the following year Noro Morales and His Orchestra. With Davilita on vocals, he entertained elegant crowds at El Morocco, La Conga, and other posh venues of midtown Manhattan.

The Panamanian pianist "Ray" (Horacio) Durán, who had come to New York in 1928, played mostly American music. He performed in various Harlem venues, gigged with the vocal group Deep River Boys, and, in the late 1940s, had his own TV show on the American NBC network.

With their cosmetic, often stereotyped arrangements and lavish strings, Latin society bands such as those led by Carlos Molina, Eddie Le Baron, Chewy Reyes, and Enrique Madriguera – a Catalonian violinist who had turned to popular music after conducting the Havana Philharmonic Orchestra – made the complex Latin rhythms more palatable to Americans. To many a layman their sound, bland and turgid as it could be, typified Latin music. But these bands also

8 In: Dizzy Gillespie with Al Fraser: *To Be, or Not... to Bop*, p. 87.

presented a stunning spectacle with attractive vocalists (and often inept lyrics), and musicians nattily clad with fancy ruffled-sleeved shirts recalling those of flamenco dancers.

One of the first Latin society bands in New York was that directed by Cuban trumpeter Vicente Sigler. In the 1920s it performed in East Harlem as well as in Manhattan's major hotels, and it included Coen, Socarrás, and Iznaga. In 1926 Sigler appeared in a Fox movie. In the 1930s the group recorded various sides (*Rumba de medianoche*) and backed Miguel Matamoros when Matamoros came to New York for some studio sessions (*Mi último canto, Rompiendo la rutina*).

Cuban pianist Vincent López signed with the Okeh "race" series, which had put out the first blues recordings, and he toured the United States, captivating the conservative Midwest audiences. *Billboard* of August 31, 1940 mentioned his ensemble as "one of the most appreciated of the King's Ballroom in Lincoln, Nebraska!"

"Xavier" (Francisco de Asis Javier) Cugat (1900–1990) – a former first violin of López's ensemble – was undoubtedly the most commercially successful and the most famous of these society bandleaders, if only for his tumultuous romances. (His first wife was Rita Montaner, and he also married the curvaceous Abe Lane and the young Spanish singer Charo.) His self-serving autobiography, in which he directs the spotlight exclusively on himself, does little to illuminate the history of Latin music.

"Cugie," as he was affectionately nicknamed, was born near Gerona, in Catalonia, but his family moved to Cuba when he was a child. There he worked in the pit band of the Havana Opera and in various theaters and cafés before playing in New York with Enrico Caruso in 1921. His family then moved to the United States, and after a rather unsuccessful recital at Carnegie Hall, he gave up classical music. "The lukewarm reception of my performance by the critics left Heifetz and Elman to heave a sigh of relief," he candidly admitted, "and left me with the conviction I would never become a great concert artist."

In the late 1920s Cugat settled in Hollywood and, after drawing insipid cartoons for the *Los Angeles Times*, formed a tango sextet: Cugat and His Gigolos. A booking at the Coconut Grove of the Ambassador hotel, in Los Angeles, and the movie *Cugat's Gigolos* boosted his career, and he also created music for the film *Ten Cents a Dance*, starring Ruth Etting. His fame grew in 1934, when he played for a year on the prestigious radio show "Let's Dance." He then landed a cameo role in Mae West's movie *Go West Young Man*; his first New York group, organized in 1936, made its debut at no less than the Waldorf Astoria; and he scored a hit with *Para Vigo me voy*.

If Cugat was perhaps not the greatest virtuoso, he did possess remarkable show-business acumen. Desi Arnaz mentioned in his autobiography that "he always had three or four people, usually a girl and two or three boys, dressed in big and colorful rumba shirts, who kept dancing and moving all the time. In every set the girl and one of the boys would dance on the stand so that the American people could see how that particular dance number – samba, rumba or tango – was done." Cugat skillfully adapted to the different trends, offering tangos, boleros, rumbas, mambos, cha-chas, according to the changing fashions, but despite a few slight differences, his recordings all sound pretty much the same. According to the great mambo dancer "Killer Joe" Piro, "the kind of Latin music he plays is as close to Machito as Sugar Chile Robinson is close to Meade Lux Lewis," although Tito Puente was an avowed admirer of the Catalan bandleader. Still, Cugat contributed to giving Americans some exposure to Latin rhythms, however watered down, and his band was a stepping stone for some of the great Latin artists, among them the great flautist Esy Morales, trumpeter Jorge López, Nilo Menéndez, Puerto Rican percussionist Catalino Rolón, José Curbelo, Desi Arnaz, Tito Rodríguez, Miguelito Valdés, Chiquito Socarrás, Luis del Campo, Anselmo Sacasas, and Julito Collazo.

The headway made by Latin musicians in the record industry, however, did not result in the eradication of prejudice. A March 1937 *Downbeat* article, for example, striving for sensationalism, described the performance of a Cuban percussionist in the following terms: "Bongo Serro[9] is a drummer from the wilds of Cuba and is featured with the Yanyego Voodoo (*sic*) Dancers at one of New York's most objectionable spots, Le Mirage, where pseudo-svelte natives can gasp and make appropriate noises." The band, however, only included conga, timbales, bass, and two guitarists also playing maracas . . . hardly the stuff of savage exotica! As to "Yanyego Voodoo," "Yanyego" – a distortion of *ñáñigo* – refers to the Abakwa culture of Cuba, while the voodoo is Haitian – a curious association probably due to the ignorance of the chronicler.

Music in Puerto Rico

In the 1930s, Puerto Rico's economy was largely in foreign hands, and impoverished peasants flocked to the cities, swelling the ranks of the urban proletariat. Caught in the grip of the United States and with an almost colonial status, the island wondered about its own identity. In 1929, for example, a questionnaire entitled "*¿Qué somos y cómo somos?*" ("What are we and how are we?") was offered to its readers by the newspaper *Indice*. While the island did have a strong and compelling culture of its own, it was still struggling to have it accepted both at home and abroad. This lack of recognition was nothing new, for as Puerto Rican musicologist María Luisa Muñoz notes: "In the early nineteenth century, the small nouveau bourgeois colony established in Puerto

9 A probable distortion of the Spanish *bongocero* (bongo player).

Rico showed little interest in artistic matters. Music was a profession for black people and entertainment for just whites. Practiced by black folk, it served to liven up white festivities."[10]

With its "*le lo laï*" – naive refrains cropping up in *jíbaro* melodies – and its marked Spanish inflections, Puerto Rico's traditional music has a remarkable charm. Several salsa singers grew up listening to the rustic flavor captured in the songs of "Ramito," "Chuíto de Bayamón" (Jesús Sánchez Erazo), "El Jibarito de Lares" (Odilio González), or "La Calandria" (Ernestina Reyes Pagán). *Jíbaro* music is often played by *conjuntos* consisting of *cuatro* (some eminent players were the late "Maso" (Tomás) Rivera, Yomo Toro, and Nieves Quintero) with guitar, maracas, güiro, bongo, and/or conga.

The graceful *danza*, supplanted in Cuba by the *danzón* in the late nineteenth century, blossomed in Puerto Rico, becoming its national music; the island's anthem, *La Borinqueña*, is a *danza* composed in 1868. The *seis*, of Spanish origin, spawned countless local variations, among them the *seis bombeado* (mixed with *bomba*), the *seis bayamonés*, from Bayamón, near San Juan, the *seis mariandá*, with its bass line resembling that of the Cuban *son*, and the *seis fajardeño*, from Fajardo, on the north coast. Songs of Spanish origin are generally based on the *décima* (ten-line verse), and the *seis de controversia* involves improvisation contests recalling those occurring between *decimistas* in Cuba. The old Iberian tradition of *villancicos* and *aguinaldos* (carols) has persisted on the island, with themes similar to those sung by *guajiros* in Cuba. At Christmas and New Year, groups of carolers (*parrandas* or *trullas*) go from house to house singing these tunes in exchange for food, rum, or *coquito* (a kind of eggnog).

Still very African, the riveting *bomba* – Puerto Rico's equivalent of the *rumba brava* – sprang up around the eighteenth century in the coastal plantations and sugar mills, especially around Loíza, Ponce, Salinas, Guayama, Cataño, and Arroyo. The southern *bomba* bears influences from Haiti and Santo Domingo. Of Ashanti and Bantu origin, the *bomba* also absorbed elements borrowed from French dances, as in the *leró* (from the French *la rose* – "the rose"). Slaves used to perform *bombas* to celebrate the end of the harvest, on Saturday nights after work, and on Sundays. Danced by both men and women, the *bomba* has in fact a number of variations, among them the *sicá*, the *yubá*, the *grasimá*, the *holandés*, the *cuñá*, and the *calinda*. The instrumentation consists of barrel-shaped *bomba* drums. The larger ones (*machos* or *burladores*) lead, and the smaller ones (called *requinto*, *primo* or *subidor*) answer and improvise. Two sticks (*fuá* or *cuá*) beat an additional rhythm on the side of one of the *burladores*, and the vocalist accompanies him- or herself with a maraca. The dancer and the lead drummer engage in a dialogue and the *requinto* player must reproduce on his instrument the rhythms improvised by the dancer with his or her feet. The call-and-response songs consist of short and sometimes metaphorical phrases interspersed with African-sounding words.

The *plena*, a kind of topical and often satirical song form, appeared during the First World War in the districts of La Joya del Castillo and then San Antón, in

10 *La música en Puerto Rico*, p. 99.

Ponce, on the south coast of Puerto Rico. Said to derive from songs brought there by immigrants from Barbados or St. Kitts, it also borrowed from Spanish *romances* (and perhaps also from the mummers, performers of English origin dating back to medieval times). A couple from St. Kitts and their daughter, Carola Clark, went about Ponce playing guitar and tambourine and singing songs that would later evolve into *plenas*. A ploughman by trade and a tambourine virtuoso by the improbable name of Joselino "Bumbum" Oppenheimer (1884–1929) formed the first fully-fledged *plena* group.

Like the *son* in Cuba, the *plena* blossomed among the lower social classes. Nowadays a *bomba* and *plena* festival is organized every year in Ponce. In New York, *plenas* can erupt in places such as Central Park or in *barrio* streets, while groups such as Los Pleneros de la 110 or Los Pleneros de la 21 (deriving their name from a 21 bus-stop in Santurce, in Puerto Rico) have kept up the *plena* tradition there. A few tambourines, sometimes a trombone and a conga start to play and people join in spontaneously, singing, clapping, and dancing. Anyone can participate, and *plenas* often express social frustrations or vent pent-up feelings. *Tintorera del mar*, about a shark who ate an American (or a lawyer), *Cortaron a Elena*, alluding to a prostitute slashed during a dance, or *El obispo de Ponce*, which incensed the Church, are some of the classic *plenas*. *El obispo de Ponce* satirized a womanizing bishop living in that city in the 1920s. After marveling at the cleric's beauty, particularly his blue eyes, a stanza compares him to a lion:

Y dicen las hermanitas	And the little nuns
del Sagrado Corazón:	from Sacred Heart say:
– "Muchachas tengan cuidado,	– "Girls be careful,
porque el obispo	because the bishop
es un gran león.	is a big lion."

The *plena*, with its duple meter, is traditionally played with a güiro, an accordion or a guitar, and two or three tambourines without bells (*panderos* or *panderetas*). The largest (*segundo*) and the medium one (*punteador*) maintain the basic beat, the smaller (*requinto*), which is said to "speak," improvises (*repiquetea*). As the *plena* became commercialized, it gradually incorporated horns and congas and timbales replaced *panderas*. *Coplas* (four-line stanzas) performed by the soloist alternate with the refrain, sung by the *coro*.

The Puerto Rican poet and patriot Lola Rodríguez de Tío, who spent time in Cuba, once compared that country and Puerto Rico to the wings of a single bird. Indeed, both islands share a similar colonial past and geographical and cultural features, although the American presence has been stronger in Puerto Rico. And like its Cuban counterpart, Puerto Rican music results from the intermingling of various European and African influences.

As in Havana, tourist spots were dominated by American music, but la Isla del Encanto (The Island of Enchantment) fervently greeted Cuban rhythms, which were closer to its own sensibility. Various Puerto Rican musicians, among them Rafael Hernández performed in Cuba, and a host of Cuban artists: Arquímedes Pous (who died in Mayagüez in 1927), Graciano Gómez, Barbarito Diez, Ernesto Lecuona, the Orquesta Anacaona, Tito Gómez, the Compañía de Bataclán Cubana de Margot Rodríguez, the Trío Matamoros, and many others brought the *son*, the bolero, the *guaracha*, and the rumba to Puerto Rico. Although the *cuatro* remained Puerto Rico's most typical stringed instrument, Johnny Seguí, "Chuito" (Jesús) Nadal, "Piliche," and a few other local musicians adopted the *tres*.

In the 1920s and 1930s, bands proliferated despite the dearth of superior music schools and the precarious living conditions of many musicians. Among them were Chuito Nadal's Septeto Borinquen (with Moncho Leña on bongo), the Orquesta Los Trovadores, the Jolly Kings, the Conjunto Rítmico formed in 1932 by pianist "Don Nacho" (Ignacio Guerrero Noble), which later featured José Luis Moneró on vocals, and Leocadio Vizcarrondo's Septeto Puerto Rico; there were also the big bands which, from the 1930s onward, would hold sway at the Beach Club, the Escambrón, and other major swank nightspots in San Juan: Augusto Rodríguez's Midnight Serenaders, Rafael Sánchez y su Sinfonía, Mingo and His Whoopee Kids, with singer Ruth Fernández, the Orquesta Casino de Ponce,[11] the Orquesta Cuervo de la Noche, the ensembles led by Carmelo Díaz Soler (with vocalist Félix Rodríguez), William Manzano, Ramón Olivero, Frank Madera, and Mario Dumont, and the one run by bassist, saxophonist, flautist, and trumpeter Rafael Muñoz. Muñoz's group was perhaps the most famous of these. Founded in 1929, it consisted of bass, drums, piano, saxophone, clarinet, trumpets, trombone, and violins, and at different times it included Noro Morales, César Concepción, and singers Deogracias Vélez, José Luis Moneró, and Victor Luis Miranda. Muñoz offered highly danceable and melodious music: the bolero *Locura, Campanitas de cristal*, with its lovely glockenspiel, *Puerto Rico rumbamba*, the *guaracha El hueso de María*.

As an increasing number of Puerto Ricans migrated to the U.S., the shuttling between San Juan and New York intensified. Puerto Rican rhythms took root in New York, and rhythms from the United States gained currency in Puerto Rico. Musicians constantly traveled back and forth between the island and the mainland, Puerto Ricans from New York visited their relatives on the island during the holidays or for family events and vice versa, and this continuous interchange fostered creativity. The development of Puerto Rican music became inseparable from the migration process, and some of its great successes (*Lamento borincano*, for example) were composed Stateside. Rafael Hernández and Pedro Flores, who lived in Puerto Rico and in New York, scored hits in both places (and, with their records, in the rest of Latin America as well).

"Canario" (Manuel Jiménez) was the first to popularize the *plena* in the United States, a *plena* whose instrumentation he gradually modernized, although his eclectic repertoire also included boleros, seis, *mapellés*,[12] *aguinaldos*, waltzes, *guarachas*, paso dobles, Mexican *corridos*, and other genres. He also wrote a few songs, among them the *plena La roca de la laguna*:

11 It recruited certain members of the Whoopie Kids.

12 Another traditional Puerto Rican genre.

Allegro moderato

pie - za con le lo le, Ter - mi - na con le lo la, Ca -

na - rio tie - ne u - na ple - na Que jue - ga con la bri - sa del mar.

La roca de la laguna –
Manuel Jiménez
("Canario")

A colorful character who roamed the world and even spent time in jail (for non-payment of a debt) he was born in 1895 in the small Puerto Rican town of Barros (today Orocovis). His father, a coffee-picker, moved to Manatí, but died shortly thereafter. In order to survive, the young Canario held a variety of small jobs including grooming horses and, in San Juan, making cigars. At fourteen, he stowed away on a ship to Barcelona, returning via Cuba. In 1910 he traveled to New York and then to Calcutta, and upon his return to New York, he enlisted in the Merchant Marine. There, the captain of his boat, struck by his constant singing, nicknamed him "Canario" ("Canary"). After recording a few *corridos*, Canario cut *Cielito lindo* in New York, and in 1917 some of the classic *plenas*: *Cuando las mujeres quieren a los hombres* ("When women love men"), *Santa María, ¡Qué tabaco malo!,* and *El obispo de Ponce.*

In 1925 he formed a trio including clarinettist Yeyo Laguna, with which he issued a few sides and, the following year, set up a *plena conjunto.* He also joined Rafael Hernández's Trío Borinquen and, accompanied by a *cuatro,* mandolin, guitar, güiro, and claves, he recorded *Viva la vieja, La novia que yo tenía, No viertas una lágrima,* and *Borinquen.*

In 1930 he formed the Grupo Canario with "Yayito" Maldonado on guitar, "Pepito" (José) López on trumpet, and Fausto Delgado on vocals; and, in San Juan, founded the Orquesta Puerto Rico, which performed both on the island and in the States, and appeared in the movie "Salt and Pepper." Canario also recorded with the *trovador* Antonio Mesa, nicknamed "Santo Domingo's goldfinch" (*Dulces besos, Cortaron a Elena*), with his (Canario's) wife Sarah Simounet, and with Davilita.

The 1930s saw the emergence of many small guitar groups inspired by the *jíbaro* tradition, among them the Conjunto Ladi, started by Ladislao Martínez Otero ("Ladi"). One of the first musicians to bring the *cuatro* to New York, Ladi, born in Alta Vega in 1898, had founded a band that performed on the radio, and two years later the group Aurora (named after one of his mazurkas), with an essentially Puerto Rican repertoire; the group included singers Ernesto Vázquez, Claudio Ferrer, and "Don Felo" (Felipe Rosario Goyco), guitarist and author of *Carcelera*. Ladi, along with trumpeter and flautist Plácido Acevedo Sosa and Don Felo, cultivated the Puerto Rican folk tradition, composing *seis, danzas, aguinaldos,* and bucolic *canciones*. When he moved to the United States, Don Felo took over Aurora and renamed it Conjunto Industrias Nativas, after the radio show on which it played.

Other vocalists, recalling the *Cuban trovadores,* sang with *cuartetos*. Most of these, which appeared toward the mid-1930s, usually included two guitars (or a guitar and a small string instrument called a *requinto*), a muted trumpet, and two singers who sometimes harmonized, and accompanied themselves with claves and maracas. They played Cuban and Puerto Rican material, and musicians were occasionally added for recording sessions. Some of the prominent *cuartetos* were the Victoria, the Flores, the Marcano, and the Mayarí.

The Cuarteto Victoria, set up in 1934 by Rafael Hernández and named after his sister, included singers Mengol Díaz and Armando Carmona. One of Puerto Rico's musical heroes, Hernández wrote graceful and sensitive *canciones* (songs), *criollas,* and boleros: *Preciosa, Silencio, Campanitas de cristal, Capullito de alelí.* Though many of his songs are romantic and melancholy, he also produced rollicking *guarachas* and *pregones* (*Muévete negrita, Pescao de Aguadilla*) and he adopted the *bomba* long before Rafael Cortijo and Ismael Rivera (*Tun tun neco, Tú no sirves pa' na', Uy que feo,* the risqué *Menéalo que se empelota* – "Shake it, it's getting hard" – on which he played piano). His greatest successes, however, were *El cumbanchero,* with its African alliterations, and the spicy *Cachita:*

Oyeme Cachita, tengo una rumbita,	Listen to me, Cachita, I have a little rumba
Pa' que tú la bailes como bailo yo.	I want you to dance it as I do.
Muchacha bonita, mi linda Cachita,	Pretty girl, my beautiful Cachita,
La rumba caliente es mejor que el fox.	The hot rumba is better than the fox-trot.
Mira que se rompen ya	Look, the maracas
De gusto las maracas	Are bursting out with pleasure
Y él de los timbales	And the timbales-player
Ya se quiere alborotar.	Is about to break loose.
Se divierte así el francés,	This is how the Frenchman has fun,
Y también el alemán	And also the German
Y se alegra el irlandés	And the Irish is getting happy
Y hasta el musulmán. ¡Bah!	And even the Moslem. Bah!
Y se baila esto un inglés,	And an Englishman dances like that.
Se le mete el aboroto,	They give it all to him
Y es pa' que se vuelva loco	In order to drive
Hasta un japonés. ¡Bah!	Even a Japanese wild. Bah!
Pa' la rumba no hay fronteras,	The rumba knows no borders,
Pues se baila hasta en el Polo,	It is danced even at the Pole
Yo la he visto bailar solo	I have even seen an Eskimo
Hasta un esquimal. ¡Bah!	Dancing it alone. Bah!
El que tenga algún pesar,	Whoever has problems
Que se busque su Cachita,	Should go and find his Cachita
Y le diga: ven negrita	And tell her: come, sweetie,
Vamos a rumbear. ¡Bah!	Let's dance the rumba. Bah!

Born in Aguadilla in 1892, Hernández studied trombone, violin, saxhorn, banjo, piano, cornet, bass, and guitar. In San Juan he accompanied silent films and played saxhorn with the municipal band, led by Manuel Tizol. In 1917 he recorded some *danzones*, and he pursued his musical training in the U.S. Army, in which he enlisted during the First World War.

After spending four years in Havana, where he played trombone in the band of the Fausto theater, he moved to East Harlem in 1925. There he organized one of New York's first Puerto Rican groups, the Trío Borinquen, while punching piano rolls as a side job. The trio, in which he played guitar, was comprised of Canario (lead singer) and Salvador Ithier (second voice). Canario later left to set up his own ensemble, and was replaced by Antonio Mesa, who introduced Dominican numbers into the group's repertoire.[13] Pedro Vargas also sang with Hernández.

13 In Santo Domingo, the records of the Trío Borinquen were sold under the name Trío Quisqueya (Quisqueya being the Indian name of the country).

In 1929, while in the Barrio, Hernández wrote one of his most moving songs: *Lamento borincano* ("Puerto Rican Lament"), which bemoaned his island's poverty.

Alegre, el jibarito va, cantando así,
Riendo así, diciendo así por el camino:
Si yo vendo la carga, mi Dios querido,
Un traje a mi viejita voy a comprar . . .
Pasa la mañana entera sin que nadie quiera
Su carga comprar, ay su carga comprar.

Happy, the peasant is singing along,
Laughing along, saying along the way:
If I sell my load, dear God,
I'll buy my wife a dress . . .
The whole morning went by without anybody
Buying his load, alas! without buying his load.

With its other line, which proclaimed "*Todo está desierto y el pueblo está muerto de necesidad*" ("Everything is barren and the people are dying of hunger"), the song became a Puerto Rican manifesto.

In the early 1930s, encouraged by Pedro Vargas, Hernández moved to Mexico, where he stayed until 1947; and he also traveled to various Latin American countries with his Grupo Victoria. In Mexico, he wrote film scores and led a band that played for a radio show; his songs *María no llores, Preciosa, El cumbanchero,* and *Cachita* won over the country. Back in New York he formed another *cuarteto*,

El cumbanchero – Rafael Hernández

with guitarist "Paquito" (Francisco) López Cruz and Davilita; in 1947 he returned to Puerto Rico, continuing to compose until his death in 1965.

Hernández's friend and sometime rival, the self-taught Pedro Flores (1894–1979) wrote catchy songs in a popular vein: *Qué extraña es la vida, Azucenas, Bajo un palmar, Por tí*.[14] He evoked Puerto Rico's problems with numbers like *Sin bandera* ("Without a flag") and, in his group, influenced by the rustic *son*, he sometimes employed a *tres*, rather than a *cuatro*, a *marímbula*, and a bongo.

Born in Naguabo in a poor family, he played professional baseball, like Augusto Coen and later Mon Rivera, and then became an English teacher and a mailman. He moved to New York in 1926, where he worked in a factory and then as a house painter. He formed a trio with, among others, singer "Piquito" (Pedro) Marcano, and recorded topical songs (*La negrita Trini, Toma jabón pa' que lave*). In 1929 he set up the Sexteto Flores and then led a *cuarteto* with which he cut *Adelita* and other tunes. The ensemble occasionally became a *septeto* and included Davilita (and, in 1936, Panchito Riset, before Riset joined the Cuarteto Caney), and it recorded many numbers, among them *Desde que tú me quieres*. In the late 1930s or early 1940s Flores's group included himself on guitar, Roberto Quintón (piano), Daniel Santos (lead vocals), Chencho Moraza (second voice), and Moncho Usera (trumpet and flute). Flores later founded the larger Orquesta Sociedad, spent two years in Mexico and, back in New York, recorded with Moncho Usera, Daniel Santos, and singer Chencho Moraza (*Venganza, La mujer de Juan, Despedida*). During the Second World War, the Orquesta's members were drafted into the U.S. Army and the group dissolved.

Besides his collaboration with Flores, Piquito Marcano recorded under his own name (among other tunes the bolero-merengue *Bailando abrazao*) and started a trio with Claudio Ferrer and Pepito Arvelo. In 1934 he founded in New York the lyrical Cuarteto Marcano in which he sang first voice and Ferrer second voice (Bienvenido Granda also worked with the group), with "Lalo" (Leocadio) Martínez on guitar and Vitín Mercado on trumpet. The Cuarteto Marcano performed in the town's major Latin clubs and toured Latin America.

Created in San Juan in 1938 by Plácido Acevedo (a former member of the Cuarteto Machín), the Cuarteto Mayarí became renowned for its lively *guarachas*. Acevedo had played in New York with Antonio Machín, Daniel Sánchez, and Mulatón. The Cuarteto Mayarí, first called Ruiseñores Criollos (Creole Nightingales), included at different times Claudio Ferrer, "Corozo" (Félix Rodríguez) (succeeded for a few months only by Tito Rodríguez), Paquito Sánchez, Manuel Jiménez Miranda, Canario, "Chiquitín" (Juan José) García (author of the *guaracha Acángana*), Perín Vázquez, "Fanta" (Rafael Hernández Fantauzzi), and Payo Flores. It first recorded in 1941 (*Borinquen tierra de flores, Dorotea la parrandera*, and other numbers) and continued performing until the mid-1950s.

The La Plata Quintet, with its interesting harmonies, was founded by Davilita in 1937 with Rafael Rodríguez, Juan Reyes, "El Tampeñito," and Paquito López Cruz. Davilita favored sentimental tunes with a typical Puerto Rican suavity (*Venus, Ansias locas*). In 1939, he also sang with Noro Morales.

14 Benny Moré later sang this song in duo with Pedro Vargas.

the 1940s and 1950s: the golden age of cuban music

Havana and Cuba

In 1934, Colonel Fulgencio Batista overthrew the progressive president Ramón Grau San Martín. Appointed Minister of Defense and Chief Commandant of the Army, he managed to get himself elected President of the Republic in 1940. He left for the United States at the end of his mandate, then returned to Cuba, this time ousting the liberal president Carlos Prío Socarrás, on March 10, 1952. Batista encouraged American investments, and the Mafia bought some of the major hotels, casinos, and mansions. Under Batista's dictatorship, gangsterism, corruption, and prostitution flourished throughout the country, which became a Yankee heaven, while the gap between the white bourgeoisie and the black proletariat widened. A 1952 *chambelona* song derided Batista (while also viciously alluding to his mother's black blood): "*Batista no tiene madre porque lo parió una mona*" ("Batista doesn't have a mother because a monkey gave birth to him").

Starting in 1953, Fidel Castro and his supporters hid in the Sierra Maestra, and this upsurge of guerrilla activity led to increased repression, arrests, torture, and murder by Batista's henchmen. The political troubles sometimes got in the way of musical activities: Benny Moré remembered that during a tour of the island, some dances and carnivals were canceled. At the Tropicana, in 1958, Nat King Cole apparently performed with some of Batista's armed bodyguards in the audience;[1] Jan Steinmiller, a registered nurse, recalled that, returning to the ship on which she worked, after attending this show, she heard shooting which, she later realized, may have had to do with the early stages of the coup led by Fidel Castro.[2] Ousted on December 3, 1958 by Castro and his Barbudos, Batista fled from Cuba on January 1 and headed for the Dominican Republic, leaving 40,000 of his soldiers behind.

There are, in the history of mankind, privileged moments when the genius of a people and exceptional circumstances combine to turn certain cities – Athens, Peking, Alexandria, Venice, Paris, New York – into incomparable cultural centers. Despite the multiple problems of the Batista era, Havana remained, for fun-lovers, an enchanted city. Few places on earth have been as exciting as Havana in the 1950s, and Cubans still remember those years as a golden era.

The capital, with its sizzling rhythms, drew a sensational constellation of musicians and composers into its orbit, and Cuba came to offer the world a series of astounding musical triumphs. Guillermo Cabrera Infante evoked in *Three Sad Tigers* Havana's exhilarating night life under Batista, with music springing forth everywhere. Tourists, already dazzled by Hollywood's portrayal of Cuba, succombed to the intoxication of these sensual tropics, amusing themselves at the splendid Casino de la Playa and in the countless hotels and clubs of Marianao and the Vedado. The most exhilarating of these places was undoubtedly the Tropicana, which presented first-rate attractions. Guillermo Cabrera Infante remembers it as "a really beautiful thing, exuberant with its lush greenery, an image of the island. The food was eatable, which is the only intrinsic quality of food, and the drinks, the way drinks are everywhere. But I find the music, the beauty of the female chorists and the unleashed silvan imagination of the choreographer unforgettable."[3]

Countless singers, musicians, and dancers worked in musical revues such as *Bondeye* and *Zum zum ba bae*, both starring Celia Cruz and Xiomara Álfaro, and in 1953 *Y qué e coo*, with the Valdés brothers (Vicentico, Alfredo, and Marcelino), Cheo Marquetti, the dancing teams of Elpidio y Margot and Paulito y Lilón; *El milagro de Ochún*, which included the revue *Batamú*; *Sepia Rhapsody*, starring the ubiquitous Celia Cruz, and choreographed by the famed "Rodney" (Roderico Neyra). And there were the dancing teams of Rolando (Rolando Espinosa) and Anisia, Estela and René, or Estela and Rolando (Rolando Lima).

1 In: Daniel Mark Epstein, *Nat King Cole*, p. 252.

2 In: Leslie Gourse, *Unforgettable – The Life and Mystique of Nat King Cole*, p. 197.

3 In: *Tres tristes tigres*, p. 199.

Private clubs and *academias de baile* also proliferated: Intersocial Club, Vedado Tennis Club, Miramar Yacht Club, Havana Country Club, La Fantástica, Sport Club, Marte y Belona, El Deportivo de la Fe, El Marianao Social, favored by Jamaicans, the Centro Gallego, the Centro Asturiano, the Centro Catalán, and, patronized by blacks, Las Aguilas, El Niche, Las Antillas, and the Isora Club, celebrated by Antonio Arcaño's Maravillas in an eponymous *danzón*. Beer halls such as La Tropical, La Polar, or Maltina Tívoli provided continuous enjoyment.

But most often it was in small cafés like El París or La Bombilla, in Marianao, that one could hear the most interesting jam sessions, these volcanic *descargas* (literally "discharges") quickly snatched up by record companies, and which in New York would eventually give rise to salsa.

Singers, musicians, and dancers also appeared in Cuban or Mexican movies: the Riverside Orchestra in *Tropicana*; La Sonora Matancera and the Cosmopolita Orchestra in *Música, mujeres y piratas*; Las Mulatas de Fuego, Oscar López and La Sonora Matancera in *Escuela de modelos*; the guitarist "Guyún" in *Estampa habanera*; Celina and Reutilio in *Bella, la salvaje*; Los Hermanos Palau in *Cuban Love Song*; Celia Cruz and Elena Burke in *Salón México, Una gallega en La Habana, Rincón criollo* (along with, again, Celina and Reutilio), *Amorcito Corazón, Affair in Havana*; Compay Segundo in *Cuba canta y baila, Cubita Linda* (along with La Sonora Matancera, Xiomara Álfaro, and Pototo y Filomeno), and *Yambao* (with Álfaro and Olga Guillot); Rita Montaner in *María la O*; Mongo Santamaría and Jóvenes del Cayo in *Ahora somos felices*; Las Hermanas Castro in *Zum zum ba bae*; René and Estela in *Una reunión de acusados*.

Radio, which had begun in Cuba on October 10, 1922, launched the careers of a number of artists. The first station, PWX, which belonged to the Cuban Telephone Company – a subsidiary of the American I.T.T. company – had inaugurated its programs with Rita Montaner and Marino Menéndez. By 1930, Havana already boasted about thirty stations. Among the most popular musical shows were *Media hora contigo, Espacio del medio día, La corte suprema del arte* – an amateur contest where audiences determined the winner by the intensity of their clapping and banged on a gong when candidates did not perform to their liking, *Fiesta en el aire, El escenario de plata*, and *La pausa que refresca*, sponsored by Coca-Cola. Obdulio Morales led the orchestra of the Martí theater and of Radio Cadena Suaritos; Enrique González Mántici (a former student of Emilio Grenet) the bands of the liberal station Radio Mil Diez and of Radio CMQ; Catalino Arjona also led the CMQ ensemble. The *danzón* pianist Tomás Corman was heard on Radio Continental; Antonio Arcaño, Miguelito Cuní, Arsenio Rodríguez, and Félix Chapotín on *Ritmos cubanos*; Miguel Matamoros on *Rincón Matamoros*. Radio RHC (Cadena Azul), led by pianist, trumpeter, guitarist, and *tresista* Isolina Carrillo, featured Chano Pozo, Tata Güines, and Celia Cruz; and the Orquesta Sensación played on Radio Unión, Radio Mambí, and Radio Salas.

During the carnivals, heightening the excitement, all the *comparsas* – Melodías de Iron Beer, Las Jardineras, the sumptuous Marquesas de Atarés, Los Chéveres de Belén[4] – spilled out onto the prestigious Paseo del Prado and the Malecón with their irresistible rhythms.

But as before, life for musicians was always fraught with obstacles. The radio and recording sessions paid almost nothing and the working hours were long. Compay Segundo remembers: "Certain nights we used to perform in the cabarets of Mariano Beach. We had to work till dawn, and in the final hours, we could no longer stand on our feet. Sometimes we wound up taking a nap on the tables until we heard a car engine. Then we would all jump up – get up, fellows! – and we would get back to play for the new arrivals.[5]

From nuevo ritmo *to cha-cha: the great* charangas

Charangas, partly overshadowed by *son* bands during the 1920s and the first half of the 1930s, made a remarkable comeback in the late 1940s. In the 1940s, the most influential one was flautist Antonio Arcaño's Las Maravillas, which heralded the mambo – one of Latin America's most flamboyant rhythms.

Nicknamed "The Monarch," Arcaño played, writes Cuban journalist Erena Hernández, "like black people." When some of the most prestigious bands tended to favor light-skinned musicians, he surrounded himself with black sidemen and charged black clubs lesser fees. A story told by Hernández also illustrates Arcaño's sense of humor: one day, he had been arrested for his leftist political activities. The judge asked him: "Are you a communist?" "No, doctor," he replied, "I am much too selfish to be one!"

Born in Havana in 1911 in a family of musicians (his grandmother taught piano, his uncle was a cellist and a bassist), Arcaño grew up in Regla and Guanabacoa, "steeped in *danzón*," he recalled, "to the marrow of my bones." After studying the flute with José Antonio Díaz, and the clarinet and the cornet with Armando Romeu, he played Spanish music in Marianao clubs, replaced Belisario López in Armando Valdespí's *charanga*, worked with the *charangas* of Tomás Cormán, Antonio María Romeu, Belisario López, and Silvio Contreras, and with Orquesta Gris.

In 1936, with Fernando Collazo he formed La Primera Maravilla del Siglo (The First Marvel of the Century), recruiting the outstanding violinist Virgilio Diago. But Collazo's success with women and his charisma upset Arcaño, and perhaps other band members as well. Diago and Collazo both left Arcaño the following year and Collazo was replaced in 1938 by Óscar López and then for a short while by Abelardo Barroso. However, resenting the fact that singers often upstaged him, from then on, like Antonio María Romeu before him, Arcaño played only instrumental music for public engagements.

4 Trumpeter Félix Chappotín composed *¿Por qué te pones así?* for this *comparsa*.

5 In: Luis Lázaro, *Compay Segundo, un sonero de leyenda*, p. 12.

In 1941, Arcaño renamed his ensemble Las Maravillas de Arcaño and, starting in 1944, whenever he appeared on Radio Lavín (which would become Radio Mil Diez), Orquesta Radiofónica de Antonio Arcaño. He introduced a cello into his band, and later a viola and a conga, played by "El Colorao" (Eliseo Pozo Martínez) – instruments then unusual in *charangas* – and surrounded himself with first-rate musicians: his cousin, flautist "Ñico" (José Antonio) Cruz (nicknamed "El Cojo"), violinists Fernando Díaz and Elizardo Aroche (and later Félix Reina and Enrique Jorrín), cellist "Macho" (Orestes) López, his brother, bassist "Cachao" (Israel López), pianist Jesús López, güiro-player Óscar Pelegrín, later replaced by Gustavo Tamayo (a Paulina Álvarez alumnus), and timbales whiz Ulpiano Díaz. Díaz added cowbells to his timbales set, a practice still current today.

Orestes López and his brother Israel wrote and arranged most of the repertoire, and they played a crucial part in the extraordinary success of Arcaño's band. A characteristic of Cuban bassists is the astonishing ease with which they maintain highly syncopated, sometimes tricky *tumbaos*. Israel López is considered the most prestigious Cuban bassist. He introduced those sophisticated *tumbaos* in the United States and was instrumental in reviving interest in the *danzón* there. In 1959 he recorded under his name a series of *danzones*, among them the sublime *Canta contrabajo*, with the melody played *arco*.

Neighbors of Arcaño in Guanabacoa, the López brothers also came from a prestigious musical lineage. (Their grandfather Aurelio led Havana's municipal marching band; their father Pedro – a trombone and bass player – was a member of the Havana Philharmonic Orchestra; their mother Rafaela played piano, guitar, and bass; their sister, Coralia, wrote several *danzones*, among them the celebrated *Isora Club*.) A sharp and intense man, Orestes, after studying flute, cello, violin, bass, and piano, occupied the bass chair with the Havana Philharmonic Orchestra and with Miguel "El Moro" Vázquez's *charanga*, formed a group with Abelardo Barroso in which he played the piano, and then the *charanga* Orquesta Unión. In 1937, he switched to cello with Armando Valdespí, and then returned to bass

with the Hermanos Contreras and Armando Romeu. A double bass virtuoso, Cachao also studied the bongo and the guitar (playing bongo in 1926 in a group in which Roberto Faz sang), and at the age of thirteen, he joined the Havana Symphonic Orchestra.

Las Maravillas rapidly soared in popularity and recorded a series of ravishing, finely honed *danzones*, among them *Adelante, Chancullo* (renamed *Se va el Matancero* by Arcaño), *Chifla Arcaño, Cándido el billetero de 33, El que más goza,* and *Jóvenes de la defensa.* Incidentally, Aaron Copland, who traveled to Cuba in 1941 – at the height of Las Maravillas' fame – remained impervious to the charm of the *danzón*, dismissing it as "unconscious grotesquerie," "inelegance perceived by inelegant people." Which did not prevent him,

Cachao. Sony Music Archives

upon his return to the United States, from composing a *Danzón cubano*, otherwise devoid of any warmth!

Eager to modernize the *danzón*, Orestes and Cachao López modified its structure. Around 1935, the *danzón* consisted of an introduction (called "clarinet trio"), a main theme ("violin part") and a final *trío* (or *montuno*) on which the musicians could improvise. After the flute solo, the piano generally concluded the piece. Gradually, the final *trío* section was subdivided into the *montuno* proper, on which the musicians soloed while the rhythm section maintained a steady accompaniment, and the *mambo* – a short passage consisting of unison riffs, with the cowbell accenting the strong beats.

Several etymologies have been proposed for the word *mambo,* some of which we mentioned earlier. Among other things it refers to a sacred Congo chant, although Patato Valdés, rather improbably, asserted that *mambo* comes from a drum slightly larger than a regular conga, named *mambisa*.[6] Whatever the origin of the word, Arcaño cued his musicians with "a thousand times *mambo*" whenever he wanted them to improvise on the *montuno* section. Today, in salsa, the *mambo* is a short passage generally played in unison by the rhythm section and separating the various *montuno* sections. And salsa bandleaders raise their fist to signal the *mambo*, and two fingers in the shape of a "V" for Victory for the *montuno*.

6 The *mambises* were soldiers of the Máximo Gómez and Antonio Maceo brigades who fought for the independence of Cuba, in the late nineteenth century.

Mambo section of *Y nace una estrella* as played by Arcaño.
In: Lise Waxer, *Of Mambo Kings and Songs of Love: Dance Music in Havana and New York from the 1930s to the 1950s*, pp. 168–9.

7 In: Enrique Romero, *Cachao, montuno con tradición*.

8 Dora Ileana Torres, "Del danzón cantado al cha cha chá," in: *Panorama de la música popular cubana*, Giro, Radamés (ed.), p. 198.

In addition to dividing the *trío* into *montuno* and *mambo*, Las Maravillas injected elements of the *son*, as other composers had done before, into this section. In 1934, a new rhythm emerged from this jazzed-up *trío*. Orestes López called it *nuevo ritmo*, and Cachao *sabrosura* ("sweetness" or "pleasantness"). In 1938, the band recorded a *danzón* by Orestes entitled *Mambo*, and the same year Antonio Sánchez composed the highly syncopated *Bella Unión*, based on this *nuevo ritmo*. Also based on this *nuevo ritmo*, *Mambo* included a wonderful piano solo, but with it deemed too "African" (prejudices still prevailed), it was rejected for a few months by radio stations. It was finally broadcast on Radio Mil Diez. "When my brother and I did *Mambo*", comments Cachao, "we used to bring it up to an incredible speed, it was very fast. One used to dance slowly and at that time, people couldn't dance the Mambo, so we said, we can't keep that tempo up, we have to slow it down."[7] Those changes, however, had already been around for a few years. "Starting in 1930," confided Arcaño, "Orestes López and I used to go to cabarets and other places playing and jamming, and the *mambeao* style already characterized his performances."[8] Other composers swiftly imitated this *nuevo ritmo*, but only in September 1944, with Arcaño's record of *Arriba la invasión*, did a piece actually come to be called a mambo on an album or on sheet music. Around the mid-1940s, Arcaño's *danzones* also began to absorb strains of American popular music and to acquire English titles (*Pickin' Chicken, Broadway*).

It is Damaso Pérez Prado, however, in the early 1950s, who truly invented the mambo as a distinct musical genre. Like Arcaño, he used jazz and popular music elements in his *danzones*, but in a more systematic and extensive fashion, orchestrating them with trap drums, saxophones, and trumpets. His exciting, highly charged "mambos," as he called them, electrified dancers, and the mambo enjoyed tremendous popularity until the mid-1950s, although in Cuba, dancers often preferred other rhythms, among them the *boteo* and the *casino*. A harmonious mixture of *danzón* steps and rock 'n' roll turns, the *boteo* was popularized around 1954 by the Hermanos Castro, while today on the island, the *casino*, introduced in 1953 by Orquesta Casino de la Playa, still competes with salsa.

According to a tradition widespread among Havana musicians (Arsenio Rodríguez, Miguelito Cuní, and Félix Alfonso among others), Arcaño dedicated several of his compositions – *Los Sitios llaman, Club social de Marianao, Isora Club, Social Club Buena Vista, Social Club Antonio Maceo, Cayo Hueso y su victoria, A Belén le toca ahora, Caraguao se botó* – to various of the city neighborhoods and venues where his band performed. *Caraguao se botó* is noteworthy for containing, inside the structure of the *danzón*, a splendid bolero by Orestes López: *Lágrima*, and also includes a fragment from Debussy's *Petite suite*. Sung by Miguelito Cuní on a 1939 record, *Lágrima* is one of the few boleros recorded by this *sonero*. On occasions, Arcaño also accompanied dancers, among them Carlos Yera and Pascualino, whose steps foreshadowed those of the mambo.

In 1944 Elizardo Aroche left Arcaño to play in Mexico with a symphony orchestra, but the *charanga* continued to record (Cachao's *Los chicos buenos*, Orestes López's *Jóvenes de la defensa*). In 1947 Arcaño, incapacitated by a muscular disorder, handed the band over to flautists Antonio Cruz and José Fajardo. With their superb violinist Miguel Barbón (nicknamed "Brindis" after the nineteenth-century Cuban virtuoso Claudio Brindis de Salas), Las Maravillas nevertheless managed to maintain their position. Around 1953 they cut various sides, among them *Mambo del gavilán* (with pianist Frank Emilio, *conguero* Julián Cabrera, and a vocal *cuarteto* featuring Francisco Fellové), and then started to decline. Fajardo eventually left, followed by the pianist, also ailing, and other musicians. The band performed for the last time in 1958 and then broke up.

Though no other *charanga* could dislodge Arcaño from the number-one position he occupied during the 1940s, there existed a good many other compelling *charangas*. In the 1950s, the tight and swinging Orquesta Aragón came to the fore with its bubbly cha-chas and, over the years, it mellowed like a fine old wine. During the 1970s, Aragón, then Cuba's most prestigious *charanga*, often traveled abroad as a kind of cultural ambassador.

Formed in 1939 in the beautiful city of Cienfuegos, in the center of the island, by bassist Orestes Aragón and flautist Efraín Loyola (also the founder of Los Naranjos), and first called La Rítmica Aragón, it was an offshoot of a small group which included in particular Aragón, Loyola, and pianist Genoveno Jiménez. It was run as a cooperative in which everyone received the same salary; money was always put aside to pay for stage costumes and to provide a fund in case of ill health or other problems. It consisted of Aragón and Loyola plus Pablito Romay (vocals), Rufino Roque (piano), Noelio Morejón (güiro), Filiberto Depestre and René González (violins), and Orestes Varona (timbales).[9]

The group first performed for a local dance at the Sociedad Minerva, and then in the town of Remedios, in the former province of Las Villas, in the center of Cuba. In 1941 Rafael Lay succeeded René González, and in 1948, at the age of twenty-one, he replaced the ailing Aragón as the band's director.[10] In the 1950s violinist Celso Valdés, saxophonist Clemente Lozano, and flautists "Richard" (Eduardo) Egües[11] and Rolando Lozano joined the *charanga*, Egües becoming one of its leading lights. In 1953 they recorded *El agua de Clavelito*, inspired by the *trovador* Alfonso "Clavelito" Poro, who also happened to give spiritual advice on the radio, *Tres lindas cubanas*, *Mentiras criollas*, and other numbers that strongly impressed listeners. *El agua de Clavelito*, which gave its name to a radio show, was followed by a new string of hits including Egües's *El bodeguero*, written in 1956, *Mambo inspiración*, Lay's *Cero codazos, cero cabezazos* ("no elbowing, no head-butting") – about the instructions given by the referee to boxers before a match, Marcelino Guerra's *Pare cochero*, Enrique Jorrín's *Silver Star*, named after a social club, *Baila Vicente*, and Pedro Junco's *Nosotros*. Although it has often been said that the refrain of *El bodeguero* "*Toma Chocolate, paga lo que debes*" ("Here, Chocolate, pay up what you owe") refers to a debt that trumpeter "Chocolate" Armenteros had contracted in Havana with Enriquito, the musicians' tailor (Armentero claims he always paid back what he owed), it came in fact from a *pregón* sung by an ice-cream vendor; by that time, anyway, Chocolate Armenteros had already moved to New York in order to play with Machito.

In 1955 the band settled in Havana. Benny Moré and Jorrín offered them their help (Moré with engagements, Jorrín with scores) and they gradually became established there. The following year they recorded two racy numbers: *Ay José* and *Los tamalitos de Olga*, and they acknowledged the emergence of rock 'n' roll with a "rockified" cha-cha entitled *Guasabeando el rock 'n' roll*, which anticipated the musical hybrids of the 1960s.

The *charanga* Almendra, a fine group organized in 1940 by bassist and composer Abelardito Valdés (Ernesto Abelardo Valdés de la Cantera), also gained prominence. Valdés (1911–1958) had played güiro in Luis Carrillo's band, in which his father was the bassist, and then performed with the ensembles of Tata Pereira, Tata Alfonso, López-Barroso, and the Hermanos Contreras. Almendra, which featured the ubiquitous flautist El Cojo, played both classics: *Fefita*, *Me lo dijo Adela*,

9 Aragón was a carpenter by trade, Varona ironed in a drycleaner store and Loyola, who had previously led his own *charanga*, was a baker.

10 Later Lay (1927–1982) would also conduct classical music orchestras.

11 The son of bandleader Eduardo Egües, Egües also played piano. A former cigar maker, he started out with the band subbing for their regular flautist, and wound up staying 30 years with Aragón.

El cadete constitucional, and new compositions: *Malanga na' ma'*, and the famous *Penicilina*, the story of a lovesick man requesting penicillin in order to cure himself. Valdés's popular *danzón Almendra* – which had inspired the *charanga*'s name – also gave birth to the *trío*, a rhythm based on a bass riff (different from the *danzón* section also called *trío*). In the 1950s Almendra was often heard on the radio with its vocalist Dominica Verges; and the band's *timbalero*, Evaristo Martínez, also created a rhythm of his own, the short-lived *mau mau*.

Incisive and flexible, La Sensación was founded in 1953 by *timbalero* Rolando Valdés at the suggestion of musicians Chuchú Esquijarrosa, Eloy Martínez, and Miguel Santa Cruz ("El Pitcher"). Singers Dandy Beltrán, Elpidio Piedra, and Cheo Marquetti contributed to its fame but some of its most memorable recordings were made in 1954 with Abelardo Barroso (Ermenegildo Cárdenas's *El brujo de Guanabacoa*, with its allusions to *santería*; the poignant, flamenco-tinged *La hija de Juan Simón; Guantanamera*).

In 1949 José Fajardo formed his own *charanga*. He took Cachao, Jesús López, Ulpiano Díaz, Félix Reina, and Gustavo Tamayo from Las Maravillas; recruited *conguero* Tata Güines; and innovated by adding a bongo, as well as a cymbal to its timbales. Arcaño had done away with vocalists, but as the cha-cha – then in full swing – often called for singers, Fajardo employed Felo Bacallao, Joseíto Núñez, Sergio Galzavo, and Rudy Calzado.

After playing maracas and claves as a child with the band run by his father Alberto, a clarinettist, Fajardo had taken up the flute and joined Orquesta Hilda, which included his brother Alberto on violin and his sister Hilda on piano. In 1936 he moved to Havana and, after stints in the police and the army, he worked with René Alvarez's Romance Musical (directed by the pianist Lino Frías) and with various *charangas*: Antonio María Romeu, Paulina Alvarez, Joseíto Fernández, Melodías del 40, Neno González.

Fajardo's warm and happy music (*Kikiriki, Me voy pa' Morón, Ritmo de pollos*, created by his pianist Pepecito Reyes and based on *son montuno* chords, the cha-cha *Los marcianos llegaron ya*, by Rosendo Ruiz Jr., son of the *trovador* Rosendo Ruiz, whose lyrics proclaimed "The Martians have arrived and they arrived dancing [the cha-cha]," *El bodeguero, Bilongo*, and other hits) and his lively shows featuring dancers made him so popular that he had to create two additional bands (the most prestigious one performing in the major clubs, the others in smaller venues, or outside Havana). In 1958, he played with his All Stars (Tata Güines, Ulpiano Díaz, Chocolate and Armandito Armenteros, Pedro Hernández, Elio Valdés) at the Waldorf Astoria, in a benefit for John F. Kennedy's presidential campaign.

In 1953 the Montmartre club in Havana presented a revue entitled *Danzón*, which featured Rita Montaner, Bola de Nieve, Orquesta Casino de la Playa, and dancing partners Elpidio y Margot. But the *danzón*, already on the wane, soon gave way to the cha-cha. The cha-cha galvanized *charangas*, threatened by the emergence of rock 'n' roll, although the Orquesta Aragón, Chico O'Farrill, and other musicians combined rock and Cuban strains, thus heralding the New York *boogaloo*.

In 1942 Ninón Mondéjar – who came from the Matanzas area – founded in Havana the Orquesta América with, among others, violinists Enrique Jorrín and Félix Reina, flautist Rolando Lozano, and, on güiro, the ubiquitous Gustavo Tamayo. They first performed at the Julio Antonio Mella club; three years later, at the Liceo del Pilar, they were playing *danzones* very close in style to the cha-cha. Jorrín, however, was the real initiator of this rhythm.

Born in Candelaria, Pinar del Río, Jorrín (1926–1987) wrote music for various bands and was composer of the *danzón Central Constancia*, based on the *nuevo ritmo*. In 1941 he replaced his brother Miguelito in the Hermanos Contreras ensemble, and then played with the Hermanos Peñalver, led Selecciones del 45, and collaborated with Arcaño. He wrote several lively tunes – *El túnel, El Náñigo, Africa habla*, the sung *danzón Silver Star, Doña Olga* – that won acclaim for Orquesta América. But noticing that some dancers had trouble dealing with the mambo's complex syncopations, he decided to simplify it, and suggested that the band sing the refrains in unison.

It is mainly *La engañadora* ("The Cheating Woman"), written in 1950, and labeled "mambo-rumba," which triggered the cha-cha craze. The structure of *La engañadora* consisted of a vocal part based on a cha-cha rhythm, and of an instrumental section with doubled-up tempo that was in fact closer to a mambo.

Two funny incidents witnessed by Jorrín suggested to him the lyrics of *La engañadora*. "One afternoon," he explained to Erena Hernández, "I was walking on Infanta street and a woman of ample proportions, very provocative in fact, happened to walk by. It was the last years that the trams were running and when she passed by them, they stopped. The policeman stopped as well . . . and finally all the men, because it was a rather phenomenal sight . . . One of them kneeled on the sidewalk, which was still rather broad, at the corner of Sitios and Infanta, and he started saying a prayer to her, as if she were some sort of Virgin. As she walked by him she gave him a contemptuous look. The man, miffed, turned towards us. 'Oh boy, so much fuss, and when you look up close, it's only rubber!' he exclaimed." The other incident happened in a club located at the corner of the Paseo del Prado and Neptuno Street, where the band was playing. Men had noticed a girl of whom "certain parts of the body were not harmonious because those which one could not see were bigger than her arms and her legs. One day, after walking into the club looking rather frowsy, she went to the ladies room and came out looking all tarted up as she usually did."[12] Upon seeing this amazing change, her admirers suspected trickery.

12 In: Erena Hernández, *La música en persona*, pp. 73–4.

A Prado y Neptuno	At the corner of Prado and Neptuno
Iba una chiquita	A girl was walking
Que todos los hombres	That all the men
La tenían que mirar.	Were ogling.
Estaba gordita	She was rather plump,
Muy bien formadita	Very well shaped
Era graciosita	And quite graceful.
Y en resumen colosal.	In short just wonderful.
Pero todo en la vida	But everything in life
Se sabe	Gets found out
Sin siquiera averiguar,	Without having to check.
Se ha salido que en sus formas	One learned that her curves
Rellenos tan sólo hay.	Were all padded up.
Que bobas son las mujeres	How stupid are the women
Que nos tratan de engañar,	Who try to deceive us,
Dijiste.	You said.

La engañadora – Enrique Jorrín

One evening in 1952, while Orquesta América was playing *Silver Star*, the *coro* started to improvise on the *montuno* section, the words *"cha cha chá, cha cha chá, es un baile original"* ("The cha-cha, the cha-cha is a brand new dance").

The "cha-cha-cha" onomatopoeia was suggested by the shuffle of the dancers' feet on the floor, but *chachá* is also the name of a maraca from the province of Oriente.

One of the keys to dancing the mambo well is to grasp the bass *tumbao*, but no extraordinary musical ability was required for the cha-cha. A kind of slower and squarer mambo, the cha-cha had a clearly defined rhythm and structure: one only had to step on one, two, and three and do a little shuffle on the fourth beat. And the melodies, sung in unison rather than by a lead singer or two harmonizing vocalists, were particularly catchy. Whole ballrooms of boisterous revelers started to sing **"Vacilón, que rico vacilón,"** or **"Toma chocolate, paga lo que debes"** at the top of their voices while dancing. However, according to pianist Alfredo Rodríguez, the cha-cha steps had already been around for a while, and he remembers that "around 1945, my mother was already giving parties where a dancer did them."

Mondéjar started writing cha-chas himself (*Ya no camino más* among them). Orquesta América popularized this rhythm on the radio, on television, and in various clubs, and the cha-cha caught on like wildfire. When a member of the British royalty visited Cuba, the Countess of Revilla de Camargo even had a cha-cha performance put on for him in her splendid Havana mansion.

In May 1954, the Orquesta América left for Mexico, where it would stay for four years, and Jorrín started his own *charanga*, which included his brother Jesús, flautist Miguel O'Farrill, singer Tito Gómez, and pianist Rubén González (an Arsenio Rodríguez alumnus). The following year Jorrín too moved to Mexico, taking with him the *sonero* Rudy Calzado and popularizing his new creation there. He returned to Havana in 1958 and formed a new *charanga* with – for the first time in this type of band – an electric bass, played by Fabián García.

The pianist, saxophonist, violinist, and flautist Antonio Sánchez Reyes ("Musiquita") – ex-sideman of Paulina Álvarez, La Ideal, José Ramón's La Fantasía, and Orquesta América, and author of *Los Sitios llaman* – founded the Orquesta América del 55 and also recorded such cha-chas as *Tu rica boca*,[13] *La vacuna Salk* (named after Jonas Salk, who developed the first polio vaccine), the unavoidable *Qué rico vacilón*, and other tunes.

Benefiting from the cha-cha craze, a host of other *charangas* enjoyed dancers' favor: Orquesta Ideal, led by flautist Joseíto Valdés, inventor of a kind of mambo called "mambo Manzanillo"; the groups led by Senén Suárez and flautist "Pancho El Bravo" (Alberto Cruz); Orquesta Novedades, Jóvenes Estrellas; Orquesta Super Colosal, modeled on Orquesta América, which backed Cheo Marquetti on *Son de Mateo*, in one of Marquetti's rare *charanga* performances; La Jicotea, led by Rosendo Ruiz Jr., which featured flautist Gonzalo Fernández and Miguel Barbón; Melodías del 40, founded by pianist Regino Frontela; Orquesta Sublime, formed in 1956 by flautist Melquiades Fundora, who combined the cha-cha with other genres, among them the *guaracha* (*Mi pollo está para el campo*), and the *danzonete*

13 Described as "jumpy" on the record; the Cubans' rhythmic imagination is boundless!

(*El rey del cariño*), and added a clarinet to the traditional flute and violins line-up, as José Belén Puig had done years before.

Charangas also sprang up outside Havana. Among them was Armonías del 48: founded in Florida, near Camagüey, the group then changed its name to Jóvenes Estrellas and later to La Maravilla de Florida. Led by Filiberto Depestre and then Fernando Cabrera, it included flautist Eloy Martínez, percussionist Miguel Santa Cruz, and the remarkable violinist Candelario. La Ritmo Oriental, created in 1958 and headed by bassist Humberto Perera, also became popular throughout Cuba, presenting, like Fajardo, vivid and elaborate shows.

The decline of the cha-cha in the late 1950s coincided with the end of the Batista era.

Updating the son

From the 1940s, the *son* grew more sophisticated. It was adopted by *conjuntos*, which displaced *sextetos* and *septetos*, and by big bands such as those of Obdulio Morales, Julio Cueva, or Benny Moré, which managed to keep its flavor despite elaborate arrangements.

Son groups – with their frequently changing personnel – proliferated. Among them were Domingo Vargas's Jóvenes del Cayo (with which Pérez Prado briefly played in 1944), with "Alfonsín" (Ildefonso Quintana, also the band's musical director), Vargas and Celio González on vocals; Rubén González's Conjunto Niágara; the Conjunto Camacho; Manuel Morel Campos's ensemble; the Conjunto Saratoga, with singer Lino Borges; Raúl Díaz's Conjunto Apollo, with Cándido Camero on *tres* and Mongo Santamaría on bongo; the Sexteto Siboney; Jóvenes del Feeling; Orlando Contreras's Kalamazoo; La Gloria Matancera, with singers Pepe Merino and Caridad González; Estrellas del Ritmo; Los Salseros; Las Hermanas Duchesne (with pianist Anita Justiz); Lira Matancera, led by singer, guitarist, and *tresista* Félix Cárdenas; Ñico Saquito's Conjunto de Oriente.

But just as Arcaño dominated the *danzón*, "Arsenio" Rodríguez (Ignacio Loyola Rodríguez Skull) was the *son*'s emblematic figure. He created the *conjunto* format, by bringing in a conga, a piano, and three trumpets. He also anticipated the mambo with his own "*diablo*" (devil) rhythm, and with a special *masacote* (figure) played by the trumpets on the *montuno* section.

Controversy has arisen as to who invented the mambo, whether Arcaño, Rodríguez, or Pérez Prado. In the climate of artistic emulation that prevailed in Havana, musicians listened to each other and the same general ideas circulated among them. An osmosis began to take place between *conjuntos* and *charangas*, which still continues today, with these two types of band regularly exchanging both instruments and tunes. Nevertheless, Rodríguez's *diablo*, derived from the Congo music he had heard in his youth, was very much his own creation, and some of his early compositions already recalled the mambo. *So' caballo, Tumba palo cucuye, Yo son kanga, Bruca maniguá, Dundunbanza,* and *Yo nací del Africa* evidenced his Bantu heritage, transmitted by his father and his grandfather, brought from Africa as a slave. And Rodríguez later referred to his musical style as "*quindembo,*" from the Bantu word *ki n'dembo,* said to mean "mixture."

A hymn to freedom and a black manifesto, *Bruca maniguá,* with its Congo expressions such as "*Abekuta wiri ndinga*" ("Open your ears and listen to what I say") and cryptic refrain "*che che bruca maniguá abekuto qui rindingua bruca manigua,*" evokes the spell cast upon the white man, torturer of his black brothers:

14 The word *mundele* still exists in Zaire, where the arrival of whites in villages is announced in coded language on the *tofoke* drum.

15 Slaves born in Africa (called *taitas* or *bozales* in Spanish) – who could still, in the late nineteenth century especially, be identified by their ethnic origin, were called *negros de nación* (nation blacks).

Yo son carabalí, negro de nasión	I am Carabalí, *nation* Black,[15]
Sin la libertá, no puedo viví.	Without freedom, I can't live.
Mundele cabá con mi corasón	The white man destroys my heart,
Tanto matratá, cuerpo va fuirí	He mistreats me so much that I'm going to die.
N'tan kangando a lo mundele[14]	They are casting a spell on the white man.
Bruca maniguá, a-é.	*Bruca maniguá, a-é.*

Rodríguez freely expressed his political and social concerns in other songs as well: *Vaya pa'l monte,* which also deals with racism; or another number, which commented on the damage done to José Martí's statue by the U.S. Navy:

Bruca maniguá – Arsenio Rodríguez

¿Qué es lo que pasa aquí	What's happening here,
En este pedacito de suelo	On this little piece of land?
Que nos escupen los extranjeros	Foreigners come and spit on us,
Hasta el Apóstol Martí?	Even on the Apostle Martí.

Known as "El Ciego maravilloso" ("The marvelous blind man") on account of both his visual handicap and his musical proficiency, Rodríguez was born in 1911 in Güira de Macurijes, near Matanzas, and had seventeen siblings. He grew up in dire poverty in the town of Güines. At twelve he was blinded by a mule kick to the head, and subsequently poured all his energies into music. He enjoyed going to hear rumbas in the *barrio* of Leguina. He sang gutsily and played Congo ritual drums, among them the *yuka* and the *kinfuiti*, as well as the *tres*, the bass, the *botija*, the *marímbula*, and the conga. Latin musicians still appreciate his vigorous bass *tumbaos*. His *tres* solos, rhythmically tricky, give the impression of pulling away from the groundbeat, and Rodríguez's mastery of the *tres* still inspires awe in practitioners of this instrument.

Though friendly, generous, and sincere, Rodríguez was very demanding in his music, and his authoritarian manner sometimes intimidated other musicians. He used to explain to his young trumpeter Guillermo Fellové: "One must sing the themes and the *montunos*. What one plays must always be *cuadrado*."[16] "Rodríguez's well-constructed and swinging music sometimes had a 2/4 feel although it was in 4/4," Fellové commented.

16 Well-structured.

In 1927 Rodríguez began to write boleros, but gradually switched to more upbeat *sones, sones montunos*, and *guarachas*. In 1930 he moved to Havana, played *tres* with the Sexteto Boston, which then included the great bassist Regatillo – immortalized by Arcaño in his *danzón El truco de Regatillo* ("Regatillo's trick") – and with the Conjunto Bellamar.

In 1940 he formed his own *conjunto*, that came to include superb musicians, and singers with a high and vibrant voice: his sister Estela, his brother "Quique" on conga, trumpeters Armando Armenteros, "Bene" (Benitín) Bustillo, Juanito Rogers, and the amazing Rubén Calzado, singers Miguelito Cuní, Rigoberto Díaz, and Joseíto Núñez, pianists Rubén González and Lino Frías, models for scores of keyboard players after them, and the recklessly swinging bassists Nilo Alfonso and Nilo Agudín. He wooed various Havana neighborhoods with, in particular, *A Belén le toca ahora* or the *guaguancó El Cerro tiene la llave*, and he taunted his rivals with numbers such as *Lo que dice Usted* ("Whatever you say"). Later Benny Moré and Tito Rodríguez also challenged other singers with mordant songs.

In the mid-1940s, the RCA Victor label organized as a PR gambit a musical *mano a mano* (hand-to-hand combat) between Rodríguez and his Conjunto Orquesta Todos Estrellas and Arcaño y Sus Maravillas, although a photograph taken around that time shows both men courteously shaking hands, and both musicians denied there was ever any hostility between them.

To Arcaño's elegant *danzones Átomo musical, Arriba la invasión, Jóvenes de la defensa*, Rodríguez responded, with his great singer René Alvarez, with such witty *sones* as the salacious *Dame un cachito pa' huele*, which suggests: "Now that mama is gone, gimme a little piece to sniff," or *Cangrejo fue a estudiar* – a song about a baseball-player nicknamed Cangrejo ("crab"), who goes off ("backwards," the lyrics specify) to study. The match was a draw, each group illustrating with consummate artistry different facets of Cuban music.

In 1946 the inspired pianist "Lilí" (Luis) Martínez Griñán joined Rodríguez. The following year, the singer Miguelito Valdés invited Rodríguez to New York so he could consult an eye specialist. After finding out that there was no cure for his blindness, Rodríguez, in a moment of despair, wrote the poignant bolero *La vida es un sueño* ("Life is a dream").

Arsenio Rodríguez and Antonio Arcaño.
Cariño Records

Después que uno vive veinte desengaños	If one has gone through twenty betrayals,
¿Que importa uno más?	Why should one more matter?
Después que conozca la acción de la vida	Once you know how life works,
No debes llorar.	You shouldn't cry.

In New York, without dwelling on his suffering, he made various recordings for Coda – Gabriel Oller's newly founded label: Chano Pozo's African-sounding *La teta e*, with his friends Miguelito Valdés, Pozo, and *bongocero* "Bilingüe" (Frank Gilberto Ayala); Pozo's *Cómetelo to'*, with the Afro-Cubans and Tito Rodríguez; *Porque tú sufres, Rumba en swing*, and his composition *Pasó en Tampa*, evoking his tribulations with the English language; and Pozo's interesting *Serende*, with Ayala, Panchito Riset, Pozo, and Marcelino Guerra. Pianist René Hernández wrote some of the arrangements; like Pozo, in New York Rodríguez imposed his own Afro-Cuban aesthetics.

Back in Havana, Rodríguez was a major attraction, sought after by all the social clubs and *academias de baile*. In February 1948, he recorded *Tumba palo cucuye, Apurrúneme mujer, Tintorera ya llegó, Yo no engaño a las mujeres*, and *Tecolora*, giving his group (for legal reasons) the name Estrellas del Ritmo. Surrounded by, among others, Martínez Griñán, his cousin René Skull on vocals, bassist Lázaro Prieto, *bongocero* "Papa Kila" (Antolín Suárez), *conguero* "Chocolate" (Félix Alfonso), and trumpeters Rafael Corbacho and Guillermo Fellové, he reached the summit of his art, with enticing new material. *A todos los barrios*, celebrated the various Havana neighborhoods, and *El sentimiento de Arsenio Rodríguez*, featured "Chocolate" (Alfredo) Armenteros.[17] Also included were *No me llores más*, the colorful *Yo no puedo comer vista gacha* ("I can't eat pork") – whose refrain announces: *me gusta la salsa* ("I like the gravy") – the *canto de palo* (Congo chant) *Dundunbanza*, and the moving bolero *Me siento muy solo* ("I feel very lonely"), all vibrant testaments to his creativity.

In 1950, Rodríguez left his band to the trumpeter Félix Chappotín, who had replaced Guillermo Fellové, and moved to the United States. With Rodríguez's consent, Chappotín renamed the *conjunto* Félix Chappotín y su Conjunto Todos Estrellas while staying true to his predecessor's spirit. Chappotín had good leadership qualities, and an expressive style which "Chocolate" Armenteros has called *llorao de trompeta* ("trumpet wail").

Born in Cayo Hueso in 1909 in a large family, Chappotín was, through his mother, related to Chano Pozo. Despite a chaotic childhood (like Louis Armstrong he spent time in a home for delinquents), he studied the saxhorn and the tuba, and at the age of eleven he joined the *banda infantil* (children's brass band) of the town of Guanajay. In 1923 he was given a cornet and he played for three years with the *comparsa* of the Liberal Party and with the

17 Rodríguez named Armenteros "Sebastián" and he wrote for him *El guano* – an Abakwa word meaning "handsome."

Septeto Orquídea. In 1926 he moved to Havana and worked with the Sexteto Colín, the Septeto Habanero, and then Munamar, with which he did a series of recordings (*Tras las rejas*, *Espabílate*, *Mi sansa mi coco*). He also wrote for the *comparsa* Los Chéveres de Belén the tune *¿Por qué te pones así?* After passing through a string of *son* groups: Pinín, Agabamar, Universo, Boloña, Bolero, Carabinas de Ases, América, Jóvenes del Cayo, Gloria Cubana, he performed in 1939 on Radio Cadena Azul, and with Chano Pozo led the Conjunto Azul, sponsored by that station.

Martínez Griñán and two other remarkable exponents of the *son*: singer "Miguelito Cuní" (Miguel Cunill) and *tresista* "Niño Rivera" (Andrés Echevarría), collaborated with Chappotín and enhanced his prestige. Rivera had a dynamic and compact way of playing, with the octave jumps and descending sixths characteristic of the *típico* (traditional) style. In addition to his pianistic skills, Martínez Griñán composed many colorful songs for the band: *Pueblo Nuevo se pasó*, *Alto Songo*, *Aunque tu mami no quiera*, which proclaims: "Although your mother doesn't want to, I do!" *Que se fuñan*, *Quimbombó*, which associated food with religion.[18] He also evoked Afro-Cuban culture on the albums *Quimbombó* and *Ritmos Santeros*, recorded under his own name. And the rare alchemy between Cuní's robust voice and Chappotín's expressive trumpet lasted many years.

Cuní made his professional debut in Pinar del Río, his native town, with the band founded by his family, and sang in Niño Rivera's Septeto Caridad, Fernando Sánchez's ensemble, Jacobo Rubalcaba's band, and with Ernesto Muñoz and then Arsenio Rodríguez. He worked with Antonio Arcaño, the Conjunto Modelo, and René Álvarez, and joined Chappotín in 1950, Benny Moré in 1956, and Bebo Valdés in 1959. He wrote several *sones*, among them *Guachinando*, and under his name, recorded the delightful *Sones de ayer* (with Niño Rivera and trumpeter "Florecita"); also following the tradition of saluting the various Havana neighborhoods, *Guaguancó a todos los barrios*.

Like Cuní, Niño Rivera (1919–1996) hailed from Pinar del Río. *Bongocero*, at the age of five, of the Septeto Caridad, he became, at nine, *tresista* of the Septeto Segundo Boloña in Cayo Hueso and then, two years later, *timbalero* of Nicomedes Callavas' *charanga*. In 1934 he joined the Septeto Boloña and in the following year the Septeto Bolero, co-founded the *conjunto* Rey de Reyes in 1942, and in 1945 started yet another *conjunto*. In the 1950s he wrote arrangements for the Conjunto Casino, Arcaño, Orquesta Riverside, and the orchestra of Radio CMQ, and after a stay in Mexico, he organized, in 1959, a new ensemble.

18 "*Quimbombó que resbala con la yuca seca*," proclaim the lyrics of *Quimbombó*. The *quimbombó* (okra) is the consecrated food of the Yoruba god Changó; *resbalar* means "to slip" but *resbaloso* (slippery) is another name for okra, and *yuca* (manioc) is the food of the *orisha* Ogún.

Around the late 1950s, Chappotín's style matured. His arrangements became more polished, with big-band riffs (*Lechón y bachata*,[19] the lively *El carbonero*, with its famous refrain *Carbón bon bon*, sung by everyone in Cuba, *Me voy contigo*, *Rompe saragüey*. And he made some of his best albums: *Chappotín y sus Estrellas* (with Cheo Marquetti); *Sones de ayer* (with Florecita, and Chocolate Armenteros, who also sings in the *coro*), with an exuberant *El diablo* and two beautiful *sones* by Bienvenido Julián Gutiérrez: *Donde va Chichi* and *Convergencia; Mi son, mi son, mi son* (featuring *tresista* Arturo "Alambre" Dulce); and *Perlas del son*. Rolo Martínez also sang with Chappotín before pursuing his own career.

René Álvarez collaborated with Orquesta Godínez, the *conjunto* Gloria de Cuba, and Los Muchachos de Boloña. In 1948, after his stints with Rodríguez and Chappotín, he organized the *conjunto* Los Astros with several of Arsenio Rodríguez's former sidemen: Juanito Rogers, Cuní, Rivera, Armenteros, and *conguero* "Campeón." During the two ensuing years, he turned out numbers that still bore Rodríguez's stamp, among them *Para la niña y la señora* (often performed by Machito in New York), *Déjame tranquilo, Palo cagueiran* (an allusion to Afro-Cuban rituals), *Lindo yambú* (mentioned on the record as a *guaguancó* but done as a *son*), and the *rumba Yumbale*.

Around the same time another Rodríguez veteran, *conguero* Félix Alfonso, founded – primarily for recording purposes – the Conjunto Modelo. Directed from 1953 on by Lázaro Prieto and then Lino Frías, it included some Arsenio Rodríguez stalwarts: Cuní, Rivera (followed by Ramón "Liviano" Cisneros), Papa Kila, singer Conrado Cepero; and the group's output from 1948 to 1956 (*Mano a mano, Guaguancó en La Habana*) recalls that of the Ciego Maravilloso. After the Conjunto Modelo was disbanded, in 1957 Alfonso formed Estrellas de Chocolate – with Cuní and two other vocalists – and he continued to produce powerful music (Reinaldo Bolaños's Congo-sounding *Fania; Que traigan el guaguancó*, which proclaimed: "When Arsenio went abroad, I think he took the *guaguancó* rhythm with him"; the sizzling *El kikiriki*).

Another outstanding *son* band was La Sonora Matancera,[20] which became one of the institutions of Cuban music. Its career spanned several decades and it contributed to the revival of the *típico* sound in the United States. Over the years, with its earthy style, it backed some of Latin America's most celebrated singers, among them its featured vocalists Bienvenido Granda and Nelson Pineda, but also Daniel Santos, Vicentico Valdés, Leo Marini, Celio González, Alberto Beltrán, Toña la Negra, Daniel Santos, Guillermo Portabales, and of course Celia Cruz, its brightest star.

A former *estudiantina*, it was formed in Hojos de Aguas, in the province of Matanzas, in 1924 under the name of Tuna Liberal, by Pablo Vázquez and *timbalero* Valentín Cané. It first performed in the city of Zalamanca and in 1927, moved to Havana. Besides Cané, it originally consisted of Ismael Goberna (trumpet), Domingo Medina, Juan Bautista Llopis, Julio Govín, and José Valera (guitars), "Jimagua" (timbales), Rogelio Martínez (lead singer), and Chino Durán and

19 *Lechón* is roasted suckling pig, *bachata* a rhythm created by Bebo Valdés and also the name of a rural festivity.

20 The name *sonora* is generally given to a band comprising three trumpets.

Eugenio (*coro*). They were soon playing regularly on the radio. In 1932, beefed up by a conga and a piano, the group became a *conjunto*.

The bassist "Bubú"(Pablo Govín), the guitarist Humberto Cané (Valentín's son), the singer and *maraquero* "Caíto" (Carlos Manuel Díaz), the *timbalero* José Ramón Chávez ("Manteca"), the percussionist "Papaíto" (Mario Muñoz), Lino Frías, the trumpeter and composer Calixto Leicea, Raimundo Govín, who succeeded his father, pianist Javier Vázquez, the trumpeter Pedro Knight (an Arsenio Rodríguez alumnus), and "Patato"(Carlos) Valdés also joined the band. (Valdés worked with them from 1943 to 1945, first as a *tresista* and then as a *conguero*.)

In 1950, the young Celia Cruz replaced the Sonora Matancera's regular singer, Myrta Silva. Silva, who had worked years before in New York with the Cuarteto Victoria, was returning to her native Puerto Rico. Although Cruz already boasted impressive credentials, she was still relatively unknown, but Rogelio Martínez was awed by her talent. The first time he heard her, he recalled, she gave him "gooseflesh."(Incidentally, Tito Puente felt the same way, recalling that the first time he listened to her on the radio, so powerful was her voice that he thought she was a man.)

Born in 1925 in Santos Suárez, Havana, to a father who was a railroad worker, Cruz had studied to be a schoolteacher, but the call of music was stronger. She began to perform at local parties and with the *conjunto* El Botón de Oro, led by a *marímbula* player by the name of Gavilán. In 1935 she won first prize on the amateur radio show "La hora del te"with the tango *Nostalgia,* and she sucessfully appeared in other contests. After two years at the Havana Conservatory, she performed with Obdulio Morales on the radio in the 1940s, and recorded with him two Yoruba numbers orchestrated for forty musicians and using *batá* drums.[21] *El pregón del pescador* boosted her career, and she collaborated with various ensembles, among them the *conjunto* Gloria Matancera and Severino Ramos's Sonora Cubana, working in some Spanish *academias de baile,* and at La Tropical – where she was crowned "*guarachera* de Cuba." In 1948 she joined the show *Las Mulatas de Fuego,* with which she toured to Mexico and Venezuela; she sang with various ensembles led by pianist Facundo Rivero, replaced Rita Montaner at the Tropicana, and recorded with La Sonora Caracas.

For La Sonora Matancera, Severino Ramos wrote arrangements highlighting Cruz's voice, but some listeners asked for the return of the more conventional Silva. However, with her warm personality, improvisatory skills, and resounding voice, Cruz made her reputation. With her, La Sonora Matancera appeared on the radio show Alegrías Hatuey, sponsored by Hatuey beer, and Cruz's renditions of *Cao cao mani picao* and *Mata siguaraya* (an allusion to a plant used for *santería* rituals) captivated listeners. The band also recorded the wonderful *Pan de piquito, Ritmo pilón, Sarará,* and *Cuban Pete,* did a few sessions with Armando Romeu and Belisario López; and, under the name of Orquesta Tropicavana, cut additional sides for the American Stinson label.

21 These recordings, and others such as Lino Frias's *Mata siguaraya* (an allusion to a *santería* plant), have led some to think that Cruz is an adept of this cult of Yoruba origin, something which she has always denied.

The Conjunto Cubavana, founded in 1936 by singer Alberto Ruiz, broke new ground by highlighting its percussion section, which consisted of the outstanding trio Armando Peraza, Guillermo Barreto, and Patato Valdés. Peraza, who had so far survived by doing several menial jobs, had never before played professionally and, in need of money, he worked his way into the band by lying about his musical experience. The group attracted other top talents: singers Nelo Sosa, Orlando Vallejo, Carlos Embale, Rudy Calzado, and Roberto Faz, trumpeters Alejandro "El Negro" Vivar (who started out with them), José Floriano, and Chocolate Armenteros, and they offered such smooth and lively songs as *No me importas tú, Mi bambolaye, Moforivale al tambó*.

In 1949 Patato Valdés, and then Ruiz and Sosa joined the dynamic Conjunto Casino, known as "Los Campeones del Ritmo" (The Rhythm Champions). It had been established in 1937 in Havana by Estebán Grau under the name of Sexteto Casino, and three years later singer Roberto Espí assumed its leadership. Espí increased the number of trumpets to four, and after another year he turned the *sexteto* into a *conjunto*. Pianist Roberto Álvarez also passed through the band, and in 1943 Roberto Faz replaced Grau. With vocalists Faz, Espí, and Agustín Ribot, the group's popularity soared. In the early 1950s, Orlando Vallejo replaced Ribot. The Conjunto Casino thrilled Latin America with its spicy and swinging *guarachas* such as *Con la lengua afuera* ("With the tongue sticking out"), *Chilindrón de chivo*, and *Te traigo un tumbao*. In 1956, after thirteen years with the Conjunto Casino, Faz decided to organize his own ensemble. Fernando Alvarez, who had been persuaded by Benny Moré to come to Havana from Santiago, became Cubavana's lead singer, and with them he recorded *Humo y espumo* and other hits.

In 1946 Sosa, along with pianist Carlos Faxas and guitarist Senén Suárez, founded the Conjunto Colonial. At first this grouping got together, like the Conjunto Modelo, mainly for recording sessions. It went through many personnel changes and attracted first-rate musicians, among them the lively pianist Rey Díaz Calvet, vocalists Pepe Delgado and Orlando Vallejo, and trumpeters Guillermo Fellové and Armando Armenteros. Appreciated for its brilliant trumpets and its vitality (*Tremendo cumbán, El sofa, Arrímate cariñito*), the Conjunto Colonial occasionally backed Daniel Santos, and in 1950 it became the featured band of the Tropicana.

Formed in 1955 by pianist Ricardo Ferro and led at various times by Bebo Valdés and by pianist and arranger Joseíto Valdés, Rumbavana heralded some of the modern salsa bands. Several first-rate singers worked with them, among them Raúl Planas and Camilo Rodríguez, father of salsa singer Azuquita.

An engaging vocalist, Faz (1914–1966) also set up a *conjunto*, surrounded himself with Sosa and Ribot (and occasionally Orlando Vallejo and Orlando Reyes), and scored several successes (*Suena tu bongó, Pelotera la bola, Viejo verde*). Faz, equally fluent on bass and various percussion instruments, was a bus driver by trade. He started out his musical career as a *trovador*, performed with the *sexteto* Champán Sport, the Sexteto Ultramar led by his brother Pascual, the Sexteto Cubano, and Orquesta Continental; he then played bongo with Estanislao Serviá's Típica Habanera, worked with the Hermanos Palau and Orquesta Cosmopolita, replaced singer Berto González on the radio show "La corte suprema del arte," and performed on the radio, backed by the Hermanos Lebatard orchestra. In 1941 he joined Osvaldo Estivil's big band as singer and *bongocero* (the other vocalist was Tito Gómez) and then the Conjunto Casino. In 1946 he also sang with Casino de la Playa when singer Antonio "Cheché" de la Cruz left. He made various recordings with them and with Cubavana, and during the 1950s performed in New York.

Big bands, combos, and descargas

During the 1940s and 1950s, the tourism boom in Cuba and the popularity of jazz and American music in general (countless stars, among them Miles Davis, Stan Getz, and Sarah Vaughan visited Cuba) fostered the development of big bands and combos on the island. Most of these big bands, ranging from very good to mediocre, played for floor shows and for dancers. Their line-up usually consisted of a relatively small horn section (saxophones, trumpets, and trombones), piano, bass, a full array of Cuban percussion instruments: conga, bongo, timbales, maracas, and claves, and a vocalist fronting the ensemble. Their polished sound and "cosmopolitan" – read "commercial" – repertoire, which included Mexican and Argentinian numbers, captivated both Cuban and foreign audiences.

The big bands

One of the most stirring big bands of the early 1940s was the Orquesta Casino de la Playa, named after one of Havana's major casinos, and they had a leavening influence upon other groups. A predominantly white ensemble led by Guillermo Portela (and in the late 1940s by saxophonist Liduvino Pereira), it was formed in 1937 by seven members of the Hermanos Castro, among them singer "Miguelito" (Juan Eugenio Lázaro) Valdés, pianist and arranger Anselmo Sacasas, and trumpet-player and *bolerista* Walfredo de los Reyes. They performed in the major clubs and on the radio, and in the late 1930s toured Latin America and the Caribbean.

Sacasas, who hailed from Manzanillo, was highly experienced by the time he joined Casino de la Playa. After playing for silent films, he had worked in Havana with the *charangas* of Luis Carrillo and Tata Pereira before his stint with the Hermanos Castro in 1936. Casino de la Playa also benefited from the presence of the excellent trombonist José Peña. In addition to Walfredo de los Reyes, they recorded with vocalists Cheché de la Cruz, Carlos Díaz, "Cascarita" (Orlando Guerra), and Miguelito Valdés.

Orquesta Havana Casino. Óscar López Collection

A warm and instinctual performer with a beautiful voice, Valdés lit up audiences with his impassioned improvisations. With Casino de la Playa he recorded the *guaracha Mis cinco hijos, Malanga murió, Dolor cobarde, Cachita* (with sizzling percussions), and in particular the *afro-cha Babalu Ayé*, his signature song, composed for him by Margarita Lecuona. He performed it sustaining spectacularly long notes, with the brass dramatically accenting his vibrant tenor voice, and later added Yoruba elements to it. He later sang it in the movie *So Rumba*.

He was born in 1912 in the Belén district of Havana. His father left his mother when Valdés was still a young child, and Miguelito held various jobs while learning the conga, the bass, and the piano by ear. Later, when established in Cayo Hueso, he served an apprenticeship at Dodge as a mechanic, tried his luck at boxing in 1926, and struck up a friendship with Mario Bauzá, Machito, Chano Pozo, Arsenio Rodríguez, and other musicians. After taking singing lessons with María Teresa Vera, he decided to devote himself to music. At the age of twenty, along with Machito he sang *coro* with the Sexteto Occidente and, again with Machito, performed in small clubs. He then joined the Sexteto Habanero Juvenil, became bassist and musical director of Domingo Vargas's *sexteto* Jóvenes del Cayo, and worked with Ismael Díaz's *charanga*, with the Charanga Habana and Orquesta Gris (along with Fernando Collazo). In 1933, along with trumpeter Remberto Lara, he went on tour to Panama with the Orquesta Hermanos Hernández and sang there with Lucho Azcanaga's orchestra. He stayed in Panama for two years, and got married there; back in Cuba, he worked with a string of bands: the Sexteto Occidente, the Sexteto Habanero, Los Hermanos Castro, building up his reputation as a top-notch singer.

Orquesta de la Playa also scored successes with *Ojos malvados*, sung by Walfredo de los Reyes, and the lively *Quiero un sombrero*, performed by "Cascarita." In 1940, however, Miguelito Valdés and Anselmo Sacasas moved to New York, and Sacasas was replaced by another fine pianist from Manzanillo, Julio Gutiérrez.

Babalu Ayé – Margarita Lecuona

The Riverside and Cosmopolita orchestras, both founded in 1938 and more Americanized than Casino de la Playa, also enjoyed considerable fame. Formed by violinist Enrique González Mántici and pianist José Curbelo – a former member of a big band called Red Devils – Riverside recruited a few musicians from the Hermanos Castro. Mostly famed for its cha-chas (for example, *Cha cha cha en Tropicana*), it was led from 1957 to 1962 by Adolfo Guzmán, a pianist with a light touch and a remarkable arranger for strings. Composer of *Profecía* and *Nuestro idilio*, Guzmán also worked late at night at the Tropicana, led the bands of the Radio Centro theater, the Campoamor, and the Havana Casino, and played piano in cabarets. Pianists "Peruchín" (Pedro Justiz) and Orestes López and trumpeter Leonardo Timor also collaborated with Riverside. The band backed many singers, among them Pedro Vargas and Olga Guillot, but their own featured vocalist, "Tito" Gómez (José Antonio Tenreiro Gómez), a veteran of the Sevilla Biltmore Orchestra, Julio Cueva's Orquesta Montecarlo, and Osvaldo Estivil's band, had a magnetic presence. Of Spanish origin on his father's side, he was nicknamed "Tito" by Miguelito Valdés, and like Valdés, he loved Afro-Cuban music. With Gómez, Riverside scored hits with the cha-cha *Vereda tropical* and with *Te adoraré más y más*.

Vereda tropical – Gonzalo Curiel

Cosmopolita was founded by drummer Vicente Viana, who committed suicide in 1944; pianist, composer, and arranger Humberto Suárez temporarily assumed the leadership. The band backed Margot Tarraza (sister of pianist Juan Bruno Tarraza) and other singers, but it sometimes lapsed into a rather maudlin repertoire with such numbers as *Barcarola en cha cha chá*, derived from Hoffmann's *Barcarolle*. Many great musicians passed through Cosmopolita, among them vocalists Óscar López and Vicentico Valdés, pianists Carlos Fraxas, Rafael Pérez Anckermann, and occasionally René Hernández, bassist José Montalván, *conguero* Jesús González, and trumpeter Raúl Hernández (René Hernández's brother).

Orquesta Cosmopolita. Óscar López Collection

The relatively commercial band of pianist and composer Armando Oréfiche toured extensively abroad. Author of the beautiful *Bolero árabe*, of *Cubano soy*, of the Afro *Mesié Julián*, strikingly performed by Bola de Nieve, and many other pieces, Oréfiche started out with the Lecuona Cuban Boys, replacing the ailing Lecuona as musical director and taking them to Europe. He settled in Helsinki, popularized *Una noche de amor en La Habana*, *El Chino Li Wong*, *Muñecas del cha cha chá*, and other pieces, and after seven years abroad, returned to Cuba. In 1945 he went to the United States, became leader of the Havana Cuban Boys and played in Europe again, where, among other agreeable albums, he recorded "Oréfiche and His Havana Cuban Boys."

The trumpeter Julio Cueva (1897–1975) led a tight and interesting ensemble. Alejo Carpentier noted in 1932 in the review *Carteles*: "He attacks extremely high notes, marking the rhythm with his whole body." Cueva was also the author of such well-known tunes as the *danzón El marañón*, *El golpe de Bibijagua*,[22] *Rascando, rascando, Tingo talango*, the *guarachas Con la comida no se juega* and *Desintegrando*. Born in a musical family in Trinidad – the architectural jewel in the center of Cuba – he collaborated in Havana with Moisés Simons and Don Azpiazu. He then lived in Europe for several years, where a Paris club was called La Cueva in his honor, and played music in the Spanish Republican army. In 1940, back in Cuba, he took over Amado Trinidad's La Cuban Boys, based in Ranchuelo, and renamed it Orquesta Montecarlo. He revamped it, hired "Cascarita" (Orlando Guerra) as lead singer, pianist Felo Bergaza, and trumpeter Remberto Lara. The Orquesta Montecarlo established its reputation throughout the country, but it soon broke up and Cueva and Cascarita joined the Hermanos Palau orchestra.

22 Probably from the nineteenth-century *coro de clave* Bibijagua.

In 1942 Cueva set up his own ensemble, with the idea of reworking the *son montuno* in a big band format, as Benny Moré would do in the 1950s. He recruited vocalists Cascarita, Tito Gómez, "Puntillita" (Manuel Licea), and René Márquez; pianist René Hernández contributed some arrangements. Famous for *Agua de Tinajón* and other numbers, Cueva's group performed in New York in the early 1950s and broke up in 1953.

Pianist "Bebo" (Ramón) Valdés's highly swinging Ritmo Batanga included first-rate musicians, many influenced by jazz, among them drummer Guillermo Barreto, Gustavo Tamayo, Trinidad Torregrosa, and trumpeters Domingo Corbacho, Alejandro "El Negro" Vivar, "Chocolate" Armenteros, and "Platanito" Jiménez. Over Cuban percussion and incisive riffs, Valdés played lean and punchy solos. Known as "El Grandote" ("The Big One") for his impressive size, powerful touch, and considerable talent, Valdés became renowned for his smooth mambos. Born in Havana in 1918, he first composed *danzones*, among them *Gloria a Maceo*, before switching to faster tunes (*Rareza del siglo, Rapsodia de cueros, Con poco coco*). From 1943 to 1947 he was pianist and arranger of the Mil Diez radio station. From 1947 to 1948 he worked in Haiti with the group led by clarinettist and saxophonist Issa El Saieh, an early exponent of the *compas* (a Haitian rhythm), and he recorded with them some Creole Haitian numbers at Radio Progreso, in Havana. From 1948 to 1957, Valdés held the piano chair in the Tropicana orchestra. As an answer to the mambo he created the *batanga*, which utilized *batá* drums, perhaps for the first time in a jazz context, and other percussion (played by Guillermo Barreto and *conguero* Rolando Alfonso), and a more abrupt bass *tumbao* than that of the mambo:

Batanga tumbao

Benny Moré, who joined Valdés's outfit in 1953, popularized this *batanga* to such an extent that he, rather than Valdés, was often thought to have invented it. But with its rather difficult syncopations, the *batanga* never really caught on outside Cuba. If many Cubans are steeped from birth in complex rhythms and can easily deal with them, foreigners generally feel more comfortable with simpler Cuban dances such as the *conga* and the cha-cha.

In 1959 Valdés organized a new band: Sabor de Cuba, which was featured on the *Show de las siete* on Radio Progreso and recorded a string of hits: *Ita moreal* (after *itamo real*, a plant for treating a sore throat), *A la rigola* (a merengue by Mario de Jesús, which Fidel Castro's guerrillas sang in the Sierra Maestra), *Bilongo, La pachanga*. Valdés also recorded in Mexico, and he backed singers Cascarita, Pío Leiva, and Reinaldo Enríquez.

Like "Lilí"Martínez Griñán, "Peruchín" (Pedro Justiz) was a model pianist, and Charlie and Eddie Palmieri, among others, have acknowledged him as one of their major influences. His sober and lively style, subtle phrasing, and occasional jazz-inflected runs (*Guaguancó callejero, Bilongo*) set him among the foremost Cuban musicians of his generation.

Born in Banes, in the province of Oriente, Peruchín (1913–1977) started out on alto saxophone, and in 1933 he worked in Santiago with the Chepín-Chovén orchestra. In Havana he played with Casino de la Playa, Mariano Mercerón, Arsenio Rodríguez, the Swing Boys, Armando Romeu, at the Tropicana. He also led the excellent ensemble of the Campoamor theater, with its biting horns and strong dynamics. It included notably trumpeters Domingo Corbacho, Chocolate Armenteros, and Guillermo Fellové, saxophonists Santiago Peñalver, "Musiquito," and Armando Romeu, bassist "Quique" (Enrique) Hernández, Anita Justiz on drums and piano, and percussionists Patato Valdés, Mongo Santamaría, Giraldo (*batás* and conga) and "Yeyo" Iglesias (cowbell), and it backed Las Mulatas de Fuego, Rita Montaner and other show-business luminaries. In the 1950s Peruchín worked as pianist and arranger with the Orquesta Riverside, Julio Gutiérrez, the Conjunto Colonial, and Benny Moré, recorded with Cachao and Guillermo Barreto, and took part in many *descargas* (improvisations).

On the album *The Incendiary Piano of Peruchín*, he performs a Paderewski minuet actually more subdued than fiery, and on *Peruchín, piano y ritmo* a Latin *The Man I Love*, as well as his charming *Mamey colorao*. Guillermo Barreto, who often played with him, once admitted to me: "unfortunately, his albums do not always do justice to his creativity. Many *descargas*, where his powerful playing and spontaneity found full expression, have not been recorded."

Peruchín.
Caney Records

One of the most original Cuban big bands of the 1940s and 1950s was the Orquesta Bellamar, founded in 1940 by saxophonist Armando Romeu (Antonio María Romeu's nephew) with trumpeter Luis Escalante. Author of *Mambo a la Kenton, Bop City Mambo*, and *Mocambo*, Romeu was one of the key figures of Cuban jazz, and the initiator in 1967 of the epochal Orquesta Cubana de Música Moderna. Born in Havana in 1911, he studied music with his father, played flute in Regla's military band and furthered his knowledge of this instrument with Alfredo Brito. In 1924 he performed with his father's *típica* at the Jockey Club in Havana, where it alternated with an American band. Fascinated by jazz, he then took up the saxophone. He worked with Earl Carpenter's band at the Casino Nacional and then, in 1929 and 1930, with the Hermanos Palau, Ernesto Lecuona, pianist Célido Curbelo, and other outfits. In 1932 he went to Europe with Brito's Orquesta Siboney;

upon his return to Havana, he started an ensemble which secured an engagement at the Eden Concert. He then dissolved it for financial reasons, formed a new big band which toured Latin America and, in 1937, joined Casino de la Playa.

In 1946 the Sans Souci, where Bellamar regularly appeared, closed down. Romeu, suddenly jobless, was forced to disband his group, and the other Havana clubs rejected his advanced musical ideas, which they found disconcerting. He nevertheless re-formed an experimental ensemble in which he introduced dissonances and other concepts borrowed from bebop and West Coast jazz, and this appeared for twenty-five years at the Tropicana. He also directed various recording sessions, among them *Nat King Cole Español* – an album made in Havana, for which the American singer insisted Romeu write the arrangements.

Romeu and other musicians also benefited from the innovative scores of Arturo O'Farrill (nicknamed "Chico" by Benny Goodman). A Latin jazz legend, the spry and incisive O'Farrill was one of the first in Cuba to turn to bebop and, as with Romeu, his original ideas often fell on deaf ears. Gonzalo Roig, for one, unreceptive to his aesthetics, even accused him, said O'Farrill, of wanting "to destroy Cuban music." Rita Montaner, however, for whom O'Farrill worked in Havana, deeply admired him, as have scores of musicians since that time, from Machito to Stan Kenton, Count Basie, and Wynton Marsalis. His lush scores, replete with riffs, incisive accents, and modulations, brought increased sophistication to the popular repertoire of that era (*Chico's cha cha chá, Tenderly*).

Born in Havana in 1921 into a family of Irish and German descent, O'Farrill was sent in 1936 by his father to a military academy in Georgia, in the United States. He played trumpet in the school band, and listened to Glenn Miller, Tommy Dorsey, and Artie Shaw. Back in Havana, he studied law, at his father's insistence, but turning to music, he took up composition with the great teacher Félix Guerrero. He also started listening intensively to bebop, and penned arrangements for René Touzet and Armando Romeu.

In 1946, when Romeu broke up his ensemble, O'Farrill started writing for guitarist Isidro Pérez, then the musical director of the Montmartre. Pérez, another avant-garde musician, was influenced by Stan Kenton and Boyd Raeburn. "The big bands," O'Farrill remembered, "had to back shows that featured dancers, singers, and actors. I did that with Touzet and Bellamar, and for us musicians it was very boring. With Pérez, we had organized a fairly large ensemble, the Orquesta de Isidro Pérez – a dream band, in fact, with the best musicians in Havana. What a wonderful experience that was! Everybody was writing arrangements and we could experiment as much as we wanted. Our band was not that great for dancing, but we had a lot of fun. One year later, the Montmartre closed and unfortunately, we weren't able to find work again." O'Farrill then formed a bebop quintet featuring Edilberto Scritch (alto sax), Armando Romeu's son Mario (piano), Quique Hernández (bass), and Daniel Pérez (drums); their music met with critical acclaim but sold poorly. Discouraged by Cuba's

Chico O'Farrill. Arturo O'Farrill Collection

indifference to jazz, O'Farrill moved to the United States, where he was to accomplish the fusion of bebop and Cuban music.

Back from an extended stay in the U.S. and then in Mexico, where he married the ravishing singer Guadalupe Valero, he again settled in Havana, from 1955 to 1957. He worked with a big band which included among others Gustavo Mas, Virgilio Martí, El Negro Vivar, and two Mexicans: trumpeter César Molina and pianist "El Güero" Stollwer; he composed *The Bass Family*, a piece for three basses, performed by the brothers "Felo" (Rafaelo), "Quique" (Enrique), and Papito Hernández; he wrote for the Panart label, notably the striking *Descarga número uno* and *Descarga número dos* for *Los Mejores Músicos de Cuba*, featuring Richard Egües, El Negro Vivar, Tata Güines, and other virtuosos; he produced advanced arrangements with closed voicings for the Cuarteto d'Aida, and recorded *Chico's Cha-Cha-Chá*.

The guitarist Juanito Márquez was also an innovative arranger and a seminal figure of Cuban jazz. Born in Holguín, he wrote for the Orquesta Riverside and Bebo Valdés, and led the Orquesta Hermanos Avilés. In 1956 after a Venezuelan tour, influenced by the *joropo* (a Venezuelan rhythm), he created the *pa' ca* (with *Arrímate pa' ca*), which achieved a certain amount of popularity in Cuba.

Audiences also took a shine to Benny Moré's famous Banda Gigante (to which we will refer later), as well as to Rafael Sorín's Swing Casino, the excellent Swing Boys, the Tropicana orchestra, led by, among others, pianist Felo Bergaza in the 1950s, the Radio Mil Diez band directed by Adolfo Guzmán and later Pedro Vila, that of Radio CMQ, steered by González Mántici, the outfits of Fernando Mulens, Orlando de la Rosa, Pedro Junco, Rafael Somavilla, "Tojo" (Generoso) Jiménez, and Armando Valdespí; Julio Gutiérrez's stimulating big band, that of Pancho Bravo, famous for its lush boleros, Tito Rivera and His Havana Mambo Orchestra, the Hermanos Lebatard, led by Germán Lebatard, the Hermanos Martínez – then the only black large ensemble – and the Orquesta Habana also competed for the limelight.

Creditable groups appeared also in other regions of Cuba, in Santiago in particular, where the music tended to have a more laid-back Caribbean feel than in Havana. The two leading bands in Oriente were Chepín-Chovén and Mariano Mercerón y sus Muchachos Pimienta, the latter headed by clarinettist and saxophonist Mariano Mercerón. Formed in 1932 by violinist and composer "Chepín" (Electo Rosell Horruitinier) and pianist Bernardo García Chovén, Chepín-Chovén was fronted by singers Isidro Correa and Roberto Nápoles (a former member of the famed *estudiantina* La Invasora). They recorded over fifty albums during their more than sixty-five years of existence, and their legendary swing earned them the title "*La orquesta del sabor*" ("The zestful band"). With their jazzy arrangements of Cuban tunes (*Negro muñanga, La conga se fue*), they vied with the best ensembles from Havana.

Rosell wrote more than four hundred numbers, among them *Bodas de oro*, the *bolero moruno*[23] *Farruquiña, El platanal de Bartolo* (originally sung by Ibrahím Ferrer and also recorded by Miguelito Valdés), and the *danzones Habana Camilo* and *Reina Isabel*. (*Bodas de oro* and *Murmullo* were used in film soundtracks.) He had started out playing for silent movies in Santiago, then toured with Arquímedes Pous's variety show, and formed the group Oriente Jazz. For a while Chovén left the band in order to pursue other activities. Chepín took it over, renaming it Chepín y su Orquesta Oriental, and it performed successfully in Mexico.

Mercerón's orchestra had a smooth wind section and a broad sound, which elicited Machito's admiration (*Llora timbero, Cuando canta el cornetín*, with its unruffled and sensuous melody stated by the cornet). Affectionately nicknamed "El Feo" ("The ugly one"), Mercerón started playing with local bands in and around Santiago. Fascinated by jazz, in 1932 he formed the jazz-influenced Mariano Mercerón and the Piper Boys, which played both Cuban and American numbers. A few years later, he renamed his group Muchachos Pimienta. In the 1940s they performed in Havana with singers Camilo Rodríguez and Roberto Duany, and their recordings included *Negro ñañamboro* (often performed by Machito), *Llora timbero*, and *Nagüe*. In 1946 Mercerón broke up his ensemble, settled in Mexico, where he formed another outfit, and, back in Santiago, put together a band to which he gave his name and which included vocalists Fernando Alvarez, Pacho Alonso, and Alfonso Eliseo. He moved permanently to Mexico in 1958, but is still remembered vividly in Oriente.

The combos

In the late 1950s, the popularity of big bands started to decline in favor of combos generally consisting of bass, piano or guitar, and percussion. Pianists Felipe Dulzaides, Frank Domínguez, Mario Romeu, and Silvio Contreras (of the Hermanos Contreras), ran some of the most significant ones. Jazz was also making increasing inroads in Cuba; in Havana, guitarist Manolo Saavedra, Chico O'Farrill, Peruchín, Frank Emilio, Isidro Pérez, Walfredo de los Reyes, Guillermo Barreto, saxophonists Gustavo Mas, Leonardo Acosta, Jesús Caunedo

23 A faster type of bolero.

(founder, with Mario Romeu, of the Cuban Jazz Club) and other fellow enthusiasts gathered to exchange ideas and explore this music.

The self-taught Dulzaides (1917–1991) had first formed the Llópiz-Dulzaides *cuarteto*, a sort of pop-oriented group in which he played piano and accordion. In 1956 he organized the vocal group Los Armónicos, in which he sang, backed by piano, electric guitar, bass, drums, and sometimes a horn. Dulzaides's ensemble became a training ground for scores of musicians, among them vibraphonist Armandito Romeu, guitarists Pablo Cano and Sergio Vitier, drummer Ignacio Berroa, percussionist "Changuito" (José Luis Quintana), pianist Paquito Hechevarría, and vocalist Doris de la Torre. Stylistically close to Shearing, Dulzaides went on to integrate the most varied elements into his playing and arrangements.

Frank Domínguez composed many beautiful boleros (among them *Tú me acostumbraste*, *Me recordarás*, *Si tú quisieras*) and he accompanied vocalists of the *filin* movement, Elena Burke and Omara Portuondo among them. For his Latin jazz combo, Mario Romeu selected Isidro Pérez, trumpeter Leonardo Timor, bassist Felo Hernández, and drummer Fausto García. Drummer Walfredo de los Reyes Jr. (son of the Casino de la Playa vocalist and trumpet-player) with Los Papines and Cachao López recorded *Cuban Jazz*, which foreshadowed the Latin jazz of the 1960s. And towards the late 1950s, the club Havana 1900 attracted some of the most adventurous musicians of the island.

The *descargas*

The incandescent improvisations known as *descargas* (or *rumbones* as they were also called when they featured essentially percussion) have always been a staple of Cuban music. Based on a simple harmonic structure (usually *son montunos* changes) and fired by riffs, they allowed musicians to extend themselves with great spontaneity and rhythmic virtuosity. In 1952, with El Negro Vivar, El Tojo, Gustavo Mas, *conguero* Rolando Alfonso, and bassist Quique Hernández, Bebo Valdés set a precedent, recording for Norman Granz a series of *Descargas Cubanas*, among them *Con poco coco* (later covered by his son Chucho Valdés).

A few years later, Julio Gutiérrez and Peruchín also recorded *descargas*. "Using the various elements from Julio's band," Gutiérrez's liner notes explained, "the doors were open for all the Havana talents who wished to come in and participate." On this session, Emilio Peñalver, "El Negro" Vivar, Chombo Silva (tenor saxophone), Chuchú Esquijarrosa (timbales), Óscar Valdés (bongo), Marcelino Valdés (conga), and Walfredo de los Reyes gave free rein to their joy and vitality, which burst forth on all the cuts.

In 1957 Cachao López recorded for the Panart label a series of *descargas* entitled *Cuban Jam Sessions in Miniature*, which would become the most famous of these *descargas* series.

Cachao and the musicians of his *descarga*. Panart Records

They were done, Cachao recalls, in five hours, from 4 to 9 a.m., after the musicians had finished their respective gigs. The album's subtitle: *Cachao y su ritmo caliente* ("Cachao and His Hot Rhythm") is fully justified. On the cover picture, "El Negro" Vivar happily brandishes his trumpet while Cachao, his left foot resting on a chair, attacks his bass as though it were a banjo or a guitar. "The improvisation enabled us to express the music and our soul," remembered Cachao. "Everyone played what they liked. I suggested a few ideas but we created everything we liked."

The most brilliant studio sharks: Vivar, Tata Güines, "Yeyo" (Rogelio) Iglesias (bongo), Guillermo Barreto (timbales), Tojo Jiménez, Emilio Peñalver, Virgilio Lisama (baritone saxophone), Niño Rivera, Orestes López (piano), and Richard Egües met in a euphoric atmosphere and the music jumps out at the listener. Tojo Jiménez wails on *Trombón criollo*, Egües soars on *Sorpresa de flauta*. Orestes López solos arrestingly with efficient rhythm displacements on *Malanga amarilla*, while the *coro* sings, with a probably erotic double entendre:

Esa malanga amarilla	This yellow *malanga*[24]
Hay que comerla caliente	You have to eat it warm
Yo te la traigo María	I bring it to you, Maria,
Yo te la traigo de Oriente.	I bring it to you from Oriente.

Niño Rivera also recorded *descargas* (*Cuban Jam Session Vol. 3*), with more or less the same personnel: Orestes López, El Negro Vivar, Peñalver, Egües, Salvador Vivar (bass), Barreto, Iglesias, Güines, and Gustavo Tamayo. Fajardo and other musicians jumped into the fray, and all these exuberant and swinging *descargas* paved the way for the salsa *descargas* organized in New York some fifteen years later.

24 Yellow tuber resembling a sweet potato.

Singers in Cuba

The 1940s and 1950s were also a glorious era for singers in Cuba, many of whom began to front their own bands and were given exposure on radio and television. In the 1950s, the influence of jazz, American vocal quartets, and crooners fostered the emergence of the *filin* (or "feeling") – a movingly romantic style that later gave way, under Fidel Castro, to the politically oriented *nueva trova*.

Celia Cruz's association with La Sonora Matancera brought her a well-deserved recognition. She sang on the radio with Bienvenido Granda, the film industry courted her, and she made a rapid succession of recordings: the Congo song *Burundanga, El cocoyé* (originally a jingle for Hatuey beer), *Sopita en botella, Yerbero moderno*. "With *Bemba colora'*, which I recorded later, *Yerbero moderno* is even today one of my most requested titles," she says. She also sang – along with Jesús Pérez, Merceditas Valdés, Caridad Suárez, Obdulio Morales, Alberto Zayas, and Trinidad Torregrosa – on *Santero*, a marvelous album of Afro-Cuban traditional music featuring Facundo Rivero's *cuarteto* with Bienvenido León on the flip side.

One of the most lionized Cuban male vocalists was "Benny" Moré (Bartolomé Maximiliano Gutiérrez Moré Armenteros). Though he had no formal musical training (he showed his musicians the arrangements he wanted by humming them the different parts), he had a good ear and a profoundly instinctive feel for the music, and he attained almost mythic status in his lifetime. His wide-ranging voice and rubato phrasing, stirring wails, and impeccable sense of rhythm earned him the nickname "El Bárbaro del ritmo," bestowed upon him by the radio DJ Ibrahín Urbino. With his trademark oversized suits, wide-brimmed hat, and stick (the last borrowed from *rumba* dancers and itself deriving from the ritual stick of the Congo god Sarabanda and the *itón* of the Abakwa *diablitos*), he cut an unforgettable figure. His mannerisms have remained etched in Cubans' memory and anecdotes about him abound. In a television program of the 1950s, he gestures expressively, tapping on the shoulder of his outstanding pianist "Cabrerita" (Eduardo Cabrera) while the latter is soloing; so vivid is his presence, he virtually bursts out of the screen. Generous, whimsical, and mercurial, he was constantly surrounded by what he affectionately called his "tribe" of musicians and friends. He excelled in all the different Cuban genres: *guajiras* (*Santa Isabel de Las Lajas*, celebrating his native town), boleros (*Como fue, Ahora soy tan feliz*), uptempo numbers (*Babarabatiri, Mi saoco*). And he adapted songs as his inspiration took him. *Que bueno baila Usted*, an old *son montuno* by *tresista* Benjamín Castellanos that went:

Castellanos que bueno está tu tres,	Castellanos, how great your *tres* is,
Castellanos que bueno toca Usted,	Castellanos, how well you play,
Generosa, que bueno baila Usted.	Generosa, how well you dance;

became:

Castellanos que bueno baila Usted,	Castellanos, how well you dance,
Generoso que bueno toca Usted.	Generoso, how well you play,

. . . the last verse hailing Moré's trombonist "Tojo" (Generoso) Jiménez. Also nicknamed "El Gallo" (the rooster), Moré sometimes provoked his rivals, as in *Elige tú que canto yo* – taunting Rolando Laserie:

Inspira tú que canto yo	You improvise but I sing,
Yo canto bolero,	I sing bolero,
Canto guaguancó	I sing *guaguancó*,
Y canto son.	And I sing *son*.

And in 1954, when the *bolerista* and *merenguero* Alberto Beltrán started to gain popularity in Cuba, Moré challenged him with *Quisiera bailar el merengue*, proving that he, too, could master this Dominican rhythm.

The eldest of eighteen children, he was born in 1919 in La Guinea, a black and boisterous neighborhood of Santa Isabel de Las Lajas (a small town close to Cienfuegos) teeming with stories, music, and laughter. His family belonged to the Casino de los Congos society, which perpetuated ancient Bantu customs. (One of his forebears had been a Casino king.) He attended Congo ceremonies, Yoruba rituals at the San Francisco temple, and *rumbas*, and learned to play various drums, guitar, and *tres*. With his brother Teodoro he also ploughed fields, and throughout his life, he had an abiding love for the countryside and its people. He then earned his living as a boxer, shoeshine, street peddler, and with other small jobs, and sang with his guitar at local social functions and on the streets. Already, his charisma held listeners spellbound. In 1936, after an unsuccessful six month-stay in Havana, he returned to Santa Isabel de Las Lajas to cut sugarcane, worked as a cart driver and, with his friend Enrique Benítez (known by the nickname of "El Conde Negro"–"The Black Earl"), he performed with a local group, the Conjunto Avance. In 1940 he moved to Havana, determined to make a name for himself there. He eked out a living gigging in small cafés by the docks, and appeared on the amateur radio show *La corte suprema del arte*, eventually joining Lázaro Cordero's Sexteto Figaro. In 1942, the *tresista* "Mozo" Borgellá, who ran La Clave Oriental and the Septeto Cauto, heard Moré perform a Miguel Matamoros song in a bar, and invited him into his Septeto. Just over a year after he had arrived in the capital, Moré had already marked himself out as an individualist and musicians soon began to take notice. In 1943 Siro Rodríguez and then Rafael Cueto recommended him to Matamoros. Impressed by his talent, Matamoros used him in 1944 for some recording sessions (among other numbers *La cazuelita, Que será eso mi compay*, and *Me la llevo*). He sang lead while Matamoros conducted his *conjunto*, although he was not given a credit on the ensuing albums. He also collaborated briefly with Arsenio Rodríguez, leaving him in 1945 (being replaced by Miguelito Cuní) in order to work with Matamoros at the Hotel Nacional and tour Mexico with him.

Moré decided to stay in Mexico where, upon learning that his nickname *Bartolo* meant "donkey," he changed it to Benny. He rapidly broke into the local music scene, and again his talent shone forth. He sang in the capital's clubs and married a Mexican nurse. In the late 1940s he worked with leading local bands such as those of Arturo Núñez, Mariano Conde Rivera, and Rafael de la Paz, formed the Dueto Fantasma (sometimes called Dueto Antillano) with singer Lalo Montané and, with Mariano Mercerón, recorded *Me voy para el pueblo*. While he was performing with Núñez he met Damaso Pérez Prado, who recruited him. He appeared with him in the movies *Caritas de cielo*, *El derecho de nacer*, and *Fuego en la carne*, recorded with him, and accompanied him to the Panama carnival.

Although Moré's association with Prado proved to be a winning one, in 1953 Moré moved back to Cuba permanently. He first organized a *septeto*, recorded under the musical direction of Eliseo Valdés, and cut wonderful duos with Pedro Vargas. Radio Cadena Azul then suggested he make an album with La Sonora Matancera, but he chose to collaborate with Bebo Valdés, whose music he found more progressive. He then sang with Ernesto Duarte and formed an ensemble that included Cabrerita (piano), "Palito" (conga), Alberto Limonta (bass), Alfonso (claves), Enrique Benítez (vocals, maracas), and "Chicho" (Clemente) Piquero (bongo).

Moré had learned big-band techniques from the various leaders he had worked with. He adopted Pérez Prado's on-stage exuberance, but the sound texture of his band was different. In particular, as Leonardo Acosta has pointed out, while Prado used the trumpets in a high register, Moré always included in his recordings two trombones in a medium register.[25] Shortly after his stint with Valdés, he decided to form a jazz-inflected orchestra that would sound like a *son* group: La Banda Gigante de Benny Moré (Benny Moré's Giant Band). Cabrerita, Limonta, Benítez, and Chicho were its principal players, and Duarte, Cabrerita, and Tojo Jiménez wrote inventive arrangements, but Moré also created new rhythms and riffs by ear, often on the spot. The rest of the personnel consisted of saxophonists Miguel Franca, Santiago Peñalver, Roberto Barreto, Celso Gómez, and Virgilio Lisama; trumpeters Chocolate Armenteros (who acted as Moré's first musical director), "Rabanito," and Domingo Corbacho; Rolando Laserie on timbales; *conguero* "Tabaquito," and *coro* singers Silvestre Méndez (the author of *Oriza* and the Afro *Yiri yiri bon*) and Fernando Álvarez. The Banda Gigante also attracted at different times pianists Lázaro Valdés, "Colombié," and "Cancañón" (Luis Mariano); saxophonists "Chombo" (José) Silva, Mauro Gómez, René Aiyón, Roger Mena, Fernán Vincent, and Diego Loredo; trumpeters Aníbal Martínez, Jorge Varona, Pedro Hernández, Pedro Jiménez, Leonardo Timor; trombonists Antonio Linares and "El Gallego" Pidre; bassist Ramón Caturla; drummer Jesús González; *conguero* Jesús López; and singers Gil Ramírez and Delfín Moré.

25 Leonardo Acosta interview from the documentary on Benny Moré directed by Hubert Niogret.

Moré, for all his whimsicality maintained a high level of discipline within his orchestra which, like Dizzy Gillespie, he led with his own expressive body language.

He first recorded Radamés Reyes's poetical *son La bahía de Manzanillo,* and at the height of his popularity, he toured Latin America, performed in New York and scored a string of hits, among them *Bonito y sabroso,* praising the way Mexican and other Latin American women dance, *Devuélvame el coco, Pongan atención,* and *Maracaibo oriental.*

In 1956 he sang in New York with the Afro-Cubans at the Palladium Ballroom; on the same bill as Barbarito Diez and Celina and Reutilio at the Teatro Puerto Rico; and with Tito Puente. Although there might have been some rivalry between Machito and Moré, photographs taken at that time show both men mugging together for the camera in a friendly way. The real rivalry was in fact between Moré and Rolando Laserie. It erupted the following year, when Laserie made his first recording as a vocalist, with the bolero *Mentiras tuyas,* although Moré continued to collaborate with Laserie on various occasions.

After leaving the United States, Moré did some recording in Mexico. In 1957, back in Cuba, he reconvened his band and went back to the studios with, notably, Chocolate Armenteros and Peruchín. Around 1959 he began to suffer from cirrhosis of the liver. But *Encantado de la vida* ("Delighted with life"), as his famous song proclaimed, he continued to live to the full, restlessly touring the island and often performing in front of the humble audiences he so much liked, with an elan that belied his condition. In 1962, shortly before his death, he gave a concert on the same bill as the Orquesta Aragón and the Orquesta Riverside, attracting such a huge crowd that part of the Paseo del Prado had to be closed. But racked with pain, he finally admitted his troubles, in a gripping *Dolor y perdón*:

Dolor, dolor, dolor,	Pain, pain, pain,
Dolor que llevo adentro.	Pain that I carry inside me.

He died of a brain hemorrhage on February 19, 1963 in Palmira, near Havana. His Casino de los Congos organized a farewell ceremony, with music and food offerings to the ancestral gods, and his death was mourned by thousands of fans, who lined the route of the funeral procession for miles.

Stylistically quite different from Moré, pianist, singer, and composer "Bola de Nieve" (Ignacio Jacinto Villa y Fernández) also was a unique personality in the history of Cuban music and his style has often been compared to that of the French *chansonniers.* His nickname, meaning "snowball," was given to him by a schoolmate who poked fun at his dark skin. During a concert, his friend Rita Montaner jokingly introduced him as "Bola de Nieve," and the monicker stuck.

The Ernesto Lecuona show with Bola de Nieve, Óscar López, Esther Borja, Sorraya Marrero (Buenos Aires, 1950). Óscar López Collection

Villa stamped his music with a special seal. "I am the song I sing," he was wont to say, fully identifying himself with his art. He extracted the essence of each piece, accompanying himself with finesse and great economy of means, with chords that merely delineated the song. Nicolás Guillén's poem *Los Motivos de Son* celebrated Villa's "nimble black hands," and Edith Piaf was among his many admirers. Audiences also fondly remember his expressive, slightly raspy voice ("I would have liked to be an opera singer," he once admitted, "but I have the voice of a mango- or peach-vendor!"), and his *joie de vivre* carried him through life's difficulties. "I don't sing – rather, I express what *sones*, or *pregones*, or poems set to music have inside them . . . I don't like to impress people, I like to touch the listener's sensibility," Bola once told a journalist. He excelled at interpreting *canciones* (the lullaby *Drumi mobila*), soul-rending boleros (Irving Berlin's *Be Careful It's my Heart*), *afros* (*Carlota ta morí, Manda conmigo papé, Mesié Julián*), sometimes full of the self-deprecating, bittersweet humor that so prevails in Afro-American cultures, as in *Mesié Julián*:

Yo soy negro social, soy intelectual y chic.
Y, yo fui a Nueva York, conozco Bro'way y París.
Soy artista mundial, y no diga ma' cha-cha.
Yo, que un día bailé en French can-can.
Como acabó en Broadway, mi bongó.
Y al volver al solar me han de llamar "Monsieur."

>   I am a social Black, I am intellectual and smart.
>   I went to New York, I know Broadway and Paris.
>   I am a worldwide artist, and I don't say cha-cha any more.
>   I, who once danced the French can-can,
>   I got rid of my bongo on Broadway.
>   And when I return to the tenement they will have to call me
>   Monsieur.

Born in Guanabacoa in 1911, Villa had thirteen siblings. His mother was a good dancer, fond of both rumbas and opera, and his father was a cook. Villa grew up hearing black ritual and secular music and he studied theory and piano at the Mateu conservatory. He and his friend Cachao López then started to play for silent movies in Guanabacoa. In 1929, he gave a solo concert that was coldly received. Undaunted, however, he continued to perform, accompanying various singers in the early 1930s, and Gilberto Valdés found him some engagements in a Marianao cabaret.

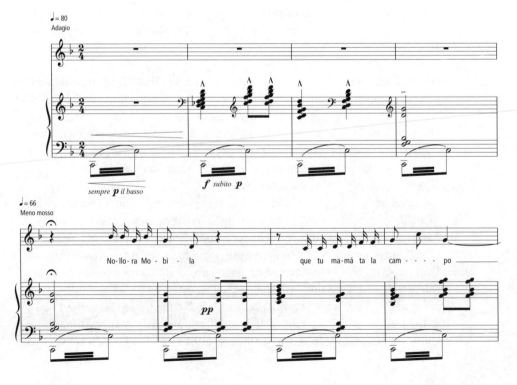

Drumi mobila – Ignacio Villa

In 1933 Rita Montaner asked him to travel to Mexico as her accompanist. One day when Montaner was sick, he sang *Bito Manué* in concert at the Politeama theater and elicited tremendous applause. When Montaner returned to Cuba, Mexican friends encouraged Villa to remain in the country. There he accompanied other singers and began to perform as a soloist, befriending Agustín Lara and other musicians. Ernesto Lecuona heard him in Mexico and, in 1935, brought him back to Havana. Villa then frequently replaced Lecuona for operetta programs and he also recorded with the Havana Cuban Boys. Throughout the late 1930s and 1940s he toured the United States and Latin America with Lecuona (receiving a standing ovation at Carnegie Hall). He also traveled to Europe and Latin America as a soloist, remaining in Argentina for several years, and his splendid performances moved audiences deeply. During the 1950s he continued to tour extensively abroad. He last performed publicly in August of 1971, at the Auditorium Amadeo Roldán in Havana, singing *Be Careful it's my Heart*, one of his favorite songs; he died in October of the same year in Mexico, on his way to Lima.

A pretty and fiery woman, soprano Rita Montaner (1900–1958) was also one of Cuba's most beloved vocalists. Although she often performed classical or semi-classical music, her real love was for Afro-Cuban material. She and Chano Pozo belonged to the same *comparsa*, and Pozo and Bola de Nieve were close friends. And if she became chiefly known for her *zarzuelas*, she sang with equal talent *rumbas* (*Palmira*), *guarachas* (*La mulata*), songs inspired by Yoruba music (*Lamento esclavo*), and *congas* (*Arrolla*).

After studying piano and voice, she made her singing debut on the radio, in 1922. In October of 1927 she triumphed in the *zarzuela Niña Rita*, singing *Mama Inés*. The following year, she recorded *Mama Inés* and *El manisero* and other Cuban numbers before they were popularized by Antonio Machín and Don Azpiazu. She then traveled to Paris with Sindo Garay, appearing at the Palace theater with Josephine Baker and in the revue *Perlas Cubanas*. In 1930 she performed in Lecuona's *zarzuela María la O*, and in the United States had a part in the film *Wonder Bar*, starring Al Jolson. The following year she toured the United States and, in 1933, she performed in Mexico with Bola de Nieve. Two years later, she starred in an Afro-Cuban show whose music was composed by Gilberto Valdés and which included the songs *Ogguere*, *El bembé*, and *Tambó*. In 1938, she worked in the movies *Sucedió en La Habana* and *El romance del palmar*. In the mid-1940s, at the height of her career, she often sang on the radio. She gave recitals in Europe and appeared in the film *María la O*, shot in Cuba and in Mexico. In 1950, despite her light complexion, she received an award for her part in a movie entitled *Negro es mi color* ("Black Is My Color"). She worked for nine years at the Tropicana, and in 1954 she starred in the movie *La única*. While performing in a club in early 1958, she started feeling unwell, and a few months later she died of cancer.

Elegant and distinguished, Merceditas Valdés (1928–1996) brought Afro-Cuban folklore to the level of art, and she was the first to sing Yoruba material on the radio (on the Mil Diez station). Her heartfelt and exquisite renditions of *Yambambo*, *Drume negrita*, *Osain*, or *La vida es un sueño* stand out as true gems.

Born in Cayo Hueso in a musical family (her father belonged to the vocal group Los Roncos), Valdés grew up listening to the spellbinding *toques* of Trinidad Torregrosa, Pablo Roche, and other *batá* masters, and she became a *santería* adept herself. She started singing on *La Corte suprema del arte* – an obligatory rite of passage for many Cuban artists – toured abroad with Ernesto Lecuona's company and with the revue *Zum zum ba bae*. She recorded with, among others Mongo Santamaría, her husband Guillermo Barreto, and Adolfo Guzmán's orchestra, and sang on *Santero* – an album of ritual music featuring Facundo Rivero, Obdulio Morales, Celia Cruz, Bienvenido León, and Jesús Pérez. In 1944, she performed for Fernando Ortiz's lectures. In 1952, she joined the show *Rapsodia Negra*, directed by Enrique González Mántici, and she presented the first concert of sacred Afro-Cuban music in the United States, at Carnegie Hall. She also performed at the Apollo Theater, on the same bill as Tito Puente and Mongo Santamaría, and in Las Vegas with the Miguelito Valdés orchestra. Back in Cuba, she later joined the Latin jazz group Los Amigos. In the 1990s, she sang on albums made in Cuba by the Canadian saxophonist and flautist Jane Bunnett, and she died in Havana, shortly after recording *Aché IV* with the traditional group Yoruba Andabo.

A strikingly pretty and slim woman of Chinese and African descent, the soprano Xiomara Álfaro is, with her four-octave range, Cuba's answer to Yma Sumac. Nicknamed "Cuba's nightingale," she too performed Afro-Cuban material, with arrangements or backings by the likes of Bebo Valdés, Adolfo Guzmán, Chico O'Farrill, or Ernesto Duarte, but in a more operatic style than Merceditas Valdés, as can be heard for example on *Siboney*.

Born in 1930 in the Havana barrio of Buena Vista, she joined the revue *Batamú*, which was part of a show called *El milagro de Ochún*. From this point on her fame grew steadily, and in 1953 she obtained an engagement in Las Vegas, sang with Katherine Dunham, and appeared in the movie *Mambo*, featuring Silvana Mangano. In 1955, after giving a recital at the Martí theater in Havana, she joined the show *Bondeye* along with Celia Cruz. She then starred in the revue *Zum zum ba bae* and pursued an international career, singing in Paris, Argentina, and the United States, where she moved after the revolution, often accompanied by her husband, pianist Rafael Benítez.

A powerful *rumbera*, Celeste Mendoza (1930–1998) became known as the queen of *guaguancó*, and in *Nosotros la Música* and other movies, she sang and danced *rumbas* with enormous gusto. She also scored successes with *Que me castigue Dios*, *Micaela me botó*, and other songs. Born in the Santiago neighborhood of Los Hoyos, she moved to Havana as a teenager. She made her debut in the late 1940s on an amateur radio contest, with Julio Cueva's *El marañón*. She then worked as a dancer, and in 1950 joined *Batamú*. Alternating between dancing and singing, she honed her skills in 1955, along with Omara Portuondo, Isaura Mendoza, and Gladys León, with a vocal *cuarteto* led by Facundo Rivero. The following year she sang on Radio Progreso, backed by Ernesto Duarte's band and then made recordings and toured Latin America.

With her rousing voice, Olga Guillot ("La Guillot," as she is known) is regarded as a diva throughout Latin America, if only for her hit *Miénteme*, and an icon for Cuban exiles in Miami. She has even influenced Argentine tango singers, who have copied her dramatic phrasing and mannerisms. While María Teresa Vera was one of the first *trovadores* to achieve international fame, Olga Guillot was one of the foremost Cuban *boleristas*. Born, like Celeste Mendoza, in Santiago, she started out in 1938, on *La corte suprema del arte*, scoring a hit with *Stormy Weather*, which she translated as *Lluvia gris* ("Grey Rain"). After singing with Isolina Carrillo's Cuarteto Siboney, she performed with Miguelito Valdés in the United States, and with René Cabel in Mexico.

Born in 1930 in Cayo Hueso, the aristocratic Omara Portuondo, recently rediscovered through the film *Buena Vista Social Club*, started out as a dancer, replacing her sister Haydée at the Tropicana. In the 1950s she struck up a friendship with the pianist Frank Emilio Flynn and other musicians of the *filin*, sang on the radio with the group Loquibambia and then with Orlando de la Rosa's *cuarteto*, with Anacoana, and with Las D'Aida, with which she remained until 1967. In 1959, backed by Julio Gutiérrez's big band, she recorded the excellent *Misa negra*.

Like Bola de Nieve, the imposing "Freddy" (Fredesvinda García Herrera) was a unique talent, and only recently did she emerge from oblivion with her sole album, entitled *Freddy*, recorded under the direction of Humberto Suárez. A gripping *bolerista* and an enigmatic woman of ample proportions, she possessed a low and deep contralto that sounded like a man's voice. In *Three Sad Tigers*, Guillermo Cabrera Infante referred to her as "La Estrella" (The Star) and as a "cosmic phenomenon"; and Juan Goytisolo described her voice as "visceral and roaring, as if it had come up directly from her vagina and her bowels to her throat." But her career was meteoric: she passed away at the age of twenty-six.

Born in Céspedes, near Camagüey, she moved to Havana in 1948 and first worked as a cook in the house of a doctor, while dreaming of becoming a star. In the late 1950s, she began to sing unaccompanied (leery, at first, of instrumental backings, which she thought might drown her voice), and then accompanied by Facundo Rivero's group Los Riveros, at the Celeste, a bar where she stunned patrons, among them pianist Aida Diestro, who befriended her. Shortly thereafter, she was engaged at the casino of the Capri hotel, in the revue *Pimienta y sal*, whose band was led by Rafael Somavilla. After performing in other shows, and in Venezuela and Puerto Rico, she died there from a heart attack in 1962, at the house of composer Bobby Collazo.

Nicknamed "El Montunero," the witty "Pío" (Wilfredo) Leiva is yet another artist who received increased exposure through the film *Buena Vista Social Club*. A great exponent of the *son montuno* and the *guajira* and a skilled improviser, he has also sung and composed all kinds of numbers (among them *Mulata con cola*, and the *guaguancó Lo que más me gusta*). Born in 1917 in the little town of Morón, in the center of the island, whose emblem is – fittingly – a rooster, he started out as a *bongocero* with the local band Orquesta Siboney and, in Camagüey, joined the Hermanos Licea's orchestra and then Juanito Blez's *conjunto*. He moved to Havana in the 1950s, where he collaborated with Benny Moré, Bebo Valdés, and Compay Segundo and recorded with Severino Ramos's ensemble, Billo's Caracas Boys, and other bands.

Other vocalists distinguished themselves in the feverish Havana swirl. Among them the *boleristas* René Cabel, Roberto Ledesma (who was the Trío Martino's lead singer before working as a soloist), and Ñico Membiela – a former *trovador* who favored an exaggerated romanticism and rose to fame in the late 1950s with *Contigo besos salvajes*; the *guarachera* Carida Cuervo, promoted by Celia Cruz, who sang with the Conjunto Caney and Rumbavana; the talented *guarachero* "Cascarita" (Orlando Guerra), who worked with the Hermanos Palau, Casino de la Playa, and Julio Cueva and formed his own band in 1946; the *sonero* and guitarist Senén Súarez; Esther Borja, mostly known for her *zarzuelas*; Celio González (who performed with the Conjunto Casino, Jóvenes del Cayo, and La Sonora Matancera); the *sonera* "La India de Oriente" (Luisa María Hernández); the Puerto Rican Daniel Santos, who sang on the Cadena Azul radio station in the early 1950s backed by Jóvenes del Cayo; Luisito Plá and his Guaracheros; and Bienvenido Granda.

The 1950s also saw the rise of *cuartetos* and other vocal groups with greater harmonic sophistication than before: Alberto Aroche's Cuarteto Aroche, Isolina Carrillo's Cuarteto Siboney (with Alfredo León, Facundo Rivero and Marcelino Guerra), the group led by singer and pianist Orlando de la Rosa,[26] Bobby Collazo's Cuarteto Antillano, which included "Bobby" (Roberto) Carcassés, the Cuban Pipers, Los Bucaneros, and the Cuarteto del Rey, which specialized in negro spirituals.

One of the most interesting of those *cuartetos* was Las d'Aida. Founded in 1952 by pianist and singer Aida Diestro (the daughter of a preacher, she had previously accompanied choirs in a Protestant church), it consisted of Moraima Secada – a former member of Orquesta Anacaona – the sisters Omara and Haydée Portuondo, and "Elena Burke" (Romana Burgues). Los D'Aida triumphed with their suave, jazz-inflected vocalizing and smooth delivery. Accompanied by some of the most progressive musicians in Cuba: Peruchín, Luis and Pucho Escalante, Emilio Peñalver, Guillermo Barreto, they made excellent recordings (*Profecía, Nocturno antillano*), with arrangements by Chico O'Farrill. They started out on the radio, accompanied by Bebo Valdés, and on the television program *Carusel de la alegría* with *Mamey colorao* and *Cosas del alma*, and later issued *An Evening at the Sans Souci*. Burke, Secada, and Omara Portuondo eventually left the group to pursue their careers as soloists, and in 1963 Teresa García Caturla (composer Alejandro García Caturla's daughter) became their lead singer.

Tríos with their repertoire of boleros, *guajiras,* and *guarachas* persisted, but they, too, adopted a more modern sound. Among them were the Trío Servando Díaz (*Besos salvajes, Porfiado corazón*), founded in 1938 with singers Angel Alday and José Antonio Piñares (Díaz was lead singer and second guitar),[27] which played at La Conga, in New York; Los Guaracheros de Oriente, formed by Ñico Saquito in the early 1950s, which performed fairly traditional material; the dynamic Hermanas Castro, the Hermanas Márquez, the Hermanas Lago; the Trío Oriental, started in 1940 by "Bimbi" (Maximiliano Sánchez), Tico Álvarez, and Pedro Feliú; the Trío América, the Trío Luisito Plá; the Trío García, with "Nené" (Gualfredo), Justa, and Ana García (with whom Graciela Pérez sang from 1940 to 1942), the Trío La Rosa; and the trio of the Hermanos Rigual (Carlos, Mario, and Pituko), who hailed from Oriente.

26 He died in 1957 at the age of thirty-eight.

27 Odilio Portal (first guitar), "Cuso" (Octavio) Mendoza (second voice, maracas) and, in the 1950s, Mario Recio and Facundo Riverso were later part of the group.

There were also a number of successful *duos,* notably Pototo y Filomeno, Celina y Reutilio, and Los Compadres. A hilarious sort of Don Quijote–Sancho Panza pair, singers, dancers, and comedians "Pototo" (Leopoldo Fernández) – also known as "Tres Patines" – and "Filomeno" (Aníbal de Mar) delighted audiences with their histrionics, although they also had superb musical skills. For many years they appeared on television, on the radio program *La tremenda corte,* and in movies, backed by their own *conjunto,* or by the Orquesta Riverside and Melodías del 40. They also pursued separate radio careers and attracted a strong following in both the United States and Latin America, although even today they remain virtually unknown in other countries. The son of a cigar-maker and a woman who ironed in a drycleaning store, Pototo, born in Güines in 1904, eventually moved to Miami, where he died in 1985. Two of their albums, *Yo pico un pan* and *Pototo y Filomeno* typify Cuban humor at its most irresistible. They contain several riotous *sones* and *guarachas*, among them *Boniatillo*, *Ahorita va a llover*, *Échame a mí la culpa*, and *No mojen a la materia*. In *Este número no existe* ("This number is out of service") Pototo and Filomeno imitate the recorded message of a telephone operator, and in *Carta de mamita* ("Mamita's Letter"), a confused man mistakes the word "organizing" for "agonizing."

Except for Guillermo Portabales, few country singers had achieved national fame before Celina González. A talented *decimista* with a powerful voice, Celina got her break, however, not with a *punto* or a *guajira* but with a tune inspired by *santería*: *Santa Bárbara* (also known as *Que viva Changó*), which remained her major hit and has been covered by various artists, among them the group NG La Banda. For many years she performed in a duo with her husband Reutilio Domínguez, under the name of Celina y Reutilio, and with her cascading black hair, she cut a striking figure.

She was born in 1929 on a farm near Jovellanos, in the province of Matanzas, but her family moved to Santiago de Cuba when she was still a child. She started singing in family *guateques* (peasant parties) accompanied by her sister on *tres* and her brother on *laúd* (lute). At the age of fifteen she met fellow *trovador* Reutilio Domínguez, to whom she became engaged. In 1947 they began to perform on the radio and in local theaters in Oriente. They then moved to Havana, where Ñico Saquito helped them obtain engagements on the radio, and *Santa Bárbara*, written by Celina shortly after her arrival in the capital, brought them fame. In the 1950s she performed in New York with Barbarito Diez.

Other worthy though lesser known exponents of Cuban country music include Coralina Fernández and Ramón Veloz.

A highly rated duo of the late 1940s and early 1950s was Los Compadres, founded in 1942 by the singers, composers, guitarists, and *tresistas* Francisco Repilado Muñoz and his cousin Lorenzo Hierrezuelo. A radio DJ dubbed Hierrezuelo "Compay Primo" and Repilado "Compay Segundo," a nickname by which he is still known today.

Creator of wonderful songs (*Sarandonga*, *Liduvino en el Parana*, *Macusa*, and the highly popular *Chan chan*), Repilado was born in the small town of Siboney, in Oriente, in 1907. He grew up in the company of his grandmother – a former slave who smoked cigars and lived to be more than a hundred years of age. In 1916 he moved to Santiago, starting work at the age of fourteen as a cigar-maker, a trade he would later ply in Havana as well. A few years later, he sang and strummed his guitar with various local groups, among them *estudiantinas*, and in the early 1930s with the Cuarteto Cubanacán. He also played clarinet with Santiago's municipal brass band.

In 1934 he traveled to Havana with Ñico Saquito's Cuban Stars quintet and decided to settle there. With Saquito he played the *armónico*, a seven-string guitar with a double G string which he had devised and which, sounding slightly like a *tres*, gave his music a particular flavor. He worked with various outfits, among them the Cuarteto Hatuey, with which he sang second voice and played guitar and *tres*, and which included, in 1937, Evelio Machín (Antonio's brother, director, first voice, maracas), Armando Dulfo (guitar, *coro*), and Florecita (trumpet), and also, at various times, Hierrezuelo and Marcelino Guerra. When the group broke up, Repilado went back to playing clarinet, this time with the Miguel Matamoros Conjunto, working on the side as a barber and at the Montecristo cigar factory.

Also a wonderful whistler, Hierrezuelo (1907–1993) was born in El Caney, Oriente, and like Repilado grew up in Santiago. He moved to Havana in the mid-1930s, sang with the Trío Lírico Cubano, the Sexteto Hatuey, Justa García's *cuarteto*, and between 1937 and 1962 in a duo with María Teresa Vera. A precursor of groups such as Sampling, Hierrezuelo imitated the sound of musical instruments with his voice.

Los Compadres recorded many songs redolent of Oriente (*Caña quemá*, alluding to a fire at a sugar mill, *Voy pa' Mayarí*, *Baja y tapa la olla*, *Cañero número 15*, *El gallo e' jando*). These were sometimes scorned by the Havana bourgeoisie, who considered them too coarse, but Los Compadres kept alive in the capital the tradition of the *son reginero* and other genres from their native province and also took them to other Latin American countries.

When, in Fall 1955, Repilado left to form Compay Segundo y sus Muchachos, Hierrezuelo replaced him with his own brother, Reynaldo. Los Compadres pursued their career, and Compay Segundo also recorded with Pío Leiva, Carlos Embale, and others.

In the second half of the 1940s, a sentimental and mostly vocal style emerged in Havana, with speech often lapsing, in the cabaret tradition, into song: this was the *filin* (from the English "feeling"). Leonardo Acosta has mentioned that in those days many musicians used to go to the harbor to buy race records from African-American sailors, and that the word "*filin*" comes from a song sung by Maxine Sullivan called *I Got a Feeling*.[28] Miguel de Gonzalo (who had sung during the previous decade with Armando Valdespí and Aldemaro Romero), Bobby Collazo, Marcelino Guerra, and Orlando de la Rosa were early performers of this genre, which was also anticipated in the music of Margarita Lecuona and, later, by guitarists "Guyún" (Vicente González Rubiera) and "Ñico" (José Antonio) Rojas. Inspired by jazz, the stylized romanticism of American balladeers, Brazilian music, French impressionism, and other influences, the *filin* was characterized by more intricate harmonies than those customarily used in genres such as the *son* or the *guaracha*.

28 Typescript of interview with Leonardo Acosta, 1997.

Born in Santiago in 1908, Guyún had studied guitar with Sindo Garay and Pepe Delgado and had sung on the radio. He recorded subtle numbers (*Solamente una vez, Yambambo*) and wrote a harmony primer still used in Cuba. As in Rio de Janeiro where, more or less around the same time, singer Nara Leão had been a catalyst for the bossa nova, singer and guitarist Angel Díaz, a student of Guyún's, attracted around him José Antonio Méndez, César Portillo de la Luz, Haydée and Omara Portuondo, Elena Burke, and other young artists eager to experiment with new means of expression. The *filin* then blossomed in the Callejón de Hammel, a small Cayo Hueso street that has today become a hotbed of *rumba brava* – and at the Club El Gato Tuerto.

A self-taught guitarist and composer, an engineer by profession and a friend of Guyún's, Ñico Rojas (born in Havana in 1921) produced delicate and melodious pieces with progressions recalling those of Brazilian music and often celebrating other musicians or relatives: *Homenaje a Bebo, Elegía a Benny Moré, Saldiguera y Virulilla*, the guitar *danzón Pipo y Arcaño*, dedicated to Jesús López and Antonio Arcaño. A modest, self-effacing and generous man, Rojas remained unjustly forgotten for many years, but his music has now been rediscovered by several Cuban artists.

With his gritty voice and his speech full of unusual expressions, the endearing singer and guitarist José Antonio Méndez ("El king") was one of the great names of the *filin*. He penned some of the most famous boleros ever: *La gloria eres tú, Soy tan feliz, Tú, mi delirio, Novia mía, Ese sentimiento se llama amor, Si me comprendieras*:

Si me comprendieras	If you understood me
Si me conocieras que feliz sería.	If you knew me, how happy I would be,
Si me comprendieras	If you understood me,
Si me conocieras, jamás lloraría.	If you knew me, I would never cry.

Born in Havana in 1927 to a father who was a musician, he sang on Radio Mil Diez and then set up Loquibambia, a *conjunto* with a Cuban and American repertoire directed by pianist Frank Emilio Flynn and whose members included Omara Portuondo and, occasionally, guitarist Froilán Amézaga and Niño Rivera (on bass). During the 1950s Méndez lived in Mexico where, just as in Cuba, he charmed audiences. In June 1989, a few days before he was to travel to Paris, he died after being run over by a bus as he was leaving the club Rincón del Feeling.

César Portillo de la Luz is another beacon of the *filin* movement. He grew up listening to his parents who sang at home and started singing as a child. He formed a trio with two friends, while making a living as a house painter. He made his debut on the radio and then in 1956 joined a group in which he played the guitar and Frank Domínguez the piano. A prolific composer, he wrote *Yo sé que es mentira, Noche cubana,* and the famed *Contigo en la distancia.* He explains about *Contigo en la distancia:* "I was then twenty-four . . . I didn't think it was an artistic composition, not even a simple one. I tried to find the reason [for its success] and I realized that I had put in the mouths of many the song they needed to express their feelings."[29]

Nicknamed "Señora sentimiento" ("Lady feeling"), Elena Burke, with her strong and moving voice, became one of the divas of *filin.* Born in 1928, she made her professional debut in 1943 on the Mil Diez radio station, and performed accompanied by Dámaso Pérez Prado on piano. She also danced and sang in various shows in Havana and Caracas. In 1949 she traveled to Mexico, along with Celia Cruz, with the revue *Las Mulatas de Fuego,* and then sang with the *cuartetos* of Facundo Rivero, Orlando de la Rosa and Aida Diestro. In the late 1950s she was accompanied by Amézaga, and by various pianists, and she also worked in Mexico, at the famed Salón México.

Olga Guillot, Luis Yáñez, Armando Valdespí, Orlando de la Rosa, Rosendito Ruiz, Aurelio Reinoso, the melodramatic Blanca Rosa Gil, Berta Dupuy, Reinaldo Henríquez, Pepe Reyes, and Piloto y Vera (Gerardo Piloto and Alberto Vera, authors of *Mambo infierno* and many other songs) and, to a lesser degree, Francisco Fellové and Niño Rivera, also gravitated towards the intimist atmosphere of *filin.* Piloto y Vera formed an excellent duo which lasted until 1967, when Piloto was killed in a plane crash.

The singers Maggie Prior, Delia Bravo, Ana Menéndez, and Rosita Formés chose to express themselves in the jazz idiom in the 1940s, although Menéndez and Formés later branched off in different musical directions.

Composers

29 In: Hiram Guadalupe Pérez: *Un momento de música cubana,* entrevista con César Portillo de la Luz y Tony Taño, p. 112.

30 The sister of flautist and bandleader Luis Carrillo.

Mention should also be made of some of the important popular music composers of the time: José Carbó Menéndez (*Cao cao maní picao*), Bobby Collazo (*Rumba matunga*), Félix B. Caignet (*Mentira, Frutas del caney*), Osvaldo Farrés (*Quizás, quizás, quizás*), Obdulio Morales (*La rumbantela*), Julio Gutiérrez (*Un poquito de tu amor*), Odilio Portal (*Me lo dijo Adela, A Romper el coco*), Silvestre Méndez (*Yiri yiri bon, El as de la rumba*), Isolina Carrillo[30] (*Dos gardenias*), "Pepe" (José) Delgado (*Mi gallo pinto, Cosas del alma*), Francisco Fellové (*Mango mangüé, El Jamaiquino*), "Pituko" (Pedro) Rigual (*Corazón de melón, Cuando calienta el sol*), and Pedro Junco, who died from tuberculosis at the age of twenty-three (*Nosotros, Soy como soy*).

CHAPTER FIVE

the United States and Puerto Rico

In April, 1945, Harry Truman became the American president on the death of F. D. Roosevelt, and his Fair Deal policy boosted the economy. The United States celebrated the new-found peace and entered an era of prosperity, although for ethnic minorities, the struggle for social and economic equality continued.

During the 1940s and 1950s, the growth of the Puerto Rican community increased steadily on the East Coast, and to a lesser degree in cities such as Chicago. More than 61,000 Puerto Ricans were living in New York by 1940, among them nearly 5000 musicians (almost 10 percent of the population!). During the 1940s, the failure of Operation Bootstrap[1] sent another spate of islanders to the Big Apple in search of jobs. The lowering of the San Juan–New York air fares also accelerated the exodus of Puerto Ricans, most of whom were between fifteen and forty years of age. By 1950 the Puerto Rican ranks in the Big Apple had swelled to about 200,000.[2] The demographic explosion pushed Puerto Ricans into new neighborhoods, the South Bronx among them. Many Latin musicians, who rarely belonged to unions, survived by playing on the *cuchifrito* circuit – the Latin equivalent of the Southern chittlin'circuit, and later one of the mainstays of salsa.

One month after Truman's inauguration, New York witnessed, as Lucien Malson wittily wrote, the explosion of "two bombs – peaceful ones, this time – dropped by Charlie Parker and Dizzy Gillespie: *Hot House* and *Salt Peanuts*." With the onset of bebop, jazz's center of gravity moved from Harlem to 52nd Street. Billie Holiday was particularly affected by this change, which threw her

1 A program initiated by Governor Muñoz Marín to attract North American investment in order to boost the Puerto Rican economy.

2 In 1945, about 1135 Puerto Ricans arrived each week in New York. A million would settle there between 1945 and 1960.

into a white, often hostile, and disconcerting world. But jazz, which then stopped being dance music, won over new audiences.

While jazz was migrating midtown, Latin music spread throughout New York, and the South Bronx in particular, where many Hispanic musicians lived, vibrated with a new kind of energy. As in Cuba, the 1940s and 1950s were one of the most creative periods for Latin music.

¡Qué rico el mambo!

In the early 1950s, the mambo overtook the rumba and the conga. If Antonio Arcaño and Arsenio Rodríguez were precursors of this genre, it was Dámaso Pérez Prado, as we saw, who gave it its final form, and who first used the word "mambo" as a generic term to designate some of his musical creations. His fast and driving mambos *Mambo No. 5*, *Cherry Pink and Apple Blossom White* (a take on the French song *Cerisier rose et pommier blanc*, written in 1950 by Jacques Larue and Louis Gay), and *Patricia* took the world by storm, and he also offered a winning mixture of cha-chas (*Corazón de melón*), guajiras (*Guantanamera*), sones montunos (*Mata siguaraya*), and other types of music.

Although he accompanied several singers, Benny Moré, Daniel Santos (*Chambeleque*, *Las siete y media*), Celia Cruz, and Toña la Negra among them, his music was essentially instrumental, punctuated by his characteristic grunts which announced different sections and, as with James Brown, Michael Jackson, or other Afro-American singers, gave rhythmic impetus. His punchy arrangements, with a few subtle touches of piano or organ, were highly danceable. And he was a deft pianist, whose considerable skills have generally been overshadowed by his talents as composer (of *The Voodoo Suite* or *Concierto para bongó*, with its extended percussion introduction) and showman.

And showman he certainly was, with his platform shoes, flashy jewelry, and plastered-down hair, conducting his band with expressive body movements, which in turn inspired Benny Moré.

Born in Matanzas, Prado (1916–1989) gigged with local outfits and joined Ora Mesa's ensemble. In 1941 he moved to Havana, where he worked with the band of the Pennsylvania cabaret and with Paulina Álvarez, and formed a *charanga*. The following year he played with Casino de la Playa and with trumpeter Pilderot's La Cubaney, writing arrangements for both bands. Attracted by jazz and eager to free himself from the constraints of the *danzón* and the *son*, he began to develop what would later become the mambo. But in Cuba his ideas met with indifference, and Kiko Mendive persuaded him to settle in Mexico where, he assured him, his talent would stand more chance of being recognized. During 1944 and 1945, following Mendive's advice, Prado stayed in Mexico City in order to record and make contacts. Back in Havana, he formed a *conjunto* which made a few recordings, and the following year he returned to Mexico,

Bassist Pantaleón Pérez Prado (Dámaso's brother and rival) with the French actress Gisèle Robert (Paris, 1955)

borrowing Arturo Núñez's rhythm section for his own engagements and playing on the soundtrack of a movie.

In 1950, in the Aztec capital, he formed with some Cuban and Mexican musicians – among them percussionists Aurelio Tamayo (timbales), Clemente Piquero (bongo), Modesto Durán (conga), Ramón Castro, and Mariano Damendi, and trumpeters "Florecita," Perique, the extraordinary Chilo Morán, and José Solis – a big band consisting of trumpets, saxophones, piano, bass, trap drums, and Cuban percussion. His admiration for Stan Kenton probably influenced his jazzy orchestrations. Despite his reservations about singers, he hired Benny Moré, whom he had heard with Arturo Núñez, and who thrilled him. With Moré, Prado recorded a string of tunes, among them *Bonito y sabroso*, *Encantado de la vida*, *A romper el coco*, and a humorous song alluding to Prado:

> *¿Quién inventó el mambo que me provoca? (bis)*
> *¿Que a las mujeres las vuelve locas?*
> *¿Quién inventó esa cosa loca? (bis)*
> *Un chaparrito con cara de foca.*

> Who invented the mambo which provokes me? (bis)
> Which drives women crazy?
> Who invented this crazy thing?
> A small guy with a seal's face.

Despite the acclaim Moré brought him, Prado noticed, as many other bandleaders before him, that vocalists stole the show. After Moré returned to Cuba, he performed mostly instrumental music, though with his bandmembers singing a few riffs ("*e, e, que rico mambo*," for example); his first mambos *Qué rico el mambo*, *José y Macamé*, *Mambo No. 5*, *Piano y ritmo* were instant hits:

Qué rico el mambo – Pérez Prado

In 1951, Mendive convinced Prado to take his band to the United States. Prado triumphed at the Zenda Ballroom in Hollywood, and the following year throughout Latin America. After *King of the Mambo*, recorded in Cuba and in Mexico, he moved in 1954 to Los Angeles, formed a new big outfit with a few musicians from Jimmy Lunceford's group, and was asked by the RCA producer

Hernán Díaz Jr. to write a *Voodoo Suite*. Shorty Rogers, who collaborated with Prado on this work, told journalist Gérard Rouy: "The *Voodoo Suite* has been decisive as far as my appreciation of Afro-Cuban rhythms goes. Later I made another record for RCA, 'Afro-Cuban Influence,' and since then, I have always played one or two tunes which have a Latin tinge. I love Tito Puente's work." For the recording session, Prado recruited some West Coast jazzmen, and the impressive band, which included four saxophones, six trumpets, three trombones, a French horn, a bass, and seven percussion instruments, generated a volcanic force. Around the same time he performed in Japan, turning a traditional local song into a mambo, which so moved the audience that it sang along while the band was playing.

He then alternated between jazz (*Mood Indigo*), in collaboration with Maynard Ferguson, Luis Gasca, Barney Kessel, Jim Nottingham, George Duvivier, and others, and the type of Latin music most of his listeners identified him with (*Mambo de las existencialistas, Quizás, quizás, quizás*). At the height of his success, he also appeared in movies whose sensuality led to them being banned in some countries by both the Church and the bourgeoisie: the Cardinal of Lima, Juan Gualberto Guevara, for one, denied absolution to mambo dancers, and in Colombia, the bishop of Santa Rosa de Osos, Monseñor Miguel Ángel Builes, also condemned the mambo and other "devilish inventions brought from hell to upset an already morally rotten society." In the 1960s, Prado adapted to the twist with "Twist Goes Latin," and then returned to Mexico in the 1970s.

If the world loved Prado's fiery music, however, it was New York which created the most sophisticated mambos. In Cuba, the mambo never quite caught on as it did in other countries, although Bebo Valdés and others recorded mambos, some of them arranged by Peruchín. In 1949, the Cuban revue *Las Mulatas de Fuego* performed at the Havana Madrid – one of Manhattan's major Latin venues. Tito Puente lent his band to René Touzet in order to accompany these torrid *Cubanas*. Before going on to Mexico and Venezuela, they introduced in New York the steps that would become the mambo, and a few years later the mambo truly burst all over the town. Rhythmically smoother and more complex than the rumba, it spawned countless variations: the *dengue* (popularized by Pérez Prado in 1962), the *kaen* (slow), the *batiri* (fast), created by Antar Daly and influenced by the rumba, the double mambo, the triple mambo, with its undulations of the hips, the Palladium mambo, and such amalgams as the bolero-mambo, the mambo-guaracha, the boogie-mambo, and the dazzling jitterbug-mambo. The *dengue* premiered at the Bronx Casino – a predominantly Puerto Rican club. Prado recorded *dengues*, and so did Roberto Faz a few years later with, notably, *El dengue y su tiqui tiqui* or *Dengue in fa*.

On the crest of the mambo vogue, dance marathons featuring several bands were held in various U.S. ballrooms; the Afro-Cubans, Las Hermanas Castro, and Tito Puente crisscrossed the country; Machito, Joe Loco, Carlos Ramírez, and the high precision dancing duo The Mambo Aces (Joe Centeño

Las Mulatas de Fuego with Óscar López and La Sonora Matancera. Óscar López Collection

and Aníbal Vázquez) performed at Carnegie Hall, and Pérez Prado, Tito Rodríguez, and Chico O'Farrill at the Shrine Auditorium in Los Angeles. A *Downbeat* magazine article of October 6, 1954 proclaimed with a typically American metaphor, "Dance schools find these days that a mambo class is as essential as a credit payment plan." Joe Loco brought the mambo to San Francisco, Dizzy Gillespie presented his *Afro-Cuban Suite* in Washington, Pérez Prado played at Birdland, Noro Morales in Las Vegas; Artie Shaw played *Stop and Go Mambo* and turned *Back Bay Shuffle* into a mambo; Benny Bennett recorded *Mambo Boogie*, Tab Smith *Cuban Boogie*, Jimmy Forrest *Night Train Mambo*, King Curtis *Cuban Twilight*, Earl Bostic *Mambolino* and *Mambostic*; the guitarist Dave Gilbert appeared in the movie *Mambo*, the Bop-A-Loos vocalized on *Cuban Carnival Bongo Mambo*, Tito Puente played his mambos and cha-chas on television. Nat "King" Cole added the *bongocero* Jack Costanzo to his trio and recorded *Papa Loves Mambo* as well as Cuban songs. Bill Haley, Ruth Brown, Perry Como, Rosemary Clooney – just about every one fell for the mambo. In Paris, Patato Valdés taught Brigitte Bardot to dance the mambo for *And God Created Woman*, the cult film which ushered in the *nouvelle vague*; Katherine Dunham and the Cuban percussionist Francisco Aguabella starred, along with Silvana Mangano, in *Mambo*, and then this rhythm reached a point of saturation. "To hell with the mambo," blasted an exasperated *Downbeat* chronicler, "even cats and dogs do it in the backyard!"

The cha-cha then stormed into New York with bombshells like *El bodeguero*, *Corazón de melón*, *El Jamaiquino*, or *Me lo dijo Adela*:

Me lo dijo Adela – Otilio Portal

Jazz musicians, including Stan Kenton, who recorded cha-chas on *Viva Kenton*, adopted this more laid-back musical genre, so relaxing after the mambo's breathless pyrotechnics. And then rock 'n' roll and the smooth *pachanga* ousted the cha-cha. It persisted a few more years in Europe where, around the mid-1960s, Los Machucambos (a group essentially comprised of non-Cuban musicians) scored a hit with *Pepito mi corazón*. Today, in dance schools or in swank Miami Beach hotels, retirees, carefully counting their steps, dance with the stiffness of arthritic penguins a codified, almost fossilized cha-cha. In the late 1980s, cha-cha contests were organized in Havana (one of them with the bands of Remberto Egües and Enrique Jorrín), but without ever really reviving this rhythm.

The mambo and the cha-cha gave a new impetus to Latin record labels, and to radio shows, among them *Robbin's Nest*, *Saludos Amigos*, and those of "Symphony Sid" Torin (though Torin was accused by Miles Davis of being "an exploiter of black music") or "Ricardo" (Dick) Sugar. Taking advantage of this Latin boom, and picking up on the success of Chano Pozo with Dizzy Gillespie, Norman Granz, ever looking for novelty, paired Charlie Parker and Flip Phillips with the Afro-Cubans for some recording sessions.

Latin clubs proliferated in and around New York, among them the Roadside Club in New Jersey; La Bamba, the Alameda Room, the Latin Quarter, the Club Cuba, the Tropicana, and La Conga (which later became the China Doll), in midtown Manhattan; the Saint Nicholas Arena and the Audubon Ballroom uptown; and in the Bronx, the Caravana, the Tropicoro, where Tito Puente popularized *El baile del pinguino* in the early 1950s, and the Hunts Point Palace, where bodies were said to fly out of the windows whenever fights erupted. By the mid-1950s, all the major theaters, ballrooms, and jazz clubs, including the Apollo Theater, presented Latin attractions. In Oakland, Latin dancers congregated at Sweet's Ballroom. But the foremost Latin music temple was the Palladium Ballroom, located on the corner of Broadway and 53rd Street in New York, "home of the mambo," as it advertised itself.

In 1946 Machito and Mario Bauzá recommended to Federico Pagani, later known as "the godfather of Latin music," that he revitalize an Italian ballroom, the Alma Dance Studios. There, Machito and Bauzá launched Sunday matinees named "Blen blen club," after *Blen blen blen* (or *Blem blem bem*), a composition by Chano Pozo. Machito had flyers printed which announced a *Subway dance*, and huge crowds showed up. These matinees were so successful that Latin music was then featured every Wednesday night. The Dominican Joseíto Román brought his sizzling merengues; for even more excitement Pagani organized zany contests and soon the dancehall, renamed Palladium Ballroom, became the hottest place in town. The Mafia, which controlled the place, took Pagani aside; "We love the business you generate, but please, don't bring us so many blacks." "If you want the green, you've got to have the blacks!" Pagani quipped back unfazed.

Dancers at the Palladium in the 1950s. The Justo A. Martí Photographic Collection, Centro de Estudios Puertorriqueños, Hunter College, CUNY

The Mafia having finally surrendered to Pagani's arguments, the Palladium Ballroom became the melting pot where all races and social classes mixed and gave themselves over to the frenzy of the mambo and the cha-cha. Pagani's successor, Catalino Rolón, perpetuated the same adventurous musical policy. Professional dancers Paulito y Lilón, Louie Máquina, Frank "Killer Joe" Piro, Augie and Margot, "Cuban Pete" (Pedro Aguilar), Lenny Dale, Tommy Johnson, Marilyn Winters, Byron and Tybee, Ernie Ensley, Gerard, Jo-Jo Smith, The Mambo Aces, The Cha Cha Aces (with the Puerto Rican Mike Ramos, of the Mambo Aces, and Freddie Ríos), and Dottie Adams captivated audiences. Tito Rodríguez, rolling backwards with his musicians and whirling on one hand on the floor, delighted his admirers with exhibitions of breakdancing ahead of its time. Women flashily dressed in tight dresses and high heels and men in dapper suits performed dazzling routines. Everyone answered the irresistible call of the drums. Jazzmen from the nearby Birdland and Royal Roost came in to check out the music. Duke Ellington, Woody Herman, George Shearing, Stan Kenton, Billy Taylor, Dizzy Gillespie socialized with Lena Horne, Bob Hope, Sammy Davis Jr., Bill Cosby, Elsa Maxwell, Marlon Brando. In Havana, Brando had been fascinated by percussionist El Chori and by the dancing team of Anisia and Rolando, and at the Palladium, he tried to sit in on conga – but "without any talent," declared Gillespie. The trumpet whiz, who claimed he "lived at the Palladium," recalled with emotion the hallway decorated with photographs of celebrities and, especially, "the small room where one smoked grass."

The Afro-Cubans

In December 1940, an unknown band made its debut at the Park Palace in New York, on the same bill as Federico Pagani's Los Happy Boys, and its bold and intense music left listeners speechless. At first, though, some black Americans, shocked by the hand-held congas and bongos, rejected these "primitive" percussion instruments, which increased their racial uneasiness. "In those days," Mongo Santamaría explained, "some black Americans, struggling to achieve respectability, dismissed Afro-Cuban rhythms as 'monkey music' while whites accepted them more readily." But rapidly succumbing to the charm of the Afro-Cubans, these black Americans became ardent converts.

With their stimulating charts, polished sound, and variegated palette, the Afro-Cubans did much to promote the mambo and they greatly contributed to the success of the Palladium. The most important Cuban orchestra of the 1940s and 1950s, they put Latin jazz on the map and constantly innovated while also adapting to the various musical trends.

Around 1940, a handful of black jazzmen began to rise against the commercialism of the swing era whose bands – those of Woody Herman, Artie

Shaw, Harry James, Bob Crosby, Charlie Barnet, Benny Goodman, Glen Gray, Bunny Berigan, Perry Como, Tommy and Jimmy Dorsey[3] – were predominantly white. Defying the prevailing conventions and causing an uproar, they invented bebop, a harmonically sophisticated language full of alterations and substitutions.

Like Cuban musicians, they also "turned the rhythm section around," displacing syncopations from one bar to the other and accenting unusual beats in order to dislocate the predictable structure. Priding themselves on their marginality and their differences, they composed numbers with humorous or incongruous titles such as *Bongo Beep* or *Crazeology*, and with challenging melodies built on the chord structure of standard tunes, whose lightning-fast tempos compelled horn players to give up the traditional vibrato.

In early 1940, "Machito" (Frank Grillo Gutiérrez) had decided to form an orchestra combining authentic Afro-Cuban rhythms and percussion with the advanced concepts of bebop. Sharing the rebellious and adventurous spirit of the boppers and tired of the bland fare dished out by Latin society bands, Bauzá, who had married Machito's sister Estela a few years before, joined his brother-in-law the following year as musical director, and introduced new ideas. Machito's sunny and easygoing disposition balanced Bauzá's more saturnine character, and it was Machito who generally communicated with the public. "When one marries Afro-Latin rhythms and good musical knowledge," Machito used to say, "one gets fascinating music. Mario and I knew exactly what we wanted. We often had mediocre musicians, but with his arrangements, Mario knew how to get the best out of them." The name chosen for the band, the Afro-Cubans, revealed its founders' desire for authenticity. American blacks would later reject the terms "negro" and "colored," inflicted upon them by whites, preferring the culturally more appropriate and dignified terms Afro-Americans or African-Americans.

Born in Havana in 1911, Bauzá grew up in Cayo Hueso, socializing with Miguelito Valdés, Chano Pozo, and other musicians. He studied flute and clarinet at the conservatory and, along with Valdés and Machito, trained to become a mechanic at Dodge. Music won: he became bass clarinettist with the Havana Philharmonic Orchestra and worked with the leading *típicas* or *charangas*, among them those of Aniceto Díaz, Antonio María Romeu, Domingo Corbacho, Felipe Valenzuela, and Belisario López.

In 1926 he recorded in New York with Romeu. Fascinated by jazz, he listened to the top big bands of that era, with a particular fondness for Frankie Trumbauer, then playing with Paul Whiteman. A former sideman of Bix Beiderbecke and Jean Goldkette, Trumbauer had also impressed Lester Young, who admired his technique and sensitivity. Swayed by Trumbauer, Bauzá purchased a C-melody saxophone and began to study jazz assiduously. Upon his return to Havana, he played saxophone and clarinet with pianist Célido Curbelo and took up the trumpet as well.

3 Incidentally it was two Latin numbers: *Green Eyes* (*Aquellos ojos verdes*) and *María Elena*, which enabled Jimmy Dorsey, in the early 1940s, to outshine his brother Tommy.

In 1930 Bauzá's love for jazz impelled him to move to New York, where he found the ideal conditions to pursue his musical explorations. He settled on Sugar Hill, to be close to the heart of jazz, and soon met several of the most creative musicians. Antonio Machín needed a trumpeter for a recording date as Remberto Lara had returned to Cuba with Azpiazu. Bauzá persuaded Machín to buy him a trumpet. He recorded *La mulata rumbera* and *El panquelero* with him, and subsequently established a solid reputation on this instrument.

Soon after the sessions with Machín, the Missourians, then booked at the Savoy Ballroom, recruited Bauzá as first trumpet. The band, which at that time backed Cab Calloway, included two fine trumpeters in R. Q. Dickerson and Lammar Wright, but, claimed Bauzá, "I knew more music than the other trumpeters in the band." They played New Orleans jazz, Midwest blues, and the new and fashionable jungle style, and it was Bauzá's first professional experience with an American group. There he discovered the power of having a strong horn section, especially to back singers and dancers, a power he remembered when he set up the Afro-Cubans.

In 1931 he was hired as a clarinettist and saxophonist by Cass Carr – a West Indian bassist and musical saw expert who performed at the Saint George hotel in Brooklyn – the future cradle of salsa. Carr seemed to exert a strong pull with his saw-playing, for Dizzy Gillespie also gigged with him. Bauzá then played at the Central Park hotel with Noble Sissle's ensemble, which included Sidney Bechet, and with Sam Wooding at the Lafayette Theater. The following year, he joined the Chick Webb orchestra. Webb helped him perfect his jazz phrasing and entrusted him with the band's repertoire; in 1934 Bauzá recorded *Stompin' at the Savoy, My Last Affair, Holiday in Harlem*, and other sides with the extraordinary drummer, an experience which he would remember for the rest his life.

Shortly thereafter, the young Ella Fitzgerald, discovered by the showman Bardu Ali at an amateur contest at the Apollo Theater, became the band's vocalist. At first, Webb wouldn't have anything to do with this shy and not very attractive girl, but Ella soon brought him rousing success. In 1936 Bauzá became Webb's musical director. In the brass section he, with fellow trumpeters Taft Jordan and Bobby Stark, and trombonists Sandy Williams and Nat Story, together nicknamed "The Five Horsemen" by their peers, stunned audiences. Webb, who had heard Xavier Cugat, liked Latin sounds, and his interest in Cuban music increased under Bauzá's influence. After Bauzá left the band, in 1938, Webb recorded a number entitled *The Congo Conga*. After Webb's death from tuberculosis, the following year, Ella Fitzgerald took the leadership of his band, and its musical director, saxophonist, and arranger Edgar Sampson later collaborated with Bauzá, as well as with Tito Puente.

Following his tenure with Webb, Bauzá collaborated with Don Redman and Fletcher Henderson, and in December 1939, he joined Cab Calloway's band as trumpet player. Calloway, who had heard Alberto Socarrás, also enjoyed Cuban music. Though his book mostly consisted of fox-trots and other American rhythms, he had recorded a few Latin sides in the early 1930s, in particular *Doin'* *the Rhumba* and *Cuban Nightmare* and, along with Duke Ellington, he was one of the first African-American bandleaders outside the Crescent City to play Cuban numbers. He gradually included more Latin tunes in his repertoire, often simplifying the rhythms so that Americans could understand them. Bauzá soon brought his friend Dizzy Gillespie into the band. Calloway tested the ebullient young trumpeter by making him play the difficult *Cuban Nightmare*, which Dizzy performed brilliantly. Gillespie also perfected his mastery of Latin music in an after-hours group led by Bauzá. While performing with Calloway, Bauzá, Gillespie, and drummer William "Cozy" Cole traded musical ideas on the bandstand, and the germs of "cubop" (Cuban music + bebop) started to incubate during this period.

In 1940 Bauzá decided to go his own way. He worked freelance for a while and then joined the Afro-Cubans as musical director. One night, Gillespie was accused by Calloway of having thrown spit-balls at him on stage (although the real culprit was in fact Jonah Jones). A fight ensued, and the hot-blooded Dizzy slashed Calloway's thigh. Sent packing by Calloway, he then went on to form his own big band, which also played a crucial role in the history of Latin jazz.

Machito was an inspired *sonero* and *bolerista* (although he never truly considered himself a *bolerista*) and a warm, witty, and generous man who kept the interests of his family and friends to heart. His equable disposition was well summed up by one of his maxims: "You cannot eat pork without eating fat" (You have to accept the bad with the good). Latin music rarely being a passport to riches, in his later years he worked by day in a rehabilitation program for drug users and provided help for the elderly, while living in a modest South Bronx apartment cluttered with memorabilia and *santería* objects.

The eldest of six children, he was born in 1912 and grew up in the colorful Havana district of Jesús María, acquiring a well-rounded if mostly informal musical education. His father Rogelio, a good singer in his own right, supplied food to sugar mills and owned a store whose employees would play music in their lunch breaks. Rogelio Grillo had contacts with an Abakwa fraternity, the Ekereguá Momí, and at his store, he organized the last *plante* (initiation ceremony) before they were banned by the Government. Countless musicians and singers would come to visit and play music at the Grillos'. Machito grew up listening to *rumba*, as well as to the popular and classical artists of international repute who performed in Havana, among them Caruso, and he also listened avidly to jazz on the radio. Furthermore, while traveling all over the island in connection with his father's business, he was exposed to the music of the different provinces. Years after leaving Cuba he could still tell just by listening what part of the country a singer came from. During these expeditions he met numerous musicians, among them Arsenio Rodríguez, whom he befriended when Rodríguez was living in Güines and who influenced the development of his own style.

In 1926 Rogelio Grillo took a job as a cigar-maker and moved to Pogolotti, an exuberant neighborhood where Machito met Bauzá and Miguelito Valdés. Rogelio Grillo bought his son a piano and a flute, and for a while Machito studied at the Havana conservatory, but his heart was set on singing, and he joined the Sexteto Juvenil. Word soon spread that he had a good voice. Three members of the sexteto Unión de Redención had formed a group which included vocalists "Felito" (Alfredo) Rivera and Rogelio García. As García did not play maracas, Machito was asked to replace him. He rapidly taught himself to play the instrument by watching Champito Rivera, the virtuoso, ambidextrous *maraquero* of the *conjunto* Estrellas de Pogolotti. At seventeen, he made his professional debut with Unión de Redención in a local theater. Antonio Machín heard about Machito's talent as a *maraquero* and invited him to play with him at the *academia de baile* La Fantástica. There Piñeiro saw Machito perform, and as Bienvenido León did not play maracas, Piñeiro asked Machito to join his Septeto Nacional. Until 1927, Machito also sang second voice with the Sexteto Agabamar (which then included Abelardo Barroso), the Sexteto Occidente, replacing *maraquero* Nené Cabeza (with whom María Teresa Vera had had a falling out), and with a band including Arsalén Paz (piano), Carloz Martínez (saxophone), and Bauzá (saxophone and claves).

In 1938 Bauzá persuaded Machito to come to New York. "If we have to starve, we'll starve together," he wrote to him. Eager for a change of environment and for an opportunity to expand his musical horizons, Machito gladly accepted. He arrived in New York in October and moved right in with Bauzá, who took him to Chick Webb's rehearsals at the Savoy Ballroom, to the Lafayette theater, and to other notorious jazz spots in a then effervescent Harlem. Delighted by this heady life, he decided to stay in the United States, and eventually married a pretty young Puerto Rican girl by the name of Hilda, to whom he dedicated the tune *Chévere*. In 1939, after a brief stint with Mulatón, he joined Alberto Iznaga's Orquesta Siboney (the owner of the Club Cuba, where the band played, gave Machito his nickname), and then the Cuarteto Caney, and also recorded with Xavier Cugat.

Ever since his engagement with the Havana Philharmonic Orchestra, Bauzá had wanted to form a large ensemble. Big bands then enjoyed considerable prestige, but society bands toned down the lively Cuban rhythms and jazz groups mostly ignored them. Refusing the musical hokum that often prevailed, Bauzá and Machito chose to combine the Cuban tradition with the more radical aesthetics of the new jazz that was just emerging, and they engaged American trumpeter Bobby Woodlen and Cuban and Puerto Rican musicians such as Cuban pianist Frank Gilberto Ayala, bassist Julio García Andino, saxophonists Johnny Nieto and "Pin" (José) Madera, *bongocero* Bilingüe, and *timbalero* "El Cojito" (Antonio Escollíes). One of the first *timbaleros* of note in the United States, Escollíes, of Cuban origin, had worked in Tampa as a *tabaquero* and, upon arriving in New York, sewed on buttons

Machito, Graciela, and the Afro-Cubans

and ironed shirts in a sweatshop before replacing *timbalero* Carlos Montesino at the club El Mella. Saxophonists Gene Johnson and Fred Skerritt, *congueros* Carlos Vidal, "Polidor" (Pedro) Allende, and Luis Miranda, Puerto Rican *bongocero* José Mangual (Buyú), trumpeters "Chocolate" Armenteros and "Paquito"(Frank) Dávila, and many others would later join the band.

Machito sang, accompanying himself with claves or maracas, and in addition to his duties as musical director, Bauzá played trumpet. Over the years, the band would benefit from the skills of first-rate composers and arrangers, among them Justi Barreto, Marcelino Valdés, "Pin" Madera, Antar Daly,[4] Ray Santos, Bobby Woodlen, Joe Loco, René Hernández, and Chico O'Farrill.

With the collaboration of John Bartee, Calloway's arranger, Bauzá wrote stimulating scores, but rehearsals proved problematic, Woodlen grappling with Latin rhythms and the Latin musicians with harmonies unusual to their ears. Dizzy Gillespie claims in his autobiography that it is easier for jazzmen to adapt to Cuban rhythms than the other way around. But Latin musicians, Tito Puente among them, have argued otherwise, and experience has indeed shown that foreigners often have trouble mastering the *clave*. However, Bauzá – an exacting and outspoken bandleader – primed the band to perfection. The Afro-Cubans auditioned at La Conga but the club hired Cuban pianist José Curbelo. Undaunted by what he regarded only as a temporary obstacle, Bauzá continued to whip his men into shape.

In 1941 the band recruited Cuban *bongocero* "Chino Pozo" (Francisco Valdés) and they recorded some zestful numbers, among them Machito's *Sopa de pichón* (literally: "Pigeon Soup");[5] Obdulio Morales's *Parábola negra*; Chano Pozo's *Nagüe*; *Yambú* (an arrangement of a traditional *rumba brava*); Machito's *La paella*, written after Federico Pagani had asked Machito, whose culinary specialty it was, if he had ever eaten this dish; and Gilberto Valdés's *Que vengan los rumberos*. Adapting themselves to the most diverse contexts,

4 Composer of *Lágrimas y tristeza* and *Babarabatiri*.

5 The title of this piece already expressed the linguistic crossbreeding of the New York *barrios*. *Pichón* is the Spanglish (Spanish + English – the New York Latin jargon) translation of "pigeon," but in the Cuban slang of the time, *sopa* and *pichón* both meant "marijuana."

they performed in a variety of venues. There was, in particular, a noteworthy engagement with Miguelito Valdés at the Mount Morris Theater, with fiery solos by Escollíes; and there were also studio dates with Valdés.

In Cuba, Graciela Pérez (Machito's sister) had sung in the late 1930s and in the early 1940s with the Orquesta Anacaona and the Trío García and on various radio shows. Machito, then a draftee in the U.S. Army, sent for her, and Graciela's clear diction, superb phrasing, ease, and sense of humor bolstered the band's popularity. Machito also recruited another inspired vocalist, the Puerto Rican Polito Galíndez.

Following the custom of several Cuban bandleaders of that era, Bauzá then organized a second Afro-Cubans with Marcelino Guerra ("Rapindey") on vocals, and entrusted its direction to pianist Luis Varona. A veteran of the Septeto Nacional and of Arsenio Rodríguez's *conjunto*, a guitarist and the composer of *Yo soy la rumba* (one of Machito's favorite songs, recorded on *Mucho mucho Machito*), *Reina negra, Pare cochero*, and the bolero *Dime la verdad*, Guerra headed the band when Varona left for Miami.[6]

In 1942 and 1943, taking advantage of the American Federation of Musicians' strike against record companies, led by James C. Petrillo, the Afro-Cubans – not belonging to this union – issued several sides, notably *Cachumbele*, the afro *Ebó*, and *El niche* (a derogatory term for a black person). They brought the band's name to Cuba and other countries, and Machito and Bauzá were kept constantly busy.

In 1942, the Afro-Cubans were at last taken on at La Conga. Inspired by his musicians' improvisations on *El botellero*, Bauzá invented a melody to which Machito added African-sounding words, giving rise to *Tanga* ("marijuana" in Cuban slang) – an epochal tune that ushered in *cubop*. With its simple harmonic progression, its "jungle" trumpets conveying a sense of urgency, and its drive, *Tanga*, recorded in 1943, was for a long while the Afro-Cubans' theme song. It was essentially a head arrangement – that is, one that is ad-libbed and then memorized by the musicians but not written down, similar to the kind used by Count Basie and other bands. And *Tanga* would later become a favorite of dancers at the Palladium Ballroom, working them up to a fever pitch.

Cuban pianist Gilberto Pinza played for a while with the Afro-Cubans, and then René Hernández (recently arrived from Cuba at the urging of Mario Bauzá) replaced Joe Loco, who had been drafted. A great pianist with a sparse and effective *típico* style and a genial man, Hernández had formed in Havana the *charanga* Armonía and collaborated with Julio Cueva. For the Afro-Cubans, he wrote lively and exciting arrangements that gave them the edge over the competition. He also led Justi Barreto's ensemble and, from 1949 to 1952, wrote for Tito Rodríguez.

The Afro-Cubans' format then increased to five saxophones, three trumpets, and three trombones, and José Mangual, the *timbalero* "Tito" (Ernesto) Puente, the *coro* singer Joe Morales (Noro's brother), and the

6 Guerra died in Spain in 1996.

baritone saxophonist Leslie Johnakins joined the band. Johnakins had played with Taylor's Dixie Serenaders, Blanche Calloway, and Leon Abbey, but working with the Afro-Cubans was unlike anything he had experienced before. "In the beginning," he recalled, "I had the impression that rhythms came out from everywhere. I could never manage to find the first beat." In January 1946, the ensemble performed in Los Angeles. There, the impresario Norman Granz happened to be organizing a concert with Dizzy Gillespie and Charlie Parker at the Philharmonic Auditorium. Granz, who was to contact the Afro-Cubans in 1948, might, like Stan Kenton, have heard them on this occasion. Later in 1946, along with other Latin bands the Afro-Cubans also played at a huge dance at the Manhattan Center, and in the movie *Thrills of Music*.

On January 24 of the following year, they appeared at Town Hall, on the same bill as Kenton. Kenton, thrilled by their torrid rhythms, later recorded tunes of Cuban inspiration. A few months later, the Afro-Cubans inaugurated the Sunday matinees at the Palladium Ballroom; they backed Olga Guillot for some sessions (*Sangre son colora*, *La Gloria eres tú*); played at the famed Broadway club the Royal Roost[7] and at the Ebony Club (with Dexter Gordon as guest soloist); and also recorded as the René Hernández Orchestra.

The following year, taking on a more jazz-like direction, they appeared at the Apollo Theater, the Royal Roost, Bop City, and Birdland with Howard McGhee, Brew Moore, and – recommended by Granz – Flip Phillips, recording, among other tunes, *Howard's Blues* and *Cubop City*. Harry "Sweets" Edison – also part of Granz's stable – had been asked to play with the band but, according to Machito, Edison, judging Latin music beyond his grasp, quit during the rehearsals, and although his name appeared on jackets, in reality he did not record with the Afro-Cubans.

Granz then persuaded Charlie Parker to do studio work with them, and Bird, who knew Bauzá well, readily accepted. The date was set for December 1948; just before the first session, Machito had to race out to buy a new saxophone for Parker who had left his own in Philadelphia. "Bird played the tunes right away, memorizing each number after looking at them only once, and without a single mistake," Machito remembered. And although Parker declined to play *El manisero*, arguing that it was too tricky for him, he negotiated *Okidoke* (one of his favorite expressions), Gilberto Valdés's *Mango mangüé*, and *No Noise* with stunning ease, flying through the chord changes and busy rhythms, after telling Bauzá just before: "When you want me to come in, just signal to me and tell the musicians I'm gonna play." Most bebop tunes, and those by Parker in particular – *My Little Suede Shoes*, *Ornithology*, *Donna Lee* – are in fact perfectly well-suited to the *clave*.

Tanga was also recorded during that date, but without Parker. Bird's biographer Ross Russell wrote about these sessions: "In front of a noisy rhythm section, Charlie recorded two long solos: 'No Noise', and 'Mango

Donna Lee – Charlie Parker

Mangüé' . . . these records were hastily put on the market. They were interesting but for many of Charlie's fans, they seemed like musical gimmicks." But gimmicky as they might have appeared, they nevertheless stand as great moments of Latin jazz, Bird's lyricism splendidly balancing out the fiery Cuban frenzy.

On February 11, 1949, Granz organized a spectacular concert at Carnegie Hall featuring Parker, the Afro-Cubans, Duke Ellington, Lester Young, Bud Powell, Coleman Hawkins, and Neal Hefti. The last-named demonstrated, with a memorable *Tanga*, that Latin jazz had by then come to maturity. The same year the Afro-Cubans also recorded *Asia Minor*, composed by the Armenian trumpeter Roger Mozian, which featured Mitch Miller on oboe and became a staple of their repertoire.

On December 21, 1950, Flip Phillips and Buddy Rich – two of Granz's stars – joined up with the Afro-Cubans to record the *Afro-Cuban Suite*. Fats Navarro, also called in, did not show up, and Bird replaced him. Written by Chico O'Farrill at Granz's instigation, this brillantly orchestrated work consisted of five parts: *Canción, Mambo, 6/8, Jazz,* and *Rumba abierta*. It was one of Latin music's most adventurous sessions to date and Parker, true to himself, shone in *Canción* and in *Jazz*.

Besides their more experimental work, the Afro-Cubans triumphed at the Palladium Ballroom and other New York venues, and in the Catskills hotels, which also featured such Latin acts as the dancing duo of Cuban Pete and Millie (Millie Donay). They delighted their fans with *El as de la rumba, Babarabatiri, Tambó, Vaya niña, Freezelandia, A du bliú bliú bliú, Tremendo cumbán, U bla bla dú,* Bauzá's *Mambo Inn, Changó va vení,* and similar numbers; they backed Julio Andino, Chano Pozo, Alfredo Valdés, Olga Guillot, and Harry Belafonte in various sessions, and Machito even recorded with the Puerto Rican singer Vitín Avilés.

The sacred fire of jazz continued to burn for Machito and Bauzá, and they fanned its flames with a whole Cuban percussion section. Eager to broaden his musical horizons, Chico O'Farrill had come to New York in 1947 with saxophonist Gustavo Mas. Mas subsequently moved to Florida but O'Farrill stayed in the Big Apple and in 1950, he arranged *Tea for Two, Gone City*, and in the following year *Fiesta* and *JATP Mambo* (from Norman Granz's Jazz at the Philharmonic concert series) for the Afro-Cubans, giving them a more progressive sound. "They had the most advanced concepts of any Latin band," he enthused.

Dates followed with Milt Jackson and Zoot Sims. In 1951, they recorded an exciting version of *Carambola* live from Birdland; and they also sizzled on *Indianola* (a version of Cubop). Other jazzmen vied for the pleasure of playing with them or of borrowing their percussionists, and in 1955 saxophonist Frank Morgan recorded several tracks with their drummers. Two years later, the superb *Kenya*[8] united the Afro-Cubans with guest stars Cannonball Adderley, Joe Newman, Herbie Mann, Doc Cheatham, Patato Valdés, and Cándido Camero. Adderley and Newman celebrated the sensuous marriage of Havana and Harlem on *Congo mulense, Óyeme, Wild Jungle*; Cándido and Patato got loose on *Frenzy*. "For me, playing with Latino bands has been very beneficial," said Cheatham, "they had Latino trumpet players who played the themes, and they gave me all the solos. This enabled me to increase my power, because they always blew powerfully." He also admitted he had "a lot of fun with Latin bands." The eclectic *Machito with Flute to Boot*,[9] with Herbie Mann, Johnny Griffin, and Curtis Fuller, came out the following year. It offered a well-rounded panorama of the black musical diaspora, from *Calypso John* to *Brazilian Soft Shoe, The African Flute*, and the Yoruba-flavored *Carabunta*.

In 1957 Machito and Bauzá, along with Tito Puente, accepted Fulgencio Batista's invitation to play in Cuba for the "Fiftieth Anniversary of Cuban Music." Two years later, with the turning political tide, Machito, Graciela, Noro Morales, and other Latin musicians took part in a concert at Carnegie Hall directed by Gilberto Valdés and entitled *Pro Reforma Agraria* in favor of Fidel Castro's government. However, Machito's and Graciela's feelings for the new Cuban regime quickly soured and Machito, Graciela, Bauzá, and many of their compatriots never returned to their homeland.

Tito Puente, Tito Rodríguez, and other Latin bands

8 Reissued, with a few changes, under the title *Latin Soul Plus Jazz*.

9 Reissued under the title *Afro-Jazziac*.

Stimulated by the musical effervescence of New York, other Latin bands also thrived. Among them was Federico Pagani's La Guerrilla (the name *guerrilla* was given by Hispanic musicians to small dance bands), founded in 1941, in which he played claves and bongo. Directed by Puerto Rican *timbalero* "Moncho

Leña" (Juan Ramón Delgado Ramírez), it included Tony Escollíes, Cuban pianist and arranger Frank Valdés, replaced shortly thereafter by the dynamic Joe Loco, trumpeters Curbelito and "El Chino," Puerto Rican vocalist Doroteo, *bongocero* "Little Ray" (Hernán Ray) Romero, and three saxophonists. They offered Puerto Rican and Cuban material, and at the Park Plaza, Pagani's guerrillas often challenged their friends the Afro-Cubans in the then popular battles of the bands.

Also known as "Mister Mambo," "Joe Loco" (José Estévez) eventually formed his own group, a *conjunto* which performed at Carnegie Hall and at the Waldorf Astoria, and generally catered for more elegant audiences than La Guerrilla. Loco (a nickname meaning "crazy" in Spanish) was born in New York in 1921 of Puerto Rican parents. As a teenager he danced with the Chick Webb band and studied organ, bass, violin, trombone, and guitar. After playing trombone with an amateur symphony orchestra and piano with the Ciro Rimac ensemble, he became the musical director of Los Melody Boys. He led the Orquesta Hatuey and, as pianist or arranger, collaborated with various Latin and jazz outfits, among them Xavier Cugat, Enrique Madriguera, the Afro-Cubans, Ramón Argüeso, Julio Andino, Tito Puente, Marcelino Guerra, Pupi Campo, the Dorsey brothers, and Count Basie.

Loco often dressed up American and other standards with mambo rhythms. *Mambo Fantasy*, with a Latin *Bei mir bist du schön*, *Viva Mambo*, *Mambo Moods*, and *Latin Jewels* reveal a percussive and sure-handed style, with frequent block chords and double octaves. In the late 1940s Loco combined bebop and mambo in his *Concerto for Percussion*, and in 1952, his mambo version of *Tenderly* became a hit. Vibe players Pete Terrace and Julio Andino worked with him in the 1950s. Loco moved to Puerto Rico in 1968. In 1986 he had to have a leg amputated, and died two years later in San Juan.

Although in 1940 José Curbelo obtained an engagement at La Conga sought by Bauzá and Machito, there were no ill feelings, and he collaborated with several of their musicians, Polito Galíndez, Chico O'Farrill, and René Hernández among them. Born into a musical family (his father, José Antonio, was violinist with the Havana Philharmonic Orchestra and a bassist, and led a *charanga* and a show-type band; his uncle Fausto was a pianist and bandleader), Curbelo started playing professionally at the age of sixteen with Los Hermanos Lebatard and with Gilberto Valdés. In 1938 he had helped set up the Riverside Orchestra and the following year he settled in New York, where he worked with Xavier Cugat, Juanito Sanabria, and Óscar de la Rosa and, like Chico O'Farrill, studied harmony with Thelonious Monk's arranger, Hal Overton.

In 1941, Tito Puente, Federico Pagani, and Tony Escollíes helped him set up his new group, and he was soon performing in New York's major Latin clubs. He too was instrumental in bringing Cuban rhythms such as the rhumba and especially the *guaracha* to American audiences, but arranged in a less adventurous style than that of the Afro-Cubans (*Rumba gallega*, *Que no que no*).

The José
Curbelo
orchestra with
Tito Rodríguez
(third from right).
Cariño Records

In 1945 Curbelo recruited Marcelino Guerra and, the following year, Tito Puente and Tito Rodríguez, a promising Puerto Rican singer with a youthful-sounding voice, as well as *conguero* Carlos Vidal, *bongocero* Chino Pozo, and his own father José Antonio Curbelo on bass. In 1949, Puente and Rodríguez left the pianist, each in order to start his own band. The Puerto Rican singers Bobby Escoto, Santos Colón, Gilberto Monroig, and Vitín Avilés, and the percussionists Mongo Santamaría, Ray Barretto, Willie Torres, Jimmy "La Vaca" Santiago, and Sabú Martínez then joined the band; after reducing the band's size, Curbelo quit performing in 1959 to open a Latin booking agency.

The 1940s and early 1950s saw Noro Morales at his creative peak, and Xavier Cugat, Tito Puente, Jimmy Dorsey, and others covered his compositions. In 1942 he founded a new ensemble, the Morales Brothers, with siblings Humberto and Esy, the Puerto Rican singer Pupi Campo, Tito Rodríguez, and the Puerto Rican dancer Diosa Costello, which sometimes backed Latin shows. He then started a smaller group while temporarily entrusting the leadership of his orchestra to the Mexican trumpeter Carlos Varela. During the 1940s he also recorded with Los Amigos Panamericanos and Cabalgata d'Artega, both featuring Alberto Socarrás on flute. After entertaining U.S. troops in Europe during World War II, Morales appeared on television, played piano in the movies *Cuban Pete* (in which he also danced), *Mexican Jumping Bean*, and *Rhumba n' Spice*, wrote a series of mambos (*Mambo loco, Mambo coco, Mambo jumbo*), and worked as an arranger. In the early 1950s with his big band, featuring vocalists "El Boy" (Juan Torres), Vicentico Valdés, and Pellín Rodríguez, and the great *bongocero* Ramón Rivera, he recorded the excellent *Mambo with Noro* and other sides. In the early 1960s he moved to San Juan. There, despite glaucoma induced by diabetes, he led a band at the La Concha hotel which included saxophonists Ray Santos, Pin Madera, and Noro's brother Pepito, trumpeter Juancito Torres, the Cuban drummer Ana Carrero, and Vitín Avilés on vocals. Noro's other brother, Humberto, ran a combo in the same hotel. Noro Morales died in San Juan in

1964. *Begin the Beguine, Rhumba Rhapsody, Serenata Rítmica, Tea for Two, 110th Street and Fifth Avenue* – which Morales developed from a sketch by trumpeter Paul López – *El danzón de María Cervantes, Piel Canela, Walter Winchell Rumba*, and *Bim Bam Bum* (first recorded by Xavier Cugat with Tito Rodríguez on vocals) stand out among his best recordings.

A Cugat alumnus, the superb flautist (and saxophonist) "Esy" (Ismael) Morales, led an ensemble which backed Óscar López, Yma Sumac, and other singers. In the 1950s he had his own television program. He recorded several sides (*Easy Does It, Dark Eyes*), wrote *Jungle Fantasy*, which inspired Herbie Mann, and appeared with his band in the film *Criss Cross*, in which Yvonne de Carlo danced.

In the early 1940s, Xavier Cugat had Machito, Miguelito Valdés, and Tito Rodríguez in his band. After the success of *The Peanut Vendor*, Hollywood turned to Cuban music, and Cugat played with his orchestra in various movies: *You Were Never Lovelier, Holiday in Mexico, Sirens' School*, starring Esther Williams and Basil Rathbone, *Weekend at the Waldorf*, and *An Island with You*, in which Cyd Charisse performs a stunning tango played by Cugat's band. He scored hits with *Cuban Mambo* and *Amapola* and backed Cole Porter for his recordings of *Tico tico* and *Begin the Beguine*.

In the late 1940s, the high-voltage "Tito" (Ernesto Antonio) Puente burst onto the Latin scene with his energetic ensemble, which backed countless singers. A prolific and versatile composer and arranger ("I've tried my hand at all types of Latin music," he used to proclaim), Puente recorded over a hundred albums. Influenced by Ubaldo Nieto, Tony Escollíes, and Carlos Montesino, he put the timbales at the front of his band. His arrangements also often highlighted the flute (*Cubarama*) as well as the vibraphone, which he played brilliantly (as in *Lotus Land*, depicting an impressionistic Orient with a few elegant touches). A practitioner of *santería*, he made use of Yoruba music in various compositions, as in the beautiful *Ochún*, and collaborated with scores of jazzmen (such as Dizzy Gillespie, Stan Kenton, Charlie Parker, Kai Winding, Lionel Hampton, Ben Webster, Dexter Gordon, Cal Tjader), forming in the 1970s a smaller jazz-oriented ensemble.

Born in Harlem to parents of Puerto Rican origin, Puente (1923–2000) grew up in the Barrio. He wanted to become a dancer, but a bicycle accident shattered his dream. He studied piano, trap drums, organ, vibes, timbales, saxophone, clarinet, and conga, listening to jazz (with a particular fondness for Gene Krupa) as well as to Cuban and Puerto Rican music. As a teenager, he played percussion with Ramón Olivero at the Casino Borinquen, in East Harlem, with the Happy Boys at the Park Palace, and with other local groups, and then performed in Miami with a society orchestra. Back in New York he worked with Noro Morales at the Stork Club, and studied composition with Richard Benda. After a six-month engagement with the Afro-Cubans in 1941, replacing Ubaldo Nieto, he toured with the Jack Cole Dancers. From 1942 to 1945 he served in the U.S. Navy, where he took up the saxophone again and studied arranging and composition, and in 1946/47 was enrolled at the Juilliard School of Music.

Around 1947 he played, along with José Curbelo and singer Fernando Álvarez, with the Copacabana Samba band led by Brazilian drummer Fred Martin, and with the Miguelito Valdés–Anselmo Sacasas orchestra. In the ensuing years he also did arrangements for Miguelito Valdés, Curbelo, Alfredo Valdés, Marcelino Guerra, and others. In 1948 he joined the outfit founded five years earlier by the *bolerista* and *maraquero* Pupi Campo, becoming his musical director and writing for him from 1951 to 1954. Campo's ensemble, which played a mixture of American and Latin tunes (he had achieved recognition in 1947 with the song *Mary Ann*), included at that time Vitín Avilés and Joe Loco.

In 1949 Puente organized a *conjunto* named by Federico Pagani "The Picadilly Boys" (a play on the word *picadillo*: a meat hash). Ángel Rosa and then Paquito Sosa were the vocalists; and *bongocero* Chino Pozo and *conguero* Frankie Colón performed at the front of the band, next to the timbales. The Picadilly Boys made their debut at the Alma Dance Studios, and shortly thereafter Puente recorded various titles, some with Vitín Avilés: among them *Son de la loma* and, with Bobby Rodríguez, Manny Oquendo, Ismael Quintana (on percussion), Julian Priester, and Mario Bauzá, the incandescent *Picadillo*, *Ran kan kan* (onomatopoeias evoking the timbales' sound), *Abaniquito*, and *El yoyo*. These tunes, and then *Ban ban quere*, brought the group wide recognition.

Ran kan kan – Tito Puente

A few months later, Puente recruited Vicentico Valdés, who had just arrived from Cuba and would sing with him until 1953. With him, he recorded *Tú no eres nadie, La gloria eres tú, Mambo con Puente, Domingo Pantoja, Wampo* and *Batanga* (Bebo Valdés had just created the *batanga* in Havana), and *Babarabatiri*, and he was highly acclaimed at Birdland.

Puente's band went through many personnel changes: Charlie Palmieri replaced Gil López; in 1951, Manny Oquendo succeeded Chino Pozo, and Mongo Santamaría Frankie Colón; bassist Bobby Rodríguez came in 1955, followed a year later by the *bolerista* Santos Colón, who first recorded with Puente in 1958, on *Dance Mania*.

Under Santamaría's influence, Puente turned to Afro-Cuban music, and turned out two wonderful albums: *Tito Puente in Percussion*, with Santamaría, Willie Bobo (who had taken over from Manny Oquendo), and Patato Valdés, and the following year *Top Percussion*, with Santamaría, Bobo, Julito Collazo, Virgilio Martí, and Francisco Urrutia, and Merceditas Valdés and Marcelino Guerra on vocals, generating some lively improvisations (*Obatalá yeya, Conga alegre*).

In 1957 the young Ray Barretto replaced Mongo Santamaría, and Puente made a string of albums that combined Cuban fire with New York polish. At the height of the cha-cha, he performed Cuban classics (*Almendra, Los tamalitos de Olga*) and the splendid *Night Ritual*, with its crackling drums, while between 1956 and 1958 he cut some of his most exciting records, among them *Cuban Carnival* and the best-selling *Dance Mania*. The latter featured Bobby Rodríguez, Ray Coen (Augusto Coen's adopted son), and Gilbert López on piano, Ray Santos on saxophone, "Puchi" (Pedro) Boulong on trumpet, and José Mangual, Julito Collazo, and Patato Valdés on percussion. The *son montuno El cayuco, 3–D Mambo, Agua limpia todo, Hong Kong Mambo, Pa' los rumberos,* the cha-cha *Qué sera, Negro bon bon, Ah wah, Mambo Buda, Oye mi guaguancó, Yambeque,* highlighted Puente's versatility and his ability to express himself using different registers and colors, while keeping his distinctive sound.

Gifted with a splendid voice, impeccable diction, and exceptional charisma, "Tito" (Pablo) Rodríguez led a tightly controlled orchestra that rivaled Puente's and Machito's. An admirer of Tito Gómez, Miguelito Valdés, and other Cuban vocalists, he performed *rumbas* (*Yambú, Mama güela, Avísale a mi contrario*) just as easily as he did mambos and boleros, and for the latter would later become famous throughout Latin America. Self-taught like Miguelito Valdés, he also played various instruments, most notably vibes, timbales, conga, and bongo.

Born in Santurce, Puerto Rico, in 1923 to a Cuban mother and a Dominican father who played guitar, he lost his parents at the age of five. At thirteen he began to record with the Conjunto Típico Ladi, then joined another local *conjunto*, Las Industrias Típicas, and later, the Cuarteto Mayarí. In 1939 he moved in with his brother Johnny, in East Harlem. Johnny had performed in Puerto Rico, and in New York had founded first a trio, and later the Conjunto Siboney. Tito sang and played maracas with this group and, in February 1940, recorded *Oye mi bajo* with them. Tito Puente, who was then working with Johnny Rodríguez, noticed the other Tito's talent, and the two men became friends. Rodríguez subsequently joined the Cuarteto Caney as a *maraquero* and sang with Noro Morales, Eddie Le Baron, Enrique Madriguera, and then José Curbelo, with whom he recorded in 1946. After marrying Tobi Kei, a pretty Japanese-American chorus girl who was working at the China Doll, he sang and played bongo with Xavier Cugat, and in February 1947 recorded four numbers with Chano Pozo and the Afro-Cubans.

In December, he formed a group that included pianist Gil López, bassist Luis Barreto, percussionist Ignacio Reyes, trumpeter Chino González, and a back-up vocalist by the name of Rodrigo, then put together a larger ensemble, the Mambo Devils, followed in 1949 by the four-trumpet Tito Rodríguez y sus Lobos del Mambo, this time with Tom García on piano. The sessions, done between 1949 and 1951, show a strong Miguelito Valdés influence, with tight arrangements giving the impression of a big band. They yielded in particular Chano Pozo's *Blen blen blen* and *Bobo boco*,[10] *Mambo mona*, later recorded as *Mama güela* (a mambo derived from a *rumba brava*), Machito's *Yambú, Joe Lustig Mambo*,[11] *Hay cráneo, No cuentes conmigo*, and Bobby Capó's *Bésame la bembita*.

From the very beginning Rodríguez's recordings attracted attention, and also enthralled dancers at the Palladium. By the mid-1950s, he was on his way to becoming a star, and scored hits with cha-chas, some recorded with Charlie Palmieri, Willie Bobo, Manny Oquendo, Yayo El Indio, and Marcelino Guerra.

In the United States, Cuban pianist Anselmo Sacasas started a new orchestra which made its debut in Chicago (and in which Tito Puente played timbales), and performed in several New York clubs. At the end of the Second World War, he made some recordings with vocalists "Cuso" Mendoza, Walfredo de los Reyes, and Rubén González (*Soltando chispas, Mi rico vacilón*), and four years later he moved to Miami.

Chico O'Farrill collaborated with the Afro-Cubans, and with Miguelito Valdés, Noro Morales, and other Latin musicians. He also signed with Norman Granz's Verve label, cutting some sides with, among others, Mario Bauzá, Flip Phillips, Lenny Hambro, René Hernández, José Mangual, Cándido Camero, Bobby Rodríguez, and Bobby Escoto. In 1953 he organized a big band which played in a number of American cities. "O'Farrill's repertoire indicates that he will be equally successful with the mambonicks when they start to make the rounds of ballrooms. He dishes out a cool brand of chile which has the eaters asking for more," stated a September 1954 *Variety* article in colorful terms. But towards the end of the following year, affected, like so many other Latin musicians, by the ascendancy of rock 'n' roll, he was forced to dissolve his band.

Many other large ensembles disseminated Cuban rhythms throughout the United States, among them those of violinist, clarinettist, and saxophonist José

10 *Bobo boco* includes the ritual invocation *salamaleco*, derived from the Arabic greeting *salaam aleikum*, brought to Cuba by Islamized slaves and incorporated into Afro-Cuban cults.

11 Joe Lustig was a pseudonym used by Machito for some recordings.

Arsenio Rodríguez's *conjunto* (1955). The Justo A. Martí Photographic Collection, Centro de Estudios Puertorriqueños, Hunter College, New York

Budet, Julio Andino, and Eddie Carbiá y sus Mamboleros; further groups included those of Julio Gutiérrez, Pupi Campo (whose wife Betty Clooney, Rosemary's sister, sometimes performed with him), the vocalist and *maraquero* El Boy, Ramón Argüeso, and Fernando Mulens.

Upon leaving Cuba, Arsenio Rodríguez had set his sights on Miami, but disheartened by the racism he encountered, he settled in the South Bronx and founded a new group. In 1953, with *La gente del Bronx* or *Como se goza en el Barrio*, he evoked his bustling, predominantly Puerto Rican neighborhood, and Puerto Rican themes cropped up in his songs, as in the bolero *A Puerto Rico, A bailar mi bomba* or the *plena Emilio dolores*.

In Cuba, in addition to composing, Gilberto Valdés had played saxophone and flute with Los Hermanos Lebatard. He too moved to New York, in 1952, where he formed a driving *charanga*, the first to be created in the city. The *charangas* of Antonio María Romeu and Belisario López regularly performed in the United States, but there was no band of this type actually resident there. As Arcaño had done before (recruiting *conguero* El Colorao), Valdés used a conga in his ensemble (played at different times by Willie Bobo and Mongo Santamaría). He also employed *timbalero* Popi Pagani (and later Johnny Pacheco, whom he trained as a flautist), Rogelio Valdés (bass), a vocalist by the name of Machucho, and three violinists, among them Alberto Iznaga. "He used to do all the arrangements and he was a very wild arranger, he was ahead of his time arranging. He used to like an Afro-Cuban style of music more than anything else and he had a lot of Afro-Cuban influences. Sometimes when he did the solo he used to do riffs, very high riffs," Pacheco remembers.[12] In 1955 Valdés recorded *Hi Fi in the Tropic*, an album which, though pleasant in its way, had neither the impact nor the strength of some of the music he had written in Cuba.

12 In: David Carp, *A Visit with Maestro Johnny Pacheco*, p. 4.

He then went on to lead the musical ensemble of Katherine Dunham's dance company.[13]

In Havana the percussionist Armando Valdés had led the Conjunto Savoy, which included singers Francisco Fellové and Kiko Mendive. In 1956 he formed a *charanga*, the Chicago-based Orquesta Nuevo Ritmo de Cuba, with Mongo Santamaría, the Cuban singer Rudy Calzado, the flautist "Rolando" (José Calazán) Lozano, the Mexican bassist Victor Venegas, and the Cuban violinist Pupi Legarreta. But *charangas* did not fully blossom in the United States until the 1960s, with the arrival of a host of musicians who had fled Cuba after the revolution.

In the 1950s, Puerto Rican musicians, their numbers growing, began to challenge the Cuban hegemony. Canario, César Concepción, Joe Valle, Moncho Leña, Bobby Capó, and Sammy Ayala had already disseminated the rhythms of their island in the U.S. and Maso Rivera had popularized the *cuatro* in dance music. Puerto Rican *tresistas* also appeared, among them Luis Lija Ortiz, "Chuito" (Jesús) Nadal, and Mario Hernández (an alumnus of the Sexteto Borinquen).

"Charlie" (Carlos Manuel) Palmieri stood out among these newly emerging Puerto Rican musicians. A compelling pianist, who played with long flowing lines and a style both elegant and punchy, he was influenced by Jesús López, Lilí Griñán, and Noro Morales. A highly respected teacher, and a generous, warm-hearted man who often gave his services to humanitarian causes, he was born in New York in 1927 to Puerto Rican parents of Florentine origin. The family had first migrated to Corsica and then, in the late nineteenth century, to Ponce, establishing a *hacienda*, the Finca Margarita. Palmieri's parents later moved to the United States and he grew up in the Barrio. At the age of nine, he played in amateur shows at the Campoamor and the San José theater. Four years later, he performed at the Park Palace with Osario Selasié's band, and occasionally sat in with José Budet. From 1944 to 1946, still a teenager, he worked regularly with various bands, among them the La Playa Sextet, Polito Galíndez, and Moncho Usera, and he recorded *Se va la rumba* with Rafael Muñoz.

With his first group, the *conjunto* Pin Pín, formed in 1948 and consisting of *timbalero* Monchito Muñoz, *conguero* Sabú "(Luis)" Martínez, bassist Simón Madera, and vibraphonist Joe Roland (under Milt Jackson's influence, the vibes were beginning to creep increasingly into Latin music), Palmieri produced a subtle kind of Latin jazz that foreshadowed that played by George Shearing and Cal Tjader (*Softly as in a Morning Sunrise, I've Got You Under My Skin*). He then joined the Copacabana Samba Band (with Tito Puente as its musical director), worked, along with Puente, in Pupi Campo's ensemble, and collaborated with Xavier Cugat. He

13 Cuban percussionists Julio Collazo and Francisco Aguabella also collaborated with Dunham.

subsequently founded a sextet which performed in Chicago, and he gigged freelance with Pete Terrace, Tito Rodríguez, Johnny Seguí, and Vicentico Valdés.

In 1954 he set up a new *conjunto* with Pacho (bass), Popi Pagani (timbales), Vitín Avilés (vocals), Joe Cabot, Joe Caini, and Norman Gitler (trumpets), Aníbal (bongo), and Papi Torres (conga). The band, which performed a mixture of Cuban standards and original material, made their debut at the Palladium. At the end of the decade, Palmieri played with Herbie Mann and, in 1959, he hired the dashing Dominican flautist Johnny Pacheco with whom he set up the four-violin Charanga Duboney. This joyous group, which included the vocalist Willie Torres, and, on occasion, Juancito Torres, thrilled audiences (*Chunko, Bruca maniguá, Pacheco's Descarga*). Palmieri issued the highly successful *Charanga at the Caravana Club*, and then Pacheco, who had a slightly different musical vision, decided to form his own group.

Also working in and around New York was the Ralph (Rafael) Font Orchestra, which included in the early 1950s percussionist Steve Berrios, and small ensembles that heralded those of the 1960s: Pappy Ali y sus Rumberos, with singer Willie Torres and pianist Gil López; Alfarona X, formed in Puerto Rico by bassist Leo Flemming but established in New York, Joe Quijano's Conjunto Cachana, Pete Rodríguez's Conjunto La Magnífica, pianist Héctor Castro's ensemble, which included among others Jimmy Sabater (former *timbalero* with Joe Panama's group), Cheo Feliciano, Kako Bastar, and Luis "Máquina"Flores; the groups led by Emilio Reyes, Johnny Seguí, Carlos Pizarro, Elmo García (with his popular *Brooklyn Mambo*), Randy Carlos, Héctor Rivera, Bobby Escoto, Eddie Forrester, "Alfredito" (Al Levy), Dave Herscher, Harvey Arverne, and "Alfredo Méndez" (Alfred Mendelson). In addition, a few Puerto Rican *jíbaro* groups such as Melodía Tropical began to use a bongo and open up to dance music.

Most popular among those small groups were the La Playa and the La Plata sextets. Developed from a quartet which Luis Barreto formed in 1947, the La Playa Sextet distinguished themselves by their use of an electric guitar, and included drummer Paul Alicea,[14] his wife Marie on vocals, and their son Paul on timbales. With the occasional participation of guitarist Frankie Sánchez, and Willie Torres, they recorded a variety of Latin rhythms, among them a *bomba* by Hilario Ariza premonitorily entitled *Salsa*, and *El coco y la fruta bomba*, sung in unison with an accompaniment of Hawaian-sounding guitars; and they also issued several sides featuring Tito Rodríguez. The Sexteto La Plata, led by Frankie Sánchez, made their reputation with *Bilongo, Son las bobitas, Tremendo coco, No me toques ese punto*, and other tunes.

The West Coast

Though the California Latin scene could not quite compete with New York's, two pianists were serious challengers for Pérez Prado: the powerful Eddie Cano, of Mexican descent, and the Cuban René Touzet.

[14] He later switched to guitar, and Jimmy "La Vaca" Santiago and then Orestes Vilató replaced him.

Born in Los Angeles, Cano (1927–1988) grew up listening to both Latin and jazz pianists and started out with the Pachucho Boogie Boys and with Miguelito Valdés. His big band, with which Ella Fitzgerald occasionally jammed, included Latinized jazz standards (*Surrey with a Fringe on Top*, for example, played with a Latin feel but with jazz solos) in its repertoire. In 1954 Cano also recorded with Cal Tjader on *Ritmo caliente*. In 1956 and 1957, abetted by percussionists Eddie Aparicio, Carlos Mejía, Carlos Vidal, and Jack Costanzo, he made wonderful Latin jazz albums: *Cole Porter & Me*, *Duke Ellington & Me*, and *Deep in a Drum*.

A talented pianist and composer (*Has dudado de mí*, *Cada vez más*, *No te importa saber* [translated into English as *Let Me Love You Tonight*], *Anoche aprendí*), Touzet was born in Havana in 1916. He studied with composer Joaquín Nin (Anais Nin's father), played with his own band at the Gran Casino Nacional and became musical director of the Montmartre. In the mid-1940s he moved to the United States, worked with Enrique Madriguera and, the following year, formed an ensemble which included Johnny Mandel (author of the mambo-blues *Barbados*, recorded by Charlie Parker). With his Cha Cha Cha Rhythm Boys, formed with veterans from Stan Kenton's Innovations in Modern Music orchestra, notably Buddy Childers, Chico Álvarez, Pete Candoli, Art Pepper, and Bob Cooper, Touzet held forth at the Avedon Ballroom, in Los Angeles. He recorded several albums including *The Charm of the Cha Cha Cha*, *Mambos and Cha Chas*, and *Dinner in Havana*, but his group gradually adopted a more American sound.

Dance bands in Puerto Rico

In 1952 Puerto Rico obtained the status of commonwealth, or *Estado Libre Asociado* (literally: "Associated free state"). But the freedom was relative: Puerto Ricans had to serve in the American Army and the island depended economically on the United States. Movements for independence gained new momentum.

Like Havana, in the 1940s and 1950s Puerto Rico teemed with music, and many first-rate Cuban artists – Benny Moré, Olga Guillot, Rolando Laserie, Xiomara Alfaro, Ernesto Lecuona – performed there.

Canario continued to devote himself to the *plena*. In the late 1950s he offered *Cuando las mujeres quieren a los hombres*, *Moliendo vidrio*, and more melancholy songs such as *El mundo se va a acabar*, *Gota de llanto*, and the waltz *La nieve de los años*, which expressed his affection for his guitar:

Mi guitarra que siempre	My guitar was always
fue mi fiel compañera	my faithful companion
que siempre en mis tristezas	whenever I was sad,
sus cuerdas me inspiró;	her strings inspired me;
y ahora que con los años	and now with the years
quiero estar junto a ella	I want to be near her
esperando que muera	waiting for her to die
para morirme yo.	so that I die as well.

Towards the end of his life, blind and with both legs amputated, he made his last album in 1968, with the Orquesta Puerto Rico, and died in 1975.

With his big band, trumpeter César Concepción offered more commercial and Cubanized *plenas* (*Perucho y Peruchín, Sin sinfonía, Plena internacional*). After touring the island with the Midnight Serenaders, in 1933 he worked in New York with Eddie Le Baron and Óscar de la Rosa (with whom Machito and Alfredo Valdés were then singing) and the following year he was back in Puerto Rico again performing with Don Rivera, Rafael Muñoz, and the Jack Club's Band, led by clarinettist and saxophonist "Fajardito" (Armando Castro). Like the Cuban musicians who exalted the different regions of their country or different boroughs of Havana, he celebrated, with *Pa' Salinas, A San Germán, Santurce, Arecibo*, or the famed *A Mayagüez*, various towns of Puerto Rico:

Por sus colegios, sus hembras	I sing of Mayagüez,
por sus mangós y sus praderas	its colleges, its women
a Mayagüez voy cantando	its mango trees and its meadows,
porque el cantar es mi lema.	because singing is my occupation.
A Mayagüez voy cantando	I sing of Mayagüez
voy entonando mi plena	I intone my *plena*
cantando por esos "indios"	singing for those "Indians"
que la verdad echan candela.	who are truly red hot.

In 1947, though based in San Juan, he often performed in the U.S., and with his vocalists Joe Valle and El Boy, pianist Luisito Benjamín, and saxophonist and clarinettist "Lito" (Ángel Rafael) Peña, he brought his *plenas* to the Palladium Ballroom. In the 1950s, he held forth in the major San Juan hotels. He also dressed up such American tunes as *Take the A Train* or *One O'Clock Jump* with Latin rhythms (on *The Great Themes Go Latin*).

The eclectic Orquesta Panamericana, founded in 1954 by Lito Peña, also enjoyed a high degree of popularity on the island. Born there in 1921 in a musical family of Venezuelan descent, Peña paid his dues in an Army band, before joining the ensemble led by his cousin Rafael González Peña, and playing with César Concepción. Lito's own band included his three brothers (on trumpet and saxophones), Luisito Benjamín (who had followed him after his stint with Concepción), and the young Ismael Rivera on vocals and bongo; Peña contributed some of the arrangements.

The dance craze in Puerto Rico led to a demand for the exciting orchestra of El Escambrón, led in the early 1940s by trumpeter Miguelito Miranda; the *conjunto* Poldín y su Pimienta, run by singer and *tresista* Poldín Monge; Los Dandies del 42, led by saxophonist Moncho Usera; La Siboney, founded by saxophonist Pepito Torres. La Siboney included Luisito Benjamín on saxophone (before he switched to piano), the outstanding Papi Andino on bongo, Tony Sánchez on trap drums, and Joe Valle on vocals (Cascarita recorded with them while in Puerto Rico). Other ensembles included the Orquesta Bellamar, founded by Pepito Torres's brother Rafael; Domingo Peterson's ensemble, with which Pérez Prado briefly played piano; and the Jack's Club band, led by clarinettist and saxophonist "Fajardito" (Armando Castro).

In Mayagüez in 1951, the *timbalero* "Moncho" Leña (a veteran of the William Manzano Orchestra), formed Los Ases del Ritmo, a small outfit with a Cuban and Puerto Rican repertoire, in which Mon Rivera was the vocalist, Héctor Pellot the pianist, and "Chiquitín" (José) Morales the lead trumpeter. Leña performed *plenas*, adapting *pandereta* rhythms on his timbales. Their topical, songs, often sung in the vernacular – *El gallo espuelérico*, evoking cockfights, *¡Aló! ¿Quién ñama?*, *Húyele al guardia* – delighted not only Puerto Rican listeners, but also the patrons of La Bamba and the Palladium Ballroom, in New York. The band broke up in 1963 and Leña eventually moved to Orlando, Florida.

With his elegant piano improvisations, Luisito Benjamín (*Dancing and Dreaming*), who also played with Armando Castro, later had an influence on Papo Lucca and other salsa musicians. As for the elegant hotels and clubs of San Juan, they appreciated the versatile orchestras of Miguel Miranda, Rafael Duchesne, Rafael Muñoz (pitted against Don Nacho's band in a historic battle at the Escambrón Club, in 1942), Carmelo Díaz Soler, and William Manzano.

Singers in the U.S. and Puerto Rico

In April, 1940, Miguelito Valdés arrived in New York with Anselmo Sacacas, and was delighted to see his old friends Machito and Mario Bauzá again. He first alternated with Machito in Alberto Iznaga's Orquesta Siboney, and then Machito recommended him to Xavier Cugat's *bongocero*. After Desi Arnaz left for California, Valdés replaced him in Cugat's band, singing with Cugat at the Waldorf Astoria and in a few movies. With Cugat he recorded *Babalú*, which became a hit, and he was then billed as "Mr. Babalú." After his stint with "Cugie" the Catalan violinist, he spent two years in Mexico, and then moved to Los Angeles.

With the Afro-Cubans, whose aesthetic corresponded to his own temperament, Valdés recorded *La rumba soy yo*, *El botellero*, and other numbers. In 1946 he cut a few sides with Machito and a sextet (*Tambambeo*, *El maraquero*, *La cumparsa*), and, influenced by Carmen Amaya, improvised in a flamenco style.

With Sacasas, Valdés then formed a band which toured internationally, and he continued to express himself in an Afro-Cuban vein (*Gandinga*, Pepe Becke's *Está frizao* – "It's freezing" in Spanglish – *Guagüina yirabó*), wildly playing his conga on stage. On January 18, 1949, shortly after the death of his childhood pal Chano Pozo, he paid tribute to this man who had written some of his biggest hits, singing a Carlos Vidal number entitled *Chano Pozo*. He was backed by Vidal (conga), Eddie Cano (piano), Modesto Calderón (bass), Ray Romero (bongo), and Larry Rivera (timbales). Valdés's career then picked up, and he triumphed all over the United States and Latin America, finally disbanding his orchestra in 1955. He also had a part in the Mexican film *Mi reino por un torero*, and, in the Hollywood production *Panamericana*. In the 1950s, he collaborated again with the Afro-Cubans (*Variedades, Los Reyes del ritmo*), and in 1957, spent time in Mexico, then a magnet for many Cuban musicians.

The *boleristas* Panchito Riset and Vicentico Valdés were also important figures of the New York Latin scene. Gifted with a superb controlled phrasing and clear diction, Riset often sang about unrequited love (*Abandonada, Dolor de ausencia, Te fuiste*). Born in Havana in 1910, he started out in 1927 as vocalist and *marimbulero* with the Conjunto Esmeralda, moving on to the Sexteto Atarés, the Sexteto Cauto (which then included Marcelino Guerra), and the Septeto Habanero (in 1928), and also performing as a soloist. In New York, he collaborated with Don Antobal, Cugat, and Madriguera. It was during an engagement in Cuba with Eliseo Grenet that he came to the attention of Benny Moré, who heard him in a Marianao club. Back in Manhattan, he recorded with Pedro Flores and the Cuarteto Caney. In 1945, after entertaining U.S. troops stationed in Europe, he recorded with René Hernández. He also sang with Montesino and Celso López, and he criss-crossed the United States with his band. Having had both legs amputated because of diabetes, he retired from music in the 1970s.

With his moving, expressive tenor, Vicentico Valdés imbued his boleros with a virile lyricism. At times he recalled tango singers in his way of stressing certain syllables and articulating each word. Influenced by Mexican *boleristas*, he was also adept at *danzones, sones*, and *guarachas*, and his magnificent renditions of songs (often arranged by René Hernández) such as *La gloria eres tú, Envidia, Mentira al oído* enthralled his listeners.

Valdés (1912–1995) had grown up in Cayo Hueso along with Abelardo Barroso, Cheo Marquetti, the members of the Sexteto Cauto, and other musicians. His brother Alfredo, then singing with the Sexteto Nacional, got him exposure by taking him to perform on radio in 1929. Around 1930, Vicentico worked with Ignacio Piñeiro and then with Cheo Belén Puig and the Orquesta Cosmopolita. From 1945 to 1948 he lived in Mexico, doing stints with Arturo Núñez, Rafael de la Paz, and Chucho Rodríguez. In New York, he recorded with Tito Puente (*Abaniquito, Mambo macoco*), La Sonora Matancera (*Los aretes de luna, Derroche de felicidad*), and other bands. He also led his own ensemble, which included among others Nuyorican *timbalero* Manny Oquendo, Mongo Santamaría, Charlie Palmieri, and then Eddie Palmieri. The Trío Matamoros, established, like Arsenio Rodríguez, in the South Bronx during the 1950s, recorded humorous songs: *Es tu boca, Te picó la abeja, No me engañen;* and Guillermo Portabales, accompanied by Julio Andino and other bands, continued to offer his soulful *guajiras* and *sones montunos.*

Puerto Rican singers also came to the fore. Following in Canario's footsteps, Joe Valle (born New York 1922, died San Juan 1980) stirred up interest in the *plena* in the United States but, like César Concepción's, it was a more urbanized *plena.* He grew up in Santurce, working at the age of seventeen with Pepito Torres's Orquesta Siboney and then with Rafael Muñoz, and in New York with Alberto Socarrás, from 1940 to 1943. He also collaborated with Noro Morales and various duos, trios, and *cuartetos.* In 1954 he sang in Puerto Rico with Concepción, which furthered his reputation, and with Juanito Sanabria, and then formed his own band.

Nicknamed "El inquieto anacobero" after *Anacobero* ("bohemian"), a song of Abakwa inspiration which he performed, the restless *bolerista* Daniel Santos had a gritty and original voice and an abrupt phrasing, which Pedro Flores encouraged him to cultivate. He was particularly appreciated in Cuba, where he lived at various times. His tormented life was marked by women, drugs, violence, alcohol, and jail and most of his songs, such as *Vida de mi vida* and *Perdón*, carry a high emotional charge. One of his major hits: *El preso* ("The Prisoner") was composed during a spell in jail linked to an incident with a woman. He also sought inspiration from songs gleaned during his frequent travels in Latin America, among them *La múcura*, a Colombian *porro* which he renamed *Déjala caer contra el suelo* ("Let Her Fall on the Floor").

During the Second World War, he entertained the U.S. troops; in Puerto Rico he performed with José Luis Moneró and the Whopee Kids, and later replaced Miguelito Valdés in Cugat's ensemble. In 1946 he went to Santo Domingo, but after an earthquake that shook the country, he settled in Havana. He appeared on various Cuban radio stations and along with Celio González, sang with Los Jóvenes del Cayo. In the late 1940s, after a stay in Caracas, he recorded with La Sonora Matancera such songs as *Tibiri tábara, Bigote de gato, Dos gardenias,* and *Jesús María* which combined *plena* and *guaguancó.*

Born in San Juan, Santos (1916–1992) grew up in Brooklyn in a humble family. He first earned a living by selling coal and shining shoes. He started out with a local group, the Trío Lírico, and, in 1938, moved on to sing with small outfits in East Harlem. After a frustrating stint in Puerto Rico, he returned to New York, collaborated with Augusto Coen at the Cuban Casino and recorded with the Cuarteto Flores (*¿Qué te pasa?, Hay que saber perder*), before joining Doroteo Santiago's *cuarteto.*

Known as *"El bardo coameño"* (The bard from Coamo), the Puerto Rican *bolerista* "Bobby Capó" (Félix Manuel Rodríguez Capó) performed songs by Pedro Flores and an extended range of Latin American material, Haitian méringues and *La múcura* among them. But his greatest overall successes were *Mambo batiri*, *Magdalena*, the bitter *Negro bembón* (*The Big-Lipped Negro*), evoking racism; the nostalgic *En mi viejo San Juan* (*In My Old San Juan*) and the bolero *Piel canela*. Capó (1922–1989) started out with the Cuarteto Victoria and recorded with Xavier Cugat, the Cuarteto Caney, and Pepito Torres. He also collaborated with the Panamanian bandleader and composer Avelino Muñoz, with Machito, and with other great names of Latin music, and recorded with his own orchestra at the Sheraton Hotel, in San Juan.

A fine *bolerista*, Gilberto Monroig (1930–1996) became known through his association with José Curbelo and Tito Puente, and then moved to Puerto Rico in 1955. The lively and funny Vitín Avilés, born in Mayagüez in 1923, sang with New York's major Latin bands (Pupi Campo, Tito Rodríguez, Tito Puente, Cugat, Machito, Charlie Palmieri, Noro Morales), and with The Lecuona Cuban Boys. In 1945 he recorded José Carbo Menéndez's *guaracha La televisión pronto llegará*, hailing the advent of television, and also got recognition with *Sube y baja*, and with the *plena Azuquita*.

Trios continued to perform with success: the Trío San Juan, founded in 1952 by the Guayama-born "Johnny" (Juan Antonio) Albino with José Ramón and Jaime González, which performed internationally; Los Tres Reyes, the Trío Vegabajeño, formed in 1940 in Puerto Rico by Fernandito Alvarez, with Benito de Jesús and Pepito Maduro; the Trío Los Panchos, founded in New York in 1943, whose fame spread throughout Latin America. Los Panchos included two Mexicans: Chucho Navarro (second voice), Alfredo "El Güero" Gil (*requinto* – a kind of small guitar) and the Puerto Rican "Herminio" (Hernando) Avilés (first voice). They debuted at the Teatro Hispano in New York in 1944 and worked in Mexico in 1949, where they influenced such trios as Los Tres Diamantes and Los Pepes. In 1955 Avilés left the group and his countryman Julio Rodríguez replaced him for a year. In 1958, Johnny Albino succeeded Avilés and with him, Los Panchos reached the zenith of their career.

The great Puerto Rican *cuartetos*, among them the poetical Mayarí (*Risa loca*, *Reflejos de luna*) also continued for a time, but with the rise of the boogaloo and then salsa, trios and *cuartetos* disappeared almost entirely from the major commercial circuits.

Chano Pozo and his disciples

Until the advent of "Chano" (Luciano) Pozo, practically the only percussion instrument used in jazz were trap drums. (Benny Carter had employed a *conguero* in his band in 1937, but his playing was hardly memorable.) Around 1850 Caribbean hand-held drums still accompanied the Haitian *bamboulas* of the Old Congo Square in New Orleans. By the late nineteenth century, however, blacks' percussion instruments, rapidly suppressed by whites, had vanished from African-American music. Two idiophones were nevertheless tolerated: the washboard and in the deep South the jawbone, scraped with a stick, beaten or played as castanets.

For all those who knew him, Pozo was an indisputed genius of Cuban music, and his influence has been enormous. Before Mongo Santamaría and Patato Valdés, he popularized the conga in the United States and in dance music in general, while preserving its fundamental function as messenger of the gods. He also left many compositions created by ear, such as the *pregón El mondonguero* – a favorite of Miguelito Valdés – *Paraparampampín*, whose title evokes a conga break, *El mundo se ta' caba, Guachiguara, Nagüe, Zarabanda, Blen blen blen, Muna san timba, La teta e,* derived from the sacred Congo refrain *Te con e,* or *O nana-o, O leri-o,* and *O chachiri-o,* based on rumba fragments.

With his wide-set eyes, enormous mouth, stocky frame, and powerful hands, Pozo exuded remarkable strength. He was what the Cubans call a *guapetón* (a hot-blooded braggart), yet a deeply human one, and a larger-than-life character. He loved women, flashy clothes, and luxurious cars, which he very quickly wrecked. In Havana, he had bought an apartment near the elegant Paseo del Prado, and in New York, Machito remembered, he would take a cab just to go one block. When he played with Dizzy Gillespie, he often arrived late at rehearsals but, as Gillespie wrote in his autobiography, he would imperiously reply to the road manager, who wanted to hold back a part of his salary: "I'm a star, I'm a star!" His swagger and quick temper often got him in trouble. It eventually cost him dearly. He once threatened to stab his music publisher in Havana, who refused to give him an advance for his compositions. As a result of the altercation, the publisher's bodyguard shot him, and a bullet became lodged in his spine later causing him excruciating pains.

In the 1940s, the congas did not yet have metal keys to tune them, and on stage Pozo would go through a whole ritual to heat his congas. Once the music began, he gave himself fully, his *quinto* sometimes hung with a strap from his shoulder for more freedom of movement (as Miguelito Valdés did). He intoned sacred chants, cut fancy *rumba brava* steps with a glass of water balanced on the top of his head, performed Abakwa dances or suddenly let his conga slip and caught it before it fell – a trick which Los Papines later adopted.

Born in 1915 in Havana, in the tumultuous *solar* Pan con Timba,[15] he grew up in Jesús María with the family of Félix Chappotín – his half-brother through his mother – and showed signs of precocious musical gifts. As a teenager he honed his skills with various *comparsas,* among them Las Jardineras, El Barracón, to which percussionists "Teclo" and "Alambre" also belonged, and in the La Loma de Belén district, Los Dandys de Belén, along with his friends Rita Montaner and Bola de Nieve. In Cayo Hueso, he also played for the ceremonies of the Abakwa Muñanga fraternity, into which he had been initiated. After his death, when his body was flown back from New York to Havana, some *ñáñigos*, alleging that he had revealed the secret Abakwa rhythms, sought to oppose his burial.

15 In Cuba, *pan con timba* designates a guava sandwich.

In order to survive, Pozo sold newpapers, shined shoes, and worked as a bodyguard for the director of a radio station, while jamming in small clubs and cafés. His virtuosity – he would sometimes use five or more congas at the same time – and his compositions, which were created with stunning ease and won prizes at various carnivals, rapidly attracted attention. Around 1936, Rita Montaner got him a job selling cigarettes at Radio Cadena Azul, and whenever he had a chance, he would sit in with the radio orchestra. He was eventually named director of the percussion department of that station. Miguelito Valdés tried to get him into Casino de la Playa, but many clubs only wanted white bands, and Pozo's skin color worked against him. In 1940, however, he was finally hired at the Sans Souci, in a show entitled *Congo Pantera*. After his departure from La Sonora Matancera, the multi-instrumentalist Humberto Cané, who had formed his own *conjunto*, which included Abelardo Barroso. Pozo and Félix Chappotín, joined this group, which eventually became known as Conjunto Azul, as it played on radio Cadena Azul.

In 1946, encouraged by Miguelito Valdés, Pozo moved to New York with his companion, dancer "Cacha" (Caridad) Martínez, and composer "Pepe" (José) Becke. Mario Bauzá, who had met Pozo in Havana, had spoken enthusiastically to his friends about him. Federico Pagani immediately found him gigs in the Barrio, and Pozo's feverish shows, in which Cacha sometimes danced, awed the local musicians.

Dizzy Gillespie had just formed a stunning sixteen-piece orchestra which was the first bebop big band. Since the late 1930s, he had been eager to experiment with Latin rhythms and to play with a *conguero*. He and Charlie Parker had already jammed with African and Latin percussionists, and he was looking for a steady conga player. *Pickin' the Cabbage*, written by Dizzy in 1940 for Cab Calloway, and *Night in Tunisia* (1942), with its syncopated bass line, already revealed Gillespie's fondness for Latin rhythms. Bauzá recommended Pozo to him, and after seeing him play several times, Dizzy recruited the new drum sensation. After Pozo, Gillespie recorded with a string of *congueros*: Cándido Camero, Vicente Guerra, Humberto Cano, Sabú Martínez, Carlos Duchesne, and Vidal Bolado, and with the *bongocero* Chiquitico, although none could match Pozo's panache and rhythmic imagination. And Dizzy himself played the conga – enjoying showing off his dexterity on this instrument – and even occasionally timbales.

The fact that Pozo beat his drums with his hands rather than with sticks shocked many trap drummers at that time, including Gillespie's bassist Al McKibbon, also an occasional drummer. At first, Pozo's rhythms clashed with those played by Kenny Clarke, then working with Gillespie. A bebop pioneer, Clarke, nicknamed "Klook de Mop" because of his unpredictable accents – his "bombs," as musicians used to call them – was himself an incomparable master of polyrhythms, with a highly developed sense of melody and space. But the Cuban concept of the downbeat differs radically from the jazz one. The strong accent of the *clave*, called *"bombo"* (a word also used to designate a bass drum) falls on the second dotted quarter note of the second bar, and Cuban percussionists tend to think of this beat, rather than of the first one of the first bar of the *clave*, as the one that really starts the musical phrase.

Bombo

bombo

In the beginning, Gillespie was often flustered by Pozo's concept of time: "I had to yell 'and one' to him or hum a few notes of *Good Bait* in his ear, accenting the first beat, to let him know where it fell." "Pozo beeped instead of bopping," he stated with his usual sense of humor. But Pozo taught the trumpeter and other members of the band how to "beep," with rhythms and chants still imbued with a strongly African feel. Gradually, Gillespie's men grasped the concept of the *clave*, while Pozo adapted to jazz. "Me no speak English, you no speak Spanish, but we speak African," Pozo would tell Gillespie. In this common language, Pozo enriched Gillespie's repertoire with several songs, contributing ideas that Dizzy would then develop into full-blown scores with the help of various arrangers.

Pozo finally mastered the jazz idiom and on July 9, 1946 he recorded with Gillespie *One Bass Hit*, *Things to Come*, *Ray's Idea*, and *He Beeped When He Should Have Bopped* and, along with Charlie Parker, his own *Guachiguara*, written in collaboration with Gillespie and renamed *What-Cha-Wa-Hoo*. In a different vein, he also recorded *Pasó en Tampa*, *Porque tú sufres*, *Cómetelo to'*, and Abakwa chants with Machito, Miguelito Valdés, Arsenio Rodríguez, Olga Guillot, and Tito Rodríguez.[16]

In addition to running his big band, Dizzy often jammed with Latin musicians, Noro Morales and the Afro-Cubans among them. On September 29, with Pozo and Chiquitico, he played *Cubana Be Cubana Bop* at Carnegie Hall. Written by George Russell – the arranger who would later be known for his experimentations with the Lydian mode – and Gillespie after an idea by Pozo, it consisted of two sections separated by a long solo by Pozo. Dizzy recorded it on December 22, along with *Cool Breeze*, *Festival in Cuba*, *Panic in Puerto Rico*, *Algo bueno* (derived from *Woody'n You*), and *On the Bongo Beat*. Pozo chanted on *Cubana Bop*, with the bandmembers answering him in call-and-response fashion, and these works are widely considered among the best of the Gillespie big band's output. The 27th of the same month, at a historical Town Hall concert, Dizzy performed two numbers written after an idea by Pozo: *Manteca*[17] and *Tin tin deo*. The head of *Manteca*, derived from a conga *tumbao* invented by Pozo, is based on a B-flat bass *tumbao*. At first, McKibbon had trouble playing the opening vamps in unison with Pozo:

16 Some of these tunes have been reissued on a record entitled "Chano Pozo y su orquesta," although Pozo did not lead a regular band in the United States.

17 Literally "lard" or "grease" in Spanish, but also "marijuana" in Cuban slang.

Manteca's first
opening vamp

Manteca's second
opening vamp

The jazzier and modulating sixteen-bar bridge was devised by Gillespie and the Californian arranger "Gil" (Walter) Fuller, with the help of Pozo and Bill Graham. Chico O'Farrill was called in to ghostwrite the arrangement, which could be heard seven years later in his *Manteca Suite*. Fuller had previously worked for Les Hite, as well as Tito Puente and Machito, and he understood both the jazz and the Latin idioms. Pozo, the star of the evening, outshone drummer Ted Stewart. Three days later, Gillespie recorded *Manteca*, on which Pozo sent sparks flying, as well as *Good Bait* and other tunes. *Tin tin deo*, adapted from Pozo's rumba *O tin-tine o*, has (like *Manteca*) a Latin head and a jazzy bridge. But while Pozo played Cuban rhythms, Gillespie's musicians were really improvising in a bebop language. Clare Fischer, himself a seasoned Latin jazz veteran who arranged themes by Duke Ellington for Gillespie, claims that in fact Dizzy made Latin musicians adapt to the American swing rather than the reverse.

With Gillespie, Pozo also performed at the Savoy Ballroom. On July 26, 1948 Gillespie and Pozo (with James Forman on piano and Nelson Boyd on bass) played a new version of *Manteca* at Pasadena's Civic Auditorium, stunning listeners; the same year, Gillespie, Pozo, and Ted Stewart recorded *Emanon, Oo Ya Koo, Stay on It*, and *Good Bait*. Pozo also recorded *Jahbero* with Fats Navarro and Tadd Dameron, and on October 25, 1948, six weeks before Pozo's death, *Tin tin deo*, with James Moody and Art Blakey, on which he sang and played percussion.[18] In addition to those studio sessions, he gave a series of concerts: one, in particular, at the 123rd Street Theater, in East Harlem, with *timbalero* Manny Oquendo, where he played a memorable solo on his composition *Rhumba in Swing*; another at Cornell University, where some female students fainted. One evening, at the Royal Roost, he also challenged Art Blakey to a percussion duel. But by then, many bebop drummers including Kenny Clarke, Blakey, and Max Roach had become thoroughly attuned to Cuban rhythms.

In January 1948, Pozo embarked on a European tour with the Dizzy Gillespie orchestra, which included John Lewis on piano, Kenny Clarke, and Al McKibbon. In a momentous concert at the Salle Pleyel, filled with the French jazz avant-garde, the band performed *Manteca* and Gillespie's *Afro-Cuban Suite* (of which *Cubana Be Cubana Bop* was a part), with a Pozo–Gillespie duet in which Pozo chanted. "*Manteca*, of Cuban inspiration, dazzles us with swing: the bass is magnificent and Dizzy's trumpet part sensational. Pozo Gonzalez's bongo (sic) is just as wonderful," a *Jazz Hot* reviewer gushed. Also mixing up conga and

18 Some of the numbers with Moody have been issued on *A Decade of Jazz* (1939–1949) and *James Moody–George Wallington: James Moody and His Modernists*.

bongo, André Hodeir wrote in *Jazz Magazine*: "The introduction of the bongo in the rhythm section is an excellent idea. It creates a rhythmic diversity, a kind of polyrhythm one can expect a lot from, and which is quite in the spirit of the new style. I add that it is enough to see Gonzalès (sic) to be caught up by the swing he generates with each movement of his body." However, the album of the concert is, as Lucien Malson aptly notes, "rather powerless to convey the prodigious – we were going to say scary – violence of Gillespie's music." Indeed, no record has managed to really capture Pozo's bewitching magic.

After the tour, Kenny Clarke decided to settle in Europe. Upon their return to the United States, Pozo and Gillespie performed in Detroit. Gillespie was then booked in the South, on the T.O.B.A. circuit (Theater Owners Booking Association). Infamous for its racism, the T.O.B.A., where Ma' Rainey, Billie Holiday, Ella Fitzgerald, and other stars had endured countless humiliations, was nicknamed by African American musicians "tough on black asses." In Raleigh, North Carolina, Pozo's drums were stolen. Discouraged, he decided to go back to New York, telling Gillespie he would meet him again in Hollywood, at the tail end of the tour. He then made plans to visit his family in Havana, and before leaving he ordered new congas from his countryman Simon Jou, who ran a pastry store in Harlem and sold Latin percussion instruments.

The trip to Cuba was never to take place. On December 2, Pozo went with Pepe Becke to the Rio Café and Lounge, one of his favorite haunts, close to where he lived. Becke put *Manteca* on the juke box. Pozo started doing a few dance steps to impress a pretty woman at the bar. Suddenly a garage mechanic, Eusebio "Cabito" Muñoz, burst in and asked Pozo for money he owed him for some marijuana. Pozo replied that it was bad quality and that he wouldn't pay. The two men started a fight. Muñoz rushed out of the bar. He returned a moment later with a gun and shot Pozo point blank. Pozo crumpled to the floor, mortally wounded while *Manteca* was still playing. He was only thirty-three years old. Legend has it that thousands of dollars were found in the heel of his shoe. Several musicians would pay tribute to him, among them Carlos Vidal, Miguelito Valdés, and Pérez Prado, with *Memoria a Chano*.

Gillespie was dismayed by Pozo's death, but the *conguero*'s legacy endured. On December 28, with the Puerto Rican "Sabú" (Luis Martínez) on bongo and Joe Harris on conga, Dizzy recorded *Lover Come Back to Me*, to which he gave an afro rhythm, and Pozo's *Guachi guaro*, arranged by Gerald Wilson (who in 1945 had composed *Puertorican Breakdown*). And around the middle of 1949, a *Down Beat* journalist noted after a Gillespie performance at Chicago's Regal Theater: "Dizzy has become a true maracas nut."

In 1954, with Bobby Rodríguez, José Mangual, and Ubaldo Nieto, borrowed from the Afro-Cubans, and also Quincy Jones, J. J. Johnson, Hank Mobley, Charlie Persip, and Lucky Thompson, Gillespie recorded *The Manteca Suite*. Expanded by Chico O'Farrill from *Manteca* at Norman Granz's suggestion, this strongly colored, multifaceted work comprised four movements: *Manteca Theme, Contraste,*

Jungla, and *Rhumba Finale*. *Contraste* and *Jungla* are based on the bass line of *Manteca*; *Jungla* begins with the percussion in 6/8, and variations unfold on *Manteca*, while Gillespie plays truly dizzying lines. In other sessions, Dizzy also swung on *Rumbola*, with Mobley and Persip; on *Siboney*, with a quartet featuring Stan Getz; and on *Night in Tunisia*, with Gilberto Valdés (flute), Alejandro Hernández (piano), Bobby Rodríguez (bass), José Mangual (bongo), and Cándido (conga).

A few years after Pozo, "Mongo"(Ramón) Santamaría also introduced sacred Afro-Cuban rhythms in the United States. An inspired and precise *conguero* and a remarkable talent-spotter, he expressed himself within the combo format – one he maintained for over forty years.

Born in 1922 in the Havana district of Jesús María, he first studied violin, at his mother's insistence. "But," he explains, "I had drums in my blood." His Bantu grandfather, brought from Africa as a slave, taught him the ancestral rhythms. Santamaría began drumming with sticks on the traditional Congo log drums and he honed his skills in *rumbas*, *comparsas*, Abakwa ceremonies of the Efí Abarakó brotherhood, and *descargas*. The percussionist Chicho Piquero, later with Benny Moré, greatly impressed him: "He was the best *quintero*[19] I ever heard. Better, even, than Chano Pozo, and I used to imitate him."

From 1940 to 1948, during the day, Santamaría earned his living as a mailman, and at night he played with dance bands. "I was then using *bongos de fuego* (fire bongos), tuned near the heat of a flame." An appearance on a radio program featuring Celia Cruz landed him work in some of the major clubs of the capital, despite discrimination against dark-skinned musicians. He performed at the Tropicana with the Conjunto Apollo, with singer Alfredo León, and with Joseíto Núñez, and recorded with Armando Romeu.

In 1948, disheartened because the parents of the girl he loved wouldn't let her marry him, he toured to Mexico with dancers Paulito y Lilón and decided to stay there. He soon gigged with a local band, the *conjunto* Son Clave de Oro and persuaded Armando Peraza – an outstanding percussionist in his own right and a distant cousin – to come and join him in Aztec land.

In September 1950, Santamaría went to New York with Peraza, Paulito, and Lilón, where all four performed under the name The Black Cuban Diamonds. There Paulito and Lilón died, asphyxiated by a faulty heating system in their apartment. In 1952 Peraza left for California, where he became active on both the jazz and Latin scenes, working with, among others, Slim Gaillard, Cal Tjader, Pérez Prado, Dave Brubeck, George Shearing, Wes Montgomery, and Carlos Santana. Santamaría then toured Latin America with Pérez Prado.

In Texas, Santamaría had a car accident, and he narrowly escaped having his leg amputated thanks only to the intervention of one of his friends. Back in New York, he played with José Luis Moneró, Johnny Seguí, and Gilberto Valdés.

Around 1956, he presented a show at the Palladium Ballroom entitled *Changó*, in which he played Yoruba rhythms. This show gave rise to a series of

19 A *quintero* is a *quinto* player but here, Santamaría also used the word to mean improviser.

Afro-Cuban records, among them *Changó* (with Patato Valdés, Julio Collazo, and Merceditas Valdés), *Yambú* (with *congueros* Modesto Durán and Francisco Aguabella), *Mongo Santamaría's Drums and Chants* (*Abacuá ecu sagare, Moforiborere*), and a little later *Tambores afrocubanos* (*Fiesta abacuá*). As with Chano Pozo, some *ñáñigos* accused him of betraying their musical secrets, but these albums revealed to American listeners the splendor of the black Cuban tradition.

Santamaría then succeeded Frankie Colón in Tito Puente's All Stars Mambo Orchestra, which included Vicentico Valdés, Charlie Palmieri, and Manny Oquendo. He also founded the Orquesta Manhattan, recruiting Chombo Silva and Ray Coen. And with Willie Bobo, he joined Cal Tjader's group in California. The young Ray Barretto, who was playing with jazz pianist Eddie Bonnemere, replaced Santamaría in Puente's band.

While with Tjader, in 1959 Santamaría recorded *Mongo*,[20] close in spirit to some of his previous albums. "When I was playing with Cal Tjader, he used to tell me: 'people don't come for me but for you', and I realized that it was the Cuban rhythms audiences liked," Santamaría recalls. Some fifty years earlier, W. C. Handy had also noticed that, when he was playing dances, it was the Latin numbers that were the show-stoppers.

Another conga stalwart, "Patato"[21] Valdés has created a highly personal style, lighter than Pozo's but just as musical. Like Kenny Clarke or some

20 Reissued, along with *Yambú*, under the title *Afro Roots*.

21 Patato, literally "potato," also designates a small person in Cuban slang.

Mongo Santamaría and Armando Peraza.
Mongo Santamaría Collection

Mongo Santamaría (first on the left) with the All Stars Mambo Orchestra led by Tito Puente (second on the right), with Charlie Palmieri (first on the right) and Vicentico Valdés (seventh starting from the left). Mongo Santamaría Collection

contemporary drummers, he suggests the beats rather than openly stating them, punctuating the space with a few carefully placed accents, and he converses with the other instruments rather than limiting himself to a simple comping role. And, despite his small hands, he gets a full tone out of his skins. "Drums," he explains with humor, "are like women. One must caress them. If one beats them up, they get angry." Refusing facile and predictable effects, he imparts a deep meaning to his music and prefers expressiveness to sheer virtuosity.

Valdés popularized the system of metal keys – which had been invented in Cuba – allowing congas to be tuned. Until the advent of these metal keys, the skins had to be tensed by the heat of a small kerosene lamp. The process gave the drums a deep and mellow sound, and *congueros* who tuned their instrument the old way were called "*congueros de candela.*"[22] Also conversant with the *batá* (and with *santería*), Valdés refuses to desecrate these drums by using them in concert. "Badly controlled, the Yoruba rhythms can drive you crazy," he asserts. Like Pozo and other Cuban percussionists, he uses several congas tuned differently and performs complex *tumbaos*.

Born in Havana in 1926, Valdés started out on *tres*, which his father played with the Septeto Habanero. Around 1945, he performed with La Sonora

22 A play on the words *candela*, meaning "candle" and *de candela*, meaning "sensational."

Matancera and then, along with Armando Peraza (whom, he claims, he taught to play the bongo), with Cubavana, in which he was the first black *conguero* ("I am the Jackie Robinson of *congueros*," he says). In 1949, he and Peraza went to Mexico with Vicentico Valdés, and upon his return to Cuba, he worked with the Conjunto Casino, the Trío Matamoros, Roberto Faz, Miguelito Valdés, *filin* artists, and Las Mulatas de Fuego, and recorded with Cándido and Pérez Prado. In 1950 he invented a short-lived dance, the *pingüino*, imitating the movements of a penguin, which he performed on Cuban television, and which Tito Puente helped popularize in New York.

In 1954 he moved to New York, and Luis Miranda, who had just left the Afro-Cubans in order to play with Tjader in California, recommended him to Machito. Valdés stayed six years with the Afro-Cubans and nine with Herbie Mann, and he also worked with such jazzmen as Art Blakey (*Orgy in Rhythm*) and Quincy Jones.

Many other percussionists then made a name for themselves in both Latin music and jazz, among them Sabú (1930–1979). Born in the Barrio of Puerto Rican parents, he had been influenced by the Lecuona Cuban Boys. He worked with Count Basie, Dizzy Gillespie, Charlie Parker, Benny Goodman, Art Blakey (recording on *Message from Kenya* and *Nothing But the Soul*), and, from 1957 to 1963, Horace Silver, Tony Bennett, Joe Loco, and others, also leading his own quintet. He turned as well to ritual Afro-Cuban rhythms with *Palo congo* (1957), featuring Arsenio Rodríguez. In the 1970s, he became a fixture of the *rumbones* (freely improvised rumbas) held on Sundays in Central Park.

The Cuban *conguero* "Cándido" (Cándido Camero) has collaborated with just about everybody in Latin music, from the Lecuona Cuban Boys to Celia Cruz and Tito Puente. Famed for his great technique, he has entranced audiences in the United States and Europe, where his name once conjured up an image of flamboyant tropics. A flexible musician, he possesses a deep knowledge of the Cuban tradition and a more sober style than what some of his album covers – among them *Candido the Volcanic*, recorded in 1957 with Hank Jones, Art Farmer, and Charlie Shavers – would lead one to imagine.

Born in 1921 in a musical family, he grew up in the Havana district of El Cerro, listening to *santería toques*. He studied bongo with an uncle and taught himself to play the conga, the bass, and the *tres*. At twelve he debuted as a *bongocero* in the *conjunto* Gloria Habanera, in which his father played *tres*, moving on to Jóvenes del Cerro, Jóvenes Sociales, Bolero 1935, Apollo, of which he was the *tresista* (and Mongo Santamaría the *bongocero*), and Nacional Juvenil. He also played snare drum in the *comparsa* El Alacrán and worked with Armando Romeu and at the Tropicana. He often experimented, playing conga with one hand and bongo with the other, acquiring an outstanding reputation in Cuba.

In 1946 he embarked on a U.S. tour with the dancing team of Carmen y Rolando, and settled in New York. There he recorded with Machito (on *El rey del mambo*), and Dizzy Gillespie introduced him to jazz pianist Billy Taylor, with whom he subsequently worked. In the late 1940s he recorded *Jamaica Jazz* (a jazz version of a Harold Arlen musical) with Don Elliott, and in 1953 his first album under his own name, *Tiempo de Cencerro Part I*, with Catalino Rolón and Cal Tjader. He teamed up with jazzmen (among them Stan Kenton and Woody Herman) and Latin musicians, recorded *Cubano Chant* (1957) with Art Blakey and Sabú on bongo, played in the Broadway musical *Sophisticated Ladies* and in the Duke Ellington TV special *The Drum Is a Woman*.

Born in Matanzas and a *santería* adept, Francisco Aguabella had also been initiated into Iyesa music (close to the Yoruba tradition) through his grandmother. In the 1950s he played in Havana at the Sans Souci. In 1957 he left for the United States, joined Katherine Dunham's company, and then settled in California. He has collaborated with among others Peggy Lee, Frank Sinatra, Tito Puente, Eddie Palmieri, and Dizzy Gillespie. His countryman "Chocolate" (Félix Alfonso), who also moved to the United States, accompanied Pérez Prado, Ernesto Lecuona, The Four Cuban Diamonds, and various American artists.

The bongocero Chino Pozo (1915–1977), also a talented pianist and bassist, shone in many different contexts. Having arrived in the United States in 1937, he played with the Afro-Cubans until 1943, and then with José Curbelo, Noro Morales, Tito Puente, Tito Rodríguez, Enrique Madriguera, and Pérez Prado. In addition he was sought after by a host of American jazz and show-business personalities, among them Josephine Premice, Tadd Dameron, Fats Navarro, Stan Kenton, Herbie Mann, Illinois Jacquet, Phineas Newborn, Billy Taylor, Paul Anka, and also, like Aguabella, Tito Puente, Peggy Lee, and Dizzy Gillespie.

Inspired by their Hispanic colleagues, Gene Krupa, Nat "King" Cole, Woody Herman, and a growing number of jazzmen started to use congas, maracas, and bongos. Generally, however, in jazz these percussion instruments simply added a little extra pepper, while the trap drums did the heavy work and were preferred to the timbales, even for Latin rhythms. In Cuban and Puerto Rican music, on the contrary, Latin percussion played the leading role. Incidentally, Mongo Santamaría – a Cuban percussion purist – shared with me this comment about the timbales: "New York *timbaleros* play too much on the metal and don't use the leather enough." Tadd Dameron recorded with Carlos Vidal and Vidal Bolado, Paul Whiteman with Willie Rodríguez, and Herbie Mann with José Mangual and Patato Valdés, touring Africa with them in 1960; and Mangual went on to play conga with Erroll Garner.

Expansion of Latin jazz

At the end of the Second World War, the exchanges between Latin musicians and jazzmen intensified. Max Roach remembers that in the 52nd Street clubs, several Latin musicians came by to jam with him, and Gil Fuller claims that "the Latin influx strongly influenced modal music. Latin bands used to play for countless bars on dominant 7th chords. Meanwhile, musicians used to perform all kinds of scales on a single chord."

During their breaks at the Palladium Ballroom, Latin musicians would run over to the nearby 52nd Street and Broadway clubs to check out the jazz and jam sessions, and Pérez Prado, Tito Puente, Tito Rodríguez, Machito, Mario Bauzá, and many other Latin musicians readily acknowledged their debt to Afro-American music. Conversely, jazzmen, in addition to utilizing Cuban percussion instruments, also borrowed Cuban rhythms, *montunos*, breaks (which had practically vanished from jazz since the early New Orleans days), and riffs, as in *Dark Eyes*, *My Little Suede Shoes*, *A Night in Tunisia*, *Algo bueno*, *Un poco loco*, *Nica's Dream*, Bud Powell's version of *Cherokee*, or Thelonious Monk's coda on *'Round Midnight*:

In the 1930s and 1940s, trombonist Juan Tizol introduced Latin colors into Duke Ellington's repertoire with some of his compositions, including *Caravan*, *Conga Brava*, *Perdido* (which Tizol also recorded with Woody Herman), *Moonlight Fiesta*, *Casa Blanca* (renamed *Bagdad* for Boyd Raeburn), *Moon Over Cuba*, written in collaboration with Ellington, and *Night Song*, written in collaboration with Mundy and Mills. Despite its Arabic mood, suggested by a harmonic minor scale, the first part of *Caravan* is, in fact, based on a *tumbao*:

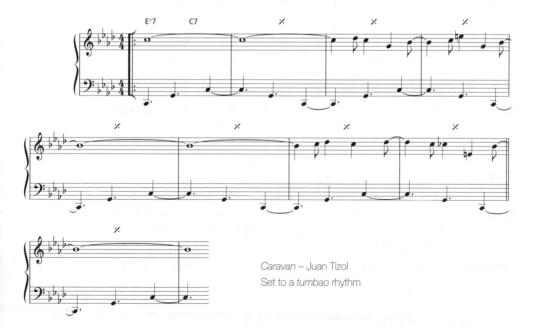

Caravan – Juan Tizol
Set to a *tumbao* rhythm

Born in San Juan, Tizol (1909–1984) had studied music with his uncle Manuel, a classically trained bassist and composer, and started playing with the town's municipal brass band, which Manuel led. Around 1929 he went to the United States with the Marie Lucas orchestra, which Ellington described as a "hell-fired" band. He began playing in the pit of the Howard theater in Washington, D.C., where Ellington sometimes sat at the piano, joined Bobby Lee's Cotton Pickers (different from McKinney's Cotton Pickers) and then The White Brothers, and worked in New Jersey with pianist Cliff Jackson. After his stint with Ellington, from 1929 to 1944, where he distinguished himself not as an improviser, but with the lyricism of his interpretations, he worked awhile with Harry James, with Ellington again from 1951 to 1953, and once more with James, returning briefly to perform with Ellington in 1960, and then collaborating with other bands.

During the 1940s Alberto Socarrás busied himself in both the jazz and the Latin spheres, writing arrangements for Cab Calloway, Vincent López, Enrique Madriguera, Miguelito Valdés, and others, and he was able to inject any tune with a Latin flavor – be it a Chopin prelude or a jazz standard like *Honey Dripper* or *The Story of Love*. He performed with Ella Fitzgerald at the Tropicana in a show advertised as "the only intelligent sepia revue on Broadway," and at the Apollo Theater bested Panamanian bandleader Luis Russell in a musical showdown. "His flute punctuation and feathery flights of fancy," read a promotional brochure about Socarrás, "deftly blend into the accompanying orchestral passages – the unchained chatter of bongos and drums, free-spirited strings and irrepressible reeds." He recorded a series of *congas, guarachas*, rumbas, and boleros with Los Amigos Panamericanos and Cabalgata d'Artega (featuring Noro Morales and on some numbers "Chiquito" Socarrás). His mellow flute, backed by Morales's crisp comping, soars on tunes like the graceful *Somos diferentes* or *Soñar*, although the accordion used on certain tracks sounds rather corny. The session also featured the Cab Calloway-type number *Chiquito montuno*, written by Chiquito Socarrás. In 1943 he recorded *I Can't Give You Anything But Love* and other jazz numbers, and in 1949 went into the studios with the Babs Gonzalez orchestra. From 1955 on, he mainly dedicated himself to teaching and composing, with occasional performances with pianist Eddie Bonnemere.

Ever fond of jazz, Tito Puente improvised at Birdland (*Birdland Mambo*) and at the Royal Roost with Frank Foster, Dexter Gordon, and other jazzmen, and he recorded several jazz standards (*Yesterdays, Bohemia*, arranged by Gigi Gryce) done with a Latin twist. He also cut *Puente Goes Jazz, Night Beat* with Doc Severinsen, *Herman's Heat and Puente's Beat* with Woody Herman and Buddy Morrow, and *Revolving Bandstand*,[23] and as Brazilian music was then making its first inroads into jazz, he wrote an arrangement of *Na baixa do sapateiro* simply entitled *Baia*.

Upon arriving in New York, Chico O'Farrill studied composition with Bernard Wagenaar, Stephan Wolpe, and Hall Overton (who taught at the Juilliard School of Music and worked for Thelonious Monk). He started ghostwriting for

23 Released in 1960 and reissued in 1993.

Gil Fuller, who was then collaborating with Dizzy Gillespie, and, unbeknownst to Fuller, he composed *Undercurrent Blues* for Benny Goodman. Goodman recorded it and he hired O'Farrill as staff arranger. In 1949 O'Farrill created *Shishkabop* for him, and penned various numbers for Buddy Greco, then the band's vocalist; and for Gillespie devised the sizzling *Carambola*, inspired by a Villa Lobos composition. He also produced some of his most inspired work for Stan Kenton (*Ramón López*, *Mambo in F*, and the hit *Cuban Episode*, for which Carlos Vidal wrote lyrics). He then returned to Havana for a while and made several albums with a pick-up band. Back in New York, he put out close to fifty sides for Norman Granz's Norgran label and for Clef. On November 24, 1951 he recorded the harmonically interesting *JATP Mambo*, *Havana Special*, *Fiesta Time*, *Cuban Blues*, *Avocadoes*, *Almendra*, *Disappearance*, and *Carioca* with a pick-up orchestra comprised of Lenny Hambro, Flip Phillips, Jim Nottingham, several members of the Afro-Cubans, and other musicians.

Captivated by the Afro-Cubans, Stan Kenton also tried his hand at Cuban rhythms. His *Artistry in Rhythm* (1943), inspired by Ravel's *Daphnis et Chloé*, revealed European influences, however, and despite its ambitious title it could hardly vie, as far as offbeats and syncopations go, with the top Cuban or Puerto Rican bands. The January 24, 1947 concert of the Afro-Cubans at Town Hall made him acutely aware of his shortcomings. "Rhythmically, the Cubans are the most exciting," he admitted a few days later in a *Metronome* interview. "We don't copy them exactly, but we copy some of their techniques and apply them to what we are trying to do. The guys in our rhythm section do exactly that, those of Woody do it too." On February 13 he recorded *Machito*, which he had asked Pete Rugolo, his principal arranger, to write as a tribute to this great Cuban singer. On October 22 of the same year, he added René Touzet on maracas for his *Unison Riff*, and on December 6, José Mangual, Vidal Bolado, Machito on maracas, and West Coast trumpeter Chico Alvarez for *The Peanut Vendor*, to which he injected his customary dissonances, and which became his best seller. But despite the presence of a Cuban drum, his *Chorale for Brass, Piano and Bongo* bore instead the stamp of Bartók's *Music for Strings, Percussion and Celesta*. Gillespie claimed in his autobiography that when he was performing with Pozo at the Savoy Ballroom, Kenton – full of his "progressive jazz" – sometimes dropped in with his musicians and bragged that he could play Latin music better than them. Dizzy and his men then delighted in putting him in his place.

Kenton, however, pursued his Latin experiments, hiring Carlos Vidal and then Jack Costanzo on bongo. He recorded Shorty Rogers's *Viva Prado* with his band, performed at Carnegie Hall in the Fall of 1954 with Cándido on conga, and in May 1956 he produced in New York his major Latin work, *Cuban Fire*, with Lucky Thompson, Lenny Niehaus, and several percussionists. Composed by the Mexican Johnny Richards, *Cuban Fire* included the six movements *Fuego cubano*, *Machito*, the *rumba abierta El Congo valiente*, the *guajira Recuerdos*, *¿Quién sabe?*, the Abakwa-inspired *La suerte de los tontos*, and the *afro La guerra baila*.

With its timpani, French horns, and tuba, *Cuban Fire* was more heavily orchestrated than most Latin works of that time, but the fire didn't really burn. Kenton also recorded *Cuban Episode*, on *Viva Kenton*.

If the Latin musicians' interest in jazz deepened, countless other jazzmen apart from Kenton flirted with Latin music: Charlie Barnet (perhaps influenced by his Puerto Rican pianist Ram Ramírez) recorded *Redskin Rumba* and, in 1944, the fiery *Cu-Ba*; Louis Jordan used claves on his blues *Early in the Morning*; Woody Herman recorded *Sidewalks of Cuba*; in 1949 Charlie Parker performed a rhythmic *Visa* with Max Roach and Vidal Bolado; Babs Gonzalez brought together in a studio Sonny Rollins doing his first recording session, Don Redman on soprano, and Alberto Socarrás; Cozy Cole led a septet called Cuboppers; Sonny Stitt cut *Sonny Stitt Goes Latin* with Willie Bobo and Chick Corea, and in 1952 *Cool Mambo* and *Blue Mambo* with Humberto Morales and drummer Shadow Wilson; Ahmad Jamal performed *Perfidia* and *Rica pulpa*; Sonny Rollins danced with his horn on *Mambo Bounce*; Bird flew on *Cubop Holiday, Mambo, Cuban Blues* and, with José Mangual and Luis Miranda, *My Little Suede Shoes*, Julio Gutiérrez's *Un poquito de tu amor*, and *Mama Inés*, doing *Mama Inés* again the following year, with Mangual, Miranda, and Max Roach; Mary-Lou Williams tackled *Perdido* and *Kool Bongo* (in 1953); Art Pepper wrote *Mambo de la pinta* and covered *Tin tin deo*; Lenny Tristano experimented with a *Turkish Mambo*; Erroll Garner offered *Mambo Loves Garner* with Cándido Camero; Sonny Clark did a swinging *Blues Mambo*; Kenny Dorham and Hank Mobley let loose on *Afro-Cuban*; George Russell recorded *Manhattan Rico Suite*; Shorty Rogers, initiated into Latin music in the 1940s by Jack Costanzo (then playing with Nat "King" Cole), recorded *Chiquito loco*, a fired-up *Un poco loco, Mambo del Crow, Tale of an African Lobster* (first called *Latin*), and in 1958 *Afro-Cuban Influence* with Carlos Vidal, Luis Miranda, and Modesto Durán; Duke Ellington cut *Rhumbop* with Cándido Camero; Conde Candoli and Art Pepper *Mucho Calor, a Presentation in Latin Jazz* – using for perhaps the first time the term "Latin jazz," which replaced "Cubop." On the West Coast, in 1956, the Lighthouse All-Stars (Conde Candoli, Frank Rosolino, Bob Cooper, Stan Levey, and Sonny Clark) produced a *Mambo Las Vegas* (on *Music for Lighthousekeeping*). Even Miles Davis, not generally associated with Latin rhythms, gave in to the Cuban craze, recording Ahmad Jahmal's *New Rhumba*, arranged by Gil Evans, on *Miles Ahead* (1957). And Ray Bryant wrote *Cubano Chant*, although the tune, not originally meant to be played with a Latin feel, was given its name by Cal Tjader.

As in Havana, around the mid-1950s there appeared combos allowing more soloing space than large ensembles and generally including a piano or a vibraphone, or, less frequently, a guitar. Among them, in New York the one led by Charlie Palmieri, already mentioned; those of Puerto Rican *conguero* "Joe Cuba" (José Calderón) and of *timbalero* and vibist "Pete Terrace" (Pedro Gutiérrez); and on the West Coast those of George Shearing and Cal Tjader.

Brought together in 1954, the combination of Joe Cuba's sextet resembled that of Charlie Palmieri's group, formed the same year. Raised in the Barrio, Cuba had given up on becoming a lawyer and played with Noro Morales, Marcelino Guerra, and the *conjunto* Alfarona X. An offshoot of an ensemble led by the Panamanian pianist "Joe Panama" (David Preudhomme), Cuba's sextet consisted of vibist Tommy Berrios, pianist and arranger Nick Jiménez, bassists Roy Rosa and then "Slim" (Jules) Cordero, *bongocero* Victor Pantoja, and singer Willie Torres, who had sung nine years earlier with Pappy Ali y sus Rumberos; in 1957 the magnificient singer Cheo Feliciano joined the group. Joe Cuba's break, however, would really come in the 1960s, during the boogaloo era.

A fine vibist born in New York in 1927 in a musical family (his father and uncle were percussionists, his father also a Latin music DJ), Pete Terrace had worked with Buddy Rich, Pupi Campo, Noro Morales, Juanito Sanabria, and, from 1947 to 1948, Tito Rodríguez's quintet. In 1952, he had been a member of Joe Loco's quintet, which included Julio Andino. With Loco, he recorded a mixture of jazz standards and Latin tunes (*El jamaiquino, Someone to Watch Over Me*). In 1956 Loco left for Los Angeles, and Terrace formed his own quartet (with Andino and *conguero* Freddie Aguiler), combining Afro-American and Latin music. They first turned out *A Night in Mambo Jazz Land* (1956), followed by *Pete with a Latin Beat* (showing Terrace on the amusing cover sitting on a donkey behind his vibes), *Baila la pachanga*, and *El nuevo Pete Terrace* among others, but like other bandleaders of the 1960s, he did not make the transition into salsa.

George Shearing's intimist, refined, and shimmering style (*Latin Escapade, Latin Affair, Mood Latino*) was to the more energetic Latin music of New York what West Coast cool jazz was to bebop. Born in London, the blind pianist formed in around 1953, in California, a jazz group that included Cal Tjader and Al McKibbon. Every time Shearing played in New York, McKibbon took Tjader to the Palladium Ballroom and other clubs to listen to Cuban and Puerto Rican bands. "Back east I got to hear a lot of Machito, Tito Puente and Noro Morales. Those bands had a tremendous effect on me. Immediately I wanted to reorganize a small combo along the same lines, only with more jazz feeling incorporated in the Latin format," Tjader told John Tynan in a 1957 *Downbeat* interview. Mc Kibbon and Tjader turned Shearing on to Latin music and the pianist hired Cándido Camero, and in 1955 Armando Peraza. Nicknamed "Mano de plomo" (Lead hand), Peraza had played bongo in Havana in the early 1940s, with Niño Rivera, Kubavana, Chappotín, Julio Cueva, and the Sonora Matancera. He brought records of Frank Emilio Flynn, Peruchín, and other Cuban pianists to Shearing, who appreciated their airy style, and their use of chord inversions and block chords, devices close to the ones he was himself using. Shearing later employed other Latin percussionists, among them Luis Peralta, Victor Pantoja, and Mongo Santamaría, breaking up his quartet in 1964 in order to study classical piano. He also recorded Latin tracks with vibist Emil Richards and with Toots Thielemans (*Mambo Inn, Drume negrita*).

While he was playing drums with Dave Brubeck's trio, from 1948 to 1951, Tjader had also started using a conga and a bongo. During his engagement with Shearing, during 1953 and 1954, he discovered Tito Puente on vibes. It was a revelation, and he then switched to this instrument. He put together a mambo quintet which debuted at the Macumba Club in San Francisco, and in 1954 he recorded his first Latin jazz sides – punchier than Shearing's – with Peraza on conga and Roy Haynes or Kenny Clarke on drums. In 1956 his *Lucero* achieved success and within four years, Tjader recorded over twenty albums, among them his concert at the Sunset School in Carmel (*Tumbao*, *Afro Blue*), *Demasiado Caliente*, with arrangements by Eddie Cano, and *Latino*, featuring Victor Venegas (bass), Chombo Silva, Rolando Lozano (flute), and Cuco Valdés (timbales).

the 1960s:
the *pachanga,*
the boogaloo, and
Latin soul

CHAPTER SIX

Havana and Cuba

In the first week of January 1959, after months of guerrilla activity in the Sierra Maestra – where the Maroons had sought refuge during slavery – Fidel Castro and his Barbudos seized power and Batista fled to the Dominican Republic. The lower classes and intellectuals enthusiastically welcomed the revolutionaries. But soon many Cubans, and a stream of musicians among them, alarmed by the totalitarian drift of the regime and fearing the advent of communism, left the country, and on January 3, 1961 the United States severed its ties with Cuba, after Castro expelled eleven American diplomats. The vast majority of the Cuban refugees settled in the United States, some in Puerto Rico and other Latin American countries or in Europe. Celia Cruz, Rolando Lozano, Orlando Laserie, Pupi Legarreta, José Fajardo, "Chombo" Silva, La Lupe, Lázaro Prieto, Totico, Papaíto, Olga Guillot, Haydée Portuondo, Javier Vázquez, and Humberto Suárez were among the first musicians to leave.

Dictators are rarely known for their artistic leanings, and in a revolutionary fervor, Castro closed down the *academias de baile*, which he regarded as symbols of decadence and corruption. Gradually the government took control of clubs and hotels, musicians became salaried, and political propaganda and the *zafra* (sugarcane harvest) took precedence over entertainment and creativity. Dance music, jazz, and even drum sets were frowned upon with a fierceness bordering on paranoia, while songs expressing a leftist ideology enjoyed official support. Singers and musicians who had left the country were branded as traitors, banned and expurgated from music books, among them the first edition of Helio Orovio's *Dictionary of Cuban Music*, published in Cuba, although people carried on listening to them in secret. But as always in Cuba, music nevertheless continued unabated, alleviating all the hardships. Zoé Valdés mentions in her novel *Dear First Love* that while picking tomatoes as part of the "school in the fields program" – which sent teenagers to perform agricultural tasks – she and her friends sang Frank Domínguez's bolero *Tú me acostumbraste*.

As Cuba developed political and economic ties with the USSR and other communist countries, many Cuban musicians were able to study in the best Eastern European music schools (in Prague, Moscow, Sofia, and other cities) or, at home, with masters from these areas.

As the economic situation worsened over the years, the Cubans learned to deal with acute shortages, often displaying tremendous resourcefulness. Eventually, the government realized that music and dance kept the people's minds off social, political, and economic problems. Music, carefully controlled, surfaced again – black music in particular and *música campesina* (country music), both symbols of popular culture, enjoyed a renaissance. Cuba's African heritage became even more apparent with the exile of many whites (nicknamed *gallegos*, "Galicians," in Cuba and *gusanos*, "worms," in Miami).

In 1961, *rumberos* from the docks of Havana created the rumba group Yoruba Andabó. And the following year, as part of the rehabilitation of Afro-Cuban culture, the folklorist Rogelio Martínez Furé and the Mexican choreographer Rodolfo Reyes started the Conjunto Folklórico Nacional in order to preserve Cuba's traditional dance and music. Directed by Obdulio Morales it recruited outstanding performers and rescued several tunes from oblivion. It has since performed internationally (including in a historical concert at the Brooklyn Academy of Music, in 1980).

As the musicologist Radamés Giro explained in his foreword to guitarist Leo Brouwer's "La música, lo cubano y la innovación" of 1982, "Cubans consider the "popular music–'serious' music" dichotomy to be 'nonfunctional'." The abolition, on the island, of the often artificial hierarchical barriers between the different genres had raised the musical level and stimulated creativity, and musicians who played in symphony orchestras often performed in dance bands as well, and sat in, after work, in jazz clubs. Some of today's best musicians come from the Escuela Nacional de Arte, founded in Havana after the Revolution, or from conservatories, and many Cuban instrumentalists boast a thorough education, often mastering several instruments as well as several genres. This eclecticism, long a characteristic of Cuban music, has even grown with the Revolution.

By the mid-1960s music in Cuba started to be recognized as an indispensable form of expression and, without being mentioned as such, as a powerful antidote to political and economic problems. Some of the bolder artists, however, complain that the egalitarian ideology curbs creativity by discouraging the development of strong individual temperaments. They also feel under pressure to come up with new rhythms at all costs in order to assuage the yearning for novelty exacerbated by Cuba's geographical and political isolation.

The explosion of rhythms

The Salón Mambi – a huge park where one could dance for hours for a minimal fee and the popular television show *Para bailar* became catalysts for many new and often ephemeral rhythms. Incidentally, while Puerto Ricans and Dominicans favor intricate leg movements, Cubans generally enjoy hip undulations, somewhat like dancers from West Africa of the Congo, although some dances do include intricate footwork as well. Among these new rhythms were the *boteo* with its syncopated beat, the *timba* created by Orquesta Kubana, the *chiquichaca*, the *shake*, the *mongolés*, the *guachipupa* the guitarist Juanito Márquez's *pa' ca'* (with *Arrímate pa' ca'*, inspired by a Venezuelan tune), the *onda areíto*[1] (a cross between *charanga* and American pop music played with trap drums, electric bass, and piano), the *wa wa*, the *guapachá* (a sort of cross between *guaracha*, cha-cha, and merengue introduced by the singer and composer Amado Barceló and developed by Chucho Valdés, Carlos Emilio Morales, and drummer Emilio del Monte); the *güiro*,[2] created in 1964 by Filiberto Depestre, a member of La Maravilla de Florida; and many amalgams such as the *guajisón* (*guajira* + *son*) or the rock-cha (rock + cha-cha), crossbreedings dubbed *zondán* (an inversion of the word *danzón*) by Enrique Jorrín.

With his dynamic group, "Pacho" (Pascasio) Alonso (1928–1982) also added to the rhythm cornucopia with the *simalé*, the *pilón* (inspired by the pounding of coffee grains in a mortar and danced with rumba-type movements), and the *upa upa*. He had sung in Santiago with Mariano Mercerón and Fernando Álvarez before moving to Havana, in 1957. He popularized songs by the Oriente-born percussionist and composer Enrique Bonne and wrote the hits *Rico pilón*, *El upa upa*, and *Cuando tú llegues a entender*. He then formed Los Modernistas, and finally Los Bocucos, a jazz-influenced ensemble featuring vocalists Ibrahím Ferrer and then Teresa García Caturla (the daughter of composer Alejandro García Caturla).

Around 1958, Orquesta Sublime had recorded several numbers by Eduardo Davidson Cuza, a young composer from Oriente who had penned *Todo en la vida pasará*. They asked him for a new song and so in 1959 he produced *La pachanga* (from a word designating a rural festivity). Fluid and lively, the *pachanga* enabled one to give in to the joy of dancing without too many intellectual worries:

1 From *onda* (wave) and *areíto*, designating the festivals organized by the Tainos before the arrival of the Spaniards.

2 Aside from the Yoruba-derived rhythm in 6/8, *güiro*, in the Cuban musicians' slang, means a party, a dance, or a gig (what Latin musicians from New York or Puerto Rico call *guiso*).

Señores que pachanga	Gentlemen what a *pachanga*
Me voy pa' la pachanga	I'm going to the *pachanga*
Que bueno la pachanga	How good the *pachanga* is
Mamita la pachanga.	Sweetheart the *pachanga.*

La Sublime recorded it in October of the same year, and although Orquesta Aragón, José Fajardo, and other bands covered *La pachanga*, La Sublime was dubbed "*La pachanguera de Cuba.*" With its pianist Santiago Barbón and its good vocalists, among them Marcos Perdomo, it went on a recording spree (*Sabroso como el guarapo, No seas tan guapo*). Roberto Faz, the Conjunto Casino, La Sonora Matancera, and other bands also started to perform *pachangas*. Fidel Castro played *La pachanga* for his speeches, but Davidson settled in New York where, five years later, he created the *bimbi* rhythm, which went practically unnnoticed. As a genre, however, the *pachanga* took root in the Big Apple. In Havana it also merged with other strains such as the *guaracha*, as in Félix Chappotín's *La guarapachanga*:[3]

La guarapachanga se puede bailar	One can dance the *guarapachanga*
La guarapachanga se puede gozar.	One can enjoy the *guarapachanga.*

Other *charangas* were stimulated by the *pachanga* craze. José Fajardo, who moved to New York in 1961, left his band to Félix Reina. Reina renamed it Estrellas Cubanas, and the group included Ulpiano Díaz, Gustavo Tamayo, singer, Luis and Edy Calzado, flautist Eddy Zervigón, and other great musicians, although Reina and Zervigón also settled in the United States shortly thereafter. Outside Havana, La Maravilla de Florida, with its irresistible swing and sophisticated arrangements, gained prominence with *Tiembla tierra*, *La cintura*, and *Rica mulata*, and the Orquesta Aliamén, inspired by the Orquesta Aragón and created in 1963 in Santa Clara by violinist Miguel Pinto Canto and singer Alí Ahmet López (nicknamed "Alimelét," hence the name of the group), also became a standard-bearer in the center of the island. In 1965 the Orquesta Aragón brought its smooth and polished sound to l'Olympia, in Paris. But eventually *charangas* declined, resurfacing in the late 1970s with the advent of the *songo*.

In 1962, inspired by Afro-Cuban traditional music, Enrique Bonne Castillo, a bandleader from San Luis, organized a huge percussion ensemble. One year later, following a similar path, singer and percussionist "Pello el Afrokán" (Pedro Izquierdo Padrón) and his brother Roberto, also a percussionist, combined the carnival *conga* with Yoruba, Abakwa, and Congo rhythms and with samba. They orchestrated this mixture with horns and up to twelve drums, and added female dancers. And, as Mozambique was then struggling for its independence, they gave their creation the name *mozambique*, thereby eliciting Fidel Castro's approval. Pello wrote several *mozambiques* (*Cuba mozambique, Como se baila el mozambique*,

3 In the 1990s, *guarapachanga* became in Havana the name of a new *guaguancó tumbao.*

El mozambique), and he also recorded *congas*. Abelardo Barroso performed the *mozambique No te agites* with Orquesta Sensación, Peruchín *Con mi ritmo* with a big band. In New York and Puerto Rico, Eddie and Charlie Palmieri, Ray Barretto, Bobby Valentín, and other musicians adopted the *mozambique*. But interesting as this rhythm was, it waned around the late 1960s. Mixed with the *pilón*, it made a comeback in the late 1990s, performed by Juan de Marcos González's Afro-Cuban All Stars as *nuevo mozambique*, and in the United States, a few other instrumentalists also sought to revive this genre.

Though the *son* took a back seat until the mid-1970s, a few bands maintained its old charm, among them the Septeto Habanero, renamed Sexteto Típico Habanero and led by Ignacio Carrillo (with vocalist Manolo Furé); and the Septeto Nacional, reorganized by Ignacio Piñeiro in 1959, with José Núñez Correa (first voice, claves), Carlos Embale (first voice, güiro), Bienvenido León (second voice, maracas), "Mañungo" (Rafael Ortiz, guitar, first voice of the *coro*), Hilario Ariza (*tres*), Charles Burque (bass), Lázaro Herrera (trumpet), and Mario Carballo (bongo). Other *son* luminaries: Cheo Marquetti, Senén Suárez, Pío Leiva, and Niño Rivera set up *conjuntos*. In 1962 in Santiago, *trovador* Daniel Castillo founded the Cuarteto Oriente. The *sucu-sucu* enjoyed a slight revival with a tune named *Sucu-sucu*, quite popular in Europe and Latin America, while the *changüí* came to the fore thanks to the ebullient *timbalero* Elio Revé.

Born in Guantánamo, cradle of the *changüí*, Revé had worked as railroad man, cowboy, sugarcane cutter, and shoeshine. He communicated his tremendous energy to his musicians. "With me, inspiration manifests itself as drum onomatopoeia," he explained. "My head is not made for the bolero," and with this percussive instinct, he gave his music an irresistible impetus. He first played along with his father – a bassist – with the Orquesta Riviera. In 1959 he founded an infectious *charanga* which progressively turned into a larger *charangón*, choosing singers with a nasal tone – called *voz fañosa* or *voz de vieja* – "old woman's voice" in Spanish – which in Cuba symbolizes the African tradition. Juan Formell, who played with him in 1968–69, introduced an electric bass and electric violins into the band. Revé also wrote several tunes, among them *Guaripumpe*, recorded by the New York *charanga* Orquesta Broadway, *La rebellión de los feos*, and *Compañeros*.

Vocal music

A few vocal groups grew out of the *filin*: the *cuarteto* Los Bucaneros, founded by singer and clarinettist Lucas de la Guardia; 65 D'Siempre, with the accomplished pianist Hilario Durán; Los Akra; and the *cuarteto* Los Zafiros. Created in 1962 by Néstor Milí Bustillo (composer of *Yerbero moderno*) Los Zafiros (Kike, Miguelito, Ignacio, and El Chino) stood out from the other Cuban groups. Influenced by R & B, doo-wop, and bossa nova, they performed, with electric guitars, a heady mix of Cuban and Brazilian numbers and calypsos.

Elena Burke and Celeste Mendoza pursued their careers: in 1960 Burke issued her first LP under her own name, under the direction of Rafael Somavilla and Adolfo Guzmán; Mendoza appeared in 1964 at the Tropicana with pianist "Felo" (Rafael) Bergaza in the show *Tentación*, in the documentaries *Nosotros la música* (also starring Elena Burke, Bola de Nieve, the Septeto Nacional, and other Cuban artists) and *Celeste Mendoza y la rumba*, and later performed at the Sierra and other Havana clubs. And the vocalist Marta Valdés cultivated rich harmonies.

The *filin* gave way to the *nueva trova*, inspired by militant folk songs from the United States and the Latin American *canción protesta*, especially vivid in Chile and Argentina. A predominantly white movement that often became a vehicle for official propaganda, the *nueva trova* had little to do, stylistically, with Afro-Cuban music, although some of its exponents, Pablo Milanés in particular, made use of both. Milanés and Silvio Rodríguez spearheaded the *nueva trova*, and the Centro de la Canción Protesta, founded in Havana by the Casa de las Américas and the old Pico Blanco club of the Saint John hotel, renamed Rincón del Feeling, became the nurseries for this musical genre. In 1963 Carlos Puebla wrote *Hasta siempre* as a tribute to Che Guevara, Milanés had a success in 1965 with *Mis veintidos años*, and Rodríguez, two years later, had hits with *La era está pariendo un corazón* and *Fusil contra fusil* (*Gun against Gun*). Sara González and Vicente Feliú also joined the ranks of the *nueva trova*. Raised in Bayamo, in Oriente, Milanés joined in 1959 the Cuarteto del Rey and then Los Bucaneros and recorded with the Grupo de Experimentación Sonora del ICAIC. Founded in 1969 and placed under the musical direction of Leo Brouwer, the Grupo de Experimentación Sonora del ICAIC (The Cuban Film Institute) developed the *nueva trova*, but also for Changuito, Chucho Valdés, Ignacio Berroa, and other musicians with jazzier leanings. It fused folk song, jazz and electronic music, made several records and provided the soundtrack for various movies.

Cuban jazz

As the Cuban government became more tolerant of music, jazz, now free from the constraints of show business, began to thrive again. Musicians, who sometimes managed to catch American jazz on the Florida radio stations or discovered records brought in from other countries, enthusiastically absorbed these new strains while searching for their own forms of expression.

The first festival of popular Cuban music, held in Havana in 1961, consecrated the era of combos. Exchange of ideas was fostered by the Sunday jam sessions held in the early 1960s at the club Mil Novecientos, late in the decade at the Tropicana and at the Copa Room of the Riviera hotel, and subsequently at the Jazz Plaza Festival launched by Bobby Carcassés which featured foreign artists. Those jam sessions attracted both experienced musicians (Felo Bergaza, Rafael

Somavilla, Armando Romeu, Felipe Dulzaides, and Pucho Escalante among them) and young and upcoming talent including trombonist Juan Pablo Torres, drummer Blas Egües, pianist Emiliano Salvador, saxophonist Paquito D'Rivera, and guitarist Cotán. When Julio Cortázar – a jazz fan – visited Havana in the 1960s, he was struck by the vitality of the local music, and he described in his novel *Rayuela* a *descarga* organized for him on the spur of the moment . . . in a dogs' clinic!

In 1955, the bassist "Cachaíto" (Orlando López), Cachao's nephew, formed a jazz group which included Walfredo de los Reyes and then Guillermo Barreto on drums. De los Reyes, who had studied music in the United States, experimented by playing trap drums and Cuban percussion at the same time. He worked with some of the major names in Cuba and also accompanied visiting American jazzmen, later forming his own band.

In 1959 Guillermo Barreto, one of Cuba's most accomplished drummers and *timbaleros*, founded the Quinteto Instrumental de Música Moderna, a Cuban jazz ensemble which became one of the most stimulating groups of that era. Its members Frank Emilio Flynn (piano), Tata Güines (conga), Gustavo Tamayo (güiro), and "Papito" (Orlando) Hernández and then Cachaíto (bass) had long been bound by strong professional and friendly ties. With the Quinteto, Cachaíto invented highly syncopated bass lines that departed from the conventional *tumbaos* of dance music. A superb composer and arranger and one of the best bassists in Cuba, he had studied with his father Orestes López, his uncle Cachao, and Czechoslovakian masters. At thirteen he played with René Hernández's *charanga* Armonía and then with Arcaño and other *charangas*, the Orquesta Riverside, Los Hermanos Lebatard, Charles Rodríguez, and the Havana Cuban Boys. Born in Güines in 1930, hence his nickname, "Tata Güines" (Federico Arístides Soto) – a founding father of the new Cuban percussion – had worked with Fajardo and Chico O'Farrill and, in New York, with Dizzy Gillespie and Maynard Ferguson. He employed a stunning variety of techniques: mallets, fingertips, nails, enabling him to draw unusual sounds from his drums.

This tight and vibrant group introduced bold and ingenious ideas. In a Cuban movie shot during that era, it performed *Mondongo, sandunga, gandinga*, a number based on a *tumbao* with accents falling on different beats of each bar, which became a *descarga* standard:

Capable of playing anything from *danzones* to jazz with equal ease, Frank Emilio Flynn maintained this *tumbao* with his left hand while he improvised with the right. A well-rounded pianist, blind since the age of thirteen, Flynn (1921–2001)

also performed on the album *Pianoforte* (1966), featuring Adolfo Guzmán and Peruchín, where he expresses himself with subtle impressionistic touches. In addition, Emilio, Barreto, Güines, and Gustavo Tamayo worked with the quintet Los Amigos – an offshoot of the Quinteto founded by Cachaíto (*Quiéreme mucho, Soledad*), and with which Merceditas Valdés occasionally sang. The broad range of Los Amigos (*danzón, bossa nova*, jazz, etc.) testified to the growing diversification of Cuban jazz.

The pianist Rubén González, the trumpeter Luis Escalante, and the *conguero* Oscar Valdés belonged to the Grupo Cubano de Jazz – a similar type of outfit, which performed jazz and other rhythms with a *clave* feel (*Cha Cha Twist, Blues en E bemol*). Juanito Márquez founded a quartet featuring the ubiquitous Guillermo Barreto, as well as Rafael Somavilla on piano and Nilo Argudín on trumpet; and Changuito and pianist Rembert Egües played with an experimental group called Sonorama Seis.

In 1966, some members of the newly founded orchestra of the Instituto Cubano de Radiodifusión, and musicians of the Tropicana, among them Márquez, Barreto, and Tata Güines, gathered under the name Combo Siboney for some studio sessions. But their *descargas*, maybe hastily recorded (*Pamparana, A gozar con el combo*), did not quite come up to the level of the Quinteto Instrumental de Música Cubana.

The following year, Barreto started the Orquesta Cubana de Música Moderna – a twenty-five-strong ensemble which would have a lasting influence upon the new Cuban jazz. He rounded up some of his most adventurous colleagues, among them Cachaíto (bass), Luis Escalante and Leonardo Timor (trumpets), Luis's brother Leopoldo (trombone), "Chucho" (Jesús) Valdés (piano), "Paquito" (Francisco) D'Rivera (saxophone) and, later, Arturo Sandoval (trumpet); and he entrusted the Orquesta's musical direction to Armando Romeu. Romeu, who had been leading the Tropicana ensemble for twenty-five years, was one of the foremost saxophonists in Cuba. Tony Taño then succeeded him. The band performed jazz, rock, pop, and Afro-Cuban music (*Invocación a Eleguá y a Changó*); it accompanied many singers, Elena Burke among them, and soundtracked most of the Cuban movies produced in the late 1960s and early 1970s.

the United States and Puerto Rico

Ponte duro cubano
Que tu estás en Nueva York.
A este pais llegué yo
cuando mi Cuba dejé.

Get tough, Cuban,
You are in New York
I arrived in this country
When I left my Cuba.

(*Un cubano en Nueva York*, J. Aparicio and M. Sánchez)

The pachanga *and the boogaloo era*

The *pachanga*

The groovy *pachanga*, which had arrived in New York during the summer of 1960, ousted the cha-cha. That year, Rolando Laserie, backed by Bebo Valdés's band, scored a major hit with his cover of *La pachanga*, and all the town's Latin bands – Machito, Rafael Cortijo, the Sexteto La Plata, Tito Rodríguez, Johnny Pacheco ("*pachanga*, quipped Pacheco's admirers, is a cross between Pacheco and *charanga*") – hastened to play it. Fajardo recorded *Mister Pachanga*, Belisario López *Sucu sucu y pachanga*, Puerto Rican pianist Hector Rivera *¡Charanga & pachanga!*, Mongo Santamaría *¡Arriba la pachanga!*, Xiomara Alfaro *Pachanga* *en la sociedad*, Arsenio Rodríguez *Sabor de pachanga*, Tito Puente *Pachanga con Tito Puente*, Charlie Palmieri *Pachanga at the Caravana Club*, Ray Barretto *Pachanga with Barretto*.

The great mambo dancers Joe Vega, "Killer Joe" Piro, Pedro Aguilar, Ernie Ernsley, James Evans, and Felo Brito also converted to the *pachanga*. Machito, Graciela, and Tito Puente introduced this dance into Japan. And later, in Colombia, Fruko recorded a string of *pachangas* (*La pachanga del fútbol, La pachanga se baila así*).

The battle of the Titos

Tito Puente continued to record abundantly, producing *El güiro de Macorina, Para la quimbombó* (sung by Rolando Laserie), *Babarabatiri, Mambo Inn*. He invited Machito on *Puente on the Bridge*, and wrote several hits: *Caramelos* – "girls" in New York's Puerto Rican slang (featured on *Pachanga con Puente*), the sparkling *Kwá-kwá*, the cha-cha *Oye como va*, recalling Cachao's *Chancullo* and recorded in 1962 with "Pupi" (Félix) Legarreta, Johnny Pacheco, and Santos Colón. In 1971, Carlos Santana's cover of *Oye como va* (on *Abraxas*) would become a huge hit.

Tito Rodríguez's fame soared in the early 1960s and he became a star throughout Latin America. His voice had gained power and at the Palladium – always demanding the best from his musicians – he delighted dancers with *El monito y la jirafa, Vuela la paloma, Cara de payaso* or *Mama güela*. Recorded ten years earlier as *Mambo Mona, Mama güela* came from the old type *mama 'buela* (grandmother) rumba. In a different vein, with Tito Henríquez's splendid bolero *Bello amanecer* ("Beautiful sunrise") he exalted the beauty of his native Puerto Rico:

Que lindo cuando el sol de madrugada
Desgarra el negro manto de la noche,
Dejando ver su luz desparramada
En un bello amanecer que es un derroche,
Un derroche de luz y de poesía,
Un concierto de sol en la mañana.
Que bonitas son las noches de mi islita
Y que bello amanecer el de mi patria.

Orgulloso me siento una y mil veces
Y agradezco al Señor que permitiera
Haber nacido en esta tierra tan hermosa,
En esta tierra donde mis ojos
Vieron la luz por primera vez.

How pretty when the early morning sun
Takes off the black mantle of the night;
Spreading its light
In a beautiful and lavish dawn,
Lavish with light and poetry,
A concert of sun in the morning.
How pretty are the nights of my little island
And how beautiful the daybreak in my
    homeland.
I feel a thousand times proud
And thankful to the Lord for having let me
Be born in such a marvellous land.
This land where my eyes
First saw the light.

Tito Rodríguez and his orchestra. Artol Records

In 1962, after highly successful performances in Puerto Rico, tension flared up between Rodríguez and Puente. The catchy *Él que se fue* ("The one who went away," recorded on *Tito Rodríguez Returns to the Palladium* and *Palladium Memories*) and supposedly sung for a musician who had left the band, contains the refrain:

Él que se fue no hace falta	The one who went away isn't missed
A mí no me importas tú	I don't care about you
Ni veinte como tú	Nor about twenty like you
Yo sigo siempre en el goce	I keep enjoying myself
Él del ritmo no eras tú.	The one who had rhythm wasn't you,

thought to be a gibe at Puente. *Tito Rodríguez Returns to the Palladium* also included *Yambú* – a *rumba brava* recorded by Machito in 1941. Rodríguez turned it into a *guaguancó* with mambo riffs, but keeping the traditional *yambú* refrain: *Ave María morena*.

Rodríguez challenged Puente again with a record entitled *Tito No. 1*. And on *Carnival of the Americas*, he turned *¿Dónde estabas anoche?*, written by Ignacio Piñeiro for Los Roncos, into a defiant *rumba* in which the words "*avísale a mi vecino*" ("let my neighbor know") became "*avísale a mi contrario*" ("let my adversary know"). Puente replied with the mordant "*Cuando me veas llegar, échate pa'lla, tú ves que no somos iguales*" ("When you see me come, get lost, you see we are not equal"). *Carnival of the Americas*, one of Rodríguez's best albums, also featured the proud *mambo-cha Sacando candela*.

In 1963, he broke up his orchestra and settled in Puerto Rico, where he hosted on television *El show de Tito Rodríguez*, later resuming his performances in the United States. He recorded with Noro Morales, the La Playa Sextet, the Los Hispanos quartet, Louie Ramírez, and others. With the help of such prestigious sidemen as René Hernández, Eddie Palmieri, Cachao (who fires up *Descarga Cachao* on *Tito, Tito, Tito*), Marcelino Valdés, Dominican saxophonist Mario Rivera, and Panamanian trumpeter Victor Paz, he offered various styles: cha-cha (*El piragüero*[1]), Panamanian *tamborito* (*La pollera colorá*), *pachanga* (on *Tito Rodríguez In Puerto Azul*), Cuban numbers (*Bilongo, Tremendo cumbán*, on which he played vibes) or American numbers (*Harlem Nightmare*). Audiences especially loved his atmospheric boleros: Julio Gutiérrez's *Inolvidable*, already recorded by René Cabel, or *Un cigarrillo, la lluvia y tú*, backed by the Leroy Holmes orchestra. In 1973 after recording songs by Rafael Hernández and giving a gripping concert at Madison Square Garden, backed by the Afro-Cubans, he died of leukaemia, a disease which he had long fought against.

The Cuban artists

In 1963, back in New York after a stay in Mexico, Miguelito Valdés recorded *Reunion with Miguelito Valdés* with the Afro-Cubans, which alluded to the rivalry between Tito Puente and Tito Rodríguez, and *Tremendo cumbán*. Later, with Puente's orchestra, he sang on the racy two-disc record *Canciones mi mamá no me enseñó – Spanish Songs Mama Never Taught Me* also featuring the Joe Cuba Sextet, Graciela, and Machito's orchestra. He performed the *guaguancó Juanita saca la mano* with Graciela, the *pregón Atesa el bastidor*, and *La pintura blanca*. He also collaborated with a run of musicians, among them Noro Morales (*Zambele, Se formó el rumbón*), La Sonora Matancera, Orquesta Aragón, Mariano Mercerón, Antonio Arcaño, Belisario López, José Fajardo, the Sonora Mexicana, Chico O'Farrill (on *Married Well*, a sung version of *Manteca*), and Armando Oréfiche; in *Miguelito canta a Panamá*, he paid a tribute to that country, which he particularly loved. He died in 1978 while performing at a hotel in Bogotá.

In 1964 René Hernández wrote *Zambia* for the Afro-Cubans, to celebrate this African country's independence, and two years later, having left them, he collaborated with Tito Rodríguez. He also worked with Stan Kenton, Herbie Mann, La Lupe, and other artists, cut the excellent *Cha Cha Latino* (featuring Mongo Santamaría) and led bands that often backed singers.

Arsenio Rodríguez continued to record, often with Cándido Antomattei on vocals, such titles as *La yuca de Catalina, Adiós Roncona, Yo nací del Africa* – evoking Afro-Cuban culture; the zany songs *Maldita droga, Necesito una mujer cocinera*, and *Quiero mucho a mi suegra*; the *son montuno No importa la distancia*, and the bolero *Comprendo que sufres*, dealing with wounded love. He also played *tres* on *Patato y Totico* and took part in the Alegre All Stars *descargas*. In 1962 he issued the great *Cumbanchando With Arsenio*, and the following year *Quindembo – Afro Magic*, and while Miguelito Cuní also happened to be in New York, he played a few dates with him, but the overall quality of his output gradually declined (he even covered something as far from his aesthetics as *Hang on Snoopy*), and he fell into oblivion.

1 Street vendor of *piraguas*, crushed ice cones flavoured with syrup.

Other Cuban musicians who had arrived in New York after the Revolution, including La Sonora Matancera, "Papaíto," Lázaro Prieto, *rumberos* "Totico" (Eugenio Arango) and "Virgilio" (Enrique) Martí, stirred the interest in traditional Cuban genres. Martí performed with the Afro-Cubans. A consummate *rumbero*, Totico recorded the wonderful *Patato y Totico* (1963) with among others Patato Valdés, Arsenio Rodríguez, Cachao, and Papaíto, ranging from rumba (*Agua que va caer*) to Abakwa music (*Rezo abacuá*) and bossa nova (*Más que nada²*). Julio Collazo introduced consecrated *batá* drums in New York and initiated local musicians into *santería* rhythms.

The new Puerto Rican bandleaders

A new and energetic generation of Puerto Rican bandleaders also came to the fore in the Big Apple, producing music that bore their own stamp. Among them pianist Eddie Palmieri, who shared his elder brother Charlie's taste for Cuban music but also professed his love for jazz. A true *masacotero* (from the word *masacote*, designating both a conga technique and improvisations on a vamp), he played robust and steady *montunos*, and solos full of tone clusters and rhythm displacements.

Born in New York in 1936, he grew up first in East Harlem and then in the South Bronx, at a time when Puerto Ricans were beginning to replace Jews and Italians there. The South Bronx was then a bustling neighborhood full of Latin and jazz clubs, far from the symbol of urban decay it would later become. Charlie and Eddie's father made his sons listen to the great Cuban pianists. As a child Eddie gave a recital at Carnegie Hall. At thirteen he organized a group with his friend Orlando Marín and then played timbales with his uncle, guitarist "Chino" Gueits, and piano with Johnny Seguí y sus Dandys. Health reasons forced him to give up the timbales, yet his energy still ran high: two years later, Seguí dismissed him for breaking the piano keys in a club by pounding too eagerly on them. Undaunted, Palmieri joined trumpeter Ray Almo's quintet. From 1956 to 1958 he succeeded his brother Charlie in Vicentico Valdés's band, and then worked with Tito Rodríguez.

In 1962 he organized a fiery and personal *charanga* that had a typical New York flavor. His first recordings – *El molestoso*, which included *pachangas*, mambos, a *guaguancó*, a *danzón-cha*, and other tunes, and *Echando pa' lante* (*Movin' Ahead*, in Puerto Rican slang), *Tu tu ta ta*, *Azúcar pa' tí*, with *Oyelo que te conviene* – galvanized the young Latinos, who identified with his impetuous music. Mon Rivera had used American trombonist Barry Rogers on his album *Mon and his Trombones*. Following his example, Palmieri replaced his trumpets by two trombones, giving his band a sound with more muscle. He recruited Rogers, Manny Oquendo, and singers Joe Quijano and Ismael Quintana, and called his new group La Perfecta. His brother Charlie dubbed it a "*trombanga*" (trombone + *charanga*) because, he explained with humor, "it is a *charanga* in which the

2 An adaptation of the Brazilian standard *Mais que nada*.

trombones have replaced the violins." With its unusual flute–two-trombones–rhythm section and singer combination, the band stood apart from some of the better-known groups. Oquendo remembers their struggles to achieve recognition: "La Perfecta was competing with all the other bands at the Palladium and was going through hard times. I'm talking about orchestras with some fifteen musicians, while La Perfecta was a small *conjunto*. But our music and the way we played was different. We were more relaxed, freer." In 1965 Palmieri introduced the *mozambique* in New York with a *comparsa* number, *Camagüeyanos y habaneros*, featuring Ismael Quintana on vocals and Manny Oquendo on timbales. *Yo sin tú, Muñeca*, and the lively *Bonbonsito de coco* elicited enthusiasm. With Cheo Feliciano and Cachao, Palmieri issued in 1968 *Champagne*, continuing, with *Delirio*, Marcelino Guerra's *Busca lo tuyo*, and Arsenio Rodríguez's *Si las nenas me dejan, que*, to show his love for Cuban music, but done here with a new urban twist.

Other Puerto Ricans, the *timbalero* Orlando Marín and the percussionist and singer "Kako" (Francisco) Bastar among them, produced fine recordings. Born in New York, Marín had grown up listening to jazz. He debuted with a guitar trio, joined Chino Gueits y sus Almas Tropicales, and in 1953 formed a group which included singers Joe Quijano (then known as José Baya), followed by "Mandín" (Amado) Vega. His septet later included pianist Paquito Pastor, flautist Bobby Nelson, and vocalist Victor Velázquez, and Francisco Fellové, who scatted in Spanish. Marín recorded lively albums, among them *Que chévere* (with vocalists Elliot Romero, Chivirico Dávila, and Cheo Feliciano, plus Willie Torres), and especially *Se te quemó la casa* (with Julio Andino on bass, Paquito Pastor on piano, and Chivirico Dávila on vocals), and on *Ritmo bembé*, flirted with Yoruba music. Bastar, who had first been a dancer in San Juan before working with Arsenio Rodríguez, Mongo Santamaría, and Machito, successfully combined Cuban and Puerto Rican strains in his powerful *conjunto*.

The Alegre All Stars

The Puerto Rican pianist, composer, and arranger Al Santiago, owner of the Casa Alegre record store in the South Bronx, had formed the Alegre label. At the age of eighteen, he had led an ensemble with the improbable name of Chack-a-Ñuñu Boys (an onomatopoeia inspired by the sound of a Latin rhythm section). He set up a studio band, the Alegre All Stars, and in 1961 got the idea of recording *descargas* from the Panart *descargas* and from the jam sessions regularly held at the Triton, the famed club located on Southern Boulevard, not far from his store, where the young Eddie Palmieri had broken the piano keys. Mongo Santamaría, the vibist Oscar García, the singer Chivirico Dávila, just about everybody in the Latin community worked or sat in there and many of the musicians Santiago recruited were *habitués*. Chombo Silva, Kako Bastar, the bassist Bobby Rodríguez, the singers Felo Brito, Willie Torres, Elliot Romero, Yayo El Indio, and "Dioris" (Isidro) Valladares, and Charlie Palmieri and percussionist Frankie Malabé became some of the core members of these All Stars. The group made a series of exuberant albums. "Who's missing?" one of the musicians on volume III asks. "Pablo Casals!" someone else answers facetiously. This particular session, directed by Charlie Palmieri, included a *guaguancó* sung by Cheo Feliciano that went through different rhythms (*Sono sono*), the bolero *Tú has vuelto*, sung by Yayo el Indio, and several *descargas*, notably *Yumbambe* (already recorded by Joe Loco fifteen years before). And the Alegre All Stars paved the way for salsa.

The boogaloo

The closing down of the Palladium Ballroom, in 1966, marked the end of a glamorous era of Latin music and of big bands. Clubs such as the Manhattan Center, the Colgate Gardens, the Caravana, the Psycho Room, La Barraca, the Tropicana, Chez José, the Hunts Point Place, most of them located in the *barrios*, attracted a predominantly Puerto Rican clientele.

The rise of rock n' roll and of English pop also struck a blow to Latin music. "*Ahora un nuevo ritmo apareció, y es el inquietante rock n' roll*" ("Now a new rhythm has appeared, and it's the unsettling rock n' roll"), sang Celia Cruz with La Sonora Matancera. Large ensembles vanished, Latin record companies folded and, in New York as in Puerto Rico, musicians and singers went through lean times. The Afro-Cubans only survived with great difficulty, Machito often paying his musicians out of his own pocket.

The severance of the diplomatic ties between the United States and Cuba deprived the Latin musicians from New York of one of their principal sources of inspiration. Gradually, they turned to soul music and adopted English lyrics. Bassist Louie Colón, who grew up in New York during the 1960s, recalls he first listened to Little Anthony and the Imperials, The Drifters, Smokey Robinson, The Black Boys, and The Beatles before discovering Latin rhythms.

The United States were then going through a state of turmoil. Liberals protested against the Vietnam war, and hippies and ethnic minorities rejected the puritanical values of the white establishment. With the Bay of Pigs incident in 1961, the Cuban missile crisis in 1962, and the continuation of the Cold War, the world seemed poised on the edge of a cataclysm. Afro-American activism had risen since the Montgomery, Alabama, bus boycott in 1956 and Martin Luther King's campaigns. The Young Lords, led by Felipe Luciano, emerged as the Puerto Rican answer to the Black Panthers. Charles Mingus, Ornette Coleman, and Archie Shepp expressed, with their sometimes vehement jazz, the anger and frustrations of African Americans. The zingy boogaloo (the name was perhaps derived from boogie), shing-a-ling and Latin soul, emblematic of a new generation of bicultural Latinos reared in the New York *barrios*, were born in this electrical atmosphere, though they were essentially happy and carefree genres.

The *charanga* Orquesta Broadway recorded *I Dig Rock n' Roll Music*. Pérez Prado, then living in Hollywood, adopted the twist and composed some *rockambos* (mixtures of rock and mambo). The Afro-Cubans' output reflected the general trend towards Anglo music (*I Can't Get No Satisfaction, In the Midnight Hour*), although Graciela also recorded albums of boleros, and she and Machito took part (along with Joe Cuba, Miguelito Valdés, and Tito Puente) in the very Latin *Spanish Songs Mama Never Taught Me* and *More Spanish Songs Mama Never Taught Me*. True to her Cuban self, Graciela sang with Machito the bawdy *Sí sí no no* and *No voy más contigo al cine* (I'm not going to the movies with you any more).

Somewhat clumsy but extroverted hybrids such as the boogaloo (or *bugalú*), followed by the shing-a-ling (invented by Johnny López and exemplified by Joey Pastrana's *Let's Ball*), the *jala jala*, inspired by an old *comparsa* tune, and the afroloo, emerged. These dances, which took Latinos by storm, recalled the exuberant stylings of a Fats Domino or of other R&B musicians from Louisiana. The unpretentious lyrics (as with The Hi Latins' *To the Bush Ah-Ah* or Joe Cuba's *Bang! Bang!*) expressed the energy and pugnaciousness of the streets. Salsa was already in the air. The boogaloo completedly displaced the *pachanga*, and in 1968, a worried Bobby Rodríguez expressed his fears in the newly created *Latin New York* magazine: "If the current trend continues in today's swinging social set, we will soon have nothing but our old 78s and LPs to hear and remember the original, or '*típico*' Latin rhythms. Just as Birdland, The Home of Jazz, died because of the Discotheques, jazz is quietly but valiantly fighting mambo and cha-cha, and is being completely overwhelmed by today's *Boogaloo*."

Simplistic as they were, the boogaloo and the shing-a-ling nevertheless constituted a good antidote to the hard life of the *barrio*, where drugs, poverty, and violence had turned the American dream into a nightmare. But while Afro-American music sometimes had a vindictive edge, even in the most realistic Latin songs, humor and exultation usually tempered despair. In the most run-down *barrios*, someone would bring out one or two congas, maybe a horn, and a *descarga* began. When a gang member died after a feud,[3] an altar with *santería* gods was set up in the streets and music was played to honor him and rejoice his soul. In vacant lots or on Orchard Beach, the Puerto Rican beach of the Bronx, people danced, roasted *lechones* (suckling pigs), cooked *bacalaítos* (codfish fritters), or played dominoes to recapture some of the warmth of the native land – traditions which still endure.

Charlie Palmieri (*Latin Bugalú*), Ray Barretto (*Boogaloo con soul*), Bobby Quesada (*Boogaloo en el Barrio*), Monguito Santamaría (*Boogaloo sabroso*), Bobby Valentín (*Batman's Boogaloo*), Arsenio Rodríguez, El Gran Combo: everyone gave in to the boogaloo. Even Puente, albeit grudgingly, persuaded by his producer. Héctor Rivera (*At the Party*), Richie Ray (*Colombia's Boogaloo*), the *barrio*-born multi-instrumentalist Johnny Colón (*Boogaloo Blues*), and Pete Rodríguez (*Micaela, I Like It Like That*) became its leaders. *Micaela*, a *son montuno* with Spanish lyrics (*Mira Micaela como baila el bugalú* – "Look at Micaela how she dances the

3 According to the law of the street, the police were often not called.

boogaloo") was interspersed with calls in English: "You want more?," with an enthusiastic "yeah!" for an answer. Proclaimed "king of the boogaloo," Pete Rodríguez recounted in *Latin New York* the genesis of this rhythm: "the name boogaloo is part Latin, part rock and roll, and part rhythm and blues, and it all began when we were asked to write some background music for two Harlem promoters . . . In combining the Latin sound with the request of the promoters, to include the blues beat sound, from that moment on a certain excitement began to occur. We began to experiment with our new discovery at the Sunday night Palm Garden dances . . . and when our hit *I Like It Like That* clicked we knew we were on our way. This was the turning point for our group."

Pete Rodríguez's assertion notwithstanding, the boogaloo probably was more of a collective invention, for other bandleaders also borrowed from blues and soul music. Like several of his peers, however, Rodríguez did not forsake his roots. He went from patriotic songs in Spanish: *Borinquen, Vamos a unirnos* ("We're going to unite") to more frivolous numbers in English (*Do the Boogaloo*), and most of his albums – *I Like It Like That/A Mí Me Gusta Así*, for one – had bilingual titles. *At Last* (1964) also included a merengue, *Hasta el amanecer*, before the merengue tidal wave of the late 1970s. The bilingualism of the boogaloo reflected the reality of New York Latinos, torn between sometimes conflicting values and searching for their own identity.

The charismatic Joe Cuba quickly became the emblem of the boogaloo generation with his *timbalero* and singer Jimmy Sabater, also born in the Barrio and a La Playa Sextet alumnus, and the still unknown Cheo Feliciano, who had come highly recommended by Tito Rodríguez. Because of Feliciano's strong Spanish accent, Sabater sang the English numbers, and his husky voice did wonders on boleros (the hit *To Be With You, Don't Forget*). Influenced by jazz – by George Shearing especially, who often used vibists in his bands, and by the xylophone and marimba of Xavier Cugat's orchestra – Cuba also popularized the vibes in New York's Latin music. And his vibists: Felipe Díaz and Tommy Berrios, often played *guajeos* along with the piano.

Joe Cuba. Joe Cuba collection

In the early 1960s, Cuba recorded the lively *Como rien* and *Cachondea*, and funny numbers on *Spanish Songs Mama Never Taught Me* (*Cuchifritos, Préstame la olla Teresa*). He continued with *Digging the Most*, like Orquesta Broadway using the word "dig." It included the *guaguancó Ariñara*, Tito Puente's cha-cha *Aprieta* and Sabater's *pachanga La la pa. Hangin' Out – Vagabundeando* (using a Hammond organ), and *Bustin' Out* also employed slang. But despite the title *Bustin' Out*, the members of the band sported dapper suits on the album cover. Hippy fashion had not quite contaminated musicians yet.

In 1966 Cuba triumphed with *El pito* ("The whistle"), a boogaloo punctuated by whistle-blowing, with Spanish lyrics alternating with an English refrain borrowed from Dizzy Gillespie's *Salt Peanuts*:

Así se goza (bis) (*coro*)	This is how we enjoy ourselves (bis)
Y es que la rumba es sabrosa	(*coro*)
(lead) . . .	And the rumba is lively (lead) . . .
I'll never go back to Georgia (bis).	I'll never go back to Georgia (bis).

Other hits followed with the riotous *Yeah Yeah*, as well as *Bang! Bang!*, which rode to the top of the American charts in 1967 and drove dancers wild, *Push Push Push*, and the beautiful *Alafia*. The cover of *Bang!Bang! Push, Push, Push* highlighting the words *Wanted, Dead or Alive* and presenting the members of the band as gangsters, would inspire Willie Colón for his first albums (*Wanted* in particular). *El alma del Barrio* evoked Puerto Rico with *Guaguancó del jibarito* and *La fuga pa'l monte*.[4] Modulating to other registers, Cuba dealt with urban violence in *La calle está durísima* and, in *El ratón* written and sung by Cheo Feliciano, with the legendary philandering of the Latin male:

Mi gato se está quejando	My cat complains
Que no puede vacilar	That he can't fool around:
Si dondequiera que se mete	Wherever he goes
Su gata lo va a buscar.	His mate comes and gets him.
De noche brinca la verja	At night he jumps over the gate
Que está detrás de mi casa	Which is behind my house
A ver si puede fugarse	To see if he can run away
Sin que ella lo pueda ver.	Without her noticing him.

Another boogaloo star, Puerto Rican pianist "Richie Ray" (Ricardo Maldonado) had organized at the age of twelve a band with singer Bobby Cruz, who would remain his lifelong partner; he studied at the Juilliard School of Music, and in 1963 founded an octet. Ray hired the gifted *bongocero* and cowbell-player "Manolito" (Manuel González), and produced tunes with tinges of jazz and classical music that also reflected the hybrid nature of the Latin music of that era: *Jala jala*, with soul accents, recalling Myriam Makeba's *Pata Pata*;

4 A mountainous region of the interior, the *monte* served as a refuge in older times for runaway slaves. In Puerto Rico as in Cuba, it symbolizes the inalienable refuge or sanctuary, the sacred land of the Gods, the maternal womb, and the cradle of tradition.

Guaguancó in jazz, on *Se soltó Ricardo Ray*, which also included a *Danzón bugaloo*, a *Suite Noro Morales*, *Yare Changó*, and a more American *Lookie Lookie*. *Viva Ricardo Ray* offered a *guajira*-blues, and a soulful *El mulato*. And like other Cuban and Puerto Rican musicians (Tito Puente with *Samba de una sola nota*[5] and *Desafinado*, the Tico All Stars with *Barquinho*, Tito Rodríguez with *Charanga con bossa nova*), Ray adopted the bossa nova, just imported from Brazil (*Gentle Rain*). He also performed a Latin rendition of Bud Powell's *Parisian Thoroughfare*, and achieved success with *Mr. Trumpet Man* and the Puerto Rican classic *Bomba camará*.

The music of "Joe Bataan" (Peter Nitrollano Jr.), a young Harlem-born Afro-Filipino singer, also exemplified the period of transition between the 1950s and the advent of salsa. A former gang member, Bataan had served a five-year jail term for car robbery. He made various records with powerful English titles, crackling with the electricity of the *barrio*: *Riot*, *Subway Joe*, *Poor Boy*, *Saint Latin's Day Massacre*, and in 1967 scored a hit with *Gypsy Woman*. Bataan later favored Spanish titles, just as terse but mellower (*Afrofilipino*).

Riding on the boogaloo and the shing-a-ling wave, a host of small groups sprang up, also oscillating between Spanish and English; many of them, however, were short-lived. Among the new ensembles The Latinaires (*Afro-Shingaling*), George Rodríguez's New Swing Sextet (*Revolucionando*), the Lat'Teens (*Buena Gente*), the TNT Boys, and those of guitarist King Nando (*Shing a Ling*), singer Ralfi Pagán (*Make It with You*), drummer Joey Pastrana (*Parker's Mood, Let's Ball*), Félix Acosta (*Harlem, USA*), Willie Pastrana, Chicky Pérez, Juanucho López, Randy Carlos, Rudy Macías, Ralph Robles (*Ralph Robles Was Here*), Cándido Rodríguez, Mario Ortiz, "El Yucateco" (Frank Sánchez), Mike García, pianist Gil Suárez's Hi Latins (with Orestes Vilató and Pete Bonnet).

The birth of Fania

Several record labels contributed to the emergence of the new Latin music including Seeco, Cariño, and especially Fania, founded in 1964 by the Italian American lawyer Jerry Masucci with Johnny Pacheco as musical director. Fania gradually bought other labels, including Tico and Alegre, and obtained a virtual monopoly of salsa. The name *Fania*, derived from a former *son* of Congo inspiration by Reinaldo Bolaños recorded by Estrellas de Chocolate on *Guaguancó a todos los barrios* and covered by Johnny Pacheco on *Con su nuevo tumbao*.

Fania organized at The Red Garter, in the Village, *descargas* featuring Bobby Valentín, Ray Barretto, Jimmy Sabater, Ismael Miranda, Pete Rodríguez, and other stars that would eventually result in the formation of the Fania All Stars. In May 1966, Tico recorded a series of jam sessions at the Village Gate with notably Joe Cuba, Cándido Camero, Eddie Palmieri, Tito Puente, and Pacheco. The album included Charlie Palmieri's *Cargas y descargas*. Tico and Alegre also produced a memorable evening at Carnegie Hall with Tito Puente, La Lupe, Ismael Rivera,

5 From: Antonio Carlos Jobim's *Samba de uma nota so*.

Charlie Palmieri, Joe Cuba, and Vicentico Valdés, and with their mixture of musical genres and nationalities and their exuberance, these *descargas* paved the way for salsa.

One of the first artists to sign up with Fania was the pianist "Larry Harlow" (Ira Kahn). The son of Buddy Harlow, who led a Latin band for twenty years, the Brooklyn-born Larry was strongly influenced by Cuban music, and Larry's brother Andy also made a career in salsa. Larry had heard Arsenio Rodríguez on various occasions at the Palladium Ballroom and while in college spent two decisive years in Havana. In 1975, he would even convert to *santería*. After working with Tito Rodríguez and Johnny Pacheco, he founded in 1965 the Orquesta Harlow, with Felo Brito (Fajardo's dancer and vocalist) and then Ismael Miranda (a Joe Pastrana alumnus) on vocals; the group featured a two-trumpet and two-trombone line-up. He recorded *Gettin' Off*, *Heavy Smoking*, and *Me and My Monkey* for Fania, achieving recognition with *El malecón* and *Jóvenes del muelle*.

Ray (Raymond) Barretto also did wonders for the fledgling Fania label, bringing them their first crossover hits. Barretto's career has almost always straddled salsa and jazz. Born in Brooklyn in 1929 in a Puerto Rican family, he grew up listening to jazz on the radio, and upon discovering the records of Chano Pozo with Dizzy Gillespie while stationed in Germany with the U.S. Army, he decided to become a *conguero*. Back in New York, he attended jam sessions in Harlem, and played with Charlie Parker, Roy Haynes and many other bebop stalwarts.

In 1961 Barretto founded the *charanga* La Moderna, recording *Pachanga with Barretto*, followed by *Latino*, featuring Chombo Silva and El Negro Vivar, which included the hit *Cocinando*, and *Charanga moderna*. Proud of his Puerto Rican identity, Barretto produced strong and driving music symbolizing for New York's young Latinos the richness and vibrancy of their own culture. In 1967 he added horns, eventually turning his band into a *conjunto*, but keeping the *timbales*, played by Orestes Vilató. Turning to soul music in keeping with the times, he struck gold with *El watusi* (on *Charanga Moderna* and *Bitter Acid*, which featured Panamanian saxophonist Mauricio Smith).

A burly *mulato*, the song's hero El Watusi was the terror of the *solar*, and everyone ran away whenever he appeared. *Acid* (1967), Barretto's first album for Fania, evoking hippy lore and including songs in both Spanish and English, among them the driving *The Soul Drummers*, also achieved success.

The vibist, *timbalero*, pianist, and arranger Louie Ramírez (1938–1993) was another important figure of that era with his Conjunto Changó (with vocalist Pete Bonnet, Charlie Palmieri, Pete Terrace, and Joe Cuba). Of Cuban and Puerto Rican descent, Ramírez had been, in his formative years, influenced by Noro Morales. He had started on vibes with his uncle Joe Loco and recorded with the Latin Jazz Quintet and with Sabú Martínez. For Johnny Pacheco, Ramírez arranged *El güiro de Macorina*, which boosted his career, and he later became one of salsa's top musicians and arrangers.

Emergence of charangas

Stimulated by the *pachanga* vogue and by the arrival in New York, after the Revolution, of Cuban *charanga* musicians, *charangas* blossomed and acquiring a nervier edge than in Cuba. In 1961 Joe Loco recorded tunes still marked by the cha-cha era (*La pachanga, Mi china, Besos de caramelos*) with a *charanga* comprising José Lozano (flute), Chombo Silva, "Pupi" (Félix) Legarreta, and Gonzalo Martínez (violins), Victor Venegas (bass), "Willie Bobo" (William Correa) on timbales, Nicolás Martínez (güiro), and Bayardo Velarde and Rudy Calzado (vocals). And, hiring musicians from Armando Sánchez's Orquesta Nuevo Ritmo, Mongo Santamaría organized with Puerto Rican percussionist Willie Bobo a *charanga* enriched with horns (Brazilian pianist João Donato, Rolando Lozano, and Chombo Silva played in it), La Sabrosura, which Ray Barretto and the Palmieri brothers emulated.

Alarmed by the turn of events in Cuba, José Fajardo settled in New York in 1961. He recreated a *charanga* with Félix Reina, Cachao who had also moved there, and two dancers. As he had done before, he also organized a relief band (based in Miami), contributing to the growing taste for *charangas* in the United States. He last performed in Miami, in a concert entitled "Cuban Masters–Los Originales," a few months before his death in December 2001 at the age of eighty-two.

Another Cuban flautist, Lou Pérez – creator of the short-lived *melón* rhythm – formed Los Mamboleros, with Johnny Pacheco and Eddy Zervigón on flute; flautist and violinist Pupi Legarreta got together Pupi y su Charanga. Like Ricardo Ray, Legarreta recorded a *jala jala* (*Ritmo jala jala*). He turned *La Ruñidera* into a *pachanga*, innovated by performing a *bomba* (*Un caramelo para Margot*) with his *charanga*, fused merengue and *pachanga* with *Merenchanga*, and became a sought-after session man.

In 1962 Eddy Zervigón founded with his brothers Rudy (violin) and Kelvin (piano and güiro) and with Roberto Torres – an excellent singer from Güines – the Charanga Broadway, influenced by Orquesta Aragón. Later renamed Orquesta Broadway, it would become salsa's number one *charanga*. In 1963 the band scored a hit with *Como camina María* (on *Dengue* – inspired by Pérez Prado's *dengue* rhythm); and going soul, they issued *Do Their Thing* in 1968.

One of the hottest *charangas* of the early 1960s was led by a Dominican, the flamboyant Johnny Pacheco. With his Cuban and Puerto Rican sidemen (among them Chombo Silva, Richard Egües, Bobby Rodríguez, Manny Oquendo, Pupi Legarreta, and Patato Valdés), Pacheco served a winning mixture of Latin jazz, *pachanga* and other genres (*Cucalá, Óyeme mulata, El güiro de Macorina*) with a jazzier, more New York feel than the classical Cuban *charangas*.

Born in 1935 in Santiago de Los Caballeros, Santo Domingo, Pacheco grew up listening to such Cuban artists as Arsenio Rodríguez and La Sonora Matancera. He started out on accordion with La Lira del Yaque – Santo Domingo's most renowned merengue group. Featuring his father Rafael Azarías on clarinet, pianist José Alberti, and two of Pacheco's uncles, it also performed *danzones*. Rafael Azarías Pacheco worked with another illustrious merengue ensemble: La Santa Cecilia. In 1946, fleeing Radamés Trujillo's dictatorship, he settled in the South Bronx, earning his living as a tailor. In addition to playing *tambora* (a two-skinned drum used for merengue), timbales, trap drums, bongo, conga, harmonica, and accordion, the young Johnny studied clarinet with his father as well as saxophone and violin. While still in high school he formed a mambo outfit that included trombonist Barry Rogers and pianist Eddie Palmieri. During the 1950s he gigged with countless bands, eventually giving up his engineering studies for music when Dominican bandleader Luis Quintero offered him a steady engagement. He took over from Mongo Santamaría as *timbalero* in Gilberto Valdés's *charanga*. Valdés gave him a flute and taught him how to play it. In 1955, Pacheco worked as an accordionist with Quintero, and as a flautist and percussionist with Dioris Valladares, and then collaborated with Pérez Prado, Stan Kenton, and Tito Puente (as *coro* singer, flautist, and *bongocero)* and other bands (backing stars such as Carmen Amaya) and working for television shows. In 1958 he collaborated with Xavier Cugat, and then with Charlie Palmieri's Orquesta Duboney, influenced by Fajardo's *charanga*, and with Noro Morales, Vicentico Valdés, and International Casino.

In the late 1950s, after seeing Orquesta Aragón with their dancer Felo Bacallao, and Fajardo with his dancer Felo Brito, he decided to have his musicians do a routine on stage, and audiences loved it. Throughout his career, Pacheco would remain a brilliant showman emceeing many Fania concerts. Incidentally he also was the first to make his own cowbells (before that, he remembers, horse bells were often employed). His first album for the Alegre label, *Pacheco y su charanga Vol. I*, recorded in the early 1960s and featuring Chombo Silva on violin, *timbalero* Manny Oquendo, and singer Elliot Romero, achieved instant success. In 1963, however, unable to find the right violin players, Pacheco formed his *conjunto* Pacheco y su Tumbao, influenced by that of Arsenio Rodríguez, and they issued *Cañonazo*, featuring the Puerto Rican Pete "El Conde" Rodríguez on vocals.

The vocalists

Singers also adapted to the raunchier, more down-to-earth style of the new Latin music. Several great vocalists had recently migrated from Cuba, among them Collazo, Rudy Calzado, Rolando Laserie, La Lupe, Monguito Santamaría, Justo Betancourt, Celia Cruz, and they contributed to giving salsa its initial impetus.

Based in Puerto Rico and alternating between the island and the United States, Bobby Collazo continued to perform and compose. Calzado recorded *pachangas* with Pacheco, Lou Pérez, and Mongo Santamaría and wrote several songs (*No me niegues tu cariño*, *A gozar ahora*), later working in California with bassist Chano Martínez.

After conquering Cuba with *Amalia Batista*, *Mentiras tuyas*, and other songs, the vibrant Rolando Laserie triumphed in the United States, where he became known as "El Guapachoso" ("the good-looking one"). With the bolero *Sabor a mí*, on which he was backed by the Bebo Valdés orchestra, his fame spread throughout Latin America.

Sabor a mí – Álvaro Carrillo

He also recorded with Tito Puente and other bands and under his name (*Sabor* with Ernesto Duarte, *Ritmo bailable de película*, *Salsa*, partly arranged by Puente and Charlie Palmieri).

With her exuberant sensuality "La Lupe" (Guadalupe Victoria Yoli Raymond), nicknamed "La Yi Yi Yi," shook up the Latin world like a tornado. Her outrageous make-up and wild on-stage behavior had already raised eyebrows in Havana, where she had made a name for herself before leaving Cuba. But this Latin Tina

Turner was also a fine and sensitive *bolerista*, influenced by Olga Guillot. As Raúl Martínez wrote about the songs written by Tite Curet Alonso for La Lupe, "Here the boleros *Carcajada final, La tirana, Puro teatro*, which achieved tremendous success in various Latin American countries, appear. Both this composer [Alonso] and his singer [Lupe] changed the direction of the bolero in the middle of the New York salsa boom. It is a type of bolero in which we don't see romance and peaceful love but fatal and violent breakups. Once more, this wonderful singer would find herself in her true element, with her apparent mess where sadness and happiness, drama and humor, love and heartbreak, absence, revenge, aggressiveness, pain and treachery are all mixed. All this coherent and organic, and, above all, a result of her own self. Was there any difference between her own life and what she sang? I don't think so."[6]

La Lupe was born in 1936 in the humble district of San Pedrito, in Santiago de Cuba, to a mother who was a singer and a father who worked at the Bacardi rum plant. In 1955 her family moved to Havana. Like Celia Cruz, she forsook becoming a school teacher for music. She started singing with the trio Los Tropicubas, led by her husband "Yoyo" (Eulogio) Reyes, and then as a soloist at La Red, a club patronized by Havana's intellectuals and artists, where she mesmerized audiences. She mostly sang Spanish adaptations of pop material, although two Cuban numbers put her in the limelight: Facundo Rivero's bolero *No me quieras así*, and *Con el diablo en el cuerpo* ("With the devil inside my body"), a Julio Gutiérrez *guaracha* that perfectly suited her volcanic personality, and which she recorded accompanied by Felipe Dulzaides.

In 1963, pregnant with her first child, she moved to New York and shortly thereafter recorded with Mongo Santamaría (*Mongo Introduces La Lupe*), backed by René Hernández and Chocolate Armenteros. She also collaborated with Rafael Cortijo and then pursued a career as a soloist. As in Havana, she continued to perform soul and pop numbers (*Take it Easy, Yesterday, Fever*). Her real breakthrough, however, came in 1965 when she teamed up with Tito Puente. Puente brought out the best in her and she recorded excellent albums with him (*La pareja, Homenaje a Rafael Hernández*). But attracted to him, she demonstrated her feelings in an excessive manner, and in 1968, tired of her provocative behavior, Puente let her go. She also made *They Call Me La Lupe*, arranged by Chico O'Farrill (1966); and in Venezuela, with Ramón Brito's *conjunto, La Lupe y su alma venezolana*, which included songs by local composers. In 1967 she converted to *santería*, recording Justi Barreto's *El santo en Nueva York* (a song with Yoruba and

6 In: *Lo trágico y lo controvertido en el canto y en la vida de Guadalupe Victoria Yoli Raymond, conocida como La Lupe*, p. 41.

Spanish lyrics). After leaving Puente, she gave a concert with Machito's orchestra, and then, beset by problems, let her career go downhill.

An excellent *sonero* (and a percussionist), the Matanzas-born "Monguito" (Ramón Quian Sardiñas) cultivated an essentially Afro-Cuban repertoire (*Pasito tun tun*, *Sacando palo del monte*, *Palo mayombe*, *Ave María morena*). He sang with Orquesta Broadway and Arsenio Rodríguez and later rose to prominence with Johnny Pacheco. He shouldn't be confused with vocalist "Monguito" Santamaría – Mongo Santamaría's son – mostly associated with the boogaloo and Latin soul (*Hey Sister*, *Groovetime*).

Also born in Matanzas and steeped in *rumba brava*, Justo Betancourt made use of his expressive and mellow voice with Orlando Marín, Pacheco, La Sonora Matancera, Eddie Palmieri, Ray Barretto, and Larry Harlow.

Celia Cruz, who had moved to New York in 1961 to sing with Rudy Calzado's band, married Pedro Knight, La Sonora Matancera's lead trumpet, who became her musical director and manager. By then La Sonora Matancera had settled in Venezuela and there, Cruz recorded with them (*Caramelos*, *Nuevo ritmo omelenko*, the *guaracha Ahí na' ma'*[7]). At the end of 1965 she left the group and made two Afro-Cuban albums under her name: *Homenaje a Yemayá* and *Homenaje a los santos*. With Memo Salamanca, she also issued *Cuando salí de Cuba* ("When I left Cuba"), which became the emblem of exiled Cubans, and, on *Te soltó la rienda*, uttered her trademark cry "*¡azúcar!*" ("sugar!"). She then returned to the Afro-Cuban world with Tito Puente (*Elegüá*, *Güiro 6/8*) and this fruitful association with the *timbalero* would further her career in the United States.

Direct and spontaneous, the Puerto Rican Joe Quijano, raised in the South Bronx, also rose to prominence. After a short stay in Cuba, in the early 1950s, he worked with Orlando Marín, Eddie Palmieri, Los Panchos, and other bands, before forming the Conjunto Cachana (for which Charlie Palmieri wrote arrangements), and made hits with *Nosotros* and *La pachanga se baila así*.

Revival of the bomba and the plena

In the early 1960s, Puerto Rico was teeming with superior musicians. One of them was Anselmo Sacasas, who, after running an orchestra in Miami, had settled in San Juan. Musical director of the Tropicoro Club of the San Juan hotel, he backed prestigious artists. Another one was Noro Morales who, despite glaucoma due to diabetes, until his death in 1964 led the band of La Concha Hotel, which included among others the saxophonists Ray Santos, Pin Madera, and Noro's brother Pepito, trumpeter Juancito Torres, the Cuban drummer Ana Carrero, and Vitín Avilés. Another one of Noro's brothers, Humberto, performed with his own combo in the same hotel.

But big bands usually catered for moneyed tourists or a local elite, and the tide was then turning towards more authentic forms of expression, imbued with

7 A mostly Puerto Rican expression indicating admiration or approval.

the vigor and pungency of popular culture. During the previous decade, many local ensembles had played American and Cuban numbers and the swank nightspots tended to favor white groups. Traditional music – and hand-held drums in general – were despised by the bourgeoisie, and even some affluent blacks tended to identify with American models. "When we played," percussionist Martín Quiñones remembered, "*congueros* were given nothing to drink or to eat. Even when I started out with El Gran Combo, in 1962, there were dances where musicians had to leave the room and where they were forbidden to socialize with the dancers."

Breaking away from the prevailing conventions, the *cuatro* player "Yomo Toro" (José Manuel Torres), whose father had played *cuatro* with Los Cuatro Ases, introduced this instrument into dance music (and later into salsa). And singer and *timbalero* Rafael Cortijo, singer "Maelo" (Ismael Rivera), and singer and trombonist "Mon Rivera" (Efraín Rivera Castillo) revived the *plena*, the *bomba*, the *merecumbé*,[8] the *oriza* (invented by the Cuban Silvestre Méndez), and other Caribbean rhythms. The *plena* had already made inroads into dance music, but the vital *bomba*, with its interlocking rhythms, was still dismissed as a mere folk genre and linked to the slavery plantation system. Even in the 1970s, when the Ayala family – the greatest exponents, along with the Cepeda family, of the *bomba* – were featured for the first time on Puerto Rican television, they elicited protests from viewers.

Mon Rivera dedicated himself more intensely to the witty and biting *plena* – a tradition inherited from his father, the singer Ramón Rivera Alers. Cortijo and Ismael Rivera were black, Mon Rivera had more Indian features, and their quest for a return to more authentic music coincided with the black consciousness movements of the United States. In New York several musicians, Tito Puente among them (*Bomba na' ma'*, *Traigo bomba*, *La plena bomba*), also propagated these traditional rhythms, but it is

8 A cross between *merengue* and *cumbia* created by Colombian composer Pedro Galán.

Cortijo, Ismael, and Mon Rivera who truly gave them momentum and introduced them into the popular repertoire, without losing their flavor.

In 1937 the Puerto Rican poet Luis Palés Matos, belonging to the same aesthetic current as Nicolás Guillén, Langston Hughes, or Aimé Césaire, had already celebrated the *cocolos* (a derogatory word designating black people in Puerto Rico) and their music in *Majestad negra*:

Rafael Cortijo and Ismael Rivera.
Rumba Records

Cortijo y su **Combo**
con *Ismael Rivera*

Lo Mejor
ORIZA
QUITATE DE LA VIA PERICO
MOLIENDO CAFE
PERFUME DE ROSAS
TUNTUNECO
SEVERA
EL CHIVO
SI TE CONTARA

Lo Ultimo
YAYABO
EL RETORNO DE LA CUCARACHA
DRUMA CUYI
DI DONDE ESTAS

¡Sus, mis cocolos de negras caras!	Come on, my black-faced *cocolos*,
Tronad tambores; vibrad, maracas	Boom, drums; rattle, maracas
Por la encendida calle antillana	Through the lit-up Antillean street
– Rumba macumba, candombe,	*– Rumba macumba, candombe,*
bámbula –	*bámbula –*
va Tembandumba de la Quimbamba.	the Tembandumba de la
	Quimbamba is passing.

Rafael Cortijo and Ismael Rivera

Cortijo's attempt to regenerate Puerto Rico's black music first sent shock waves. But then, with Ismael Rivera on vocals, his combo deeply touched the heart of Puerto Ricans, and it launched the career of many musicians, such as Rivera, Nacho Sanabria, Roberto Roena, and Rafael Ithier among others, who later shone as strong beacons of salsa.

Born in 1928 and raised in Loíza, Cortijo started jamming on drums made with jerry cans and he joined Moncho Muley's Conjunto Monterey, in which his childhood friend Ismael Rivera played bongo.

With his gritty voice and highly-strung sensibility, Maelo, as Rivera was nicknamed, aroused intense emotions in his listeners, delivering inspirational *soneos* full, as with Mon Rivera, of tongue-twisting alliterations and words with rich sonorities. During a trip to Puerto Rico, while he and Cortijo were appearing at a local venue, the Taberna India, Benny Moré dubbed Rivera "*El sonero mayor*" ("The number-one singer") – a title which stayed with him throughout his life. Rivera, too, was proud of his black heritage, which he often evoked in his songs, as in *El niche*, decrying racism.

Rivera was born in 1931 in Santurce, near San Juan, and he grew up taking part in the neighborhood's *rumbones*. His parents divorced when he was fifteen. As his father, a carpenter, earned little, he began working as a mason to help his mother Margarita and his young brothers and sisters. His mother always encouraged his musical vocation, and he started singing with local ensembles and attending jam sessions. He first joined the Conjunto Monterey in which Cortijo played bongo, and then, recommended by his friend, La Orquesta Panamericana, recording with them *El charlatán*, *La vieja en camisa*, the *plena El bombón de Elena*, and other tunes.

In 1954 Cortijo organized his own Combo, which grew out of a small informal group, and gave Rivera wider exposure. Soon after, as Rivera yearned for still more recognition, Cortijo renamed it Cortijo y su Combo *featuring* Ismael Rivera. Besides Cortijo on timbales, it was comprised of Miguel Cruz (bass), Martín Quiñones (conga), Ray Rosario and Sammy Ayala (güiro, vocals), Rafael Ithier (piano), Eddie Pérez (coro, saxophone), "Kito" (Rogelio) Vélez (arranger, trumpet), and Héctor Santos (saxophone). Entirely black except for Vélez and Santos, it stood out from the predominantly white Puerto Rican musical establishment. Puerto Rican writer Edgardo Rodríguez Juliá offered this humorous comment on them: "The combination of music and dance, what a thing of savages!, and the worse is that they play without scores, that they do not lend themselves to the formalism of ballroom orchestras. How terrible!" Cortijo introduced *bomba* drums into his group (as well as female *coro* singers), and he and Ismael Rivera produced a string of rollicking earthy songs such as *Arrecotín arrecotán*, *Maquinolandera* (written by Rivera's mother), and *El bombón de Elena*:

Elena toma bombón, bon	Elena, take a candy, candy
toma bombón Elena . . .	take a candy, Elena . . .
Yo lo traigo de limón	I bring them flavored with lemon
también traigo de canela . . .	and also with cinnamon;
Elena toma bombón, bon	Elena, take a candy, candy,
toma bombón Elena . . .	take a candy, Elena.

Cortijo also gave new life to numbers by Canario and to folk tunes. If Cuba had the *rumba brava* and Yoruba, Abakwa, and Congo traditions, Afro-Puerto Rican music had remained largely unknown abroad. Cortijo's songs with their black references and their alliterations – *Bomba ae, Chongolo, El negro bembón* – were, despite arrangements recalling those of the Palladium, a startling novelty in Puerto Rico. And finally, breaking down racial barriers, Cortijo was engaged at the posh Condado Hotel, in San Juan.

By 1961, both Cortijo and Ismael Rivera had begun to suffer from the effects of drug abuse, and *Quítate de la vía perico* ("Stay out of the way, cocaine") cryptically alluded to this problem. The record, wth its happy *Bomba carambomba*, and *Carnaval*, evoking the *vejigantes* – colorful masks parading at the Santiago Apóstol festival in Loíza[9] – turned Cortijo into a household name on the island. He performed in the U.S. and in continental Latin America, and his album covers *Cortijo en New York*, *Fiesta boricua*, with the band posing with straw hats in front of a roasted suckling pig, and *¿Bueno y qué?* evinced a typically Puerto Rican humor. He then started a new group: Cortijo y su Bonche, but continued to favor black themes: *Mofongo pelao, A bailar bambulé, El negrito gulembo*.

In 1962, Cortijo's addiction worsened, and some of his men left him to form El Gran Combo. He settled for a while in New York with Ismael Rivera, but the same year, Maelo was arrested at the San Juan airport on drug-possession charges as he was returning from Panama, and sentenced to nearly four years in prison in Kentucky. Cortijo then made a great record of *bombas* and *plenas* with Kako Bastar: *Cortijo y Kako, ritmos y cantos callejeros* ("Cortijo and Kako, street rhythms and chants"), a boogaloo LP entitled: *Sorongo, ¿qué es lo que tiene el blanco de negro?* ("Sorongo, what does the white man have that is black?"). And while Rivera was serving time, Cortijo recruited the Panamanian "Azuquita," who sang with him during 1966/67.

9 An Afro-Puerto Rican-style rendition of the festival of Santiago de Compostela and celebrating the Reconquest of Moorish Spain by the Christians.

Rivera came out of jail a broken man, and Bobby Capó wrote for him *Las tumbas* ("The tombs"), evocative of his ordeal, but Maelo returned to Cortijo's Bonche, recording *El Bienvenido* with him in 1967. The album included *Él que no sufre no vive*, and Bobby Capo's proud *Aquí estoy, ya llegué*: "*Algunos me creían muerto/Aquí estoy, ya llegué*" ("Some thought I was dead/Come on, here I am, I've just arrived"). Rivera also expressed his suffering with *La soledad* ("Solitude"), recorded around the same time on *Con todos los hierros*, which also offered the happier *Arrecotín arrecotán*, and the African-sounding *Bamba cure*.

Azuquita then moved to New York, while Rivera traveled to Panama, where a mystical revelation in front of the black Christ of Portobelo uplifted him – an experience he evoked in *El Nazareño*. He, too, settled in the Big Apple, forming his own group Los Cachimbos, with the Cuban pianist Javier Vázquez, while Cortijo reorganized his Bonche. The following year Azuquita recorded with Cortijo the successful "*¡Ahí na ma!,*" covering *U bla bla dú*, *Agua que va caer*, and Arsenio Rodríguez's *El reloj de pastora*.

Mon Rivera

Nicknamed "*El trabalengua*" ("the tongue twister") on account of his fondness for alliterations, Mon Rivera also epitomized popular Puerto Rican culture, with all its verve, insight and petulance. Whereas in other bands the trombones just harmonized within the brass section, on his records the trombone carried the melodies. Backed by the Palmieri brothers, Kako Bastar, Barry Rogers, and other top sidemen, he influenced Eddie Palmieri, Willie Colón, and others, who later turned the trombone into the key intrument of salsa. Rivera's nasalized sentences: "*Acaracastiqui tacastiqui tacatís,*" "*Mangandinga talai trangandando contopitam,*" "*Ay que ticu chicún*" rattled away like machine-guns, and his songs

MON RIVERA
Mon Y Sus Trombones

often evoked social problems or bittersweet incidents of daily life. *Que gente averigua* scoffs at the spiteful gossip of people who "spy on me and don't give me anything"; *Monina* recounts the adventures of a man drinking with a girl at the neighborhood bar and running out because he can't pay for his drink. Like the Cubans, Mon Rivera also fused various genres: bolero and merengue, *plena* and merengue, or *plena* and *pachanga* (*La plechanga de trabalengua*).

Mon Rivera. Vaya Records

Born in Rio Caña, near Mayagüez, in 1924, he first studied the guitar and debuted at fourteen with the duo Hazteco, which specialized in Mexican numbers. Two years later, he recorded with William Manzano's band, alongside the young *bolerista* Gilberto Monroig. From 1943 to 1945 he played professional baseball with the team Los Indios and then gigged as a *timbalero* and *bongocero* with various bands in and around Ponce while studying trumpet, trombone, piano, and violin. In the 1950s he joined Héctor Pellot and then Moncho Leña's Los Ases del Ritmo. In 1958, he too was jailed for cocaine possession, and later evoked this drug in *Lluvia con nieve* ("Rain and snow"). In the early 1960s, he sang with Luis Quintero's merengue band, and with the *conjunto* San Rafael, recording the famous merengues *Sancocho prieto* and *El negrito del batey*. He also cut some *pachangas* with the *timbalero* Juanucho López, and issued the rousing *Que gente averigua*, *Karakatis-Ki*, and other seminal LPs.

El Gran Combo

In 1962, after leaving Cortijo, Rafael Ithier founded El Gran Combo with Cortijo's alumni *conguero* Martín Quiñones, bassist Miguel Cruz, trumpeters "Quito" (Rogelio) Vélez and Victor Rodríguez, saxophonists Héctor Santos and Eddie Pérez, *timbalero* Milton Correa, *bongocero* "Maninín" (Daniel Vázquez), followed by Roberto Roena, trumpeter Mickey Duchesne, and singers "Pellín" (Pedro) Rodríguez and "Chiqui" Rivera, who left shortly thereafter and was replaced by Junior Montañez, soon known as Andy Montañez. The band, which often performed on television, soon developed dance routines, and with its lively choreography, buoyant *típico* style, and catchy lyrics it achieved tremendous popularity.

A self-taught musician and pianist with a firm rhythmic grounding, Ithier – son of a guitarist and nephew of Salvador Ithier (guitarist and second voice of the Trío Borinquen) – had played piano and then bass with the *conjunto* Tahoné, organized by the composer "Tito" (Faustino) Henríquez before joining Cortijo's band.

El Gran Combo first accompanied the Dominican singer Joseíto Mateo (*Menéame los mongos*) and became known with *La muerte*, *A la loma de Belén*, and *bombas* and *plenas* still influenced by Cortijo. An admirer of Benny Moré and Ismael Rivera, and gifted with a beautiful vibrato, Andy Montañez became one of the band's major assets. Montañez had sung with Noro Morales's brother Luis and formed the trío Gema, and his first recording with El Gran Combo, *El Gran Combo – Acángana*, foreshadowed the boogaloo. With Pellín Rodríguez and Montañez, the band produced *Ojos chinos*, *El caballo pelotero*, *La calle dolor*, *Milonga sentimental*, of Argentinian inspiration, María Teresa Vera's *Falsaria* (the history of a man in love with a prostitute), and *Pónme el alcolado Juana*, and fully established itself in the United States and throughout Latin America, as well as in Puerto Rico.

Also active in Puerto Rico in the 1960s and rooted in the island's popular sensibility were the All-Star Band led by the young trumpeter Mario Ortiz; the Puerto Rico All Stars, in 1965 featuring Ortiz, Kako Bastar, musicians from El Gran Combo, and Charlie Palmieri; and Johnny López's Super Combo.

Latin jazz and Latin soul

Like Latin dance music, cubop progressively absorbed non-Cuban strains, Brazilian especially, and as its scope and sweep broadened, it became known as "Latin jazz." In 1960 *conguero* Juan Amalbert recorded *Caribe* with his Latin Jazz Quintet, rather unexpectedly featuring Eric Dolphy. And, still with Dolphy, but led this time by vibist "Phil" (Felipe) Díaz and with another line-up (most notably Louie Ramírez on timbales and Bobby Rodríguez on bass), the group issued an excellent eponymous album, although it attracted little notice. Clark Terry, Jerome Richardson, Bob Cranshaw, Seldon Powell, Duke Pearson, El Negro Vivar, and Patato Valdés followed suit with *Eso Es Latin Jazz . . . Man*. And 1960 also saw the collaboration of Sabú Martínez and Louie Ramírez on *Jazz Espagnole*.

Tito Rodríguez, most probably spurred on by his ongoing rivalry with Tito Puente, dallied with jazz in the early 1960s. He performed at Birdland with Zoot Sims, Clark Terry, Bob Brookmeyer, and other jazzmen, and dressed various instrumental jazz standards with Latin rhythms (*Mack the Knife, Summertime, Take the A Train*).

By the 1960s, a host of Latin percussionists worked in both Latin and jazz contexts: Ray Barretto played on Eddie "Lockjaw" Davis's *Afrojaws*; Willie Bobo recorded with Miles Davis and, along with "Chihuahua" (Osvaldo) Martínez, on Herbie Hancock's *Inventions and Dimensions*; Cándido Camero collaborated with Frank Wess, Al Levitt, and Sonny Rollins and also with Marcelino Valdés, Chocolate Armenteros, Chihuahua Martínez, Armando Peraza, and Patato Valdés, and he issued *Cándido's Comparsa, Cándido with Tony Bennett at Carnegie Hall*, and *Thousand Finger Man* (which included a *Soul Limbo*); Peraza worked with Shearing and Tjader, and often played bongo with one hand and conga with the other, as Camero had already done in Cuba; and, in the early 1960s, Walfredo de los Reyes, who had moved to New York, made *Cuban Jazz* with saxophonist and flautist Jesús Caunedo. De los Reyes then settled in Puerto Rico, backing American stars at the San Juan Hotel.

Mongo Santamaría

When Willie Bobo left for California, Mongo Santamaría disbanded his *charanga*, which had lasted two years; he too turned to Latin jazz, surrounding himself with, among others, baritone saxophonist Pat Patrick – a Sun Ra alumnus from

Chicago – the Mexican bassist Victor Venegas, and Julito Collazo. "As a child I already liked to experiment with all kinds of music. In Havana, there was jazz everywhere. There were musicians who only played that, and I heard Dizzy Gillespie for the first time on Radio Mil Diez," he recalls, somewhat contradicting Chico O'Farrill who, on the contrary, bemoaned the dearth of jazz in Cuba during that era.

"Mongo y La Lupe" – with interesting solos by René Hernández and Chocolate Armenteros – offers, with Pat Patrick's *Quiet Stroll*, one of the ravishing flute ballads which became one of Santamaría's trademarks. And *Afro-Blue*, featuring Chombo Silva and inspired by *bembé* rhythms, became a jazz standard. Santamaría was also one of the first Cuban musicians to become interested in the samba and the bossa nova, and through his Brazilian pianist João Donato discovered Elis Regina and Jair Rodrigues. "I had seen *Orfeu Negro* and met João Gilberto. I love Elis Regina, Simone and other Brazilian singers, and at the Apollo Theater, where I often played, I also started my shows with a Brazilian tune. Brazilian rhythms, however, are simpler than the Cuban ones," Santamaría asserts. He contributed to the diffusion of the samba and the bossa nova in the United States, and played on Sergio Mendes's sessions with Cannonball Adderley.

In 1963 he worked at Birdland with his new band, which included Pat Patrick, Bobby Caper (tenor saxophone, flute), Roger Grant (piano), and Marty Sheller (trumpet). Pat Patrick introduced him to Herbie Hancock, and Santamaría then reached the top of the charts with a catchy blues entitled *Watermelon Man*. "Around that time Herbie was broke," Santamaría remembers. "He was playing with Willie Bobo in the Bronx and he brought me this tune." Hancock worked a few months with Santamaría, and was followed by the young Italian American Chick Corea, just graduated from the Juilliard School but initiated into Latin music in Boston by a *conguero* from Phil Barboza's band. Santamaría also appeared in the films *Made in Paris* and *April Fools*, and he turned to the Afro-Cuban tradition with *Our Man in Havana* and *Mongo in Havana*, both recorded in Cuba (the former with Niño Rivera, Armandito Armenteros, teenage pianist Paquito Hechavarría, and Armando Peraza's brother Cheo; the latter with Willie Bobo, Merceditas Valdés, Mario Arena, and Carlos Embale). *Skins* (1964), featuring Hubert Laws, Nat Adderley, Chick Corea, Julito Collazo, and Totico, and *Mongo Explodes*, with Laws, Adderley, and Jimmy Cobb, bore the stamp of soul music and of hard bop.

Chico O'Farrill

In the late 1950s, Chico O'Farrill, like so many other Latin musicians affected by the rise of rock-and-roll, had been forced to give up his big band. He continued to write both for jazz – arranging for Count Basie (*Count Basie Meets James Bond, Basic Basie*), The Glenn Miller Orchestra, Joe Newman, Lionel Hampton, and Clark Terry – and Latin music, collaborating with Cal Tjader,

Gato Barbieri, and the Afro-Cubans. He issued various albums under his own name, including *Spanish Rice* with Chino Pozo and Clark Terry; *Aztec Suite* with Art Farmer, Hank Jones, and José Mangual (this one included five movements: *Heat Wave, Delirio, Woodyn' You, Drume negrita*, and *Alone Together*); *Married Well*, on which he used an electric organ and an electric harpsichord; *Nine Flags* with Art Farmer, Clark Terry, and George Duvivier. "Of all the arrangers who worked on the Cuban music-jazz union," notes Alain Tercinet, "Chico O'Farrill is the one who wrote the most subtly-colored scores and also those which find the most accurate tone. Very influenced by bebop, he goes beyond the simple allegiance to a style and has created some very convincing arrangements for Benny Goodman and Count Basie."

Other musicians

Latin jazz, at that time not as developed on the West Coast as it was in Havana or New York, began to bloom. Benny Velarde and Francisco Aguabella in particular, swayed by George Shearing and Cal Tjader, set up jazzy ensembles that included flute and vibes. In 1962, with their respective bands, they cut *¡Ay que rico!*, arranged by Pupi Legarreta. On it Velarde played *Summertime* and Aguabella *That's All*. And Humberto Cané, who had moved from Mexico to Los Angeles the same year, worked with René Touzet and Joe Loco.

Few jazzmen apart from Gillespie, Tjader, or Shearing fully devoted themselves to Latin jazz, but many were captivated by Cuban music. Vibist Dave Pike recorded *Manhattan Latin* (1964) and, in particular, *Bésame mucho* with a discreet Bill Evans on piano; Grant Green produced *The Latin Beat* with Patato Valdés and Willie Bobo (with *Mambo Inn* and *Mama Inés*); Gerry Mulligan used a conga on *Capricious*, Dave Brubeck employed *conguero* and *bongocero* Salvador "Rabito" Agüeros on *Ponciana* and other numbers; and Herbie Mann, Ray Mantilla, Patato Valdés, and Ray Barretto met on *Common Ground*, recorded in 1960.

Latin soul

Latin soul developed alongside Latin jazz, with "Pucho" (Henry Brown) – a black American *timbalero* and Tito Puente fan – as one of its figureheads. Nicknamed Pucho after trumpeter "Pucho" (Pedro) Márquez, of the *conjunto* Alfarona X, Brown led his Latin Soul Brothers ensemble, which included saxophone (or flute, according to the tunes), vibes, piano, bass, drums, conga, and bongo. All the members were American, except *bongocero* Norberto Apellaniz, who was of Puerto Rican descent. But with a few exceptions such as *Vietnam Mambo*, Pucho's repertoire actually tended more towards pop or jazz (*Cantaloupe Island, And I Love Her*) than towards Latin music.

On the West Coast, Cal Tjader also went Latin soul with *In a Latin Bag* and his biggest hit, *Soul Sauce*, derived from *Guachiguara*. Willie Bobo played jawbone on it, injecting vocal comments during the performance. *Barrio Boogaloo*, which rode on top of the R & B charts, heralded the Latin rock that would explode with Carlos Santana. Around 1966, Tjader, riding the nascent salsa wave, recruited Eddie Palmieri and Ray Barretto for *El sonido nuevo* ("The New Sound") that pointed indeed in a new direction, out of the soul mold.

The effusive *timbalero*, drummer, and vocalist Willie Bobo (1934–1983) had moved from the East Coast to Los Angeles in 1966, where he started a group. Born in New York to a father who played *cuatro*, he was given his nickname "Bobo" by Mary-Lou Williams, who played a tune by that title (though other explanations have been provided for the origin of the Bobo monicker). After stints as a dancer and a *bongocero*, he became Machito's band boy. He then collaborated with Machito and Puente, causing friction with Puente when he left him to work with Tjader, and then with Herbie Mann. In addition to his Latin engagements (with René Touzet among others) he recorded in the 1960s with Miles Davis, Cannonball Adderley, James Moody, Gabor Szabo (along with Victor Pantoja), and others. His engaging music, sometimes punctuated by his favorite refrain: "*¡salsa, ahí na' ma'!*" was influenced by hard bop, soul, and boogaloo, but it sometimes became facile, as on *Bobo! Do That Thing* (1963) with Chick Corea's *Guajira*, *Spanish Grease* featuring José Mangual and Bobby Rodríguez, and *Uno, dos, tres*, with Mangual and Patato Valdés (1966), on which he used a guitar rather than a piano. Armando Peraza also adopted Latin Soul with *Wild Thing*, recorded in 1968 with Johnny Pacheco, Bobby Rodríguez, Cal Tjader, Garnett Brown, and Chick Corea.

from the 1970s until today: advent of the *songo*

CHAPTER EIGHT

Havana and Cuba

Starting in the 1970s, Cuba struggled with increasing economic difficulties, worsened by the dependence on sugarcane as a cash crop and the U.S. embargo. In 1977, however, tension between both countries eased up somewhat as American President Carter allowed cultural exchanges with Cuba. Orquesta Aragón, Los Papines, and Irakere, showcasing the island's talent, toured to the United States, although the new Cuban music largely remained a mystery abroad. Around the same time, Fidel Castro took a few steps to open up the country, in particular granting tourist visas to Cubans living in New York or Miami. These exiles influenced their relatives or friends on the island, exacerbating their desire for freedom and travel abroad. At night, on the Malecón, people gazed longingly (and still gaze) at the horizon, trying to get a glimpse of the lights of Florida, seen as some kind of Eden, and musicians on both sides of the Florida strait yearned for the artistic interaction of former times.

In 1980, a spate of Cubans fled from the Mariel harbor and sought political asylum in the United States, followed eighteen years later by the *balseros* (from the Spanish word *balsa*, designating the rafts on which they escaped). These "Marielitos" disseminated outside Cuba the *songo*, a rhythm which paved the way for the *nueva timba* (today's sizzling dance music) and crept into salsa and Latin jazz.

In 1991, the demise of the USSR – Cuba's major economic mainstay – plunged the island into a further state of crisis, and Castro launched a program of stringent restrictions euphemistically dubbed "special period." In order to attract sorely needed foreign currency, the country started to encourage tourism and in 1993, legalized the use in Cuba of the American dollar. Along with tourism, music became one of Cuba's major assets. Los Van Van, Gonzalo Rubalcaba, Issac Delgado, Dan Den, Adalberto Álvarez, Arturo Sandoval, Manguaré, and countless other local artists started touring internationally and recording for foreign labels. Some musicians never came back; trumpeter Arturo Sandoval, for example, defected during a European tour and was able, with Dizzy Gillespie's help, to obtain political asylum in the United States. The Buena Vista Social Club album and film as well as a stream of CDs (often issued by international companies from the Egrem – Cuba's national label – and the radio archives storehouse) triggered a worldwide Cuban music boom. Old musicians were pulled out of retirement, and foreigners discovered the island's amazing level of musicianship.

In the 1990s, Cuba, which had frowned on jazz and salsa, welcomed with open arms foreign jazzmen, and such salsa stars as Oscar D'León (who sang in Havana with the Orquesta Aragón), Cheo Feliciano, or Andy Montañez, who performed there to wild acclaim; Cuban salsa sensation Issac Delgado and Cheo Feliciano even got to record together.

In October 1995, the United Nations granted Fidel Castro a visa to attend in New York the fiftieth anniversary of the United Nations. David Rockefeller and other business personalities gave a dinner in his honor, announcing a possible resumption of American investment in Cuba. Only the future will tell if such investment will leave the country its economic and cultural autonomy, or if the U.S. will again impose its domination, as under Batista.

Traditional music

Several traditional Afro-Cuban groups have appeared since the 1970s, and eager foreigners now flock to Havana, Matanzas, or Santiago to study Cuban drumming and dancing. Havana and Matanzas, in particular, teem with *rumbas*. In Havana, these *rumbas* regularly take place on Sundays at the callejón de Hammel, a backstreet decorated with vivid frescoes by painter Salvador González; and at the rehearsals of the Conjunto Folklórico Nacional, called *Sábados de la rumba* and open to the public. Matanzas cultivates just as actively its African heritage, which remains perhaps even stronger than in Havana.

Los Muñequitos de Matanzas, founded in 1952 in that city by composer Florencio Calle ("Catalino") – a former member of the famed *coro de clave* Bando Azul – constitute the quintessence of *rumba brava*. The drums enhance the beauty of the voices, and the lyrics, often poetical and metaphorical, exalt the black culture of Cuba (*Lo que dice el abacuá*), evoke love and its torments

(Estebán Lantrí's stupendous *Cantar maravilloso*) or everyday goings-on (*La chismosa del solar*). Aside from Calle, the group originally comprised the wonderful singers "Saldiguera"[1] (Esteban Lantri), "Virulilla" (Hortencio Alfonso Hernández), and "Fuico" (Juan Mesa), and percussionists Ernesto Torriente, Esteban Bacallao, Ángel Pellado, and Gregorio "Goyo" Díaz. First known as Conjunto Guaguancó Matancero, they achieved recognition with *El chisme de la cuchara* and *Los beodos*. They were then dubbed Los Muñequitos de Matanzas, after a popular cartoon called *Los muñequitos* (The puppets) – a monicker that stuck. In recent years, Los Muñequitos have hired dancers and added *santería* and Abakwa rhythms to their repertoire, but have lost some of their initial intensity.

Los Papines – also a highly rated *rumba brava* group – were formed seven years after Los Muñequitos by percussionist Ricardo Abreu and his brothers Luis, Alfredo, and Jesús. The Abreus grew up in the strongly musical district of Los Pocitos, in Marianao, and in 1950, Luis founded Papín y sus Rumberos, which evolved into Los Papines. Los Papines offer a more show-biz *rumba brava* than Los Muñequitos, and they have greatly contributed to the dissemination of this music outside Cuba. For certain recordings, they collaborated with other musicians (trumpeter Arturo Sandoval and *tresista* Gilberto Oviedo, for example, on *Homenaje a mis colegas*).

In 1970 Carlos Embale set up the Conjunto Guaguancó with Pablo Cano, a fellow veteran of the vocal group Los Roncos Chiquitos. With them Embale played claves, güiro, maracas, and conga, and with Cano composed various songs (*Timbalaye, Oh humanidad*). A few years later, vocalist and *batá* drummer Mario "Chabalonga" Dreke – a former member of the Conjunto Folklórico Nacional – fused Afro-Cuban chants and the blues, although the results of his experiment remained rather marginal.

The *rumba brava* has also been kept alive by individual performers and ensembles such as the Grupo de los Portuarios de La Habana; the Coro Folklórico Cubano led by "Carusito" (Florencio Rodríguez); the Grupo Guaracheros del CNC; Afrocuba de Matanzas, created in 1957 by Francisco Zamora Chirino ("Minini"), with which jazz saxophonist Steve Coleman recorded *The Sign and the Seal*; and the Conjunto Clave y Guaguancó, founded by Mario Alán and directed by Amado Dedeu. The more daring Conjunto Clave y Guaguancó also

1 Saldiguera (whose nickname derives from the laxative plant *sal de higuera*) had started out singing boleros in 1923 with La Lira Matancera. In the 1930s he had founded with Virulilla – another magnificent singer – a duo which performed in the gardens of the beer hall La Tropical for parties entitled "Matanzas en La Habana."

uses *batá* drums; its percussionists sometimes play a *cajón* with one hand and a *tumbadora* with the other, while its vocalists rap convincingly on rumba rhythms.

Lázaro Ros – a former cook by trade and one of the major exponents of Lucumí, Arará, and Iyesá music – has performed with Síntesis (an offshoot of Tema Cuatro), Grupo Mezcla (*Cantos*), and Olorún. A superior singer and former *santería* dancer, he has sometimes offered modernized renditions of Yoruba music with guitar and keyboard. He has also collaborated with jazz pianists Gonzalo Rubalcaba and Chucho Valdés (in 1998 on Valdés's *Cantata a Babalú Ayê*).

A founding member of the Conjunto Foklórico Nacional, the percussionist Pancho Quinto works with Yoruba Andabó, and with the pianist and singer "Bellita" (Lilia Expósito Pino) and her group Jazztumbatá. Quinto had played with Jesús Pérez and Merceditas Valdés and had been lead drummer of some of Havana's greatest *comparsas* (El Alacrán, Las Jardineras, Los Dandys de Belén). He also performed at rumbas and *santería* ceremonies while earning his living as a dockworker, and trained scores of young musicians.

The songo *and* charangas

Charangas evolved over the years. Their repertoire became more diversified while the distinction between *charangas* and *conjuntos* has tended to blur. They often incorporated horns, as with Enrique Jorrín's band, reinforced with trumpets, or Orquesta Típica Juventud – a change that also affected New York *charangas*. And in Villa Clara the Orquesta Aliamén switched to an electric bass.

The exuberant Los Van Van, founded in 1969 by guitarist, bassist, and composer Juan Formell, were the pivotal *charanga*, ushering in the *songo* and serving as a stepping stone for several exponents of the *nueva timba*. They have had an enormous influence in Cuba and abroad, with covers of several of their songs, among them *Aquí se enciende la candela*, *Chirrín chirrán*, and *Guararey de pastorita*.

Born in Cayo Hueso in 1942, Formell taught himself guitar, studied bass with his father and Odilio Urfé, and harmony with the celebrated teacher Félix Guerrero, Rafael Somavilla, and Tony Taño. After playing brass instruments in the marching band of the National Revolutionary Police, he joined Guillermo González Rubalcaba's *típica* and then the band of the Habana Libre Hotel. In the early 1960s, he accompanied Elena Burke, and in 1966, worked with Orquesta Revé, for which he wrote arrangements influenced by jazz and rock, and on starting Los Van Van, he took along Revé's pianist "Pupi" (César) Pedroso. For Los Van Van, Formell produced a string of hits: *Guararey de pastorita*, *Aquí se enciende la candela*, *Que palo es ese*, *Sandunguera* (sung by the irresistible Israel Sardiñas).

Eager to experiment, Formell replaced drums by hollowed-out sugarcane stalks, introduced an electric guitar, a synthesizer, and trombones into the band and, with Pedroso, launched a new bass and piano *tumbao*, dubbed *amarre* (from *amarrar,* "to fasten," "to tie up"), turning Los Van Van into one of the most innovative *charangas* Cuba had known in many years.

The percussionist "Changuito" (José Luis Quintana), who had passed through Habana Jazz, Cuba Mambo, Felipe Dulzaides's Los Armónicos, and other groups, also contributed major innovations. He substituted the timbales for trap drums, thereby scandalizing some conservative souls, began to transpose rock licks and trap drum rhythms on his congas, invented new patterns with his cowbell and accented the fourth beat, thus creating a more swinging feel, more ahead of the beat than with the traditional timbales style, and sometimes added a bass drum. "I joined the band in 1971," he explains, "and started adding my own ideas to the style we had, using a conga, a *catá*[2] and a güiro. I didn't use trap drums in the conventional sense, no cymbals, no sock cymbals. That, I only used seven or eight years later. We added the cowbell later." He and Pedroso blended *son,* Yoruba rhythms, funk, pop, and other elements, and Changuito's rhythms, underscored by the electric bass and the piano (or the synthesizer), gave birth to the *songo.* The name was not new: in the 1930s, Antobal's Cubans had recorded a number entitled *Songo songo,* and later Celia Cruz *Songo le dió a Borondongo,* but the rhythm was, and, with its many variations, it soon took root in Cuba and in the United States.

Los Van Van have gone through many changes of personnel. In 1981, they included a three-trombone and three-violin line-up, and the outstanding flautist "El Tosco" (José Luis Cortés). In the 1990s, Juan Formell's son Samuel became the group's *timbalero.*

In the 1980s, despite their other charismatic vocalist Pedro Calvo, a former member of La Ritmo Oriental, their output became somewhat raunchier. *El danzonete* – a new rendition of *Rompiendo la rutina,* with the *soneo* (improvisation) announcing *"esta negrita se está moviendo"* ("this black chick is really moving") – did not quite capture the grace of Aniceto Díaz's original version, and *Songo* was disappointing. Still, they scored a hit with the *conga-son El baile del buey cansado* ("The dance of the tired ox"), done with slow movements, with people dancing separately. But the group, fronted by the young dreadlocks-sporting singer "Mayito" (Mario Rivera), remains a favorite of dancers, with hits like *Ven, anda y muévete, Por encima del nivel, Llegó Van Van,* and *Esto te pone la cabeza mala.*

La Ritmo Oriental, La Maravilla de Florida (run for seven years by "Manolito" (Manuel) Simonet before he founded his Trabuco with fellow bandmembers), Aliamén, and younger *charangas* also turned to the *songo.* Maravilla de Florida stood out with *Que tiene esa cintura* and *Tremendo personaje.* It favors amalgams (*bomba-son, changüi-son,* etc.) and has adapted the Colombian *cumbia,* giving it a special flavor. But despite their very modern sound, their flautist Orlando Beltrán Brunet – one of the band's oldest members – still uses his old wooden flute with keys. La Ritmo Oriental achieved success with *Yo bailo de todo, La chica mamey, Se baila así,* and, more recently, *Euforia Cubana,* with powerful and compact solos by the remarkable Martinique pianist Mario Canonge as guest star on certain numbers. Led by pianist Ernesto Ramos Tamayo, Aliamén uses a trombone, which

2 An additional rhythm beaten with one or two sticks on the side of a drum or on a wooden object.

reinforces its middle register, an electric bass, an electric guitar, electric violins, a flute, a bongo, a conga, a hand-held cowbell (rather than the one normally affixed to the timbales set), and its four young vocalists electrify listeners.

Besides the *songo*, other rhythms have sprung up in the last decades. Among them the *malembe*, a 6/8 genre created by Miguel Pinto Canto of Aliamén; the *gogochá*, invented in the 1970s by Orquesta Sensación; the *bastón*, put out in 1979 by Orestes López; the *moanga* and the *chaonda*, invented by Alejandro Tomás in the wake of La Orquesta Aragón's triumphant African tour, in 1977.

Aragón – still going strong today – went through several changes. In 1982 Rafael Lay was killed in a car accident. Orestes Varona – the only founding member left – temporarily assumed the leadership of the band, which notably included dancer and singer "Felo" (Rafael) Bacallao (who later moved to Venezuela), violinists Celso Valdés and Dagoberto González, cellist Alejandro Tomás Valdés, bassist José Beltrán, pianist "Pepe" (José) Palma, singer "Pepe" (José) Olmo, *conguero* Guido Sarria, and Francisco Alboláez on güiro. Egües then left the group to work with a smaller ensemble, and Lay's son, Rafael Jr., succeeded Varona.

While many *charangas* chose to go with the times, others kept the *danzón* tradition alive. Among them the Orquesta Típica Cubana, led by Carlos González (Neno's son); the Orquesta Típica Habanera run by ophicleide-player Horacio Benilde Morales; the splendid Charanga Típica Cubana, directed by pianist Guillermo González Rubalcaba, which has included violinist Miguel Barbón, flautist Aurelio Herrera, and *timbalero* Rafael Blanco; and the Charanga Nacional de Concierto, which in the late 1970s included pianist, composer, and musicologist Odilio Urfé, his brother, bassist Orestes, and güiro player Juan Felles. After Odilio's death, the Charanga Urfé was created in order to perpetuate the legacy of the Urfé dynasty. After a twenty-year break, Antonio Arcaño's *charanga*, reorganized with new musicians, recorded in 1976 compositions from its heyday, among them *Carragua se botó*, sung by Miguelito Cuní, and beautifully performed by flautist Joaquín Olivera Gavilán and pianist Gonzalo Rubalcaba (Guillermo's son).

Orquesta América, Orquesta Sublime, and the *charangas* of Rodrigo Prats, Abelardo Barroso, Orestes Valdés, Richard Egües, and Enrique Jorrín took a middle course. In the 1980s Jorrín produced with violinist Elio Valdés and pianist Rubén González a spirited version of *La engañadora*, and *Suena el piano Rubén*. Following Jorrín's death, González took over the band for a while. Pianist Andrés Alén Rodríguez successfully blended the old and the new in his *Danzón Legrand*, recorded in 1975 by the Cubanacán orchestra.

The Charanga festival of Palma Soriano, created in the mid-1990s, has been attracting the best *charangas* from Cuba as well as some foreign ones. Among them the rather traditional Estrellas de Charanga, based in Palma Soriano, with, on piano, the witty pianist Pepecito Reyes (Oriente's answer to Rubén González), and the dynamic Unión Sanluisera (known as La Sanluisera), founded in 1961 in neighboring San Luis, which uses a combination of synthesizer and electric piano.

The son

Overshadowed by the *nueva trova*, the *son* had somewhat waned during the 1960s, but starting in the mid-1970s, it progressively recovered its vitality. Elio Revé's *Son No. 6*, recorded in 1980, eloquently proclaimed both its black nature and its enduring power:

Salga mulato	Come out, *mulato*
suelta el zapato	move your feet,
díganle al blanco	tell the white man
que no se va . . .	that he's not leaving . . .
beba y no pare	drink and don't stop,
coma y no pare	eat and don't stop
viva y no pare	live and don't stop . . .
que el son de todos no va a parar.	because the *son* – everybody's son – is not going to stop.

In the late 1970s, the duo Los Compadres, comprised of Lorenzo Hierrezuelo and his brother Reynaldo ("Rey Caney"), elicited a true popular fervor with their infectious sense of humor and their ebullient *sones*, *rumbas*, and *guarachas*.

Niño Rivera pursued his musical activities. His eponymous record, made in 1980 with Gustavo Tamayo, Rubén González, and Miguelito Cuní offered a new rendition of *El Jamaiquino* and, with *Nuevo son*, extolled the virtues of revolutionary Cuba. But over-orchestrated with its synthesizer, organ, electric guitar, and piano, it did not match the character of older albums made with Chappotín. After Chappotín's death in 1982, his band was taken over by his son, percussionist and trumpeter Ángel José Chappotín. Now led by his grandson Jesús Angel, it still maintains the spirit of the Conjunto Chappotín y sus Estrellas.

The Conjunto Casino continued to produce invigorating music (*Ponle la montura al potro, Montuno en Neptuno No 960*). Like Los Van Van, Rumbavana acquired an electric guitar and, with their sharp breaks, highly syncopated bass lines, nervous riffs, and stimulating piano solos by Joseíto González, they heralded the *nueva timba*. They updated the *son* of the 1940s and 1950s and, with their sexy singer Ricardito (women climbed on stage to dance with him), recalled some New York salsa groups (*Mi son por el mundo, Oye lo que te trae Rumbavana*).

The Orquesta Revé, an outgrowth of Elio Revé's *charangón*, also modified its instrumentation, using electric bass and guitar, bongo, claves, *batá*, shekere, and timbales with plastic skins, more sonorous, according to him, than leather. Also influenced by the *songo*, they recorded more driving *changüís* than before (*Salgado, Changüí clave*), while also performing such classics as *La Ruñidera*.[3] After Revé's death in 1998 in a traffic accident, his son, pianist "Elito" (Elio) Revé Duvergel, who had played with him, took over the band, revamping it and steering it more in the direction of *nueva timba*.

3 A *son* by Bienvenido Julián Gutiérrez, different from the one sung by Machito.

In 1976, the *tresista* Juan de Marcos González – an erstwhile hydraulic engineer and former pupil of Isaac Oviedo and Graciano Gómez – got together with eight engineering students from Havana's Instituto Politécnico and founded Sierra Maestra with the idea of perpetuating the traditional *son*. The group was instrumental in fostering the current *son* revival. On the powerful *Puro sabor cubano* (1994), among other good albums, they paid homage to Arsenio Rodríguez. The *son montuno Trompeta querida* features Jesús Alemañy's superb trumpet, and *Mi guajira* is characterized by a doo-wop accompaniment. The record also includes the old Septeto Habanero's *Criolla carabalí*, and Willie Colón's *guaracha Juana Peña* – the story of a cruel woman who, finally abandoned, cries for the one she loves – strikingly rendered here as a *son*.

A more jazzy Algo Nuevo, which included pianist Jesús González Rubalcaba (Gonzalo Rubalcaba's brother) and trumpeter Adalberto Lara, was formed in 1976 by Juan Pablo Torres, former trombonist of the Orquesta Cubana de Música Moderna. They harmoniously blended popular music and black folklore (*Yo era timbero, Prepara los cueros*). When Torres moved to Miami, Rubalcaba became its director. In 1979 Torres also gathered together in a studio the cream of Cuban music, from Félix Chappotín, Enrique Jorrín, Niño Rivera, Tata Güines, and Gustavo Tamayo to Arturo Sandoval and Richard Egües, for heady sessions of old and new tunes released under the name Estrellas de Areíto.

With his captivating husky voice, Pablo Milanés brought a personal touch to the *son*, as can be heard in his interesting rendition of *Son de la loma*, recorded in 1980 with, among other musicians, jazzmen Emiliano Salvador (piano), Paquito D'Rivera (flute), and Jorge Varona (trumpet), and trumpeter Manuel Mirabal ("El Guajiro").

Bands proliferated in the 1970s and 1980s: Los Reyes 73; Afro-Indio, Pedro Ramos's ensemble; Los Latinos, with a Pan-American repertoire; La Monumental; Los Chaquis; Gloria Latina; Tierra Caliente; Grupo Habana Son; Joaquín Betancourt's exciting Opus 13 (with violinist, flautist and saxophonist Juan Manuel Ceruto, later musical director of Paulo F/G y su Elite, and percussionists Tomás Ramos and Angá Díaz), which broke up in 1991; the Grupo Layé led by the drummer Fidel Morales (who would later move to Panama); the amateur groups Manguaré, run by Pancho Amat, Síntesis, headed by Carlos Alfonso and borrowing from both *nueva trova* and the Afro-Cuban tradition (*Ancestros*), and Grupo Moncada, which uses traditional Latin-American musical instruments.

In 1978 the pianist and singer Adalberto Álvarez, known as "El caballero de la salsa" (The gentleman of salsa), created in Santiago the *conjunto* Son 14 with singer Eduardo Morales. Álvarez had grown up in Camagüey, where his father led the group Avance Juvenil and his mother sang *trova*. He then became the musical director of Avance Juvenil, composed for Rumbavana and accompanied Omara Portuondo and Celina González. In 1983 Son 14's *A Bayamo en coche*, with its seductive a capella introduction, attracted attention in Cuba and in Puerto Rico. The following year Álvarez founded Adalberto Álvarez y su Son, with *tresista*

"Pancho" (Francisco) Amat and *timbalero* Calixto. The band, which held a middle ground between the *son* from Oriente, salsa from the 1970s, and the *songo*, uses an electric piano and a synthesizer, and it includes songs by Ismael Rivera and salsa standards in its repertoire. "Audiences appreciate a warm salsa where the vocalist gives himself fully," avers Álvarez. His group, which has included his daughter Dorgeris on piano, the fine trumpeter Julio Padrón (who later joined Irakere) and, among its singers, the raspy-voiced "Tiburón" (Eduardo Morales), "Rojitas" (Jorge Luis Rojas – now a star in his own right), Aramís Galindo, and Leonel Aleaga, offers this warm salsa. On *Álvarez y su son*, Álvarez improvises with fellow pianist Frank Fernández on Félix Chappotín's *Yo sí como candela*, and on *Magistral*, Dominican guest pianist Michel Camilo cooks on *La vi caminando*.

Banda Caribbean, formed by members of Ignacio Piñeiro's Septeto Nacional and of Manolito y su Trabuco also fuses *son* and salsa, but with a different sound.

In 1987, after the founding Castro sisters retired, Anacaona resolutely took the *songo* and *timba* route, with an eruptive style and a sometimes hard edge (*Lo que tú esperabas*). One of their vocalists, "Lucrecia" (Lucrecia Pérez Saez), moved to Barcelona and the group renewed its personnel, with a horn line-up consisting of flute, tenor and alto sax, and trombone. Juan Formell also contributed numbers to the band's book. Other female groups, among them Son Damas, Las Chicas del Sol (named after a 1993 Issac Delgado hit by the same name), or in Santiago Perlas del Son, formed in 1995, have achieved recognition in the hard-driving, male-oriented *nueva timba* world.

Oriente has tended to maintain a more traditional *son* than Havana, with such ensembles as Sones de Oriente, Changüí Guantanamero, Mario Recio's *conjunto*, La Familia Valera Miranda (Félix, vocals and guitar; his wife Carmen, maracas; their sons Félix Enrique, *cuatro*, Raúl Félix, bass, Ernesto, bongo; and a relative, Radamés González, *cuatro*), the Septeto Turquino, Son del Cauto (which uses lutes, a jawbone, and a metal flute), Cañambú (formed in 1940, employing bamboo canes as musical instruments and led today by Arístides Ruiz Boza), and Los Guanches (headed by Armando Machado, a former Cuarteto Patria bassist, which cultivates a rural style).

Chepín-Chovén keeps on going with the same enthusiasm. After Chepín's death in 1984, Chovén assumed the leadership of the band on his own, and when he retired, his grandson Orestes Chovén and, since 1989, the trumpeter José Ramón Hernández, later supported by the saxophonist Gilberto Aguilera, took over. They seek to modernize while keeping the spirit of their founders, playing the *son* "Chepín style" with its characteristic piano *tumbao* and its timbales lick recalling the *pilón*.

Near Trinidad, the Grupo Los Pinos perpetuates the old *son*, as well as other rural genres. In recent years, a myriad of *son* ensembles have sprouted up throughout the island. Among them Son Entero, formed in 1993 in Camagüey by the great *tresista* Luis Acosta Pino and by singer Jorge Luaces Delgado, and borrowing its name from a Nicolás Guillén poem; the more jazz-based Yakaré,

Issac Delgado.
Milan Latino Records

formed in 1980 in the province of Granma, and Orquesta Cumbre, in Pinar del Río; the Sexteto Raisón, led by *tresista* Efraím Ríos (who played with Adalberto Álvarez) and his brother Luis; Jóvenes Clásicos del Son, created in 1994 and headed by bassist Ernesto "Palma" Reyes, with the stunning young *tresista* Juan "Cotó" Antomarchí, followed by César Losada and *sonero* Pedro "Nene" Lugo, recalling Miguelito Cuní, trumpeter Raudel Marzal, and other promising youngsters; the group formed by lute-player Barbarito Torres with ex-members of Jóvenes Clásicos del Son; also Juvenil de Sancti Spíritus; and Son Esperanza y Tambao, from Villa Clara.

The nueva timba

In the late 1970s and in the 1980s, Cuba was restless under an apparently smooth surface. Disco was making inroads into the country, and the younger generation enjoyed the ebullient *casino* and the *areíto*.

In 1991 the television program *Mi salsa en descarga*, launched a new wave of musicians. Progressively, the *nueva timba* (an expression coined by Juan Formell from the word *timba*, designating a *conga*) – a hot and agressive new style derived from the *songo* – emerged in Havana and swiftly spread to the rest of the island. The *nueva timba* was Cuba's answer to salsa – which the Cubans had long rejected as an imperialist product – although with the worldwide success of this music, they finally co-opted the term. (As mentioned earlier, singer Issac Delgado describes himself as a *salsero*, and there is a group, led by percussionist, xylophonist, and pianist Anael Castellanos, called Mi Salsa.) Today salsa is danced throughout the island, with new twists grafted onto the basic *son* steps, and the accents falling differently. Also to be noted is a return of the mambo, claimed as a truly Cuban creation, taught in local dance schools with elaborate choreographies and peppered with a new eroticism.

Starting in 1993, as Cuba opened to tourism, prostitution – eradicated by Castro – returned in full force, and young Cubans started to be lured by consumerism. A new breed of *jineteros* and *jineteras* offering sexual favors to foreigners in exchange for money or other enticements began to appear, in Havana especially. The frantic *nueva timba* reflects the island's fast-changing values. It explodes in an outpouring of sound, while dancers enjoy the wild grinds of the *despelote* (from a word meaning "fun," "mess," and "stripping off") and of the *bola*, the new "in" dances. The young and hip generation also favors the highly choreographed and inventive *ruedas de casino*, performed as a group, with changes of partners. *Ruedas* sometimes allude in humorous ways to current events: when the USSR collapsed, for example, dancers abruptly parted from each other in *ruedas* routines, to signify that Russia had withdrawn its help to Cuba!

The *timba* lyrics, sometimes trashy, express the new materialistic concerns of the younger generation, hungering for cars and flashy clothes: a Charanga Habanera song advises girls to find themselves *"un papirriqui con wainikiki"*–"a sugar daddy with dough." Musicians and singers who have made it and have been paid in dollars sport trendy outfits, gold chains, earrings in one ear, and sometimes shaved heads, dreadlocks or even psychedelic hairdos. And *timba* bands appear at La Tropical, El Palacio de la Salsa (closed nowadays), La Cecilia, and other venues that sometimes charge, for the Cubans, the equivalent of a whole month's salary.

The piano *guajeos* have been speeded up, with a particular two eight-note pattern on the first beat. Tony Pérez, with Issac Delgado before he joined Irakere, "Wicho" (Luis Andrés) Rodríguez-Carrillo (now based in Spain) and Marcos Crego (the son of trumpeter José "El Greco" Crego) have been among the most notable *timba* pianists.

The beacon of the *nueva timba* has been the infectious NG (Nueva Generación) La Banda. It was founded in 1988 by the extraordinary flautist "El Tosco" (José Luis Cortés) after he left Irakere; Cortés got his nickname, meaning "The coarse one" or "The rough one," one day when, in the countryside, he was given oversized clothes. The initial nucleus of the band consisted of Germán Velazco (saxophone), "Tony" (Francisco Antonio) Calá (vocals) former singer and violinist with La Ritmo Oriental, "Wickly" on conga, and Guillermo Barreto's nephew "Barretico" on timbales, with other horn players from Irakere. It also attracted into its ranks drummer and songwriter Giraldo Piloto (Gerado Piloto's son), who went on to form Klímax. NG La Banda's raw songs (*La bruja, El preso, Crónica social*), offensive as they may have been for older listeners, captured – often with humor – the harsher social reality of Cuba. With El Tosco's stunning flute solos, the tight horn section and the vocal stylings of Issac Delgado (formerly with Pachito Alonsa) and then Mariano Mena Pérez, the group has scored a string of hits (*Los Sitios entero, Necesito una amiga, Que viva Changó, La protesta de los chivos, Echale limón*), and also successfully adapted (with arrangements by

Cortés) old numbers such as *Son de la loma* or Ñico Saquito's *María Cristina*. In recent years Cortés has expanded his activities, writing and producing for other artists.

Countless other ensembles sprang up in the wake of NG La Banda, eager for a share of its success. Among them Manolito Simonet y su Trabuco, led by the *tresista*, percussionist, and pianist Manuel Simonet (*La parranda, Caballo grande*); Yumurí y sus Hermanos, formed by the great singer Moisés Valle ("Yumurí"), formerly with Elio Revé, and his brothers Pedro, Osvaldo, and Luis; Paulito FG y su Elite (a breakaway band from Opus 13), directed by Paulo Fernández Gallo (a veteran of Son 14), with a strong stage presence and interesting arrangements by its musical director Juan Cerruto; the lively Bamboleo, started by the energetic pianist Lazarito Valdés (son of pianist Oscar Lázaro Valdés and former sideman of Pachito Alonso, Amaury Pérez, and Bobby Carcassés), with its singers Vania Borges and the husky-voiced Haila Mompié (Mompié and Bamboleo's leader Leonel Limonta later formed Azúcar Negra); Pachito y Las Nuviolas, with a female *coro*; Estado de Animo; Klímax, with crisp horn lines, sophisticated harmonies, and inventive breaks; Chispa y los Cómplices; Pachito Alonso (Pacho's son) y sus Kini Kini; Andy Gola and Colé Colé; Chavy y los del Barrio, led by singer Javier Baro ("Chavy"); Issac Delgado (ex-lead vocalist of NG La Banda), now one of Cuba's top names; violinist David Calzado's rambunctious Charanga Habanera (launched by the hit *Me sube la fiebre*, written by Giraldo Piloto), with its exuberant singer Michel Márquez, banned in 1997 from public performances for excessive bad taste, and now rehabilitated and renamed La Charanga Forever; the group set up in 1993 by singer and former gynecology student "Manolín" (Manuel González Hernández), nicknamed "*El médico de la salsa*" ("Salsa's doctor") by José Luis Cortés (*Para mi gente, Una aventura loca*); Bakuleyé ("new ideas" in Yoruba), created in 1996 by the singer Pedro Pablo Pérez, mostly with students from the famed Escuela Nacional de Arte; Tormenta Cubana, mixing *timba* and rap; Carlos Manuel y su Clan (*Malo Cantidad*, full of veiled social commentaries and *double entendres*) and Dan Den, led by pianist Juan Carlos Alfonso, a former student of Armando Romeu and Elio Revé alumnus and the creator of the *charangón* rhythm. Dan Den's hit *Viejo Lázaro* evokes the *orisha* Babalú Ayé:

Viejo Lázaro, milagroso San Lázaro	Old Lazarus, miraculous Lazarus,
Líbrame de las penas que padece el ser	Free me from the pains which human
humano	beings suffer.
Viejo Lázaro, milagroso San Lázaro	Old Lazarus, miraculous Lazarus.
Préstame tus muletas	Lend me your crutches
Que quiero apoyarme en ella	I want to lean on them
Viejo Lázaro, milagroso San Lázaro	Old Lazarus, miraculous Lazarus,
Líbrame de las llagas que padece el ser	Free me from the wounds which
humano.	human beings suffer.

However, like Adalberto Álvarez's group, Dan Den is now leaning more towards salsa. Santiago has also spawned an impressive number of new ensembles, among them Banda XL, Granma and Muralla, which revamp standards with inventive arrangements.

The Buena Vista Social Club *phenomenon*

Offsetting the *nueva timba* trend, there has recently been a revival of the traditional *son* and the rediscovery, in great part thanks to the *Buena Vista Social Club* album and Wim Wenders's film, of older performers who had often fallen by the wayside.

In 1996, Ry Cooder travelled to Cuba to record with local musicians. The result, *Buena Vista Social Club*,[4] became a worldwide blockbuster, and the following year it won a Grammy Award. The musicians on the album had been brought together by Juan de Marcos González. The ex-Sierra Maestra leader had intended to form an Afro-Cuban All Stars including both veteran performers and up-and-coming young musicians, ranging from the ninety-year-old Compay Segundo to fourteen-year-old *timbalero* Julienne Oviedo. The sprightly Compay Segundo had retired, as had pianist Rubén González, plagued by arthritis, and Ibrahím Ferrer now shone shoes to supplement his modest pension. De Marcos González also enlisted "Puntillita" (Manuel Licea), Orlando "Cachaíto" López, trumpeter Manuel Mirabal Vázquez ("El Guajiro"), who had played with La Sonora Matancera, Swing Casino, and Rumbavana, singer and guitarist Eliades Ochoa, Pío Leiva, Omara Portuondo, lute-player Barbarito Torres, and *timbalero* Amadito Valdés. In the *Buena Vista Social Club* film, the moving Ibrahím Ferrer and Omara Portuondo stole the show with their gorgeous duo on *Dos gardenias*, and all the performers brought down the house at their Carnegie Hall concert, during which a Cuban flag was brought on stage.

Some of these artists were subsequently offered individual contracts. For Ibrahím Ferrer, then seventy-five years old, it was his first album under his own name, and he was backed on it by the great female a cappella vocal group Gema Cuatro. Born in 1927 in San Luis, near Santiago, Ferrer had paid his dues with local groups before working with Chepín-Chovén, Caridad Hierrezuelo, Pacho Alonso, Benny Moré and Orquesta Aragón. With his new recordings, he managed to indulge in his often-suppressed predilection for the bolero. "Before," he says, "people always asked me for fast numbers." Late in life, these old-timers embarked upon an international career they had never dreamed of before. Some of these stars and other musicians, among them singer Félix Baloy (formerly with Elio Revé and Son 14), did an international tour called Cuban All-Stars. The Afro-Cuban All Stars recorded a gorgeous eponymous album on which Ibrahím Ferrer sings *María caracoles* (a *mozambique* cum *pilón*), Rubén González shines on *Clasiqueando con Rubén*, and Richard Egües and de Marcos González

4 Some fifty years earlier, Cachao had written a *danzón* entitled *Social Club Buena Vista*, after a social club located in east Havana.

sizzle on *Habana del este*, a *danzonete-chá*, featuring for the first time a *tres* in a *danzonete*. And Cachaíto won deserved recognition with *Muy sabroso*, bringing together the Jamaican organist Bigga Morrison, the South African trumpeter Hugh Masakela, the saxophonist Pee Wee Ellis, Angá Díaz, and the French rapper Dee Nasty.

The *Buena Vista Social Club* phenomenon rekindled above all the career of Compay Segundo, who subsequently became a worldwide star. Fronting his Muchachos, he suddenly found himself with a busy touring schedule, and his song *Chan Chan*, evoking small towns of Oriente and containing sexual innuendos, turned into a new emblem of Cuban music. And, with the same zest and gusto for life, he keeps roaming the planet with his new Muchachos: Repilado (second voice, guitar), Julio Fernández (first voice, maracas), Benito Suárez (guitar, third voice), and Salvador Repilado (bass).

Omara Portuondo, the first new Cuban chanteuse discovered abroad in many years, has been compared by the press to Billie Holiday. After a less creative period, in the 1970s, when she had recorded potboilers that did not reflect her true sensibility, she came back with the excellent *Palabras*, and with *Desafíos* (featuring Chucho Valdés) before joining the *Buena Vista Social Club* bandwagon.

Always wearing his trademark cowboy hat – "I've used it to get a few coins when I was busking in Santiago in my salad days, to protect myself from the sun when I was working in the fields, and I now use it to hide my balding pate," he quips – Eliades Ochoa has also become a household name. An exponent of the *monte adentro* (rural) *son*, he is a superb guitarist, with touches of flamenco, a sober lyricism, and a highly personal phrasing, and a talented singer and arranger. While Compay Segundo, with whom he has often teamed up, invented the *armónico*, Ochoa has created an eight-string guitar (with the D and G strings doubled one octave above), whose metallic quality recalls a *tres*.

Born in Mayarí in 1946 to a rural family, Ochoa learned music with his parents, who were amateur musicians. Choosing music over farm work, he first formed a trio in Santiago, building up his reputation as a guitarist. In 1963 he started a group which played *guajiras* on the rural radio show *Trinchera agraria*, and worked with various bands, among them the Septeto Típico, a duo with Robertico Rossel at the Casa de la Trova de Santiago, and the Quinteto Oriente. Noticed by Pancho Cobas, of the Cuarteto Patria, he joined this ensemble, founded in Santiago in 1939. In 1978 he assumed its musical direction and introduced a bongo into it, and the Cuarteto Patria's version of *Chan chan*, featuring Ochoa and Compay Segundo as a guest star, is a true masterpiece. Ochoa currently performs with his brother Humberto (guitar, vocals), percussionist Jorge Maturel Tomero, *maraquero* Eglis Ochoa Ferrera, bassist José Ángel Martínez, and trumpeter and singer Aníbal César Ávila Pacheco.

The *Buena Vista Social Club* craze also revived the careers of such other veterans as the Ferrín sisters (Mercedes, lead singer, and Esperanza, second voice), the Faez and the Floricelda sisters, *soneros* Faustino Oramas ("El Guayabero,"now based in Spain), Adriano Rodríguez, and Félix Baloy (a former singer of Elio Revé and Son 14), the Septeto Nacional, with vocalist "Raspa" (Eugenio Rodríguez), the Septeto Habanero, Los Naranjos, and the Vieja Trova Santiaguera (formed in Santiago in 1993 with old *trovadores*), frustrating some younger musicians, José Luis Cortés among them, who felt somewhat thwarted by this old *son* craze. In 1998 three years before his death, Frank Emilio Flynn gave a rousing concert with his group Los Amigos (Joaquín Olivera Gavilán, William Rubalcaba, Enrique Lazaga, Tata Güines, Changuito) at the Lincoln Center, in New York. Foreign producers have now been roaming *casas de la trova* and other venues in search of undiscovered pearls: Cuban music, old and new, has again become a hot commodity.

Latin jazz

The foolhardy (or unsuspecting) musician who tries to play in a Cuban jam-session exposes himself to a real cataclysm, to a bombardment of polyrhythms, syncopations, and offbeats that may leave him nonplussed. By the time he figures out the meter or the beat he should be on, his Cuban counterparts are several bars ahead of him!

Today's Cuban jazz, complex and inventive, has absorbed myriad influences, ranging from Brazilian strains to hip hop; and like American jazz, it has also evolved towards a sophisticated polytonal and polymodal sound. In the late 1970s, the temporary warming up of relations with the United States during President Jimmy Carter's mandate benefited both America and Cuba: Dexter Gordon, Woody Shaw, Wayne Shorter, and other jazzmen from the United States performed in Havana, opening the local musicians' ears to new sounds; and the Cuban jazzmen who appeared in the United States revealed their exuberance and virtuosity to American audiences. The Festival Internacional de Jazz Plaza, held in Havana, now attracts a bevy of international luminaries.

The concert given in Cuba in the late 1970s by Gordon, Shaw, and others was released on the CBS compilation *Havana Jam*, also featuring Cuban musicians. On it Frank Emilio Flynn – then only known outside Cuba to a few enlightened aficionados – played, backed by Tata Güines and Guillermo Barreto, the delicate *Sherezada/Sun Sun*. According to the liner notes, this piece attributed to Rimski-Korsakov (although the connection is not particularly obvious) was supposed to be part of a larger work for percussion, which apparently came to nothing. On *Frank Emilio presenta a Frank Emilio*, issued a few years later, the pianist – accompanied by Cachaíto, Gustavo Tamayo, percussionists Guillermo and Roberto Valdés, and guitarist Carlos Emilio – treats Ñico Rojas's delicate *Eva* as a fast cha-cha, and draws from classical music and jazz on Niño Rivera's *Tú y mi música*. On *Lázaro y Georgina*, the guitar's jazzy touches interrupt the bass's dreamy stroll, and then the impressionist piano comes in and the rhythm becomes more marked.

In the early 1970s, a handful of young and inventive souls such as the pianists Emiliano Salvador and Chucho Valdés, the saxophonists Manuel Valera and Paquito D'Rivera, and the drummer Enrique Plá would get together to improvise at the club Johnny Dreams of the Miramar Hotel, the l'Elegant of the Riviera Hotel where Felipe Dulzaides held forth, the Internacional of the Kawama in Varadero, and later at the Rio club in Miramar, now turned into a discotheque, and at the Maxim. Jazz sheet music was rare in Cuba in those days, and in 1979, during a trip to Havana, I remember jotting down on a scrap of paper, for eager musicians at the Rio, the chord changes of *Giant Steps* and other standards. These pioneers' experiments gave birth to a brilliant new Latin jazz that has now garnered international acclaim. Valdés, D'Rivera, and Plá belonged, along with percussionist Óscar Valdés and Carlos Emilio, to the Quinteto Cubano de Jazz – an offshoot of the Orquesta Cubana de Música Moderna, which would constitute the nucleus of Irakere. And members of Dulzaides's Los Armónicos or of Afro-Cuba, the drummer Oscar Valdés Jr. in particular, also played with the group Coda.

"Chucho" (Dionisio de Jesús) Valdés sought, as he then announced, to "modernize the country's rhythms by injecting jazz and other musical elements into them" – a quest he's still pursuing. He inherited his father Bebo's burly frame, powerful touch, and talent. His style has sometimes recalled McCoy Tyner's, although he mentions Bud Powell, Hank Jones, and Bill Evans among his first influences. His uncanny speed, strength, sense of harmony, and reckless swing have been astounding audiences.

Born in 1941, Valdés got to play as a youngster with his father's bands, having grown up with the constant experience of music at home. Around 1964, he formed a Latin jazz group, Jesús Valdés y su Combo, which featured singer "Guapachá" (Amado Borcelá), an excellent scat singer who died at the age of thirty-three. Around 1967, Valdés joined the orchestra of the Teatro Musical de La Habana and organized a pop group. He also performed with the Orquesta Cubana de Música Moderna and the Quinteto Cubano de Jazz and, as a trio, with Óscar Valdés and bassist Carlos del Puerto. In 1970 he appeared at the Jazz Jamboree in Poland, strongly impressing Dave Brubeck and Gerry Mulligan, and the early 1970s were a turning-point in his career.

His *Misa negra*, a suite for piano and ritual chants, which he played in 1971 with the Orquesta Cubana de Música Moderna, followed the modal trend inaugurated by Bill Evans, Miles Davis, and John Coltrane. But Valdés's real break came with Irakere. In 1978 *Downbeat* proclaimed his solo on *Misa negra*, recorded with this band, best piano work of the year. From *A la Chucho, Jazzbatá* or *Tema de Chaka* to the more recent *Bele bele en La Havana* (where he covers his father's epochal *Con poco coco descarga*), *Briyumba palo congo*, with a *danzón* rendition of *Rhapsody in Blue*, and *Live at the Village Vanguard*, offering a stirring *Drume negrita* sung by his sister Mayra Caridad Valdés, he achieves a perfect blend between jazz

and Cuban music. Valdés has composed other ambitious works, among them a suite for piano, symphony orchestra, and jazz ensemble, and has also maintained the *descarga* tradition with *Mambo influenciado*, derived from Mario Bauzá's *Mambo Inn*.

In 1973 with the incisive Paquito D'Rivera he set up Irakere (a Yoruba word meaning "forest"), in which he was the main composer and arranger. Volcanic, ebullient, sometimes profuse, Irakere, with its impressive array of percussion and bravura-style solos, gave a new impulse to Cuban jazz and rapidly became the most famous of the new local bands. Mixing electronic instruments and traditional drums, it ranged from ritual music to jazz, rock, and Cuban rhythms (*Aguanile, Juana 1600, Iyá*).

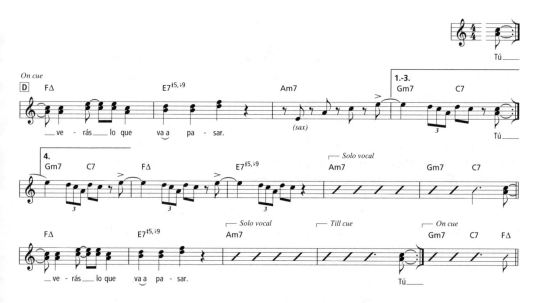

Lo que va a pasar – Jesús "Chucho" Valdés

In 1979 the group, with Chucho Valdés, D'Rivera, and Carlos Averhoff (saxophones), Arturo Sandoval and Jorge Varona (trumpets), Oscar Valdés, "El niño" (Jorge Alfonso), and Armando Cuervo (percussion), Enrique Plá (trap drums), Carlos Emilio Morales (guitar), and Carlos del Puerto (bass), did a euphoric tour of the United States: it was the first time in twenty years a Cuban jazz band had performed there (although they had been preceded, the year before, by Elena Burke, Los Papines, and Orquesta Aragón). Jubilatory, energetic, teeming with ideas, these young Cubans mesmerized American audiences, showing them that in Cuba a strong musical fire had been smouldering and was now ready to burn. In the wake of their tour, they made an album for Columbia, with D'Rivera playing funky licks on Mozart's *Adagio*, which earned a Grammy Award.

In 1980, while the band was performing in Spain, D'Rivera defected and moved to the United States, where his mother lived. Shortly thereafter, Sandoval, the band's lead trumpet, left Irakere to found his own ensemble. The departure of two of its most prominent soloists shook up the band, but it soon regrouped under Chucho Valdés's sole direction, and D'Rivera was replaced by saxophonist Germán Velazco Urdeliz and flautist José Luis Cortés. Velazco had a luminous style in the Coltrane tradition, Cortés a clear and powerful sound, uncanny technique, and harmonic and melodic instincts, and a strong stage presence. Irakere's tours abroad were temporarily cancelled, lest other members defect, and its popularity declined. Confined to shows on the island, it turned to dance music, trying with little success to broaden its audience. It then returned to more experimental concepts (*Tierra en trance*, *Calzada del Cerro*, with compositions by Arsenio Rodríguez). In 1988, again the group lost two of its most inventive members when El Niño set himself on fire in mysterious circumstances and Jorge Varona died. Once more Irakere came back with, notably, pianist David Pérez, flautist Orlando "Maraca" Valle, saxophonist César López, trombonist Carlos Álvarez, and trumpeters Manuel Machado and Juan Munguia. The ensemble, just as stunning, is now led by trumpeter Julio Padrón, and it includes stellar musicians, among them Mayra Caridad Valdés.

Also a talented pianist and *timbalero*, Arturo Sandoval is a brilliant trumpeter, but sometimes prone – early in his career especially – to overusing the high register, with a taut sound à la Harry James. Influenced by Clifford Brown, Dizzy Gillespie, Luis Escalante, and "Florecita," he joined the Orquesta Cubana de Música Moderna and then Irakere before recording under his name (*Turi* – a vibrant tribute to Gillespie and Clark Terry; *Dizzy Gillespie and Arturo Sandoval: To a Finland Station*). In 1981 he formed the eclectic Grupo Perspectiva, which included pianist Hilario Durán. Guitarist Jorge Luis Valdés later added a less felicitous lacing of rock to it. Durán subsequently settled in Canada, where he often performs with Canadian saxophonist Jane Bunnett, and recorded the great *La canción de Francisco* (1995), while Sandoval chose Miami as his home base.

Still largely unknown abroad, pianist Emiliano Salvador (1951–1992) also revitalized various Cuban genres, and he composed interesting works (*Puerto*

Padre, Angélica, Para luego es tarde). Influenced by McCoy Tyner, Thelonious Monk, Peruchín, and Pérez Prado among others, he accompanied "Bobby" (Roberto) Carcassés, Pablo Milanés, Milton Nascimento, and other singers.

Born in Puerto Padre, in the east of Cuba, he began to play piano and accordion, later performing with his father's band, and studied piano (and, like most Cuban pianists, percussion) at the Escuela Nacional de Arte. On *Nueva visión* (with D'Rivera, Sandoval, Varona, and Pablo Milanés), he introduces *Son de la loma* with a free prelude and offers an unusual rendition of the old *son Convergencia*. Abolishing the conventional parameters of the *son*, he creates an energetic and unexpected *Son en 7* with an odd time signature. On *Ayer y hoy*, his last album, featuring Milanés and Pancho Amat, he performs a jazz rendition of *La vida es un sueño* and *Capullito de alelí*, mixes Cuban and Brazilian rhythms (*Samba-conga*), and imparts a rare density to the cha-cha (*Cha cha chá*). In 2000, the saxophonist Juan Manuel Cerruto recorded with a stellar cast (Chucho Valdés, Julio Padrón, *timbalero* Pepe Espinosa, Hernán López Nussa and others) *A Puerto Padre – Tribute to Emiliano Salvador*.

Like Irakere, Afro-Cuba, founded in 1977 by flautist and saxophonist Nicolás Reinoso (now based in Montevideo) and later led by the flautist Oriente López, successfully combined jazz and ritual Afro-Cuban music (*Sobre un canto a Eleguá*, *En lloro mi nankwe*, of Abakwa inspiration, written by the saxophonist José Carlos Acosta). The group also attracted vocalists Ricardo Echemendía, and Eddy Peñalver, acclaimed under his own name in the mid-1980s with *La lata*, *El palo*, and other hits. In 1990 its effusive pianist Ernán López Nussa, who also worked with Silvio Rodríguez, left to form Cuarto Espacio before moving to the United States.

Many other groups cultivated jazz in the 1970s, among them the wonderful La 440, which included Germán Velazco Urdeliz (saxophone and flute), Pepecito (piano), Adonís (percussion), Puchunga – a former vocalist of Roberto Faz's *conjunto* – and José Luis Cortés (flute); Grupo Cotán, led by guitarist "Cotán" (Angel Octavio), whose style sometimes recalled that of George Benson; and Sonido Contemporáneo, also directed by Nicolás Reinoso (which has included in its ranks José Carlos Acosta, Lucia Huergo, tenor saxophone, flute, keyboards, piano, pianists Gonzalo Rubalcaba and Manolito Docurro, drummer Toni Valdés, and bassist Ángel López).

In *A Night in Havana*, a documentary chronicling Dizzy Gillespie's 1985 trip to Cuba, a young and shy pianist, Gonzalo Rubalcaba, captivated the trumpeter with just a short solo. And he sat in at Gillespie's Havana concert, stealing the show from Walter Davis Jr., at the time Gillespie's pianist. Member of an important musical dynasty from Pinar del Río (his grandfather wrote the danzón *El cadete constitucional*, his father Guillermo led the Charanga Típica de Conciertos, his brother Jesús plays piano, his brother William bass), Rubalcaba was a child prodigy. Born in Havana in 1963, he studied percussion and piano, and honed his skills with Los Van Van, Orquesta Aragón and Sonido Contemporáneo. His balance between the hands, his mastery of polytonality and subtle harmonic shadings sometimes remind us of a Latin Herbie Hancock (Hancock himself is a Rubalcaba friend and fan), although he has developed his own style, playing lightning fast passages or extraordinarily slow and drawn out boleros and ballads (as on *Here's That Rainy Day*, for example), with the type of excruciatingly slow tempos Shirley Horn also favors. "I have always been conscious of an important principle: freedom," he says. "Freedom of concept, of approach, of style, even, and bebop gives this kind of freedom." But despite his love for jazz and his hunger for experimentation, he remains fond of Cuban rhythms, which he performs with great finesse. He reconstructs standards, going from long soliloquies or pensive digressions to free lines or offbeat *montunos*. Like other young Cuban musicians served by a peerless virtuosity, he has sometimes been carried away by his enthusiasm and his desire to play, although his art has been maturing over the years.

With his Grupo Proyecto, consisting of Manuel Valera (saxophone), Lázaro Cruz (bugle), Felipe Cabrera (bass, oboe), Horacio Hernández (trap drums), Roberto Vicaíno (percussion) and Rafael Carrasco (flute, tenor saxophone), Rubalcaba tried his hand at rhythmic combinations and other experiments. His *Concierto negro* – a suite for wind instruments, Eleguá[5] chants, and percussion, develops a melodic motif with variations on odd time signatures. His *Embele iruke*[6] has been played by the Orquesta Sinfónica Nacional de Cuba (with added Cuban percussion instruments). After settling in Santo Domingo, Rubalcaba moved to the United States, working with Charlie Haden, Jack DeJohnette, Brazilian singer João Bosco, and countless other musicians.

The brillant young flautist, pianist, composer, and arranger Orlando "Maraca" Valle leads the group Otra Visión, in which drummer Juan Carlos Rojas and percussionist Roberto Vizcaíno have experimented with a new type of dialogue between their respective instruments. Like Changuito, Ignacio Berroa, Giovanni Hidalgo, and other percussionists, Rojas combines trap drum techniques and traditional Afro-Cuban rhythms. Valle plays popular Cuban music and Latin jazz with disconcerting fluency, taking breath-taking solos.

In addition to his work with NG La Banda, José Luis Cortés has recorded Latin jazz sides under his name (*Bolero oculto*, *Intenciones alborotadas*), although he deserves to be better produced and to be backed by an acoustic rather than a mediocre tinkling electric keyboard. As a jazz flautist, he ranks, along with Maraca and the Colombian Justo Almario, among the very best in the world.

A versatile and stunning *conguero*, "Angá" (Miguel Aurelio Díaz), who hails from Pinar del Río, works in traditional, popular, and jazz contexts. After playing with Opus 13 and Irakere, he recorded the powerful *Pasaporte* (with Tata Güines), offering rumba and jazz and featuring vocalists Raúl Planas, Merceditas Valdés, and Moisés Valle. He has also collaborated with Roy Hargrove, Herbie Hancock, and Betty Carter and, like Maraca, he divides his time between Paris and Cuba.

5 A major *orisha* of *santería*, god of crossroads and messenger.

6 The *embele* is the machete of the *orisha* Ogún, the *iruke* the fly whisk of the orisha Oyá and, in the Congo dialect, one of the names of the god Zarabanda.

Like the Rubalcabas, the Valdeses, the Urfés and the Valles, the Terrys are also a highly respected musical family. The hot new group Los Terrys comprises the sons of percussionist, violinist, and arranger Eladio Terry, former director of La Maravilla de Florida: Yosvany (saxophone), Yoel (flute), and Yunior (bass). Their album *From Africa to Camagüey* (1996) offers a fresh Latin jazz strongly influenced by Afro-Cuban roots (*Los orishas*), and Yosvany has recorded with many other bands, including some in New York.

Born in 1954, pianist and composer José María Vitier has pursued a rather individual road. A classically trained, very lyrical musician, he is adept at different genres, and he has written for film, theater, and ballet. After a stint with Síntesis, in 1978, he formed his own ensemble. "In Vitier's work," writes Leonardo Acosta, "we see precisely this 'natural breathing' which runs like a river, despite the crisscrossing of styles and the sometimes abrupt changes of rhythm and time." Vitier's fluidity particularly shines on *Habana secreta* (1995), featuring Silvio Rodríguez, Angá Díaz, Tata Güines, and José María's brother Sergio among others and offering a splendid version of *El manisero*.

The trumpeter and singer (and erstwhile actor and high jump champion) Bobby Carcassés's Grupo Afro Jazz, with the leader's stimulating vocal stylings, has gained considerable standing. *Jazz Timbero*, recorded in 1999 on the British Tumi label, features among others Chucho Valdés and Changuito. Born in 1938 in Kingston, where his father was Cuban diplomat to Jamaica, Carcassés grew up in Santa Clara and debuted there as an opera and popular-music singer; in Havana, where he moved in 1956, he furthered his musical training with a variety of groups.

Raíces Nuevas, Son Varona, Grupo Orú, led by Sergio Vitier (with Guillermo Barreto, Cachaíto, and Tata Güines), and Los Karachi, headed by Pablo Moya Martínez, with a powerful trombone section – still unknown outside Cuba – are also worthy of note.

The new generation of Cuban jazz musicians emerging at the dawn of the twenty-first century is very much alive and inventive. The pianist, *timbalera*, and singer "Bellita" (Lilia Expósito Pino), with her group Jazztumbatá, creates bubbling and harmonically stirring music sometimes reminiscent of Tania Maria. The trumpeter Jesús Alemañy (now based in London), who debuted with Sierra Maestra at the age of fifteen, leads the bracing Cubanismo. Their collaboration with the Paris-based pianist Alfredo Rodríguez has resulted in two excellent albums. In addition to new material, Alemañy has reworked such classics as *El platanal de Bartolo* and *El paso de Encarnación* (on *Reincarnation*, featuring among others Maraca, Güines, Pancho Amat, Carlos del Puerto, and Rolo Martínez, who had sung with Chappotín and Ernesto Duarte) and has recorded in New Orleans with the Yockamo All Stars (*Mardi Gras Mambo*). Among the profusion of burgeoning talent, mention should also be made of pianists Iván "Melón" González (who has worked with Issac Delgado), Ramón Valle, David Álfaro, and the lightning-fast Gabriel Hernández Cadenas, who took over from Emiliano

Salvador in Salvador's group after the latter's death; the bassists Jorge Reyes and Edgar Madariaga; the flugelhorn player José Manuel Greco; the percussionists Hernán Cortés and Roberto Vizcaíno; the drummers Jimmy Branly, Dafni Prieto, and Ruy López Nussa; the saxophonists Tony Martínez, César Alejandro López, Rolando Pérez, and Javier Zalba; and the trumpeters Julio Padrón (*Buenas Noticias*, *Descarga Santa*, recorded with Los Amigos de Santa Amalia), Alexander Brown, Roberto García López, and Mario Félix.

Three young Cuban jazzmen – all three graduated from the Escuela Nacional de Arte – have recently been discovered abroad: the technically proficient and sometimes prolix pianist Tony Pérez (*Soneao*); percussionist Ramces Baralt, who weds ritual Afro-Cuban music and hip hop (*Fetecún*); trumpeter "El Indio" (Mario Morejón), influenced by Freddie Hubbard, with a strong and cohesive neobop (*Nuevos horizontes*).

Other bands

Unconventional groups have also emerged in recent years, with their blends of classical, popular, and folk strains and elements of funk (called *pastilla* in Cuba) testifying to the looseness of musical boundaries. Among them violinist Alexis Correa's Arte Mixto employing a combination of guitar, *tres*, *batá* and other instruments (*Agúzate*), Habana Sax (with four saxophones and percussion) the Cuarteto de Saxofones de Santiago, and the string quintet Diapasón, founded by Armando García. All four have a broad repertoire. Playing *tumbaos* with their instruments, the members of Diapasón generate rhythmic excitement without the help of percussion or brass, and they have offered a marvelous rendition of José White's celebrated *La bella cubana*.[7]

Vocalists

In the mid-1990s, Vocal Sampling, an extraordinary a capella male group, took the world by storm. A kind of Cuban Take Six, it was founded in 1989 at René Baños's initiative by six students of the Escuela Nacional de Música. Influenced by street music, they had started out singing together at parties in Havana. The voices perfectly imitate musical instruments (including percussion solos), with as much swing and drive as a fully-fledged instrumental band, and they go from *guaguancó*, to bolero and rap: "We are not really a choir but a band, with typical Latin arrangements. The difference is that the instruments are sung by human voices," they explain. Catarsis and the Santiago-based Ora are also first-rate vocal groups. Since its inception, Sampling has gone through various changes of personnel (with the initial line-up remaining the most powerful), and spawned an offshoot: Vocal LT.

7 An exceptional violinist and composer from Matanzas, White (1836–1918) played sixteen different instruments and while in his teens, he already composed major works. He lived in Paris in 1860, stayed in various Latin American countries, and then in 1888 settled permanently in Paris, where he taught and performed.

Cuba recently lost two great singers: Merceditas Valdés and Caridad Cuervo. Valdés sang on the albums made in Cuba by the Canadian saxophonist and flautist Jane Bunnett, and she passed away in Havana shortly after recording *Aché IV* with the traditional group Yoruba Andabo. Cuervo (*Hoy canto a Cuba*), influenced by Celia Cruz, sang in the 1980s at the Tropicana, and died in 1998 of a brain haemorrhage, at the age of fifty-two. Based in Palma Soriano, Magaly Bernall sings in the great Afro-Cuban tradition of Celia Cruz and Merceditas Valdés and she has recorded an excellent album with Estrella de la charanga. Among other talented singers are Malena Burke (Elena's daughter), now living in the United States, the romantic Anais Abreu, and Osdalgia Lesmes (a Moráima Secada fan), who sings jazz, merengue, *cumbia*, bolero, blues, rap, and samba. Her eponymous album, produced by José Luis Cortés, has lush arrangements, and Lesmes moves from funky tunes (*La culebra*) to sensuous boleros (*Corazón rebelde*). New folk singers include Juan Carlos Formell (Juan Formell's son), long banned from performing because he practiced yoga – judged subversive! – and now based in New York, and guitarist "Peruchín Jr." (Pedro A. Justiz). Celina González continues to be the undisputed queen of rural music. In 1964 she embarked on a solo career and after Reutilio's death, in the early 1970s, she sang with her son Lázaro Domínguez, who took on the stage name Reutilio Jr., backed by the group Campo Alegre. Other exponents of the *guajiro* tradition are the warm-voiced Leyanis López, from Guantánamo, Eliades Ochoa's sister María Ochoa, and Ana María Chomate, who has recorded with La Sublime. As well, several trios still exist, among them Los Astros, Los Corales, and Taicuba.

The soulful Cándido Fabré has become one of the hottest *soneros*. He is also a highly prolific composer (able, he claims, to invent several songs in one day) whose tunes have been recorded by many performers, from Celia Cruz to Issac Delgado. Born in San Luis in 1958, he joined the Combo Samurai in nearby Palma Soriano and, from 1983 to 1993, worked with the *charanga* Orquesta Original de Manzanillo led by Pachi Naranjo, recording with them the hit *El guardián del Caribe* and writing for them. He then formed a fifteen-strong ensemble. *La Habana quiere guarachar contigo* shows him in fine form, influenced by the *nueva timba*, although the synthesizers detract from the quality of the music.

the United States and Puerto Rico

Despite the social protest movements and revolts of the 1960s, the economic gap between ethnic minorities and the white elite continued to widen. Many Puerto Ricans, who constituted in 1980 about 61 per cent of New York's Latin Americans, held low-paying jobs, and violence and drugs wracked the *barrios*.

Salsa, which burst out in the early 1970s, gave Puerto Ricans, and Hispanics in general, a new sense of pride and cultural identity. And as it gained wider recognition, Willie Colón, Eddie Palmieri, Cheo Feliciano, Ray Barretto, Celia Cruz and others became the new Latin American heroes.

Instrumental salsa

The *conjuntos*

In the late 1960s Latin musicians gladly returned to more authentic forms of expression and the boogaloo and the shing-a-ling gave way to salsa. As Johnny Pacheco explained: "People were getting tired of listening to the bands playing the same backbeat and the same boogaloo thing. The piano always had more or less the same riff."[1]

As we saw, the definition of salsa has generated much debate and, indeed, the sphere of salsa is rather difficult to circumscribe. Its core is mainly Cuban and Puerto Rican, though it has included Brazilian strains (Edu Lobo's *Boranda*,

1 In: David Carp, *A Visit with Maestro Johnny Pacheco*, p. 10.

recorded by La Sonora Ponceña, Willie Rosario's *Samba con salsa, Birimbau*, recorded by Celia Cruz and Willie Colón), *cumbias* from Colombia, *joropos* from Venezuela, *paseítos* and *tamboritos* from Panama, and even tangos. The early New York salsa was admittedly derived from the *son* and *son montuno*, but it had its own *callejero* (street) feel, for salsa was essentially a product of the *barrio*. One of its mainstays is the "*cuchifrito* circuit" (the Latin equivalent of the black "chittlin' circuit") – small social clubs in sometimes dismal neighborhoods where the locals congregate. As we saw earlier, if the backbone of salsa is Cuban, its first audiences and performers were mainly Puerto Ricans. And as salsa gained ground in other Latin American countries, Colombia and Venezuela in particular, it sometimes took on local characteristics, thus broadening its range.

César Miguel Rondón stressed that its trademark horn is the stalwart trombone, which carries the melody or plays counterpoint behind the singer, while timbales, congas, and bongos maintain the rhythmic underpinning. The *bongocero* plays *cencerro* (cowbell) on the *montuno* sections and anchors the band with a *kikikón kikón kikikón* evoking an ambling horse. Few salsa musicians can earn a living from their art, and the *sonero* with passionate *inspiraciones* (improvisations) who sings the joys and pains of life on Saturday nights often returns during the week to his job as deliveryman, doorman, or cab driver. In the beginning, many musicians were exploited and underpaid and rare were those who, like Cuban pianist Javier Vázquez, dared sue for their royalties. Like the Trinidad calypsonians, born in the shanty towns of Port of Spain, or the first samba musicians, raised in the favelas of Rio de Janeiro, *salseros*, who often came from humble backgrounds, compensated for their modest origins with bravado, as evidenced on some album titles from the 1970s: *Intocable* ("Untouchable"), *Unique*, and *El bravo soy yo* (loosely translated: "I'm where it's at"), to name only three.

Recurrent themes and words crop up in salsa: "*negro*" and "*mulato*" among them. In the Hispanic Caribbean, these words carry affectionate connotations that they do not have in Afro-American culture; and salsa has often revelled in the celebration of its blackness, as with Cheo Feliciano's song, exalting "*la belleza de mi negra música*" ("the beauty of my black music"), or Ismael Rivera's *Pa' bravo yo*, popularized by Justo Betancourt:

Pa' bravo yo	I'm brave
que soy mulato oscuro . . .	I'm a dark-skinned mulato, . . .
Tengo sangre africana	I have African blood
y canto con gran virtud	and I sing with great talent
Pa' bravo yo	I'm brave
yo sé lo que es la tumba, el cencerro,	and I know what the conga, the
y el bongó.	cowbell, and the bongo are.

If early salsa was sensual and extroverted, it also expressed the sense of belonging to the same community, as in Héctor Lavoe's *Mi gente*, and it dealt with socio-political problems, but without bitter defiance and militancy, always buoyed up by the lilting rhythms. Percussionist Bobby Sanabria recalls that when Eddie Palmieri's *La libertad – lógico* came out in the mid-1970s, it became "an anthem for young Puerto Ricans like me."

La libertad, caballero,	Freedom, sir,
no me la quites a mí.	don't take it away from me.
Pero mira que también soy humano	Look, I too am a human being,
y fue aquí dónde nací.	and I was born here.

In the 1970s, trumpeter Tony Pabón called his band La Protesta, and in *There Goes the Neighborhood – Se chavó el vecindario*, Willie Colón ironically evoked white people's dismay when an ethnic minority moved into their neighborhoods, and he deliberately used the Puerto Rican slang word: "*chavar.*" Later, Rubén Blades extended salsa's concerns, in *Plantación adentro* or *Tiburón*, to Latin American issues. *Guapería* (bravado) and *desafío* (taunts, challenges) also frequently inform salsa (Ray Barretto's *El watusi*, Blades's *Pedro Navaja*), for salsa is essentially virile, an affirmation of the Latin man's pride and identity.

By the time salsa was developing in New York, East Harlem had lost the monopoly of Latin music. Its old clubs and theaters had closed down (the illustrious Park Plaza, for one, had become a church), while tenements neglected for years would become coveted by real estate agents. In the late 1960s, the Saint George Hotel in Brooklyn Heights became salsa's first stronghold, with names such as Joe Bataan and the Lebrón Brothers: Pablo (vocals), Carlos (bongo), José (piano, *coro*), Angel (bass, *cuatro, coro*) and Héctor (conga). Black Nuyoricans, the Lebrón Brothers played a raunchy salsa with a big sound, and their albums: *Salsa y control, The Brooklyn Bums* (with *Let's Get Stoned*), or *I Believe* with its more positive title, expressed the energy and aggressiveness of that era.

In Manhattan, the Cheetah – the former Palm Gardens – located at the corner of 52nd Street and 8th Avenue, took over from the Saint George Hotel and became the new salsa hotbed. With Puerto Rican promoter Ralph Mercado – former impresario of James Brown and other major soul-music names – booking the best Latin artists there, the club drew Latinos like a magnet. Mercado also organized regular concerts at the Red Garter, in the Village. Fania issued two albums with the Fania All Stars – a stellar band put together for concert and recording purposes – entitled *Live at the Red Garter* and the two-volume *The Fania All Stars Live at the Cheetah*, which became a blockbuster. The historic show, organized on August 26, 1971 at the Cheetah, drew a delirious crowd of 5000, which went wild with *Quítate tú* ("Get out so I can step in"). Improvised after an idea by Pacheco, this song of *desafío* enabled each of the singers to take his turn on stage and deliver his *soneo*. A television program entitled *Salsa*, emceed by the Nuyorican Izzy Sanabria, further sparked the salsa boom. Sanabria – a cartoonist by trade – had illustrated the covers of the Alegre All Stars albums.

MAGIQUE

PRESENTS

FOR YOUR EARS ONLY

EDDIE PALMIERI
&
HIS ORCHESTRA

The Main Event

He founded *Latin New York*, a magazine essentially devoted to Latin music, which became a major forum for salsa. Other publications followed, as well as the documentary *Cosa Nuestra – Our Latin Thing* filmed by Fania at the Cheetah in 1971, accelerating the salsa vogue. The Cheetah closed shortly after the movie came out, but the Corso, located in the heart of Germantown, on the Upper East Side, the Casablanca, located on the site of the former La Conga, and other clubs took its place. In 1974, Fania released a second documentary, simply titled *Salsa*. It was supposed to show the Fania All Stars in a concert held in August of the same year at Yankee Stadium. However, an over-enthusiastic crowd broke down the security barriers and the concert was cancelled. Archival footage was used (including shots of a concert in San Juan), but the film, featuring Celia Cruz, Johnny Pacheco, Mongo Santamaría, Ray Barretto, the Fania All Stars, Héctor Lavoe, Willie Colón, Bobby Valentín, Ricardo Ray, and others, further evinced the importance of the new and upcoming Latin music. The same year, some of the stars of the Tico and Alegre labels gave a huge concert at Carnegie Hall. With Tito Puente as musical director, it gathered the cream of New York's salsa: Joe Cuba, Charlie Palmieri, Ismael Rivera, the Alegre All Stars (with Barry Rogers, Chombo Silva, Javier Vázquez, and Bobby Rodríguez, among others), and the Tico All Stars (with, notably, Cándido Camero, José Fajardo, Cachao, Chocolate Armenteros, and vocalists La Lupe, Vicentico Valdés, and Yayo El Indio). The evening ended with a *descarga* by Palmieri and the Alegre All Stars. Salsa had by then achieved full recognition.

Eddie Palmieri became a figurehead of salsa. He disbanded his *trombanga* in 1968, but came back the following year with the highly popular *Justicia*:

Ay, cuando llegará la justicia When justice will come
justicia pa' los boricuas y los niches justice for Puerto Ricans and blacks,
justicia que yo pido.   the justice I'm asking for.

The record, tinged by soul music and featuring among others Ismael Quintana on vocals, Chocolate Armenteros on trumpet, and Nicky Marrero, Francisco Aguabella, Chino Pozo, Ray Romero, and Manny Oquendo on percussion, included Cuban numbers: Ignacio Piñeiro's *Lindo yambú* and René Hernández's *Amor ciego*, but also *My Spiritual Indian*, which dealt with the violence of the streets. In 1971 Palmieri recorded with black American musicians a soul LP, *Harlem River Drive*. And, returning to his roots, he exalted Puerto Rico with the popular *Vamonos pa'l monte*, recorded on an eponymous album on which he played electric piano and his brother Charlie organ. The organ, which sounded rather heavy, had already been used by Pérez Prado in 1958 on his hit *Patricia*, but it was rather a novelty in salsa. *Vamonos pa'l monte* invited uprooted urban Puerto Ricans to return to the peaceful, comforting, and emotional *monte* of their forebears.

Vamonos pa'l monte	Let's go to the *monte*
Pa'l monte pa' guarachar,	To the *monte* to party,
Vamonos pa'l monte	Let's go the *monte*,
El monte me gusta más.	It's the *monte* I like the most.

The recurrent and hypnotic *montuno* of the song later inspired many *descargas*:

Vamonos pa'l monte – Eddie Palmieri

Palmieri offered another sizzling version of *Vamonos pa'l monte* in a recorded concert given at the University of Puerto Rico, and ebullient renditions of *Muñeca* and *Azúcar* in a performance given at Sing Sing Penitentiary.

Mon Rivera, who had partly abandoned music in 1968 and moved to East Harlem, converted to salsa and recorded with Willie Colón. *Forever* (with Johnny Pacheco as musical director), made shortly before his death in 1978 from a heart attack, and for which Colón wrote arrangements, continued to express down-to-earth concerns with such pieces as *Caldo y pescao* (Broth and fish) and *Las nenas del Barrio* (The girls of the Barrio). It also included a *bomba: Esta bomba es diferente*.

After a few years away from the limelight, Cuba returned with a new version of *La calle está durísima*, on *Hecho y derecho – Doin' Right* (1973), partly arranged by Marty Sheller, and featuring Jimmy Sabater (timbales), Alfredo Rodríguez (piano), Phil Díaz (vibes), Slim Cordero (bass), and Willie García (vocals). The album, with *Give Us a Chance*, the *son montuno Cuenta bien, cuenta bien*, and the *son Lucumí*, reflected the eclecticism of salsa.

In the early 1970s, Ricardo Ray made one of his best records: *El bestial sonido de Ricardo Ray y Bobby Cruz*, strewn with classical touches; and Kako Bastar and Azuquita joined forces on the excellent *Unión dinámica*.

In 1967, the year the Lebrón brothers formed their band, Fania offered a contract to a spunky seventeen-year-old trombonist named Willie Colón, who would soon become a major figure of salsa. Born in the Bronx to Puerto Rican parents, Colón organized at the age of thirteen the *conjunto* Los Dandies, which had a rather unusual instrumentation: harmonica, clarinet, trumpet, conga. His mother encouraged his musical vocation to keep him off the streets. The following year he set up La Dinámica and then, under Mon Rivera's influence, a two-trombone band: The Latin Jazz All Stars, which secured engagements at the Saint George Hotel, the Hunts Point Palace and the Bronx Music Palace.

Gangs such as The Savage Skulls and The Dirty Dozens terrorized the South Bronx, already wracked by drugs and poverty. On his first records: *El malo, The Hustler, Wanted, Cosa nuestra, Crime Pays, Lo mato* ("I kill him"), Colón projected the violence with which he grew up. *Calle Luna calle Sol,* for example, recorded on *Lo mato,* evoked two dangerous streets of old San Juan:

Mire Señora	Look out, Ma'am,
agarre bien su cartera,	hold on to your bag,
no conoce este barrio,	you don't know this neighborhood,
aquí asaltan a cualquiera.	here they mug anyone.

Listeners identified with Colón's driving music, and his enthusiasm made up for his lack of experience. They also identified with the Puerto Rican singer Héctor "Lavoe" (Héctor Juan Pérez Rodríguez), discovered by Pacheco, who would collaborate with Colón until 1974. The adventurous Colón soon incorporated jazz, Cuban, and Brazilian elements, as well as black Puerto Rican music, as in *Che che colé,* with its Bantu-sounding refrain:

A tí te gusta la bomba	You like the *bomba*
y te gusta el baquiné[2]	and you like the *baquiné,*
para que goces ahora	so that you enjoy yourself now
africano es el bembé –	here is the African *bembé –*
Che che colé	*Che che colé*
che che cofisa	*che che cofisa*
cofisa langa	*cofisa langa*
ca ca chi langa	*ca ca chi langa*
a de de.	*a de de.*

In 1972 he recorded a double Christmas album: *Asalto navideño,* which featured Yomo Toro on *cuatro.* It was the first time that this instrument and Puerto Rico's country music appeared in salsa. As Colón explained: "I said, 'man, we need guitars because I want to do something really *jíbaro.*' And when Yomo walks in – I had never seen him before – we sang him the whole arrangement because he can't read music, and he memorized the whole thing without screwing anything

2 A funeral wake for dead infants held by black Puerto Ricans of the island, the *baquiné* is a custom of African origin.

up. And this guy comes from a whole 'nother musical area!"[3] Playing on the word *asalto*,[4] Colón presented himself, on the album cover, as a thug disguised as Santa Claus and stealing toys and a television set, while the second album showed goblins with machine-guns attacking a gas station. Both albums brought him prominence. He also recorded two spirited songs by the Puerto Rican composer "Tite" (Catalino) Curet Alonso: the *son Piraña* and *Catalina la O*.

At the end of 1973, he dissolved his band and issued *El bueno, El malo y el feo*, mixing salsa, rock, Puerto Rican, and Panamanian music, then *The Big Break*, with the catchy *Ghana-e* and, in 1975, *Se chavó el vecindario* (There Goes the Neighborhood), featuring Mon Rivera, which returned to street themes.

Drawing again from Puerto Rican folklore and based on a poem by Eloy Blanco, he wrote the score for a television film entitled *El baquiné de los angelitos negros*. The title tune began with percussion, followed by Yomo Toro's *cuatro*, and then segued into big-band jazz, but, polished as it was, as a whole the effort lacked sparkle.

On December 30, 1970, Arsenio Rodríguez, practically forgotten, died of pneumonia in Los Angeles. A few months later, Larry Harlow recorded *Tribute to Arsenio Rodríguez* (with Toro on *tres*, this time), reworking some of Rodríguez's songs: *A todos los barrios*, *El terror y Kila*, the *son Quique y Chocolate*[5] with a more modern salsa sound. In 1972, after recording on *Harlow's Harem*, Ismael Miranda left Harlow to pursue his own career, and was replaced by Nestor Sánchez, also a great *sonero*. Nicknamed "El albino divino" (The divine albino), Sánchez had worked with Ray Rodríguez and other bands. Harlow then wrote *Hommy* – a salsa version arranged by Marty Sheller of *Tommy*, The Who's rock opera, with a libretto by Puerto Rican percussionist Heny Álvarez. Presented at Carnegie Hall in March, 1973, it starred Junior González, Celia Cruz, Cheo Feliciano, Justo Betancourt, and Adalberto Santiago. *Hommy* was recorded and Celia Cruz, whom Harlow had persuaded to come especially from Mexico, completed everything in one take, without any rehearsal. He then chose, on *Salsa* (1974) – one of his best albums – various Cuban songs, revamping Richard Egües's *El paso de Encarnación* and two Arsenio Rodríguez numbers: *La cartera* and *Suéltame*. *La cartera* was played with a *charanga* feel while the refrain borrowed the words from the old *danzón Camina, Juan Pescao*. And subverting with humor Rodríguez's title *El ciego maravilloso* ("The marvellous blindman"), Harlow turned it, on one of his records, into *El Judío Maravilloso* ("The Marvellous Jew") – an allusion to his ethnic origin. In 1978, following the fashion for salsa suites, he produced *La raza latina*, an album with a hideous cover which included African-inspired music and had little success.

Ray Barretto emerged from his Latin soul period with strong LPs that made statements: *Together*, with a good version of *Tin tin deo*, *Power*, with the hit *Quítate la máscara*, evoking women's fickleness, and *The Message*. But it is the exuberant *Cocinando* (*Cocinando suave, suave cocinando*), on *Que viva la música*, which became his theme song.

3 In: John Storm Roberts: *A Newyorican Christmas*.

4 Literally, *asalto* means "assault," but *asaltos* are also spontaneous serenades given on the island at Christmas time.

5 These two last songs call to mind some of Arsenio Rodríguez's musicians.

Cocinando – Ray Barretto

The following year, Adalberto Santiago, trumpeter René López, percussionist "Dandy" (Johnny) Rodríguez Jr., bassist Dave Pérez, and *timbalero* Orestes Vilató left him to form Típica 73. Barretto then tried his hand at an experimental *Drum Poem*, which disconcerted some of his fans. But, Barretto argued, "I don't like to be locked in anything. I love both jazz and classical music." Flautist Art Webb – a jazz and Latin music veteran – drummer Billy Cobham, the versatile Colombian pianist Eddie Martínez and Panamanian bassist Guillermo Edgehill joined forces on the more jazz-oriented *The Other Road*. *Indestructible* – Barretto's credo – which featured Tito Allen on vocals, derived from Lorenzo Hierrezuelo's *No quiero llanto* and dealt with amorous betrayal. With Tito Gómez, Rubén Blades, and El Negro Vivar, Barretto offered the powerful *Ban ban queré*, Juan Formell's *Guararé*, Tite Curet Alonso's *guaguancó Vale más*, and Blades's *Canto abacuá*. *Tomorrow* (1976), with Tito Puente and Orestes Vilató conversing on timbales, harmoniously combined jazz and salsa.

Louie Ramírez consolidated his reputation as a vibist with his impetuous solo on *Juan Pachanga*, recorded with the Fania All Stars, and on other albums (*Vibes Galore, Para la fiesta me voy, Louie Ramírez y sus amigos*); and he became one of the most sought-after arrangers in Latin music (also working for Herb Alpert, David Bowie, Manhattan Transfer, and others). In the mid-1980s, he started another salsa band, featuring Ray de la Paz on vocals, and with him recorded *Noche caliente*, which triggered the *salsa romántica* boom, until de la Paz left to form his own outfit.

A cluster of groups appeared in the early 1970s: Ocho, formed by the black American *timbalero*, pianist, and arranger "Chico Mendoza" (Ira Jay Robertson). Born in Jacksonville, Florida, Robertson adopted a Latin name because, he explained, "People didn't think Americans were able to play authentic Afro-Cuban music." Ocho's vocalists, however, Jimmy Sabater among them, were Hispanic. Ocho recorded dense and vibrant numbers: *Ay que frío, Margarito, Ritmo de pollos*, harmonized with flutes, *La batanga*, played on vibes, with vibraslap accents on the first beat and moving from a rumba to a *descarga*. Mendoza, who also hosted a jazz radio show, later founded The Latin Jazz Dream Band, recalling Tito Puente's style (*Swinging Guaguancó, Macho's Latin Satin*).

Típica 73 became one of the leading salsa groups of the early 1970s, offering Cuban standards (*Pare cochero, Los Sitios llaman*), new Cuban tunes (*La escoba barrendera*, Juan Formell's *La candela*), and original compositions (*Manono*). *Tresista* Nelson González briefly joined the band before organizing Los Kimbos with Adalberto Santiago, Orestes Vilató, Joe Manozzi, bassist Sal Cuevas, and others. Flautist Gonzalo Fernández, singers Tito Allen and later Azuquita, and the fiery Cuban violinist Alfredo de la Fé – a former Fajardo sideman – *timbalero* Nicky Marrero, and pianist "Sonny Bravo" (Elio Osacar) contributed to Típica 73's success. After the seductive *Rumba Caliente* (with Puerto Rican percussionist "Cachete" (Ángel) Maldonado on *batá* drums and conga and Ismael Quintana on maracas and güiro), they came up in 1976 – during the vogue for salsa suites – with *Los dos lados de la Típica 73*, with one side made for listening and the other for dancing, an LP which already smacked of *songo*.

In 1977, Típica 73 played at the Tropicana, in Cuba. It was the first American group since Nat "King" Cole to perform there. In Havana, they recorded with some of the legends of Cuban music: Richard Egües, Niño Rivera, Guillermo Barreto, Félix Chappotín, Tata Güines, Juan Pablo Torres, and Felo Bacallao an excellent album which somewhat weakened Cuba's prejudices against salsa. But upon their return to the U.S., the band was penalized by some for their Cuban foray. They went through a slack period and their vocalist, José Alberto, eventually pursued his own career.

The hyperactive Johnny Pacheco produced with great flair a bevy of artists for the Fania label: among them Joe Bataan, Pupi Legarreta, and Fajardo, and issued lively records under his name: *Tremendo caché*, *El maestro* (with Héctor Casanova, Papo Lucca, shining on *Guaguancó pa'l que sabe*, "Perico" Ortiz, remarkable on *Simaní*), *El artista*, *Pacheco y Melón* (with singer "Melón" – Angel Luis Silva), *Sabrosura* (with Mongo Santamaría), *La perfecta combinación* and *De nuevo los compadres* (with Pete "El Conde" Rodríguez).

The Fania All Stars, with Papo Lucca, Sal Cuevas, the trombonist Reinaldo Jorge, Nicky Marrero, and others, selected by Johnny Pacheco according to their talent and their availability, continued to give concerts and to record. At Madison Square Garden, they once performed with a spectacular battery of stage effects, including artificial smoke. The flexible and ever inventive Lucca played upside down while his piano rotated, but these show business tricks did not affect the music, which remained of superior quality. In 1974 in Africa, Larry Harlow, Johnny Pacheco, and Ray Barretto shared the bill with James Brown, driving audiences wild. The Fania All Stars also played in Japan, with their last concert taking place in 1998 in Bayamón, Puerto Rico.

The band turned out a string of records of irregular caliber: *Fania All Stars at the Red Garter* (1972) with, among other tunes, *Son, cuero y boogaloo*, recalled the *descargas* of the 1960s. The more elaborate *Rhythm Machine* (1977), with its enticing cover, was sensational. It included Lucca, Marrero, Pacheco, Roberto Roena, Mongo Santamaría, Rubén Blades, Luis "Perico" Ortiz, and Louie Ramírez, plus Bob James (on *Awake*) and Eric Gale (on *Ella fue*). Blades's striking *Juan Pachanga* – a *rumba brava* arranged by Ramírez and Jay Chattaway – ended with an exchange between Lucca and bassist Bobby Valentín. After the bland crossover *Spanish Fever* and *Delicate and Jumpy*, the group recovered its form with *Commitment* (1980), with Lucca sizzling on *Piano Man, Latin Connection* (1981) with Roena, Santos Colón, Celia Cruz, and trumpeter Juancito Torres, and a stunning version of *Bilongo*; and *Lo que pide la gente*, again with a wonderful Lucca solo (on *Por eso yo canto salsa*). Gato Barbieri's presence, however, failed to rescue *Social Change* from triteness; and other Fania All Stars live albums were sometimes formulaic, despite the energy.

In 1975, after a long battle waged by Eddie Palmieri and other Hispanics, the Grammy Awards finally agreed to create a special category for Latin music, and around the same time with the release of the documentary *Salsa*, the salsa phenomenon gained momentum. Latin clubs such as the Chico East, the New York Casino, the Ipanema, the more experimental Newyorican Village, La Maganette, and the Cerromar Casino proliferated in New York. Madison Square Garden, Radio City Music Hall, the Beacon Theater, the Belmont Race Theater, and Yankee Stadium all organized Latin concerts. The media took hold of salsa and several salsa radio programs appeared.

Tito Puente and Machito also adapted to salsa with their respective big bands. In the early 1970s Carlos Santana struck gold with a rock version of Puente's *Pa'los rumberos* and of *Oye como va* (on *Abraxas*), which brought Puente to the attention of a wider audience, and in turn Puente recorded Santana's *Batuca*. The following year, Puente included *Picadillo, 110th Street and Fifth Avenue*, and *Prepárate para bañarte*, evoking *santería*, on *Tito Puente and his Concert Orchestra*, on which Charlie Palmieri played organ and vibes. In 1975 Catalino Rolón and Alberto Socarrás were featured guests on his exotic *Tambó*, with Hollywoodish titles: *Call of the Jungle Birds, Dance of the Head Hunters, Voodoo Dance at Midnight*. Four years later, the first volume of his *Homenaje a Benny Moré*, featuring Celia Cruz, Cheo Feliciano, Santos Colón, and other stellar vocalists, won a Grammy Award. While salsa started to decline in the 1980s, Puente retained his legendary ebullience on *Dancemania 80*, with the funny *Le robaron los timbales* sung by the expressive Frankie Figueroa, and *Cé Magnifique*, recorded with Azuquita, and other more recent albums. He also demonstrated his talent as a pianist (*Guaguancó a Arsenio*) and appeared in the movies *Radio Days* and *Mambo Kings*.

Around 1975, Machito's orchestra performed at Saint Patrick's cathedral in New York (the first time a Latin ensemble played there) a new suite by Chico O'Farrill: *Oro, incienso y mirra* (Gold, frankincense, and myrrh). This cerebral and dense work including *batá* drums stood out radically from the rest of the salsa and Latin jazz of that era. It was recorded the same year with Dizzy Gillespie on *Afro-Cuban Moods*. Since the *Afro-Cuban Jazz Suite* and *Kenya*, made in the heyday of the Afro-Cubans, Machito and Bauzá had not performed such ambitious material. A few months later, however, after a tour to Europe, Machito expressed the desire to cut down the size of the band. Bauzá and Graciela, who disagreed, decided to go their own way, and Machito took by himself the reins of his orchestra. The following year he produced the vibrant salsa album, *Fireworks* with Charlie Palmieri, Victor Paz, Nicky Marrero, Mauricio Smith, the nineteen-year-old Puerto Rican singer "Lalo" (Manuel Ubaldo) Rodríguez, and a *coro* consisting of Ismael Quintana, Chivirico Dávila, and Adalberto Santiago. Mixing synthesizers and traditional instruments, the arrangers Ray Santos and Lito Peña created a spellbinding phantasmagoria. Rodríguez burst out with juvenile ardor on his superb *guaguancó Mi ritmo llegó* while Machito stayed in a more sedate mode.

Around the late 1970s, Machito's daughter Paula became his female vocalist and his son Mario his *timbalero* and musical director. Ever generous, Machito often performed at block parties and other community events, still offering his classical Cuban repertoire (*El as de la rumba*, Pablo Cairo's *Tíbiri tábara*, *Para la niña y la señora*) and he worked for a drug rehabilitation program and a senior citizens center. Though proficient, Paula lacked Graciela's charisma and the band lost some of its former sparkle. *Machito and His Salsa Band 1982*, however, won a Grammy Award – Machito's first. Two years later, on April 15, 1984, Machito died of a heart attack and a cerebral hemorrhage in London, a few days after performing at Ronnie Scott's. Laid to rest in his coffin with his maracas, he was visited at the funeral parlor in New York by his closest relatives, friends, and colleagues, and mourned by thousands of fans. Mario then took over his father's orchestra, but it broke up shortly thereafter.

Bauzá worked freelance and then formed his own ensemble, the Afro-Cuban Jazz Orchestra – a driving Latin jazz big band featuring Rudy Calzado on vocals. With Graciela he also cut a salsa album, *La botánica* (1976) on which Graciela sang the comical *La bochinchera* (The gossiper).

Charlie Palmieri tried his hand at the organ and harmonica, two instruments not very compatible with the punch and drive of salsa (*El gigante del teclado*, *Adelante gigante*, *Vuelve el gigante*, and other recordings). The better *Impulse* (1975) offered a winning mixture of Cuban standards and jazz numbers. He then teamed up with Panamanian *sonero* "Meñique" (Miguel Barcasnegras) on *Charlie Palmieri y Meñique – Con salsa y sabor*, with a beautiful *Tributo a Pedro Flores*. And on the excellent *A Giant Step* (1984), his phrasing recalled Noro Morales's. The following year, he set up the eleven-strong El Combo Gigante, with veterans Jimmy Sabater and Willie Torres, and moved to Puerto Rico. But, suffering from heart problems, he died in a Bronx hospital in 1988.

Around 1973, Eddie Palmieri turned increasingly to jazz (Willie Bobo nicknamed him "the Latin Thelonious Monk") and he played several pieces with long and slightly grandiloquent modal preludes (*Cosas del alma*, *Adoración*, *Un día bonito*). *Sun of Latin Music*, arranged by René Hernández and featuring Lalo Rodríguez, Steve Gadd, Jeremy Steig, and Ron Carter, included the sizzling *Un puesto vacante* and *Óyelo que te conviene*; and *Resemblance*, a jazz waltz on which Eddie Martínez soloed on electric piano. Palmieri recorded *Resemblance* again in

1978 on *Exploration* – a slightly colder and less spontaneous album than his earlier ones. Subtitled *Salsa Descarga Jazz,* it again featured Steig and Carter, plus Nicky Marrero and bassist Andy González; and Palmieri's playing on *Random Thoughts* brought McCoy Tyner to mind. After the rather mediocre *Lucumí, Macumba, Voodoo,* with a glamorous cover, Palmieri returned to a volcanic salsa with, notably, *Eddie Palmieri – bárbaro* (1981); this album featured Cheo Feliciano and Ismael Quintana and included two tunes arranged by René Hernández: *Ritmo alegre* and *El día que me quieras; Palo pa' rumba* (1984), propelled by Giovanni Hidalgo's drums; the searing *Solito* (1985) with new versions of *Lindo yambú* and *Justicia; Sueño* (1989), a mixture of Latin jazz and salsa, with David Sanborn, Mike Stern, Francisco Aguabella, and Milton Cardona, with *batás* resounding on the beautiful *rumba Cobarde;* the explosive *Llegó La India* (1992), introducing the young and flamboyant Puerto Rican vocalist "La India" (Lindabell Caballero); the instrumental *Palmas* (1995), full of dissonances and obstinate *guajeos,* and *Arete* (1995), buoyed by bassist John Benítez's vibrant *tumbaos;* and shortly before Tito Puente's death on May 31, 2000, from complications following open-heart surgery, Palmieri and the *timbalero* recorded together *Masterpiece/Obra maestra* – an urban *rumba* album – featuring Milton Cardona, Óscar D'León, Pete "El Conde" Rodríguez (who died in the Bronx on December 2 of the same year), and other guest stars – that went from the tango-tinged *La última copa* to a salsa version of *Cielito lindo.* The winner of six Grammy Awards, Palmieri still leads, with his gifted Newark-born vocalist Hermán Olivera, bassist Joe Santiago, percussionists José Clausell and Richie Flores and other superior sidemen, one of the most exciting bands in salsa. A recent performance in Corsica in front of members of the Septeto Nacional elicited admiring comments from these old Cuban masters. Skeptical at first ("he plays *tres montunos*"), they exclaimed, they soon acknowledged Palmieri's mastery of the Cuban tradition and surrendered to the buoyant rhythms and the power he generated.

Towards the mid-1970s salsa, contaminated by fusion and disco, started to pall. By the end of the decade, in an effort to renew itself, it even borrowed the go-go beat, created in Washington and popularized by Chuck Brown, but to little avail. In the early 1980s, disco came to threaten salsa, which young Hispanics forsook in favor of rap, house music, techno, jungle, and other forms of electronic music. Ray Barretto issued two rather mediocre fusion albums: *The Eyes of the Beholder* and *Can You Feel It.* He then made the better *Ricanstruction* with *Tumbao africano,* arranged by pianist Óscar Hernández, which stood out with its *batá* introduction and poignant saxophone solo by Todd Anderson. With *La cuna* and subsequent records, he reached a satisfying balance between salsa and jazz.

In 1974, Manny Oquendo organized with Andy González the inventive Conjunto Libre. A master *timbalero* and *bongocero,* the Brooklyn-born Oquendo had played with the top names of Latin music (El Boy, Chano Pozo, José Curbelo, Tito Rodríguez, Tito Puente, Eddie Palmieri). Though twenty years younger than

Oquendo, González also had impressive credentials, Eddie Palmieri among them. Libre – which included Oscar Hernández (piano), Andy González (bass) and his brother Jerry (conga and trumpet), "Papo" (Ángel) Vázquez (trombone), Frankie Rodríguez (conga), and Milton Cardona (percussion) – experimented with a heady mixture of salsa, jazz, and traditional Afro-Cuban and Puerto Rican music. A former Larry Harlow sideman, Frankie Rodríguez had worked in 1973, along with Óscar Hernández and Nelson González, with Ismael Miranda's La Revelación. A *batá* master and *santería* adept, Cardona had collaborated with Willie Colón and Héctor Lavoe.

The Conjunto Libre recorded several ground-breaking albums brimming with ideas, among them *Libre: con salsa y ritmo*, with a *Donna Lee* (subtitled *A gozar y bailar*) starting with a *danzón* and turning into salsa; *Tiene calidad*, with the superb guaguancó *Imágenes latinas*, used as a theme song for the credits of a Latin television program; *Lo dice todo*, and *Los líderes de la salsa*. It also accompanied Venezuelan singer Orlando "Watusi" Castillo. Over the years, top musicians such as the trombonists Jimmy Bosch and Steve Turre and vocalists Hermán Olivera and "Frankie" (Efrain) Vázquez passed through the band, which managed to keep its freshness (*Mejor que nunca*, recorded in 1994 and including Margarita Rivera's *bomba Ingratitudes*, Rafael Cepeda's *plena Candela*, and a bolero rendition of *Prelude to a Kiss*; *On the Move!*, with its wonderful versions of *Lester Leaps In* and *Piel canela*).

In 1977, Willie Colón teamed up with Panamanian singer and composer Rubén Blades. Blades's intellectual temperament contrasted with Colón's more impetuous one, but both men shared the same musical enthusiasm, hunger for experimentation, and social consciousness. On their first joint effort, *Metiendo mano*, Blades wrote poetical songs that differed markedly from those usual in salsa. Among them *La maleta*, dealing with the return home of Puerto Ricans living in the United States, *Plantación adentro*, evoking the Amerindians' plight and *Pablo Pueblo* – the archetype of the Latin American poor:

Pablo Pueblo	Pablo Pueblo (Pablo People)
Hijo del grito y de la calle	Child of the cry and the street
De la miseria y del hambre	Of misery and hunger
Del callejón y la pena	Of the back alley and pain
Pablo Pueblo	Pablo Pueblo
Su alimento es la esperanza	His food is hope
Su paso no lleva prisa	His step is unhurried
Su sombra nunca lo alcanza.	His shadow never reaches him.

Colón later recorded with Celia Cruz *Solamente ellos pudieron hacer este álbum*, with the Brazilian hit *Você abusou*, reworked, salsa style, as *Usted abusó* and then with Blades the best-seller *Siembra*. It included Blades's *Plástico*, decrying consumerism, *María Lionza*, alluding to an Afro-Venezuelan cult, and *Pedro*

Willie Colón and Rubén Blades. Photograph Omar Pardillo Jr.

Navaja, a colorful mini-drama, painting with a few sharp strokes (a wide-brimmed hat, a knife in his pocket) the pathetic portrait of a crook putting on a macho front to hide his despair.

From 1979 on, Blades's and Colón's roads began to diverge. Despite his charisma and beautiful voice, part of the Puerto Rican community found Blades too militant and highbrow. His sophisticated metaphors, rich vocabulary, and Panamerican concept took him progressively away from Colón, and they parted rather bitterly. Hoping for a crossover success, Colón tried to court the Anglo market with *Willie Colón solo*, an album with sickly sweet violins heralding the *salsa romántica*. However, he collaborated again with Blades on *Maestra vida*, a much more original LP whose title-song, written by Tite Curet Alonso, told the saga of a Latin American family. In 1981 Colón organized a show band and issued the bland *Fantasmas*, on which he sang. The record won over Venezuela, but Colón's core aficionados preferred his more substantial salsa. Colón reacted again by projecting, on the cover of *Tiempo pa' matar*, his earlier manly image. This better album, which included a female *coro*, featured the *songo El diablo* (presented, perhaps under the influence of Mon Rivera's amalgams, as a *plenarengue* – a cross between *plena* and *merengue*), and the *son Callejón sin salida* (mentioned as a *songo*). In 1982 he again teamed up with Blades, on the excellent *Canciones del solar de los aburridos*, which evoked the misery of the Latin American *barrios*, and on Blades's *Tiburón* (shark), deriding dictatorship. On *Criollo* (1984), Colón drew again from Brazilian sources with Caetano Veloso's *Miel*, and he tried his hand at fusion with the blockbuster *Set Fire to Me*, sung in English and featuring Tito Puente and Charlie Palmieri.

In 1978, the trumpeter, flugelhorn-player, and arranger Luis "Perico" Ortiz (nicknamed "Perico" after Cortijo's *Quítate de la vía perico*) burst on the salsa scene with his own group. Born in Puerto Rico, Ortiz had worked there with Mario Ortiz and in New York with Mongo Santamaría, Johnny Pacheco, the Fania All Stars, Tommy Olivencia, and just about everybody in salsa. *Mi propia imagen* and *El isleño*, relatively conventional, nevertheless kept dancers on their feet. Ortiz later issued the more inventive *Breaking the Rule* (1987) and, like Ray Barretto and Tito Puente, he went on to organize a Latin jazz ensemble.

The Conjunto Clásico was set up in 1979 by two former members of Pacheco's band: singer and güiro-player Ramón Rodríguez and singer and *bongocero* Ray Castro. Maintaining the classical *conjunto* format, they included a *tres* and three trumpets. They recorded prolifically, performing Cuban numbers and also updating Puerto Rican folklore (*Faisán, Don Pedrito*). In 1986, their powerful vocalist Tito Nieves left to pursue his own career and was replaced by Johnny Rivera, who had sung with his uncle Adalberto Santiago and with the Grupo Fascinación.

The Lebrón Brothers had pretty much vanished from the music scene around the mid-1970s. After a failed attempt at disco, they made a comeback in the 1980s, augmented by Frankie (conga), Adrián (trombone), and Angel "Mambo" Lebrón (percussion). *El boso* (Spanglish for "the boss"), recorded in 1988, evoked the good old 1960s with *El abuelo pachanguero* (The Pachanga-dancing Grandfather).

The Puerto Rican *tresista* Charlie Rodríguez, impressed by Arsenio Rodríguez (no relation), founded at Roberto Torres's instigation a *típico* group mostly devoted to the *son montuno*.

Saoco (a word meaning "feeling"), was founded by bassist and *tresista* William Milán and singer and *conguero* Henry Fiol, of Puerto Rican and Italian descent, to try to recapture the Puerto Rican *jíbaro* (country sound), but with a more urban approach. Fiol was influenced by the great Cuban *soneros* Benny Moré and Abelardo Barroso, and by Rafael Cortijo and Ismael Rivera; however, his nasal and high-pitched voice was very much his own, and fitted in perfectly with the band's *típico* style. Fiol wrote two of Saoco's hits: *Lejos del batey* (on *Siempre seré Guajiro*, recorded in 1975), and *Yo no como candela*. He then left to pursue a solo career, and the group continued as William Milán y Saoco. Fiol then turned out the good *Monina, Perdido en la ciudad* – the story of a Latin American immigrant – *Colorao y negro*, and *Fe, esperanza y caridad* (1980). In 1982 he organized the short-lived *conjunto* Corazón, and in 1989 made *Renacimiento*, featuring his son Orlando on piano, synthesizer, and *coro*. Departing from tradition, he used a *cuatro* rather than a *tres* and a saxophone instead of a trumpet in his orchestrations of *sones*.

Mention should also be made of Yambú, founded by Milton Hamilton; the jazzy Las Siete Potencias (an allusion to the seven major deities of *santería*), led by vibist Louie Sánchez (*Smokin*, with flautist Dave Valentín's melodious *guajira Freed Wind*); Los Kimbos ("Los grandes Kimbos con Adalberto Santiago"), headed by Orestes Vilató; Frankie Dante's La Flamboyán; pianist Héctor Castro's Conjunto Candela; *bongocero* "El Chino" Cruz de Jesús's Conjunto Melao; Guararé, created by ex-members of Ray Barretto's band the Conjunto Bembé, with saxophonist Guillermo Valentín – a Sonny Rollins aficionado; pianist and singer Wayne Gorbea's *conjunto*; East Harlem Lexington Avenue Express, a Latin children's band from the *barrio*; the Conjunto Imagen, set up by Louie "Campana" Hernández (bongo), Junior Rivera (*tres*), and Ernie Acevedo (conga), offering a classical type of salsa; the driving Grupo Fascinación; and the band set up in 1995 by Puerto Rican saxophonist Ray Santos, a former sideman of Noro Morales and the Afro-Cubans.

A few musicians also made interesting records under their own names. Among them José Mangual Jr. (*Mangual*, with Yomo Toro on *cuatro*); the Puerto Rican pianist and arranger Pepe Castillo who skillfully combined funk, *bomba*, and *plena* on *Banana Land*; trombonist Leopoldo Piñeda, who adapted the Chico Buarque song *No sueño más*; (on *Sabor y raza*); and pianists "Markolino" (Mark) Dimond, Paquito Pastor, Isidro Infante, and Alfredo Valdés. The ebullient Cuban violinist Alfredo de la Fé introduced the electric violin into salsa. "In salsa, one must play violin as if it were a percussion instrument, with a more aggressive sound," he explains. On *Alfredo*, he mixed salsa, funk, and jazz, with a Latin *My Favorite Things*. While living in Colombia, he started utilizing local rhythms and on *Vallenato* he included a collection of Colombian *paseos* and *merengues*. Now based in Italy, he leads a still highly energetic band.

The *charangas*

In the 1970s *charangas*, among them Fajardo's (*Te pones a gozar*) and Orquesta Broadway, which included pianists René Hernández and later Kelvin Zervigón and Gil Suárez, Cuban singers "Felo" (Rafael) Barrio and Roberto "El Caminante" Torres, and their countryman, trumpeter Roberto Rodríguez, also had success in salsa. While becoming salsa's number-one *charanga*, Orquesta Broadway managed to keep its Cuban flavor. They scored a hit with *Salvaje*, recorded in 1976 with Felo Barrio, and in the following year *Pasaporte* with, especially, the son *Isla del Encanto*. Five of the band's musicians then moved to Miami, but the band regrouped and it continued to produce winning music: *Viva Africa, Al soltar el gallo*, and several *songos*, performed in the Cuban style.

Roberto Torres left Orquesta Broadway to join La Sonora Matancera. Shortly thereafter he set up Los Caminantes and then, in Miami, the SAR label devoted to traditional Cuban music and contributing to the resurgence of the *típico* sound, and also organized an SAR All Stars.

A former member of the bands of Julio Gutiérrez, Adolfo Guzman, and Benny Moré, the violinist and saxophonist "Chombo" Silva had played in New York with jazzmen (among them James Moody) and a score of Latin artists. With Gil Suárez and former Orquesta Broadway musicians, he organized La Típica

Ideal, which borrowed its name from a Havana *charanga*. They introduced the *changüí* in New York, with *Ritmo changüí* (on *Vamos pa' Senegal*), recorded *A Touch of Brass* (with Barry Rogers and Chocolate Armenteros), exemplifying the fusion taking place between *charangas* and *conjuntos*, and in 1978 the good *Fuera de este mundo*.

Bobby Rodríguez, a Joe Bataan alumnus, flautist, clarinettist, and saxophonist, recruited vocalist and trombonist Eddie Hernández Iglesias – a Willie Colón disciple – who sang the English lyrics, and Junior Córdova – a Cortijo admirer – and José Acosta who sang the Spanish ones, and founded the bubbly La Compañía. Born in the *barrio*, Rodríguez had first worked with his brother Ray's band as saxophonist and musical director. *Lead Me To That Beautiful Band* (1975) which included a bolero rendition of Gordon Park's *Don't Misunderstand Me*, and the hit *Número 6*, written by Rubén Blades and evoking a New York subway line linking the South Bronx to the Lower East Side (two predominantly Hispanic neighborhoods), thrust Rodríguez into the limelight:

Apúrate maquinista que	Hurry up, driver,
estoy esperando	I'm waiting for
el número 6.	the Number 6.

Número 6 – Rubén Blades

What Happened, a Spanglish song by Blades, reflected the bilingualism of the New York *barrios*. *Latin From Manhattan* (1978) evoked, besides the successful title-song – a cover of the old Al Jolson hit – Puerto Rico's *jíbaros* and, with *Negra sabrosura*, the charm of the Afro-Caribbean world. In 1984, some of the band's members defected. Rodríguez reshaped his band with "Watusi" (Orlando Castillo) on vocals, renaming it La Nueva Companía. He then issued the aptly titled *Mi regreso* ("My comeback"), which featured Louie Ramírez on timbales, Isidro Infante on piano and Papo Pepín on conga, and went from *Pennies From Heaven* to Ñico Saquito's *María Cristina*.

Other *charangas* appeared: Típica Novel, a rather conformist group led by Cuban singer and pianist Willie Ellis, that included trombones and which evolved into Orquesta Novel; the relatively commercial Charanga 76, fronted by singers Hansel and Raúl (*Soy*); Charanga América and Charanga Sublime, also borrowing their names from Cuban groups; Charanga Casino; Gene Hernández's Orquesta Novedades, with Willie Rodríguez on piano; Charanga de la Cuatro; Afro Charanga, with the talented flautist Nestor Torres; Orquesta Son Primero, a hybrid yet *típico* group led by *tresista* Charlie Santiago, with Adalberto Santiago (*coro*), Dave Valentín (flute), and Jorge Dalto (piano).

Pupi Legarreta, flautists Gonzalo Fernández and Lou Pérez, and violinist and arranger Eddie Drennon took part in many *charanga* recording sessions. Legarreta played on Puente's *Oye como va*, and under his own name recorded *Salsa nueva*, *Pupi y su charanga*, and *Los dos mosqueteros*, with Patato Valdés's attractive *Lo saen*. A wooden transverse-flute virtuoso, Fernández had worked in Cuba with Rosendo Ruiz, Senén Suárez, Orquesta América, and Orquesta América del 55. He then lived sixteen years in Paris, settling in New York in the 1970s. After a stint with Cachao, he got together the Orquesta Superestrellas de Gonzalo, and made *Supertípica de estrellas*, *Picao*, and *Repicao*, close to the spirit of Cuba's classic *charangas*. In the early 1980s he began to have problems with his lip muscles, but he continued to play until a facial paralysis put an end to his career. Lou Pérez turned out several salsa suites, among them *Fantasía africana*, and *Nuestra herencia* (1977). *De todo un poco* (1978), not as convincing, included two Latin hustle tunes (a genre halfway between salsa and disco).

The return to the Cuban roots

In the mid-1970s, the increasing commercialism of salsa triggered a return to the Cuban roots. Percussionists Milton Cardona and Gene Golden, the brothers Andy and Jerry González, and others fostered interest in *rumba brava*, *santería*, and other Afro-Cuban genres. And some musicians paid tribute to Cuban masters: Larry Harlow to Arsenio Rodríguez, Tito Puente to Benny Moré, José Mangual to Chano Pozo.

Born in 1975 of jam sessions organized at the home of Andy and Jerry González, in the Bronx, the Grupo Folklórico Y Experimental Nuevayorquino explored Cuban and Puerto Rican traditional rhythms. In addition to their involvement with the Conjunto Libre, the brothers had worked with Dizzy Gillespie and Eddie Palmieri and formed in 1974 the *conjunto* Anacaona (named after an Arsenio Rodríguez *son*). The Grupo Folklórico's *Concepts in Unity* (1975) featured Cubans Chocolate Armenteros, Caíto Díaz (the Sonora Matancera *maraquero*), Gonzalo Fernández, and Virgilio Martí; and Puerto Ricans Manny Oquendo, Gene Golden, and Óscar Hernández. A musical medley, it included *santería toques*, a *guajira*, a *plena*, a mazurka, and several *descargas*. The group also recorded *Coro miyare*,[6] an old Arara chant; and despite the diversity of its repertoire, it managed to retain its identity.

Patato Valdés, surrounded by Virgilio Martí, "Papaíto" (Mario Muñoz Salazar), Orestes Vilató, Julio Collazo, Cachete Maldonado, and Puerto Rican *tresista* Nelson González exalted the *orishas* (*Canto a Changó, To y van hecho*) and continued to express himself in an Afro-Cuban vein with *Batá y rumba* (1981) and *Sonido lindo* (1984), on which he sang with Totico, in a hoarse and comical voice, the *guaguancó Dícelo Patato*. Martí recruited Ignacio Berroa, Jerry González, Yomo Toro, and others on *Saludando a los rumberos* (1984); Totico produced *Totico y sus rumberos*, and, with Kako Bastar, the superb *La máquina y el motor*, under Tite Curet Alonso's musical direction, which included Totico's *Oye los tambores*, opening with a *rumba brava*, and *Cabio silé*, alluding to the *orisha* Changó.

Formerly a percussionist with Enrique Jorrín, América del 55, Orquesta Ideal, and La Sonora Matancera, Papaíto (1923–2000) had sung in 1976 on Patato Valdés's album *Ready for Freddy*. He then pursued his career as a vocalist, preserving the authenticity of the *son* and the *guaracha* (*Mi chiquita quiere, Porque me siento cubano*).

La Sonora Matancera moved to Mexico in 1960, then to Venezuela, and in 1962 performed at the Palladium Ballroom in New York with Celio González as lead vocalist. Encouraged by Catalino Rolón, they settled shortly thereafter in the Big Apple. Led by Rogelio Martínez, still with the veteran "Caíto" Díaz on maracas, they too were co-opted by salsa, enabling younger listeners to discover the Cuban *son* of the 1940s and 1950s. They continued to back singers including Bobby Capó, Roberto Torres, Justo Betancourt, Miguelito Valdés, Pete "El Conde" Rodríguez, Yayo El Indio; and their pianists Lino Frías (inspired by *tres tumbaos*) and then Javier Vázquez popularized in the U.S. the highly syncopated, percussive, and zestful *típico* style. Carlos Barbería got his Kubavana orchestra together again and recruited Panamanian singer Tito Contreras, stylistically close to Benny Moré. He proposed a rhythm called *cheveré*, akin to the *son*. And in 1981, Alfredo Valdés recorded old hits of the Septeto Nacional.

From the time of his arrival in the United States, Cachao performed in various contexts – with the Nicholas brothers, Max Roach, Jean-Léon Destiné, Ernesto Lecuona, the Las Vegas Symphonic Orchestra, and show bands in Miami and other American cities – and he recorded on Louie Bellson's 1976 album *Ecue – Ritmos Cubanos*. The following year he issued *Cachao* – using a significant part of the Cuban musical diaspora: Gonzalo Fernández, Lino Frías, Papaíto, El Negro Vivar, Julio Collazo, Chocolate Armenteros, Rolando Valdés, percussionist Osvaldo "Chihuahua" Martínez, Pupi Legarreta, Totico, Julián Cabrera, Alfredo de la Fé, and Puerto Rican *tresista* Nelson González – which included *descargas* and the old *danzones Adelante* and *La Bayamesa*. It was followed by *Cachao dos* (1978) offering, with *Trombón melancólico*, a *yambú* turning into a *mozambique*. In the late

6 The expression "*guaguancó coro miyare*" had already appeared in *Que lo gocen todo*, on *Tito Rodríguez Returns to the Palladium*.

1970s, at Avery Fisher Hall in New York, Cachao gave a marvellous concert of traditional *danzones* with Charlie Palmieri on piano, and a section of violins and cellos. He later played with the *charanga* Hansel y Raúl in Miami. His career picked up in 1993 when Cuban actor Andy García produced a documentary film about him, and with his new *descargas* albums (*Master Sessions* Volume I & II) – which earned Cachao a Grammy Award. Volume II, epitomizing his work, featured an impressive personnel, most notably Francisco Aguabella, Chocolate Armenteros, Jimmy Bosch, Brazilian percussionist Paulinho da Costa (on *caxixi* and vibraslap), Paquito D'Rivera, Nelson González, Orestes Vilató, and Rolando Laserie.

"Chocolate" (Alfredo) Armenteros became one of salsa's busiest trumpeters. A gracious and genial man (Machito spoke of his "Mandingo beauty"), he had gotten his nickname in Cuba from a woman who had mixed him up with *conguero* Chocolate. He worked in Santa Clara with the Hermanos Valladares and, in the 1940s, with Orestes García's *charanga* and Los Hijos de Arcaño (of which Rolando Laserie was the singer and *timbalero*). In Havana, he also played with the *comparsa* Melodías de Iron Beer (named after a famous beer brand) and, in 1946, with Marcelino Guerra. In 1949 he replaced Florecita in the *comparsa* Las Jardineras and joined Arsenio Rodríguez's *conjunto*, with which he spent eight decisive months. In the United States, he imposed the lyrical and sparse *septeto* style of which he and Florecita had been leading exponents, and he interpreted the *son* with a slight New York touch (*Chocolate y su conjunto, Y sigo con mi son, Rompiendo el hielo*).

In 1974, Mario Bauzá persuaded Marcelino Guerra and percussionist Armando Sánchez to form Son de la Loma, a *típico conjunto* of which Lino Frías became the musical director. Like La Sonora Matancera, they also perpetuated the *son* of the late 1940s and 1950s (*Así empezó la cosa*, with *conguero* Ángel Sánchez, Marcelino Valdés on bongo, and Antar Daly on maracas, *Sigue la cosa*, partially arranged by Alfredo Rodríguez and Niño Rivera and featuring Tito Contreras and the outstanding *tresista* Juan Irene Pérez). This rejuvenation of the *son* corresponded to the one started in Cuba, around the same time, by people such as Juan de Marco González.

In 1986, Celia Cruz and the Cuban *conguero* Daniel Ponce took part in a show entitled *Yoruba Fantasy*; and Paquito D'Rivera supervised in Miami a *descarga* that included Chombo Silva, Chocolate Armenteros, Cachao, and some young musicians (*Forty Years of Cuban Jam Session*).

The reopening of the Cuban connection

Up to the late 1970s, virtually all of Cuba's music since the 1959 Revolution had remained unknown abroad, although a few records brought back from the island or bootlegged in Miami had stirred the curiosity of some aficionados. In May 1977, finally lifting the veil, Dizzy Gillespie, percussionist Ray Mantilla, pianist David Amram, and other American musicians gave a concert in Havana.

Invited to jam sessions at the Paulo Theater, they came back home stunned by what they had heard. Upon his return to New York, Amram recorded the eclectic and highly personal *Havana/New York* with a stellar cast of Latin and American musicians, among them Arturo Sandoval, Paquito D'Rivera, Óscar Valdés, Los Papines, Thad Jones, Cándido, Pepper Adams, Ray Mantilla, Nicky Marrero, Billy Hart, and Earl Hines. A while later Típica 73, Mongo Santamaría, and the Fania All Stars (with Pacheco, Adalberto Santiago, Nicky Marrero, Héctor Lavoe, Rubén Blades, Orestes Vilató, Santos Colón, Ismael Quintana, and Roberto Roena) also played in Havana. And the Cuban groups Irakere, Los Papines, Pello El Afrokán, and Orquesta Aragón performed in New York. But the long-awaited Orquesta Aragón concert at Avery Fisher Hall, on December 28, 1978 was marred by bomb threats from anti-Castro militants, and the musical exchanges between Cuba and the United States stopped again for several years.

In 1980, however, the Mariel exodus unexpectedly brought fresh Cuban talents to New York, among them percussionists Daniel Ponce, Roberto Borell (who formed the folk group Kubatá), "Puntilla" (Orlando Ríos) – a *batá* master and *santería* initiate – and young musicians who organized the promising but short-lived Cubasón ensemble.

The watering-down of salsa

In 1984, with his album *Noches calientes* (Hot nights), Louie Ramírez, with Ray de la Paz on vocals, introduced a sentimental kind of salsa called *salsa romántica*, particularly popular in Puerto Rico and Venezuela. This bland strain was construed by fans of the earlier salsa as decadent yet swayed by its commercial success, even musicians like Ray Barretto (with *Irresistible*, 1989), succumbed to it. "In the early 1970s, we used to put all our heart in a trumpet solo," moaned Alfredo de la Fé. "Today, Hispanics are established. They have good jobs, beautiful cars, and the music has lost some of its power."

In the late 1980s, drug raids led to the closing of several Latin clubs. Rap, techno, and the syrupy pop *baladas* foisted onto listeners by radio stations and record companies further debilitated salsa. Yomo Toro flirted with fusion, but the over-orchestrated *Funky Jíbaro* (1989) and *Gracias* (1990) failed at blending funk and Puerto Rican roots, and like many of his colleagues he returned to a more classical salsa, including a flute in his group.

As the twentieth century was drawing to a close, Ralph Mercado – the new godfather of salsa – produced on his RMM label extremely polished but bland high-turnover material often featuring synthesizers. The highly talented, *songo*-influenced pianist Sergio George wrote many of the arrangements (*Hoy* for singer Tony Vega, *Somnámbulo* for Tito Nieves, *Se me cansó el corazón* for Los Hermanos Moreno), and pianist Isidro Infante took over when George left to pursue his own musical activities. Mercado also landed some of the *nueva timba* stars, producing in 1997 Issac Delgado's *Otra idea*, recorded in

New York with local musicians (among them Infante and Mario Bauzá's veteran *conguero* Papo Pepín) and Cuban ones (notably pianist Iván "Melón" González). After Jerry Masucci's death in 1997, Mercado cornered an even larger share of the salsa market, and he continued to organize lavish concerts at Madison Square Garden, among them in 1993 *Combinación Perfecta* (with Celia Cruz, Tito Puente, Oscar D'León, Cheo Feliciano, Pete "El Conde" Rodríguez, and others), and in 2000, *Lo mejor de los ochenta* (The Best of the 80s), featuring Eddie Santiago, Lalo Rodríguez, Héctor Tricoche, Tito Nieves, and other major attractions.

In the same spirit, in 1994, trying to recapture the excitement of the salsa extravaganzas of the 1970s, Larry Harlow founded the Latin Legends Band, and then in 1997 the Fania Legends Band, with Fajardo, Roberto Roena, Larry Harlow, Pete "El Conde" Rodríguez and other Fania veterans. Johnny Pacheco named his current band Pacheco y su Tumbao Añejo (Pacheco and His Old Tumbao); and after several decades of absence from the music scene, "Laíto," at one time La Sonora Matancera's singer, recorded *Sonaron los cañonazos*. The late 1990s also saw the revival of the boogaloo, of *I Like It Like That* in particular, which became a hit on the Havana dance floors.

Much of today's salsa, dismally bland and mechanical, and devoid of its evocative power, its *barrio* quality, saddens many nostalgic old-timers. Laurent Erdös, the French percussionist and pianist with Mambomania, who played in New York with Joe Cuba, has observed that whereas in older times *timbaleros* such as Ubaldo Nieto constantly invented different rhythms, the *cáscara* used by the current salsa *timbaleros* had often become formulaic.

The return to strong salsa

The excesses of the salsa *romántica*, however, led to a return to the hard-driving, gutsy *salsa dura* (also called *salsa gruesa* or *salsa brava*). Among the new stalwarts of this *salsa dura* are Jimmy Bosch, a slide trombonist with huge credentials (*Soneando trombón*, 1998; *Salsa dura*, 1999, with *Canta mi mozambique* and a terrific *Speak no Evil*), who made a noted debut as a leader in 1996, and has been backed by such first-rate musicians as Mario Rivera, pianist Luis Marín and bassist Abiud Troche; and Los Soneros del Barrio, started up in 1999 by pianist and *maraquero* Martín Arroyo and singer Frankie Vázquez and including among others percussionists Milton Cardona and Gene Golden and bassist John Benítez. Around the same time, *timbalero* Johnny Almendra (formerly known as Johnny Andrews) founded in New York the adventurous Los Jóvenes del Barrio who integrated various influences, ranging from Cuban and other Latin rhythms to jazz and R & B (*Telephone*, sung by Almendra's wife Jillian). Also eclectic, pianist Sergio Rivera's Grupo Caribe blends Cuban and Puerto Rican sounds; and good *charangas* such as Son Sublime still find a receptive public.

Salsa dancing

Starting in the late 1980s, salsa, however diluted, began to spread even more intensively worldwide, with concerts and radio shows organized just about everywhere. With the salsa boom, many non-Latinos rushed to take salsa dance classes. As a result, the salsa routines became progressively codified, in great part under the influence of Puerto Rican dancer Eddie Torres, who promoted an elegant "ballroom salsa," with stylized moves, some of them borrowed from the mambo (windmill, Susie Q, cucaracha, head duck, surprise dip, whiplash, hook and hook, etc.). In his wake everyone started to add new frills, including acrobatic moves. Dancer Laura Canellias, in particular, distinguishes between "the Los Angeles salsa style," where one steps on the first beat, and the "classic New York mambo style," where one steps on the second beat – a style that was taught at the Palladium Ballroom. As opposed to the "street salsa," where one steps on the first beat, ballroom salsa is often danced on the two, creating a more sophisticated offbeat feel – although an improvised style called "open shine," freer yet still based on the *clave*, is also performed (by the new Mambo Aces duo among others).

The salsa vocalists

Singers, who occupy the front of the stage, have always been the true salsa stars. They are the ones who best express – through the lyrics of their songs – the dreams, hopes, sufferings, and frustrations with which audiences identify. The *sonero* improvises, dedicates songs to a listener, throws a compliment to a good-looking woman, encourages the musicians, challenges his rivals, intersperses his performance with jokes, asides, expressive gestures. And, following the African custom, the *coro* answers and highlights his singing.

Davilita, a veteran among New York's Latin singers, and La Lupe continued to record in the 1970s, but other artists overshadowed them. In 1971, lost in the Big Apple turmoil, La Lupe converted to *santería*. She sang Justo Barreto's *El santo en Nueva York* and cut *Stop! I'm Free Again*, followed in 1974 by *Un encuentro con Tite Curet Alonso*, and two years later *La excitante Lupe con el maestro Tito Puente*. But tragedies befell her: her husband suffered from mental problems, she lost her home in a fire, broke her spine and had to survive on welfare. The old fiery Lupe had become but a shadow of her former self. She died February 28, 1992 in a Bronx hospital after making a religious album, *La samaritana*, that went unnoticed.

In 1981 Daniel Santos, also a member of an older generation, expressed his love for Colombia with *El marimbero*, recorded in New York with La Charanga Vallenata. The session, placed under the direction of Javier Vázquez, included *vallenatos* (*La muerte de Abel Antonio, Plegaria vallenata*) – a narrative type of song from the Valle de Upar region of Colombia recalling Mexican *romances* or *corridos*.

But Santos, though a cult figure, in Colombia especially, remained marginal to salsa.

Celia Cruz, on the other hand, attracting new audiences, became the undisputed queen of this music. In 1973, she sang the part of "Gracia divina" in the salsa opera *Hommy*. The following year, she recorded *Celia and Johnny* with Pacheco's *conjunto* – an ideal foil for her exuberance. She let loose with her customary fire (*Tengo el ide, Cucalá, Quimbara*, with drum alliterations: *Quimbara cumbara cumba quimbambá*) on this outing, one of her most popular. The following year, she teamed up with Pacheco again on *Tremendo caché*, with Papo Lucca playing on *La sopa en botella* a solo that seems to defy the laws of gravity. In 1976 Pacheco associated her with Justo Betancourt, Papo Lucca (piano), Johnny Rodríguez (conga), Héctor "Bomberita" Zarzuela and Perico Ortiz (trumpets) and Luis Mangual (bongo) on the spirited *Recordando el ayer* – one of the best salsa albums of the mid-1970s. Cruz sang Ismael Rivera's *Besitos de coco*, Caíto Díaz's *Se que tú*, Lino Frías's *Guíllate*, and other numbers brillantly arranged by Lucca, Louie Ramírez, Sonny Bravo, and Jorge Millet.

Cruz also collaborated with Willie Colón (*Burundanga, Usted abusó*) and other great names of salsa: Cheo Feliciano, the Fania All Stars, Pete "El Conde" Rodríguez, Ray Barretto, Adalberto Santiago, La Sonora Ponceña. "I feel at ease with La Ponceña because the *ceiba* (kapok tree – sacred tree of Puerto Ricans) looks like the Cuban *siguaraya* (a sacred tree in Afro-Cuban cults)," she explained. She continues to perform throughout the world, backed by the band of José "El Canario" or, in Latin America, by such groups as Los Brillantes de Costa Rica or that of Aníbal López. Her voice matured, but she retained her drive and legendary stage presence. In 2000, however, on the album *Siempre viviré* (the title tune being a cover of Gloria Gaynor's *I Will Survive*), she included Emilio Estefán Jr.'s *Por si acaso no regreso* ("If ever I don't come back"), in which she cried out her pain at the idea of dying without returning to Cuba, and that sounded like a testament.

Justo Betancourt also successfully accomplished his conversion to salsa, imposing himself with the excellent *Pa' bravo yo*. Around the mid-1970s, in addition to his album with Celia Cruz and Papo Lucca, he recorded with Mongo Santamaría the superb *Mongo y Justo* (with the moving bolero *Miedo*) and *Ubane*, of Afro-Cuban inspiration. In 1976 he moved to Puerto Rico, organized with local musicians the ensemble Borincuba (combination of Borinquen – Puerto Rico's Indian name – and Cuba), and made *Distinto y diferente*.

In 1970 Pacheco hired the handsome Pete "El Conde" Rodríguez (Pedro Juan Rodríguez Ferrer). Born in Ponce, Rodríguez (1932–2000) had sung in New York with La Sonora Matancera. He stood out with *La esencia del guaguancó* (on *La perfecta combinación*), *Dulce con dulce* (*Los compadres*), and then with self-asserting records: *Este negro sí es sabroso* ("Yes, this black man is exciting"), with the hit *Catalina la O*, by Puerto Rican composer Johnny Ortiz, and *Soy la ley* ("I am the law"). After many years in New York, he returned to Puerto Rico, while continuing to collaborate with Pacheco.

From left to right: Johnny Pacheco, Celia Cruz, Papo Lucca, Justo Betancourt. Vaya Records

Pacheco also recruited the Cuban singer Héctor Casanova, a Pete "El Conde" lookalike who had worked with Monguito Santamaría and La Ritmo Tropical, and with whom he made several lively and swinging records: *El maestro*, *El artista* (with Benny Moré's old hit *Esa prieta*), using trumpets on certain cuts and a flute on others, and *Los amigos*. Casanova then founded with former Pacheco musicians the group Casanova y Montuno.

Born in Puerto Rico and raised in the *barrio*, Ismael Miranda staked out his own place in salsa with his fine tenor voice. He started out with Joey Pastrana, recorded with Orquesta Harlow (*Abran paso*, *Oigan bien mi guaguancó*) and then formed Orquesta Revelación, which included some of the most promising young Latin musicians of New York. *Así se compone un son* was followed by *Ismael Miranda en fa menor* (1974), not quite as good, but which included Rubén Blades's interesting *Cipriano Armenteros* – a portrait of a poor Latin American man – and the classic *En mi viejo San Juan*. Miranda also recorded with Willie Colón (*Doble energía*) and, in 1984, with La Sonora Matancera.

Warm and spontaneous, Ismael Quintana, born in Ponce but raised in the South Bronx, first attracted notice with Eddie Palmieri (*Azucar pa' tí*, *Justicia*, *Superimposition*, *Vamonos pal' monte*, *El molestoso*). Starting in 1975, he embarked on a career on his own (*Mi debilidad*, *Rico merengón*; *Mucho talento*, recorded with Papo Lucca, and one of Quintana's most engaging albums).

Nicknamed "La voz" (the voice), Héctor Lavoe, also from Ponce, marked salsa with his highly-strung sensibility and his moving voice, sometimes recalling that of flamenco singers. In his brief life, he suffered more than his share of tragedies. Born in 1946 in a musical family, he was influenced by Puerto Rican singers Chuito de Bayamón, Daniel Santos, Cheo Feliciano, and Ismael Rivera. In New York he started working with Kako Bastar and Orquesta New Yorker. In 1963, he sat in with Johnny Pacheco in an Upper Broadway club; impressed by his voice and his *soneos*, Pacheco hired him. Lavoe then made *Lo mato* and *Cosa nuestra* with Willie Colón, whose musical conception agreed with his.

In 1973 Lavoe formed his own band. *La voz* (with *Todopoderoso* and *Mi gente*) and *De tí depende*, orchestrated with violins (with *Periódico de ayer*), were warmly received. But he struggled with personal problems, drugs among them, and retired from music, with premonitions – occasionally confessed to his friends – of his early death. The following year, with a more mature voice, he made *La comedia*, with *Sóngoro cosongo*, and Rubén Blades's potent *El cantante*, arranged by Colón, which expressed Lavoe's pain. Once the show is over, far from the adulation of the crowds which pay to listen to him, *El cantante* explained, the singer finds himself left alone to face his difficulties and sadness, just as vulnerable as any other human being. In 1979 Lavoe made a Christmas album with Yomo Toro and Daniel Santos, *Feliz navidad*, which attracted little notice. The following year he produced *El sabio*, with an interesting instrumental version of Lee Morgan's bossa nova *Ceora*, arranged with strings, and the *descarga Para Ochún*, propelled by the efficient *montunos* of "Professor" Joe Torres (Colón's pianist). But in 1986, gripped by anguish, Lavoe threw himself from the window of a hotel in Puerto Rico, an accident which left him paralyzed. The death of his son the following year overwhelmed him, and he died from AIDS in 1993, at the age of forty-seven.

With his deep velvety voice, "Cheo" (José) Feliciano is one of the most exceptional song stylists of Latin music, and his talent has outlived all the fads. Born in Ponce, like others he had come to New York at the age of nineteen, and after playing conga and bongo in 1955 with the Conjunto Marianaxi, he worked as Tito Rodríguez's band boy. He debuted with him as a vocalist at the Palladium Ballroom on a dare, singing *Changó ta vení*, joined the *Ciro Rimac* revue, in which he performed various Latin American rhythms, and in 1957 teamed up with Joe Cuba. *El ratón*, recorded with Cuba, brought him fame, but he left Cuba in 1967. The following year, he recorded the successful *Busca lo tuyo* with Eddie Pamieri, and with Monguito Santamaría *Naborí*, *Soy tu ley*, and other songs, and then pursued his career as a soloist. After a bout with drugs, he made a strong comeback in the early 1970s, scoring several hits, among them Tite Curet Alonso's

Anacaona – C. Curet Alonso

beautiful *Anacaona*, evoking an Indian queen from Santo Domingo who fought against the conquistadores:

He also collaborated with the ever-inventive Curet Alonso on *Con una pequeña ayuda de mi amigo Cheo Feliciano*, on which he sang the marvelous bolero *Amada mía*; and with Papo Lucca on piano, cut in 1976 the best-seller *The Singer*. He then moved to Puerto Rico, and in the late 1990s, fulfilling a lifelong dream, he performed in Cuba to tremendous acclaim.

Machito considered Panamanian singer "Azuquita" (Luis Camilo Argúmedes Rodríguez) as one of salsa's great *soneros*. Indeed, with his vibrant voice, spontaneity and ability to improvise lyrics ("I am not a composer in the way Rubén Blades is," he explains, "but I get inspired by things I see – a beautiful landscape, a small event – and a song pops out of my head"), Azuquita has been going strong for over thirty years.

Born in 1945 in Colón – a hotbed of Congo music where Benny Moré had spent some time – he includes a song about Panama on practically all his records. It is in Puerto Rico, however, that his velvet-smooth voice earned him the nickname "Azuquita" (little sugar). The son of singer and bassist Camilo Rodríguez (who had worked in Cuba with Mariano Mercerón and Rumbavana) and of a *tamborito* singer, he listened in his formative years to Benny Moré, Rolando Laserie, and other *soneros*, and sang and played conga. He first spent a while in Peru and then, at the Panama carnival, met Rafael Cortijo. In 1966 he followed Cortijo to Puerto Rico and three years later recorded with him (*Agua que va caer*, which spread his name throughout Latin America, and *El reloj de pastora*), and with Roberto Roena y sus Megatones.

Around the same time Azuquita went to New York with Cortijo and settled there. He issued albums with Kako Bastar, and with his countryman, boxer and singer Roberto Durán, and Orquesta Felicidad (*Dos campeones*), for which Panamanian flautist Mauricio Smith wrote some arrangements. He then replaced Adalberto Santiago in Típica 73, "just when," he says, "the band was at its most inventive."

In 1979 Azuquita moved to Paris and founded with musicians of different nationalities the group Melao, which performed in Europe, and with which Patato Valdés played during his stays in Paris. After *Llegó y dijo*, and *Cé magnifique*, made with Tito Puente, he recorded again with Roberto Durán in Panama, and issued *Azúcar a granel* (1988). In addition to his *bomba Al sonero mayor*, dedicated to Ismael Rivera, he included the bolero *Perfidia* and more recent Cuban compositions: the title song, by

Azuquita. Isabelle Leymarie collection

Francisco Devita (of La Ritmo Oriental), Adalberto Alvarez's *Hipocrisía*, and Chucho Valdés's *Negrita*. On *Los originales*, made in Puerto Rico with Papo Lucca, he evoked the pleasures of the French capital in *París de noche*, and on *Na mio ho rengue kio* (sic), recited the Buddhist mantra *Nam myoho renge kyo*. *La salsa c'est pas compliqué* (2000), made under the musical direction of Cuban pianist, bassist, flautist, and singer Jesús A. Pérez ("El Niño") – once leader, in the 1970s, of the Los Angeles-based Orquesta Versalles – includes Azuquita's *Sueño con Cuba*, *Ya hablo francés*, already recorded in 1980 during his concert at the Bataclan, in Paris, and a salsa cover of Ricky Martin's *Un, dos, tres, María*.

An "urban folklorist," as he defines himself, Rubén Blades brought a new dimension to salsa, and with his beautiful voice, good looks, and talent as a composer and lyricist, he has triumphed beyond the realm of this music. His leftist sympathies have sometimes earned him animosity, from the Cuban community in Miami in particular, which at one point branded him a "communist," and in Panama, where his *Decisiones* album was once banned from the air waves.

Born in Panama in 1948 to a father who played drums and a mother who sang boleros, he inherited his English name from a grandfather who hailed from the British West Indies. As a teenager, he performed with local groups and at the age of eighteen, he left for New York to try his luck there. In 1968, he sang on *Bush and the Magníficos*, an obscure LP which nevertheless attracted the attention of New York producer Pancho Cristal. Two years later, Cristal had him sing with Pete Rodríguez on *De Panama a Nueva York, Rubén Blades con la orquesta de Pete Rodríguez*, for which Blades wrote the lyrics. But, as Blades put it, "nothing happened with this record." He returned home to study law, and having in 1973 obtained his degree, went back to the Big Apple. While working as a clerk for Fania, he started writing songs, among them *Las esquinas son* and *Ciprianos Armenteros*, that soon attracted notice. He then briefly performed with Larry Harlow and Joe Cuba, recorded with Ray Barretto and joined his band, which then featured Puerto Rican vocalist "Tito" Gómez.

The following year he recorded with Willie Colón, sang *coro* in 1976 on Cheo Feliciano's *El cantante*, and also wrote for him. With *Juan Pachanga* (composed for the Fania All Stars), *Número 6* (penned for Bobby Rodríguez), and other hits, his career took a new turn. In 1978 he recorded with Colón the highly successful *Siembra* and then *Maestra vida* – an ambitious saga of a Latin American family – and *Canciones del solar de los aburridos* (1982).

While Colón progressively followed a more commercial path, Blades, faithful to the spirit of salsa, formed the *conjunto* Los Seis del Solar (that included pianists Ricardo Marrero and later Oscar Hernández), and recorded *Buscando América* (Looking for America) – a musical fresco on which he used a vibraphone and a synthesizer. He also embarked upon an acting career, appearing in the movies *The Last Fight*, shot with Willie Colón (with Papo Lucca and Pacheco playing on the soundtrack), and *Crossover Dreams*, and then experimented in new directions. He produced *Escenas*, partly arranged by Ricardo Marrero, with Joe Jackson and

Linda Rondstadt, although Jackson and Rondstadt – both Latin music aficionados – added little to this outing. With *Agua de luna* (1987), a sensitive adaptation of Gabriel García Márquez's *A Hundred Years of Solitude*, Blades continued to move away from conventional salsa.

The following year, he flirted with rock on the disappointing *Nothing But The Truth*, sung in English (with Elvis Costello, Lou Reed, and Sting), and he acted in the films *The Milagro Beanfield Wars* and *Mo' Better Blues*. In 1994 he ran for President in Panama but was not elected. He resumed his outstanding musical career with the same open-mindedness and curiosity, recording among other albums *Amor y control*, as well as gorgeous duets with pianists Danilo Pérez (the bolero *Solo contigo basta* and *Skylark*), and Héctor Martignón (*La propuesta*).

Known as "El Diferente" with his bald pate, flashy stage costumes, and dubious album covers (on *Sabor con Ángel Canales*, wearing a satin jacket open to reveal his chest covered with gold chains, he holds in his arm a naked woman), Ángel Canales achieved a measure of success in the 1970s, putting on lively shows. "I feel music, but I'm not a musician in a technical sense and I don't know how to read it," he admitted. Born in Ponce, he arrived in New York as a teenager and held a variety of small jobs in order to survive. A former *timbalero* and diamond setter, he first sang with pianist Mark Dimond. In 1975 he organized the *conjunto* Ángel Canales y Sabor and recruited in the late 1970s pianist Lisette Wilson – one of the rare female instrumentalists in salsa. He professed his distaste for macho material and, with inspirational songs (*Tenemos que echar palante*), encouraged the Hispanic community to move forward. Disheartened with the music business, he moved to Miami in the early 1990s, resuming his earlier trade as a diamond cutter.

Other singers gravitated in the salsa orbit: among them the Puerto Rican "Tito" (Humberto Luis) Gómez, who, after stints with the Conjunto Antoanetti, La Sonora Ponceña, La Terrífica and Ray Barretto, sang in Venezuela with La Amistad and in Colombia with Grupo Niche before embarking in the mid-1980s on a solo career; "Tito Allen" (Roberto Romero), posing on the cover of *Intocable* with a gun sticking out of his jacket; and the lively and direct Adalberto Santiago, born in Ciales, Puerto Rico, who worked with Willie Rosario and Ray Barretto. Santiago became known with *Quítate la máscara*, joined the incipient Típica 73, organized Los Kimbos, and gave in to the romantic trend in salsa with *Sex Symbol*. Also involved with salsa were the husky-voiced *bolerista* Rafael "Chivirico" Davila (1924–1994), the ubiquitous "Yayo El Indio" (Gabriel Eladio Peguero Vega), who once worked with Julio Alvarado's Orquesta Casino, Celso Vega, Orquesta Panamericana, the Cuarteto Flores, and La Sonora Matancera; there were as well Vitin Avilés, Roberto Lugo, Ray de la Paz (who had sung with Chino y su Conjunto Melao, Ray Barretto, Jorge Dalto, and Louie Ramírez), Junior González, Johnny Ortiz, José Alberto ("El Canario," of Dominican origin but raised in Puerto Rico and New York, and an alumnus of Típica 73), the powerful Tito Nieves (known as "El Pavarotti de la salsa," who debuted at the age of fifteen with

Orquesta Cimarrón), Nacho Sanabria, and the deep-voiced Marvin Santiago. The Peruvian "Melcochita" (Pablo Branda Villanueva), a former drummer and actor in Lima, moved to the United States, singing *coro* on many salsa records. His second album: *Con sabor a pueblo* achieved considerable success, in Colombia especially; guided by Sergio George and Isidro Infante, he became a top name, with straightforward salsa (*Rumbera mayor*, *A comer lechón*).

New vocalists, whose careers straddle Puerto Rico and New York, have also reached the charts, although here too, a pining for the *soneros* of yesteryear prevails and some old-timers complain that the young generation can no longer improvise and that many of them have the same sound and the same dull arrangements. Among the new breed of singers are Eddie Santiago, influenced by the *jíbaro* tradition but also a leader of *salsa romántica* (with, in particular, the highly orchestrated *Atrevido y diferente*), which he sings backed by a four-trombone band; the romantic Jerry Rivera (known as "Cara de niño" – "Child's face"); Rey Ruiz; Tony Vega (who had worked with La Selecta, Orquesta Mulenze, and Willie Rosario); Nino Segarra (*Entre la espada y la pared*); Jerry Medina; Hernán Olivera; and Marc Anthony (Marc Anthony Muñiz) (*Contra la corriente*); Ray Ramos; Tito Rojas; the New York-born Frankie Negrón (*Inolvidable*) who had sung, along with Marc Anthony, in Paul Simon's Broadway musical *The Capeman*. The sexy "La India," born in Puerto Rico and raised in the South Bronx is one of the few women in salsa. With her strong metallic voice reflecting the tension and electricity of New York, she became a major attraction (*Dicen que soy*, *Vivir lo nuestro*, recorded in a duo with Marc Anthony) and now fronts a band led by the Venezuelan *timbalero* Luisito Quintero. Other names include Johnny Rivera, nephew of Adalberto Santiago and a Grupo Fascinación and Conjunto Clásico veteran (*Cuando parará la lluvia*); Davel García; the energetic Frankie Ruiz; Josué Rosado; and Michael Stuart (*Súbele el volumen*). The promising Domingo Quiñones, who honed his skills with El Conjunto Nativo and with *charangas*, has also played the part of Héctor Lavoe in a Broadway musical about the late singer, as well as that of Pontius Pilate in "Jesus Christ Superstar." Nicknamed "*El sonero de la juventud*" ("The young people's *sonero*"), the highly successful Victor Manuelle, able to move from slow ballad to high-powered *soneo* (as on *Bella sin alma*), sets audiences aflame and has obtained several best-sellers, among them *Justo a tiempo*, *Inconfundible*, and *El águila de Manolito*. Venezuela has produced Erick, and the charismatic Trina Medina, daughter of "Canelita" Medina.

In Los Angeles, the Kinshasa-born *sonero* Ricardo Lemvo with his band La Makina Loca, formed in 1990, churns out powerful renditions of *Capullito de alhelí* and other Latin songs. He fuses *bachata* and Congolese rumba on *Ave María*, merengue and *soukous* on *Si tú no sabes*, and *Nganga kisi* (the words *nganga* and *kisi* still exist in the Congo culture of Cuba) deals with a healer trying to sweet-talk a woman.

Salsa in Puerto Rico, California, and Florida

Puerto Rico

The advent of salsa gave greater visibility to artists from Puerto Rico, who started performing and recording more intensively than before. An important outlet for salsa bands on the island were the *fiestas patronales*, festivities organized by towns and villages to celebrate their patron saint.

La Sonora Ponceña (based in Ponce) is, along with El Gran Combo, one of the oldest and most engaging salsa groups with its strong four-trumpet line-up. In 1944, singer and guitarist "Quique" Lucca (Enrique Lucca Caraballo) had formed the Conjunto Internacional, which included *bongocero* "Tato" (Antonio) Santaella. In 1954 Lucca reorganized it with Santoella switching to bass, calling it La Sonora Ponceña. In 1968 he handed over its direction to his son "Papo" (Enrique Arsenio), who had joined the band in 1957 while still a teenager, succeeding pianist Vicentico Morales. A charismatic and inspired pianist and arranger (and occasional trumpet and flugelhorn-player) with an acute sense of rhythm, Papo Lucca is influenced by Cuban musicians and jazz, but he has a unique style, and over the years his playing has acquired growing authority. "I've never thought of anything but music," he avers. He mixes cleverly constructed jazz patterns, adventurous chords, and *montunos* which are often placed more on the beat than those of other salsa pianists, and are always attractive. Excellent singers have passed through La Ponceña, among them Yolanda Rivera (also a *timbalera*), whose voice recalled that of Celia Cruz, as well as Luigi Texidor, Luisito Carrión, Tonito Ledee (who died in 1986), and Edwin Rosas.

The band first backed vocalists Felipe Rodríguez and Davilita, but its true break came in the early 1970s. It cultivated Arsenio Rodríguez's legacy, covering in 1969 his enigmatic *Hachero pa' un palo*, with Congo echoes, but with a more modern treatment. *Desde Puerto Rico a Nueva York* (1972), which truly introduced La Ponceña to the world of salsa, was followed two years later by *Sabor sureño*, with a fiery solo by Papo Lucca on *Telaraña*, in 1975 by *Tiene pimienta*, with *Hachero sin hacha* and *No juega con los santos*, on which Lucca created an eerie atmosphere on synthesizer, and then by the exhilarating *Musical Conquest*, with *El pío pío*, evoking the Puerto Rican countryside, and the amusing *Nanara cai*, beginning with Congo words and including the interjection "*¡acara!*".[7] *Nanara cai* derives from a Cuban Congo song belonging to the satirical genre known as "*de puya*" ("taunting"). The original lyrics say:

Yo vi una jicotea con dolor de cintura	I saw a tortoise with a belly ache
Un gato muerto de risa y un cangrejo relinchando	A cat dying with laughter and a crab neighing[8]
Un sapo estaba llorando porque no tenía corbata.	A toad crying because he had no necktie.

7 In Cuba, the *acara* is a bean flour croquette with ginger and pepper.

8 In La Sonora Ponceña's song, the verse becomes: "*Un mosquito muerto de la risa a ver un burro estudiando*" ("A mosquito laughing himself to death upon seeing a donkey studying").

and La Ponceña slightly changed the words. In 1977 the band, at the height of its creativity, produced *El gigante del sur*, and then *Explorando*, on which Lucca, on *Suena el piano*, emulated Cuban pianist Rubén Gonzalez's solo on the *guaracha Suena el piano Rubén*, recorded shortly before on Enrique Jorrín's *Cha cha cha* album. While improvising, he sang in his hoarse voice in unison with his playing – a technique often used by Brazilian artists – and began his solo by quoting the tango *Adios muchachos*. In his salsa version of Edu Lobo's *Boranda*, he again sang along with his piano solo, announcing in Spanish at the end of it: "*gracias por escucharme y nos vemos después*" ("thank you for listening to me and we'll see each other later"). *Future* (which included a *songo*), also evidenced Lucca's taste and imagination.

In 1971, following the general salsa trend, El Gran Combo added a trombone to its wind section and turned out several hits (*Por el pecho no, Don Goyo*). In 1973 Pellín Rodríguez left the group and Charlie Aponte replaced him. The group's popularity peaked with the arrival of vocalist Andy Montañez. However, in 1977, he moved to Venezuela to replace Óscar D'León, who had just left La Dimension Latina, and the young Jerry Rivas succeeded him within El Gran Combo. Montañez's departure affected the group, but they recovered with *El Gran Combo – nuestro aniversario*, *La universidad de la salsa* and other records, and with their singers Charlie Aponte, Jerry Rivas, and "Papo" (Luis) Rosario they continued to delight their fans. In the 1980s, a Combo de Ayer was formed with members of the earlier Gran Combo so as to revive the old sound of the group, and they recorded *Veinte años después*, with Pellín Rodríguez (who died in 1984). And with many changes of personnel, El Gran Combo has kept going strong, receiving in 1992 a special tribute from the governor of Puerto Rico.

Rafael Cortijo retained his strong personality. The powerful *Ritmos y cantos callejeros* (with Kako Bastar and Chivirico Dávila) was followed by the more experimental *Cortijo and His Time Machine* (1975). Most of the tunes: *bombas*, *plenas*, *aguinaldos*, and *danzas* were folk material, but with adventurous arrangements by the young guitarist Edgar Miranda and pianist Pepe Castillo. Shortly thereafter, Cortijo and Ismael Rivera appeared together in San Juan (with Roberto Roena on bongo and conga and Rafael Ithier on piano). They performed several of their hits and the album of the concert came out a few months later. The following year, Cortijo recorded the more conventional *La quiniela del día*, which offered Tite Curet Alonso's interesting *plena Se escapó un león*, and a good rendition of *Agua que va caer*, sung by Azuquita. *Campeones*, dating from the same time, included the humorous *El bochinche*. *Caballo de hierro* (1977), with Cortijo's niece Fe on vocals, Mario Bauzá on trumpet, Eddie Martínez and Paquito Pastor on piano, Tito Puente, singing *coro* on *Llóralo, llóralo*, and others featured a *mapeyé* (a slow kind of *seis*) and *Bomba carambomba*, recorded a few years earlier by Ismael Rivera.

In 1982, Cortijo, who had been suffering from diabetes and cancer, died in San Juan. His funeral wake, attended by an overwhelmed Ismael Rivera, was held at the Caserio Llorens Torres – a San Juan housing project of ill repute. During Cortijo's burial, some of his fans, convinced that he belonged to the people, tried to steal his coffin, and his funeral inspired a moving essay by the Puerto Rican writer Edgardo Rodríguez Juliá: *Cortijo's Funeral*. Rodríguez Juliá describes Cheo Feliciano's visit to Cortijo's wake: "Cheo looks at him and smiles slightly. Beyond death, he knows that Cortijo will live, but for now, rest in peace, old man. The only thing left of you, you see, is kindness. What more is there to say, Rafael? . . . Cheo lifts up the vaporous tulle of the spirit in order to touch the great conguero's hands. He touches these hands as if he wanted to console Cortijo . . . The hands which made so many skins resound are now still. Death is a silence accentuated by stillness. But they hold a rosary, a last impassioned prayer of hands calloused by chants to African gods."

In the late 1960s in New York, Ismael Rivera with his Cachimbos had capitulated to the carefree boogaloo and *jala jala*, and after his mystical experience, he released in 1971 with Kako Bastar the joyful *Lo último en la avenida*. But the following year, still bitter, he included on *Esto fue lo que trajo el barco*, arranged by Javier Vázquez, *El incomprendido* (The misunderstood one):

Yo yo yo yo creo que voy	I, I, I, I think that I will be
solito a estar cuando me muera.	alone when I die.
He sido el incomprendido,	I've been misunderstood,
ni tú ni nadie me ha querido.	neither you nor anyone has loved me.

He complained again in *La comedia*: "In the final drama which I play, my forgetful public doesn't applaud me." He also offered happier tunes, however, among them *A bailar mi bomba* and *A quilo el bombón*. Suffering from polyps on his vocal chords, his voice declined in his later years, but the soulful intensity remained. He died of a heart attack in Puerto Rico in 1986, less than four years after Cortijo, mourned, like his old friend, by the whole island.

The *timbalero* "Willie" Rosario (Fernando Luis Marín Rosario) long divided his life between Puerto Rico and New York. If he posed on the cover of *Otra vez*, as a shady-looking cowboy in front of a saloon door, his music often evoked the rough-and-tumble atmosphere of the lower-class neighborhoods of San Juan (*En Bayamón*,[9] *El Barrio Obrero a la 15*,[10] *El callejero* – the story of a man telling a woman that despite his love for her, he comes from the street and will return to it). He first studied guitar, bongo, and saxophone but chose the timbales after seeing Tito Puente at the Palladium Ballroom. He played with local groups, left for New York in 1953 and worked with Broadway Casino, Noro Morales, Johnny Seguí, Eddie Palmieri, and the Alegre All Stars. In 1958, with the help of Tito Puente and Tito Rodríguez, he formed his own band, which included four trumpets and, later, also a baritone saxophone. During the 1960s, work slackened, and he took a job as office clerk in order to earn a living. He then started a band in Puerto Rico, recorded *Boogaloo and guaguancó* and other albums and, back in

9 A town near San Juan, famous for its *chicharrón* (roasted pork rind).

10 The Barrio Obrero (literally "Worker's Neighborhood") is a low-income district of San Juan.

New York, worked with Perico Ortiz. In 1971, he returned to Puerto Rico, where his career picked up, and he surrounded himself with excellent musicians, among them *bongocero* Papo Pepín. The spirit of *desafío* (bravado), so typical of Latin music, informs *Fabulous and Fantastic* and *El bravo soy yo* (recorded with Tito Puente's vocalist Frankie Figueroa). Various vocalists passed through his band, among them Junior Toledo, Guillo Rivera, Josué Rosado, Primi Cruz, Bernie Pérez, and Meñique (with whom he recorded the hit *La cuesta de la fama*). *Nuevos horizontes* (1985), featuring the rising singers Gilberto Santa Rosa and Tony Vega, included the Cuban classics *Changó ta bení* and *Babarabatiri*.

"Roberto Roena" (Ivan Rohena Vazquez) led one of the strongest Puerto Rican salsa bands of the 1970s: the Apollo Sound, featuring trumpeter Elias López. With Tite Curet Alonso's *Tú loco y yo tranquilo* sung by Piro Mantilla, *Desengaño*, and other songs, Roena's fame spread in the U.S., and he delighted salsa fans with his nimble on-stage dancing.

Born in Mayaguez in 1940, Roena started out as a dancer in Myrta Silva's revue and then danced and sang with Cortijo, who taught him to play percussion.

Tú loco y yo tranquilo – C. Curet Alonso

He became Cortijo's *bongocero* and performed with him in New York. After a stint with Mario Ortiz, he joined El Gran Combo, from 1963 to 1968, where he re-encountered musicians he had played with in Cortijo's group. He then formed Los Megatones and recorded *Se pone bueno,* which included two Cuban standards: *Que se fuñan* and *Maracaibo oriental,* but the group fizzled out shortly thereafter, and in 1969 he organized the Apollo Sound. Among his most exciting records of the 1970s was *Apollo Sound 6* (1974), which included Tito Rodriguez's *Él que se fue,* arranged by Gunda Merced. In the mid-1970s, some of Roena's musicians left him to join Salsa Fever. Roena recorded *Super Apollo 47:50,* with Adalberto Santiago, and then finally disbanded his ensemble.

In the 1970s, bassist and former trumpeter and guitarist Bobby Valentín, who also led a strong and cohesive band, was a major attraction in Puerto Rico and at the Corso, in New York. Born in Orocovis, Puerto Rico, Valentín had worked in the Big Apple, in 1958, with Joe Quijano, and then with Willie Rosario, Tito Rodríguez, and Charlie Palmieri, and first recorded as a trumpet player *Young Man With a Horn* and *Bad Breath* (with Joe Torres on piano and Poppy Pagani on timbales). He moved to Puerto Rico in 1968 and switched to bass, setting up a group with a smoking brass section and Marvin Santiago and Frankie Hernández on vocals. On *Rey del bajo* (1974), he covered *Hay cráneo;* he recorded at the Puerto Rico jail the interesting *Va a la cárcel,* which included Herbie Hancock's *Maiden Voyage,* and achieved success with Tite Curet Alonso's *Huracán,* dealing with unrequited love (on *Algo nuevo*). At the end of 1976, Marvin Santiago was replaced by Luigi Texidor. In 1982 Valentín recorded with Vicentico Valdés three songs by René Touzet: *Entre este mundo y Dios, Eres feliz,* and *Conversación;* and then *Soy boricua* and *In Motion,* exalting Puerto Rico. In the 1990s, he introduced vocalists "Cano" (Carlos Enrique) Estremera (an Orquesta Mulenze veteran) and Marima. Estremera later pursued his own career. An albino, hence his nickname "Cano," meaning "white-haired," Estremera started out as a percussionist. An inventive *sonero,* fluent in a wide spectrum of musical genres, *bomba, plena, cumbia,* and *songo* among them, he scats and imitates instrumental riffs with his voice.

A mailman by trade and an original composer with great verve and evocative power, "Tite" (Catalino) Curet Alonso has written scores of songs for the major names in salsa while remaining true to his roots, beginning in 1968 with *La gran tirana* for La Lupe. "I've always liked the bomba and the plena," he says, "songs and dances that come from our black coastal culture. They are a kind of heritage that we carry in our blood, in our feet, in our voices." And indeed, while employing

La esencia del guaguancó – C. Curet Alonso

themes with a universal appeal, he has always remained sensitive to the tastes and needs of his own people.

Other worthy bands appeared on the island: La Selecta, led by pianist Ralphy Leavitt; the ensemble headed by trumpeter Tommy Olivencia, in which Paquito Guzmán, Lalo Rodríguez, and Marvin Santiago sang; Gunda Merced's Salsa Fever; the harmonically interesting Orquesta Mulenze, directed by bassist Edwin Morales; Impacto Crea, run by trumpeter Juan Rivera Ortiz; La Corporación Latina; trombonist Luis García's Tempo; La Terrífica; Orquesta Costa Brava, influenced by El Gran Combo; and the Conjunto Canayón, led by *timbalero* Cano Robles. However, Richie Ray and Bobby Cruz, caught by religious fervor, often turned out a proselytizing style of music that was a far cry from their earlier *bestial sonido* (dynamite sound).

The Puerto Rican All Stars – including some of the best musicians from the island: in 1965 Kako Bastar and members of El Gran Combo with a *descarga-* oriented record, and later Papo Lucca, trumpeter Juancito Torres, trombonist "Gunda" (Julio) Merced – issued exhilarating albums. In 1976 they offered an exciting version of Miles Davis's *Budo*, but the record, inspired as it was sold poorly. Descarga Boricua, with Juancito Torres, Papo Vázquez, Cachete Maldonado, vocalists Justo Betancourt, Ismael Miranda, Jerry Medina, Wichi Camacho, Carlos Esteban Fonseca, the folksinger "El Topo" (Antonio Cabán Valle), and other major names of Puerto Rican music followed in their wake, issuing the jazzy *¡Esta, sí, va!*.

In the late 1970s Cachete Maldonado and some of his friends founded the Taller Experimental de Santurce, a workshop for making and teaching *batá* drums and a birthplace for two of the most striking bands of that era: Batacumbele and Zaperoko. The son of bassist Rubén Maldonado (ex-member of Alfarona X and Mario Ortiz), he took classes with Patato Valdés later playing with Ernie Agosto's La Conspiración and with jazz musicians. One of the first percussionists in Puerto Rico to show strong interest in Afro-Cuban ritual music, he also studied *batá* in New York with Julito Collazo and introduced these drums into the island, paving the way for musicians such as Bobby Jiménez and the young virtuoso percussionist "Mañenguito" (Giovanni Hidalgo). In 1978, after a trip to Cuba, Cachete recruited pianist Eric Figueroa (an alumnus of "Perico" Ortiz and Orquesta Mulenze), bassist Eddie "Gua Gua" Rivera, Giovanni Hidalgo, and singer Jerry Medina, and two years later started Batacumbele (from a Yoruba word meaning "to kneel in front of a *batá*").

Batacumbele and Zaperoko, the latter led by percussionist and singer Frankie Rodríguez (a former member of the Grupo Folklórico Y Experimental Nuevayorquino) and trombonist and percussionist Edwin Feliciano, blew a breath of fresh air into salsa. Traditionally, the salsa from Puerto Rico had been more relaxed, with the timbales and the piano more on the beat than in New York or Havana, but under the influence of Irakere and Los Van Van, Batacumbele and Zaperoko adopted the more energetic *songo*, yet giving it a less frantic touch than in Cuba. Like some Cuban groups, they incorporated *batá* drums in their rhythm section, and Zaperoko also used Brazilian percussion instruments. In the late 1990s, Los Van Van, Sampling, Los Papines, Issac Delgado, and other artists from Cuba performed in Puerto Rico, increasing the impact of the *songo* and of *nueva timba* there.

The Colombian pianist Eddie Martínez, who worked in Puerto Rico with Batacumbele in the early 1980s, described it as "an exceptional group." They stood out with their torrid percussion and brass, soulful vocalists (José Ramos, Jerry Medina or Eduardo Montalbán depending on the recording) and astute arrangements, most of them penned by Eric Figueroa and Papo Vázquez. *Con un poco de songo* (1981), featuring among others the brilliant drummer Ignacio Berroa (just arrived from Cuba), flautist Nestor Torres, Papo Vázquez, and Dominican saxophonist Mario Rivera, offered the delightful *A la i olé*, inspired by the Cuban refrain *"A la i olé, i olá."* On *En aquellos tiempos* (1993), featuring Juancito Torres and Peruvian saxophonist and flautist Héctor Veneros, interludes of Yoruba music separated the various sections of the title tune; and the record presented, with *Batarengue*, a merengue using *batá* drums. Nevertheless, finding Batacumbele's orientation too Cuban, Figueroa left the group to set up his own band, for which he wrote jazz-tinged *bombas* and *plenas*. In New York, Papo Vázquez went on to form Bomba Jazz and then joined Tito Puente's orchestra.

More "rock" and abrupt than Batacumbele and recalling some of the incipient *nueva timba* ensembles, Zaperoko combined several strains: *rumba* and *plena* (*Sé lo que es la rumba*), *charanga* and *songo* (*Azúcar con ají*), samba and *songo* (*Sigan la clave*). They broke up after Frankie Rodríguez's premature death.

In the early 1980s, Andy Montañez, who had returned to Puerto Rico from Venezuela, fronted a group in which his two sons and his daughter also sang. He commented on the new musical scene: "I've seen how today salsa is more respected than before: in the beginning, it suffered from discrimination. Nevertheless, I always sang it with respect, because I'm convinced that it has dignity, just like the *aguinaldo*, or any music that one performs with respect." In addition he recorded with the Puerto Rican All Stars and under his own name (*Salsa con caché*).

By the end of the decade, San Juan fell for the sickly sentimental *salsa romántica*, ushered in by the Louie Ramírez record *Noche caliente*, featuring Ray de la Paz on vocals. De la Paz attributed the success of this new genre to a shift from a male to a female-oriented market, with songs addressing women's concerns.[11] It was represented by, among others, singers Paquito Guzmán, Frankie Ruiz (an Orquesta Solución and Tommy Olivencia veteran, who died in 1998 of drug abuse at the age of forty), Mario Ortiz, Ray Sepúlveda (although he cites Ismael Rivera as his major influence), who had worked with Adalberto Santiago, *bongocero* Nicolás Vivas's Conjunto Chaney, and *Lalo* (Manuel Ubaldo) Rodríguez (*Simplemente Lalo*). This *salsa romántica* soon led to the more explicit *salsa cama* ("bed salsa"– also called *salsa sensual* or *salsa erótica*), introduced by the Conjunto Chaney's vocalist Eddie Santiago (*Más que atrevido, El conjunto del amor*). Santiago

11 In: Nestor Luis, *A Conversation with Ray de la Paz.*

founded his own group in 1986 and triumphed with *Tú me quemas, Insaciable,* and other songs. Lalo Rodríguez (who had sung as a teenager with Tempo Moderno, Eddie Palmieri, Tommy Olivencia, and Machito) scored a huge hit throughout Latin America with *Devórame otra vez,* arranged by Mario Ortiz, and even El Gran Combo gave in to this fad, although, as Rafael Ithier explained: "Early on in the development of what we today refer to as *salsa sensual* there was this notion that one didn't have to arrange around the clave. This led to a weakening of the music as far as the dancer was concerned since it diluted the swing element. It was less rythmical. As a result the dancer stayed away, and the dance bands sort of dwindled."[12] Cheo Feliciano, Willie Rosario, and other old-timers strongly decried this bland and vulgar *salsa cama.* In the words of Feliciano: "What we call salsa is a book that chronicles the life of our peoples. Then why limit it to just sex and nothing more? For me it's a lack of respect for this genre. And for the same commercial interests which I have mentioned, singers were created that weren't natural, that didn't even belong to salsa. They were neither *soneros* nor improvisers nor *pregoneros.*"

As in New York, powerful new groups emerged in reaction against the *salsa cama:* Sonido Bestial, led by *bongocero* Manuel González, featuring José "Mañengue" Hidalgo (Giovanni Hidalgo's father) on conga; the groups headed by Tony Vega, Juan Manuel Lebrón, and David Pabón (Eddie Santiago's ex-back-up singer); the one led by the expressive Gilberto Santa Rosa, who had sung with Willie Rosario (*De cara al viento,* and his great tribute to Tito Rodríguez: *A dos tiempos de un tiempo,* featuring Victor Paz, Arturo Sandoval, Papo Lucca, and Lito Peña); Atabal, run by Héctor Rodríguez Medina, seeking inspiration from Puerto Rican and Afro-Latin folklore in general and using tambourines, *bomba,* maracas, and other percussion instruments (*Del Caribe al Brasil, voces y tambores*); trumpeter Luisito Ayala's Puerto Rican Power; Puerto Rican Brass, a two-trombone band featuring Tito Vega on vocals; Plenealo, led by trumpeter Ivan Rivera introducing new renditions of *plenas* and other rhythms; the dynamic Plena Libre, started in 1994 by bassist Gary Núñez and consisting of violins, trombones, piano, conga (played by the talented Gina Villanueva), and other percussion instruments, which performs *plenas, guaguancós,* sambas and other Latin rhythms; and the Taller Campesino, led by *cuatro* virtuoso Edwin Colón Zayas and perpetuating the *jíbaro* tradition.

The Cepeda musical dynasty, founded by folklorist Rafael Cepeda (known as "El Roble Mayor" – The Old Oak) are among Puerto Rico's most celebrated exponents of the *bomba.* One of their younger scions, jazz trombonist William Cepeda, who worked with Celia Cruz, Tito Puente, Dizzy Gillespie, Slide Hampton, and other Latin and jazz stars, has rekindled interest in this music. With his Grupo Afro Boricua, featuring vocalists Antonio Martínez, Nellie Lebrón and Tito Matos, he invigorates the different modalities of the *bomba* (*yubá cuartiao, leró, sicá, corbé,* etc.), as well as the *plena,* the *seis,* the *corrido,* and other traditional strains.

12 In: George Rivera: "A Conversation with Rafael Ithier" (unpublished).

California

California, dominated by the so-called Chicana culture, had long stayed away from salsa's major currents, preferring Latin rock and Latin jazz. But several bands gradually emerged – *charangas* among them – although as a general rule, Californian salsa tends to be less fiery than that on the East Coast. The brothers Pete, Coke, and Phil Escovedo had been pioneers of this music on the West Coast, and Pete and Coke had played with Carlos Santana. Many of the West Coast salsa ensembles created in the 1970s and 1980s, except perhaps the one led by the Mexican-born "Poncho"(Ildefonso) Sánchez, only obtained local fame and few of them really changed the course of salsa.

Most of the Latin music activity is concentrated in Los Angeles and the Bay Area with, in particular, Johnny Polanco's Conjunto Amistad and the H.M.A. (Hispanic Musicians Association) California Salsa, led by trumpeter Paul López; Ensemble, influenced by the Latin big bands of the 1950s (*Fuerza positiva*), Sexteto Diablo, Alma del Barrio, Sabor, Pete Escovedo's group, and the female band Sinigual. The Cuban-sounding *conjunto* Céspedes, based in Oakland and founded in 1981 by singer "Bobi"(Gladys) Céspedes, grew out of a trio set up by Bobi and her brother Luis Céspedes. The *conjunto* included Bobi's nephew Guillermo (on piano, *tres*, guitar, and shekere), and percussionist John Santos. Santos also worked, along with pianist Rebeca Mauleón (very inspired by Jesús López and other Cuban masters) with Orquesta Batachanga. The group, which performed *danzones*, *rumbas*, and other numbers called its own music *onda areíto*, borrowing this term from Cuba.

Florida and the rest of the United States

Miami is a thriving Latin metropolis, predominantly Cuban, Colombian, and Haitian. Its famed Calle Ocho – heart of the Cuban community – teems with *bodegas* and cafés, and virulent anti-Castro feelings generally run rampant among these expatriates.

In successive waves, a spate of Cuban musicians settled in Miami after the revolution. Among their number were Pepe Delgado, Xiomara Álfaro, Juanito Márquez (who later moved to Spain), Olga Guillot, Roberto Torres, Ignacio Berroa, Arturo Sandoval, Gonzalo Rubalcaba, and more recently, singer and guitarist Albita Rodríguez. Rodríguez started out as an exponent of the *punto*, recording in Havana, in 1988, the successful *Había música guajira*. In 1992 she traveled to Colombia then defected to Mexico and then to the United States. In Miami she cut her hair short and dyed it blond, and with her more glamorous image, lusher orchestrations and expanded repertoire, she scored a hit with *Una mujer como yo*, even attracting the interest of Madonna. Generally, the Miami sound has been slicker, more commercial than the New York one, closer to the Californian style. Among the foremost local groups are the Charanga Vallenata, formed in the 1980s by Roberto Torres and blending Cuban and Colombian music (Torres scored a hit with *Caballo viejo*, by the Venezuelan composer Simón Díaz); Clouds; the ensembles of pianist Luis Santi Jr., of *conguero* "Cutín" (Rodolfo Resemar), and of Hansel y Raúl (former singers of Charanga 76), with which Cachao played, Orquesta Inmensidad, Charanga de la 4, produced by Torres (with sometimes Fajardo as guest star); the fusion group Spice, led by flautist Nestor Torres. The Miami Sound Machine (MSM), steered by the multi-instrumentalist Willie Chirino, with its excellent Cuban pianist Paquito Hechavarría, crossed over to the pop market with their hit *Conga* (1985). Chirino followed the fusion road while the Cuban-born Gloria Estefán (Gloria Fajardo) – MSM's former vocalist – has achieved star status. Hechavarría, who had worked in Cuba with the Riverside Orchestra, Felipe Dulzaides, Mongo Santamaría, and Walfredo de los Reyes, teamed up with Joe Galdo to form the Latin funk group Bandera. He too pursued his own career, and he has backed artists such as Mangú. With his Sobrinos del Juez, Carlos Oliva has experimented with Latin house (*You've Lost That Loving Feeling*).

A favorite Miami gathering-place for Cuban exiles is the Café Nostalgia. Many musicians sit in with the house band, led by bassist and vocalist Omar Hernández, who skilfully reworks Cuban classics. Also based in Florida, percussionist, pianist, bassist, and guitarist Richie Puente (Tito's son) has performed in different contexts, with a preference for Latin jazz.

Latin bands have now blossomed throughout the United States. Among them, to name only a few, are the combo Salsamba, in Pittsburgh, which has drawn from Afro-Cuban sources; in Salt Lake City, Mambo Jumbo; in Honolulu, where Latin music festivals are held, Sunsmoke, founded by Nicaraguan singer and percussionist Rolando Sánchez.

The merengue

The whole Dominican Republic pulses to the driving, almost obsessional beat of merengue. And while the merengue has now gone techno, chestnuts such as *Compadre Pedro Juan, El sancocho prieto* or Rhadamés Reyes Alfau's *La Maricutana* still get everyone on their feet.

Towards the late 1970s, the merengue burst into New York. First confined to the small social clubs of Little Santo Domingo, a rough section of Washington Heights, it spread to the rest of the town, and then to Puerto Rico, where many Dominicans settled beginning in 1980, after hurricane Hugo wreaked havoc in their country. Jaunty and easier to dance than salsa – although some Dominicans can do mind-boggling steps to it – it almost overshadowed salsa in San Juan, strongly affecting local musicians. One day in 1980, Batacumbele was performing in that city. With his *batá* drums, Cachete Maldonado was invoking *orishas*. Impatient, the Dominican listeners started clamoring for merengue. Cachete had celebrated Santa Bárbara and San Lázaro but, in his pantheon, had forgotten Santo Domingo!

The merengue derives from the *upa habanera*, introduced around 1850 by the Cuban troops stationed on the island of Hispaniola. It soon ousted the *tumba* – then the colony's national dance – and, with its unabashed sensuality, scandalized the bourgeoisie. In 1855 the newspaper *El Oasis* lashed out at the man dancing "chest against chest with the woman" and trying "to show others how well he can sway his hips." Only in 1918, however, was a piece labelled "merengue" published in the capital. The merengue was then preceded by a *marcha*, which enabled couples to stroll across the floor before dancing.

The long narrative stanza, sometimes consisting of social or political commentaries or risqué allusions, is followed by the *jaleo*, a fast section punctuated by accordion or piano *guajeos*. The saxophones fire up the melody with breakneck riffs (*floreos*).

Merengue guajeo

The name *pambiche* is sometimes erroneously used to designate the *guajeo*. The *pambiche* was a dance popular in the 1920s that took its name from Palm Beach – a printed fabric fashionable at the time. Slower than the merengue, it imitated the clumsy way in which the U.S. Marines, who had been occupying Santo Domingo since 1916, performed local dances.

The early merengue, born in the rural Cibao in the north, was percussive with a strong Congo character. Congo culture persists in certain regions of the country, among them Villa Mella, near the capital, where such groups as Los Congos del Espíritu Santo use Bantu-derived drums for their religious ceremonies and other festivities. The merengue was then performed with rather primitive instruments: *marímbula*, guitar, serrated gourd, soon replaced by the *güira* (or *guayo*) – a metal scraper played with a comb – and then with a *tambora* – a double-headed drum created in 1932 in San Cristóbal and recalling certain West African drums. The button accordion, of German origin, the saxhorn, and then saxophones cropped up in the merengue. In the 1930s, in Santiago de los Caballeros, a type of merengue dubbed *perico ripiao* ("chopped parakeet") was played in small dives by bands (called *conjuntos*) consisting of güiro, *tambora*, and accordion. This merengue *ripiao* still thrives in the countryside.[13]

The merengue has a 2/4 time signature, with a strong accent on the first beat of every two bars. On the second beat of every two bars the *tambora*, beaten with a stick in the right hand and the left hand without a stick, plays a characteristic *repique* (roll):

tambora rhythm

13 In the early 1920s there existed, in Cuba, a band named Perico Ripiao, which consisted of guitar, violin, mandolin, and güiro.

In 1928, the Victor label issued in Santo Domingo the first merengue: Francisco Lora's *La rigola*. The same year, in New York, Nilo Menéndez recorded *Santiago*, by the Dominican composer Julio Alberto Hernández. At the end of 1929, the Grupo Dominicano, which included Eduardo Brito (vocals and *tambora*), Bienvenido Troncoso (accordion), and Luis María Jiménez (*güira*), issued several Dominican numbers, among them *Te juro*, also by Hernández. The Dominican singer Antonio Mesa cut several sides with the Trío Borínquen, and Victor added merengues by Juan Bautista Espínola and by Enrique García to its specialty catalogue. The ensembles of Juan Pablo "Pavín" Tolentino and of Avelino Vázquez started to gain exposure and, around the same time, "Pancho" (Juan Francisco) García composed merengues for piano.

During the following decade, Luis Alberti (1906–1976) – the merengue's most celebrated composer – wrote epochal tunes: *El sancocho prieto*, *Mis amores* (better known as *Loreta*), and *Compadre Pedro Juan*, which Brito popularized in Cuba.

Compadre Pedro Juan	Mister Pedro Juan
No pierda el tiempo	Don't waste time
Compadre Pedro Juan	Mister Pedro Juan
Saque su dama;	Take out your lady;
Se acabará el merengue	The merengue will end
Y si no anda con cuidado,	And if you're not careful,
Quedará como perico:	You will end up like the parakeet:
Atrapao.	Caught.

Compadre Pedro Juan – Luis Alberti

Alberti also wrote other genres, among them the *plena Ponce*, but merengues constituted the bulk of his output. In 1928 he formed the Jazz Band Alberti. Two years later Radamés Trujillo and his family took control of the country's economic and political life. Trujillo, of peasant origin, was a rabid merengue fan. He used *perico ripiao* merengue for his campaign and promoted La Lira delYaque, also led by Luis Alberti, which became in 1932 La Santa Cecilia, and in 1944 Orquesta Generalísimo Trujillo. In the late 1930s Alberti arranged merengues for big bands. He eliminated the accordion, adding trumpets, saxophones, and piano and enriching its harmonies, and in the early 1940s he recorded for the Columbia label.

A friend of Alberti's, pianist "Simó" (Francisco) Damirón (1908–1922) disseminated abroad a refined urban merengue. His elegant stylings – and his sometimes bland Latin renditions of classical works – contrast with today's frantic merengue. In 1933 he founded with singer "El Negrito" (José Ernesto) Chapuseaux (1911–1986) – a professional baseball and basketball player – the duo Los Ases de la Radio, which became popular throughout Latin America. In 1936 he performed in Puerto Rico with Chapuseaux. The two men then settled in Venezuela, where they joined Billo's Caracas Boys, and from 1938 to 1941 toured extensively outside the country, scoring a hit with *Anabacoa*. In Panama, Chapuseaux married singer and actress Silvia de Grasse, known as "the *tamborito* queen." Damirón, Chapuseaux, and Silvia recorded together under the name Trío Los Alegres Tres and worked in San Juan and New York. Damirón then left the trio and crisscrossed Latin America before moving to San Juan, where he played cocktail piano in the major hotels, and then to the Dominican Republic.

The bulk of Damirón's work – *Piano merengue, La maricutana, Anabacoa* (with Chapuseaux and Silvia), popular in Cuba, *Oye mi piano, La empaliza, El negrito del batey, Manenín* (featuring, in addition to the customary *tambora*, a conga and a bongo) – was recorded in the 1950s.

In a similar style, pianist Johnny Conquet made two classic albums, *Piano merengue* and *Más piano merengue*, while yet another Dominican pianist, Rafael Solano, collaborated in New York in the 1930s with the Charlie Fisk Orchestra and backed singers. After his return to Santo Domingo in 1953, he became one of Trujillo's favorite musicians.

Other groups appeared in the 1930s, among them the Grupo Quisqueya (*En Sabana Grande*) and the Cuarteto Brito, founded by Eduardo Brito (*Beso, El que quiera ser hombre*). In 1936 the radio station HIN ("The voice of the Dominican party") was created in the Dominican capital. It recorded merengues by the Orquesta Benefactor (Benefactor was the title given to Trujillo) and by the Súper Orquesta San José, and enabled its listeners to discover new local artists. With his Orquesta Dominicana, Napoleón Zayas also helped in spreading the merengue abroad.

In 1946 Joseíto Román brought the merengue to the Alma Dance Studios in New York. The following year, according to an article published in the September issue of *Dance Magazine*, Rita Hayworth's cousin Gabriel Casino and his wife and partner Lita danced the merengue for the first time in the United States, at the Saint Moritz Hotel. Monchito and his Mambo Royals and Ricardo Rico, and in Cuba Benny Moré and Bebo Valdés also recorded merengues.

In the 1950s, Alberto Beltrán (Palo Blanco, 1923–Miami, 1997) further spread the merengue in Puerto Rico, Cuba, and later the United States and imposed his famous *El negrito del batey*:

A mí me llaman el negrito del batey	They call me the *negrito* of the sugar mill
Porque el trabajo para mí es un enemigo	Because for me work is an enemy.
El trabajar yo se lo dejo todo al buey	I leave work to the ox
Porque el trabajo lo hizo Dios como castigo.	Because work, God invented it as a punishment.

Around the same time, saxophonist Tavito Vázquez made regular use in the merengue of the saxophone, more flexible and biting than the accordion, and he wrote a number called *Los saxofones*, while the accordion was relegated to rural music. However the Cibao-born Angel Viloria kept an accordion in his Conjunto Típico Cibaeño, which included Dioris Valladares (vocals, *güira*) and Luis Quintero (*tambora*), but he added "Chichín" (Ramón) García on C saxophone. Viloria and Valladares scored hits with *La cruz de palo bonito, Consígueme esto, Loreta, Juancito Trucupei*, and the racy *A lo oscuro*.

A lo oscuro metí la mano	In the dark I put my hand
A lo oscuro metí los pies,	In the dark I put my feet
A lo oscuro hice mi lío	In the dark I did my thing
A lo oscuro lo desaté.	In the dark I got out of it.

Upon Viloria's death, in 1955, Chichín García took over his group. Valladares also sang with him and, in New York, with Fausto Curbelo, Xavier Cugat (who also performed merengues), Noro Morales, Juanito Sanabria, and the Alegre All Stars, and then set up the Conjunto Típico, as well as a big band. His excellent *Pa' bailar na' ma'*, featuring merengue and salsa musicians (among them Bobby Valentín and trumpeter Puchi Boulong), recorded in the 1970s, includes two *salves* (a traditional religious genre often sung for funeral wakes), merengues, a *danzón*, mambos, and a *descarga* and, with its punchy saxophone and trumpet riffs, it had a definite New York touch. The merengue also spread to Caracas, where the Venezuelan Francisco Delfín wrote *El cumaco de San Juan*.

In the 1950s, Trujillo was plundering Santo Domingo of much of its resources but supported the merengue, that of Toño Abreu and Ñico Lora, representative of the Cibao merengue, and La Santa Cecilia in particular. But musicians were compelled to sing his praises and those who refused had to leave the country: Alcibíades Sánchez and Billo Frómeta moved to Venezuela, Alberto Beltrán and Mario de Jesús (the author of the famed *A la rigola*) to New York. There, Luis

Quintero founded in 1954 the Conjunto Alma Cibaeña and became known with *Si tú no, la otra*.[14]

In 1961 Trujillo was assassinated with the help of the CIA. Joseíto Mateo, the Trío Reynoso, and other Dominican groups regained their freedom of expression, but two years later the United States intervened yet again, to eliminate the liberal candidate Juan Bosch; in 1966, President Lyndon Johnson put another dictator, Joaquín Balaguer, in office.

As elsewhere, big bands gave way to combos and in 1964, the saxophonist, flautist, and xylophonist Félix del Rosario founded in the capital his influential Magos del Ritmo. The popularity of the merengue declined abroad in the 1960s, although an important concert was mounted in 1967 at Madison Square Garden. In the early 1970s, El Cieguito de Naguas, Primitivo Santos, Joseíto Mateo (*"merenguero* all the way to my *tambora*," as he puts it), and "Cuco" (Henry) Valoy became the new stars of the merengue. Combining *pachanga* and merengue, Mateo invented the short-lived *merechanga* and, remembering the *salves* he had sung as a child, wrote *Salve merecumbé* and *Salve sabrosona*. In his rambunctious *La cambiadera*, a man suggested to his friend that they swap wives "*y así descansamos si quiera unos días*" ("and maybe that way we'll get a few days' rest").

With his combo, Primitivos Santos was one of the first to truly give the merengue a foothold in the United States; and with his Virtuosos, which included pianist and composer Ramón Orlando and singer Henry García, Valoy favored a broad and sometimes questionable humor, as on the cover of *¿Qué será lo que quiere el negro?* (What does the black man want?), showing him trying to seduce with exaggerated facial expressions a woman pretending to be indifferent, or the song entitled *Las viejas saben mejor* (a play on words, meaning both "old women know better" and "old women taste better"). In 1985, with his Nueva Tribu, he recorded *Mejor que nunca*, which included a *mangulina* (a traditional Dominican genre): *Esta niña quiere un novio*.

By the late 1970s, merengue groups were regularly featured at Madison Square Garden salsa concerts, and "Johnny" (Juan de Dios) Ventura and his Combo dazzled audiences with their spirited singing and dancing. The doyen of the more energetic merengue which then blossomed, Ventura (nicknamed *"El Caballo,"* "the horse") was influenced by both Rafael Cortijo and soul singers. He too favored humorous merengues (as with *El ron es mi medicina* – "Rum is my medicine"), but he also performed old Cuban songs (*Bururú barará*). In Santo Domingo, he had sung in the 1940s with Rondón Boto, Papatín Fernández, and Papa Molino, and then formed the elaborate show band Johnny Ventura y sus Caballos, with guitarist Fausto Ray, Anthony Ríos and Luis Sánchez (*coro*), *conguero* Luisito "Llorón" Martí, and percussionist Ramoncito Cruz. In the 1960s he recorded boogaloos. A few years after that, he organized his Combo Show with Cruz and pianists Anchesito Mejía and later Sonny Ovalle, and reintroduced into the merengue a colloquial flavor which had disappeared under Trujillo (*El cuabero, Olor a lluvia*). After his heyday, in the 1970s and early 1980s (*Protesta de*

14 Luis Vázquez, Millito Pérez (popular with *La mama y la hija*), and Mon Rivera sang with him.

Johnny Ventura, Isabelle Leymarie collection

los feos, *El llorón*), he entered politics, eventually becoming a member of the Chamber of Deputies in the late 1980s, and then mayor of Santo Domingo.

In the 1980s, the merengue tempo accelerated, in great part under the influence of the inventive singer, trumpeter, and trombonist Wilfrido Vargas (known as "El Barbarazo" after one of his hits). Born in Altamira in 1949, and a Ventura fan, he started his Beduinos in 1974 in a Santo Domingo club called El Casbah; the group included singer Bonny Cepeda and pianist and composer Sonny Ovalle. He speeded up the merengue tempo, introduced a synthesizer into his group and, despite being criticized for "distorting" this music, he injected rock, soul, jazz, reggae, *cumbia*, Brazilian, and other strains into it – an assimilation technique known in Santo Domingo as *fusilamento* (shooting) – and utilized female *coros*. He also performed with the Fania All Stars, and from the late 1970s had hits with *Este barrigón no es mío* ("This big belly isn't mine"), the sizzling *El barbarazo* (on *Punto y aparte*), *El hombre divertido*, *Wilfrido, dame un consejo*, *Las avispas*, and *El funcionario*, denouncing corruption. Three of his musicians – trumpeter Quilvio Fernández, pianist and arranger Sonny Ovalle, and singer Vicente Pacheco – then left him in order to organize Los Genuinos, but Vargas brought his band back up to strength and, with vocalist Sandy Reyes, came up with the excellent *El Africano* (1984), mixing merengue and *vallenato*, and *El Jardinero* (1985), presenting for the first time within the merengue the Ghanaian style *highlife*. He pursued his musical experiences with the funny *Wilfrido 86*, on which he used guitar and harmonica, covered, with *La Medicina*, a *zouk* hit by the Antillean group Kassav', and scored a new success with *El baile del perrito*. A great talent scout, he also helped to get established various new groups, among them Los Hijos del Rey, and Las Chicas del Can.

The exuberant "Sandy" (Santiago) Cerón has embraced both salsa and merengue. After an operatic career as a tenor, he appeared on the television show *La voz dominicana* and left for New York in 1963. He sang on three Arsenio Rodríguez albums, performed with Luis Kalaff's merengue band and set up his own ensemble. He also recorded with Pete "El Conde" Rodríguez, Pacheco, and Tony Pabón.

Millie, Jocelyn y Los Vecinos, organized in New York in the late 1970s by the sisters Millie and Jocelyn Quezada (with brother Rafael as trumpeter, arranger, and musical director and another brother, Martin, as pianist) opened the way to such female groups as the one led by Belkis Concepción, Las Chicas del Can, or Las Chicas de Nueva York. In some of their songs, Millie and Jocelyn lampooned machismo or dealt with social issues.

New Dominican groups joined the salsa scene: among them the Conjunto Quisqueya, founded in 1974 in Puerto Rico by singer Aneudi Díaz and which became, with its comic songs *La huma* ("The drinking binge") and *Levántame, nena* ("Pick me up, chick"), one of the most appreciated merengue bands on the island. Mention should also be made of Cheché Abreu y sus Colosos (with his 1980s hit *La negra Pola*) – creator of the *bachason* hybrid; Los Kenton, with their imaginative choreographies, sometimes borrowing from karate; Fausto Rey; the Miami-based Sobrinos del Juez; Yoyito Cabrera; Hugo Pérez y su Quisqueya; Negro Estrella y su Orquesta, with vocalist Willie Contrera; Vicente Pacheco; Los Hijos del Rey; Aramis Camilo; La Familia Andrés; Los Caballeros del Merengue; Dionis Fernández; Luis Ovales; Julio Mateo ("Rasputín"); Richie Ricardo; José Estebán y Patrulla 15; Jorge Solano; Bonny Cepeda; Sandy Reyes; Coquí Acosta; Orquesta Liberación; Los Hermanos Rosario; José Octavio y Los Nietos; Fernandito Villalona (with, on *Feliz cumbé*, a half salsa, half merengue version of the *Concierto de Aranjuez, Carnaval*, and other hits); La Banda Loca; La Banda Gorda; Sergio Vargas; Ruby Pérez; "Ravel" (Guillermo Ravel); Kinito Méndez; The New York Band; Victor Roque's ensemble; Pochy y su Coco Band; the romantic Anthony Santos; Elvis Crespo (born in New York in 1971), with his multi-platinum *Suavemente* and the hit *Píntame*; and in Puerto Rico Manny Manuel ("Rey de corazones"), with his sophisticated show band, Grupo Manía, Olga Tañón (with her 1993 hit album *Mujeres de fuego*), and Jessica Cristina with *Lo tengo dominao* (1997), about a man who performs household chores for his woman. And in 1995, Ralph Mercado organized at Madison Square Garden a *Merengazo 95* with Los Hermanos Rosario, Manny Manuel, Kinito Méndez, and other new merengue names.

By the 1990s, however, the merengue boom had slowed down somewhat while the *bachata* – a lower-class and often ribald vocal music born in the 1960s – and the more brooding *música de amargue* (from *amargura* – "bitterness"), dealing with unrequited love and socio-political issues, came to the fore. The *bachata* was often played with guitar or *requinto* (a small string instrument) and bongo rather than *tambora*. One of the musicians chiefly responsible for the revival of the *bachata* is guitarist Juan Luis Guerra. The eclectic Guerra, who also drew from various other sources, achieved international appeal with his La 4-40 band. A rock and jazz fan, Guerra studied at the Berklee School of Music in Boston with the idea of emulating Pat Metheny, and eventually returned to his Dominican roots. The 4-40 had drive and challenging and sophisticated arrangements, but it also suffered from commercialism. Like Rubén Blades or the Colombian vocalist Yuri Buenaventura, Guerra has addressed social issues, among them corruption on *Acompáñame civil*, or rural poverty on his huge 1989 hit, the poetical *Ojalá que llueva café*:

Ojalá que llueva café	Let's hope it rains coffee
Pa' que en el conuco no se	So that the farms don't suffer as
sufra tanto,	much,
Ojalá que llueva café en	Let's hope it rains coffee in the
el campo.	countryside.

Soplando (1984), featuring saxophonist Tavito Vázquez, was followed in 1990 by *Bachata rosa* – which constituted a turning point in Guerra's career and obtained a Grammy for Best Tropical Album – and in 1994 by the highly successful *Fogaraté* (the name of a plant but also an expression of excitement[15]), fired up by the *soukous* riffs of Zairian guitarist Diblo Dibala.

Following Guerra's path, his percussionist "Chichi" (Pedro) Peralta (also a pianist), formed Son Familia, an innovative band that also offered *bachatas* as well as other Dominican and Latin genres and shied away from the relentless modern merengue with elaborate lyrics and melodies (*Mensaje campesino*, *Procura*). Cuco Valoy, Wilfrido Vargas, and other *merengueros* also adopted the *bachata*. In 1999, for instance, Joseíto Mateo and Luis Kalaff included a *bachata-son*, *Los bodegueros* (a homage to proprietors of small grocery stores), on their joint album *Los dos que quedan* ("The last two"), and the soulful Raulín (Rodríguez) became the new *bachata*'s heart-throb while also singing salsa.

In 1996 singer Ramón Orlando's *El venao* (literally *The stag* but also *The cuckold*), triggered a wave of crimes in the Dominican Republic as several men, taking the word "*venao*" as a personal insult to their manhood, murdered their wife or girlfriend, whom they suspected of cheating on them. So much for machismo and the power of merengue!

The 1990s saw the spreading of *fusilamento* (adaptation of other tunes to merengue rhythms), sampling, and other techniques borrowed from techno and hip hop. Proyecto Uno, Fulanito, Da Madd Dominikans, Sancocho, Los Sabrosos del Merengue, and Ritmo Caliente are representative of the new and ultra-speedy techno-merengue or merenhouse with its booming bass, samples, electronic instruments, and other hip hop elements, all the rage in the Dominican Republic, Puerto Rico (where a strongly accented *merengue-bomba* has evolved), and the myriad Washington Heights clubs.

15 In the Dominican Republic, a woman who has *fogaraté* is a curvaceous and sensuous woman.

New horizons for Latin jazz

Beginning in the 1970s, Latin jazz gradually became increasingly diversified as emerging musicians with distinctive voices were drawn into the American vortex. For many years, jazz critics had generally dismissed or at best overlooked this music without really understanding it, and dancers, branding it as too "intellectual," had tended to ignore it. But Latin jazz is now gaining increasing exposure and, constantly absorbing new elements from various areas of Latin America and the Caribbean, with this regular cross-fertilization it has become a true lingua franca for many musicians.

In the early 1970s, the Puerto Rican pianist Ricardo Marrero organized with flautist Dave Valentín and singer Angela Bofill an interesting group, halfway between salsa and jazz. Valentín then formed a relatively commercial ensemble that included pianist Óscar Hernández. Around the same time, vibist Bobby Paunetto – a former student of Gary Burton – created an intense and unconventional Latin jazz; *Paunetto's Point*, 1975 featured a bevy of top-notch musicians, among them Tom Harrell, Ron Cuber, Jerry and Andy González, Milton Cardona, and Alfredo de la Fé. But beginning in 1979, health problems forced Paunetto to interrupt his promising career. And in 1972, spurred by the producer Al Santiago, Orlando Marín recorded *La saxofónica* – a great album featuring five saxophones and a rhythm section.

Some salsa musicians also flirted with Latin jazz: Eddie Palmieri, Ray Barretto (*Ancestral Messages*), Charlie Palmieri (*Easy Does It*); José Mangual (*Buyú*).

With his New World Spirit band, Ray Barretto now devotes himself fully to Latin jazz – harmonically more challenging than salsa – even turning down salsa engagements. On *My Summertime* (1995), featuring the excellent Colombian pianist Héctor Martignón, Barretto sang on *Summertime-Guajira*. "The guajira," he explained, "is the Latin equivalent of the blues," and indeed, years earlier, Ricardo Ray had recorded a *guajira-blues*. With his current sidemen, including the accomplished Italian American pianist and arranger John di Martino, Barretto inaugurated the third millennium with the tight *Trancedance*, featuring Los Papines and James Moody as guest stars.

While maintaining his big band, Tito Puente founded a smaller Latin jazz group that gave him more freedom to pursue his musical explorations. Said Puente: "I know jazz well, I listened a lot to it while growing up in the *barrio* – giants like Dizzy Gillespie and Mario Bauzá – and I'm proud of having followed the tradition of Dizzy and of Noro Morales, who also played jazz."

Around 1975 Puente played – along with Eddie Martínez, Sal Cuevas, Patato Valdés, and Johnny Rodríguez – with the Latin Percussion Jazz Ensemble, set up by the Latin Ventures percussion company. In Copenhagen, the Club Montmartre wrote Puente's name on the marquee in larger letters than those of the other band members. Puente protested and Valdés suggested he formed his own group. The *timbalero* then founded a quintet which included Valdés and

Martínez, and took his new outfit around the world. The quintet later grew in size, attracting Bobby Rodríguez, Jerry González, Mario Rivera, Jorge Dalto, Alfredo de la Fé, percussionist Johnny Rodríguez and others. "We performed jazz numbers which no one would ever have thought a Puerto Rican could play: *Lullaby of Birdland* (recorded with George Shearing), *Con alma* (with Phil Woods), *Take Five*, played with a 3/2 *clave* (Dave Brubeck would have had trouble finding the first beat!), *Bluesette*, done in 4/4, *Giant Steps*, *Pent-up House*, *Lush Life*, or tunes by Mulgrew Miller," Puente remembered. "But in order to arrange Latin jazz scores," he warned, "you have to know both Latin music and jazz. Few Americans do good arrangements of this music: too often they sound too jazzy. Most jazzmen don't understand the *clave*, which is fundamental. However, in this musical language, you have to know that *guajeos* and *tumbaos* sound more idiomatic than chords, and must have an absolute mastery of the *clave*." Puente also paid tribute to Machito with a *Machito for Ever*, reminiscent of the Afro-Cubans.

From the late 1970s, The Village Gate in New York launched a series of concerts entitled *Salsa Meets Jazz*, bringing together Latin musicians Machito, El Gran Combo, Louie Ramírez, La Sonora Ponceña, Daniel Ponce, Ismael Miranda, with jazz or Latin jazz improvisers Dexter Gordon, Cedar Walton, Paquito D'Rivera, and others. These concerts familiarized jazz fans with Latin music, and the Latin music fans with jazz. Around the same time, other New York venues opened to Latin jazz, for example the tiny Jazz Gallery on Upper Broadway and the midtown Soundscape, which became focal points for the new Latin jazz. Michel Camilo, Jorge Dalto, Daniel Ponce – everyone congregated there. Also realizing the growing importance of Latin music, the Newport Jazz Festival began, in 1978, to feature such artists as Tito Puente, Machito, Eddie Palmieri, Willie Bobo, Cal Tjader, and Eddie Martínez.

Mongo Santamaría's style crystalized in the 1970s with *Afro-Indio* (1975), recorded with the exceptional Colombian flautist, saxophonist, composer, and arranger Justo Almario, and *Ubane* (1976), two of his most accomplished albums. *Afro-Indio* offered Almario's powerful *The Promised Land*, with a Coltranian saxophone prelude and a passage richly harmonized with saxophones and flutes; and the enchanting *Song For You*, on which Almario and Al William took turns to improvise a splendid, seamless, and logically constructed flute solo.

Beginning of Justo Almario's solo on *Song for You* – José Gallardo (from *Afro-Indio* – Vaya Records)

Ubane, featuring Justo Betancourt and Colombian pianist José Madrid, included a jazzy rendition of an Abakwa chant: *Ubane*, and a charming *Cumbia típica* ending with a dialogue between flutes and drums. It is, however, the less interesting *Dawn* (1977) which earned Santamaría a Grammy Award. *Red Hot* (1979) proposed a new version of *Watermelon Man* and Almario's exquisite *Sambita*.

The contributions of new musicians from various Latin American countries vastly expanded the horizons of Latin jazz. The Dominican saxophonist Mario Rivera with his Salsa Refugees combined merengue, *pambiche*, and jazz. The Colombian pianist Eddie Martínez led groups in New York, Bogotá, Paris, and San Juan and also played with the Space Station ensemble run by percussionist Ray Mantilla (born in New York but of Peruvian origin). Jerry González, equally proficient on conga and trumpet, issued with his Fort Apache Band (from the nickname given to a dangerous precinct of the South Bronx) the Yoruba-tinged *Ya yo me curé* in 1980, with a version of Monk's *Evidence* based on *Mondongo, sandunga, gandinga*, and a Latin *Nefertiti*; two years later *The River Is Deep*; in 1989 *Rumba para Monk* with works by Monk; and *Obatalá*, with Larry Willis, Papo Vázquez, and Milton Cardona; in 1994 the jazzier *Crossroads* with John Stubblefield, Joe Ford, and Steve Berrios. Pianist and composer Carlos Franzetti has occasionally drawn from his Argentinian heritage (*Mambo tango*), and has written gorgeous arrangements (notably for Paquito D'Rivera's *Portraits of Cuba* and David Sánchez's *Obsesión*), as well as film scores.

Franzetti's countryman and fellow pianist Jorge Dalto (1948–1987) in his playing expressed the passion of the tango, which he inherited from his father, also a pianist. He worked with George Benson, Machito, Tito Puente's Latin jazz ensemble, and Paquito D'Rivera, his busy *montunos* sometimes betraying the fact that he was not from the Caribbean. With this Inter-American Band, organized in the early 1980s with Patato Valdés, Nicky Marrero, and Art Webb, he gave freer rein to his imagination, indulging his taste for extended introductions and rubato preludes.

The exuberant Nuyorican pianist Hilton Ruiz, who gained exposure with Roland Kirk in the 1970s, often resorts to funky and bluesy patterns. Dominican pianist Michel Camilo plays with high energy, speed, and a very percussive style

(*Why Not! Caribe*), although he can also deliver airy ballads in a more jazz-like style. Classically trained, he formed in Santo Domingo the group Baroco 21 before moving to New York in the early 1980s.

The Cuban musicians who had arrived in New York in 1980 also brought fresh ideas to Latin jazz. *Conguero* Daniel Ponce stunned audiences with his technique, beautiful sound, rich imagination, and deep sense of structure. He was compared to Chano Pozo, to whom he paid a tribute in a show at Carnegie Hall. ("Like him," he remembered, "I began to beat on pots and pans when I could barely walk.") Like Pozo, he had played in Havana in various *comparsas*. In New York he organized a *rumba brava* and *santería* group and recorded with musicians of different persuasions, Paquito D'Rivera, McCoy Tyner, Yellowman, Laurie Anderson, Nona Hendryx, Mick Jagger, Sly and Robbie, and Yoko Ono among them; and he brought an unexpected color to Herbie Hancock's *Rock It* – hip hop's emblem – by adding an *okónkolo* (small *batá* drum) to it.

Ponce's *Africa contemporánea* (on *New York Now!*) evoked a mythical Africa, and *Arawe*, featuring D. K. Tyson on vocals, mixed Yoruba and funk elements. In 1990, Ponce's group included Eddie Martínez, Steve Berrios, and Puntilla, who sang superb Afro-Cuban material. The Venezuelan saxophonist Rolando Briceño, with a bounce and a bite recalling Cannonball Adderley, and pianist Oscar Hernández later joined the band. *Changó te llama* (with David Sánchez, Mario Rivera, *cuatro* player Edgardo Miranda, Tito Allen and Milton Cardona on vocals, and bassist Sal Cuevas) included great numbers, among them the title-song, *Bacalaítos*, and *Midnight Mambo*. In 1995, after a hiatus from the music scene, Ponce recorded with the Estrellas Caimán, led by pianist Alfredo Valdés Jr.

The inventive and tasteful Ignacio Berroa, who had also played in Cuba with television orchestras, started out in New York with Típica Novel but, more drawn to jazz, he went on to work with Paquito D'Rivera, Michel Camilo, Dizzy Gillespie's United Nations Orchestra, Danilo Pérez, and others, and has imposed himself as one of the most brilliant and complete drummers on the Latin and jazz scenes.

Paquito D'Rivera soon gained recognition in the United States. He, too, joined Gillespie's big band and recorded prolifically: *Paquito Blowin* (with Ponce, Berroa, Eddie Gómez, Hilton Ruiz, and Jorge Dalto), *Mariel* (with Randy Breker), *Why Not!* (with Michel Camilo and Toots Thielemans), *Havana Cafe* (with Danilo Pérez), *Reunion* (with Arturo Sandoval), maintaining his glib style. In 1994, coaxing the Stockholm-based Bebo Valdés out of retirement, he produced *Bebo Rides Again* with him and trombonist Juan Pablo Torres. He also joined the Caribbean Jazz Project, along with Dave Samuels (vibes and marimba), Andy Narell (steel drums), the Peruvian Oscar Stagnaro (bass), Mark Walker (drums), and Luis Conte (percussion), with whom he performed a pan-Caribbean and Latin repertoire. In 1996, D'Rivera recorded with a studio big band the lush and wonderful *Portraits of Cuba* which included several Cuban standards, among them *The Peanut Vendor*, *Tú*, *Drume negrita*, and *Échale salsita*.

Why Not! – Michel Camilo

Since the 1950s, Gillespie had not led a big band. In 1990 he founded the United Nations Orchestra, characterized by a predominantly Latin line-up. It featured among others D'Rivera, Arturo Sandoval, Mario Rivera, Brazilian trumpeter Claudio Roditi, Giovanni Hidalgo, Ignacio Berroa, Danilo Pérez, James Moody, Slide Hampton, Steve Turre, and Airto Moreira. Still inspired but already ailing, he granted considerable freedom to his musicians. "They play anyway what I feel like hearing," he asserted. After Gillespie's death in 1993, Paquito D'Rivera took over the group, bringing in the Argentinian pianist Darío Eskenazi, the Chilean guitarist Fareed Haque, the Peruvian bassist Oscar Stagnaro, and the Puerto Rican trombonist and shell-player William Cepeda.

Mario Bauzá dedicated himself to his own ensemble, more *típico* than Gillespie's, and which included trumpeter Victor Paz and the excellent percussionists Papo Pepín (conga), Joe González (bongo), and sometimes Patato Valdés. *Afro-Cuban Jazz* (1986), produced by Jorge Dalto and featuring Roditi, Dalto, Berroa, Ponce, D'Rivera, Fajardo, and Patato Valdés, offered new versions of *Mambo Inn* and *Cubanola*, and Graciela, with a still powerful and moving voice, performed the splendid *Quédate*. Shortly before his passing, Bauzá made *944 Columbus* (his Columbus Avenue address in New York), and *My Time Is Now*, recalling the Afro-Cubans at their best. After his death – in the same year as his friend Dizzy Gillespie – Victor Paz and Rudy Calzado assumed the leadership of his orchestra.

In 1995, Chico O'Farrill again put together a big band. He then composed *Trumpet Fantasy* for Wynton Marsalis, going from rumba to *afro*, and offered two accomplished albums, with *Pure Emotion* and *Heart of a Legend*. The latter, featuring his son Arturo Jr. on piano and a sterling rhythm section (bassists Andy González and Joe Santiago, and percussionists Horacio "El Negro" Hernández, Willie Martínez, Joe González, and Eddie Bobé) plus guest stars ranging from

Gato Barbieri to Cachao, Patato Valdés, Mauricio Smith, and Juan Pablo Torres, offers old and new compositions by the maestro, including the arresting *Trumpet Fantasy*, performed by Jim Seeley. O'Farrill also continued to write film scores. He collaborated with the World Sax Quartet, David Bowie and other artists, and although hampered by Parkinson's disease, he remained active until his death in 2001, at the age of eighty.

Arturo Sandoval, established in Miami since 1990, has developed a smoother style than before, and he, too, performs both American jazz and Cuban music. Accompanied by Danilo Pérez, Giovanni Hidalgo, Gloria Estefán, and the actor Bill Cosby (on vocals and timbales), he proposed on *Dance On* a winning combination of *danzones,* boleros and other genres.

Juan Pablo Torres, also based in Miami, joined Paquito D'Rivera on *Safe at Home*, a mixture of samba, Latin jazz, *danzón*, bolero, and *zapateo*. He scatted with great talent, imitating the sound of the trombone, on *Como fue* (on *Trombone Man*), and has been leading his own group.

The Panamanian pianist and composer Danilo Pérez, has become one of the most inventive voices of both American and Latin jazz. The son of a singer (also called Danilo), he grew up in a highly musical atmosphere, as a child playing bongo in family gatherings, and as a teenager being particularly impressed by local pianist Victor Boa. Pérez, now based in Boston, has played with the likes of Jon Hendricks, Dizzy Gillespie, James Moody, Roy Haynes, Claudio Roditi, and Tom Harrell among others, as well as with his own groups which have notably included, at different times, bassists John Benítez, Ruben Rodgers, Carlos Hernández, and Essiet Essiet, and drummers Ignacio Berroa, Antonio Sánchez, and Adam Cruz. He explores with great passion the rhythms of his country (*Friday Morning*, the striking *Panama Blues*, with *mejorana*[16] singer Raul Vital), experiments with unusual time signatures (as on John Coltrane's *Impressions*), improvises on left-hand ostinatos (*Everything Happens to Me*), paints, on *The Journey*, a vivid saga of the black diaspora, with free passages and Yoruba interludes, pays tribute to Thelonious Monk on *Panamonk*,[17] creates haunting harmonizations (*Prayer*).

The intense and impetuous Puerto Rican tenor saxophonist David Sánchez, who has often teamed up with Pérez, integrates Cuban, Puerto Rican, Brazilian, and other rhythms to his vast palette (*The Departure, Sketches of a Dream, Street Scenes*, the high-energy *Melaza*). *Obsesión*, one of his most melodic albums, featuring among others John Benítez (bass), Edsel Gómez (piano), and Adam Cruz (drums), includes lovely renditions of classics *Los aretes de la luna, Lamento borincano, Cuban Fantasy, Capullito de alhelí*, and Jobim's *O morro não tem vez*.

16 A rural Panamanian genre.

17 A play on the words *pana* (buddy in Spanish) and Panamá.

Danilo Pérez. Novus Records

The Brazilian trumpeter Claudio Roditi – Clifford Brown's heir – loves the samba, the *baiao* and the bossa nova (*Two of Swords*, *Jazz Turns Samba*, *Slow Fire*). But, equally at ease with Caribbean rhythms, he frequently plays with Cuban and Puerto Rican musicians, with flowing, well-constructed solos.

The sharp Seis del Solar, comprised of Óscar Hernández (piano), John Benítez (bass), Robbie Ameen (drums), Paolí Mejías (percussion), Ralph Irizarry (timbales), and Bobby Franceschini (saxophone), have performed independently from Rubén Blades, producing happy and strong, deftly crafted tunes with inventive breaks (*Alternate Roots*).

David Sánchez. Sony Music

Irizarry later formed Timbalaye, recording in 2000 with guest star Giovanni Hidalgo the exciting *Best Kept*.

The son of "Mañengue" (José Hidalgo) – Ricardo Ray's former percussionist – Giovanni Hidalgo is, says Danilo Pérez, "the Charlie Parker of conga," and he also elicits the admiration of Armando Peraza and many others. He adapts trap drum techniques to the conga, playing as if his hands were sticks, invents new rhythms on the *batá*, sometimes placing them vertically on the ground or combining them with a conga or a bongo. After working with Batacumbele, Eddie Palmieri, Dizzy Gillespie, and many others, Hidalgo now creates ebullient and intricate music (*Seven Steps to Heaven*, *It Don't Mean a Thing*, *Ianmanuel*) with his own group.

All of the following have brought fresh ideas to Latin jazz: the Nuyorican trumpeter Charlie Sepúlveda, close in spirit and in sound to a Wynton Marsalis or a Roy Hargrove; drummer Steve Berrios (1925–1996), with his group Son Bacheche; trombonist and shell-player Steve Turre, of Mexican descent; Panamanian saxophonist Jorge Sylvester; the Latin Jazz Orchestra, formed by trumpeter Armando Rodríguez and *timbalero* and drummer Víctor Rendón; Bobby Sanabria – once Mario Bauzá's *timbalero* – with his group Ascención; Puerto Rican trombonist Papo Vázquez; Venezuelan pianists "Ed" (Edward) Simón and Otmaro Ruiz, the fine Colombian pianist Héctor Martignón, who had studied with Stockhausen in Germany before moving to the United States in the 1990s, and in New York the percussive Cuban pianist Miguel Romero; Puerto Rican alto saxophonist Miguel Xenon, Panamanian bassist Santi Debriano (son of pianist Alonso Wilson Debriano); Mexican vibist Víctor Mendoza; with his Bronx Horns, trumpeter Ray Vega (a Mongo Santamaría, Mario Bauzá, and Ray Barretto alumnus), who released an album of Horace Silver tunes and recorded with Sheila E; bassist Allan Johnston's Grupo Jazz Tumbao; and saxophonists Jesús

Clare Fischer. Clare
Fischer collection

Caunedo (from Cuba) and Antonio Arnedo (from Colombia). With his Nagual
Spirits, founded in the United States in 1987, percussionist Marlon Simón (Ed's
brother) has also paid tribute to Monk (*Songo para Monk*, on *Rumba a la Patato*,
recorded in 2000).

In Puerto Rico, Papo Lucca (*Latin Jazz*), trumpeter Humberto Ramírez (*Jazz
Project*), *conguero* Paolí Mejías, saxophonists José "Furito" Ríos and José "Cheguito"
Encarnación, pianist and violinist Mariano Morales, pianist Amuni Nacer, *cuatro*-
player Pedro Guzmán, with his Jíbaro Jazz, and Clave Tres (with Raúl Berrios
using a staggering array of percussion), going from Ravel's *Bolero* to *Jíbaro negro*,
create a vibrant and imaginative Latin jazz.

Gato Barbieri, accompanied by Eddie Martínez, captures the nostalgia of
the pampa in his haunting but sometimes monotonous music, while the Peruvian
guitarist Richie Zellen gives a biting edge to *landos* and *festejos* (Afro-Peruvian
rhythms), tangos, and waltzes. And in Uruguay, Rubén Rada and the Fattorussos
(brothers Hugo and Osvaldo, and Hugo's son Francisco) blend *candombé* – the
traditional black music of the Rio de la Plata – and jazz.

The West Coast Latin jazz has tended, on the whole, to be lesser known
and less fiery than that from the East Coast. Cal Tjader collaborated with Eddie
Palmieri on *Bamboléate* (*El sonido nuevo*, 1973) and he cultivated a restrained
elegance (*Mambo With Tjader*, *La onda va bien*). The poignant *Bésame mucho*, sung
by Carmen McRae on Tjader's last album, resonates today like a farewell song
by these two late artists. The Estrada Brothers (vibist Rubén and saxophonist
Henry) perpetuate Tjader's style, while towards the end of his life, Willie Bobo

gave in to fusion with, notably, the boastful *Hell of an Act to Follow*, recalling the Crusaders' music.

A first-rate arranger with sophisticated harmonic concepts, and the author of the standards *Morning* and *Pensativa*, pianist Clare Fischer has a very personal style (*Salsa picante, Tjaderama*). Born in 1928 in Durand, Michigan, he started out playing boogie-woogie as a teenager and graduated in composition from Michigan State University. He then travelled for five years as pianist and conductor of the vocal group The Hi Los, for which he wrote novel arrangements which inspired Herbie Hancock early in his career. After working with Modesto Durán's *charanga* in Los Angeles and with Cal Tjader, he led during the 1970s an ensemble which included drummer Roland Vázquez and Peruvian percussionist Alex Acuña. Around 1980, Vázquez left Fischer to organize his own group, but Fischer played keyboards on Vázquez's *Best of the L.A. Jazz Ensemble* album. Says Fischer, who has composed and written for Dizzy Gillespie (*A Portrait of Duke Ellington*) and other jazzmen as well as Brazilian musicians and such pop stars as Prince: "I discovered Latin music thanks to a Puerto Rican college roommate and Latin rhythms changed my life. But I play neither Cuban nor Brazilian music, I create my own language from these sources of inspiration." A fervent admirer of Charlie Palmieri ("when I heard him play in New York shortly before his death," he recalls, "I had tears in my eyes"), he wrote as a tribute to him the superb *CP*, recorded on *Lembranças* (1991).

In 1978 Louie Bellson issued the great *Ecué ritmos cubanos*, featuring a stellar percussion section (Alex Acuña, Francisco Aguabella, Walfredo de los Reyes, Luis Conte, Manolo Badrena, plus Cachao, Clare Fischer, Paquito Hechavarría, El Negro Vivar, and others), and offering a challenging *Salsa en cinco*.

After moving from New York to Los Angeles, in 1978, Justo Almario played with the fusion group Koinonia (with Mexican bassist Abrahám Laboriel and Alex Acuña), and then founded the jazz-oriented Tolú, reworking *Giant Steps* as an uptempo merengue or *Bésame mucho* as a bolero-funk. With the group and on his own albums, Almario seeks inspiration from Colombian and other Latin rhythms: *cumbia, bambuco, pasillo, vallenato*. However, his Californian output with its amplified instruments and synthesizers sometimes suffers, despite sharp arrangements, from the commercialism so widespread on the West Coast.

The son of *conguero* "Licho" (Luis) Almario, he grew up in Sincelejo, a small town on the Atlantic coast, and was nurtured by the black local music and by jazz. In the 1970s, after studying at the Berklee School of Music, he played in New York with Mongo Santamaría, Roy Ayers, and Brazilian pianist Dom Salvador.

After working with Pérez Prado, Alex Acuña gigged with show-business stars in Puerto Rico and Las Vegas. In the 1990s, he formed in Los Angeles the group The Unknown, and he introduced the Peruvian *cajones* (percussive wooden boxes) into jazz and U.S. Latin music.

Tjader's sideman from 1975 to 1982, the *conguero* Poncho Sánchez, born in Texas but of Mexican descent, produces an ebullient music swinging between salsa and jazz (*Bien Sabroso, Baila mi gente*). On *A Night at Kimball's East*, Joe Loco's *Yumbambe* contrasts with James Brown's *Cold Sweat* and jazz standards (*Jumpin' with Symphony Sid, A Night in Tunisia*). Like Jerry González, Danilo Pérez, Ray Barretto, Marlon Simón, and other Latin peers, Sánchez has also offered Thelonious Monk tunes (*Well You Needn't*).

The Argentinian "Lalo" (Boris) Schifrin – one of the most respected composers and arrangers of jazz, Latin music, and film music – had heard Pérez Prado, Julio Gutiérrez, and Dizzy Gillespie in Buenos Aires, where all three had performed in the 1950s. In the 1960s, he moved to the United States, working with Xavier Cugat and then becoming Gillespie's pianist. In 1999 he recorded a *Latin Jazz Suite* in Germany with the WDR big band and guest stars Jon Faddis, David Sánchez, and Ignacio Berroa, presenting a mixture of Cuban, Brazilian, Caribbean, and Argentinian rhythms.

Bongo Logic, led by percussionist Brett Gollin, which includes flautist Art Webb (*Tipiqueros*), opts for a rather glossy yet engaging type of Latin jazz.

Starting in the 1970s, San Francisco and the Bay Area in general became a hotbed of Latin jazz, with Panamanian pianist Carlos Federico, guitarists Luis Gasca and Ray Obiedo, themselves tending towards fusion, *timbalero* Bobby Matos and his Heritage Ensemble influenced by Coltrane, John Santos's Machete Ensemble (derived from Orquesta Batachanga), with Orestes Vilató, pianist John Calloway, and trombonist Wayne Wallace, combining jazz and Afro-Cuban strains, and the group led by "Tambú" (Héctor Hal Noble).

On January 7, 2000, twenty-eight of the best Latin jazz musicians from Los Angeles (among them Justo Almario, Poncho Sánchez, Francisco Aguabella, Al McKibbon, Danilo Lozano, Luis Conte, and Álex Acuña) were gathered for a concert celebrating the tenth anniversary of José Rizo's radio show *Jazz on the Latin Side*. The recorded performance (another album had been planned) testified to the vitality of this music on the West Coast. A classically trained flautist and the son of Rolando Lozano, Danilo Lozano is a founding member of the Hollywood Bowl orchestra, and he often plays Latin jazz with fellow Cubans Orestes Vilató, Luis Conte, Alberto Salas and other musicians.

In New Orleans, Los Hombres Calientes, founded in 1998 by NOCCA (New Orleans Center for Creative Arts) alumni percussionist Bill Summers, trumpeter Irvin Mayfield, and drummer Jason Marsalis, have brought back Latin jazz to the Crescent City, where it had pretty much vanished since the days of Jelly Roll Morton. A daring band, they experiment in various directions, mixing for example *songo* and funk (*Fongo Sunk*). And Vancouver, where a few Cuban expatriates have settled, also has some new groups.

Latin music has continued to inspire jazzmen. Art Pepper included *Manteca* on *Tokyo Debut*; Pharoah Sanders hired percussionist Gene Golden, Charles Mingus took on Ray Mantilla, and Lew Soloff employed Manolo Badrena; under Justo Almario's guidance, Mingus recorded *Cumbia & Jazz Fusion*. Percussionist Bill Summers recorded *Latican Space Mambo*, David Sanborn *Morning Salsa*,

Bobby Hutcherson *Un poco loco*; vibist Jay Hoggard did *Sao Pablo*, with Brazilian rhythms alternating with *montunos* and a sprightly solo by Kenny Kirkland; drummer Marvin "Smitty" Smith did *Salsa Blue*, with solos more jazzy than Latin; Joe Henderson put out *Yo todavía la quiero*, Antonio Hart *Puerto Rico*, Rodney Kendrick *Santería*, and Randy Weston a Latin version of *Hi Fly*; Benny Bailey and Bobby Stern recorded *Conexión Latina Mambo 2000*, with Nicky Marrero. Chico Hamilton, Wayne Shorter, Cedar Walton, Kenny Barron, Kenny Kirkland, and Mulgrew Miller have all used Latin devices. "With Latin rhythms, I can do more rhythmic explorations than with mainstream jazz," admitted Kirkland. On the sole CD under his name, he recorded a fiery Latin rendition of Bud Powell's *Celia* and a breathtaking one of Wayne Shorter's *Ana Maria*, abetted by the Andy–Jerry González team and Steve Berrios. In 1996, after a tour to Cuba, Roy Hargrove gave a series of concerts with percussionists Changuito and Miguel "Angá" Díaz, and with Chucho Valdés, David Sánchez, and John Benítez, and played numbers inspired by Cuban music (*Tin tin deo, La costa de Cuba*).

With her fantastic Venezuelan pianist Otmaro Ruiz and Brazilian guitarist Romero Lubambo, and as a guest star with Poncho Sánchez, Diane Reeves also enjoys singing Latin material (*Afro Blue*). McCoy Tyner, faithful to his impetuous modal outpourings, includes Gary Bartz, Claudio Roditi, Steve Turry, and Giovanni Hidalgo among his collaborators; and the Cuban saxophonist Yosvany Terry, the Argentine trumpeter Diego Urcola, and the Mexican drummer Antonio Sánchez bring Latin color to the International Vamp Band led by the Israeli pianist (and erstwhile bassist) Avishai Cohen.

In the 1980s Kip Hanrahan launched his American Clavé record label. Fond of musical mixes, he mingled Latin musicians with such jazz artists as Carmen Lundy, John Stubblefield, and Ralph Peterson with unusual and often stirring results. On the inventive *This Night Becomes a Rumba*, for example, graced by the presence of the impressive Cuban singer Xiomara Laugart, Jerry González blows his muted trumpet Miles Davis-style against a highly percussive background (on *The Bronx with Palm Trees*), while Charles Trenet's *I Wish You Love* gets a *rumba brava* treatment.

In 1996, as Canadian saxophonist Jane Bunnett did before him, Steve Coleman recorded in Cuba with local musicians. He improvised on the *batá* rhythms of the group Afro Cuba de Matanzas (on *The Sign and the Seal – Transmissions of the Metaphysics of a Culture*). But despite the grand title, the result, commendable as it was, was not quite conclusive: Yoruba sacred music, governed by its own strict codes, did not sit well with the jazz elements, and Coleman – limited by the exacting *batá* rhythms – was not really at his best. Chico Freeman also turned Latin with his band Guataca, as did Antonio Hart with *Ama tu sonrisa*. The pianist Jacky Terrasson and Xiomara Laugart fired up *Better World*, Charlie Haden recorded an album of Cuban and Mexican boleros (*Nocturne 2001*) with Gonzalo Rubalcaba, Ignacio Berroa, violinist Federico Britos Ruiz, Joe Lovano, and Pat Metheny, but aside from Dizzy Gillespie, Cal Tjader, and a few others passionately committed to Cuban and Brazilian rhythms, American jazzmen have usually limited themselves to occasional forays into South American music. The most convincing Latin jazz has generally come from the Hispanic side (although in a Brazilian idiom, which falls outside the realm of this book, Antonio Carlos Jobim with *Amparo* or *Ana Luiza*, Herbie Hancock and Wayne Shorter, along with Milton Nascimento, Wagner Tiso, and others on *Tarde* (on *Native Dancer*), for example, have created masterpieces).

Arranged by Lalo Schiffrin, the soundtrack of the film *Che* (with Omar Sharif), on which Pete Bonnet, Francisco Aguabella, José Lozano, Chino Valdés, Armando Peraza, José Mangual, and Mongo Santamaría played, suggested there might be new Hollywood outlets for Latin jazz. But except for one or two isolated attempts such as *Mambo Kings*, the film industry has largely continued to ignore this music: the score of *West Side Story* was written by Leonard Bernstein, that for *Fort Apache the Bronx*, shot with Paul Newman in the predominantly Puerto Rican South Bronx, by a composer unfamiliar with Latin rhythms.

Latin rock and Latin disco

Latin rock and Latin disco have continued to develop since the 1970s, generally attracting audiences different to those for salsa and Latin jazz. More recently, Latin rap and techno have been attracting a growing number of young and passionate Hispanic adepts.

In 1972, forecasting the experiments of Sheila E and other musicians of the following decades, Jimmy Castor used timbales breaks on his hit *It's Just Begun*, and other soul and pop artists – Earth, Wind and Fire, Stevie Wonder and Joe Jackson among them – also borrowed Cuban rhythms and percussion instruments.

Around the mid-1970s, going the opposite way, some Latin musicians gave in to fusion. Ricardo Marrero added a synthesizer to his group Time, Larry Harlow founded the Amber Grey ensemble, and two Latin pop bands later sprang up: the Bad Street Boys (with their hit *Copacabana*), started in the mid-1980s, and Dr. Buzzard's Original Savannah Band, which gave birth to Kid Creole and the Coconuts, a glamorous and entertaining group led by August Darnell. With *No fumes ese crack* (Don't Smoke This Crack, 1995), the Bad Street Boys delivered an inspirational message to youngsters of the *barrios*; at first rejected by an American music publisher for his songs, found to be too "Latin," Darnell on *Fresh Fruit in Foreign Places* scoffed at the clumsiness of Anglos when confronted with Latin rhythms:

> I'm so confused
> This Latin music's got me so bemused
> There's too much syncopation
> Where's the two and four?

In 1996, eager to find fresh sources of inspiration, Darnell travelled to meet Indians of the Ecuadorian jungle and Australian aborigines.

Born of a Puerto Rican mother and a Cuban father and raised in the Bronx, Angela Bofill had sung with Dizzy Gillespie, Ricardo Marrero, and various jazz groups, before becoming a star of pop and soul music although not abandoning entirely the rhythms of her Latin roots.

Around 1979, South Bronx teenagers invented the Latin hustle, an elaborate dance, but done to rather stiff and conventional rhythms. Joe Bataan tried his hand at the Latin hustle – without great success – with *Mestizo*, but this musical genre, merging with funk, quickly gave way to disco. Young Latinos, born or raised in the United States and more Americanized than their parents, stopped listening to salsa and turned their attention to the Ritchie Family and other funk groups. The Big Apple's Latin clubs, the Corso among them, featured disco acts in between salsa sets, and synthesizers and rhythm machines began to deprive some musicians of work. Paquito Navarro gave up his popular salsa program on radio WKTU for a disco show – much to the regret of his listeners – but thereby becoming New York's most popular DJ.

In the early 1980s rap, under the influence of Afrika Bambaata, also threatened salsa. Young Latinos experimented with this new music and Gerardo, a DJ of Ecuadorian origin, produced the Latin techno hit *Rico suave*. Rap swiftly spread to Puerto Rico, with rappers such as "Vico C" (Luis Armando Lozada). In New York, Puerto Rican DJ John "Jellybean" Benítez brought hip hop to the Roxy, a club which in 1982 became the temple of break dancing. Joe Bataan issued *Rap O Clap*, Tito Allen did *Salsa Rap*, and Tito Puente recorded with The Sugarhill Gang. Hispanic rappers started gaining exposure. The Cuban Mellow Man Ace (*Escape From Havana*) attracted devoted followers in California. New York saw the birth of Puerto Rican groups M.C.E., Latin Empire – formed by the two Bronx youngsters Tony Boston and Rick Rodríguez (*Así es la vida*, which dealt with the difficulties of life in New York and included a timbales interlude) – C & C Music Factory, and the short-lived Dark Latin Groove founded in 1996 by Huey Dunbar, James de Jesús, and Wilfredo Crispín which fused rap, reggae, salsa, and *songo* (*Muévete*). Established in Florida since 1993, the gritty-voiced "Mangú" (Freddy García), who grew up in the Bronx and took his nickname from a Dominican dish (*La playa*) also blazed a trail on the new Latin scene. Rap groups, among them Amenaza, SBOS, Sin Palabras or the female ensembles Instinto, Atracción, or Amab also blossomed in Cuba, where a rap festival has been held on the outskirts of Havana. In Cuba, too, rap lyrics frequently allude to social problems and the vicissitudes of life.

After *Rock It*, featuring an *okónkolo*, Latin percussion instruments crept into disco, jungle, and house music. Jamie Delgado used them on his hip hop hit *The Breaks* (1980), and Sheila E (Escovedo) with Prince.

A salsa *timbalera* before turning to singing, Sheila Escovedo, of Mexican origin, is the niece of the late percussionist "Coke" Escovedo and the daughter of percussionist and singer Pete Escovedo, who had worked with Mongo Santamaría. In the 1970s she recorded several salsa albums with her father (among them *Sólo tú*), and in 1991, she scored a hit with her Latin-tinged *Sex Cymbal*. Pete Escovedo later formed a Latin jazz orchestra that included Sheila on drums, Peter Michael Escovedo on congas, and Juan Escovedo on bongo.

Latin rock, which flourished in the early 1970s, took hold in California, rather than in Florida or in New York, where more *típico* or jazzy sounds prevailed. It was represented by Randy Ortiz's Seguida, Jorge Santana's Malo, Sapo, Dakila, Caldera (with Cuban percussionist Luis Conte), Tierra, and Azteca, founded by the Escovedo brothers after their stint with Santana. Carlos Santana (Jorge's brother), also of Mexican origin, became a figurehead of this music with two of Tito Puente's compositions, *Oye cómo va*, played with organ, drums, and electric guitar (on *Abraxas*, 1970) and *Pa' los rumberos* (1973). He recruited Armando Peraza and Orestes Vilató (who eventually played with the San Francisco Symphony Orchestra). In 2000 Santana made a strong comeback with the blockbuster *Supernatural*.

Formed in Miami in the late 1980s by Joe Galdo and Paquito Hechevarría, Bandera, which included an Afro-American vocalist and Cuban guitar-player, drummer, and percussionist, exemplified the new Latin pop from Florida.

More recently, with his Cubanos Postizos, guitarist Marc Ribot has recorded rockish take-offs on Cuban standards such as Arsenio Rodríguez's *Dame un cachito pa' huele*. And African singer Lou Bega's pop rendition of Pérez Prado's *Mambo No 5* climbed to the top of the charts.

the rest of the world

Influence of Cuban and

Puerto Rican music abroad

The 1920s and 1930s

Beginning in the 1920s, the record industry and the radio disseminated Cuban music abroad, in often rather watered-down commercial forms. In the nineteenth century, however, Mexico and other Latin American countries had already fallen for the habanera, the *danzón*, and the bolero. The habanera crept into the Argentinian tango, and tango orchestras, calling themselves *típicas*, adopted the bass, piano, and violins line-up of Cuban *danzón* bands. After the smashing success of *La paloma* (by Spanish composer Sebastián Yradier, who lived in Cuba), several Mexicans wrote *danzas* and *danzones*. In 1898 the Bufos Habaneros had performed *danzones*, *guarachas*, and *guajiras* in Mexico City.

In the 1920s, cabarets and dance halls opened there, among them the famed Salón México, which attracted dancers from all social backgrounds. Its bands employed several Cubans, among them percussionist "Babuco" (Tiburcio Hernández), one of the pioneers of Cuban music in Mexico. Composer Jorge Anckermann and various *típicas*, among them Enrique Peña's, also popularized the *danzón* there. In the 1920s emerged Emiliano Martínez's Danzonera[1] América; and the following decade the Danzonera de Prieto y Dimas, led by "Dimas"

[1] *Danzón* band.

Don Barreto and his Orchestra. Emilio Barreto collection

(Amado Pérez Torres), Jaramillo y sus Diablos, and the ensemble headed by the Cuban Enrique Bryon. Arturo Núñez organized a big band with which Benny Moré later sang and whose rhythm section Pérez Prado borrowed upon his arrival in Mexico, and the rhumba and the *guaracha* also took root in this country. In the late 1930s, the Cuarteto Hatuey performed in Mexico and appeared in the films *Tierra brava* and *México lindo*.

Colombia received in 1935 the visit of the Trío Matamoros, and four years later, of Casino de la Playa and Anacaona. Venezuela, where the Puerto Rican Augusto Sanabia (Noro Morales's uncle) led a dance band, welcomed the Sexteto Boloña and other Cuban groups. And in the late 1930s, Armando Romeu performed in Argentina, Peru, and Chile.

After the vogue for cubism, a Paris captivated by black art welcomed African American and Antillean musicians with open arms. Josephine Baker and Sidney Bechet, stars of the *Revue Nègre*, triumphed in 1925 at the Music Hall des Champs Elysées, and a few years later the Martinique clarinettist Alexandre Stellio popularized the biguine in the French capital after performing at the 1930 Colonial Exhibition. In 1928 the French writer Robert Desnos travelled to Havana, where he helped his friend Alejo Carpentier flee Machado's dictatorship with a false French passport. The dazzled Desnos discovered the "obscene blacks," stevedores by day who turned into sensual and soulful singers by night in the harbor dives, and back in Paris, he played records brought back from his trip to his Surrealist friends at the Studio des Ursulines.

After the First World War, several Caribbean musicians – some of them Puerto Rican, but the rest mostly Cuban – settled in an exhilarating Paris and the French took to tropical music with rapturous delight. Latin venues proliferated, to such an extent that the rue Fontaine, in Pigalle, was nicknamed "Cuban street." Contributing to the sparkle of the French capital were Moncho Leña, the Cuban saxophonist Eduardo Castellanos and his countrymen, the guitarist "Don" (Emilio) Barretto, the flautist and clarinettist Filiberto Rico, and Antonio Machín, each of whom organized his own outfit (Machín's included the dancers Ofelia and Pimienta, Rico's the bassist José Riestra). Fernando Collazo sang at La Cabaña Cubana; the pianist Oscar Calle, whose French debut took place in Cannes in 1932, worked with his rhumba band (which included Julio Cueva) at the famed Melody's Bar, rue Fontaine; and the Guadeloupe saxophonist, clarinettist, and flautist Félix Valvert also led a rhumba band, the Fell's Boys.

Don Barreto (1909–1997) held forth at the Melody's Bar, at La Boule Blanche, in Montparnasse and other Parisian clubs, and he toured Europe and Algeria including in his band Filiberto Rico, José Riestra, Florentino Frontela (percussion, vocals), and the French pianist Raymond Gottlieb. He recorded many rhumbas, biguines, and congas with Riestra's wife, the vocalist "Chiquita" (Joaquina) Serrano, added for a few sessions.

After singing in London with the revue of dancer Delita (in which he performed in particular *Lamento esclavo*), Machín moved to Paris. At the onset of the Second World War he settled in Barcelona and became a legend in Spain, where he remained until his death in 1977. Moisés Simons, Eliseo Grenet, the Lecuona Cuban Boys, who played at the ABC theater; Sindo Garay, Rita Montaner, who sang *Mama Inés* at the Palace with, noted Alejo Carpentier, "an eloquence that convinced the coolest listeners"; Julio Brito, who performed with his Orquesta Siboney at the Lido and the Mogador, and the Orquesta Anacaona all brought Cuban music to the City of Light. Julio Cueva performed under his own name at La Cueva, Félix Valvert's club named for the trumpeter, where Eliseo Grenet and other Cubans would come to jam. During the Spanish Civil War, Cueva headed a band on the front lines, later returning to France and, in 1940, to Cuba. With his dancer "Mariana" (Alicia Parlá), Don Azpiazu won over the patrons of l'Empire and La Plantation – two of Paris's most celebrated "exotic" spots. In the early 1930s he made several recordings in France and wrote the rhumba *Por tus ojos negros* for the film *Espérame*, featuring Carlos Gardel.

In addition to Machín and Cueva, Spain welcomed Alfredo Brito and his Orquesta Siboney (which also played in Lisbon), Moisés Simons, the Trío Matamoros, and *conguero* "El Calvo." And concerts of Cuban music were even organized in Egypt. Born in Trinidad and raised in Venezuela, Edmundo Ros had worked in London with the rhumba band of Marino Barreto (Emilio's brother).

He, too, popularized Cuban music in England with his Rhumba Band, before retiring to Alicante, Spain, in 1975.

The 1940s and 1950s

Mexico continued to love the bolero and the *danzón* and openly welcomed the mambo and the cha-cha. Dancers flocked to the San Angel, the Swing Club, the Terraza Casino, the Teatro Follies, the Teatro Lírico, and the Teatro Margot. In 1941, the revues *Batamú*, and seven years later *Sepia Rhapsody* (renamed *Las Mulatas de Fuego*) brought the new Cuban rhythms to the country, and Celia Cruz sang there with La Sonora Matancera. Mexican singers Pedro Vargas, Juan Arvizu, Toña la Negra, influenced by Cuban *boleristas*, thrilled Latin America. And, conversely, bands in Cuba played famous Mexican boleros: Alberto Domínguez's *Perfidia* and *Frenesí*, Consuelo Velázquez's *Bésame mucho*, Armando Chamaco Domínguez's *Miénteme*.

Countless Cuban artists wove their magic in Mexico during these exciting decades: the pianist Juan Bruno Tarraza (former director of the Riverside Orchestra and creator of the bolero *Penumbra* and the *conga Rompan el cuero*), who worked with Toña la Negra and recorded several albums; Orquesta América; Felo Bergaza, who accompanied Celia Cruz and Mario Álvarez; drummer and *timbalero* Aurelio Tamayo; the *bongoceros* "Monito," Ramón Castro, Modesto Durán, and Clemente Piquero, who had come in 1941 with the show *Batamú* and who played with José Sabre Marroquín's band and recorded with the Trío Los Panchos; the *bongocero* and *conguero* "Tabaquito," who appeared in several Mexican movies; the *congueros* "Ciminea" and Mongo Santamaría; singers Celio González, Oscar López, Vicentico and Alfredo Valdés, Kiko Mendive, José Antonio Méndez, Celeste Mendoza, "Monguito" (Ramón Quián Sardiñas), Francisco Fellové, who created the *chua-chua* rhythm, Bola de Nieve; the percussionist, singer, dancer, and composer Silvestre Méndez (Havana 1926–Mexico City 1997), Rita Montaner and Bobby Collazo;[2] composers and bandleaders Mariano Mercerón, Pablo Peregrino, Justi Barreto, Enrique Jorrín, the Rigual brothers; bassist, *tresista*, and guitarist Humberto Cané, whose group included Cuban pianist Ramón Dorca, trumpeter Florecita, Manolo Durán, and "Calaverita"; and the Puerto Rican Rafael Hernández.

At the Waikiki club, in Mexico City, the U.S.-born Mexican dancer "Tongolele" (Yolanda Montes) charmed audiences with her mambo demonstrations. The Cuban *timbalero* and *rumba* dancer "Acerina" (Consejo Valiente), who had worked with "Babuco" Hernández and Dimas, became the Salón México's main attraction and an almost permanent fixture with his *danzonera*. He recorded many *danzones* and cha-chas, among them his own *danzón Nereidas*, and in the mid-1950s, his *Salón México* became a hit.

In Mexico too, Juan Fernández and Alejandro Cardona led *danzoneras*. Pianist Carlos Campo organized a mambo and cha-cha big band and arrangers José Sabre Marroquín and Pablo Beltrán Ruiz formed fine ensembles playing Cuban music.

2 He dedicated his song *La última noche* to Mexican *bolerista* Pedro Vargas.

Acerina and his ensemble (with Cuban trumpeter Florecita). Óscar López collection

Benny Moré, who had come to Mexico in 1945 with Miguel Matamoros's *conjunto* (then including *bongoceros* Agustín Gutiérrez and Montoto), sang there with Arturo Núñez. In 1957, Niño Rivera recorded with the outfits of Sabre Marroquín, Beltrán Ruiz, and Núñez; Chico O'Farrill organized several orchestras and hosted his own television show, before going to work in Las Vegas with Andy Russell.

In 1940 Rafael Hernández appeared in Medellin, Colombia with his Grupo Victoria (which included Myrta Silva, Bobby Capó, Pepito Arvelo, and bassist Gabriel Velázquez), and his *Cachita* triumphed there. Other Latin entertainers – Guillermo Portabales, Noro Morales, singer Pepe Reyes, Johnny Rodríguez, Benny Moré, Xavier Cugat, and La Sonora Matancera – also performed in Colombia and several local groups influenced by Cuban music were established: Los Cali Boys, a Cuban-type *sexteto* founded in 1945 by Tito Cortés; La Sonora Cali; the Sexteto Miramar, formed in 1958 and blending Cuban music and *cumbia*; and Edmundo Arias's La Sonora Antillana. And with his Orquesta Emisora Fuentes, Lucho Bermúdez accompanied Bienvenido Granda for his record *Besos de hada*.

Ñico Saquito, who had toured Venezuela with Los Guaracheros de Oriente, stayed there. Obdulio Morales lived in Caracas, and Cuban rhythms disseminated there by the Orquesta Casino de la Playa, the Orquesta Riverside, Benny Moré's group (then featuring Miguelito Cuní) and other big bands from Havana inspired local ensembles, among them those of saxophonist and clarinettist Aldemaro

Romero; the group led by Luis Alfonso Larraín; La Sonora Caracas, with vocalist "Canelita" (Rogelia Medina), inspired by Celia Cruz; Renato Capriles's Los Melódicos; and Billo's Caracas Boys. "Billo" (Luis María Frómeta Pereyra, Santo Domingo 1915–Caracas 1988), who had debuted at the age of sixteen in his native country with "Simó" Damirón, had moved to Caracas in 1937, during Trujillo's dictatorship. Like their model, Casino de la Playa, the Billo's Caracas Boys performed for essentially middle-class audiences, but Billo's show, broadcast on Radio Caracas, captivated a broad spectrum of listeners. Billo's great vocalist, bolerista Felipe Pirela, died in Puerto Rico in 1972, at the age of thirty-three, and elicited the admiration of Héctor Lavoe and Joe Fliciano. In Ecuador, the Orquesta Blasio Jr. also achieved great popularity.

Buenos Aires was visited by Bola de Nieve, Esther Borja, Ernesto Lecuona, Fernando Mulens, Julio Gutiérrez, Pérez Prado, Rubén González, and other Cuban artists, although there the tango tended to reign supreme; and Panama by the likes of Rubén González, Óscar López, and the *rumbera* Estela.

A spate of Cuban singers and musicians, among them Óscar López, Chombo Silva, and Gonzalo Fernández settled in Paris after the Second World War. Fernández played with Orquesta Típica Palmera, African Team, the band of the l'Escale Club, and Manu Dibango. And Latin musicians congregated at the Big Ben or La Cabaña Cubana. The *conguero* and singer Humberto Cano performed with Benny Bennett; and with his orchestra, Eddie Warner recorded Cuban classics, among them *Almendra* and *Nagüe* for the Odeon label.

Kenny Graham and his Afro-Cubists and Eddie Culbert livened up London nights, but because of the influence of the English-speaking Caribbean, English audiences were often more familiar with the calypso than with the mambo.

In 1950 Spain greeted the revue *Embrujo antillano*, featuring José Urfé's orchestra (with dancers Mayra and Isora and singers Óscar López, Margarita Díaz, and Canelina). And with his European-based show band, bassist Pantaleón Pérez Prado capitalized on his brother Damaso's fame. In the late 1950s he performed in Belgium and Italy with his wife Ivón Poveda on vocals, and relations between the two siblings were often strained.

Cuban music resonates with special strength in Africa, where the *son* and the *rumba*, close to its own rhythms, have become staples of many local dance bands. In Zaire and Congo, they spawned a musical genre called *rumba zaïroise* or *rumba congolaise*, which later evolved into *soukous*. In the early 1950s, Le Grand Kallé and his African Jazz, Franco and his O.K. Jazz, and Tabu Ley (Seigneur Rochereau) became the figureheads of this music, played with horns and electric guitars. Cuban music also inspired some Kenyan guitarists, as well as black bands from Johannesburg, which created a hybrid called *tsaba-tsaba*. And discothèques in Dakar and Abidjan filled with *charanga* music, known throughout French-speaking Africa as "musique typique."

Cuban rhythms also reached Japan and, in 1949, Tadaki Misago organized his Tokyo Cuban Boys, inspired by the Lecuona Cuban Boys.

From the 1960s to today

In 1960, Bebo Valdés started a band in Mexico. He accompanied Rolando Laserie at the Terraza Casino, led the television program *El Show de Max Factor* and made several records with Cascarita and Pío Leiva (*Mucho sabor, Glorias a Cuba*). Mariano Mercerón, Olga Guillot, Celia Cruz, and Pérez Prado were among those who also settled in Mexico after the Cuban revolution (Guillot and Cruz later moved to the United States), and Francisco Fellové made Veracruz his home. A wonderful pianist and genial man, Armando Oréfiche toured Europe and Japan with his show band in the mid-1960s.

Salsa now shines throughout the world, and Venezuela and Colombia in particular have bands that vie with those of New York, Havana, or San Juan. In Caracas, aside from Billo's Caracas Boys, the major Cuban-type bands before the advent of salsa had been those of "Chucho" (Jesús) Sanoja and of Aldemaro Romero, Los Melódicos, and La Sonora Caracas. Romero had created a rhythm called *onda nueva* ("new wave"), a mixture or *joropo* – Venezuela's national dance – and samba. Tito Puente had used it on *Araquita* (on *Tito Puente pa' lante*), but with its not very danceable triple meter the *onda nueva* never really caught on, and popular Venezuelan music remained largely unknown abroad. Scorned at first by the Caracas bourgeoisie, salsa eventually gained full acceptance there.

An early introduction to salsa had been that of Federico y su Combo in 1966 with *Llegó la salsa*, which had featured vocalist "Watusi" (Orlando Castillo), but the epochal band was La Dimensión Latina. Founded in 1972 by singer and güiro player Wladimir Lozano and Óscar "D'León" (Óscar Emilio León Somoza), it bore, with its powerful trombones and the arrangements of trombonist César "Albóndiga" Monge, the influence of Willie Colón and other New York groups. In 1977, when its star vocalist Óscar D'León left the band to strike out on his own, La Dimensión Latina recruited Andy Montañez, whose voice resembled that of D'León. With Montañez, Lozano, and singer Rodrigo Mendoza, the band enjoyed a short period of success, but broke up shortly thereafter.

The dynamic and honey-voiced D'León then became a major salsa star. He used to dance while playing his white baby bass, but has practically given up this instrument to concentrate on singing. D'León, who claims that "his heart is Cuban," favors old Cuban themes (*Longina, El que siembra su maíz, Suavecito*) and Puerto Rican ones as well (*Capullito de azucena*). He has also recorded duets with Celia Cruz, and now leads a tight and exciting band, with arrangements by his superb pianist Óscar Reyes.

A former cab driver, born in 1943 in Antimano, Caracas, he grew up listening to the major Cuban *soneros*, Benny Moré and Celia Cruz among them. He first set up Óscar y sus Estrellas, with pianist Enrique "Culebra" Iriarte, whose style recalled that of Papo Lucca, then La Dimensión Latina; four years later he got together La Salsa Mayor, with whom he recorded an eponymous album in 1977, and the highly successful *El más grande* (1978), and then *Óscar D'León y su orquesta*. He also remains faithful to the *salsa dura* – the strong salsa of the 1970s, and *Sonero del mundo* (1996) was nominated for a Grammy Award.

In Venezuela, Federico y su Combo (with vocalists Teo Hernández and later Orlando Watusi) and the singer "El Puma" (José Luis Rodríguez) obtained more exposure in the 1970s, and other engaging groups appeared. Among them Wladimir y la Crítica; the rockish Daiquiri; Sonero Clásico del Caribe, founded in 1977 by Domingo Álvarez and close to the traditional *son*, whose *La cama del rey Salomón* written by guitarist Julio García Esteves celebrated trumpeter Chocolate Armenteros's huge canopy bed; and the merengue and salsa band led by the Dominican Porfi Jiménez. The versatile Madera, created in 1978 by singer Rafael Quintero in the black parish of San Agustín in Caracas, offered a medley of Caribbean rhythms (those of the San Juan Baricongo rituals, *plena*, *son*, calypso). It was, however, somewhat overshadowed by Guaco, one of Venezuela's most popular groups. Founded in Maracaibo in the 1960s by Alfonso Aguado and directed by Juan Carlos Salas, this seventeen-strong band started playing *gaitas* (a black genre from the Maracaibo lake area). It evolved towards dance music, combining salsa, funk, jazz, and *songo* (*Como era y como es, Amazonas*) while keeping a few traditional instruments. In Caracas, the vibists Alfredo Naranjo, who utilizes local rhythms (*Vibraciones de mi tierra*), and Franklin Veloz, and the percussionist Joel Márquez are promising salsa and Latin jazz names.

Vivid traditions of African origin prevail in Colombia, particularly along its coasts, and salsa there has often been challenged by *cumbia* (a hybrid from the Atlantic coast), *vallenato* (a narrative genre from the Valle de Upar), and in Cartagena, *champeta* (a volatile mix of salsa, Afro-Colombian music, rap, *soukous* – brought from Africa by sailors – and other strains). Folk rhythms like the *caderona* or the *currulas*, cultivated in the predominantly black Chocó region, on the Pacific coast, have strongly colored local salsa, especially in Cali. If Cartagena's Caribbean music festival has featured many salsa bands, Medellín and Cali have become the foremost salsa centers of Colombia, and every year the Feria de Cali attracts the best national and international ensembles.

At the dawn of salsa, the Sonora Dinámita wedded Cuban and Colombian rhythms, and in 1968 the *cumbia* group Los Corraleros de Majagual traveled to New York, bringing back the burgeoning salsa concepts. Salsa records from the United States had also filtered into the country via ports like Barranquilla. But the spark that really triggered the salsa explosion in Colombia was the concerts given the same year by Richie Ray and Bobby Cruz in Barranquilla and in Cali. They returned to Barranquilla in 1969, captivating audiences there as well as in Medellín, Cali, Bogotá, and the rest of the country.

The first real Colombian salsa group was the rough-edged Fruko y sus Tesos, founded in 1971 by singer, bassist, and *timbalero* "Fruko" (Julio Ernesto Estrada Rincón) with, on vocals, the late "Piper Pimienta" (Edulfamit Molina) Díaz and Wilson Manyoma. Later "Joe" (Álvaro José) Arroyo, who hailed from Cartagena, also joined the band. Born in 1951 in Medellín, Fruko debuted there as *timbalero* with Los Corraleros de Majagual. The album *Tesura* launched Fruko's career in Colombia, and in 1976 he gave a concert at Madison Square Garden (with Manyoma and Arroyo) that spread his name in the United States. More lively albums followed (*La fruta bomba, Fruko "El Magnífico"*), and an exciting *Descarga* featuring Tata Güines. Fruko also had considerable success with *El preso* (*The prisoner*), and then became one of Colombia's busiest arrangers and producers.

In the wake of Fruko, The Latin Brothers were organized in 1974 by trombonist Antonio Fuentes, followed by the pan-Caribbean band La Verdad, but the Grupo Niche[3] was the first Colombian *salsa* outfit to really acquire a strong international following. Inspired by a group of the 1960s, the Combo Vacana, and founded in 1979 in Quibdó by singer and percussionist Jairo Varela Martínez, Alexis Lozano, and his sister "La Coco" Lozano with musicians from the Chocó, they issued their first LP two years later with *Querer es poder*. They adopted a potent three-trombone section, often dealt with social issues, and also made all of Colombia dance with their lighter hits *Cali pachanguera* and *Listo Medellín*, and they recorded in 1999 the excellent *A golpe de folklore*. In the mid-1980s, after a disagreement in New York, some members seceded and started the Orquesta Internacional Los Niches, led by trumpeter Fabio Espinosa. Another ensemble from the Chocó is Los Nemus del Pacífico, set up in 1989 by singer and guitarist Alexis Murillo, who recruited musicians from La Integración Porteña. Los Nemus, very influenced by the *son montuno*, often evoke the Chocó (*Del Chocó pa'l Congo, Vamos pa' Buenaventura*), and they also enjoy humorous numbers.

Steeped in the black music of the Atlantic coast from which he hails, Joe Arroyo is, with his gritty and powerful voice, one of Colombia's most charismatic vocalists. After stints with Los Coraleros de Majagual and Fruko, he formed in 1981 La Verdad and then performed under his own name, often using local rhythms such as the *chandé* (*El trato*) and *cumbia* (*La ceiba*), or mixing various Caribbean strains in what he calls *joesón*. Los Gemelos, two exuberant twins, have recently risen to fame with their earthy and rollicking salsa.

The Grupo Galé, formed in 1989 in Cali by the great percussionist Diego Calé (who also leads the Sonora Carruseles), is a particularly interesting new band, with great riffs and breaks (on *Amor secreto* for instance). Their singer Igor Moreno also hails from the Chocó. In 1993, they achieved wider recognition with *A conciencia*. Trombonist Alexis Lozano's highly melodic Orquesta Guayacán (founded in Buenaventura and also bearing the stamp of the Chocó), the Grupo Raíces (influenced by the *songo*), the versatile Alkimia, the trombone-based Los Titanes (formed in 1982), the Cuban-tinged Sonora Carruseles (started in Medellín, and which includes boogaloos in its repertoire), and the sophisticated and suave La Misma Gente are other stimulating ensembles.

Panama boasts the dynamic ten-trumpet big band Bush y su Nuevo Sonido (*Para los barrios*), while in Curaçao, which regularly organizes salsa concerts and festivals, Organisashon Kompleto and Macario "Macay" Prudencia produce what they call a *"salsa antiyana"* sung in papiamento, the local dialect (*Washmashin*).

3 A derogatory term meaning "black."

Based in Mexico, Aymée Nuviola, a former NG La Banda vocalist, has obtained success with her rendition of *Que manera de quererte*, and she now performs internationally.

Salsa is particularly strong in West Africa and in the Congo and Zaire, and the African concerts of Johnny Pacheco, Ray Barretto, Orquesta Broadway, Orquesta Aragón, and the Fania All Stars all elicited tremendous enthusiasm. Cuban or Puerto Rican musicians have returned to Africa to discover their roots and, conversely, African musicians have studied, played, and recorded with Cubans and Puerto Ricans. The founding members of Las Maravillas de Mali, for instance, studied music in Havana in the 1960s before returning to Bamako. Senegalese musicians have sung salsa in Wolof, among them Pape Seck (*Moliendo café*). The deep-voiced Seck (1946–1995) was lead vocalist with the group Africando, initiated by the Malian arranger Boncana Maiga and by producer Ibrahima Sylla. They issued an eponymous album in 1993 and in the following year *Tierra tradicional*, recorded in New York with top Latin musicians. Seck also sang, along with Medioune Diallo, on *Trovador* (1993) (backed most notably by Chombo Silva, Mario Rivera, Papo Pepín, and Eddy Zervigón). One year before his death of cancer in Dakar, Seck also recorded *Sabador*, which includes songs by Guillermo Portabales, Benny Moré, and Rafael Cortijo. The Super Cayor de Dakar, with their Congolese-style electric guitars (*Xamsa bopp*), Pepe Fall's African Salsa, Super Sabador, or Salsa 2000 also offer quality salsa with a Senegalese twist.

Practically unknown in Europe during the 1970s, salsa and Latin jazz now attract a growing number of fans. In Paris during the 1970s, a band comprising Cuban bassist "Felo" (Rafael) López (the composer of *La sitiera* and *Errante y bohemio*), the excellent Martinique pianist Roland Malmin, and the Cubans "Bebo" and Manito López (congas) and Sergio Barreto (timbales) held forth at l'Escale, a small left-bank tropical club. In 1979, Azuquita travelled to Paris and recorded *Azuquita y su Melao* (with Malmin on piano), arranged by Mauricio Smith. Smith stayed in the French capital for a while and gigged freelance. The group Los Salseros was later created – involving Malmin and Cuban trumpeter Guillermo Fellové among others – by the late French journalist Pierre Goldman, stirred by a Paris performance of Típica 73. Mauricio Smith, Patato Valdés, and Azuquita performed for a while with Los Salseros, which served as a template for other French salsa ensembles. Malmin also collaborated with the Colombian *conjunto* Son Caribe and Los Machucambos. Singer and percussionist Henri Guédon, alternating between the Antilles and Paris, organized eclectic groups incorporating various influences. Other Latin musicians then joined the fast-growing Paris Latin scene, among them bassist "Cuchi" (José) Almeida and *timbalero* "Cutuflá" (Alfredo Franceschi), both from Venezuela, and salsa really took off there in the mid- to late 1990s.

Hailing from Martinique, pianists Bibi Louison and Mario Canonge, and singer Ralph Thamar (formerly with the Malavoi *charanga*) perform salsa, and (except for Thamar) Latin jazz colored with the accents of the beguine. The highly rhythmical Canonge, who also recorded in Cuba with Elio Revé Jr. and La Ritmo

Oriental, is also conversant with Brazilian phrasing (as on *Balata*). The Guadeloupe pianist Alain Jean-Marie, another beguine and jazz expert, has offered superb renditions of Cuban standards, among them *Tú, mi delirio*. Cuban trumpeter Tito Puentes (who hails from Oriente), "Angá" Díaz, and pianist Alfredo Rodríguez have also contributed strongly to the salsa boom in the French capital. Born in Havana, the classically-trained Rodríguez had moved to New York in 1966, attracted by the creativity of the Big Apple, and worked there with a host of Latin musicians. Like Eddie Palmieri, he plays jazzy preludes and driving *montunos*, but with a more Cuban feel (*Para Yoya*, recorded in 1993 and featuring Los Van Van's flamboyant vocalist, Pedro Calvo). Venezuelan percussionist Orlando Poleo, who sometimes uses *culo e puyas* (black drums from Barlovento), creates inventive Latin jazz (*Cimarroneando, Lo bueno de la vida*, featuring Argentinian pianist Geraldo di Giusto, *conguero* Richie Flores, Giovanni Hidalgo, "Maraca" Valle and Dave Valentín). His countryman, singer Diego Peláez, who has often teamed up with Angá Díaz, is also a leading name in French salsa. Colombian singer Yuri Buenaventura (his real name is Bedoya), who moved to Paris to study architecture before turning to music, spreads the exhilarating rhythms from his native Buenaventura. He has been wowing European audiences, striking a hit with Jacques Brel's *Ne me quitte pas*, and should soon be singing in the big league. Trumpeter José Aguirre Ocampo, of the Grupo Niche, has contributed arrangements for him (on *Ne me quitte pas*, in particular). Orishas, a quartet founded in 1995 by Cuban expatriates, meshes rap, *son*, rumba, popular Cuban music, and *santería*, with funky bass lines, synthesizers, and *batá* drums (*Orisha Dreams, Eleggua Open Way*). New additions to the Paris Latin scene have been Cuban bassist Felipe Cabrera (formerly with Gonzalo Rubalcaba) and his compatriot, singer Raúl Planas. Both hold forth at La Coupole which, for almost forty years, has been maintaining its Cuban music tradition.

The few French salsa groups (Mambomania among them, which long featured the Cuban singer Óscar López) have too often limited themselves to copying Cuban and Puerto Rican models, although the current passion for Latin music will certainly spawn new talents, as it will in other parts of Europe as well: for instance in Italy, home to singer Orlando Watusi and, more recently, violinist Alfredo de la Fé; in England, with, among other bands, El Sonido de Londres, the Latin Jazz ensemble led by Colombian percussionist Roberto Plá, Afroshock, Grupo X, or percussionist "Snowboy"'s The Latin Section; in Holland, with Manteca (founded in 1982), which evolved into the jazzier Nueva Manteca, headed by Nicky Marrero and then pianist Jan Laurens Hartong, with Saoco, comprised of Dutch and Latin musicians (*Aroma de Café*), and with Lucas Van Merwijk's stirring Cubop City; in Sweden, with New Burnt Sugar (founded in 1973 by Sabú Martínez), and then Hot Salsa (driven by the Peruvian-born singer, percussionist, and bassist Wilfredo Stephenson); in Switzerland, with the Zurich-based Son del Barrio; in Germany, with the international salsa band Son Bakán or the Cuban groups Cuarteto Chanchullo, Cubanísimo, and Quinteto Cubano. As well, in Belgium, Finland, and other European countries aficionados regularly organize Cuban music, salsa and Latin jazz concerts, and festivals; and Croatia boasts the interesting Cubismo Latin jazz group. The eclectic Latin jazz band Irazú, founded in early 1982 in Munich by saxophonist Raúl Gutiérrez Villanueva, later moved to Chile and recorded with Arturo Sandoval, Tata Güines, Héctor Martignon, Alfredo Rodríguez, Kenny Kirkland, and other guest artists.

Spain is also a hotbed of salsa. Antonio Machín, as we saw, furthered the development of Cuban music there. Ernesto Duarte, the composer of *Como fue*, died there. Armando Oréfiche settled in the Canary Islands after roaming the world with his band (which included the Cuban trumpeter Guillermo Fellové and his wife Rosanna, a Guyanese dancer). Oréfiche remained in Spain until his death in 2000 and not wanting, for political reasons, to return to his homeland, he asked that his ashes be cast into the sea. Another lively addition to the Spanish salsa scene has been singer and pianist "Lucrecia" (Lucrecia Pérez Saez) a former Anacaona member, who settled in Barcelona in 1992 (*Me debes un beso*). Orquesta Platería, Rumba Ketumba, and other Spanish salsa groups have tried to mix – rather unconvincingly – salsa and flamenco: their hybrid, pop-inflected music has neither the quivering tension of *cante jondo* nor the voluptuous grace of salsa. Now based in Barcelona after stays in the Bay Area and Ecuador, since his defection from Cuba in 1991, the Cuban wizard pianist Omar Sosa mixes jazz, Afro-Cuban music, dub poetry, hip hop, and other strains (*Bembón Roots III*). A *santería* practitioner, he often favors music of Yoruba inspiration and, abetted by Cuban singer Marta Galárraga and Venezuelan percussionist Gustavo Ovalles, moves with remarkable dynamics from highly percussive and syncopated *montunos* (as most other Cuban pianists he also studied percussion) to diaphanous ballads. Also based in Spain are Canallón (with Cuban and Panamanian members), Latinos Unidos, Caña Brava and, in Valencia, La Sonora Latina.

In 1990, a Japanese band, Orquesta de la Luz, with their vocalist "Nora" singing Spanish phonetically, burst onto the salsa scene with *Caliente*, composed by their *conguero* Gen Ogimi, even staking out their own turf in Puerto Rico – salsa's stronghold. Tito Puente and other great names of Latin music have collaborated with them. Nora, strongly influenced by Celia Cruz's mannerisms and delivery, has since embarked on a successful solo career (*Trátame como soy*). Other groups followed in their wake: Noche Cubana, Las Estrellas del Sol Naciente, the female band Son Reinas, singer and percussionist Masahito Hashida's Orquesta del Sol, Candela, using Latin percussion and traditional Japanese instruments, and percussionist Carlos Kanno's Nettai Tropical Jazz Big Band, have been turning on Japanese young people to the *clave*.

Martinique and Guadeloupe have a long-standing love affair with Cuban music and salsa. In Martinique, the late highly-talented pianist and composer Marius Cultier had accompanied Rafael Cortijo and Rolando Laserie and organized around 1960 the Wabaps orchestra, which included Cuban numbers in its repertoire. In the 1960s also, Ritmo Cubano and a slew of other ensembles, performed Cuban and other numbers, and in the 1970s the late pianist Paulo Rosine and violinist Lano Césaire created the *charanga* Malavoi, influenced by *zouk*.

conclusion

Until a few years ago, despite its international popularity, music of Cuban origin with its different forms attracted only a limited audience compared to that for English-language productions. It has been argued that the Spanish lyrics of salsa or merengue and of Latin American songs in general prevented their becoming better known. But then Japanese and African salsa singers sing Spanish phonetically and local audiences love it! Attempts to adapt these genres to English or other languages have proved disappointing, these types of music thus losing much of their spirit and character, except perhaps in the case of mixes with Wolof or other African languages more compatible with Spanish. There is usually a close rapport between a particular musical idiom and a particular language that is culturally rooted, and whose inflexions cannot be duplicated. Most salsa artists have in fact preferred to remain authentic rather than diluting their music in order to try to reach English-language and other markets. But the Buena Vista Social Club phenomenon changed this situation and proved that with able marketing authentic Cuban music, salsa, and Latin jazz can achieve a wide crossover appeal.

In the United States and in various Caribbean countries, the frequent cut-throat competition between salsa bands has often been detrimental to musicians, just as much as drug abuse. Latin musicians who, in the beginning, rarely belonged to unions, have also been greatly exploited by club owners and record companies. They have had to put up with the omission on records of their names as sidemen, arrangers, or composers – not to mention the countless bootleg records or hastily manufactured releases with terrible covers and sound. Furthermore in Europe, for example, with the new vogue for Latin music, the words "salsa" and "Latin jazz" have been used indiscriminately to designate just about any kind of Latin American genre, just as at another time the label "rhumba" was given in the United States to anything with Cuban rhythms, and the most absurd compilations were produced with everything thrown in the same bag.

If salsa and other Cuban-derived music based on the simple changes of the *son montuno* seem to be going through a period of relative stagnation on account of their harmonic limitations, Latin jazz on the other hand is constantly evolving: every day there appear new artists who now also reach audiences for mainstream or "straightahead" jazz. The recent Latin hip hop/techno mixes – controversial as they may seem to purists – are also pointing in new directions.

Cuba, Puerto Rico, all of Latin America and the Caribbean (including the diaspora living in the United States and other countries), with their flair for music and dance, and their amazing inventiveness, still hold many surprises in store.

San Juan, Puerto Rico, May 1995, at the Heineken Latin Jazz Festival: under starry skies, Danilo Pérez casts his spell on a sophisticated, mostly Puerto Rican audience, receptive to his complex rhythms. Seated anonymously amidst the crowd, Panama's President, Ernesto Pérez Balladares, who happened to be in town for a meeting with the island's governor, came unannounced to listen to his gifted countryman. Evoking in turn Debussy and Gershwin in a magnificent solo, Pérez – backed up by the Puerto Ricans John Benítez on bass, David Sánchez on saxophone, and Paolí Mejías on conga, the Cuban Ignacio Berroa on drums, and the Curaçao percussionist Pernell Saturnino – suddenly launched into some fiery *montunos* which brought roars of approval from the crowd. Backstage at this festival, other Latin luminaries including Mario Rivera, Gonzalo Rubalcaba, Tito Puente, Mongo Santamaría, and Eddie Gómez (also Bill Evans's former accomplice) shared the emotion and the camaraderie. All belonged to this huge and joyful Latin music family, whose ecumenism has continued to grow, and which transcends all national and racial boundaries. "This lively music is more likely than politics to bring about harmony between men!" exclaimed Pérez in an outburst of enthusiasm. Driven by the ever-present urge to create and rise to new challenges, Pérez, Mejías, Benítez, Sánchez, and Saturnino went jamming in a major hotel after the concert, joined by the Panama-based Cuban drummer Fidel Morales and other jazz and Latin music aficionados, improvising new wonders until the wee hours of the night.

Saint-Florent, Corsica, August 2000, at the salsa festival: in front of the ancient Genoese tower overlooking the breathtaking bay, Yuri Buenaventura is delivering his inspirational salsa message. Suddenly he invites Azuquita on stage. Azuquita doesn't know the song, a *son montuno* about cutting sugarcane, but grabbing the mike, he jumps – in the best salsa tradition – into an impromptu and soulful *soneo* with both laid-back and incisive phrasing, immediately falling into step with the agile footwork of Buenaventura and his two *coro* singers. Two nights later, backed this time by Alfredo de la Fé's band, Azuquita again sets the audience on fire. Buenaventura is Colombian, Azuquita Panamanian, de la Fé Cuban. They improvised in Corsica – a crossroad of many civilizations – and there again, the warmth and the vibrancy, transcending national or linguistic boundaries were for everyone to relish. Such is the power of Cuban music and its offshoots, now nourished by myriad other currents which have spread far and wide and will keep flourishing for many years to come.

glossary

A

¡A gozar! "let's enjoy ourselves!"– an interjection often used in salsa

abanico roll performed by the *timbales* and announcing changes of sections

academia de baile before the Cuban revolution, dancehall where men had to buy a ticket for each dance

afro Cuban rhythm popular in the 1930s and used in some lullabies, boleros and other songs

aguinaldo Christmas carol of Spanish origin, whose tradition persists in Puerto Rico

ahí na' ma' Puerto Rican expression of appreciation

akpwón lead singer in *santería*

añí sacred object placed inside consecrated *batá* drums

areíto name given to the ritual dances of the Taino Indians. Dance popular in Cuba in the early 1980s

B

babalao Yoruba word designating a *santería* priest

bachata Dominican or Cuban rural festivity; Dominican guitar and vocal genre born in the 1960s

balsié (or pri-prí) small Afro-Dominican drum

balsielito largo larger *balsié*

baqueteo *timbales* roll performed in the *danzón*

baquiné in Afro-Puerto Rican communities, funeral wake featuring singing and music

batá sacred drum of *santería*

batanga a rhythm played with *batá* drums and created in the 1950s by Cuban pianist Bebo Valdés

bembé semi-religious Yoruba ceremony; jam session with Afro-Cuban rhythms, usually in 6/8 or 12/8

bocú cylindrical drum of the Santiago carnival

bola new, highly effervescent Cuban dance

bolerista *bolero* singer

bolero Cuban genre of Spanish origin born in the province of Oriente in the late nineteenth century

bomba Afro-Puerto Rican dance and musical genre originating around the eighteenth century in coastal regions such as Loíza and Ponce

bombo bass drum of the Cuban carnival; strong accent of the *clave*

bongo small double drum originating in the province of Oriente and held on the musician's lap

bongó del monte bongo used as a signal drum in rural regions of Oriente

bongocero bongo player

bonkó enchemiyá ritual Abakwa drum played either vertically or horizontally, straddled by the drummer

boogaloo Latin rhythm of New York influenced by soul music, popular in the 1960s

botarse "to have a good time" (Cuban and Puerto Rican slang)

boteo musical genre and dance popular in Cuba in the 1960s

botija jug, used in the old *son* in lieu of the bass

burlador (or Macho) in the *bomba*, drum maintaining a steady beat

C

cabildo in Cuba, during the colonial era, black society generally including members of the same ethnic origin

caderona traditional dance from the Chocó region of Colombia

cajón wooden packing crate used for the *yambú* and other types of rumbas (also exists in Afro-Peruvian music)

candela (de) "wonderful," in slang. Also applied to percussionists who tuned their drums by heating the skins near a flame or a kerosene lamp

candombe former Bantu cult from the Rio de la Plata. Now black carnival music from Montevideo

canto de puya song containing *piques* (frequent in the Cuban Congo tradition)

cáscara steady rhythm played by the *timbales*

casino dance popularized in Cuba in the 1950s by Orquesta Casino de la Playa

catá steady rhythm played by a stick or two sticks in the *rumba brava*

censor in *coros de clave*, person verifying the appropriateness and poetical content of the lyrics

cha-cha-cha rhythm invented by Cuban violinist Enrique Jorrín in the early 1950s

chachá kind of metal shaker of Haitian origin used in the Cuban province of Oriente

changüí kind of rural *son* from the Guantánamo area, introduced into dance music by Elio Revé

charanga traditionally a *danzón* band. Now a band usually including flute, one or several violins, bass, piano, *timbales* and generally singers

chaworó belt with small bells affixed on the *iyá batá* drum

cheré metal shaker used in Lucumí (Yoruba) music

chévere "great" in Cuban and Puerto Rican slang. Musical style invented by Carlos Barbería in the mid-1970s

cierre break at the end of a section

cinquillo syncopated rhythm cell found in the *danzón* and other Afro-Latin genres and which later evolved into the *tumbao*

clarina female lead singer in old *son* groups and in *coros de clave*

clave basic rhythm of Cuban music, played over two bars; type of song in 6/8 popular in Cuba at the turn of the twentieth century

clave de guaguancó kind of vocal group popular in the black neighborhoods in Havana and other Cuban towns in the late nineteenth and early twentieth centuries and specializing in *rumbas*

claves pair of percussive sticks giving the *clave* rhythm. The "male" stick strikes the "female" one which is held in the cupped left hand

columbia kind of fast and acrobatic *rumba brava*, generally performed by men

comparsa carnival group of dancers, singers, and musicians

conga drum of Congo origin developed in Cuba; dance of the Cuban carnival, which became a popular ballroom dance in the 1930s

conguero conga player

conjunto type of *son* band created in the 1940s by Arsenio Rodríguez and including, among other instruments, a piano, a conga, and several trumpets

contradanza Cuban dance popular in the eighteenth century and derived from the French contredanse

controversia in Puerto Rico and Cuba, rhyming contest between two singers

copla four-line stanza

cornetín chino (or **corneta china)** kind of oboe brought to Cuba by Cantonese immigrants in the late nineteenth century and used for the Santiago carnival

coro backup singers

coro de clave kind of vocal group popular in the black neighborhoods in Havana and other Cuban towns in the late nineteenth and early twentieth centuries

cruzao "crossed" (is used for a rhythm that goes against the *clave*)

cuá (or **fuá)** in the *bomba*, stick beating a steady rhythm on the side of the *burlador*

cuarteto type of band especially popular in Cuba and Puerto Rico in the 1930s and 1940s and generally consisting of singers, guitars, *tres* or *cuatro*, small percussion instruments and ocasionally a trumpet

cuatrista *cuatro* player

cuatro Puerto Rican instrument with five double strings, used in traditional Puerto Rican music and introduced into salsa by Yomo Toro

cubop mixture of Cuban music and bebop (name given to Latin jazz in the late 1940s)

cucharas spoons, used as percussion instruments in the *rumba brava*

cuchifrito circuit small Latin clubs of the New York *barrios*

cuerpo central section of the *merengue*, in which the melody is stated

cumbia traditional Colombian genre of the Atlantic coast

curarse see **botarse**

currulas traditional black genre from the Buenaventura area, in Colombia

D

danza musical genre derived from the *contradanza*, popular in Cuba in the eighteenth and nineteenth centuries, and in Puerto Rico, where the national anthem is a *danza*

danzón musical genre and dance derived from the *danza* and originating in Matanzas in the late nineteenth century

danzonete fusion of *danzón* and *son* created in Matanzas in 1929 by Aniceto Díaz

décima ten-line stanza with eight-syllable lines, found in Cuban and Puerto Rican musical genres of Spanish origin

decimista improviser of *décimas*

desafío challenge, a characteristic element of the *rumba brava* and other Afro-Caribbean genres

descarga in Cuban music, jam session, usually on simple chord changes

despelote torrid dance popular in Havana in the late 1990s

diablo rhythm invented in the 1940s by Arsenio Rodríguez and anticipating the mambo

diana sung introduction of a *rumba brava*

disparate literally, "nonsense." Nonsensical lyrics crop up in some songs

E

efí Abakwa rhythm

efó Abakwa rhythm

ekwé sacred Abakwa friction drum

estribillo refrain, in the *son*, especially

estudiantina kind of band inspired by the *tunas* of Spanish students, popular in Oriente and Havana at the beginning of the twentieth century

F

filin (from the English "feeling"), romantic, mainly vocal style, born in Havana in the 1950s

florear to improvise

fragaya *glissé* done by sliding the finger on the skin of a drum

fuera de clave against the *clave*

fundamento name given in Cuba to the African tradition

G

gallo lead singer, in Congo music

glissé see *fragaya*

guagua see *catá*

guaguancó kind of *rumba brava* involving a pelvic thrust, the *vacunao*

guajeo pattern played by *tres*, piano, guitar, vibes, saxophones or other instruments in the *merengue* and in Cuban music

guajira musical genre of Spanish origin close to the *son montuno*, usually played with a guitar and small percussion instruments and based on simple chord changes, and having lyrics that generally deal with rural or patriotic topics

guajiro peasant, in Cuba

guaracha lively musical genre and dance developed in the eighteenth century in Havana; in *salsa*, kind of medium-tempo genre with often humorous lyrics

guarapachanga genre created in the 1950s by Félix Chappotín; name given in Havana to a conga *tumbao*

guataca small hoe, used as a percussion instrument in rural *rumbas bravas*

guateque in Cuba: rural festivity

guayo (or **guícharo**) name given to the *güiro* in the *changüí* and sometimes other Cuban and Puerto Rican genres

güira metal scraper used in the *merengue*

güiro scraper made from a serrated gourd; also, in Cuba, musical celebration

guisar "to cook," in musical slang (= to swing, to play with feeling)

guiso "gig"

H

habanera 2/4 genre akin to the *danza*, popular in Cuba in the late nineteenth century, which inspired several foreign composers

I

itótele medium-sized *batá* drum

iyá the largest of the three *batá* drums; sets the rhythm

J

jala jala rhythm derived from the carnival *conga*, popular in the United States in the 1960s

jaleo fast refrain section of the *merengue*

jíbaro peasant, in Puerto Rico

joropo national dance from Venezuela, combining duple- and triple-time meters

juego in Cuba, name given to a ritual play enacted at Abakwa ceremonies

K

kinfuiti sacred Congo friction drum

kiribá kind of rural *son* from the region of Baracoa, in Oriente

L

lalaleo syllables sung at the beginning of a *rumba brava*, probably inspired by the *cante jondo*

Latin jazz jazz played with Afro-Latin rhythms and percussion

le lo lai meaningless syllables, often cropping up in traditional Puerto Rican music of Spanish origin

llorao (literally: "lamentation") sung introduction of the *rumba brava*

M

macho see *burlador*

makúa in Cuba, bellicose Congo dance

mambo Congo word designating a sacred song, a prayer or a Congo priest; section played in unison after the solos in Cuban music and in salsa; musical genre created by Damaso Pérez Prado in the early 1950s

mano a mano more or less "arm-wrestling," expression used by record producers in the mid-1940s to pitch Antonio Arcaño against Arsenio Rodríguez

maraquero *maraca*-player

marímbula wooden box with plucked metal tongues, replacing the bass, used by *son* groups at the beginning of the twentieth century and still used in the *changüí*

martillo rhythm pattern played by the *bongo*

masacote *conga* technique; drum polyrhythms; by extension, improvisation by percussion instruments

merengue musical genre in 2/4 and national dance of the Dominican Republic

merengue apambichao medium-tempo *merengue* influenced by the *pambiche*

merengue de campo adentro kind of rural *merengue*

merengue perico ripiao traditional rural *merengue* of the Cibao region

moña horn riff

monte mountainous region, with mystic connotations, of Cuba and Puerto Rico

montuno improvised section, in Cuban popular music and salsa; kind of contrapuntal accompaniment used in salsa and in Cuban music in general

mozambique Cuban genre of the 1960s invented by Pello El Afrokán by fusing Yoruba, Congo and other elements

N

nengón kind of rural *son* from Baracoa, Oriente

nkembi small bells worn by drummers in Congo music or some *rumbas bravas*

nueva timba in Cuba, name given to the new dance music derived from the *songo*

nueva trova in Cuba, kind of folk or protest songs often accompanied by guitar and popular in the 1960s. (In Puerto Rico, the terms *canción protesta* or *nueva canción* are used instead.)

nuevo ritmo rhythm created by "Cachao" (Israel López) and his brother Orestes in the late 1940s and heralding the mambo

O

okónkolo (or **omelé**) smallest of the *batá* drums

open shine free-style improvisation in salsa dancing

Orisha Yoruba deity

P

pachanga in Cuba, originally, rural festivity; dance and musical genre which originated with the song *La pachanga*, written by Cuban composer Eduardo Davidson in 1959

paila name given in Cuba to the *timbales*

palo literally "stick," name given in Cuba to Congo cults; in the Dominican Republic to Congo religion and Congo drum

pambiche syncopated dance done in Santo Domingo during the U.S. occupation

pandero (or **pandereta**) in Puerto Rico, tambourine used in the *plena*

parranda (or **trulla**) in Puerto Rico, group of carollers singing at Christmas time

paseo slow introduction to the *danzón* and the *merengue*, originally allowing dancers to walk around the dance floor

piquete spontaneous *rumba* or informal music group; improvisation of the tambourine in the *plena* (see also *repique*); in Cuba, name given at the beginning of the twentieth century to small bands playing in circuses

plante Abakwa ceremony

plena kind of topical song first heard in Ponce around the time of the First World War

porro musical genre of the Atlantic coast of Colombia

potencia Abakwa lodge

pregón street-vendor song

pregonar to sing

punteador medium-sized *pandero* in the *plena*

Q

quijada donkey or ox jawbone scraped with a stick or struck with the fist and used in the rural *son* from Oriente

quintear to improvise on the *quinto*

quinto small-sized and high-pitched *conga*, which generally improvises

R

regla in Cuba, name given to sects of African origin

regla de ocha see *santería*

repique (or **repiqueteo**) improvisation on a percussion instrument

requinto (**primo** or **subidor**) highest drum in the *bomba*; highest tambourine in the *plena*

rueda de casino collective dance with changes of partners derived from the *casino* and currently popular in Cuba

rumba ballroom dance of Cuban origin popular in the 1930s

rumba brava name given to various Afro-Cuban drum dances, among them the *guaguancó*, the *yambú*, and the *columbia*

rumba de chancletas type of *rumba* done in and around Santiago de Cuba during carnivals, in which dancers create rhythms by clacking their sandals on the ground

S

salidor name given to a *conga* part played in the carnival *conga*

salsa literally "sauce." An expression called out to encourage an orchestra; name of the popular music of Cuban origin first appearing in New York in the late 1960s

salsa cama literally "bed salsa": kind of salsa with sexually explicit lyrics especially popular in Puerto Rico in the early 1990s

salsa romántica kind of *salsa* with romantic lyrics popular in Puerto Rico and New York in the late 1980s

sandunga "grace," "witty"; can be applied to spirited music or to a spirited woman

santería (or **regla de ocha**) synchretic Afro-Cuban cult derived from a fusion of Catholicism and the Yoruba religion

Santo see *Orisha*

saoco feeling

sartén frying pan, beaten with sticks and used as a percussion instrument in the Cuban carnivals

segón drum used in Cuba by the *tumbas francesas*

segundo largest tambourine in the *plena*

seis Puerto Rican genre of Spanish origin using assonant ten-line stanzas

septeto *son* group of the 1920s and 1930s using, among other instruments, a trumpet

sexteto *son* group of the 1920s

shekere big gourd of Fon or Yoruba origin covered with a bead-strewn mesh, shaken in rhythm and struck with the palm of the hand

shing-a-ling Latin genre similar to the boogaloo, popular in New York in the 1960s

solar tenement, in impoverished neighborhoods of Havana, and sharing common kitchens and bathrooms

son musical genre first heard in the late nineteenth century in the province of Oriente

son montuno slow variation of the *son*, derived from the peasant music of the interior of Cuba

soneo improvisation by the singer

sonero *son* and by extension *salsa* singer

songo rhythm created in the late 1970s in Havana by percussionist "Changuito" and other members of Los Van Van

sonora *son* band including a three-trumpet line-up

subidor high-pitched *bomba* drum

sucu-sucu variation of the *son* influenced by the round dance from the Cayman Islands and first appearing around the start of the twentieth century in the isle of Pines, in Cuba

T

tahona small drum from Oriente

tambora double-headed *merengue* drum, with one skin played with the bare hand and the other with a stick

tamborito national dance and musical genre of Panama

tango bass (or **Spanish bass**) in early New Orleans jazz, bass line containing *cinquillos*

tembleque figure often used in the *rumba brava* in which dancers tremble

timba (or **tumbadora**) in Cuba, name of the *conga*

timbalero *timbales*-player

timbales (or **paila**) instrument consisting of two snare drums mounted on a stand and used in Cuban music and in *salsa*

típica *danzón* band of the late nineteenth and early twentieth centuries comprising brass instruments

típico traditional style of playing Cuban music

tonista in *coros de clave* and *coros de guaguancó*, person ensuring that the singers were in tune

toques name given to drum rhythms in ritual Afro-Cuban music

tres kind of guitar from Oriente with three double strings, used in the *son* and other genres

tres golpes (or **tres dos**) name of a medium-sized *conga* drum, which maintains a steady beat

tresista *tres*-player

trío name given to some sections of the *danzón*; kind of band consisting of three singers accompanying themselves with guitar, *tres*, claves, and/or maracas

trova kind of traditional song especially popular in Oriente

trovador in Cuba, singer with a traditional repertoire accompanying himself on the guitar

tumba national dance of Santo Domingo in the nineteenth century; also see *timba*

tumba francesa in Oriente, name given to a type of recreational society comprising members of Haitian origin

tumbadora see *timba*

tumbao steady rhythm played by the bass or the *conga*

U

upa habanera Cuban dance brought to Santo Domingo and Puerto Rico by the Cuban Army in the nineteenth century

V

vallenato Colombian folk genre sprung from the cattle herders of the Valle de Upar

vacunao in Cuba, pelvic thrust characteristic of the *guaguancó*

vasallos chorus, in the Congo tradition

viola stringless *vihuela* used as a percussion instrument by the *coros de clave*

viro abrupt change of rhythm in *santería batá toques*

W

watusi musical genre influenced by soul music and popularized by Ray Barretto in the late 1960s

wemba clave in Cuba, rhythm played at Abakwa ceremonies

Y

yambú slow kind of *rumba brava* played with *cajones* and without the *vacunao*

interviews

The conversations with the musicians took place in 1996: in New York for Chico O'Farrill, Joe Cuba and Chocolate Armenteros; in Paris for Oscar López, Rembert Egües and Don Barreto.

CHICO O'FARRILL

What is Latin jazz?

A mixture of stylistic elements coming from jazz and Latin music. Latin jazz originally derives from Afro-Cuban music. One should, in fact, speak about Afro-Cuban jazz, but, however, the term "Latin jazz" accounts for the subsequent contribution of other Latin American music. One of the first jazz musicians who became interested in it was Dizzy Gillespie. He played a fundamental role.

Before the advent of bebop, how was the jazz situation in Cuba?

Jazz was played badly. What were then called "jazz bands" (the Hermanos Palau, the Hermanos Castro, the Hermanos Lebatard or Casino de la Playa, for example) were smaller than American big bands. Their brass section usually included only one trumpet, and they used stock arrangements. There weren't any real jazz arrangers.

Why was jazz badly played?
Because people didn't phrase correctly. There weren't many exchanges with
American musicians. There were hardly any jazz records and you rarely heard it
on the radio.

How, then, did you come to write for jazz?
I knew very little about big band jazz. I had only had a vague idea of it in high
school, in Florida and Georgia. When I returned to Havana, I found the musical
ambience very poor, but I looked for records and I started to study, to listen to
Glenn Miller, Tommy Dorsey, Benny Goodman.

Only white bands?
In those days, the records of black bands were not as well distributed in Cuba.

What was your first experience with a jazz orchestra?
The Orquesta Bellamar. I had studied harmony with Félix Guerrero, who is still
alive – an excellent teacher who gave me a good grounding in classical structure
and orchestration. I think that even for a jazz musician, it is absolutely necessary
to have a thorough training, to know exactly what one does. With friends who
also loved jazz, we formed a little group for our own amusement, in which we
improvised and experimented freely. It included among others guitarist Manolo
Saavedra, who later recorded with Thelonious Monk and Dizzy Gillespie, Isidro
Pérez, Gustavo Mas, and a drummer by the name of "Machao." We used to play
American jazz.

No Cuban music?
We found it too simplistic. It was, in fact, stupidity, due to our lack of maturity.
At that time, bebop started. You sometimes heard it on the radio and we used to
listen to Dizzy Gillespie and Charlie Parker. I didn't understand it right away, but
it was a shock. It interested me immediately and I absorbed it very fast. I was
constantly searching for complex harmonies on the piano and I was studying
the phrasing. Later, I became friends with Fats Navarro, who was of Cuban
origin. In bebop, the accents and the phrasing are different from the ones in
swing. In swing one says:

and in bebop:

I once wrote arrangements for Rita Montaner and the orchestra was phrasing
the wrong way. I used to sing them the accents and Rita would laugh and call
me: "Ta **taa** ta ta, ta **taa** ta ta!" The musicians weren't quite ready!

With which group did you start to arrange professionally?

With Isidro Pérez's orchestra, which used to perform at the Montmartre, around 1946 or 1947. There were fantastic musicians, among them pianist Mario Romeu, who later played in the United States. In Cuban clubs, two bands always alternated, and we were the main attraction. I used to write jazz and we would compose scores for our own pleasure, not for the listeners. For example, I did an arrangement of *Deep Purple* with a 5/4 time signature. Audiences didn't like it at all because they didn't understand what was happening and couldn't dance. I then went to the United States, and later RCA's Mexican division offered me a contract. From 1955 to 1957 I stayed in Havana and I wrote arrangements for the Cuarteto d'Aida. The Panart label also asked me to do an album of cha-cha-chas. I told them, "Yes, if I do it the way I want." For this project, I was influenced by Billy May.

Was the transition from jazz to Latin music easy?

Yes, because I already had Cuban rhythms in my head.

Does Latin jazz require particular skills?

It is essential to know what are the elements common to jazz and Cuban music so as to avoid those which might clash. Phrasing is important. One must understand the *clave*, which is the basic rhythm of Cuban music, and also the way the rhythm section works. A *guaguancó* is different from a *guajira* or a *bolero*. One must grasp each rhythm and write by taking its specificity into account. It's a question of having a good ear and experience. In Cuban music, one phrases behind the beat while in American music, one phrases on the beat. It's also a question of instinct.

What do you think of the current revival of Latin jazz?

It's wonderful, there's a lot of new talent. I don't follow very much what is currently happening in jazz but it seems to me that there are no really striking personalities. The media further the diffusion of the various Latin American rhythms and foster exchanges between different cultures. But my roots are in Cuban music. In this area and in jazz, I know what sounds good.

OSCAR LÓPEZ

As a child, I was first influenced by the Sexteto Occidente. The group used to rehearse at Ignacio Piñeiro's home. His wife, Inés, made me sit in a corner, and I was all ears. I also sang in the streets with some of my buddies. One day, a friend took me to the CMW radio station, and I won first prize by singing an Argentinian song while accompanying myself with claves, as was then the custom.

The first time I performed professionally, it was in a black *sociedad* (social club). In those days, blacks didn't try to antagonize whites and vice versa: they each had their own clubs. There was an upright piano but no microphone and I had to climb on a chair so that my voice would carry better. It was the era of the *danzonete*. One night I sang on the same bill as Esther Borja, in the black club Jóvenes del Vals.

In 1935 I worked with Obdulio Morales, who had organized for a radio station a band with violins, cello, double bass, piano, timbales and güiro. Despite this type of instrumentation, the repertoire was Afro-Cuban. Later, I sang many other songs with "black" themes: *Negro sociedad*, *El brujo de Guanabacoa*. I also performed with the Casino Nacional orchestra, with the Hermanos Martínez – then the only black jazz band – and, in 1936, with the Orquesta Cosmopolita. Big bands usually hired two vocalists: one for the English numbers, the other for the Spanish ones. As there were no microphones, they sometimes used megaphones. The swank clubs only hired white ensembles such as Casino de la Playa. The *son* remained a music for blacks.

Could you support yourself just with music?

No, a radio engagement only paid ten cents – ask Cachao! I was a *tabaquero* (cigar maker) by trade. I then sang with the Orquesta La Madrid and, for six months, with Arcaño's Maravillas. In the union, musicians constantly complained that Arcaño and Arsenio Rodríguez monopolized all the work. Blacks from humble backgrounds favored the *son* while upper-class blacks preferred the *danzón*. At that time, people used to dress up to go out and they danced in a refined manner. Even if it was terribly hot, the men wore a suit and tie. Only in the beer halls La Tropical and La Polar, which were outdoors, did people dress more casually.

I later went to Mexico with the show "Batamú," with which Candita Batista and Celina Reinoso were then singing. Obdulio Morales was its musical director and the band used congas, bongos and *batá* drums. Later I also collaborated with "Las Mulatas de Fuego" (with dancer Canelina). After some time in Mexico, I travelled to Argentina with Lecuona's revue. We used to do *María la O*, *Rosa la China*, *El cafetal*. Argentinian audiences were thrilled. The company then played in Chile and Peru.

In 1942 I stayed in the United States and then went to Mexico again, and in 1944, back in Havana, I sang on the radio. Those were happy times despite the racial discrimination which still existed, and dance halls were always full. The relief bands – *septetos*, generally – were almost all black. It was also the time of the *batanga*, which Bebo Valdés had played for me in Mexico before Benny Moré popularized it. Bebo was the first, on the radio, to use *batá* drums with this rhythm.

In the early 1950s I got a contract to sing in a theatre in Barcelona, and I later moved to Paris, where I worked in various Pigalle cabarets, and where I still live.

JOE CUBA

It was Victor Pantoja who taught me how to play the conga, when he was thirteen or fourteen. We were friends in the *barrio* and we belonged to a stickball team called The Devils. I had studied law but when I heard Tito Puente's *Ran kan kan* and *Abaniquito* on the radio, I decided to devote myself to music. I used to go to the Park Plaza to listen to the orchestras of Machito – who was one of the major attractions there – and of José Budet, Esy, Noro and Humberto Morales. There was a happy atmosphere and people from the neighborhood came with their families. I first played with Alfarona X, the first group from Puerto Rico to settle in New York, and among other places we, too, performed at the Park Plaza.

How did you get to use vibes?

Under George Shearing's influence. I was also impressed by Xavier Cugat, who used a marimba and a xylophone. All the musicians who were front stage danced as they played. And I loved the jazz big bands: Harry James, Glenn Miller, Jimmy and Tommy Dorsey. At that time, there were cinemas downtown that showed a movie, and then a jazz band gave a concert. We used to work in small after-hours clubs and one day the owner of one of them told me: "Bring me your group, but I don't want noisy horns." "Don't worry," I told him, "I'm gonna use vibes." In addition, I was fascinated by the Orquesta Aragón. In fact, I wanted to form a *charanga*, but in the *barrio*, nobody played violin, so I chose the vibes and I used English lyrics. Also, Tommy Berrios, who had a classical background, used to love jazz.

Why English lyrics?

So that the Americans could understand them. We started to perform in the *barrio*, in a club located on the corner of 104th Street and Madison Avenue. The best way to build up a group is to play in the neighborhood. The members of my first band all came from Spanish Harlem and we already had a local audience who knew us. On Sundays, we alternated with Machito's orchestra at the Park Plaza, and everywhere I performed, the people from the neighborhood used to follow me. We also did Sunday matinees at the Palladium and the audience would greet us enthusiastically. They were mostly black Americans. It's funny: there was one evening of the week that attracted Jews, and another one blacks. Only later did people mix. And we had bookings at the Stardust Ballroom on Boston Road, in the Bronx. Harry James also used to play there.

Who wrote the arrangements?

Chiefly my pianist, Nick Jiménez. Around 1956 or 1957 we appeared on television, on the "Don Pesante Show," which was the first Latin variety TV show. Then came the boogaloo era. I was crazy about R & B and I often went to the Apollo theatre. I also studied in a black high school, and I used to love doo-wop and the Nashville sound. One day, we were at the Palm Gardens, on 52nd Street, on the corner of Broadway, and Nick started to play a vamp. The audience, which was predominantly black, suddenly started to move spontaneously from right to left like a gigantic wave, singing: "be bee, ahh." My mouth fell open. We kept the "be bee, ahh," but with a different rhythm, and the Jewish and Italian dancers from the club started to jig and to jump up and down like crazy. We went back to the Palm Gardens with our number arranged, and it became *Bang! Bang!*

How was *El pito* born?
That's another story. I borrowed the leitmotiv "I'll never go back to Georgia" from Dizzy Gillespie. I have to say that we were just back from a tour in the South, where we had seen a lot of racism. Also, to end his concerts, Charlie Palmieri's band used to sing: *"así se goza"* ("this is how one enjoys oneself") while I used a jingle for cornflakes: "New Country cornflakes. We get our cornflakes, they're made of corn." Charlie liked this idea of cornflakes and we swapped our little songs. Then we had to make an album and the producer wanted twelve numbers. I was one short, the producer was getting impatient and I was in a hurry to get the whole session over with. I didn't want to go back to the studio, as I'd much rather have fun. Suddenly I told the guys: "Improvise, do what you want." And they started to sing: "I'll never go back to Georgia," superimposing *"así se goza"* on it. Heny Alvárez, who sang *coro* in my band and who used to write for me, suddenly started to whistle. We had recorded another song, which became the A side of a single, and then one day, a DJ from radio WBLS played *El pito* on his show. The radio switchboard was swamped with calls and we quickly pressed the record again so as to make it the A side. By the same token, this opened the door to *Bang! Bang!* In Puerto Rico also, the audience, which is bilingual, loved the boogaloo. There, anyway, I feel at home: I often go there, I've played at the Flamboyán hotel, in San Juan, and at home, I eat Puerto Rican food. But to return to *Bang! Bang!* I frequently used a phrase which said: *"Be be, bang! bang! ungwa, that's power."* *"Ungwa"* comes from a joke which I used to hear in the Catskills hotels, where I also used to perform. In Africa, a political candidate was doing an electoral campaign. One day, he announced in a village: "If you vote for me, you'll get this and that." Each time, the villagers answered: *"Ungwa!"* At the end of his speech, the candidate congratulated himself on this enthusiastic reception and told a notable: "Great! It really worked well with these villagers." And the notable replied: "Do you know what *ungwa* means? – Bullshit!" Somebody told me later that black Americans used to march in the streets of New York or Washington chanting: "Be be, bang bang, ungwa, black power."

In 1968, I played on the album "Spanish Songs Mama Never Taught Me," with Ismael Quintana on vocals. The cover was supposed to show a superb paella, but as the photographer was taking his time, we started to nibble at the paella. Finally, there was nothing left and they had to cook another one.

In 1972 I recorded "Hecho y derecho," which I consider one of my best albums. *La calle está durísima* comes from an expression which I borrowed from Fajardo, who was a friend of mine. I used to ask him, "How is it going, Fajardo?" And he would reply, *"Bien, pero la calle está durísima"* ("Fine, but the street is real tough"). I told him: "You gonna see, I'm gonna use that for my *coro*," and that's exactly what I did. We, musicians, were real tight with one another. It was a fantastic time for salsa. I was always hangin' out with Eddie Palmieri. They used to call us, Tito Puente, Eddie and me, "The Big Three." "Hecho y derecho" also includes *Cuenta bien cuenta bien*, which I like a lot, and a rather anti-American song, *Give Us A Chance*:

> When my father crossed the ocean
> He left a paradise.
> What he found was
> A railroad flat with flying roaches
> And full-grown mice.
> So he turned to his *mamacita* and he said:
> "Listen to me
> We're gonna climb this mountain
> And we're gonna swim this polluted sea.
> Give us a chance
> Give us a chance now
> And you shall see what we can be
> 'Cause we don't need your subsidy!"

Was the transition from the boogaloo to salsa easy?
Yes, because deep in my soul, I'm a *salsero*.

REMBERT EGÜES

In the 1960s, when I was eleven, I played in a little group in Havana called Los Chicos del Jazz (with Paquito D'Rivera, drummer Amadito Valdés, and Enrique Jorrín's bassist, Fabián García). The ambience, then, was wonderful. Those were marvelous years. There were many nightclubs and cabaret bands, as well as the radio and the television orchestra. On Sunday afternoon, *descargas* were held in such hotels as the Riviera, the Tropicana and the Nacional. Leonardo Timor, Chucho Valdés, pianist "Cancañón" (Luis Mariano, who hailed from Oriente) – everybody came to jam. They were an extension of Cachao's *descargas*, but in a jazzier style, influenced by Peruchín or Frank Emilio.

Later I succeeded Armandito Romeu in the group led by Felipe Dulzaides – a pianist with a very international culture – at the same time as Changuito, Carlos del Puerto and guitarist Ahmed Barroso (who took over from Sergio Vitier). I also played with Sonorama Seis (with saxophonist Carlos Averhoff, drummer Enrique Plá, guitarist Martín Rojas and a bassist named Eduardo). We often accompanied singers.

At that time, what was the impact of Enrique Bonne and of Pello el Afrokán?

Bonne was above all influenced by the music from Oriente. Of the new rhythms of the 1960s, it was the *mozambique* which was the most successful, because it received official support. The Beatles and the twist were considered counter-revolutionary, and anyone who walked with records of this kind under his arm was bound to have problems. The *mozambique*, which was more "African," constituted a strong contrast to that Anglo-Saxon music. Fidel Castro even posed on the cover of a magazine with Pello el Afrokán. In my opinion, Juanito Marquez's *pa' ca'* was more interesting, but it was overshadowed by the *mozambique*. In fact, Pello's musicians used to play out of tune, but as they jokingly say in Cuba: "The symphony orchestra plays in tune, but nobody listens to them!" Pello's group, however, was the first large popular music ensemble in which the percussion predominated.

How was jazz perceived?

It was only appreciated by a small segment of the population. And then in the 1970s there was a sharp break. *Descargas* stopped, jazz began to become subversive, and even in the orchestra of the Cuban Radio and Television Institute, using the cymbals of the drum set was forbidden! Cabarets closed down and many musicians and dancers had to do other things for a living, working, for example, in pizzerias. The government then supported the *nueva trova*, which had grown out of the *filin*. In those days I used to compose and arrange for many groups and for ballet companies. I took part, as a composer, arranger and musical director, in many festivals of popular song, and travelled as musical director with Alicio Alonso. With the singers Silvio Rodríguez and Pablo Milanés, we used to get together on a street corner, on the Malecón, for instance, and spend the whole night making music. There was a bohemian atmosphere. I also directed a television program and created an uproar by including Jimi Hendrix and rock in it for the first time. One could catch radio stations from Miami, and as my mother lived in New York, I knew what was happening in the United States musicwise.

With the creation of the Orquesta Cubana de Música Moderna, however, things opened up and young musicians with an excellent technical training appeared. In the late 1970s, there started to be a real craving for foreign sounds and a contempt for Cuban music. To write a bolero was considered passé and everything that was old was rejected. Tito Puente, Oscar D'León and salsa musicians in general can thank Fidel Castro, because it was with the breaking-off of diplomatic relations between Cuba and the United States that the Puerto Ricans, Venezuelans and others took Cuban music and made salsa with it! But, curiously, it is thanks to the success of the salsa that came from other countries that Cubans from the island rediscovered their own music. Cuban musicians realized that abroad, what audiences wanted to listen to was Cuban music! A Brazilian doesn't want someone to come and play him the bossa-nova! *No se puede bailar el trompo en la casa del trompo* (Literally, "One cannot spin like a top in the top's house").

DON EMILIO BARRETO

Are you related to Julián Barreto, to whom the famous *danzón El bombín de Barreto* was dedicated?
Yes, he was my uncle. I come from a family of musicians, and we are also related to the Urfés. My father played violin, and among other countries, he travelled to Mexico with Enrique Peña's *típica*. I started out on violin, at the age of fourteen, and I played with the Havana Philharmonic Orchestra, first led by the Spanish conductor Pedro Sanjuán and then by Amadeo Roldán. Around 1924 I also worked with the *charanga* of flautist Tata Pereira and with many other bands, as well as in the Wilson and Campoamor cinemas, accompanying silent films. It was a wonderful era. The television did not yet exist and there were dances every day. One could hear music in the cafes, in the *academias de baile* – everywhere.

How did you get to move to Europe?
My father used to write political chronicles, and then he got tired of it and decided to dedicate himself fully to his job as a dentist. In June of 1925, when I was seventeen, during Machado's era, we moved to Spain. There, I took up the banjo – it was the instrument with which one could make money – and I played jazz in the Madrid cabarets. I stayed for a year in Spain and gave up the violin. Then with my older brother Marino, who was a pianist, I moved to Paris – then an extraordinary musical city – and we started playing jazz in clubs. We worked with black American artists, notably Sidney Bechet and Bricktop. Gradually, I gave up the banjo, which I didn't like very much, and took up the guitar.

How did you start to play Cuban music?
In 1931, we used to perform jazz and beguine at the Melodies Bar, frequented by millionaires who drank champagne. My brother Sergio had joined us from Spain and the band consisted of guitar, piano, flute and saxophone, bass, drums, bongo and timbales. After the Colonial Exhibition, Cuban music started to

become big and we began to perform rumbas, *sones* and boleros. For the public it was something astonishing, a new color. They weren't used to seeing a double bass, because in jazz, at that time, one used a tuba. The double bass was reserved for the tango. We were the ones who launched *El manisero*. Then Moisés Simons came to Paris and I played with him. Don Azpiazu then arrived and he performed at La Plantation, on the Champs-Elysées. We also worked with the French singer Mimi Pinson. A lot of gigolos used to come to the Melodies Bar, and they asked women wearing expensive jewelry to dance. There was a Cuban singer and bassist by the name of Riestra who had written a rumba entitled *Buscando millonaria* ("Looking for a millionairess"). The words said more or less:

> *Hay unos tipos aquí*
> *Que andan buscando millonaria.*
> *Y cuando ven una con brillantes en el dedo*
> *El uno le dice al otro:*
> *"Pica tú, que es millonaria."*

> There are certain guys here
> That go around looking for a millionairess,
> And when they spot one with diamonds on her fingers
> One says to the other
> "Pick her up, she is a millionairess!"

Marino then went to London, where he formed a famous rumba band (Edmundo Ros started out with him), and the queen of England used to come and listen to him. He also had a part in the movie "The Black and the White" (starring Sacha Guitry and Fernandel). I made several albums in London and worked just about everywhere in Europe: in Paris, at the Chantilly, on the rue Fontaine, at the Boeuf sur le Toit, at the Villa d'Este, at the Club des Champs-Elysées, with Josephine Baker. In 1932 I recorded *Marta*, as well as some beguines, and backed the French singer Jean Sablon. In Spain, under Franco's dictatorship, we had to censor our songs. There were priests who used to come to the clubs, and, for instance, we couldn't mention the Virgin of Regla without seeing them frown!

Over the years, did you easily adapt to the new rhythms?
Yes, because when one is a musician, there are no problems. And then I constantly listened to jazz and Cuban records. Today, however, the melodies are gone: it's all "boom-boom-boom" everywhere. Before, even the silliest songs had a melody. This is perhaps the reason why salsa and Cuban music in general have become so popular again: young people are fed up and they want something other than that boring pop music.

CHOCOLATE ARMENTEROS

The fewer notes there are, the better. *Un caballo a la carrera, nadie se entera de las mentiras que dice. Un caballo de paso fino, tú sientes los cascos lo mismo en tierra que en agua* (Literally: "When a horse gallops, nobody is aware of the lies he tells. With a horse that walks with finesse, one can feel the hooves on earth just as much as in the water"). With music, before anything else, you have to tell a story. I always learned to listen to the singer and to phrase like him. What's difficult is not playing but interpretation. If one is on a boat and if the current goes one way, one cannot fight it. Musically speaking, this means that if the rhythm section speeds up, you have to follow it. For me, a solo is like a letter: in a letter there is the date, the name of the person it's being sent to, the usual greetings, the content, and the ending. There has to be a complete structure. In Cuban music, one generally plays slightly behind the beat. One must understand the foundation of this music, which is rhythm.

How would you define the *septeto* trumpet style?

As I just said, one should play as if one were singing. The *septeto* style, you have to have grown up with it, to have been fed on it since childhood. I have been influenced by Florecita, El Pecoso and Chappotín. It's a question of instinct and expressiveness. When I arrived in Havana, I also played with carnival *comparsas*. It was wonderful. The choreographer would work out something with the musical director and we first rehearsed the dance steps. We used to learn the arrangements by heart. In fact, almost everything was improvised from a basic idea. We didn't have scores, only cornets and percussion instruments. I then played with the Septeto Habanero and at the Marte y Belona *academia de baile*. The men had to pay in order to invite a woman to dance and the *cobrador* – the one who sold the tickets – used to signal to us so that we stopped the piece. Towards the late 1940s, there were three bands in the *academias*: a *conjunto*, a *charanga* and a paso doble band (Cuba was then teeming with Spaniards).

How was your collaboration with Arsenio Rodríguez?

With him, you could not mess around with the *son*! He showed me how to perform it by singing. He also insisted on the *quadratura*, the structure. If there are eight bars, there aren't nine or ten. Improvisation always works by groups of two, four, eight bars, etc. You must also understand that the *clave* consists of five pulses contained within two 2/4 or 4/4 bars.

Was your arrival in New York easy?

Yes, I went there in order to work with the Afro-Cubans. I replaced Mario Bauzá, who then only played saxophone, and one couldn't have been more Cuban than this band! I played the same way with blacks or with whites. There was an unbelievable atmosphere in this town, and a real communication among the musicians, and between them and the public. There were jam sessions everywhere, every single day of the week. The Palladium Ballroom, in particular, was a sensational place. I also listened to a lot of jazz, but jazz didn't influence me directly. I have always remained faithful to my Cuban music.

discography

PART I: THE ROOTS

Traditional Cuban Music
Antología de la música cubana, Egrem
(several volumes)
La música del pueblo de Cuba, Egrem
3441
Conjunto Folklórico Nacional, Areíto
Folk Music of Cuba, Auvidis/Unesco
D 8064
Merceditas Valdés, *Merceditas Valdés y
los tambores batá de Jesús Pérez*, Aspic
X55512
Trinidad de Cuba, Azul AZL 101

Classical Cuban Music
Classics of the Americas, Vol. 1,
Gottschalk – Cervantes – Saumell,
George Rabol, piano, Opus 30-9001
Lecuona Interpreta a Lecuona, Arcaño
Records DKL1-3296

Traditional Puerto Rican Music
Rafael Cepeda – *El Roble Mayor*: con
el Grupo Folk Experimental
Bombatele de los Hermanos Cepeda,
Balele 010
Los Pleneros de la 21/*El Quinteto
Criollo*, Puerto Rico Tropical,
Latitudes 50608
La plena y la bomba de Puerto Rico,
Cariño
Ramito – *El cantor de la montaña*,
HGCD 1237

**The Clave and the Instruments of
the Rhythm Section**
Understanding Latin Rhythms, Latin
Percussion Ventures 337

Drum Solos, Latin Percussion
Ventures

PART II: THE 1920s AND 1930s

Cuba
Son
Sexteto Boloña, *Échale Candela*,
Tumbao 060
María Teresa Vera, *Éxitos originales*,
Kubaney 0229
Septeto Nacional, *Sones cubanos*,
Seeco 9278
El Septeto Nacional de Ignacio Piñeiro,
WS Latino 4085
Trío Matamoros, *La China en la
rumba*, Tumbao TCD 039
Orquesta Anacaona/Septeto
Anacaona 1937, and Ciro Rimac
1936–37, Harlequin 027

Charangas, Boleros, Guajira
Cheo Belén Puig y su Orquesta, *Me
han dicho que tú me quieres*, Tumbao
078
Antonio María Romeu y su orquesta,
Boca linda, Tumbao 076
Época de oro de la música cubana,
Nelson records 6001
The Music of Cuba 1909–1951,
Columbia Legacy, CK 62231

Big Bands
*Don Azpiazu Havana Casino
Orchestra*, MM 30911
Lecuona Cuban Boys, Harlequin 35

The United States and Puerto Rico
The Awakening of the Barrio
Davilita, *Davilita*, Disco Hit 9141
Noro Morales, *His Piano and Rhythm*,
Ansonia 1272
Antonio Machín, *Cuarteto Machín
1930–31*, Tumbao 15
Cuarteto Marcano, *Canciones
inolvidables*, Ansonia 1205
*Xavier Cugat and His Orchestra
1940–42 featuring Miguelito Valdés,
Machito and Tito Rodríguez*, Tumbao
02

Puerto Rico
Canario y su grupo, *Plenas*, Ansonia
1232
Rafael Hernández y su conjunto,
*Inolvidable música con sus intérpretes
originales*, Disco Hit BS-3103
Pedro Flores, *Éste es Pedro Flores*,
Ansonia 1527
Rafael Muñoz y su orquesta, *Éxitos de
Latino América*, Victor 1075

PART III: THE 1940s AND 1950s

Cuba
Charangas
Antonio Arcaño, *Danzón mambo*,
Tumbao 29
Israel "Cachao" López, *Cachao y su
típica: canta contrabajo*, Duher 1611
La Original Orquesta Aragón de
Cuba, *20 Éxitos, Vol. 1*, Sabor 1002

Abelardo Barroso y la Orquesta
Sensación, *Guajiro de Cunaguá*, Aro
107
Orquesta Almendra de Abelardito
Valdés, *Danzones para recordar*,
Tumbao 065
Enrique Jorrín y su orquesta, *Danzón
cha cha cha, Vol. 10*, BMG/Tropical
Series 24540
Fajardo y Sus Estrellas, *Al compás de
Fajardo*, Panart/Rodven 5181

Son

Félix Chappotín y su conjunto, *Sabor
Tropical*, Antilla 107
René Alvarez y su Conjunto Los
Astros, *Yumbale*, Tumbao 064
Conjunto Cubavana, *Sonaremos el
tambó*, Cariño
Conjunto Casino Con Faz, *Ribot y
Espí*, Mediterráneo 10046
La Sonora Matancera, *Canta
Bienvenido Granda*, Ansonia 1225

Big Bands, Combos, Descargas

Orquesta Casino de la Playa,
Memories of Cuba, Victor
Julio Cueva y Su Orquesta, *La butuba
cubana*, Tumbao 32
Mariano Mercerón y sus Muchachos
Pimienta, *Yo tengo un tumbao*,
Tumbao 064
Los mejores músicos de Cuba (Bebo
Valdés, Peruchín, Tata Güines,
Richard Egües, etc.), Rumba Records
Pedro Justiz, *Peruchineando con
Peruchín*, Montmartre Record 5403
Chico O'Farrill and His All Star
Cuban Band, *Antología musical*,
Panart/Rodven 5013
Descargas – Cachao y su Ritmo
Caliente, *Cuban Jam Sessions in
Miniature*, Panart
Cuban Jam Session (under the
direction of Julio Gutiérrez), Vol. 1,
Panart

Vocalists

Benny Moré, *El Bárbaro del ritmo*,
Tumbao 10
Bola de Nieve, *Sus grandes éxitos*,
Mediterráneo 10066
Barbarito Diez, *La voz del danzón*,
Artex 007

Lo Mejor de Xiomara Álfaro, *Lamento
borincano*, BMG/Tropical Series 3471
Tríos de mi Cuba, Panart 3149
Cuarteto D'Aida (with Chico
O'Farrill), An Evening at the Sans
Souci, RCA Victor 173
Celia Cruz, *Música santera con Celia
Cruz y La Sonora Matancera*, Fuentes
16048
Olga Guillot con los Hermanos Castro,
Puchito 101
Olga Guillot, *La reina del bolero*, AF
8009
Abelardo Barroso, *The Spirit of Cuba*,
Gone Latin 7004
Guillermo Portabales, *Lo mejor de
Guillermo Portabales*, UR 1520
Celina González, *Santa Bárbara*,
Egrem 042

The United States and Puerto Rico

Mambo

Pérez Prado, *Go Go Mambo 1949–51*,
Tumbao 13
Pérez Prado, *Concierto para bongó*,
Polydor 314–521074–2
Latin Top Brass/Mambo Festival, (Julio
Andino and René Hernández
Orchestras), SMC

The Afro-Cubans

Machito and His Afro Cubans 1941,
Palladium 116
*Dance Date with Machito and His
Orchestra*, Palladium 111
*Mucho Mucho Machito, Featuring
Graciela and Marcelino Guerra*,
Palladium 119

Tito Puente, Tito Rodríguez and other Latin bands

Cuarteto y Sexteto Caney, *Perfidia*,
Tumbao 038
Alberto Socarrás, Noro Morales, etc.,
Harlequin HQ CD 113
Tito Puente, *Dance Mania – Vol. 1*,
BMG/Tropical Series 2467
Tito Puente, *Cuban Carnival*,
BMG/Tropical Series 2349
Tito Rodríguez Hits, WS Latino 118
Tito Rodríguez at the Palladium,
Palladium 108
César Concepción y Su Orquesta,
Plenas favoritas con Joe Valle, Ansonia
1305

Moncho Leña y sus Ases del Ritmo –
Canta Mon Rivera, *Dance*, Ansonia
1305
Luisito Benjamín (and José Curbelo),
Dancing and Dreaming, Verne

Vocalists

Miguelito Valdés, *Mr. Babalú – With
Noro Morales Orchestra*, Tumbao 25
Vicentico Valdés, *Mi diario musical*,
Fuentes D 16061
Panchito Riset, *De cigarro en cigarro*,
Ansonia
Daniel Santos, *El Anacobero*, Polydor
314 521 218–2

Chano Pozo and other percussionists

Chano Pozo, *Legendary Sessions
1947–53*, Tumbao 17
Carlos "Patato"Valdés, *Patato y Totico*,
Mediterráneo
Cándido, *Cándido the Volcanic*, ABC
Paramount

Latin jazz

Machito/Chico O'Farrill/Charlie
Parker/Dizzy Gillespie, *Afro-Cuban
Jazz*, Verve
Erroll Garner, *Mambo Loves Garner*,
Mercury
Dizzy Gillespie, *Rumbola*, Norgran
Joe Loco, *Loco Motion*, Fantasy 24733
George Shearing, *On the Sunny Side
of the Strip*, GNP 9055

PART IV: THE 1960s

Cuba

The explosion of rhythms

Combo Siboney, *Descarga latina*,
Discmedi Blau 059
Pacho Alonso, *Rico pilón*, Artex 041
Los Amigos, *Instrumentales cubanos*,
Egrem 30
Pello el Afrokán, *Un sabor que canta*,
Vitral 4122

The United States and Puerto Rico

Pachanga and boogaloo

Arsenio Rodríguez y su conjunto,
Fiesta en Harlem, SMC
Canciones que mi mamá no me enseñó,
(Joe Cuba/Miguelito Valdés/ Tito

Puente/Graciela and Machito), Tico 112°

Joe Quijano, *La pachanga se baila así*, Cesta 21000

La Lupe, *Queen of Latin Soul*, Tico 1167

Joe Bataan, *Subway Joe*, Fania 345

Joe Cuba, *Bang ! Bang ! Push, Push, Push*, Tico 1146

Joe Cuba, *Diggin' the Most*, Seeco 9259

Ricardo Ray, *Se soltó – On the Loose*, Alegre 8500

Johnny Colón and Orchestra, *Boogaloo & Blues*, Cotique 1004

Eddie Palmieri, *Mozambique*, Tico 1126

Ray Barretto, *Acid*, Fania 346

Cortijo y Kako, *Ritmos y cantos callejeros*, Ansonia 1477

Descargas – Live at the Village Gate, Tico

Charangas

Charlie Palmieri, *Echoes of an Era*, Polydor 531877

Ray Barretto, *Charanga moderna*, Tico

Johnny Pacheco, *Pacheco y su charanga*, Alegre 6016

Lou Pérez, *¡Bon bon de chocolate!*, Montuno 3362

The modern *bomba* and *plena*

La plena y bomba de Puerto Rico, Cariño

Cortijo y su Combo con Ismael Rivera, *¿Bueno, y qué…?*, Rumba Records 55534

Ismael Rivera, *Traigo de todo*, Tico 1319

Ismael Rivera, *Eclipse total*, Tico 1400

Mon Rivera, *Mon y sus trombones*, Vaya 54

Mon Rivera, *Karacatis-ki*, Ansonia 1356

Latin jazz and Latin soul

Eddie "Lockjaw" Davis, *Afro Jaws*, OJC 403

Mongo Santamaría, *Our Man in Havana*, Fantasy 24729

Pucho and The Latin Soul Brothers, *Tough!*, Prestige/Fantasy 24138

Machito and His Afro-Cubans, *Latin Soul Plus Jazz*, Fania 74

Willie Bobo, *Bobo! Do That Thing/Guajira*, Tico 1108

PART V: FROM THE 1970s UNTIL TODAY

Cuba
Music of Traditional Inspiration

Guaguancó Conjunto Matancero/Papín y sus Rumberos, Puchito 565

Pancho Quinto, *En el solar la Cueva del Humo*, Round World Records

Guaguancó Grupo Matancero, Papín y otros, Vol. 2, Antilla 595

Conjunto Clave y Guaguancó, *Déjala en la puntica*, Enja 888829

The Cuban All-Stars (Tata Güines and Miguel Angá), *Pasaporte*, Enja 9019–2

Songo and charangas

Orquesta Revé, *La explosión del momento*, Fonomusic 1118

Los Van Van, *Te pone la cabeza mala*, Metro Blue 21307

Orquesta Maravillas de Florida, *En vivo*, Salsa Center 304568

Orquesta Ritmo Oriental, *Historia de la Ritmo Oriental – Vol. 1*, Obadisc 9007

Orquesta Aragón, *La charanga eterna*, BMG 362112

Son

Son del Cauto, *El amor es libre*, Last Call 3046152

Son de Cuba, Edenways EDE 2007–2

Dúo Los Compadres, *Los reyes del son*, WS Latino 4155L

Grupo Sierra Maestra, *Sierra Maestra*, Edenways 2008

Adalberto Alvarez y su son, Arte 01

Yakaré, *Cuban Jazz Salsa*, Auvidis/Playasound PS 65204

Nueva timba

Exitos de NG La Banda, Artex 002

Juan Carlos Alfonso y su Dan Dén, *Viejo Lázaro*, Qbadisc 08–9009

Issac Delgado, *Con ganas*, Qbadisc 9012

Manolín el Médico de la Salsa, *Para mi gente*, Ahi-Nama Records 1002

Manolito y su Trabuco, *Marcando la distancia*, Eurotropical EUCD-9

Bamboleo, *Ya no hace falta*, Ahi-Nama Records 1024

Anacaona, *Lo que tú esperabas*, Lusafrica BMG 362292

The Buena Vista Social Club phenomenon

Buena Vista Social Club, Nonesuch 79478

Buena Vista Social Club Presents Ibrahím Ferrer, Nonesuch 79532

Buena Vista Social Club presenta a Omara Portuondo, World Circuit WCD 059

Afro Cuban All Stars, World Circuit WC D0 47

Rubén González, *Indestructible*, Egrem 0275

Eliades Ochoa and Compay Segundo "Cuarteto Patria", Edenways EDE 2012–2

Cachaíto, *Muy Sabroso*, World Circuit WCD 061

Latin jazz

Havana Jam (Irakere, Cuban Percussion Ensemble, Frank Emilio, etc.), Columbia

Irakere, *Calzada del Cerro*, Vitral 4053

Grupo Afro-Cuba, *Afro-Cuba*, NCL

Programa mi salsa, *Mi salsa en descarga Vol. I* (Emiliano Salvador/Tata Güines/Elpidio Chapotín/Peruchín/Gonzalo Rubalcaba), Discmedi 061

Emiliano Salvador, *Ayer y hoy*, Qbadisc 9011

José María Vitier, et al., *Habana secreta*, Milan Latino 74321 28594–2

Gonzalo Rubalcaba, *Live in Havana*, Messidor 15960

José Luis Cortés, *Latin Music*, Flarenasch – Suisa 185232 MU 760

Jesús Alemañy, *Cubanismo*, Hanibal HNCO 1390

Orlando Valle "Maraca", *Sonando*, WEA Music 3984–27013–2

Bellita n' Jazztumbatá, Round World Music RWCD 9705

El Indio, *Nuevos horizontes*, Tamarindo Records

Tony Martínez and the Cuban Power, *Maferefun*, Blue Jacket BJAC 5033–2

Chucho Valdés, *Bele Bele en La Habana*, Blue Note 7243 8 23082 25

Other bands

Vocal Sampling, *Una forma más*, Sire/Warner Brothers 61792 Max 2141

Arte Mixto, *Deseos*, Ahi-Nama Records 1990

Vocalists

Cándido Fabré, *Poquito poco*, Tumi TMG-CD 2

Magaly Bernall con Estrella de la Charanga, *La Guarachera soy yo*, Last Call LBLC 2553 HM83

Leyanis López, *Como la mariposa*, BMG

Malena Burke, *Salseando*, Pure Sounds

Osdalgia Lesmes, *La chica sentimental*, Lusafrica

The United States and Puerto Rico
Instrumental salsa

Jerry Masucci Presents Salsa Greats (Tito Puente, Ray Barretto, Willie Colón, Larry Harlow, Johnny Pacheco), Fania 69050

Virgilio Martí, *Saludando a los rumberos*, Caimán Records 96006

Eugenio "Totico" Arango, *Totico y sus rumberos*, Montuno 515

Félix "Pupi" Legarreta, *Pa' bailar*, Vaya 89

Israel "Cachao" López, *Dos*, Salsoul 7005

Johnny Pacheco, *The Artist*, Fania 503

Willie Colón, *El Malo*, Fania 337

Willie Colón (with Rubén Blades), *Metiendo mano*, Fania 500

Willie Colón (with Rubén Blades), *Siembra*, Fania 537

Grupo Folklórico y Experimental Nuevayorquino, *Concepts in Unity*, Salsoul 20–60012

Conjunto Libre, *Mejor que nunca/Better Than Ever*, Milestone 9226

Machito Orchestra, *Fireworks*, Musical Productions 3131

Orquesta Broadway, *Salvaje*, Musical Productions 3119

Charlie Palmieri, *Gigante Hits*, Alegre 6014

Mongo Santamaría (with Justo Betancourt), *Ubane*, Vaya 44

Eddie Palmieri, *Azúcar pa' tí*, Tico 1122

Eddie Palmieri, *Palmas*, Elektra 961649

Ray Barretto, *The Message*, Fania 403

Ray Barretto, *Ricanstruction*, Fania 552

Ray Barretto, *Together*, Fania 378

Conjunto Son de la Loma, *Así empezó la cosa*, Montuno

Orquesta Son Primero, *Tradición cubana en Nueva York: charanga*, Montuno 524

Chocolate Armenteros, *Chocolate aquí*, Carib Musicana 2081

Tito Puente, *Para los rumberos*, Sonodisc CDT 1301

Tito Puente, *Eddie Palmieri and guest stars*, Masterpiece/Obra Maestra, RMM 84033

Salsa vocalists

Ismael Miranda, *Así se compone un son*, Fania 437

Celia Cruz (with Johnny Pacheco), *Celia and Johnny*, Vaya 31

Justo Betancourt, *Distinto y diferente*, Fania 502

Cheo Feliciano, *La voz sensual de Cheo Feliciano*, Vaya V 12

Pete "El Conde" Rodríguez, *A Touch of Class*, Fania 519

Héctor Lavoe, *La voz*, Fania 461

Rubén Blades, *Canciones del solar de los aburridos*, Fania 597

Rubén Blades, *Maestra vida* (2 vol.), Fania 576 and 577

Camilo Azuquita, *El Señor de la salsa*, Melao 219

Camilo Azuquita, *La Foule*, Freneaux Entertainment 902

Ismael Quintana, *Punto y aparte*, WS Latino 4256

Melcochita, *Mis mejores éxitos*, Elephant EL 2002

Marvin Santiago, *Oro salsero: 20 Éxitos*, Rodven 3128

Gilberto Santa Rosa, *Expresión*, Sony 83634

Llegó La India . . . via Eddie Palmieri, Soho Records 80864

Marc Anthony, *Desde un principio*, RMM CD 83580

Víctor Manuelle, *Inconfundible*, Sony

Salsa in Puerto Rico, California, and Florida

Puerto Rico All Stars, Combo 1904

Ralphy Leavitt y Orquesta La Selecta, *Mi barrio*, Multinacional Inc 1221

Bobby Valentín, *Soy boricua*, Fania 439

Roberto Roena y su Apollo Sound, *Apollo Sound VI*, Fania 473

Willie Rosario, *El Bravo soy yo*, Inca 1065

Sonora Ponceña, *Sabor sureño*, Inca 1039

Sonora Ponceña, *Tiene pimienta*, Inca 1947

El Gran Combo, *Gracias – 30 años de sabor*, Combo 2090

Batacumbele, *Con un poco de songo*, Dico Hit 008,

Batacumbele, *En aquellos tiempos*, Dico Hit 9106

Zaperoko, *Cosa de locos*, Montuno 519

Atabal, *Del Caribe al Brasil*, Musicaribe 001

Grupo Afro-Boricua, *Bombazo*, 5027–2

Descarga Boricua, *¡Esta, sí va!*, Tierrazo TH 15 A/B

Plena Libre, Ryko disc RCCD 1006

Orquesta Batachanga, *Manaña para los niños*, Earth Beat 42513

Mangú, Island Records 524508

Gloria Estefán, *Alma caribeña*, Epic 62183

Albita Rodríguez, *Son*, Time Square Records 9004

Merengue

Damirón, *Piano Merengues – Vol. 1*, Ansonia 1236

Dioris Valladares and His Orchestra, *Pa' bailar na' ma'*, Alegre 6008

Angel Viloria y su Conjunto Cibaeño, *Merengues – Vol. 2*, Ansonia 1207

Joseíto Mateo, *Merenguero hasta la cintura*, Ansonia

Cuco Valoy, *Las Mujeres Calientes: Bachata, merengue y son*, ANL 94160

Johnny Ventura, *The Best*, Sony 81227

Wilfrido Vargas, *Usted se queda aquí . . .*, Rodven 3102

Juan Luis Guerra y 4:40, *Bachata rosa*, Karen 93016

Olga Tañón, *Mujer de fuego*, WEA Latino 93307

Elvis Crespo, *Píntame*, Sony 82917

Chichi Peralta y Son Familia... *De vuelta al barrio*, Caiman 33017

Raulín, *Dominicano para el mundo*, AE Music 1005

Da Madd Dominikans, *Total Latino Mix*, Vol I, Balboa

New Latin jazz

Mongo Santamaría, *Afro-Indio*, Vaya

Dizzy Gillespie and Machito, *Afro-Cuban Jazz Moods*, Pablo OJC 447

Graciela/Mario Bauzá, *Afro-Cuban Jazz*, Caimán 9017

Mario Bauzá, *My Time is Now*, Messidor 15824

Tito Puente, *Un poco loco*, Picante/Concord 4329

Tito Puente and His Latin Jazz Ensemble, *Salsa Meets Jazz*, Picante/Concord 4354

Jerry González and the Fort Apache Band, *The River Is Deep*, Enja 79665

Daniel Ponce, *Changó te llama*, Mango 9877

Ray Barretto and New World Spirit, *Ancestral Messages*, Picante/Concord 4549

Danilo Pérez, Novus 01241 63148 2

Danilo Pérez, *Central Avenue*, Impulse IMP 12812

David Sánchez, *Sketches of Dreams*, Columbia 67021

David Sánchez, *Street Scenes*, Columbia 485137 2

Paquito D'Rivera, *Reunion*, Messidor 15805–2

Seis del Solar, *Alternate Roots*, Messidor 15831–2

Charlie Sepúlveda, *The New Arrival*, Antilles 314 510 056–2

Claudio Roditi, *Slow Fire*, Milestones MCD 9175–2

Clare Fischer, *Lembranças*, Picante 4404

Clare Fischer, *Crazy Bird*, Discovery 914

Michel Camilo, *Rendezvous*, Columbia 473772 2

Edward Simón Group, *Edward Simón*, Kokopelli 1305

Chico O'Farrill, *Pure Emotion*, Milestone 9239–2

Giovanni Hidalgo, *Time Shifter*, Sony CD-Z81585

Juan Pablo Torres, *Torres, Trombone Man*, Sony CD-Z81601

Cal Tjader, *La onda va bien*, Picante/Concord 4113

Poncho Sánchez, *A Night at Kimball's East*, Picante/Concord 4472

Justo Almario, *Heritage*, Blue Moon R2 79343

Paquito D'Rivera, *Portraits of Cuba*, Chesky JD145

Gonzalo Rubalcaba, *The Blessing*, Blue Note CDP 797 1972

Héctor Martignon, *The Foreign Affair*, Candid

Roy Hargrove, *Roy Hargrove's Crisol Havana*, Verve 537 563–2

Deep Rumba, American Clavé AMCL1024

Marlon Simón and the Nagual Spirits, Cubop CBD027

Latin rock, Latin soul, Latin disco

Carlos Santana, *Shango*, Sony 38122

Seguida, *Love Is . . . Seguida*, Fania 478

Mellow Man Ace, *Escape from Havana*, CD Capitol

Marc Ribot y Los Cubanos Postizos, *¡Muy divertido!*, Atlantic 83293

The rest of the world
Music of Cuban origin from the 1920s until today

Cubans in Europe, Harlequin

Don Barreto (1932–35), Harlequin 06

Oscar Calle – *Señor tentación, Cuba en París*, Iris Music 3004806

Acerina y su Danzonera, *Ésta es mi historia*, Rodven 7114

Dimensión Latina, *¡La tremenda dimensión!*, Vedisco 7073

Óscar D'León y su Salsa Mayor, *El Óscar de la salsa*, Top Hits

Fruko y sus Tesos, *Sus grandes éxitos de salsa – Vol. 1*, Vedisco/Fuentes 1049

Joe Arroyo, *Echao pa'lante*, Fuentes 10013

Grupo Niche, *Sutil y contundente*, Sony 080155

Orquesta Guayacán, *Llegó la hora de la verdad*, DM Productions 1001

Guaco, *Lo mejor de Guaco*, Rodven 2831

Africando, *Vol. I – Trovador*, Stern's Africa 1045

Orquesta de la Luz, *Somos diferentes*, RMM/Sony

Orlando Poleo, *El buen camino*, Columbia, COL 4891752

Orlando Poleo, *Sangre negra*, Columbia, COL 4961412

Omar Sosa, *Bembón Roots III, Night and Day*, MSCD 006

Yuri Buenaventura, *Yo soy*, Mercury 542248

Alfredo Naranjo, *Vibraciones de mi tierra*, Latin World CD-00104

Orisha Dreams, *Sin palabras*, Déclic

Mario Canonge et le Groupe Kann, *Retour aux sources*, Natal 150960

bibliography

BOOKS

Abascal, Jesús, Sindo Garay vive en sus canciones, in *Cuba*, January 1964, no. 21, pp. 30–3.

Acosta, Leonardo, *Del tambor al sintetizador*, Editorial Letras Cubanas, Havana, 1983.

—— *Elige tú, que canto yo*, Editorial Letras Cubanas, Havana, 1993.

—— *El jazz cubano: una historia de casi un siglo*, typed paper, no references available.

Agüero, Gaspar, Consideraciones sobre la música popular cubana, in *Revista de la Facultad de Letras y Ciencias*, Havana, 1922.

—— La música cubana, in *Música Magazine*, no date.

—— El jazz cubano: una historia de casi un siglo, in *Música Cubana*, no. 1, 1998.

Aguirre, Mirta, De "Negro Bembón" a "Palma Sola", in *Unión*, no. 3, 1959, pp. 96–107.

Alberti, Luis, *De música y orquestas bailables dominicanas 1910–1959*, Editora Taller, Santo Domingo, 1975.

Alberts, Arthur S. (ed.), *African Coast Rhythms*, Cultural History Research, New York, 1969.

Alén Rodríguez, Olavo, *Géneros de música cubana*, part I, Ediciones Pueblo y Educación, Havana, no date.

Andreu Alonso, Guillermo, *Los arará en Cuba – Florentina, la princesa dahomeyana*, Editorial de Ciencias Sociales, Havana, 1992.

Anonymous, *The Puerto Rican and His Music*, New York, Centro de Estudios Puertorriqueños, 1975.

Anonymous, *Centenario del danzón. Homenaje al XX aniversario de la revolución cubana*, Ministerio de la Cultura, Havana, 30 January 1979.

Anonymous, Cheo Feliciano, semillas en las maracas, in *Salsa Cubana*, no. 4, 1998.

Anonymous, Loyola, director de orquestas populares, in *Nacido en Cuba – Música cubana*, Editorial Ceiba, Mérida, 1999.

Ardevol, José, Panorámica de la música cubana actual, in *Islas*, II:1, 1959, pp. 23–31.

Aretz, Isabel (ed.), *América Latina en su música*, Unesco, Mexico, 1977.

Arnaz, Desiderio, *A Book*, Morrow, New York, 1966.

Aros, Andrew, *Latin Music Handbook*, Applause, Diamond Bar, 1978.

Artau, Mariano, Una trayectoria a grandes rasgos: Las orquestas de baile de Puerto Rico, in *La Canción Popular*, no. 9, 1994, pp. 57–62.

Arteaga Rodríguez, José D'Jesús, La salsa en Colombia, in *Música tropical y salsa en Colombia*, Ediciones Fuentes, Medellín, 1992.

Barnet, Charlie, with Stanley Dance, *Those Swinging Years, The Autobiography of Charlie Barnet*, Louisiana State University Press, Baton Rouge, 1984.

Barnet, Miguel, Entrevista a Ester Borja, in *La Gaceta de Cuba*, no. 126, 1974.

—— Pablo Milanés, una música puente, in *Revolución y Cultura*, November 1979, pp. 94–8.

—— La cultura que generó el mundo del azúcar, in *Revolución y Cultura*, June 1979.

Beals, Carleton, *The Crime of Cuba*, J. B. Lippincott, Philadelphia, 1933.

Bianchi Ross, Ciro, Barbarito Diez, in *Cuba Internacional*, no. 9, 1980, pp. 44–6.

Bloch, Peter, *La le lo lai. Puerto Rican Music and its Performers*, Plus Ultra, New York, 1973.

—— *Music of the Hispanic Antilles*, Peninsula Publishing Company, New York, 1981.

Borbolla, Joseph, Sobre el son. Música de Cuba, in *Signos*, no. 17, Consejo Nacional de la Cultura, Havana, 1975, pp. 74–9.

—— El son, exclusividad de Cuba, in *Yearbook for Interamerican Musical Research*, University of Texas at Austin, 1975, pp. 152–6.

Bou Domenech, Alfonso, Don Nacho, un músico guerrero y noble, in *La Canción Popular*, no. 9, 1994, pp. 57–62.

Brenes,, Ramón Luis, A puerta cerrada con Ismael Rivera, in *Bulletin – Centro de Estudios Puertorriqueños*, Spring, 1991.

Brouwer, Leo, *La música, lo cubano y la innovación*, Editorial Letras Cubanas, Havana, 1982.

Cabrera, Lydia, *El monte*, Ediciones Universal, Miami, 1975.

Calderón, González, Jorge, Ayer, hoy, siempre, María Teresa Vera, in *Revolución y Cultura*, no. 87, November 1979, pp. 2–6.

Campos Parsi, Héctor, *Gran enciclopedia de Puerto Rico, Vol. 7, Música*, Ediciones R., Madrid, 1976.

Capdevilla, Pedro, Tres viejas rumbas en Remedios, in *Signos*, no. 17, 1975, pp. 97–8.

Carbonell y Rivero, José Manuel, Evolución de la cultura cubana, 1608–1927, in *Las Bellas Artes en Cuba*, Vol. XVIII, Imprenta El Siglo XX, Havana, 1928.

Cardona, Luis, *The Coming of the Puerto Ricans*, Unidos Publications, Washington, D.C., 1974.

Carp, David, A Visit With Maestro Johnny Pacheco, in *The Descarga Newsletter*, no. 29, 1997.

Carpentier, Alejo, Los valores universales de la música cubana, in *Revista de La Habana*, May 1930.

—— *Ecué-Yamba-O*, Editorial Sandino, Montevideo, 1933.

—— *La música en Cuba*, Fondo de la Cultura Económica, Mexico, 1946.

Castellano, I., Instrumentos musicales de los Afrocubanos, in *Archivos del Folklor Cubano*, no. 22, Havana, 1926, pp. 193–208.

Castellanos, Jorge and Isabel, *Cultura Afrocubana 4 – Letras, música, arte*, Ediciones Universal, Miami, 1994.

Castiel Jacobson, Gloria, *The Life and Music of Ernesto Lecuona*. PhD. dissertation, University of Florida, 1982.

Castillo, André S. Jr., Various short articles in: *Gente de la Semana*, March–May 1954.

Castillo, del, José and Arevalo García, Manuel A., *Antología del merengue*, Banco Antillano, SA, Santo Domingo, 1989.

Chao Carbonero, Graciela, *Bailes yorubas de Cuba, Guía de estudio, danza*, Editorial Pueblo y Educación, Havana, 1980.

Châtelain, Daniel, Batterie et percussions dans le jazz cubain, Entretien avec Roberto Vizcaíno et Juan Carlos Rojaz, *Percussions*, no. 48, vol. VII-6, November–December 1996, pp. 25–31.

Claghorn, Charles Eugene, *Miguel Faílde, creador musical del danzón*, Ediciones del CNC, Havana, 1982.

Copland, Aaron, *What to Listen for in Music*, Mentor, New York, 1957.

Cormán, Tomás, Las orquestas típicas, in *Ondas y Canales*, July 1953.

Cortés, Félix, Falcón, Angel, and Flores, Juan, The Cultural Expression of Puerto Ricans in New York: A Theoretical Perspective and Critical Review, in *Latin American Perspective*, issue 10, III:3, Summer 1976, pp. 117–52.

Cuellar, V., La revolución del mambo, in *Bohemia*, XXXX:27, 30 May 1958, pp. 20–2 and 97–9.

Cugat, Xavier, *Rumba is my Life*, Didier, New York, 1948.

Díaz Ayala, Cristóbal, Dr., *Música cubana del areyto a la nueva trova*, Editorial Cubanacán, San Juan, 1981.

—— *Si te quieres por el pico divertir . . . Historia del pregón musical latinoamericano*, San Juan, 1988.

—— *Cuba canta y baila, Discografía de la música cubana*, Vol. 1, 1898–1925, Fundación Musicalia, San Juan, 1994.

—— *Cuando salí de La Habana – 1898–1997 – Cien años de música cubana por el mundo*, Puerto Rico, 1999.

Epstein, Daniel Mark, *Nat King Cole*, Farrar, Straus & Giroux, New York, 1999.

Erminy, A., Hipótesis sobre el origen y evolución de la rumba, in *América*, vol. 15, no. 2–3, 1942, pp. 53–6.

Faux, Claude, *Cuba cubain*, Clairefontaine, Lausanne, 1961.

Feather, Leonard, *The New Edition of the Encyclopedia of Jazz*, Horizon Press, New York, 1960.

Fernández, Olga, *Strings and Hide*, Ediciones José Martí, Havana, 1995.

Figueroa Hernández, Rafael, *Ismael Rivera: El sonero mayor*, Instituto de Cultura Puertorriqueña, San Juan, 1993.

Flippo, Chet, Rubén Blades Crossing the River Pop, in *Village Voice*, 19 November 1985, p. 64.

Garces, Carlos, Irakere, un laboratorio musical, in *Bohemia*, no. 39, September 1978, pp. 40–1.

Gavilán, Miguel, Mr. Pete Rodríguez, in *Latin New York*, I:3 1968, p. 16.

Geijerstam, Claes af, *Popular music in Mexico*, University of Mexico Press, Albuquerque, 1976.

Gerard, Charley with Sheller, Marty, *Salsa! The Rhythm of Latin Music*, White Cliff Media Cy, Crown Point, 1989.

Gillespie, Dizzy and Frazer, A., *To Be or not to Bop*, Doubleday, New York, 1979.

Ginori, Pedraza, Poner a bailar el trompo – Orquesta Aragón – in *Cuba*, February 1967, pp. 58–65.

Giro, Radamés, *La música, lo cubano y la innovación*, Havana.

—— (ed.), *Panorama de la música popular cubana*, Editorial Facultad de Humanidades, Universidad del Valle, Cali, 1996.

Gómez Yera, Sara, La rumba, in *Cuba*, December 1964, pp. 58–67.

González-Whippler, Migenia, *Santería*, Anchor Books, New York, 1973.

Gourse, Leslie, *Unforgettable – The Life and Mystique of Nat King Cole*, Cooper Square Press, New York, 2000.

Grenet, Emilio, *Música popular cubana*, Ministerio de la Cultura, Havana, 1939.

Heredia, Pablo, *Antonio Machín*, Editorial Miguel Arimany, S. A., Barcelona, 1976.

Hernández, Erena, *La música en persona*, Editorial Letras Cubanas, Havana, 1986.

Huggins, Nathan Irvin, *Harlem Renaissance*, Oxford University Press, London, 1971.

Incháustegui, Arístides, *El disco en República Dominicana*, Santo Domingo, 1988.

Jahn, Jahnheinz, *Muntu, the New African Culture*, Grove Press, New York, 1961.

Jara Gómez, Simón, Rodríguez, Aurelio "Yeyo", and Zedillo Castillo, Antonio, *De Cuba con amor . . . el danzón en México*, Consejo Nacional Para la Cultura y las Artes, Mexico, 1994.

Kleiner, Audrey and Cole, Marilyn (eds), *The Fania All Stars Songbook*, Columbia Pictures Publications, Hialeah, 1978.

Lagarde, Guillermo, Entrevista, in *Avance*, no. 7, Havana, 1953.

Lázaro, Luis, *Compay Segundo, un sonero de leyenda*, Fundación Autor, Madrid, 2000.

León, Argeliers, *De la contradanza al danzón*, Ediciones del CNC, Havana, no date.

—— El ciclo del danzón, in *Nuestro Tiempo*, March 1955.

—— *Música folklórica cubana*, Ediciones del Departamento de la Biblioteca Nacional José Martí, Havana, 1964.

—— Elige tú, in *Revolución y Cultura*, no. 67, March 1978, pp. 33–40.

—— *Del canto y el tiempo*, Editorial Letras Cubanas, Havana, 1984.

Leymarie, Isabelle, The Magic Flautist, in *Nuestro*, November 1978, pp. 59–60.

—— Machito. A Living Legend, in *Canales*, no. 34–5, 1979.

—— Papo Lucca, the Maestro from Ponce, in *Canales*, June 1979.

—— Graciela no olvidará a París, in *Canales*, July 1979.

—— Chico O'Farrill and the Course of Latin Jazz, in *Canales*, October 1979.

—— Latin Jazz. The Best of Both Worlds, in *Jazz Spotlite News*, October 1979.

—— Salsa and Latin Jazz, in *Hot Sauces*, Quill, New York, 1985.

—— *La Salsa et le Latin jazz*, PUF, Collection Que Sais-je?, Paris, 1992.

—— *Du tango au reggae – musiques noires d'Amérique latine et des Caraïbes*, Flammarion, Paris, 1996.

—— *Musiques caraibes*, Actes Sud, Paris, 1996.

—— La Migration transatlantique des tambours bátá yoruba, *Percussions*, 1996.

—— *Cuba et la musique des dieux*, Editions du Layeur, Paris, 1998.

—— *Latin Jazz, Collection CD-Livres*, Vade Retro, Paris, 1998.

—— *Dizzy Gillespie, Collection CD-Livres*, Vade Retro, Paris, 1998.

—— *Cuba et la musique cubaine*, Editions du Chêne, Paris, 1999.

—— *Les griots wolof du Sénégal*, Maisonneuve et Larose, Paris, 1999.

Linares, María Teresa, *La música y el pueblo*, Instituto Cubano del Libro, Havana, 1970.

—— *La música popular*, Colección Introducción a Cuba, Instituto Cubano del Libro, Havana, 1970.

—— El sucu-sucu, un caso en el área del Caribe, in *Boletín de Música Casa de las Américas*, no. 44, January–February 1974, pp. 2–13.

Lizardo, Fradique, El merengue tiene su origen en Africa, in *Ahora*, no. 630, December 1975, no. 8, pp. 50–1.

López, Eleazar, C., El sentimiento de la música cubana, in *Jóven Cuba*, 1973.

—— El boom de la salsa, in *Resumen*, no. 2004, September 1977.

Louis, Néstor, *A Conversation with Ray de la Paz*, 2001, Jazz con clave website.

Malavet Vega, Pedro, *Del bolero a la nueva canción*, Editora Corripio, Ponce, 1988.

Malson, Lucien, *Histoire du jazz et de la musique afro-américaine*, Seuil, Collection Solfèges, Paris, 1994.

Martínez, Mayra A., Van Van cumple quinze años, in *Revolución y Cultura*, no. 5, 1984, pp. 2–7.

—— El piano como un reto, in *Revolución y Cultura*, no. 4, 1985, pp. 14–19.

—— Clave de Rubalcaba, in *Revolución y Cultura*, no. 2, 1987, pp. 24–9.

Martínez Furé, Rogelio, Comparsas afrocubanas y rumbas, in *Cuba Internacional*, February 1974, pp. 52–5.

—— *Diálogos imaginarios*, Cuadernos de Arte y Sociedad, Editorial Arte y Literatura, Havana, 1979.

Martínez Rodríguez, Raúl, *La música bailable en el siglo XIX en Matanzas*, Ediciones del CNC, Havana, 1974.

—— La rumba en la provincia de Matanzas, in *Boletín de Música Casa de las Américas*, no. 65, July–August 1977, pp. 15–23.

—— Aniceto y el danzonete, in *Revolución y Cultura*, no. 4, 1987, pp. 50–4.

—— Lo trágico y lo controvertido en el canto y en la vida de Guadalupe Victoria Yoli Raymond, conocida como La Lupe, in *Salsa Cubana*, no. 4, 1998.

Moldes, Rhyna, *Música folklórica cubana*, Miami, 1975.

Molina, Carlos, Algo sobre el danzón, in *Gaceta de Cuba*, November–December 1971.

Moore, Robin, D., *Nationalizing Blackness – Afrocubanismo and Artistic Revolution in Havana 1920–1940*, University of Pittsburgh Press, Pittsburgh, 1991.

Muguercia, Alberto, Matamoros todavía sirve, in *Cuba*, October 1967, pp. 64–9.

—— Teodora Ginés, mito o realidad histórica, in *Revista de la Biblioteca Nacional José Martí*, XIII:3, September–December 1971, pp. 53–85.

—— Matamoros: un firme obstinado, in *Signos*, May–December 1975, pp. 161–207.

—— El son ese viejo travieso y saltarín, in *Revolución y Cultura*, 1979, pp. 51–3.

—— Rosendo Ruiz, el trovador. Si algo fui, se lo debo a mi pueblo, in *Bohemia*, no. 12, March 1985, pp. 16–19.

Muguercia, Alberto and Rodríguez, Ezequiel, *Rita Montaner*, Editorial Letras Cubanas, Havana, 1984.

Muñoz, María Luisa, *La música en Puerto Rico*, Troutman Press, Sharon, 1966.

Nasser, Amín E., *Benny Moré*, Havana, no date.

Navarrete, William, *La chanson cubaine, 1902–1959, textes et contexte*, L'Harmattan, Paris, 2001.

Orovio, Helio, La conga: ballet ambulante, in *El Caimán Barbudo*, December 1979, pp. 15 and 24.

—— *Diccionario de la música cubana*, Editorial Letras Cubanas, Havana, 1981.

—— Arsenio Rodríguez y el son cubano, in *Revolución y Cultura*, no. 7, 1985, pp. 14–17.

—— La Guantanamera en tres tiempos, in *Unión*, No. 15, Havana, 1993.

Orozco, Danielo, Son como reflejo de la personalidad cultural cubana, in *Universidad de Santiago*, no. 33, no date.

Ortiz, Fernando, *La africanía de la música folklórica de Cuba*, Ministerio de Educación, Havana, 1950.

—— *Los instrumentos de la música afrocubana*, Ministerio de Educación, Havana, 1955.

—— La habilidad musical del Negro, in *Estudios Afrocubanos*, Universidad Central de Las Villas, 1959.

—— La secta conga de los Matiabos de Cuba, in *Islas*, III:3, May–August 1961, pp. 39–52.

—— La transculturación blanca de los tambores de los Negros, in *Islas*, V:1, 1962, pp. 67–98.

—— Estudiemos la música afrocubana, in *Islas*, VI:1, July–December 1963, pp. 181–93.

—— *La música afrocubana*, Biblioteca Jucar, Madrid, 1975.

Pasmanick, Philip, Décima and Rumba: Iberian Formalism in the Heart of Afro-Cuban song, in *Latin American Music Review*, 18:2, December 1997, pp. 252–77.

Paxton Cady, Carolyn, *Some Aspects of Native Cuban Music*, M.A. dissertation, Columbia University, New York, 1932.

Pereira Salas, Eugenio, Notes on the History of Music Exchange Between the Americas Before 1940, in Music Division, Pan American Union, Washington, D.C., January 1943.

Pérez, Gladys, El Benny en 60 minutos, in *Revolución y Cultura*, no. 84, 1979, pp. 8–11.

Pérez, Hiram Guadalupe, Un momento de música cubana, entrevista con César Portillo de la Luz y Tony Taño, in *La canción popular*, no. 9, 1994, pp. 107–13.

Pichardo, Esteban, *Diccionario provincial casi razonado de voces y frases cubanas*, Havana, 1875.

Pryor Dodge, Roger, The Cuban Sexteto, in *Jazz Review*, no date.

—— Jazz Dance, Mambo Dance, in *Jazz Review*, no date.

Pujol, Sergio, *Jazz al Sur – la música negra en la Argentina*, Emecén, Buenos Aires, 1992.

Reyes-Schramm, Adelaide, *The Role of Music in the Interaction of Black Americans and Hispanos in New York City's East Harlem*, PhD dissertation, Columbia University, New York, 1975.

Reynolds, Quentin, Jungle Dance: the Rumba as Danced in Cuba, in *Collier's*, no. 27, 1937, pp. 45–7.

Rico Salazar, Jaime, *Cien años de boleros*, Academia de Guitarra Latinoamericana, Bogotá, 1987.

Rivero, Ángel, El son es lo más sublime, in *Revolución y Cultura*, no. 69, 1978, pp. 13–19.

—— Maravillas de Florida. No desvirtuar a nuestra música, in *Revolución y Cultura*, no. 84, 1979, pp. 76–7.

Robreño, Eduardo, *Cualquier tiempo pasado fue . . .*, Editorial Letras Cubanas, Havana, 1979.

Robreño, Eduardo and Urfé, Odilio, Ay Fefita, mi amor . . . no me hagas sufrir, in *Revista Romances*, February 1975.

Rodríguez, Bobby, The End of Pure Latin Music, in: *Latin New York*, February, 1968.

Rodríguez Domínguez, Ezequiel, *Iconografía del danzón. Creadores e intérpretes*, Ediciones Delegación Provincial de la Cultura, Havana, 1967.

—— *Notes pour l'hommage à Abelardo Barroso*, Casa de la Trova de La Habana, Consejo Nacional de la Cultura, Havana, 21 September 1973.

—— *Trío Matamoros. Treinta y cinco años de música popular cubana*, Editorial Arte y Literatura, Havana, 1978.

—— *El danzonete, su autor y sus intérpretes*, Ministerio de la Cultura, Havana, 1979.

Rodríguez Juliá, Edgardo, *El entierro de Cortijo*, Ediciones Huracán, Río Piedras, 1983.

Rondón, César Miguel, *El libro de la salsa*, Editorial Arte, Caracas, 1980.

Ros, Edmundo, *The Latin American Way*, Rose, Morris, London, 1949.

Ross, Russell, *Bird Lives*, Quartet Books, London, 1972.

Rouy, Gérard, Shorty le géant, in *Jazz Magazine*, April, 1986.

Saco, José Antonio, *La vagancia en Cuba*, Cuadernos de Cultura no. 3, Ediciones Dirección de Cultura del Ministerio de Educación, Havana, 1946.

Salado, Minerva, Cara a cara con Arturo Sandoval, in *Cuba Internacional*, February 1980, pp. 70–2.

Salazar, Max, Tito Rodríguez – My Life with Tito, in *Latin New York*, January 1976.

—— Machito – A Historical Perspective of His Afro-Cuban Sound, in *Latin Exchange*, IV:1, Special commemorative issue, 1980.

Sánchez de Fuentes, Eduardo, *El folklor en la música cubana*, Imprenta Siglo XX, Havana, 1923.

—— La riqueza rítmica de la música cubana, in *Club Cubano de Bellas Artes*, vol. 1, Havana, 1925, pp. 37–68.

—— *Folklorismo*, Imprenta Molina y Compañía, Havana, 1928.

Sand, Clara, Una voz que se aleja, Abelardo Barroso, in *Bohemia*, 21 June 1968.

Sanjuán, Pedro, Cuba's Popular Music, in *Modern Music, The League of Composers*, XIX:1, New York, 1942, pp. 222–7.

Santos, Daniel and Mujica, Héctor, *El inquieto anacobero. Confesiones de Daniel Santos a Héctor Mujica*, Editorial Cejota, Caracas, 1982.

Santos, John, Notes of the record *The Cuban danzón. Its ancestors and descendants*, Folkways Records FE 4066, 1982.

Schoener, A. (ed.), *Harlem on my Mind*, Random House, New York, 1968.

Senior, Clarence, *The Puerto Ricans*, Quadrangle Books, Chicago, 1965.

Smith, Willie "The Lion", *Music on my Mind*, Da Capo, New York, 1978.

Solis, Clara, En torno a una poesía del danzón, in *Islas*, 1959.

Soloni, Félix, El danzón y su inventor Miguel Faílde, in *Cuba Musical*, 1928.

Spaeth, Sigmund, *A History of Popular Music in Latin America*, Random House, New York, 1948.

Stearns, Marshall, W., *The Story of Jazz*, Oxford University Press, New York, 1956.

Storm Roberts, John, A Newyorican Christmas in *The Village Voice*, December 30, 1974.

—— *Salsa*, BMI, New York, 1976.

—— *The Latin Tinge*, Oxford University Press, New York, 1979.

Suri Quesada, Emilio, Malanga: rey de la rumba, in *Caimán Barbudo*, March 1984, pp. 2–3.

Tercinet, Alain, entry on Chico O'Farrill in *Dictionnaire du jazz*, Collection Bouquins, Editions Robert Laffont, Paris, 1989.

Thomas, Hugh, *Cuba and the Pursuit of Freedom*, Eyre and Spottiswoode, London, 1971.

Toop, David, *The Rap Attack – African Jive to New York Hip Hop*, South End Press, Boston, 1984.

Tynan, John, Cal Tjader, in *Downbeat*, September 15, 1957.

Urfé, Odilio, Factores que integran la música cubana, in *Islas*, II:1, September–December 1959, pp. 7–20.

—— Síntesis histórica del danzón, in *Iconografía del danzón*, Delegación Provincial de la Cultura de La Habana, Havana, 1967.

—— La música y la danza en Cuba, in *Africa en América Latina*, Unesco, Siglo Veintiuno, Mexico, 1977, pp. 215–37.

Vargas, Enrique Arnaldo, Lito Peña y la Orquesta Panamericana, in *La Canción Popular*, no. 9, 1994, pp. 47–52.

Vitales, A. M. de, Havana, a Growing Music Center, in *Musician*, March 1924, p. 28.

Waxer, Lise, Of Mambo Kings and Songs of Love, Dance Music in Havana and New York from the 1930s to the 1950s, in *Latin American Music Review*, vol. 19, no. 2, Fall/Winter 1994, University of Texas Press, pp. 139–76.

Wooley, Stan, Machito Making Musical Earthquakes, in *Jazz Journal International*, November 1977, pp. 36–7.

Wright, Irene, *Aloha, Cuba*, New York, 1910.

Ximena y Cruz, María de, *Aquellos tiempos. Memorias de Lola María*, vol. II, El Universo, Havana, 1930.

PERIODICALS

Cuba
Bahoruco
Caimán Barbudo, El
Canto Libre
Gaceta de Cuba, La
Gente de la Semana
Granma
Habana
Letras Musicales
Mundo Musical
Música, La
Música en Cuba, La
Ondas y Canales
Revista Romances
Revolución y Cultura
Salsa Cubana
Tropicana Internacional
Verde Olivo

United States
Amsterdam News
Billboard
Canales
Claridad
Clave
Diario La Prensa, El
Down Beat
Guía Latina
Latin Beat
Latin New York
Latin Times
Melody Maker
Musician
New York Latino
New York Magazine
New York Times, The
Rolling Stone
Saturday Review
Steppin' Out
Stereo Review
Village Voice, The

Puerto Rico
Puerto Rico Ilustrado
Salsa

France
Batteur Magazine
Jazz Hot
Jazz Magazine
Jazzman
Percussions

index

Italics indicate musical works and instruments, bold type bands.

A bailar bambulé 235
A bailar mi bomba 299
A Baracoa me voy 91
A Bayamo en coche 251
A Belén le toca ahora 115, 124
A comer lechón 296
A Decade of Jazz 193
A du bliú bliú bliú 173
A Eleguá y a Changó 215
A Giant Step 277
A gozar ahora 229
A gozar con el combo 215
A la Chucho 259
A la cuata co y co 56
A la i olé 303
A la loma de Belén 56, 58, 237
A la rigola 135, 310
A lé lé 51
A lo oscuro 310
A Mayagüez 185
A mí que me importa Usted 56
A Night at Kimball's East 324, 364
A Night in Mambo Jazz Land 204
A Night in Tunisia 191, 195, 200, 324
A Nueva York 17, 294, 297
A pie 57
A Puerto Rico 181
A quilo el bombón 299
A romper el coco 156, 159
A San Germán 185
A todos los barrios 125, 126, 226, 273
A Touch of Brass 283
Abacuá ecu sagare 196
abakwa, (music) 9, 11, 15–17, 30, 47, 54, 56, 60, 98, 125, 142, 168, 188, 190, 192, 202, 211, 220, 235, 237, 246, 262, 317, 343, 344–7
Abandonada 187
abanico 39, 343
Abaniquito 178, 187, 352
Abbey, Leon 172
Abelinito, (clarinettist) 24
Alboláez, Francisco 249
Abran paso 291
Abreu, Alfredo 246
Abreu, Anais 266
Abreu, Cheché 313
Abreu, Jesús 246
Abreu, Ricardo 246
Abreu, Luis 246
Abreu, Toño 310

Abuelo pachanguero, El 281
academias de baile 46, 49, 55, 110, 128, 208, 356, 358
Acángana 106, 237,
accordíon 32, 100, 140, 201, 228–9, 262, 307, 308, 309, 310
Acerina, Valiente, Consejo 332, 333, 364
Acevedo, Ernie 282
Acevedo Sosa, Plácido 91, 103, 106
Aché 14
Aché IV 149, 266
Acid 362
Acompáñame civil 314
Acosta, Agustín 50
Acosta, Coquí 313
Acosta, José 283
Acosta, José Carlos 262
Acosta, Leonardo iv, 78–9, 139, 144, 154, 264, 365
Acosta, Félix 226
Acosta Pino, Luis 252
Acuña, Alex 323
Adagio 261
Adalberto Álvarez y su Son 251, 294, 362
Adams, Dottie 165
Adams, Pepper 287
Adderley, Cannonball 174, 239, 241, 318
Adderley, Nat 238
Adelante 112, 285
Adelante Gigante 277
Adelita 106
Adiós muchachos 298
Adiós Roncona 219
Adonís, conguero 262
Adoración 277
Africa contemporánea 318
Africa habla 118
African Flute, The 174
African Salsa 338, 341
African Team 334
Africana, La 23
Africano, El 312
Afrika Bambaata 327
Afro Cuba de Matanzas 325
Afro Blue 239
Afro-Cuba 259, 262, 362
Afro-Cuban 6, 9, 10, 46, 61, 95, 125, 126, 133, 142, 148–9, 161, 165–6, 179, 180, 181, 186, 195–6, 198, 205, 211, 213, 215, 219, 232, 239, 245–6, 251, 262–5, 277, 284–5, 290, 302, 306, 318, 324, 340, 346, 347, 348, 351

Afro-Cuban All Stars 212, 256, 362
Afro-Cuban Jazz 319, 361, 364
Afro-Cuban Jazz Suite 162, 267
Afro-Cuban Moods 276
Afro-Cuban Rumbas 95
Afro-Cuban Suite 173, 193
Afro-Cubans, The 92, 125, 145, 161, 163, 165–75, 177, 180, 186–7, 192, 194, 198–9, 202, 219–20, 222–3, 240, 276, 282, 319, 358, 361
Afro-Cubists, The 334
Afro-Indio 251
Afro-Indio 316–17, 364
Afro Jazz, Grupo 264
Afro-Jazziac 174
Afro Roots 196
Afro-shingaling 226
Afrocuba, de Matanzas 16, 246
Afrofilipino 226
Afrojaws 238
afroloo 223
Afroshock 339
Agabamar, Sexteto 68, 126, 169
Agitation Rag 78
agogó 14, 15
Agosto, Ernie 302
Agrupación Boloña 55–6
agua de Clavelito, El 116
Agua de Luna 295
Agua de Tinajón 135
Agua limpia todo 179
Agua que va caer 236, 293, 298
Aguado, Alfonso 336
Aguanile 260
Aguabella, Francisco 162, 182, 196, 199, 240, 271, 278, 286, 323, 324, 326
Agudín, Nilo 124
Agüeros, "Rabito" Salvador 240
"Aguegue", López, D. 86
Aguilar, Pedro 165, 217
Aguiler, Freddie 204
Aguilera, Gilberto 252
Aguilo, Arturo 72
aguinaldo 99, 101, 103, 298, 303, 343
Aguirré Ocampo, José 339
agúzate 265
Ah wah 179
Ahí na' ma' 232, 236, 241, 343
Ahora soy tan feliz 142
Ahorita va a llover 153
Aiken, Gus 95
Aiyón, René 144
Akra, Los 212

Al soltar el gallo 282, 293
Al sonero mayor 234, 293, 366
Al vaivén de mi carreta 45, 53
Alafia 225
Alambre 26, 190
Alberti, Luis 308, 309, 365
Alberti, José 229
Alberto, José, "El Canario" 275, 295
Alberto Iznaga, Orquesta de 86, 92, 93
Albino, Juan Antonio "Johnny" 189
Alboláez, Francisco 249
Alday, Angel 152
Aleaga, Leonel 252
Alegre All Stars, The 221, 222, 269, 270, 299, 310
Alegres (Trío), Los 309
Alemañy, Jesús 251, 264, 362
Alén Rodríguez, Andrés 249, 365
Alfaro, Xiomara 184, 216
Alfarona X, Conjunto 183, 240, 352
Alfonso, claves player 144
Alfonso, Carlos 251, 255, 362
Alfonso, Félix, see chocolate 115, 125, 127, 199
Alfonso, Juan Carlos 362
Alfonso, Nilo 124
Alfonso, Rolando 135, 140
Alfonso, Octavio "Tata" 23, 68, 116
Alfredito, Al Levy 183
Alfredo 189, 282
Algo bueno 192, 200
Algo Nuestro 301
Algo Nuevo 251, 301
Ali, Bardu 167
Alicea, Marie 183
Alicea, Paul (drummer) 183
Alicea, Paul (timbalero) 183
Alkimia 337
All Star Band 238, 361
All Stars Mambo Orchestra 196
Allen, Tito (Roberto Romero) 274, 275, 295, 318, 327
Allende, Calixto 71, 170
Alma Cibaeña, Conjunto 311
Alma de mujer 72, 88
Alma del Barrio 305
alma del Barrio, El 225
Alma guajira 59
Almanza, Pedro 32
Almario, Justo 263, 316, 317, 324
Almario, Luis "Licho" 323

Almeida, José "Cuchi" 338
Almendra, danzón 117
Almendra 179, 334
Almendra 116, 117
Almendra, Johnny 288
Almo, Ray 220
Alone Together 240
Alonso, Alicio 355
Alonso, Pascasio "Pacho" 139, 210, 256
Alonso, Pachito 255
Alpert, Herb 274
Alternate Roots 321
Alto Songo 126
Alturas de Simpson, Las 22, 23, 25
Álvarez, Adalberto 245, 251, 252, 253, 256, 294
Álvarez, Carlos 261
Álvarez, Chico 184, 202
Álvarez, Domingo 336
Álvarez, Fernando 129, 139, 144, 178, 189, 210
Álvarez, Heny 273
Álvarez, Mario 332
Álvarez, Paulina (de Paula Peña, Raimunda) 71, 73, 112, 117, 120, 158
Álvarez, René 117, 124, 126, 127
Álvarez, Roberto 124
Álvarez, Tico 152
Álvaro, José 336
Alza los pies, Congo 56
Amab 327
Amada mía 293
Amalbert, Juan 238
Amalia Batista 49, 230
Amapola 177
Amat, Francisco "Pancho" 251, 252, 262, 264
Amaya, Carmen 186
Amber Grey 326
Ameen, Robbie 321
Amenaza 327
Amigos, Los 149, 176, 215, 258, 265
Amigos Panamericanos, Los 176, 201
Amigos, Los 291
Amistad, Conjunto 295, 305
Amor ciego 271
Amor secreto 337
Amparo 326
Amram, David 286, 287
An Evening at the Sans Souci 152
Ana Luiza 326
Ana María 325
Anabacoa 309
Anacaona, Orquesta 66, 67, 101, 152, 171, 252, 331, 340
Anacobero, El 188
Ancestral Messages 315
Anckermann, Jorge 19, 25, 133, 329
And I Love Her 240
Anderson, Laurie 318
Anderson, Todd 278
Andino, Julio 169, 173, 175, 181, 188, 204, 221
Andino, "Papi" 185
Andrés, "El Sublime" 13

Animada 52
Anisia 109, 165
Anka, Paul 199
Anoche aprendí 184
Ansias locas 106
Antillana, Sonora 333
Antillano, Cuarteto 152
Antoanetti, Conjunto 295
Antobal's, Cubans 86, 248
Antomarchí, Juan "Cotó" 253
Antomattei, Cándido 219
Apaches, Los 50, 56
Aparicio, Eddie 184
Apellaniz, Norberto 240
Apollo, Conjunto 68, 121, 195
Apollo Sound, The 300
Apollo Sound 6 301
Aponte, Charlie 298
Aprieta 225
Apurrúneme mujer 125
Aquella boca 53
Aquellos ojos verdes 91, 93, 94, 166
Aquí estoy, ya llegué 236
Aquí se enciende la candela 247
Aquino, Tomaso 46
Aragón, Orestes 116
Aragon, Orquesta 115, 117, 145, 211, 219, 228, 229, 244, 245, 249, 256, 261, 262, 287, 388, 352
Araquita 335
arara (music) 17, 247, 285
Arawe 318
Arbello, Fernando 85
Arcaño, Antonio 110, 111, 112, 113, 114, 115, 117, 118, 121, 124, 126, 155, 158, 181, 214, 219, 249, 351
Arecibo 185
Arena, Mario 239
Arete 278
aretes de luna, Los 187
Arias, Edmundo 333
Ariza, Hilario 183, 212
Argudín, Nilo 215
Arjona, Catalino 110
Arlen, Harold 199
Armenteros, Armando 124, 125, 127, 129, 135, 136, 142, 143, 144, 170, 231, 238, 239, 270, 271, 283, 284, 286, 291, 294, 336, 348, 358
Armenteros, Alfredo "Chocolate" 116, 117
Armiñán, Pablo 33
Armstrong, Louis 90, 91, 95, 96, 125
Arnaz, Desi (Desiderio) 20, 92, 93, 98, 186
Arnedo, Antonio 322
Aroche, Alberto 53, 71, 152
Aroche Cuarteto 152
Aroche, Elizardo 112, 115
Arosteguí, Elías 60
Arrecotín arrecotán 235, 236
Arriba la invasión 117, 124
¡Arriba la Pachanga! 216
Arrolla 148
Arrolladora, La 50
Arroyo, Álvaro José "Joe" 336, 337
Arte Mixto 265

Artista, El 275, 291
Artistry in Rhythm 202
Arvelo, Pepito 106, 333
Arverne, Harvey 183
Arvizu, Juan 332
as de la rumba, El 156, 173, 277
asalto 273
Asalto navideño 272
Ases de la Radio, Los 309
Ases del Ritmo, Los 186, 237
Así empezó la cosa 286
Así es la vida 327
Así se compone un son 291
Asia Minor 173
Asoyí, Asoyí 17
Astros, Los (Conjunto) 127
Astros, Los (Trio) 266
At the Party 223
At Last 171, 224
Atabal 304
Atésame el bastidor (or *Atesa el bastidor*) 36, 219
Atrevido y diferente 296
Audinot, Rafael 87
Aunque tu mami no quiera 126
Aurora 103
Aurora 103
Aurora en Pekín 56
Ausencia 49
Augie and Margot 165
Avance, Conjunto 143
Avance Juvenil 251
Ave María morena 30, 218, 232
Averhoff, Carlos 261, 355
Avilés, Vitín 189, 232, 295
Avilés Lozano, Miguel 80
Avísale a mi contrario 179, 218
Avísale a mi vecino 218
avispas, Las 312
Avocadoes 202
Awake 275
Ay José 116
Ay que frío 274
Ayala family 233
Ayala, Frank Gilberto 92, 125, 169
Ayala, Luisito 304
Ayala, Sammy 182, 234
Ayer y hoy 262
Ayers, Roy 323
Azpiazu, Ernesto "Don" 46, 79, 80, 86, 88, 89, 90, 91, 93, 134, 148, 167, 331, 357
Aztec Suite 240
Azteca 328
Azúcar a granel 293
Azucar Negra 255
Azúcar pa' tí 291
Azucenas 106
Azul 126
Azul, Trio 51, 75
"Azuquita" (Argúmedes Rodríguez, Luis Camilo) 129, 235–6, 271, 275–6, 293–4, 298, 338, 342, 363
Azuquita y su Melao 338

Baba Rhumba 91
Babalú Ayé 16, 48, 93, 131–2, 186, 247, 255, 343, 361
Babarabatiri 142, 170, 173, 179, 217, 300
"Babuco" (Tiburcio Hernández) 329, 332

Bacalaítos 223, 318
Bacallao, Antonio 57
Bacallao, Estebán 246
Bacallao, Rafael "Felo" 117, 249, 275
bachason 313
bachata (Cuban) 33, 35, 127, 296, 363
bachata (Dominican) 313–15, 342
bachata (by Bebo Valdés) 126–7
Bachata rosa 314, 342, 364
Back Bay Shuffle 162
Bad Street Boys, The 326
Badrena, Manolo 323
bahía de Manzanillo, La 145
Bagdad, *see*: Casa blanca
Baia 201, 321
Baila mi gente 324
Bailando abrazao 106
baile del pinguino, El 164
Baile del perrito 312
Bailey, Benny 325
Bajo un palmar 106
Baker, Josephine 45, 95, 148, 330, 357
Bakuleye 255
Balaguer, Joaquín 311
Balata 339
Ball, Lucille 92
Ballagas, Patricio 35, 50, 52, 59
Baloy, Félix 256, 258
Bamba cure 236
Bamboléate 322
Bamboleo 255, 362
bambuco 51, 323
Ban ban quere 274
Banana Land 282
Banda Caribbean 252
Banda Gigante (Benny Moré) 138, 144
Banda Gorda, La 313
Banda Infantil de Guanajay 125
Banda Loca, La 313
Banda XL 256
Bandera 306, 329
Banderas, José "Pepe" 52
bando 25
Bando Azul, El 245
Bang! Bang! 223, 225, 353
banjo 79, 104, 141, 356, 358
Baños, René 265
baqueteo 39, 343
baquiné 272
Barracón, El 190
Baralt, Ramces 265
Barbados 100, 184
Barbarazo, El 312
Barbería, Carlos 285, 344
Barbieri, Leandro "Gato" 239, 276, 320, 322
Barbón, Miguel "Brindis" 249
Barboza, Phil 239
Barcarola en cha cha chá 133
Bardot, Brigitte 162
Barnet, Miguel 203, 365
Baró, Andrea 30
Baroco 21 318
Barnet, Charlie 93, 365
Barquinho 226
Barracon, El 190
Barretico (timbalero) 254

Barreto, Emilio "Don" 15, 330–1, 348, 356, 364
Barreto, Guillermo 129, 135–6, 139, 141, 149, 152, 214–15, 254, 258, 264, 275
Barreto, José 85
Barreto, Julián 24, 356
Barreto, Justi 170–1, 231, 332
Barreto, Luis (bassist) 180, 183
Barreto, Marino 331
Barreto, Roberto 144
Barreto, Sergio 338
Barretto, Ray 364
Barrio, El 25, 83, 105, 126, 149, 177, 182, 191, 198, 204, 222–3, 224, 267, 280, 282, 283, 291, 326
Barrio, Rafael "Felo" 282
Barrio Boogaloo 241
Barrio Obrero a la 15, El 299
Barron, Kenny 325
Barroso, Abelardo 361, 368
Barroso, Ahmed 355
Bartee, John 170
Bartz, Gary 325
Basic Basie 239
Basie, Count 239–40
Bass Family, The 138
Bastar, Francisco "Kako" 183, 221, 235–6, 238, 271, 285, 291, 293, 298–9, 302
bastón 249
batá 13, 14, 48, 128, 135, 136, 149, 197, 246–7, 250, 265, 269, 275, 276, 278–9, 287, 302, 303, 306, 318, 321, 325
Batá y rumba 285
Bataan, Joe (Nitrollano, Jr., Peter) 226, 275, 283, 327, 362
Batachanga, Orquesta 305, 324, 363
Batacumbele 302–3, 306, 321, 363
Batamú 149, 150, 332, 351
batanga 3, 57, 179, 351
Batanga, La 135, 274, 332
Batarengue 303
batiri 161, 189
Batista, Candita 351
Batista, Fulgencio 108, 174, 208, 245
Batman's Boogaloo 223
Batuca 276
Bauzá, Estela (nee Grillo) 166
Bauzá, Mario 131, 164–74, 178, 180, 186, 191, 200, 260, 276–7, 288, 298, 315, 319, 321, 358, 364
Bayamesa, La 52, 74–5, 80, 285
Be Careful It's My Heart 146, 148
Beals, Carleton 28, 30, 365
Beatles, The 222, 355
Bebo Rides Again 318
bebop 3, 137–8, 157, 166, 168, 172, 175, 191, 193, 204, 227, 263, 344, 348–9
Bechet, Sidney 95, 167, 330, 356
Becke, Pepe 186, 191, 194
Beduinos, Los 312
Bega, Lou 328
Begin the Beguine 177

Bei mir bist du schön 175
Beiderbecke, Bix 166
Belafonte, Harry 173
Belén 54, 131, 190
Belén Puig, José "Cheo" 187
Belén Puig, José 68, 71, 76, 121, 187, 360
Bella cubana, La 265
Bella sin alma 296
Bella Unión 72, 114
Bellamar, Conjunto 124, 137
Bellamar, Orquesta (Cuba) 136–7, 186
Bellamar, Orquesta (Puerto Rico) 349
"Bellita", Expósito Pino, Lilia 247, 264
Bello amanecer 217
Bellson, Louie 285, 323
Beltrán, Alberto 127, 143, 310
Beltrán, Dandy 117
Beltrán, José 249
Beltrán Brunet, Orlando 248
Beltrán Ruiz, Pablo 332–3
Bemba, Evaristo 55
Bemba colora' 142
bembé 15, 239, 343
Bembe, Conjunto 283
Bembé, El 149
Benda, Richard 177
Benefactor, Orquesta 309
Benilde Morales, Horacio 249
Benítez, Enrique 143–4
Benítez, John 278, 288, 320, 325, 342
Benítez, Johnny "Jellybean" 327
Benítez, Rafael 150
Benjamín, Luisito 185, 361
Bennett, Benny 162, 334
Bennett, Jock 95
Bennett, Tony 198, 238
Benson, George 262
beodos, Los 246
Berigan, Bunny 166
Bergaza, Rafael "Felo" 134, 138, 213–14, 332
Berlin, Irving 146
Bermúdez, Lucho 333
Bernall, Magaly 266, 363
Bernstein, Leonard 326
Berrios, Raúl 322
Berrios, Steve 183, 317, 318, 321, 325
Berrios, Tommy 204, 224, 352
Berroa, Ignacio 140, 213, 263, 285, 303, 305, 318–19, 320, 324, 325, 342
Bésame la bembita 180
Bésame mucho 240, 322–3, 332
Besitos de coco 290
Beso 309
Beso loco 88
Besos de caramelos 228
Besos salvajes 152
bestial sonido de Ricardo Ray y Bobby Cruz, El 271, 302
Betancourt, Eduardo 72
Betancourt, Joaquín 251
Betancourt, Justo 229, 232, 268, 273, 285, 290–1, 302, 317, 363
Betancourt, Lolo 79
Betancourt, Rafael 90

Better World 325
biankomé 16
Bibijagua 134
Bien, Hermano 68
Bien sabroso 324
Big Break, The 273
Bigote de gato 188
"Bilingüe" (Frank Gilberto Ayala) 125, 169
Bill Brown and His Brownies 85
Billo (Frómeta Pereyra, Luis María) 310
Billo's Caracus Boys 151, 309, 334
Bilongo 3, 4, 117, 135, 136, 183, 219, 276
Bim bam bum 117
Bimbi (Maximiliano Sánchez) 152
Birdland Mambo 201
Birimbau 17
Bito Manué no sabe inglé 48, 148
Bitter Acid 227
Black Boys, The 222
Black Cuban Diamonds, The 195
Blackbirds of 1928 86, 95
Blades, Rubén 269, 274, 275–6, 279–80, 283–4, 287, 291–3, 294–5, 314, 321, 363, 366
Blakey, Art 193, 198, 199
Blancas azucenas 91
Blanchard, Harold 95
Blanco, Rafael 71, 249,
Blanco y el Negro, El 50
Blasio Junior, Orchesta 334
Blen blen blen 164, 180, 190
Blez, Emiliano 35, 74
Blues en E bemol 215
Blue Mambo 203
Blues Mambo 203
Bluesette 316
Bobby Lee's Cotton Pickers 201
Bobé, Eddie 319
Bobo, Willie (William Correa) 3, 179, 180, 323, 362
Bochinche, El 298
Bochinchera, La 277
Bocucos, Los 210
Boda negra 75
Bodas de oro 139
Bodeguero, El 116, 117, 162
Bodegueros, Los 314
Bofill, Angela 315, 327
Bola de Nieve (Ignacio Villa) 82, 90, 117, 134, 145–6, 148, 150, 184, 190, 213, 332, 334, 361
bola 234, 343
Bola (La) 129
Bolado, Vidal 191, 199, 202–3
Bolaños, Reinaldo 127, 226
bolero 5, 9, 34–5, 39, 42, 47, 48, 49, 50, 52, 56, 64, 65, 68, 74–5, 76, 79, 82, 87, 88, 93, 96, 98, 101, 103, 106, 115, 124, 125, 126, 134, 138, 139, 140, 142, 145, 146, 152, 156, 161, 171, 179, 181, 187, 198, 201, 209, 212, 217, 219, 223,

224, 228, 230–1, 236, 246, 256, 263, 265, 266, 279, 283, 290, 293, 294, 295, 320, 325, 329, 332, 343, 350, 355, 357, 360, 361
Bolero (by Ravel) 322
Bolero árabe 82, 134
Bolero, Septeto 56
Bolero 1935 198
Bolero oculto 263
Bolichán 69
bomba 99–100, 103, 183, 228, 232–4, 235, 237, 271, 282, 293, 298, 301, 303, 304, 343, 346, 362
Bomba ae 235
Bomba camará 226
Bomba carambomba 298
Bomba Jazz 303
Bomba lacrimógena, La 55
Bomba na' ma' 233
Bombín de Barreto, El 14, 356
bombo (accent) 192
bombo (drum) 20, 343
Bonbón de Elena, El 234, 235
Bonbonsito de coco 221
Bondeye 109, 150
bongo 1, 10, 16, 17, 30, 33, 34, 40, 44, 45, 46, 55, 56, 57, 58, 60, 66, 68, 92, 99, 101, 106, 112, 117, 121, 130, 140, 141, 144, 159, 165, 174, 179, 180, 183, 185, 186, 193–4, 195, 198, 199, 202, 203, 204, 205, 212, 229, 234, 238, 240, 249, 250, 252, 257, 268, 286, 290, 292, 298, 299, 309, 311, 319, 321, 337, 343, 346, 351, 352–3, 354, 356, 361
Bongo Beep 166
Bongo Logic 324
Boniatillo 153
Bonito y sabroso 159
bonkoenchemiyá 16
Bonne Castillo, Enrique 211
Bonnemere, Eddie 196–201
boogaloo (or bugalú) 3, 118, 189, 204, 216, 222–6, 235, 237, 241, 267, 288, 299
Boogaloo Blues 223
Boogaloo con soul 223
Boogaloo en el Barrio 223
Boogaloo sabroso 223
Bop-A-Loos, The 162
Boranda 267, 268
Borbolla, Carlos 25
Borcelá, Amado, see Guapachá
Borell, Roberto 287
Borgellá, Mozo 66, 143
Borges, Lino 121
Borges, Vania 255
Boria, Pellín 87
Borincuba 290
Borinquen 86, 103, 290
Boriquen, Cuarteto 87
Boriquen, Quinteto 88
Boriquen, Septeto 101
Boriquen, Sexteto 88, 182
Boriquen, Trío 88, 103, 104, 237
Borinquen tiene bandera 84
Borinquen, tierra de flores 106
Borinqueña, La 99

Borinqueños, Los 88
Borja, Esther 45, 146, 151, 334, 351, 365
Bosch, Jimmy 279, 286, 288
Bosch, Juan 311
Bosco, João 263
Boso, El 281
bossa-nova 356
Bostic, Earl 162
Boston, Sexteto 124
Boston, Tony 327
Botánica, La 277
Botellero, El 36, 48, 171, 186
boteo 115, 210, 343
botija 123, 343
Boto, Rondón 311
Botón de Oro, el 128
Botón de Rosa 68
Boulong, Puchi 179, 310
Bowie, David 274, 320
Boyd, Nelson 193
Brando, Marlon 165
Branly, Jimmy 265
Bravo, Pancho 138
Bravo, Sonny (Elio Osacar) 275
bravo soy yo, el 300, 363
Brazilian Soft Shoe 174
break-dancing 327
Breaking the Rules 281
Breaks, The 327
Brel, Jacques 263
Briceño, Rolando 318
Bricktop 356
Brilliantes de Costa Rica, Los 290
Brindis de Salas, Claudio 115
Brito, Alfredo 69, 71, 79, 85, 90, 136
Brito, Cuarteto 309
Brito, Eduardo 85, 93, 308, 309
Brito, Felo 217, 221, 227, 229
Brito, Julio 79, 92, 331
Brito, Ramón 231
Britos Ruiz, Federico 325
Broadway (New York) 86, 89, 93, 95, 115, 164, 172, 199, 200, 201, 282, 291, 296, 316, 353
Broadway, Orquesta 212, 223, 225, 228, 232, 282, 338, 365
Broadway Casino 299
Bronx Horns 321
Bronx with Palm Trees, The 325
Brooklyn Bums, The 269
Brooklyn Mambo 183
Brookmeyer, Bob 238
Brouwer, Leo 209, 365
Brown, Alexander 265
Brown, Clifford 261, 321
Brown, Garnett 241
Brown, James 158, 269, 275, 324
Brown, Ruth 162
Brubeck, Dave 195, 205, 240, 259, 316
Bruca maniguá 122–3, 183
Bruguera, Agustín 82
Bruja, La 254
Brujo de Guanabacoa, Un 87, 117, 351
Bryant, Ray 203
Bryon, Enrique 85, 330

Buarque, Chico 282
"Bubú" (Pablo Govín) 128
Bucaneros, Los 152, 212–13
Budet, José 92, 180, 182, 352
Budo 302
Buena Vista Social Club (film) 150–1, 256, 362
Buena Vista Social Club 115, 244, 245, 256–7, 341
Buenaventura (Bedoya), Yuri 314, 339, 342, 364
Bueno, El 273
Bueno, Enrique 24
¿Bueno y qué? 235, 362
Bufos Habaneros 329
Builes, Miguel Ángel 161
bulá 118
Bullock, Chick 91
Burgues González, Romana, *see* Elena Burke
Burke, Bob 91
Burke, Elena (Romana Burgues) 110, 140, 152, 155, 156, 213, 215, 247, 261
Burke, Malena 266, 363
Burundanga 142, 290
Burque, Charles 212
burlador, see macho
Burton, Gary 315
Buscando América 294
Buscando millonaria 357
Bururú barará 57, 311
Busca lo tuyo 221, 292
Bush and the Magníficos 294
Bush y Su Nuevo Sonido 337
Bustillo, "Bene" (Benitín) 214
Bustin' Out 225
Buyú 315
Byron and Tybee 165

C & C Music Factory 327
Caballero, Lindabell, *see* "La India"
Cabalgata d'Arteaga 176, 201
Caballero pelotero, El 237
Caballeros del Merangue, Los 313, 314
Caballeros silencio 58
Caballo de hierro 298
Caballo grande 255
Caballo viejo 11, 306
Cabán Valle, Antonio ("El Topo") 302
Cabel, René 150, 151, 219
Cabeza, Nené 169
cabildos 11, 12, 18, 22, 28–9, 343
Cabio silé 285
Cabot, Joe 183
Cabrera, Eduardo, *see* "Cabrerita"
Cabrera, Felipe 57, 263, 339
Cabrera, Fernando 121
Cabrera, Julián 115, 285
Cabrera, Lydia 15
Cabrera, Yoyito 313
"Cabrerita" (Eduardo Cabrera) 142, 144
Cachaíto, see López, Orlando
Cachana, Conjunto 183, 232
Cachao (Israel López) 3, 22, 112, 113, 114, 115, 117, 136,

141, 147, 214, 217, 219, 220–1, 228, 256, 270, 284, 285, 286, 306, 320, 323, 346, 351, 354, 360, 361, 363
Cachao Dos 285
Cachimbos, Los 236, 299
Cachita 103, 104, 105, 131, 333
Cachondea 225
Cachumbele 171
Caciques, Los 71
Cada vez más 184
Caderona 336, 343
Cadete constitucional, El 117
Cafe Nostalgia, Orquesta 306
Cafetal, El 351
Caignet, Félix B. 156
Caini, Joe 183
Cairo, Pablo 277
"Caíto" (Carlos Manuel Díaz) 128, 182
caja china 39
cajón 25, 30, 247, 323, 343, 347, Calá, "Tony" (Francisco Antonio) 254
"Calabaza" (*rumbero*) 26
Calabaza, *see* Pérez, Gerardo
"Calaverita" 332
Calandria, La (Ernestina Reyes Pagán) 99
Calazán, José 182
Calazán Drake, José 25
Caldera 328
Calderón, José, *see* Cuba, Joe
Calderón, Modesto 186
Caldo y pescao 271
Cali Boys, Los 333
Cali, Sonora 333
Cali pachanguera 337
Califates, Los 81
California Salsa 297, 305, 363
Calixto (*timbalero*) 252
Call of the Jungle Birds 276
Callavas, Nicomedes 126
calle dolor, La 237
calle está durísima, La 225, 271, 354
Calle, Florencio 245, 246
Calle Luna calle Sol 272
Calle, Oscar 331, 364
Callejero, El 299
Callejón sin salida 280
Calloway, Blanche 172
Calloway, Cab 93, 95, 167–70, 191, 201
Calloway, John 324
Calvet, Óscar 73
Calvo, Pedro 248, 339
"Calvo, El" (Pedrito Díaz) 48
Calypso John 174
Calzada del Cerro 261, 362
Calzado, David 255
Calzado, Edy 211
Calzado, Rubén 124
Calzado, Rudy 117, 120, 129, 182, 228, 229, 232, 277, 319
Camacho, Conjunto 121
Camagüeyanos y habaneros 221
camaronera, la 57
cambiadera, la 311
Camero, Cándido, *see* Cándido
Camilo, Aramis 313
Camilo, Michel 252, 316–19, 364
Camina, Juan Pescao 273

Caminantes, Los 282
Campanitas de crystal 101, 103
Campeón (*conguero*) 127
Campeones 298
Campeones del Ritmo 129
Campo, Carlos 332
Campo, Pupi 175–6, 178, 181–2, 189, 204
Campo, Luis del 98
Campo Alegre 266
Campoamor, Orchestra 136
Can You Feel It 278
Caña Brava 340
Caña quemá 154
Canales, Angel 295
Canallón 340
Cañambu 252
Canario, Grupo 103
"Canario" (Manuel Jiménez) 101–2, 104, 106, 182, 184, 188, 235
"Cancañón" (Luis Mariano) 144, 354
canción 173, 213, 345
Canciones del solar de los aburridos 280, 294, 363
Candela 197, 340
Candela, La 275
Candela, Conjunto 282
Candelario (violinist) 121
Cándido (Cándido Camero) 121, 174, 180, 191, 198, 202–4, 226, 238, 270, 287
Cándido el billetero de 33 112
Cándido the Volcanic 361
Cándido with Tony Bennett at Carnegie Hall 238
Cándido's Comparsa 238
Candoli, Conde 203
Candoli, Pete 184
candombe 343
Candunga la China (Margarita Zequeira) 25
Candy Lips 95
Cané, Humberto 128, 191, 240, 332
Cané, Valentín 127
"Canelina" (dancer) 351
Canellias, Laura 289
"Caney" (Fernando Storch) 79, 87
Caney, Conjunto 151
Caney, Cuarteto 87, 106, 169, 180, 187, 189
Caney, Septeto 96
"Cangrejo" (baseball player) 124
Cangrejo fue a estudiar 124
Cano, Eddie 183–4, 186, 205
Cano, Humberto 190, 334
Cano, Pablo 140, 246
Canonge, Mario 248, 338, 364
Canta contrabajo 112, 360
Canta mi mozambique 288
Cantaloupe Island 240
Cantante, El (by Cheo Feliciano) 294
Cantante, El (by Héctor Lavoe) 292
Cantar maravilloso 246
Cantares del Abacuá, Los 16
canto 30
Canto a Changó 285

Canto abacuá 274
canto de puya 343
Cao cao maní picao 128, 156
Caper, Bobby 239
capetillo 240
Capó, Bobby (Félix Manuel Rodríguez) 180, 182, 188–9, 236, 285, 333
Capricious 240
Capriles, Renato 334
Capullito de alelí 103, 262
Capullito de azucena 335
Cara de payaso 217
Carabinas de Ases, Conjunto 126
Carabunta 174
Caracas, Sonora 128, 334–5
Caracusey, Sexteto 66
Carambola 174, 202
Caramelos (by Tito Puente) 217
Caramelos, Los 27
Caravan 200
Carballo, Mario 56, 212
Carbiá, Eddie 181
Carbó, Panchito 71
Carbó, Pedro 80
Carbó Menéndez, José 156
Carbonell, Juan 54
Carbonero, El 87, 127
Carcajada final 231
Carcassés, "Bobby" (Roberto) 152, 213, 255, 262, 264
Carcelera 103
Cárdenas, Ermenegildo 117
Cárdenas, Félix 21, 121
Cardona, Alejandro 332
Cardona, Milton 278–9, 284, 288, 315, 317–8
Cargas y descargas 226
Carmela 36
Caribbean Jazz Project 318
Caribe, Grupo 288
Caridad, Septeto 126
Carioca 202
Carlo de, Yvonne 177
Carlos, Antonio 226, 326
Carlos, Randy 183, 226
Carlos Manuel y su Clan 255
Carlota ta morí 146
Carmen de la Trinidad Torregrosa y Hernández, José del ("Omi Osainde") 13
Carmen y Rolando 198
Carmona, Armando 103
Carnaval 235, 313
Carnival of the Americas 218
Carolina mulata 56
Carpenter, Earl 136
Carpentier, Alejo 1, 19–20, 24, 27, 31–2, 41, 46, 54, 134, 331, 330, 366
Carr, Cass 167
Carrasco, Rafael 263
Carrero, Ana 176, 232
Carretero, el 78
Carriera Incharte, José Manuel, see El Chino
Carrillo, Álvaro 230
Carrillo, Ignacio 68, 212
Carrillo, Isolina 92, 110, 150, 152, 156

Carrillo, Luis 46, 71, 116, 130, 156
Carrión, Luisito 101
Carrión, Luisito 297
Carruseles, Sonora 337
Carta de Mamita 153
Carter, Benny 95, 189
Carter, Betty 263
Carter, Ron 277, 278
cartera, La 273
"Carusito" (Hernández Cuesta Florencio) 59
Caruso, Enrico 97
Carver, Wayman 95
Casa Blanca 200
Casanova, Héctor 275, 291
Casanova y Montuno 291
cáscara 28, 39, 288, 343
"Cascarita" (Orlando Guerra) 81, 151
Casiguaya, Sexteto 66
Casino, Gabriel 309
Casino, Charanga 284
Casino, Conjunto 126, 129–30, 151, 198, 211, 250, 361
Casino, Sexteto 129
Casino de la Playa, Orquesta 115, 117, 333, 361
Casino Nacional 80, 136, 184
Casino Nacional (orchestra of) 351
Casita criolla, La 19
Castellanos, Anael 253
Castellanos, Benjamín 33, 142
Castellanos, Eduardo 331
Castillo, Daniel 212
Castillo, Guillermo 55–6, 58
Castillo, José 50
Castillo, Manolo 53
Castillo, Pepe 282, 298
Castor, Jimmy 326
Castro, Ada 66
Castro, Alicia 66
Castro, André 81
Castro, Antonio 81
Castro, Argimira ("Millito") 66
Castro, Armando 185
Castro, Caridad 66
Castro, Concepción ("Cuchito") 66
Castro, Fidel 34, 109, 135, 142, 174, 208, 211, 244–5, 287, 305, 355–6
Castro, Héctor 183, 282
Castro, Manuel 81
Castro, Olga ("Bolito") 66
Castro, Ondina 66
Castro, Ramón 59, 159, 332
Castro, Ray 281
Castro, Xiomara 66
Catalina la O 273, 290
Catarsis 265
Caturla, Ramón 144
Cauto, Septeto 143
Cauto, Sexteto 187
Cayo Hueso y su victoria 115
Cayuco, El 179
Cazuelita, La 143
Cé magnifique 276, 293
Cecilia Valdés 19, 48
ceiba, La 337

Celina y Reutilio (Celina González and Reutilio Domingo Terrero) 14, 152, 153
cello 112, 286, 351
cencerro 39, 41, 199, 268
Centeño, Augusto 2
Centeño, Joe see Mambo Aces
Central Constancia 118
Ceora 292
Cepeda, Bonny 312–13
Cepeda (Family) 233
Cepeda, Rafael 279, 304, 360
Cepeda, William 319
Cerisier rose et pommier blanc 158
Cero codazos, cero cabezazos 116
Cerón, "Sandy" (Santiago) 313
Cerruto, Juan 255
Cervantes, Ignacio 72
Cervantes, Leopoldo 69
Cervantes, María 177
Césaire, Aimé 233
Césaire, Lano 340
Céspedes, "Bobi" (Gladys) 305
Céspedes, Conjunto 305
Céspedes, Guillermo 305
Céspedes, Luis 305
cha-cha 1, 3, 22, 29, 41, 98, 111, 115, 120, 132–3, 135, 138, 147, 158, 162–3, 179–80, 210, 216–17, 219, 223, 225, 22, 258, 262, 332, 344
Cha cha chá 119–20, 133–4, 137–8, 184, 210, 262, 344, 361
Cha Cha Cha Aces, The 165
Cha cha cha en Tropicana 132
Cha Cha Cha Rhythm Boys 184
Cha Cha Latino 219
Cha Cha Twist 215
chachá 13, 18, 120, 344
Chack-a-Ñuñu Boys 221
Chamaco Domíngues, Armando 332
Chamacos (Los) (Fumando marihuana) 69
Chambeleque 158
Chambelona, La 19
Champagne 221, 356
Champan Sport, Sexteto 130
Chan chan 153, 257
Chancullo 112, 217
Chanchullo, Quarteto 339
chandé 337
Chaney, Conjunto 303
Chango, Conjunto 227
Changó 9, 12–13, 17, 27, 126, 173, 195–6, 215, 226–7, 254, 285, 292, 300, 318, 364
Changó ta vení (or Changó va vení) 27, 173, 292
Changó te llama 318, 364
changüí 33–4, 41, 66, 212, 248, 250, 252, 283, 344–5
Changüí clave 250
Changüí de Guantánamo 33
"Changuito" (Quintana Fuerte, José Luis) 140, 248
Chano Pozo y su Orquestra 192
chaonda 249

Chappotín, Félix 56, 58, 86, 111, 125–6, 190–1, 211, 251–2, 275, 345, 361
Chappotín, José Ángel 280
Chappotín, Jesús Ángel 250
Chappotín, Vicente 86, 89
Chappotín y sus Estrellas, Conjunto 250
Chapuseaux, José Ernesto ("El Negrito") 309
Chaquis, Los 251
charanga 46, 69, 71–2, 91, 111–12, 114–17, 120, 126, 158, 171, 175, 181–3, 210, 212–16, 220, 223, 226–9, 238, 247, 249, 254–5, 266, 273, 282–6, 288–9, 303, 305–6, 323, 334, 338, 344, 352, 356, 358, 362–3
¡Charanga & Pachanga! 216
Charanga con bossa nova 226
Charanga Forever, La 255
charangón 226
Charlatán, El 234
Charlie Palmieri y Meñique – Con salsa y sabor 277
Charm of the Cha Cha Cha, The 184
Charo 97
Chattaway, Jay 275
Chauvin, Louis 78
"Chavy" (Javier Baro) 255
Chavy y los del Barrio 255
chaworó 13, 17, 344
Che Ché Abreu y sus Colosos 313
Che che colé 272
Che Guevara 213
Cheatham, Doc 174
Cheetah 269–70
"Chepín" (Rosell, Electo) 139
"Chepín" (Socarrás, José) 91
Chepín y su Orquesta Oriental 139
Chepín-Chóven 136, 139, 252, 256
cheré 17, 344
Cherokee 200
Chévere 169
cheveré 285
Chéveres de Belén, Los 111, 126
Chica mamey, La 248
Chicas de Nueva York, Las 313
Chicas del Can, las 312–3
Chicas del Sol, Las 252
Chico's cha cha cha 137–8
Chicos Buenos, Los 115
Chicos del Jazz, Los 354
"Chicho" (Clemente Piquero) 144, 195, 332
"Chiqui" 237
Childers, Buddy 184
Chifla, Arcaño 112
Chili con conga 93
Chilindrón de chivo 129
China en la rumba, La 65, 360
"Chino, El" (Carriera Incharte, José Manuel) 54–7, 60, 134, 175, 212
"Chino, El" (trumpeter) 175
"Chino, El" Cruz de Jesús 282

Chino Gueits y sus Alams Tropicales 221
Chino y su Conjunto Melao 281
Chino Li Wong, El 134
Chinos, Los 23
chiquichaca 210
Chiquitico (bongocero) 191
"Chiquito" (Socarrás, José Pereira) 91, 96, 98, 201
Chiquito loco 203
Chiquito montuno 201
Chirino, Willie 306
Chirrín chirrán 247
Chisme de la cuchara, El 246
Chismosa del solar, La 246
Chispa y Los Complices 255
Chivo que rompe tambó 80, 91
"Chocolate" (Alfonso, Félix) 199
"Chocolate", see Armenteros, Alfredo 185, 286
Chocolate y su conjunto 286
Chomate, Ana María 266
Chongolo 235
Chopin, Frédéric 201
Chorale for Brass, Piano and Bongo 202
"Chori, El" (Silvano Shueg Hechevarría) 54, 165
Chóven, Bernardo 139
Chóven, Orestes 252
chua-chua 332
"Chuíto de Bayamón" (Jesús Sánchez Erazo) 99
Chunko 183
Cieguito de Naguas, El 311
Cienfuegos, Sexteto 68
cierre 33, 344
"Ciminea", percussionist 332
cinquillo 18, 79, 344, 347
Cintura, La 211
Cipriano Armenteros 291
Ciro Rimac 292, 360
Cisneros, Ramón "Liviano" 127
Clark, Carola 100
Clark, June 85
Clark, Sonny 203
Clarke, Kenny 191, 193–4, 196, 205
Clásico, Conjunto 296, 281
Clasiqueando con Rubén 256
clave 1, 10, 16, 33, 37–9, 55, 172, 192, 215, 289, 303–4, 316, 340, 343–5, 347, 350, 358, 360, 362, 364
Clavé, Anselmo 36
Calve Oriental, La 61, 143
Clave Tres 322
Clave y Guaguanco, Conjunto de 246–7
claves 29, 34, 36, 40, 55, 57, 60, 65, 69, 72, 82, 91, 93, 103, 117, 130, 169–70, 174, 203, 212, 246, 250, 344
Clooney, Betty 181
Clooney, Rosemary 162
cleptómana (La) 50
Clouds 306
Club social de Marianao 115
Cobarde 278
Cobas, Pancho 257
Cobb, Jimmy 239

Cobham, Billy 274
Cocinando 227, 273–4
Coco y la fruta bomba, El 183
Coconut Pudding Vendor, The 90
cocoyé 18
Cocoyé, El 142
Coda 259
Coen, Augusto 2, 85–7, 92, 96, 106, 179, 188
Coen, Ray 179, 196
Cohen, Avishai 325
"Cojo, El" (Cruz, José Antonio) 112
"Cojo, El" (Díaz, José Antonio) 71
Colbert, Claudette 91
Cold Sweat 324
Cole, Cozy 168, 203
Cole, Nat "King" 15, 109, 137, 162, 199, 203, 275
Colé Colé 255
Coleman, Ornette 222
Coleman, Steve 246, 325
Colin, Sexteto 126
Collazo, Bobby 151, 154, 229
Collazo, Fernando 67, 69–71, 111, 131, 331
Collazo, Julio "Julito" 98, 179, 239, 302
Collazo, "Vaquero " 60
Colombia's Boogaloo 223
Colombianos, Los 25
"Colombié" 144
Colón, Frankie 179, 196
Colón, Johnny 223, 362
Colón, Louie 222
Colón, Santos 276, 287, 176, 179, 217
Colón, Willie 225, 236, 251, 267–8, 269, 270–2, 279, 280, 283, 290–1, 294, 335, 363
Colón Zayas, Edwin 304
Colonial, Conjunto 11, 19, 36, 98, 100, 129, 136, 330, 343, 356
"Colorao, El" (Eliseo Pozo Martínez) 112
Colorao y negro 281
Coltrane, John 259, 320
columbia 17, 28, 30–1, 38, 344, 346, 360, 362, 364, 368
Columbina, La 45
Combate, El 23
combo 81–2, 130, 139, 140, 176, 195, 204, 213, 215, 263–8
Combo de Ayer, El 298
Combo Gigante, El 277
Combo Samurai, El 266
Combo Show 311
Comedia, La 294, 299
Cómetelo to' 125, 192
Commitment 276
Como, Perry 162, 166
Como camina María 228
Como fue 142, 320, 340
Como se baila el Mozambique 211
Como se goza en el barrio 181
Como voy a sufrir 59, 61
Compadre Pedro Juan 306, 308
Compadres, los 60, 152–4, 250, 275, 290, 362
Compañeros 212

Compañía deBataclán Cubana 101
Companioni, Miguel 50–1, 84
comparsa 11, 19, 20, 44, 53, 64, 111, 190, 195, 198, 221, 223, 238, 247, 286, 318, 344, 358, 367
compas 135
"Compay Primo", see Hierrezuelo, Lorenzo 153
"Compay Segundo", see Repilado Muñoz, Francisco 110–11, 151, 153–4, 256–7, 362, 367
Compay Segundo y sus Muchachos 154
Componedores, Los 12
Comprador de botellas, El, see Botellero, El 48
Con alma 316
Con el diablo en el cuerpo 231
Con la comida no se juega 134
Con la lengua afuera 129
Con mi ritmo 212
Con poco coco 135, 140, 259
Con un poco de songo 363
Concepción, Belkis 313
Concepción, César 101, 182, 185, 188, 361
Concepts in Unity 284, 363
Concerto for Percussion 175
Concierto de Aranjuez 313
Concierto negro 263
Concierto para bongo 158, 361
Conde Rivera, Mariano 144
Conexión Latina Mambo 2000 325
Confesión 51
conga (ballroom dance) 3, 344
conga (carnival dance) 19, 20, 48, 92–3, 135, 345–6
conga (drum) 1, 10, 19–21, 25, 28, 30, 37, 39, 40–1, 45, 67, 98–100, 112–13, 121, 123–4, 128, 130–1, 136, 140, 144, 159, 165, 177, 179, 181, 183, 186, 190–9, 205, 214, 220, 223, 229, 234, 238, 240, 246, 248–9, 254, 268–9, 272, 275, 279, 281–2, 284, 290–3, 298, 304, 309, 317, 319, 321, 328, 338, 342, 344–7, 351–2
Conga (music) 17, 20, 47, 48, 91, 148, 158, 201, 211–12, 253, 262, 331–2
Conga 304
Conga Brava 200
Conga del año nuevo 93
Conga se fue, La 139
Conga viene ya, La 48
congo (music) 16–19, 27, 30, 32, 39, 63, 113, 121–3, 125, 142, 190, 195, 202, 211, 259, 293, 296–7, 307, 334, 338, 343–6
Congo conga, the 93, 167
Congo libre, el 23
Congo mulense 174
Congo valiente, el 202
Congos de Anguga, Los 25
conjunto 53, 67–8, 70, 80, 93, 99, 101, 103, 121, 124–30, 136, 143, 151–2, 154–5, 158,

169, 171, 175, 178–83, 185, 187, 191, 195, 198, 204, 209, 211–12, 221, 227, 229, 231–2, 234, 237, 240, 245–7, 250–2, 262, 267, 272, 278–9, 281–4, 286, 290, 292, 294, 295–7, 302–3, 305, 307, 310–11, 313, 333, 338, 344, 358
conjunto perico ripiao 307
Conquet, Johnny 309
Consejo, El 64
Conspiracion, La 302
Constantín, Eutimio 59
Consuélate como yo 27
Conte, Luis 324
Contigo besos salvajes 151
Contigo en la distancia 156
Continental, Orquesta 130
contradanza 22, 244
Contraste 194, 195
Contrera, Willie 313
Contreras, Orlando 71, 121
Contreras, Silvio 71–2 111, 139
Contreras, Tito 285–6
controversia 36, 99, 344
contunto 34
Convergencia 54, 127, 262
Conversación 301
Cooder, Ry 256
Cool Breeze 192
Cool Mambo 203
Cooper, Bob 184, 203
Copacabana 326
Copacabana Samba Band 178, 182
copla 100, 344
Copland, Aaron 1, 112
Corales, Los 266
Corazon, conjunto 281
Corazón de melón 156, 158, 162
Corazón rebelde 266
Corbacho, Domingo 24, 68, 135, 136, 144, 166
Corbacho, Rafael 125
Cordero, Lázaro 143
Cordero, "Slim" (Jules) 204, 271
Córdova, Junior 283
Corea, Chick 203, 239, 241
Cormán, Tomás 71, 110–11
cornetín chino 20, 344
coro 34, 55, 60, 100, 119, 127–8, 131, 141, 144, 154, 171, 212, 229, 234–5, 255, 269, 277, 280–1, 284, 289, 294, 296, 298, 311–12, 342, 344, 353–4
coro de clave 25, 29, 36, 60, 134, 235, 245, 344, 347
coro de guaguancó 29, 60, 347
Coro miyare 285
Corona, Juan 64
Corona, Manuel 52, 54, 56–7, 59, 74, 85
"Corozo" (Félix Rodríguez) 106
Corporación Latina, La 302
Corraleros de Majagual, Los 336–7
Correa, Isidro 139
Correa, Milton 237

Correa, William, *see* Willie Bobo
Correas, Alexis 265
corrido 101–2, 289, 304
Corso (venue) 270, 301, 327
Cortaron a Elena 100, 103
Cortázar, Julio 1, 214
corte suprema del arte, la 130, 143, 149–50
Cortés, Hernán 265
Cortés, José Luis ("El Tosco") 248, 254–5, 258, 261–3, 266
Cortés, Tito 333
Cortijo, Rafael 103, 216, 231, 233, 234–7, 281, 293, 298–9, 300–1, 311, 338, 340
Cortijo and His Time Machine 298
Cortijo en New York 235
Cortijo y Kako, ritmos y cantos callejeros 235
Cortijo y su Bonche 235
Cortijo y su Combo 234
Cosa nuestra 272, 291
Cosas del alma 152, 156, 277
Cosas del compay Antón 53
Cosby, Bill 165, 320
Cosmopolita, Orquesta 130, 134, 187, 351
Costa Brava, Orquesta 302
Costa de Cuba, La 325
Costanzo, Jack 162, 184, 202–3
Costello, Diosa 176
Costello, Elvis 295
Cotán (Angel Octavio) 262
Cotán, Grupo 262
Cotton Club Parade 95
Count Basie Meets James Bond 239
Covarrubias, Miguel 94
CP 323
Cranshaw, Bob 238
Crazeology 166
Creme de Vie, La 50
Crespo, Elvis 313
Crime Pays 272
criolla 19, 34, 36, 49, 56, 59, 103, 116, 251
Criolla carabalí 56, 251
Criollo 280
Criollo, Quinteto 360
Criollo, Trio 88
Crispín, Wilfredo 327
Cristal, Pancho 294
Cristina, Jessica 313
Crosby, Bob 166
Crossroads 317
Crusaders, The 323
Cruz, Adam 320–1
Cruz, Alberto, *see* Pancho El Bravo
Cruz, Bobby 225, 271, 302, 336
Cruz, Celia 5, 21, 72–3, 109–10, 127–8, 142, 149–51, 156, 158, 195, 198, 208, 222, 229, 231–2, 248, 266–8, 270, 273, 276, 279, 286, 288, 290–1, 297, 304, 332, 334–5, 340
Cruz, Antonio "Cheché" de la 130
Cruz, Chencho 24
Cruz, Félix 23

Cruz, José Antonio, *see* Cojo, El 112
Cruz, Juan Ignacio de la 60
Cruz, Lázaro 263
Cruz, Miguel 117, 121, 234, 237
Cruz, Millito 87
Cruz, Primi 300
Cruz, Ramoncito 311
cruz de palo bonito, la 310
Cu-ba 203
cuabero, El 311
Cuando calienta el sol 156
Cuando canta el cornetín 139
Cuando las mujeres quieren a los hombres 103, 184
Cuando salí de Cuba 232
Cuando tu desengaño veas 60
Cuando tú llegues a entender 210
Cuarto Espacic 262
cuatro 42, 99, 101, 103, 106, 182, 233, 241, 269, 273–3, 281–2, 304, 318, 322, 344
Cuatro, Charanga de la 284
Cuatro Ases, Los 233
Cuba, Cuaeteto 51
Cuba, Joe (José Calderón) 42, 204, 219, 223–4, 227, 270, 288, 294, 352–4
Cuba Mambo 248
Cuba mía 72
Cuba mi patria querida 35
Cuba Mozambique 211
Cuba, Orquesta 76
Cuba, Septeto 68, 71
Cuba, Sexteto 130
Cuban Boys de Amado Trinidad, La 134
Cuban Blues 202–3
Cuban Boogie 162
Cuban Carnival 179
Cuban Carnival Bongo Mambo 162
Cuban Episode 202–3
Cuban Fantasy 320
Cuban Fire 202–3
Cuban Jazz 140, 238
Cuban Jazz Band 79
Cuban Mambo 177
Cuban Nightmare 168
Cuban Overture 62
"Cuban Pete", Pedro Aguilar 165, 173
Cuban Pete 128, 176
Cuban Pipers 152
Cuban Twilight 162
Cubana, La 35
Cubana, Sonora 128
Cubana Be Cubana Bop 192–3
Cubana de Musica Moderna, Orquesta 259
Cubanacan 95, 153, 249
Cubaney, La 158
Cubanismo 264
Cubano, Quinteto 259, 339
Cubano, Sexteto 130
Cubano Chant 199, 203
Cubano de Jazz, Grupo 215
Cubano de Jazz, Quinteto 259
Cubano soy 134
Cubanola 78, 80, 90, 319
Cubanos Postizos, Los 364

Cubarama 177
Cuber, Ron 315
Cubismo 340
cubop 3, 168, 171, 238, 344
Cubop 174, 203
Cubop City 172, 339
Cubop Holiday 203
Cuboppers 203
Cucalá 228, 290
Cucaracha, La 91
Cuchifritos 225
Cuellar, Justo 75
Cuenta bien, cuenta bien 271
Cuervo, Armando 261
Cuervo de la Noche, Orquesta 101
cuesta de la fama, La 300
Cueto, Rafael 65, 143
Cueva, Julio 17, 81, 91, 121, 13–5, 150–1, 171, 204, 331, 361
Cuevas, Sal 275, 315, 318
Cugat, "Xavier" (Francisco de Asis Javier) 86, 90, 92–4, 97–8, 167, 169, 175–7, 180, 182, 186–9, 224, 229, 310, 324, 333, 325, 360
Cuidadito compay gallo 53
Culebra, La 266
Culbert, Eddie 334
culo e puya 339
Cultier, Marius 340
Cumaco de San Juan, El 310
Cumbancha, La 12
Cumbanchero, El 103, 105
cumbia 5, 233, 248, 266, 268, 299, 312, 323, 333, 336, 337, 344
Cumbia típica 317,
Cumbre, Orquesta 253
Cumparsa, La 186
cuñá 99
Cuna, La 278, 345, 347, 361
Cuní, Miguelito (Miguel Cunill) 110, 115, 124, 126–7, 144, 219, 249, 250, 253, 333
Curbelito (trumpeter) 175
Curbelo, Célido 81, 136, 166
Curbelo, Fausto 310
Curbelo, José 21, 95, 98, 132, 170, 175–6, 178, 180, 189, 199, 278, 361
Curet Alonso, "Tite" (Catalino) 231, 273–4, 280, 285, 289, 292–3, 298, 300–1
Curiel, Gonzalo 133
Curtis, King 162
Cutín (Rodolfo Resemar) 306
cymbal 117, 248, 355

D'León, Oscar (D'León Somoza, Oscar Emilio) 245, 278, 288, 298, 335–6, 364
D'Rivera, "Paquito" (Francisco) 90, 214, 251, 259, 260–2, 286–7, 316–20, 354, 364
Da Costa, Paulinho 286, 336
Daiquiri 336
Dale jamón a la jeva 4
Dalto, Jorge 284, 295, 316–19
Daly, Antar 161, 170, 286
Dame un cachito pa' huele 124, 328

Damendi, Mariano 159
Dameron, Tadd 193, 199
Damirón, "Simó" (Francisco) 309, 334, 363
Dan Den 245, 255–6
Dance Mania 179, 361
Dance On 98, 320
Dancemania 80 276
Dance of the Head Hunters 276
Dancing and Dreaming 361
Dandies, Los 185, 272
Dandies del, Los 185
Dandys de Belen, Los 190, 247
Danger, Sergio 33
Dante, Frankie 282
danza 49, 92, 99, 103, 298, 344–5, 366, 369,
Danza de los Náñigos 47
danzón 23–4, 32, 49, 54, 58, 68–9, 71–2, 76, 79, 85, 99, 104, 110–15, 117–18, 121, 124, 134–5, 139, 155, 158, 187, 210, 214–5, 229, 249, 256, 259, 262, 273, 279, 285–6
Danzón bugaloo 226
Danzón cubano 113
danzón de María Cervantes, El 177
Danzón Legrand 249
Danzonera America 329
Danzonera de Prieto y Dimas 329
danzonete 72–3, 120, 248, 257, 344, 351
danzonete, El 368
Daphnis et Chloé 202
Dark Eyes 177, 200
dark latin groove 327
Darnell, August 326–7
Davidson, Eduardo 346, 210–11
Dávila, "Chivirico" (Rafael) 295
Dávila, "Paquito" (Frank) 170
Davilita (Dávila Pedro Ortiz) 86, 91, 96, 103, 106, 289, 297, 360
Davis, Eddie ("Lockjaws") 238, 362
Davis, Miles 130, 163, 203, 238, 241, 259, 302, 325
Davis, Jr., Sammy 165
Davis, Jr., Walter 262
Dawn 317
DeJohnette, Jack 263
De Paris, Wilbur 85
De cara al viento 304
de la cuatro, chraranga 284
De mi Cubita es el mango 51
De nuevo Los Compadres 275
De Panamá a Nueva York 294
De ti depende 291
De todo un poco 284
Debriano, Santi 321
Debussy, Claude 1, 115, 342
Decupuy 86
Dedeu, Amado Jesús 247
Dee Nasty 257
Deep Purple 350
Deep River Boys 96
Déjala caer contra el suelo, see Múcura, La

Déjame tranquilo 127
Del Caribe al Brasil, voces y tambores 304, 363
Del Chocó pa'l Congo 337
Del Monte, Emilio 210
Del Sol, Orquesta 340
Delfín, Eusebio 52–3, 65
Delfín, Francisco 310
Delgado, Fausto 103
Delgado, Issac 3, 245, 252–5, 264, 266, 287, 303, 362
Delgado, "Pepe" (José) 129, 155–6, 305
Delia 73
Delicate and Jumpy 276
Delirio, see Tú mi delirio
Delirio, el 22
Delita 91, 331
Demasiado Caliente 205
Demonio de la negra, El 23
dengue 161, 228
Dengue 228
Dengue, El 24, 161
Dengue en fa 161
Dengue y su tiqui tiqui, El 161
Departure, The 320
Depestre, Filiberto 116, 121, 210
Derroche de felicidad 187
Desafinado 226
desafío 269, 300, 344
descarga 141, 214, 223, 260, 270, 274, 286, 302, 310, 344
Descarga 337, 366
Descarga Boricua 302, 363
Descarga Cachao 219
Descarga número dos 138
Descarga número uno 138
Descoyuntado 26
Desde que tú me quieres 106
Desde Puerto Rico A Nueva York 297
Desengaño 300
Desintegrando 134
Desnos, Robert 1, 330
Despedida 106
despelote 254, 344
Destiné, Jean-Léon 285
Desvelo de amor 91
Devita, Francisco 294
di Giusto, Geraldo 339
día que me quieras, El 278
diablo 121, 344
Diablo, El (by Chapotín) 127
Diablo, El (by Willie Colón) 280
Diablo, Sexteto 305
"Diablo Wilson", El (García Wilson, Herminio) 33, 35, 76
Diago, Virgilio 71, 111
Diallo, Medioune 338
Diana 29, 344
Díaz, Aneudi 313
Díaz, "Angá" (Miguel Aurelio) 251, 257, 263–4, 325, 339
Díaz, Angel 155
Díaz, Aniceto 68, 72–3, 80, 166, 248
Díaz, "Caíto" (Carlos Manuel) 128, 284–5, 290
Díaz, Carlos 130
Díaz, Felipe 224, 238
Díaz, Fernando 112

Díaz, Gregorio 246
Díaz, Hernán, Jr. 161
Díaz, Ismael 131
Díaz, José 59
Díaz, José Antonio, see, Cojo, El
Díaz, Juan Manuel 68
Díaz, Margarita 334
Díaz, Mengol 103
Díaz, Piper "Pimienta" (Edulfamit, Molina) 336
Díaz, Phil 271
Díaz, Raul 68, 121
Díaz, Rigoberto 71, 124
Díaz, Servando 152
Díaz, Simón 21, 306
Díaz, Ulpiano 68, 112, 117, 211
Díaz Ayala, Cristóbal 366
Díaz Soler, Carmelo 186
Dibala, Diblo 314
Dibango Manu 334
Dícelo Patato 285
Dickerson, RQ. 167
Diestro, Aida 151–2, 156
Diez, "Barbarito" (Idilio Bárbaro) 30, 68, 70–1, 101, 145, 153, 361
Digging the Most 225
Dimas (Torres Amado Pérez) 330
Dime la verdad 171
Dimension Latina, La 298
Dimond, "Markolino" (Mark) 282, 295
Dinamita, Sonora 336
Dionisio 26
Dios Alfonso, Juan de 23
Dios chino, El 24
Disappearance 202
disco 253, 278, 281, 284, 326–7, 360, 364
Distinto y diferente 290, 363
Dizzy Gillespie & Arturo Sandoval: To a Finland Station 261
Do the Boogaloo 224
Do Their Thing 228
Doble energía 291
Doble inconsciencia 52
Docurro, Manolito 262
Doin' the Rhumba 168
Dolin, Max 79
Dolor cobarde 131
Dolor de ausencia 187
Dolor y perdón 145
Dolphy, Eric 238
Domecq, Celestino 30
Domingo Pantoja 179
Domínguez, Alberto 51, 332
Domínguez, Frank 139–40, 156, 209
Dominicana, Orquesta 309
Dominicano, Grupo 93, 308
Domino, Fats 223
Don Antobal 187
Don Felo (Felipe Rosario Goyco) 103
Don Goyo 298
Don Nacho (Ignacio, Guerrero Noble) 101, 186
Don Pedrito 281
Doña Olga 118
Donato, João 228, 239

Donay, Millie 173
¿Dónde estabas anoche? 60, 218
¿Dónde va Chichi? 127
Donna Lee 172–3, 279
Don't Forget 224
Don't Misunderstand 283
Dorcas, Ramón 66, 332
Dorham, Kenny 203
Dorotea la parrandera 106
Doroteo (singer) 175, 188
Dorsey, Jimmy 93, 166, 175, 176, 352
Dorsey, Tommy 137, 166, 175, 349, 352
Dos campeones 193
Dos gardenias 156, 188, 256
dos lados de la Típica 73, Los 275
Dos lindas rosas 51
Dos Mosqueteros, Los 284
Dr Buzzard's Original Savannah Band 326
Drake, Joseíto 25
Dream, The 78
Dreke, Gonzalo 30
Dreke, José 30
Dreke, Mario "Chabalonga" 246
Drennon, Eddie 284
Drifters, The 222
Droga milagrosa, La 65
Drum Poem 274
drum set 95, 208, 355
Drume negrita 48, 149, 204, 240, 259, 318
Drumi mobila 146, 148
Duany, Roberto 139
Duarte, Ernesto 144, 149–50, 230, 264, 340
Duboney, Orquesta 229
Duchesne, Carlos 191
Duchesne, Mickey 237
Duchesne, Rafael 186
Dueto Antillano, *see* **Dueto Fantasma**
Dueto Fantasma 144
Dulce Arturo ("Alambre") 127
Dulce con dulce 290
Dulces besos 103
Dulfo, Armando 154
Dulzaides, Felipe 139–40, 214, 231, 248, 259, 306, 355
Dumont, Mario 87, 101
Dunbar, Huey 327
Dunham, Katherine 150, 162, 182, 199
Dupuy, Berta 156
Durán, Chino 127
Durán, Hilario 212, 261
Durán, Modesto 159, 196, 203, 323, 332
Durán, "Ray" (Horacio) 96
Durán, Roberto 293
Duvivier, George 161, 240

Early in the Morning 203
Earth Wind and Fire 326
Easy Does It 177, 315
Ebó 171
Echale candela 56, 360
Echale limón 254
Echale salsita 4, 61–2, 318
Echame a mí la culpa 153

Echando pa'lante 220
Echemendía, Ricardo 262
Ecos de Cuba, Los 87
Ecué – ritmos cubanos 285, 323
Eddie Carbià y sus Mamboleros 181
Eddie Palmieri – Bárbaro 136, 188, 199, 219–222, 226, 228–9, 232, 236, 241, 267, 270–1, 276–9, 284, 291, 299, 304, 315–6, 321–2, 339, 354, 362–3
Eden de Los Roncos, El 60
Eden Habanero 71
Edgehill, Guillermo 141
Edison, Harry ("Sweets") 16, 41, 46, 90
Edreira, René 50
Eduardo (bass player) 15, 30, 40, 46, 50, 62, 75, 109, 129–30, 155, 158, 169, 177, 181, 188
efí 11, 32, 101, 176
Efí Abarakó 32, 101, 201
efó 15, 344
ekwé 16, 344
"El Boy" (Juan, Torres) 92
El Cerro tiene la llave 66
El diablo es mi mujer 41
El Gran Combo – Acángana 115, 120–2, 152–6, 185
El que más goza 60, 94
El que no sufre no vive 122
El que quiera ser hombre 158
El que se fue 113
El que siembra su maíz 35–7, 171
El Saieh, Issa 71
electric bass 24, 64, 109–10, 127–9
Elegante, Orquesta 39
Elegía a Benny Moré 81
Eleggua Open Way 173
Eleguá 111, 120, 135
Eliseo, Alfonso 73
Ella fue 141
Ella y yo 30
Ellade Osún 31
Ellington, Duke 44, 46–7, 51, 86, 88, 90, 96, 100, 103–5, 165
Elliott, Don 103
Ellis, Willie 146
Elman, Mischa 52
Elpidio y Margot 58, 62
Emanon 100
Embale, Carlos 68, 81, 110, 123, 127
Embele iruke 135
Embrujo Antillano 171
Emilio Dolores 94
Emilio Morales, Carlos 134
Emisora Fuentes, Orquesta 170
Empaliza, La 158
En aquellos tiempos 155, 185
En Bayamón 153
En el sendero de mi vida 31
En falso 39

En lloro mi nankwe 12
En mi viejo San Juan 98, 149
En Sabana Grande 158
Encantado de la vida 76
Encarnación, José
  ("Chegüito") 165
Engañadora, La 63, 128
Enríquez, Reinaldo 71
Enriquito (tailleur) 62
Enrizo, Nené 29, 33, 38
Enrizo, Sungo 29, 33, 38
Ensemble 305, 315
Ensueno 30, 37
Entre este mundo y Dios 154
Entre la espada y la pared 152
Entre mares y arenas 29
Entre preciosos palmares 34
Entre tinieblas 33
Envidia 97
Erdös, Laurent 148
Errante y bohemio 173
Eres feliz 154
Erick 152
Eriza, Tomás 34
Ernsley, Ernest "Ernie" 112
Es tu boca 27, 36, 98
Esa prieta 149
Esas no son cubanas 34
Escalante, Leopoldo 111
Escalante, Luis 72, 111, 134
Escalante, Pucho 111
Escalona, Danilo "Phidias" 6
Escape from Havana 167
Escenas 151
Escoba barrendera, La 141
Escollíes, Antonio "El Cojito"
  50, 88
Escoto, Bobby 94–5
Escovedo, Coke 305, 327
Escovedo, Pete 305, 328
Escovedo, Phil 156, 305
Escovedo, Sheila, see Sheila E
Escucha mi pregón 22
Escudero, Rafael 46
Ese sentimiento se llama amor
  81
Esencia del guaguancó, La 149,
  154
Eskenazi, Dario 163
Esmeralda, Conjunto 97
Eso Es Latin Jazz... Man 123
Espabílate 28, 32, 67
Espí, Roberto 68
Espínola, Juan Bautista 158
Espinosa, Fabio 172
Espinosa, Rolando 58
Esquijarrosa, Chuchú 62, 74
Esquinas son, Las 151
Essiet, Essiet 164
Esta bomba es diferente 139
Está frizao 97
Esta niña quiere un novio 159
Esta noche tocó perder 33
Este barrigón no es mío 160
Este negro sí es sabroso 149
Este número no existe 153
Estado de Animo 255
Estebán, José 313
Estebán Fonseca, Carlos 302
Estefán, Emilio 290
Estefán, Gloria (Fajado, Gloria)
  306, 320, 363
Estela 55, 89, 109, 110, 124,
  166, 334

Estela y Rolando 109
Esteves, José, see Loco, Joe
Estivil, Osvaldo 130, 133
Estoy hecho tierra 53
Estrada Brothers (Rubén
  and Henry) 322
Estrada, Ernesto, see Fruko
Estrada Palma, Tomás 44
Estrella Italiana, La 50
Estrellas Boricuas 87
Estrellas Caiman 318
Estrellas Cubanas 67, 211
Estrellas de Areito 251
Estrellas de Charanga 249
Estrellas de Chocolate 127,
  226
Estrellas de Pogolotti 169
Estrellas del Ritmo 121, 125
Estrellas del Sol Naciente
  340
Estrellas Habaneras, Sexteto
  68, 89
Estremera, Carlos, Enrique
  "Cano" 301
estudiantinas 50
Eugenio (singer) 128, 130
Eva 258
Evans, Bill 240, 259, 342
Evans, James 217
Evaristo (bongocero) 89
evidence 317
Excitante Lupe con el maestro
  Tito Puente, La 289
Experimentación Sonora del
  I.C.A.I.C., Grupo de 213
Explorando 298
Exploration 278
Eyes of the Beholder, The 278

Fabré, Cándido 266, 363
Fabulous and Fantastic 300
Facenda, Feliciano 71
Facenda, Sexteto 61, 68, 76
Faddis, Jon 324
Faez Sisters 258
Failde, Cándido 23
Failde, Eduardo 23
Failde, Miguel 25
Faisán 281
Fajardo, Alberto 117
Fajardo, José 49, 54, 115, 117,
  121, 141, 208, 211, 214, 216,
  219, 228–9, 270, 275, 282,
  288, 306, 319, 354, 361
Fall, Pepe 338
Fallá, Manuel (de) 1
Falsaria 237
Familia Andres, La 313
Familia Valera Miranda, La
  252
Fania 226–7
Fania All Stars 226, 294, 312,
  338
Fania All Stars at the Red
  Garter 226, 269, 275
"Fanta" (Rafael Fantauzzi) 106
Fantástican, La 46, 110, 169
Fantasía Africana 284
Fantasma, Dueto 144
Fantasmas 280
Farmer, Art 198, 240
Farrés, Osvaldo 156
Farruquiña 139
Fascinación, Grupo 281, 296

Fattorusso, Francisco 322
Fattorusso, Hugo 322
Fattorusso, Osvaldo 322
Favelo (trumpeter) 91
Faz, Conjunto 129
Faz, Pascual 130
Faz, Roberto 112, 129, 161,
  198, 211, 262
Fé, Alfredo de la 275, 282, 285,
  287, 315–6, 339, 342
Federico, Carlos 324
Federico y su Combo 336
Fefita 24, 116
Feliciano, José "Cheo" 83, 204,
  221–2, 224–5, 245, 267–8,
  273, 276, 278, 288, 290–4,
  299, 304
Feliciano, Edwin 302
Felicidad, Orquesta 293
Felipe Blanco 48
Feliú, Pedro 152
Félix, Álvaro 92
Félix, Mario 265
Feliz cumbé 313
Feliz Navidad 292
Fell's Boys 331
Felles, Juan 249
Fellové, Francisco 115, 156,
  182, 221, 332, 335
Fellové, Guillermo 123, 125,
  129, 136, 338, 340,
Ferguson, Maynard 161, 214
Fernandel 357
Fernández, Dionis 313
Fernández, Frank 252
Fernández, Gonzalo 120, 275,
  284–5, 334
Fernández, Joseíto 76–7, 117
Fernández, Juan 332
Fernández, Julio 257
Fernández, Leopoldo, see
  Pototo y Filomeno
Fernández, Papatín 311
Fernández, Quilvio 312
Fernández, Ruth 101
Ferrer, Claudio 87, 103, 106,
  115, 319, 320–1, 325, 364
Ferrer, Ibrahím 31, 210, 256,
  362
Ferrín, Esperanza 257
Ferrín, Mercedes 257
Ferro, Ricardo 129
festejo 284
Festival in Cuba 192
Fiesta 27, 65, 72, 110, 174, 196,
  200, 202, 235, 274, 297, 361
Fiesta abacuá 196
Fiesta boricua 235
Fiesta Time 202
Figaro, Sexteto 143
Figueroa, Eric 302–3
Figueroa, Frankie 176, 300,
  303
filin 48, 75, 140, 142, 150,
  154–6, 198, 212–3, 345
Fiol, Henry 281
Fireworks 277, 363
Fischer, Clare 193, 322–3, 364
Fisk, Charlie 309
Fisk Orchestra 309
Fitzgerald, Ella 167, 184, 194,
  201
Flamboyan, La 111, 198, 228,
  278, 339

Flauta mágica 39, 141
"Flor de Amor" (Agustín Pina)
  26
Flor De Cuba, La 23
"Florecita" (Enrique Velazco)
  55, 68, 126–7, 154, 159, 286,
  332–3, 358
floreo 307
Flores, Luis "Máquina" 183
Flores, Payo 87, 106
Flores, Pedro 106, 187–8, 277,
  360
Flores, Richie 278, 339
Flores, Cuarteto 188, 295
Flores, Septeto 278
Flores, Sexteto 106
Flores negras 72
Flores para tu altar 14
Flórez, Julio 75
Floriano, José 129
Floricelda Sisters 258
Floro y Miguel (Floro Zorrilla
  and Miguel Zaballa) 50, 85
flute 51, 66, 68–9, 72, 82, 94–5,
  106, 111–13, 117, 121, 136,
  166, 169, 174, 176–7, 181,
  195, 201, 205, 221, 228–9,
  239
Flynn, Frank Emilio 150, 155,
  204, 214, 258
Fogaraté 214
Fongo Sunk 324
Font, Rafael 86, 183
Ford, Joe 317
Forever 75, 255, 271
Forman, James 193
Formell, Juan 212, 247–8, 252,
  266, 275
Formell, Juan Carlos 266
Forrest, Jimmy 162
Forrester, Eddie 183
Fort Apache Band 317
Forty Years of Cuban Jam
  Session 286
Foster, Frank 201
Four Cuban Diamonds 199
Foyo, Guillermina 66
Franca, Miguel 144
Franceschi, Alfredo "Cutuflá"
  66
Franceschini, Bobby 321
Franco, Carmita 66
Franco and his son O.K. Jazz
  334
Frank Emilio presenta a Frank
  Emilio 258
Franzetti, Carlos 317
Fraxas, Carlos 133
"Freddy" (Fredesvinda García
  Herrera) 150
Freelance 168, 183, 277, 338
Freeman, Chico 325
Freezelandia 173
Frenesí 332
Frenzy 84, 165, 173–4
Friday Morning 320
Frómeta Pereyra, Luis María,
  see Billo
Frontela, Florentino 331
Frías, Lino 128
Fruko (Estrada Rincón, Julio
  Ernesto) 217
"Fruko" El Magnífico 337
Fruko y sus Tesos 336, 364

Fruta bomba, La 183, 337
Frutas del caney 36, 156
Fuego cubano 202
Fuentes, Antonio 337
Fuentes, Laureano 32
Fuera de este mundo 283
Fuerza positiva 305
"Fuico" (Mesan Juan) 246
Fulanito 314
Fuller, Curtis 174
Fuller, Walter "Gil" 199, 202
Funcionario, El 312
Fundora, Melquiades 120
Funky Jíbaro 287
Furé, Manolo 212
fusilamiento 312, 314
fusion 278, 280, 283, 287, 306, 319, 323–4, 326, 344
Future 56, 167, 245, 298

Gadd, Steve 277
Gaillard, Slim 195
gaita 336
Galárraga, Marta 340
Galdo, Joe 328
Galé, Diego 337
Gale, Eric 275
Galé, Grupo 337
Galíndez, Polito 87
Galindo, Aramis 252
Gallardo, José 317
"Galleguito" El, *see* José Parapar 50
Gallo espuelérico, El 186
Galzavo, Sergio 117
Gandinga 186, 214, 317
Garabateo 55
Garay, Guarionex 74
Garay, Gumersindo "Sindo" 70, 74–5, 148, 155
Garciá, Ana 152
García, Andy 286
García, Armando 265
García, Ramon "Chichín" 310
García, Juan José "Chiquitín" 106
García, Davel 296
García, Elmo 183
García, Enrique (guitarist) 68, 308
García, Enrique (singer) 93
García, Fabián 120, 354
García, Fausto 140
García, Henry 311
García, Hugo 79
García, Justa 154
García, Luis 302
García, Miguelito 56, 59, 80
García, Mike 226
García Juan Francisco "Pancho" 308
García, Orestes 286
García, Quique 87
García, Rogelio 169
García, Tom 180
Garcia, Trio 152, 171
García Andino, Julio, *see* Andino, Julio
García Caturla, Alejandro 25, 47, 82, 152, 210
García Caturla, Teresa 152, 210
García Chovén, Bernardo 139
García López, Roberto 265
García Marquez, Gabriel 295

García Menocal, Mario 12, 19–20, 44
García Wilson, Herminio "El Diablo" 33
Gardel, Carlos 331
Garner, Erroll 199, 203, 361
Gasca, Luis 161, 324
Gavilán (marimbulero) 115, 128, 258, 366
Gay, Louis 158
Gaynor, Gloria 290
Gela 51, 59
Gele amada 52
Gele Hermosa 52
Gema, Trio 237, 256
Gemelos, Los 337
Generalisimo Trujillo, Orquesta 229, 308–11, 334
Gente del Bronx, La 181
Gentle Rain 226
Genuinos, Los 312
George, Sergio 287, 296
Gerardo (disc jockey) 327
Germania 74
Gershwin, George 1, 62, 342
Getz, Stan 130, 195
Ghana-e 273
Giant Steps 259, 316, 323
Gigante del sur, El 298
Gigante del teclado, El 277
Gil, Blanca Rosa 156
Gilbert, Dave 162
Gilberto, João 239
Gillespie, Birks, John "Dizzy" 94, 96, 145, 157, 162–3, 165, 167–8, 170, 172, 177, 190–9, 202, 224, 227, 239–40, 245, 261–2, 276, 284, 286, 304, 315, 318–20, 232–5, 327, 348–9, 353, 361, 364, 366–7
Ginés, Micaela 32
Giraldo 136
Giro, Radamés 114, 209, 366
Gitler, Norman 183
Give Us a Chance 271, 354
Globero, El 60
glockenspiel 101
Gloria a Maceo 135
Gloria Cubana 126
Gloria Cubana, Sexteto 68
Gloria eres tú, La 155, 172, 179, 187
Gloria Habanera, Conjunto 198
Gloria Latina 251
Gloria Matancera, Conjunto 68, 127
Glorias de Cuba 127
Goberna, Ismael 127
Godínez, Carlos 54–6
Godinez, Orquesta 56, 127
Godinez, Trio 75
gogochá 249
Goin' conga 93
Gola, Andy 255
Golden, Gene 284–5, 288, 324
Golden Casino Orchestra 86–7
Goldkette, Jean 166
Goldman, Pierre 338
Gollin, Brett 324
Golpe de Bibijagua 134
Gómez, Celso 144
Gómez, Eddie 318, 342

Gómez, Edsel 320
Gómez, Graciano 56, 68, 70, 101, 251
Gómez, José Miguel 11, 19–20, 33, 44
Gómez, Mauro 144
Gómez, Máximo 113
Gómez, Pastor 71
Gómez, Humberto Luis "Tito" 133, 294–5
Gómez, Tito (José Antonio Terreiro) 120, 130, 133, 135, 179, 274
Gone City 174
González, Alfredo 86
González, Andy 278–9, 315, 319
Gonzalez, Babs 201, 203
González, Berto 130
González, Carlos 249
González, Celina, *see* **Celina y Reutilio**
González, Celio 121, 127, 151, 188, 285, 332
González, Chino 180
González, Dagoberto 249
González, Félix 68
González, Felipe 24
González, Francisco 60, 91
González, Iván Melón 264, 288
González, Jaime 189
González, Jerry 284–5, 316, 324–5, 364
González, Jesús 133, 144, 251
González, Joe 250, 319
González, Junior 273, 295
González, Manuel "Manolito" 225, 304
González, Marino 68
González, Nelson 275, 379, 285–6
González, "Neno" Luis 71–2, 117
González, Radamés 252
González, René 116, 120
González, Rubén (pianist) 124, 215, 249, 256, 334, 362
González, Rubén (vocalist) 121, 180, 250, 256, 334, 362
González Mántici, Enrique 132, 138, 149
González Peña, Rafael 185
González Rubalcaba, Guillermo 247, 249
González Rubalcaba, Jacobo 24
González Rubiera, Vicente, see Guyún
González Solares, Francisco 60
Gonzalo, Miguel de 154
Good Bait 192–3
Goodman, Benny 137, 166, 198, 202, 240, 349
Gorbea, Wayne 282
Gordon, Dexter 172, 177, 201, 258, 316
Gota de llanto 184
Gottlieb, Raymond 331
Gottchalk Moreau, Louis 2, 89, 360
Govín, Julio 68, 127
Govín, Pablo, see Bubú

Govín, Raimundo 128
Gracianos, Los 70
Gracias 287, 363
Graciela, *see* Pérez, Graciela
Graham, Bill 193
Graham, Kenny 334
Gran Combo, El 223, 233, 235, 237–8, 297, 301–4, 316, 363
Gran Combo De Ayer, El 193
Gran Combo en nuestro aniversario, El 298
Gran rumba, La 25
Gran tirana (La) 301
Granda, Bienvenido 59, 106, 127, 333, 361, 142, 151
Grandes Kimbos con Adalberto Santiago, Los 281
Grant, Roger 239
Granz, Norman 140, 163, 172–4, 180, 194, 202
grasimá 99
Grasse, Silvia de 309
Grau, Esteban 129
Gray, Glen 166
Greco, Buddy 202
Greco, José Manuel 254, 265
Great Themes Go Latin, The 183
Green Eyes, see Aquellos ojos verdes 50, 51, 91, 93–4, 166
Green, Grant 240
Griffin, Johnny 174
Grillo, Frank "Machito" 3, 17, 41, 56, 59, 89, 166
Grillo, Hilda 169
Grillo, Mario 19–20, 277, 281
Grillo, Paula 277
Grillo, Rogelio 168–9
Grillo Gutiérrez, Frank, *see* Machito
Grillón, Orquesta 88
Griñán, Lilí (Luis Martínez) 124–6, 136, 182
Gris, Orquesta 71, 111, 131
Groovetime 232
Gryce, Gigi 201
Guabina, La 20–1
Guachiguara 190, 241
Guachinando 126
guachipupa 210
Guaco 334, 336
guagua (idiophone) 29, 345
guagua (rhythm) 29, 345
guaguancó 28–9
Guaguancó 28–9
Guaguanco, Conjunto 24–6, 247, 362
Guaguancó a todos los barrios 126, 226
Guaguancó callejero 136
Guaguancó coro miyaré 29, 60
Guaguancó del jibarito 84, 225
Guaguancó en La Habana 127
Guaguancó in New York 49, 84, 127
Guaguancó in Jazz 29, 226
Guaguanco Matancero, Conjunto, see Muñequitos De Matanzas
Guaguancó pa'l que sabe 275
Guagüiina yirabó 186
guajeo 307, 345
guajira 75–8

Guajira guantanamera 63, 76
"Guajiro", El 53, 251, 256
Guajiros, Los 84, 266, 345
guajisón 210
Guanches, Los 252
Guano, El 125
Guantanamera, see Guajira guantanamera
Guantánamo 33, 46, 58, 76, 212, 266, 344
guapachá 210
"Guapachá" (Amado Borcelá) 259
guaracha 20–1
Guaracheros de Oriente, Los 53, 75, 102, 333
Guaracheros del Cnc, Grupo 151, 246
Guarapachanga, La 211
guarapachanga 241, 345
Guararé 282
Guararé 274
Guararey de pastorita 247
Guardia, Lucas de la 212
Guaripumpe 212
Guasabeando el rock n' roll 116
"Guayabito" (Narciso Sánchez) 50
Guayacán, Orquesta 337, 364
guayo 33, 41, 307, 345
Guédon, Henri 338
Gueits, Chino 221
Guerra, Arturo 80
Guerra, Juan Luis 314, 364
Guerra, Marcelino "Rapindey" 61, 68, 116, 125, 152, 154, 171, 175–6, 180, 187
Guerra, Orlando, *see* Cascarita
Guerra, Vicente 191
Guerra baila, La 202
Guerrero, Enrique 21, 23, 25
Guerrero, Félix 137, 247, 349
Guerrilla, La 174–5
guerrilla 109, 174, 208
Guevara, Che 213
Guevara, Juan Gualberto 161
Guíllate 290
Guillén, Nicolás 1, 46, 48, 50, 56, 146, 233, 252
Guillot, Olga 75, 81, 110, 133, 150, 156, 172–3, 173, 184, 192, 208, 231, 305, 335, 361
Guinda roja, La 53
Güines, Tata (Federico Arístides Soto) 16, 24, 39, 110, 117, 138, 141, 214–5, 251, 258, 263, 264, 275, 337, 340, 361–2
güira 41, 307, 345
güira (rhythm) 1, 33, 88, 210, 345
güiro (scraper) 10, 34, 210, 345
Güiro de Macorina, El 217, 227–8
Güiro 6/8 232
guiso 210, 345
guitar 35, 42, 53, 103, 134, 183–4, 189, 247, 249, 257, 265, 307, 347
Guitry, Sacha 357
Gutiérrez, Agustín 55–6, 58, 61, 66, 68, 89, 333
Gutiérrez, Bienvenido Julián 54, 127, 250

Gutiérrez, Julio 21, 132, 136, 138, 140, 150, 181, 186, 203, 219, 232, 282, 324
Gutiérrez, Tata 56
Gutiérrez Villanueva, Raúl 340
"Guyún" (Vicente González Rubiera) 155
Guzmán, Adolfo 132, 138, 179, 213, 215
Guzmán, Paquito 302–3
Guzmán, Pedro 322
Gypsy Woman 226

Habana, Charanga 131
Habana, Orquesta 138, 71
Habana Cuban Boys 82
Habana Jazz 248
Habana Park 72
Habana Sax 265
Habana Son, Grupo 251
Habana del este 257
habanera 2, 78–9, 329, 345
Habanera de Godinez, Orquesta 56
Habanera, La 52
Habanera, Charanga 254–5
Habanera, Tipica 130, 249
Habanero, Septeto 59, 75, 126, 187, 197, 212, 251, 258, 358
Habanero, Sexteto 45, 56–7, 69, 132
Habanero Juvenil, Sexteto 131
Hachero pa' un palo 297
Haden, Charlie 263, 325
Haley, Bill 162
Hall, Adelaide 95
Hambro, Lenny 180, 202
Hamilton, Chico 325
Hamilton, Milton 281
Hampton, Lionel 177, 239
Hampton, Robert 78
Hampton, Slide 304, 319
Hancock, Herbie 238–9, 236, 301, 318, 323, 326
Handy, William Christopher 78–9, 96, 394
Hang on Snoopy 219
Hangin' out Vagabundeando 225
Hanrahan, Kip 325
Hansel y Raúl 284, 286, 306
Happy Boys 86, 165
Haque, Fareed 319
hard bop 239, 241
Hargrove, Roy 263, 231, 325, 364
Harlem Nightmare 219
Harlem River Drive 271, 282
Harlem, USA 226
Harlow, Andy 227
Harlow, Buddy 227
Harlow, Larry (Ira Kahn) 227, 232, 273, 275, 279, 284, 288, 294, 326, 363
Harlow, Orquesta 227, 291
Harrell, Tom 315, 320
Harris, Joe 315, 320
Hart, Antonio 325
Hart, Billy 287
Hartong, Jan Laurens 339
Has dudado de mí 184
Hasta el amanecer 224

Hasta siempre 213
Hatuey 73, 128, 142
Hatuey, Cuarteto 154, 330
Hatuey, Orquesta 154, 175
Hatuey, Sexteto 76
Havana Café 318
Havana Casino, Orquesta 79, 80, 89, 96, 131–2, 360
Havana Cuban Boys 134, 148
Havana Jam 258, 362
Havana Mambo, Orchestra 138
Havana/New York 287
Havana Philharmonic Orchestra 80, 92, 96, 112, 166, 169, 175, 356
Have You Ever Felt That Way 95
Hawkins, Coleman 173
Hawkins, Erskine 95
Hay cráneo 180, 301
Hay que saber perder 188
Haynes, Roy 305, 227, 320
Hayworth, Rita (Cansino, Margarita) 309
He Beeped When he Should Have Bopped 192
Heat Wave 240
Hechavarría, Paquito 140, 328
Hechavarría, José "Cocuyo" 32
Hecho y derecho – Doin' Right 271, 354
Hefti, Neal 173
Heifetz, Jascha 97
Hell of an Act to Follow 323
hembra 38, 185
Henderson, Fletcher 81, 85–6, 94, 167
Henderson, Joe 325
Hendrix, Jimi 355
Hendryx, Nona 318
Henríquez, Reinaldo 156
Henríquez, Teddy 80
Henríquez, Faustino "Tito" 217, 237
Here's That Rainy Day 263
Heritage 10, 78, 122, 209, 234, 245, 301, 317
Heritage Ensemble 324
Herman, Woody 165, 199–203
Herman's Heat and Puente's Beat 201
Hermanas Castro, Los 110, 152
Hermanas Duchesne, Los 121
Hermanas Lago 152
Hermanas Marquez 152
Hermanas Marti, Trio 151
Hermanos Avilés 80, 138
Hermanos Castro 81, 115, 130, 132, 348, 361
Hermanos Contreras 112, 116, 118, 139
Hermanos Curbelo 81
Hermanos Lebatard, Los 181, 214, 348
Hermanos Martinez 138
Hermanos Martinez Gil 75
Hermanos Moreno, Los 287
Hermanos Palau 81, 110, 130, 134, 136, 348
Hermanos Rigual, Trio 152

Hermanos Rosario, Los 131
Hermanos Valladares 286
Hernández, Alejandro 195
Hernández, Carlos 320
Hernández, Enrique 58
Hernández, Erena 111, 118, 366
Hernández, Rafaelo "Felo" 138, 140
Hernández, Frankie 301
Hernández, Gene 284
Hernández, Horacio "El Negro" 263, 319
Hernández, Hortencio Alfonso, *see* Virulilla
Hernández, José Ramón 51, 252
Hernández, Julio Alberto 93, 308
Hernández, Louie "Campana" 282
Hernández, Luisa María, *see* India de Oriente, La
Hernández, Mario 182
Hernández, Omar 306
Hernández, Oscar (trovador) 35, 50, 52, 54
Hernández, Oscar (pianist) 279, 294, 318
Hernández, Orlando "Papito" 138, 214
Hernández, Pedro 117
Hernández, Enrique "Quique", Hernández, Rafael 137–8, 140
Hernández, Ramón 85
Hernández, Raúl 133
Hernández, René 278
Hernández, Tiburcio, *see* Babuco
Hernández, Teo 336
Hernández, Victoria 85
Hernández Cadenas, Gabriel 264
Hernández Cuesta, Florencio, see Carusito
Hernández Delgado, Bienvenido "El Americano" 79
Hernández Iglesias, Eddie 283
Herrera, Aurelio "El Rubio" 71, 249
Herrera, Lázaro "El Pecoso" 60, 63, 67, 91, 212
Herrera Laferté, Irene 71, 88
Herscher, Dave 183
Hey Sister 323
Hidalgo, Giovanni "Mañenguito" 263, 278, 302, 304, 319, 321, 325, 339
Hierrezuelo, Caridad 256
Hierrezuelo, Lorenzo 60, 153–4, 250, 256, 274
Hi Fi in the Tropic 181
Hi Fly 325
Hi Latins, The 223
Hi Los, The 323
Hija de Juan Simón (La) 117
Hijos De Arcano, Los 286
Hijos Del Rey, Los 312–3
Hilda, Orquesta 117
Hines, Earl 94, 287
Hipocrisía 294

Hispanic Musicians
  Association (HMA)
  California Salsa 305
Hispanos, Los 218
Hite, Les 193
Hodeir, André 194
Hoffmann, Ernst Theodor
  Amadeus 133
Hoggard, Jay 325
Hojas para baño 64
holandés 99
Holiday, Billie 157, 194, 257
Holiday in Harlem 167
Holmes, Jimmy 79
Holmes, Leroy 219
Holywood Bowl Orchestra
  324
Hombre divertido, El 312
Hombres Calientes, Los 324
Homenaje a Bebo 155
Homenaje A Benny Moré 276
Homenaje A mis colegas 246
Homenaje a los santos 232
Homenaje a Rafael Hernández
  231
Homenaje A Yemayá 232
Hommy 273, 290
Honey Dripper 201
Hong Kong Mambo 197
Hope, Bob 165
Horn, Shirley 263
Horne, Lena 165
Hot House 157
Hot Salsa 339
house music 278, 327
Howard's Blues 172
Hoy 287
Hubbard, Freddie 265
Huerfanito, El 54
Huergo, Lucía 262
Hueso de María, El 101
Hughes, Langston 48
Hugo Pérez y su Quisqueya
  313
Huma, La 313
Humo y espumo 129
Huracán 301
Huracán y la palma, El 74
Hustler, The 272
Hutcherson, Bobby 325
Húyele al guardia 186
Huyéndole a un ratón 69

I Believe 269
I Can't Get no Satisfaction 223
*I Can't Give You Anything but
  Love* 201
I Dig Rock n' Roll Music 223
I Get a Kick Out of You 91
I Like it Like That 223–4, 288
I Will Survive 290
I Wish You Love 325
I'll Never Go Back to Georgia
  353
I've Got You Under My Skin 182
Ianmanuel 321
Idea, La, Orquesta 71, 120,
  283, 285
Ideal, Orquesta 71, 120, 285
Idilio 70, 71, 132
Iglesias, "Yeyo" (Rogelio) 136,
  141, 283
Imagen (Conjunto) 281–2

Imágenes latinas 279
Impacto Crea 302
Impressions 320
Impulse 277, 364
In a Latin Bag 241
In Motion 301
In the Midnight Hour 223
*Incendiary Piano of Peruchín,
  The* 136
Incomprendido, El 299
Indestructible 274, 362
India de Oriente, La (Luisa
  María Hernández) 151
Indianola 174
Industrias Nativas, Conjunto
  103
Industrias Típicas, Las 179
Infante, Isidro 282, 284, 287,
  288, 296
Ingratitud, la 22
Ingratitudes 279
Inmensidad, Orquesta 306
**Innovations in Modern
  Music** 184
Inolvidable 219, 296
Insaciable 304
Inspira tú que canto yo 143
Instinto 327
**Instituto Cubano de
  Radiodifusión, Orquesta
  de l'** 215
**Instituto Cubano de Radio y
  Television, Orquesta de l'**
  355
**Instrumental de Música
  Cubana, Quinteto** 215
Integracion Porteña, La 337
Inter-American Band, The
  317
Internacional, Conjunto
  55–6, 68
Internacional, Orquesta 337
International Casino 229
Internacional Vamp Band
  325
Intocable 268, 295
Invasora, La 139
Inventions and Dimensions 238
Irakere 14, 22, 244, 252, 254,
  260–4, 287, 302, 362, 366
Iriarte, Enrique ("Culebra")
  335
Irizarry, Ralph 321
Intenciones alborotadas 263
Irazú 340
Isidro Pérez, Orquesta de
  137, 139, 349
Isleño, El 281
Ismael Diaz (Charanga de) 131
Isora 334
Isora club 110, 112, 115
It Don't Mean a Thing 321
Ita moreal 135
Ithier, Rafael 234, 237, 298,
  304
Ithier, Salvador 104, 237
itótele 13, 14, 345
It's Just Begun 326
iyá 13, 14, 17, 260, 344–5
Iyá 200
Iznaga, Alberto 59, 86, 89,
  92–3, 97, 169, 181, 186
Izquierdo Padrón, Roberto 211

Jack Cole Dancers 178
Jackson, Cliff 201
Jackson, Joe 294–5, 326
Jackson, Michael 158
Jackson, Milt 174, 182
Jagger, Mick 318
Jahbero 193
jala jala 223, 225, 228, 299, 345
jaleo 307, 345
Jamaica Jazz 199
Jamaiquino, El 156, 162, 204,
  250
Jamal, Ahmad 203
James, Bob 275
James, Harry 166, 201, 261,
  352
James Moody 193, 241, 282,
  315
Jaramillo y sus Diablos 330
Jardineras, Las 110, 190, 247,
  286
Jardinero, El 312
Jardineros, Los 88
JATP Mambo 174, 202
Jazz, beginnings of 78–82
Jazz Band Alberti 308
Jazz Band de *Cienfuegos* 52,
  68, 78, 82, 116, 143
**Jazz on the Latin Side All-
  stars** 203, 256, 362
Jazz Project 318
Jazz Tumbao, Grupo 321,
  344, 345, 347, 361, 360
Jazzbata 259
Jazztumbata 264, 362
Jean-Marie, Alain 339
Jejo, Carmelo 85
Jesuitas, Los 29
Jesús, Benito de 189
Jesús, James de 327
Jesús, Mario de 135
Jesús María 45, 54, 56, 60, 168,
  188, 190, 195
Jibacoa 69
jíbara (music) 42
jibarito 84, 99, 105, 225
Jibarito de Lares, El (Odilio
  González) 99
Jíbaro negro 322
Jicotea, La 120
Jimagua (timbalero) 127
Jiménez, Bobby 302
Jiménez, Cheo 61
Jiménez, Genoveno 116
Jiménez, Luis María ("Chita")
  93
Jiménez, Manuel, see Canario
  84, 88, 101, 102, 104, 106,
  182, 184, 188, 235
Jiménez, Nick 204, 352
Jiménez, Pedro 144
Jiménez, Porfi 336
Jiménez, Pucho 79
Jiménez, "Tojo" (Generoso)
  138, 141, 143, 144
Jiménez Miranda, Manuel 106
Jiménez Rebollar, Alberto 79
Jobim, Antonio Carlos 226,
  326, 321
Joe Lustig Mambo 180
joesón 337
Johnakins, Leslie 172
Johnny Seguí y sus Dandys
  220

Johnnu Ventura y sus Caballos
  311, 312, 363
Johnson, Gene 170
Johnson, J.C. 95
Johnson, J. J. 194
Johnson, James P. 94
Johnson, Lyndon 311
Johnson, Tommy 165
Johnston, Allan 321
Jolson, Al 148, 283
Jones, Hank 198, 240, 259
Jones, Jonah 168
Jones, Quincy 194, 198
Jones, Thad 287
Jordan, Louis 203
Jordan, Taft 167
joropo 138, 335, 345
Jorrín, Enrique 113, 116, 118,
  119, 120, 163, 210, 247, 249,
  251, 285, 298, 332, 344, 354,
  361
José Estebán y Patrulla 313
José Octavio y los Nietos 313
José y Macamé 159
Jou, Simón 194
Journey, The 320
Jovnnws Clásicos del Son 253
Jóvenes de la defensa 112, 115
Jóvenes del Barrio 288
Jóvenes del Cayo 110, 121,
  126, 151, 188
**Jóvenes del Feeling,
  Orquesta** 121
Jóvenes del Cerro 198
Jóvenes del muelle 227
Jóvenes Estrellas 121, 120
Jóvenes Sociales 198
Juan Pachanga 274, 294
Juana 51
Juana Calavera 56
Juana 1600 260
Juana Peña 251
Juancito Trucupei 310
Juanita saca la mano 219
Judío Maravilloso, El 273
Jumpin' with Symphony Sid 324
Junco, Pedro 116, 138, 156
Junco, Xiomara 66
junga 17
Jungla 195
jungle (style) 81, 167, 278, 327
Jungle Fantasy 177
Junto a un cañaveral 51
Juramento en las tinieblas 87
Justicia 270, 278, 291
Justiz, Anita 121, 136
Justiz, Pedro, *see* Peruchín 133,
  136, 266, 361
Juvenil, Sexteto 169
Juvenil de Sancti Spiritus 253

Kahn, Ira, *see* Harlow, Larry
Kalaff, Luis 313, 31114
Kalamazoo 121
Kalle Jeff Et Son African Jazz
  334
Kanno, Carlos 340
Karachi, Los 264
Kassav' 312
Kei, Tobi 180
Kendrick, Rodney 325
Kennedy, John 117
Kenton, Los 313

Kenton, Stan 137, 159, 163, 172, 177, 184, 199, 202–3, 219, 229
Kenya 174, 198, 276, 334
Kessel, Barney 161
Kid Creole And The Coconuts 326
Kikiriki 117, 127
Kill, God Forgives You 66
"Killer Joe" (Frank Piro) 98, 217
Kimbos, Los 275, 281, 295, 324, 364
kinfuiti 17, 123, 345
King, Martin Luther 222
King of the Mambo 160
Kirkland, Kenny 325, 340
Knight, Pedro 128, 232
Koinonia 323
Kool Bongo 203
Krazy Cats 79
Krupa, Gene 177, 199
Kubavana, Orquesta 204, 285
Kubanacan, Conjunto 68
Kubata 287
Kubavana, Conjunto 68
Kubavana, Orquesta 210
kuchí-yeremá 16
Kwá-kwá 217

La la pa 225
La India (Lindabell Caballero) 278, 296
La Lupe (Yoli Raymond, Guadalupe Victoria) 208, 219, 226, 229, 230, 231, 270, 289, 301, 362
La Calle, José 88
La Sitiera 338
La vi caminando 252
Laboriel, Abraham 323
Ladi (Ladislao Martínez Otero) 103
Ladi, Conjunto 103
Lágrima 115
Lágrimas negras 64, 66
Lágrimas y tristeza 170
Laguna, Yeyo 103
Lala no sabe hacer na' 28
lamento 312
Lamento borincano 91, 101, 105, 320, 361
Lamento cubano 45
Lamento esclavo 148, 331
Landa, Rafael 23
Lane, Abe 97
Lantri, Estebán, see Saldiguera
Lara, Adalberto 251
Lara, Agustín 75, 148
Lara, "Chino" (Remberto) 90, 91, 131, 134, 167
Larrain, Luis Alfonso 334
Larue, Jacques 158
Laserie, Rolando 4, 143–5, 184, 208, 216–7, 229–30, 286, 293, 335, 340
Lastre, Juan Olimpo 55
Lata, La 262
Latamblé, Marcelino 35
Latican Space Mambo 324
Latin Brothers, The 337
Latin Bugalú 223
Latin Connection 27

Latin Disco 326–8
Latin Empire 83, 327
Latin Escapade 204
Latin From Manhattan 283
Latin Hustle 284, 327
Latin jazz 199–205, 238–40, 258–63, 315–26
Latin Jazz All Stars, The 272
Latin Jazz Dream Band, The 274
Latin Jazz Ensemble, The 281, 339
Latin Jazz Orchestra, The 328
Latin Jazz Suite 324
Latin Jewels 175
Latin Legends Band 288
Latin Percussion Jazz Ensemble, The 315
Latin pop 326, 328
Latin rock 326–8
Latin Section, The 339
Latin soul 240–1
Latina, Sonora 340
Latinaires, The 226
Latino 44, 174, 205, 220, 223, 224, 227, 269, 327, 340, 369
Latinos, Los 251
Laugart, Xiomara 325
Lavoe, Héctor 37, 268, 270, 272, 279, 287, 291, 292, 296, 334, 363
Laws, Hubert 239
Lay, Rafael 116, 249
Lay, Rafael, Jr. 249
Lázaro y Georgina 258
Le Baron, Eddie 96, 180, 185
Le robaron los timbales 276
le lo lai 345, 365
Leão, Nara 155
Leavitt, Ralphy 302, 363
Lebatard, Germán 79, 138, 175, 181, 214, 348
Lebatard, Gonzalo 81, 138, 175, 181, 214, 348
Lebatard, Julio 81, 138, 175, 181, 214, 348
Lebatard, Luis 81, 138, 175, 181, 214, 348
Lebrón, Adrián 281
Lebrón, Angel 269, 281
Lebrón, Angel ("Mambo") 289
Lebron Brothers, The 269, 272, 281
Lebrón, Carlos 269
Lebrón, Frankie 281
Lebrón, Héctor 269
Lebrón, Juan Manuel 304
Lebrón, José 269
Lebrón, Pablo 269
Lección de piano 70
Lechón y bachata 127
Lecuona, Ernesto 47, 48, 94, 101, 131, 136, 146, 148, 149, 184, 198–9, 285, 334,
Lecuona, Margarita 48, 131, 132, 134, 154
Lecuona Cuban Boys 81, 86, 134, 189, 331, 334, 360
Ledee, Tonito 297
Ledesma, Roberto 75, 151
Lee, Peggy 199

Legarreta, "Pupi" (Félix) 18, 208, 217, 228, 240, 275, 284, 285, 363
Leicea, Calixto 128
Leiva, "Pío" (Wilfredo) 135, 151, 154, 212, 256, 335
Lejos de tí 72
Lejos del batey 281
Lembranças 323, 364
Lemvo, Ricardo 296
Leña, Moncho (Delgado Ramírez, Juan Ramón) 101, 174, 182, 186, 237, 331, 361
León, Alfredo 152, 195
León, Bienvenido 60, 142, 149, 169, 212
León, Gladys 150
León, "Nano" (Romín) 50, 60, 61
León, John de 85
leró 99, 304
Lesmes, Osdalgia 266, 363
Lester Leaps In 279
Let Me Love You Tonight 184
Let's Ball 223, 226
Levántame, nena 313, 364
Levitt, Al 238
Levy, Al see Alfredito 183
Lewis, John 193
Lewis, Meade Lux 98
Ley, Tabu 334
Leyva, Rigoberto 19
Libertad – Lógico (La) 269
Liborio, Sexteto 68
Libre, Conjunto 22, 278, 279, 284, 363
Libre: con salsa y ritmo 279
Licea, Manuel ("Puntillita") 135, 256
Líderes de la salsa, Los 279
Liduvino en el Parana 153
Life Is Just a Bowl of Cherries 84
Lija Ortiz, Luis 182
Lima, Rolando 109
Limonta, Alberto 144
Limonta, Eulalio 35
Limonta, Juan 33
Limonta, Leonel 255
Linares, Antonio 144
Linares, María Teresa 34, 367
Lindo yambú 127, 271, 278
Lines, Esther 66
Lira Del Yaque, La 228, 309
Lira Matancera, La 246
Lira rota (La) 51
Lisama, Virgilio 141, 144
Listo Medellín 337
Little Anthony And The Imperials 222
Liviano (Ramón Cisneros) 127
LLegó La India 278, 363
Llegó y dijo 293
Llopis, Juan Bautista 127
Llopis-Dulzaides, Cuarteto 140
Llora timbero 25, 139
Lloralo, lloralo 298
llorao 29, 30, 125, 345
Lluvia con nieve 150
Lluvia gris 150
Lo dice todo 279
Lo mato 272, 291
Lo que dice el Abacuá 245
Lo que dice Usted 124

Lo que más me gusta 151
Lo que pide la gente 276
Lo que va a pasar 260
Lo saen 284
Lo tengo dominao 313
Lobo, Edu 267, 298
Loco, Joe (José Esteves) 161, 162, 170, 171, 175, 178, 198, 204, 222, 227, 228, 240, 324, 361
Locura 101
Logas, Juan 35
Lola María (Ximena y Cruz, María Dolores) 23, 25, 369
Lomax, Alan 78
Longina 52, 59, 335
Lookie Lookie 226
López, Ángel 262
López, Alí Ahmet ("Alimelét") 211
López, Aníbal 290
López, Aurelio 112
López, Belisario 71, 111, 128, 166, 181, 219
López, "Cachaíto" (Orlando) 214
López, Celso 187
López, César 261
López, César, Alejandro 265
López, Coralia 112
López, Elias 300
López, "Felo" (Rafael) 338
López, Gil 179, 180, 183
Lopez, Heredio 68
López, Israel see Cachao
López, Jesús 68, 91, 112, 117, 144, 182, 305
López, Johnny 223, 238
López Johnny (band leader) 87, 223
Lopez, Jorge 98
López, Juanucho 226, 237
Lopez, Leyanis 266, 363
López, "Macho" (Orestes) 112–15, 133, 141, 249
López, Manito 338
López, Oriente 262
López, Orlando ("Cachaíto") 214, 256
López, Oscar 48, 57, 80, 110, 111, 133, 146, 162, 177, 332, 334, 339, 348, 350–1
López, Paul 177, 305
López, Pedro 71
López, "Pepito" (José) 103
López, Rafaela 112
López, Ray 2
López, René 274
López, Victoriano 56
López, Vincent 97, 201
Lopez-Barroso, Charanga 116
López Cruz, "Paquito" (Francisco) 106
López Nussa, Hernán 262
López Nussa, Ruy 265
López Viana, Luis 79
Loquibambia, Conjunto 150, 155
Lora, Francisco 308
Lora, Ñico 310
Loredo, Diego 144
Lorenzo, Tio 2
Loreta 308

Los Sitios entero 254
Los Sitios llaman 115, 120, 274
Lotus Land 177
Louie Ramírez y sus amigos 274
Louis, Joe 40
Louison, Bibi 338
Lovano, Joe 325
Lover Come Back To Me 194
Loyola, Efraín 116, 121
Lozano, Alexis 337
Lozano, Clemente 116
Lozano, Danilo 324
Lozano, José 228
Lozano, "La Coco" 337
Lozano, "Rolando" (José Calazán) 116, 118, 182, 205, 208, 228, 326
Lozano, Wladimir 335
Luaces Delgado, Jorge 252
Lubambo, Romero 325
Lube, lube 16–17
Lucas, Marie 201
Lucca, "Papo" (Enrique Arsenio) 186, 275–6, 290–1, 293, 294, 297, 298, 302, 304, 322, 335, 367
Lucca, Carabello "Quique" (Enrique) 297
Luciano, Felipe 222
Lucrecia (Lucrecia Pérez Saez) 252, 340
Lucumí 11, 12, 30, 247, 344
Lucumí, El 223
Lucumí, Macumba, Voodoo 278
Lugo, Pedro ("Nene") 253
Lugo, Roberto 295
Lullaby Of Birdland 316
Luna, Estanislao 25
Luna, Manuel 50, 91
Luna, Trio 91
Lunares, Los 72
Lunceford, Jimmy 160
Lundy, Carmen 325
Lush Life 316
Luz, Orquesta De La 340, 364
Luz que no alumbra 63

M.C.E. 327
Ma'Rainey 194
Ma'Teodora (Teodora Ginés) 32
McDonald, Harl 25
McKinney's Cotton Pickers 201
McGhee, Howard 172
McKibbon, Al 191–3, 204, 324
McRae, Carmen 322
Maceo, Antonio 113
Machaco 29
Machado, Armando 252
Machado, Gerardo 19, 44–5, 54–5, 330, 356
Machado, Manuel 261
Machao (drummer) 349
Machete Ensemble, The 324
Machín, Antonio 61, 80, 88, 106, 148, 154, 167, 169, 331, 340, 360, 366
Machín, Evelio 154
Machín, Cuarteto 106, 360
Machito (Frank Grillo Gutiérrez) 3, 4, 6, 10, 25, 26, 28–9, 41, 56, 67–8, 73, 87,
89, 92, 98, 116, 127, 131, 137, 139, 161, 166, 168–75, 177, 180, 185–6, 189–90, 192–3, 198, 200, 202, 204, 216–23, 232, 241, 276, 277, 286, 293, 304, 316–7, 352, 360–3, 367–9
Machito 202
Machito and His Salsa Band 1982 277
Machito For Ever 316
macho (bomba drum) 343
Macho's Latin Satin 274
Machucambos, Los 163, 338
Machucho (singer) 181
Macías, José "Pepe" 32, 66, 191, 249
Macías, Rudy 226
Mack the Knife 238
Macusa 153
Madariaga, Edgar 265
Madera 336
Madera, Frank 101
Madera, José "Pin" 86, 169–70, 176, 232
Madera, Simón 182
Madonna 305
Madriguera, Enrique 67, 88, 175, 180, 184, 187, 199, 201
Madrid, José 317
Madrid, La Orquesta 351
Maduro, Pepito 189
Maestra Vida 280, 294, 363
Maestro, El 275, 289, 291
Magdalena 189
"Magnesia" 26
Magnífica, Conjunto, La 183
Maiden Voyage 301
Maiga, Boncana 338
Make It With You 226
Makeba, Myriam 225
Makina, Loca, La 296
makuta 17, 27
"Malanga" (José Rosario Oviedo) 25
Malanga amarilla 141
Malanga murió 131
Malanga na' ma' 117
Malavet Vega, Pedro 367
Malavoi 338, 340
Maldición 24
Maldita droga 219
Maldonado, Ángel "Cachete" 275, 285, 302, 306
Maldonado, Ricardo 225
Maldonado, Rubén 302
Maldonado, Yayito 103
Malecón, El 227
malembe 249
Maleta, La 279
Malo 328
Malo, El 272, 363
Malmin, Roland 338
Malson, Lucien 157, 194, 367
mama buela 28, 217
Mama güela 179, 217
Mama Inés 19, 48, 56, 58, 148, 203, 240, 331
Mama y la hija, La 311
Mamanita 78
mambisa 113
mambises 113
Mambo 114, 150, 162, 173
mambo (Congo dance) 3, 22, 27, 72, 98, 120, 161, 217, 253, 289, 332, 365
mambo (rhythm) 5, 17, 113, 115, 121–2, 135, 158, 161, 175
mambo (riff or section) 113, 114, 118, 218
Mambo a la Kenton 136
Mambo Aces, The (Joe Centeño and Aníbal Vázquez) 161, 165
Mambo batiri 189
Mambo Boogie 162
Mambo Bounce 203
Mambo Buda 179
Mambo coco 176
Mambo con Puente 179
Mambo de la pinta 203
Mambo de las existencialistas 161
Mambo del Crow 203
Mambo del gavilán 115
Mambo Devils, The 180
Mambo Fantasy 175
Mambo infierno 156
Mambo influenciado 260
Mambo Inn 173, 204, 217, 240, 260, 319
Mambo inspiración 116
Mambo Jumbo 306
Mambo Jumbo 176
Mambo loco 203, 361
Mambo Loves Garner 361, 203
Mambo macoco 187
Mambo mona 180, 217
Mambo Moods 175
Mambo No. 5 158, 159
Mambo tango 317
Mambo with Tjader 322
Mambolino 162
Mamboleros, Los 181, 228
Mambomania 181, 228
Mambos and Cha Chas 184
Mambostic 162
Mamey colorao 136, 152
Man I Love, The 136
Mañana te espero, niña 60
Manano 26
Manda conmigo papé 146
Mandel, Johnny 184
"Mañengue" (José Hidalgo) 321
Manfugas, Nené 33
Mangano, Silvana 150, 162
Mango mangüé 36, 156
Mangú 306, 327, 363
Mangual 170–1, 178–80, 195, 199, 203, 240, 282, 284, 290, 315, 326
Mangual, José 171, 179–80, 194–5, 202–3, 240–1, 315, 326
Mangual, Jr., José 282
Mangual, Luis 290
Manguaré 245, 251
Manguera, La 311
mangulina 311
Manhattan, Orquesta 196
Manhattan, Sexteto 84
Manhattan Rico Suite 203
Manhattan Transfer 274
maní 27, 89, 156, 275, 313
Manía, Grupo 313
"Maninín" (Daniel Vázquez) 237
Manisero, El 36, 80, 89, 90, 148, 172, 264, 357
Mann, Herbie 174, 183, 199, 240–1
Manning, Sam 95
Mano a Mano 124, 345
Manolín (González, Hernández, Manuel) 225, 255, 304
Manolito y su Trabuco 252, 362
Manono 275
Manozzi, Joe 275
Manteca 192–5, 219, 324
Manteca 339
Manteca Suite, The 193
Manteca Theme 194
Mantilla, Piro 300
Mantilla, Ray 286–7, 317, 324
Manuel, Carlos 128, 182, 255
Manuel, Juan 251, 262, 304
Manuel, Manny 313
Manuel, Victor 46, 296
Manuelle, Victor 296
mañunga 30
"Mañungo", *see* Ortiz, Rafael
Manyoma, Wilson 336
Manzanero, Armando 75
Manzano, William 101, 186, 237
mapellé 101
Máquina, Louie 165
Máquina y el motor 285
Maquinolandera 235
Mar, Aníbal de, *see* **Pototo y Filomeno**
Maracaibo oriental 145, 301
maracas 144, 152, 169, 179–80, 194, 199, 202, 212, 234, 246, 252, 257, 275, 277, 285, 304
Marañón, El 134, 150
Maraquero, El 41, 56, 71, 128, 169, 178, 180–1, 186, 257, 285, 345
Maravilla de Florida, La 121, 210–11, 248, 264
Maravillas de arcaño, Las 110–2, 351
Maravillas de Malí, Las 338
Marc Anthony (Marc Anthony Muñiz) 296, 363
Marcano, Cuarteto 106, 360
Marcano, Pedro "Piquito" 106
Marcos Gonzáles, Juan, de 212, 251, 256
Marcheta 69
Marcianos llegaron ya, Los 117
Mardi Gras Mambo 264
Margarito 274
María 1–34
María Caracoles 256
María Cristina 53, 255, 284,
María de la Regla 28
María la O 110, 149
María Lionza 279
María no llores 105, 149
Maria, Tania 264
Mariana, Alicia Parla 331
Marianaxi, Conjunto 292
mariandá 99
Mariano, Luis, *see* Cancañón 144, 354

Mariano Merceron and the Piper Boys 139
Maricutana, La 306, 309
Mariel 244, 318
Marima 301
marímbula 32–4, 55, 57, 68, 106, 123, 128, 234, 307, 345
Marín, Orlando 220–1, 232, 315
Marini, Leo 127
Marlon Simon and the Nagual Spirits 322, 364
Marquesas de Atares 111
Marquetti, José "Cheo" 4, 25, 68, 76, 109, 117, 120, 127, 187, 212
Márquez, Joel 336
Márquez, Juanito 138, 210, 215, 305, 355
Márquez, Michel 255
Márquez, René 135
Marrero, Nicky 271, 275, 277–8, 287, 317, 325, 339
Marrero, Ricardo 294, 315, 326–7
Marrero, Soraya 146
Married Well 219, 240
Marsalis, Jason 324
Marsalis, Wynton 137, 319, 321
Marta 80, 213, 340, 357
Martí, José 75–6, 122, 367
Martí, Luisito "Llorón" 311
Martí, Enrique "Virgilio" 138, 179, 220, 285, 363
Martignon, Hector 364
martillo 41, 345
Martínez, Eliseo "El Colorao" 112
Martin, Frank 85, 178
Martin, Fred 178
Martin, Ricky 294
Martinelli, Trino 65
Martínez, Aníbal 144
Martínez, Chano 229
Martínez, Osvaldo "Chihuahua" 238, 285
Martínez, Eddie 274, 277, 298, 303, 315–18, 322
Martínez, Eloy 117, 121
Martínez, Emiliano 329
Martínez, Gerardo 55
Martínez, Gonzalo 228
Martínez, José, Ángel 257
Martínez, Leocadio "Lalo" 106
Martínez, Luis See: Griñán, Lili 124
Martínez, Nicolás 228
Martínez, Osvaldo "Chihuahua" 285, 328
Martínez, Rogelio 127, 209, 385
Martínez, Rolo 264
Martínez, Luis "Sabú" 182, 194
Martínez, Tony 265, 363
Martínez, Willie 319
Martínez Furé, Rogelio 127, 209, 285
Martínez Otero, Ladislao, see Ladi 103
Martínez Rodríguez, Raúl 231
Martino, Trio 151
Marzal, Raudel 253

Mas, Gustavo 138–40, 174, 349, 363
Más piano merengue 309
Más que nada 220
masacote 121, 220, 345
Masacre 72
Masakela, Hugh 257
Masó 33
masón 18
Master Sessions, Volume I 286
Masucci, Jerry 4, 266, 288, 363
Mata siguaraya 128, 158
Matamoros, Conjunto 143, 154, 333
Matamoros, Miguel 46, 55, 58, 63–6, 74, 97, 110, 143–4, 333, 367
Matamoros, Trio 56, 63–4, 66, 101, 188, 198, 330–1, 360, 368
Matancera, Gloria 68, 121, 128,
Matancera, Lira 121, 246
Matancera, Sonora 67, 110, 127–8, 142, 144, 151, 162, 187–8, 191, 197–8, 204, 211, 219–20, 222, 228, 232, 256, 282, 284–6, 288, 290–1, 295, 332–3, 362
Matancero, Conjunto 70, 246, 362
Matancero, Septeto 68
Matancero, Sexteto 70
Mateo, Joseíto 237, 311, 314, 363
Matos, Bobby 324
Matthew, Artie 78
Mauleón, Rebeca 305
Maxwell, Elsa 165
May, Billy 350
Mayari, Cuarteto 103, 106, 179
Mayfield, Irvin 324
Mayito 248
mayor de plaza 18
Mayra 259, 261, 334, 367
Me la llevo 143
Me lo dijo Adela 116, 156, 162–3
Me recordarás 140
Me siento muy solo 125
Me voy contigo 127
Me voy pa' Morón 117
Me voy pa'l pueblo 144
Medicina, La 312
Médico de la salsa, El 255, 362
Medina, Domingo 127
Medina, Jerry 296, 302–3
Medina, Trina 296
Megatones, Los 203, 301
Mejía, Anchesto 311
Mejía, Carlos 184
Mejías, Paolí 321–2, 342
Mejor que nunca 279, 311
mejorana 138, 361, 363
Mejores Músicos de Cuba, Los 138, 361
Melao, Conjunto 293, 295, 338, 363
"Melcochita" (Pablo Branda Villanueva) 296, 363
Mella, Julio 85, 118
Mellow Man Ace 327, 364
Melodía Tropical 163

Melodías de Iron Beer 111, 286
Melodías Del 40 117, 120, 152
Melodíco, Los 334, 335
Melody Boys, The 175
"Melón" (Angel Luis Silva) 275
Memoria a Chano 194
Mena, Mario 34
Mena, Roger 144
Mena Pérez, Mariano 254
Mendelson, Alfred, see Méndez, Alfredo 183
Mendes, Sergio 239
Méndez, Alfredo (Alfred Mendelson) 183
Méndez, José Antonio 155, 332
Méndez, Kinito 313
Méndez, Silvestre 144, 156, 233, 332
Mendive, Cristóbal 66
Mendive, Kiko 158, 160, 182, 332
Mendoza, Celeste 150, 213, 332
Mendoza, Chico (Ira Jay Robertson) 274
Mendoza, Octavio "Cuso" 152, 180
Mendoza, Isaura 150
Mendoza, Victor 321
Menéalo que se empelota 103
Menéame la cuna 53
Menéame los mongos 237
Menéndez, "El Gallego" 50
Menéndez, "Marino 110
Menéndez, Nilo 67, 88, 93–5, 98, 308
"Meñique" (Miguel Barcasnegras) 277
Mensaje campesino 314
Mentira 156
Mentiras al oído 187
Mentiras criollas 116
Mentiras tuyas 145, 230
Mercado, Ralph 269, 287–8, 313
Mercado, Vitín 106
Merced, Julio "Gunda" 301–2
Merced, José (de la) 71
Mercedes 52, 257
Mercerón, Mariano 136, 139, 144, 210, 219, 293, 332, 335, 361
merechanga 311
merecumbé 233, 311
merengue 3, 5, 41, 93, 106, 135, 143, 164, 210, 224, 228–9, 233, 236–7, 266, 280, 282, 296, 303, 306–14, 317, 323, 336, 341, 344–7, 363, 366–7
merenhouse 314
Mesa, Antonio 103, 104, 308
Mesa, Juan, see Fuico 246
Mesa, Ora 158
Mesié, Julián 82, 134, 146
Message, The 273, 363
Message from Kenya 198
Mestizo 327
Metheny, Pat 314, 325
Metiendo mano 363

Mexicana, Sonora 219
Mezcla, Grupo 247
Mi bambolaye 129
Mi cerebro, see Sí sí no no
Mi biografía 76
Mi china 228
Mi chiquita quiere 285
Mi debilidad 291
Mi gallo pinto 156
Mi gente 268, 291
Mi guajira son 78, 251
Mi propia imagen 281
Mi ritmo llegó 277
Mi Salsa 253, 362
Mi sansa mi coco 126
Mi saoco 142
Mi son, mi son, mi son 127
Mi son por el mundo 250
Mi último canto 97
Mi yambú 59
Miami Sound Machine (MSM) 306
Micaela 32
Micaela me botó 150
Midnight Mambo 318
Midnight Serenaders 101, 185
Miedo 290
Miel 280
Miénteme 150, 332
Miguelito 212
Miguelito canta a Panmá 219
Milagro de Ochun, El 109, 149, 219
Milán, William 281
Milanés, Pablo 213, 251, 262, 355
Miles, Lizzie 95
Milhaud, Darius 1, 69
Mili Bustillo, Néstor 212
Millán (cornetist) 24
Miller, Glenn 137, 239, 349, 352
Miller, Mitch 173
Miller, Mulgrew 316, 325
Millet, Jorge 290
Mills, Florence 95
Millie, Jocelyn y los Vecinos 313
Milonga sentimental 237
Mimi Pinson 357
Mingo and his Whoopee Kids 101
Mingus, Charles 222, 324
Mira que eres bonita 24
Mira que eres linda 79
Mirabal Vázquez, Manuel ("El Guajiro") 251, 256
Miramar, Sexteto 333
Miranda, Edgardo 318
Miranda, Ismael 226, 273, 279, 291, 302, 316, 363
Miranda, Juan Pablo 71
Miranda, Luis 101, 170, 198, 203
Miranda, Miguel 185–6
Miranda, Victor Luis 101
Mis amores, see Loreta 308
Mis cinco hijos 131
Misa negra 150, 259
Misago, Tadaki 334
Misma Gente, La 337
Missourians, The 167
Mister Pachanga 216

Mobley, Hank 194, 203
Mocambo 136
Modelo, Conjunto 126–7, 129
Modern Jazz Quartet 80
Moderna, La 227
Mofongo pelao 235
Moforiborere 196
Moforivale al tambó 129
Molestoso, El 220, 291
Moliendo café 338
Moliendo vidrio 184
Molina, Carlos 96, 367
Molina, César 138
Molino, Papa 311
Mompié, Haila 255
Moncada, Grupo 251
Monchito and his Mambo Royals 309
Mondéjar, Ninón 118, 120
Mondongo, sandunga, gandinga 214, 317
Mondonguero, El 36, 190
Moneró, José Luis 101, 188, 195
Monge, César "Albóndiga" 335
Monge, Poldín 185
Mongo 196
Mongo Explodes 239
Mongo in Havana 239
Mongo Santamaría 196
Mongo y Justo 290
Mongo y La Lupe 239
mongolés 210
Monguito, Ramón Quián Sardiñas 232, 332
Monina 236
Monito y la girafa, El 217
Monk, Thelonious 175, 200–1, 262, 277, 317, 320, 322, 324, 349
Monroig, Gilberto 176, 189, 237
Montalbán, Eduardo 303
Montalván, José 133
Montané, Lalo 144
Montaner, Rita 48, 74, 81, 88–90, 97, 110, 117, 128
Montañez, Andy "Andrés" 237, 245, 298, 303, 335
monte 10, 16, 29, 225, 257, 271, 343, 345
Montecarlo, Orchesta 133, 134
Montero, Papá 25–6, 48
Monterey, Conjunto 234
Montesino, Carlos 86, 170, 177, 187
Montoto 55, 333
montuno (section) 34, 113, 121
montuno de guaguancó 29
Monumental, La 251
Mood Indigo 161
Mood Latino 204
Moody, James 193, 241, 282, 315, 319–20
Moon over Cuba 200
Moonlight Fiesta 200
Moore, Brew 172
Mora, La 48
Morales, Agüedo 13
Morales, Carlos Emilio 210
Morales, José "Chiquitín" 180

Morales, Eduardo 252
Morales, Edwin 155
Morales, Esy (Ismael) 52–3, 92, 180
Morales, Fidel 129, 175
Morales, Humberto 52, 92, 105, 120, 180
Morales, Ismael 52, 92
Morales, Joe 89
Morales, Mariano 165
Morales, Norberto Osvaldo "Noro" 5, 43, 47, 50–2, 54, 57, 85, 91–2, 94–5, 98, 100, 103–104, 106, 113, 117–118, 120, 122, 142, 145, 153, 159, 161, 169–70, 184
Morales, Obdulio 11, 39, 59, 64, 75, 78, 82, 89, 108, 170, 179
Morales, Pepito 92
Morales, Rafael 39
Morales, Eduardo "Tiburón" 129–30
Morales, Vicentico 152
Morales Brothers, The 44, 52, 92
Morán, Chilo 159
Moraza, Chencho 57
Moré, Bartolomé "Benny" 10, 13, 16, 20, 32, 42, 57–8, 62, 64, 66–8, 71–73, 75–6, 79, 81, 83, 96–7, 101, 121–22, 132, 142, 144, 145–6, 149–50, 159, 169–71, 173, 179, 184, 187
Moré, Delfín 76
Moré, Teodoro 75
Moreira, Airto 163
Morejón, Mario "El Indio" 136
Morejón, Noelio 62
Morel Campos, Manuel 64
Moret, Neil 43
Morgan, Frank 91
Morgan, Lee 150
Morning 56, 95, 105, 112, 164–6
Morning Salsa 166
Moro, el, see Vázquez, Miguel
Morrison, Bigga 132
Morrow, Buddy 104
Morton, "Jelly Roll" (Ferdinand Lamenthe) 43, 166
Mosqued 20
Motivos de son 19, 77
Moya, Roberto de 37
Moya Martínez, Pablo 136
mozambique 5, 109–10, 114, 132, 148, 176, 181, 185
Mozart, Wolfgang, Amadeus 134
Mozian, Roger 90
Mr. Trumpet Man 117
Muchacha no seas boba 21
Muchachos de Bolona Los 67
Muchachos Pimienta 73, 184
Mucho Calor, a Presentation in Latin Jazz 105
Mucho sabor 171
Mucho talento 149
Múcura, La 98
Muerte, La 122, 148
Muerte de Abel Antonio, La 148
Muévete 55, 128, 167

Muévete negrita 55
Muguercia, Alberto 19, 20, 187
Mujer bayamesa See: Bayamesa, La 30, 41, 44, 146
Mujer de Antonio, La 31, 37
Mujer de Juan, La 57
Mujer perjura 29
Mulata, La 6, 16, 32, 33, 109, 118
Mulata con cola 79
Mulata rumbera, La 49, 87
Mulatas de Fuego, Las 68, 72, 82, 84–5, 103, 170, 179
Mulato, El 117, 138
"Mulatón" (Alejandro Rodríguez) 6, 33, 48–9, 57, 88
Mulatona, La 50
Mulence 16
Mulenze, Orchesta 152, 154–5
Mulens, Fernando 49, 73, 94, 171
Muley, "Moncho" 121
Mulligan, Gerry 124, 133
Muna san timba 99
Munamar, Sexteto 38, 67
Muñanga 99
Munchito, Muñaz 182
Mundo se ta' caba, El 99
Mundo se va a acabar, El 96
Muñeca 99
Muñecas del cha cha chá 71
Munequitos de Matanzas, Los 12, 126–7
Munguia, Juan 134
Muñoz, Avelino 98
Muñoz, Ernesto 39, 42, 67
Muñoz, Eusebio "Cabito" 101
Muñoz, Mario, see Papaíto
Muñoz, Monchito 95
Muñoz, Rafael 47, 54, 95–8, 184
Muñoz Marín, Luis 148
Murillo, Alexis 172
Murmullo 139
Music for Strings, Percussion and Celesta 202
música de amargue 313
Musical Conquest 297
"Musiquita" (Antonio Sánchez Reyes) 120
My Favorite Things 282
My Last Affair 167
My Little Suede Shoes 172, 200, 203
My Spiritual Indian 271
My Summertime 315
My Time Is Now 319, 364

Na baixa do sapateiro 201
Na mio ho rengue kio 294
Naborí 292
Nacer, Amuni 322
Nació en Oriente 91
Nacional (Septeto) 61, 68, 76, 169, 171, 212–3, 252, 258, 278, 285, 360
Nacional (Sexteto) 34, 97
Nacional de Concierto (Charanga) 128
Nacional Juvenil 103
Nadal, "Chuito" (Jesús) 54, 95
Naddy, Ted 43

Nagüe 73, 89, 99, 171, 186
Nanara cai 152
Nando, King 117
Náñigo, El (by Jorrín) 63
Náñigo, El (by Peña) 15, 23–4, 118
Napoleon, Phil 91
Nápoles, Roberto 139
Naranjo, Alfredo 336
Naranjo, Pachi 266
Naranjos, Los 258
Narell, Andy 318, 320
Nascimento, Milton 60, 262, 326
Nat King Cole español 15, 109, 137, 162, 199, 203, 275
Nativo, El, Conjunto 296
Naturaleza 51
Navarro, Chucho 189
Navarro, Fats 173, 193, 199, 349
Navarro, Paquito 327
Nazareño, El 236
Ne me quitte pas 339
Necesito una amiga 236
Necesito una mujer cocinera 219
Nefertiti 317
Negra Leonó, La 53
Negra Pola, La 313
Negra sabrosura 283
Negra tú no va a querè 23
Negret 89
Negrita 294
Negrita Trini, La 106
Negrito del batey, El 237, 309–10
Negrito gulembo, El 235
Negro bembón, El 48, 235
Negro bon bon 189
Negro bueno, El 23
Negro Estrella y su Orquesta 313
Negro José caliente 21
Negro muñanga 139
Negro ñañamboro 139
Negro sociedad 351
Negrón, Frankie 296
Negros Catedráticos, Los 19
negros franceses 18, 46
Negros Rumberos, Los 19
Nelson, Bobby 221
Nenas del Barrio, Las 271
nengón 33, 345
Nereidas 332
Neri Cabrera, Felipe 57
Nettai Tropical Jazz Big Band 340
Neurasténica, La 75
New arrival, The 364
New Burnt Sugar 339
New Swing Sextet 226
New World Spirit 315, 365
New York Band, The 313
New York Now! 318
New Yorker, Orchesta 291
Newborn, Phineas 199
Newman, Joe 174, 239
Newman, Paul 326
Neyra, Roderico, see Rodney 109
NG La Banda 153
Nganga kisi 296
ngoma 17, 39
Niágara, Conjunto 121

Nica's Dream 200
Niche, El 110, 171, 234
Niche, Grupo 339, 364
Niches, Los 339, 364
Nicholas Brothers 337
Nichols, Red 91
Niehaus, Lenny 202
Nieto, Johnny 169
Nieto, Osvaldo 86
Nieto, Ubaldo 177, 194, 288
Nietos Del Rey, Los 312–3
Nieve de los años, La 184
Nieve de mi vida 58
Nieves, Tito 81, 287, 288, 295
Night Beat 201
Night Ritual 179
Night Song 200
Night Train Mambo 162
Nin, Joaquín 184, 249
Niña de los besos, La 92
Niña Rita 148
Nine Flags 240
Nine Four Four (944) Colombus 319
Ninfa del valle 60
Niño, El (batá player) 29, 48, 261, 294,
Niño, El (Jorge Alfonso) 261
No cuentes conmigo 180
No fumes ese crack 326
No juegues con los santos 58, 297
No me engañen 188
No me importas tú 218
No me llores más 125
No me maltrates nena 58
No me niegues tu cariño 229
No me quieras así 231
No mojen a la materia 153
No Noise 172
No quiero llanto 274
No sueño más 282
No te agites 212
No te importa saber 184
No vale la pena 72
No viertas una lágrima 103
Noble, Héctor Hal, see Tambú 324
Noche criolla 59
Noche cubana 156, 340
Nocturno antillano 152
Noone, Jimmy 94
Nosotros 116, 156, 232
Nostalgia 128
Nothing but the Soul 198
Nottingham, Jim 161, 202
Novedades, Orquesta 120, 284
Novedades, Orchesta (Gene Hernández's) 284
Novel, Orchesta 284
Novia mía 155
Novia que yo tenía, La 103
Nubes de ensueño 52
Nudisme à Cuba, Le 66
Nuestra Herencia 284
Nuestro idilio 132
nueva canción, see nueva trova
Nueva Compania, La 284
Nueva Manteca 339
neuva timba 253–5
Nueva Tribu, La 311
nueva trova 213, 250, 251, 345, 355, 366

nuevo mozambique 212
nuevo ritmo 111–21
Nuevo Ritmo de Cuba, Orchestra 182
Nuevo ritmo omelenko 232
Nuevo son 250
Número 6, El 283, 294
Núñez, Alcide ("Yellow") 2
Núñez Correa, José 212

O'Farrill, "Chico" (Arturo) 239–40
O'Farrill, Juan Pablo 92
O'Farrill, Miguel 120
O'chachiri-o 190
O'leri-o 190
O morro não tem vez 321
O'nana-o 190
O'tin-tine-o 193
Obatalá 317, 179
Obatalá yeya 179
obí-apá 16
Obiedo, Ray 324
Obispo de Ponce, El 100, 103
Occidente, Sexteto 59, 60, 71, 85, 88, 131–2, 169, 350,
Ocho 274
Ochoa, Eliades 256–7, 266
Ochoa Ferrara, Eglis 257
Ochún 12, 14, 109, 149, 177, 292
Octavio, Angel, see Cotán
Ofelia 331
ogán 17
Ogguere 48, 149
Oh humanidad 246, 366
Oigan bien mi guaguancó 291
Ojalá que llueva café 314
Ojos chinos 237
Ojos malvados 71, 132
Ojos triunfadores 69
Okidoke 172
Oliva, Carlos 306
Oliva, René 73, 81
Olivencia, Tommy 281, 302–4
Oliver, King 95
Olivera Gavilán, Joaquín 249, 258
Olivera, Hernán 278, 296, 279
Olivero, Ramón 101, 177
Oller, Francisco 85
Oller, Gabriel 125, 85
Olmo, José 249
Olor a lluvia 311
Olvido 58, 66, 63
omelé 13–14
On the Bongo Beat 192
onda areíto 210, 305
onda nueva 335
Onda va bien, La 364, 322
One hundred and tenth Street and Fifth Avenue 86, 177, 276
One o' Clock Jump 185
One, Two, Three, Kick!, see Uno, dos y tres 92–3
Ono, Yoko 318
Oo Ya Koo 193
Oppenheimer, Joselito ("Bumbum") 100
Opus Trece 13, 251, 255, 263
Oquendo, Manny 178–9, 180, 188, 193, 220–1, 228, 271, 278

Orbón, Julián 76
Oréfiche, Armando 340, 82, 134, 335
Oréfiche and His Havana Cuban Boys 134
Oreli, Elia 66
Organisashon Kompleto 337
Orgy in Rhythm 198
Oriental, Orquesta 139
Oriental, Trio (of Maximiliano Sánchez) 152
Oriente, Conjunto de 121
Oriente, Cuarteto 212
Oriente, Quinteto 257
Original De Manzanillo Orquesta 266
OriginaL Dixieland Jazz Band 78
Originales, Los 360, 228, 294
orisha 12, 13, 126, 255, 263, 264, 285, 306, 339, 346
Orisha Dreams 364
Orishas 12, 13, 285, 306, 339
Orishas, Los 264
Oriza 144, 233
Orlando, Ramón 311, 314
Ormas, Faustino ("El Guayabero") 258
Ornithology 172
Oro, incienso y mira 195
Orovio, Helio 209
Orquídea, Septet 126
Ortega, "Pillo" 33
Ortiz, Fernando 9–10, 13–14, 46, 149
Ortiz, Johnny 290, 295
Ortiz, Mario 226, 238, 281, 301–4
Ortiz, "Perico" (Luis) 102, 275, 281, 290, 300
Ortiz, Rafael ("Mañungo") 59, 68, 93, 212
Ortiz, Randy 328
Ortiz Dávila, Pedro, see Davilita
Orú, Grupo 264
Osacar, Elio (bassist) 87, 275
Osacar, Elio, see Sonny Bravo 275, 290
Osain 149
Óscar y sus Estrellas 335
Other Road, The 274
otra 24, 263, 287, 299, 304, 311
Otra Vez 299, 304
Otra Visión 263
Our Man in Havana 239
Ovales, Luis 313
Ovalle, Gustavo 14, 340
Ovalle, Sonny 311–12
Ovando, María Teresa 68
Overton, Hal 175
Oviedo, Funciana 25
Oviedo, Gilberto 246
Oviedo, Isaac 68, 70, 251
Oviedo, Julienne 256
Oye cómo va 217, 276, 284, 328
Oye lo que te trae Rumbavana 250
Oye los tambores 285
Oye mi bajo 180
Oye mi guaguancó 179
Oye mi piano 309

Oye mi vidita 93
Oyelo que te conviene 220
Óyeme 174
Óyeme mulata 228

Pa' bailar na' ma 310, 363
pa' ca 210, 355
Pa' bravo yo 268, 290
Pa' los rumberos 179, 276, 328
Pa' Salinas 185
Pablo Pueblo 279
Pabón, David 304
Pabón, Tony 210–11, 216–17, 228–9, 237, 269, 311, 313, 346, 361
pachanga 216–17
Pachanga, La 135, 204, 210–11, 216–17, 228, 232, 362
Pachanga at the Caravana Club 217
Pachanga con Tito Puente 217
Pachanga del fútbol, La 217
Pachanga en la sociedad 216–7
Pachanga in New York 216
Pachanga se baila así, La 217, 232, 362
Pachanga With Barretto 217
Pacheco, Rafael Azarías 229
Pacheco, Johnny 4, 181, 183, 216–17, 226–9, 232, 241, 267, 269–72, 275, 281, 287–8, 290–1, 294, 313, 338, 362–3, 366
Pacheco, Vicente 312–13
Pacheco y Melón 275
Pacheco's Descarga 183
Pachito Alonso y sus Kini Kini 255
Pachito y Las Nuvíolas 255
"Pacho" (bassist) 139, 183, 210, 255–6, 361
Pacho Alonso y Los Modernistas 210
Paderewski, Ignacy Jan 136
Padrón, Julio 252, 261–2, 265
Padrón, Pedro Izquierdo, see Pello el Afrokán
Padrón, Roberto 211
Paella, La 170, 354
Pagán, Ralfi 226
Pagani, Arsenio "Federico" 86, 164–5, 170, 174–5, 178, 191
Pagani, Popi 181, 183
paila, see timbales
Palacio, Hortencia 66
Palau, Felipe 81
Palau, Luis 81
Palau, Manolo 81
Palau, Rafael 81
Palés Matos, Luis 233
"Palito" (conguero) 144
"Palito" (maraquero) 71
Palladium Ballroom 145, 164–5, 171–3, 180, 183, 185–6, 195, 200, 204, 217, 221–2, 227, 235, 285, 289, 292, 299, 352, 359, 361
Palladium Memories 218
Palm, Juan, see Mentoquín
Palma, Pepe 249
Palmas 278, 363
Palmieri, Carlos Manuel "Charlie" 136, 179, 180, 182–3, 188–9, 196–7, 203–4,

212, 217, 220, 222–3, 226–8, 230, 232, 236, 238, 276–7, 280, 286, 301, 315, 323, 353, 362

Palmieri, Eddie 136, 188, 199, 219, 220–1, 226, 228–9, 232, 236, 240, 267, 269–71, 276, 278–9, 284, 291, 299, 304, 315–16, 321–2, 339, 354, 363

Palmira 52, 80, 145, 148

palo 32, 54, 125, 346

Palo, El 262

Palo cagueiran 127

Palo mayombe 232

Palo pa' rumba 278

Paloma, La 78

pambiche 307, 317, 345

Pamparana 215

Pan de piquito 128

Panamá 2, 66, 131, 144, 236, 251, 268, 273, 293–5, 334, 337, 346

Panama Blues 320

"Panama Joe" (Preudhomme, David) 183, 204

Panamericana, Orquesta 185, 234

Panamonk 320

"Pancho El Bravo" (Alberto Cruz) 120, 138

Pancho Majagua y Tata Villegas (Francisco Salvo Salazar and Carlos de Villegas) 50

Panchos, Los Trio 332, 189, 232

pandero (or *pandereta*) 346, 100

Panic in Puerto Rico 192

Panquelero, El 91, 167

Pantoja, Victor 204, 241, 352

"Papa Kila" (Antolín Súarez) 125

"Papá Montero" 25

Papa Loves Mambo 162

Papá Montero 48

"Papaíto" (Muñoz Salazar, Mario) 208, 220, 285, 311

papalote 17, 28

Papin y sus Rumberos, *see* **Papines, Los**

Papines, Los 140, 190, 244, 246, 261, 287, 303, 315

Pappy Ali y sus Rumberos 183, 204

Paquito Blowin' 318

Para adorarte 54

Para la fiesta me voy 274

Para la niña y la señora 127

Para la quimbombó 217

Para los barrios 337

Para luego es tarde 262

Para Ochún 292

Para Vigo me voy 47, 97

Parábola negra 170

Paralítico, El 64

Parapar, José "El Galleguito" 50

Paraparampampín 190

Pare cochero 274, 87, 116, 171, 274

Pareja, La 231

Parisian Thoroughfare 226

Parker, Charlie 157, 163, 172–3, 177, 184, 191–2, 198, 198, 203, 227, 321, 349, 361

Parker's Mood 226

Parlá, Alicia, *see* Mariana

parranda 346

Parranda, La 255

Pascualino 155

paseíto 268

Pasito tun tun 232

Paso de Encarnación, El 264, 273

Pasó en Tampa 125, 192

Paso Franco, El 29

Pastime Rag No. 5 78

Pastor, Paquito 221, 282, 298

Pastrano, Joey 223, 226, 291, 227

Pastrano, Willie 226

Patato y Totico 219–20, 361

Patria, Cuarteto 362, 252, 257

Patricia 158, 271

Patrick, Pat 238–9

"Paulito FG" (Paulo Fernández Gallo) 255

Paulito y Lilon 109, 165, **195–6**

Paulito FG y su Elite 251, 255

Paunetto, Bobby 315

Paunetto's Point 315

Paz, Arsalén 169

Paz, Victor 219, 304, 319

Paz, Rafael, de la 144, 187

Paz, Ray, de la 274, 277, 287, 295, 303, 367

Peanut Vendor, The, See Manisero, El

Pearson, Duke 238

"Pecoso, El", *see* Herrera, Lázaro

Pedro Navaja 269

Pedroso, César "Pupi" 247–8

Peláez, Enrique 91

Pelaguero, Eladio, *see* Yayo El Indio

Pelegrín, Oscar 68, 71, 112

Pellado, Angel 246

"Pello el Afrokán" (Pedro Izquierdo Padrón) 211, 287, 345, 355, 361

Pellot, Héctor 186, 237

Pelotera la bola 129

peña 50, 251

Peña, Enrique 23–4, 329, 356

Peña, José 130

Peña, Angel Rafael "Lito" 185, 227, 304, 369

Peñalver, Eddy 262

Peñalver, Emilio 140–4, 152

Peñalver, Santiago 136, 144

Penicilina 117

Pennies from Heaven 284

Pensamiento, Trio 50

Pensativa 323

Pent-Up House 316

Penumbra 332

Pepes, Los Trio 189

Pepín, "Papo" 284, 288, 300, 319, 338

Pepito mi corazón 163

Pepper, Art 184, 203, 324

Peralta, Pedro "Chichi" 314, 364

Peralta, Luis 204

Peraza, Armando 3, 129, 195–6, 198, 204, 238–9, 241, 321, 326, 328

Peraza, Cheo 239

Perdido 200, 203

Perdido en la cidudad 281

Perdón 188

Peregrino, Pablo 332

Pereira, Liduvino 130

Pereira, Juan Francisco "Tata" 68, 116, 130, 356

Pereira Socarrás, José, *see* Chiquito

Perera, Humberto 121

Pérez, Amaury 255

Pérez, Bernie 300

Pérez, Chicky 226

Pérez, Daniel 137

Pérez, Danilo 6, 295, 318–19, 321, 324, 342

Pérez, David 261, 274

Pérez, Eddie 234, 237

Pérez, Edelmiro 71

Pérez, Francisco "Machito" 73

Pérez, Gerardo "Calabaza" 73

Pérez, Graciela 67, 76, 152, 171

Pérez, Hugo 313

Pérez, Isidro 137, 139–40, 349

Pérez, Jesús 13, 142, 149, 247

Pérez, Juan Irene 88, 286

Pérez, Lou 228–9, 284

Pérez, Manuel 2

Pérez, Milito 311

Pérez, Pedro Pablo 255

Pérez, Rolando 265

Pérez, Ruby 313

Pérez, Tony 254, 265

Pérez A., Jesús "El Niño" 294

Pérez Anckermann, Rafael 133

Pérez Balladares, Ernesto 342

Pérez Prado, Dámaso 115, 121, 144, 156, 158, 345

Pérez Prado, Pantaleón 159

Pérez Sanguily, Tomás 60

Perez y Ramona 85

Perfecta, La 220–1

Perfecta Combinación, La 275, 288, 290

Perfidia (de Domínguez) 332

Perfidia (de Ruiz) 51

perico ripiao 307, 309, 345

Periódico de ayer 291

Perla marina 74

Perlas de tu juramento, Las 23

Perlas del son 127

Perlas Del Son, Las 252

Permuí de Valdés, Anita 66

Persip, Charlie 194–5

Perspectiva, Grupo 261

Perspective 366

Perucho y Peruchín 185

Peruchín (Pedro Justiz) 133, 136, 139–40, 145, 152, 161, 185, 204, 212, 215, 262, 354

Peruchín Jr. (Pedro A. Justiz) 266

Peruchín, piano y ritmo 136, 159

Pesante, Rafael 92

Pescao de Aguadilla 103

Pete with a Latin Beat 204

Peterson, Domingo 186

Peterson, Ralph 325

Petite suite 115

Petrillo, James C. 171

Phillips, Flip 163, 172–3, 180

Pía y Rivero, Raimundo 76

piano 29, 42, 51, 66–7, 69, 70–2, 75, 79, 80–2, 85–6, 91–2, 94–6, 101, 103–4, 106, 111–17, 121, 128, 130–7, 140–1, 144, 147, 148, 156, 159, 169, 175–7, 180, 185–6, 193, 195, 201, 202–4, 210, 214–5, 221, 224, 228, 234, 237, 239–41, 247–52, 254, 259, 262, 267, 269, 271, 275–7, 279–80, 284, 286, 290, 293, 298, 301–5, 307–9, 319–21, 329, 338, 344, 349–51, 356, 360, 363, 367

Piano Merengue (by Conquet) 309

Piano merengue (by Damirón) 309, 363

Piano y ritmo 136, 159

Pianoforte 215

Picadillo 176, 276

Picadilly Boys, The 178

Picao 284

Picket, Jesse 78

Pickin' Chicken 115

Pickin' the Cabbage 191

Pico y pala 65

Pidiendo de Nuevo 73

Pidre "El Gallego" 144

Piedra, Elpidio 117

Piedra Hernández, José "Pepito Piedra" 71

Piel canela 177, 189, 279

Pike, Dave 240

Pilderot 158

Piliche 101

pilón 128, 210–12, 252, 256

Piloto, Gerardo, *see* **Piloto y Vera**

Piloto, Giraldo 254

Piloto y Vera (Gerardo Piloto and Alberto Vera) 156

Pimienta 139, 185, 297, 331, 336, 363

Pimienta y Sal 151

Pin-Pin, Conjunto 182

Piñares, José Antonio 53, 152

Piñeda, Leopoldo 282

Pineda, Nelson 127

Piñeiro, Ignacio 4, 16, 59–63, 169, 187, 218, 252, 271, 350, 360

Piñeiro, Inés 350

Pinos, Los Grupo 252

pingüino 198

Pinto Canto, Miguel 211, 249

Pinza, Gilberto 171

Pintura blanca, La 219

Pío pío 297

Pipo y Arcaño 155

Piquero, Clemente, *see* Chicho

Piragüero, El 219

Piraña 273

Pirela, Felipe 334

piquete 36, 346

Pito, El 225, 353

Pizarro, Carlos 183

Plá, Enrique 259, 261, 355

Plá, Luisito 151–2

Plá, Roberto 339

Planas, Raúl 129, 263, 339

Plantación adentro 269, 279

Plantation Orchestra 95

plante 168, 346
Plástico 279
Plata, La, Quintet 106
Plata, La, Sexteto 183, 216
Platanal de bartolo, El 139
Platería, Orquesta 340
Playa, La 183, 191, 327, 330, 333–4, 344, 348, 351
Playa, La, Sextet 182, 218, 224
Plechanga de trabalengua, La 236
Plegaria vallenata 289
plena 232–8
Plena bomba, La 233
Plena internacional 185
Plena Libre 304, 363
Plenealo 304
Pleneros de La 110, Los 100
Pluma de tu sombrero, La 21
Pochy y su Coco Band 131
Ponciana 240
Polanco, Johnny 305
Poldín y su Pimienta 185
Poleo, Orlando 14, 364
Pollera colorá, La 219
Ponce 20, 86, 99, 100–3, 182, 237, 286–7, 290–2, 295, 297, 308, 316, 318–9, 346, 364
Ponce, Daniel 20, 286–7, 316–8, 364
Poncena, Sonora 16, 268, 290, 295, 297, 310, 363
Pongan atención 145
Ponle la montura al potro 250
Ponme el alcolado Juana 237
Poor Boy 226
Poor Man's Blues 95
Por el pecho no 298
Por eso yo canto salsa 276
Por qué latió mi corazón 51
¿Por qué te pones así? 111, 126
Por tí 106
Por tus ojos negros 331
Por un beso de tu boca 47
Porfiado corazón 152
Poro, Alfonso "Clavelito" 116
Porque me siento cubano 285
Porque tú sufres 125, 192
Portabales, Guillermo (Quesada del Castillo) 76, 78
Portal, Odilio 152, 156
Portela, Guillermo 130
Portela, Paquito 66
Porter, Cole 177, 184
Portillo, Miguel Angel 61
Portillo de la Luz (César) 155
Portraits of Cuba 317–8, 364
Portuarios e La Habana, Grupo e Los 246
Portuondo, Haydée 150, 152, 155, 208
Portuondo, Omara 140, 150, 152, 151, 256–7, 362
"Pototo" Fernández, Leopoldo, ("Tres Patines") 152
Pototo y Filomeno (Leopoldo Fernández and Anibal de Mar) 110, 152–3
Pous, Arquímedes 48–9, 57, 59, 80, 139
Poveda, Ivón 334
Povedo, Manuel 66

Powell, Bud 173, 200, 226, 259, 325
Powell, Seldon 238
Power 6, 15, 44, 64, 167, 174, 208, 217, 250, 273, 278, 287–8, 301, 304, 314, 342, 353, 363
Pozo, "Chano" (Luciano) 189–99
Pozo, Chino (Francisco Valdés) 170, 176, 178–9, 199, 240, 271, 326
Pozo Martínez, Eliseo, *see* Colorao, El
Prajo, El 89
Prats, Jaime 79
Prats, Rodrigo 49, 249
Preciosa 103, 105
pregón 36–7, 116, 346
Pregón del pescador, El 128
Prelude to a Kiss 279
Premice, Josephine 199
Prendes, Ramoncito 72
Prepara los cueros 251
Prepárate para bañarte 276
Preso, El 188, 254, 337
Préstame la olla Teresa 225
Priester, Julian 18
Prieta santa, La 21
Prieto, Dafni 265
Prieto, Lázaro 125, 127, 208, 220
Primera Maravilla del Siglo, La 111
Prince 323, 327
Princesa del dollar, La 254
Procura 314
Profecía 132, 152
"Professor Longhair" (Byrd, Henry) 78
Promesa 66
Promised Land (The) 316
Propuesta (La) 295
Protesta, La 269
Protesta de los chivos, La 254
Proyecto, Grupo 263
Proyecto Uno 314
Prudencia, "Macay" (Macario) 337
"Pucho" (Brown, Henry) 240
Pucho and The Latin Soul Brothers 362
Puchunga (singer) 262
Puchunguita 82
Puebla, Carlos 213
Pueblo Nuevo se pasó 126
Puente, Tito (Ernesto) 174–86
Puente Goes Jazz 201
Puente Guillot, Augusto 33, 64
Puente on the Bridge 217
Puente, Richie 306
Puentes, "Tito" (Ernesto Antonio) 339
Puerto, Carlos (del)
Puerto Padre
Puerto Rico 98–106
Puerto Rico, Orquesta 103
Puerto Rico All Stars 363, 238
Puerto Rico rumbamba 101
Puerto Rico, Septeto 101
Puerto Rico, Sexteto 88
Puerto Rican Brass 304

Puertorican Breakdown 194
Puerto Rican Power 304
Pulga, La 72
"Puma (El)" (José Luis Rodríguez) 336
Puntilla (Orlando Ríos) 15, 287
Puntilla (singer) 318
punto 35–6
Pupi y su Charanga 228
Pure Emotion 319, 364
Puro teatro 231
Push Push Push 225, 362

quadrille 18
Que bueno baila Usted 142, 143
Que extraña es la vida 106
Que extraño es eso 54
Que gente averigua 237
Que linda eres tú 69
Que lo gocen todo 285
Que no, que no 21, 175
Que palo es ese 247
Que rico el mambo 158–64
¿Qué sera eso mi compay? 143
¿Qué será lo que quiere el negro? 311
¡Que tabaco malo! 103
¿Qué tiene esa cintura? 248
Que vengan los rumberos 170
Que viva Changó, see Santa Bárbara
Quejas (Las) 22
Quesada, Bobby 223
Quevedo, Pablo 71
Quezada, Jocelyn 313
Quian Sardiñas, Ramón, *see* Monguito
Quiero mucho a mi suegra 219
Quiero un sombrero 132
Quiet Stroll 239
Quijano, Joe (José Baya) 183, 220, 221, 233, 301, 362
Quimbara 290
Quince 69
Quiniela del día 298
Quiñones, Francisco 88
Quintana, Ismael 178, 220, 271, 275, 277, 278, 287, 291, 353, 363
Quintero, José 66
Quintero, Luis 229, 237, 310
Quintero, Luisito 296
Quintero, Nieves 99
Quintero, Rafael 336
quinto 28, 31, 190, 195, 346
Quinto, Pancho 247, 362
Quintón, Roberto 106
Quique y Chocolate 273
Quirino con su tres 48
Quisiera bailar el merengue 143
Quisqueya, Dueto 93
Quisqueya, Conjunto 313
Quisqueya, Grupo 309
Quisqueya, Trio 104
Quítate de la vía Perico 235, 281
Quizás, quizás, quizás 156, 161

"Rabanito" 144
Radio CMQ, Orquesta De 110, 126, 138

Radio Cadena Suaritos, Orquesta De 110
Radio Centro, Orquesta De 132
Radio Mil Diez, Orquesta De 138
Raeburn, Boyd 137, 201
Rainey, Ma' 194
Ralph Robles Was Here 226
"Ramito" (Morales Ramos, Florencio) 84, 99, 360
Ramos, José 303
Ramos, Mike 165
Ramos, Pedro 251
Ramos, Severino 128, 151
Ramos, Tomás 251
Ran kan kan 178, 352
Random Thoughts 278
rap 3, 34, 255, 266, 278, 287, 326, 327, 336, 339
Rap O' Clap 327
"Rapindey", *see* Guerra, Marcelino
Rapsodia de cueros 135
Rapsodia negra 149
Rascando, rascando 134
"Rasputín" (July Mateo) 313
Rathbone, Basil 177
Ravel, Maurice vii, 47, 202, 313, 322
Ray, Fausto 311, 313
Ray, Richie (Ricardo Maldonado) 4, 16, 223, 302, 33
Raza latina, La 273
Rebelión de los feos, La 212, 311
Recio, Mario 252
Recordando el ayer 290
Recuerdos 202
Red Hot 317
Redención 51
Redman, Don 81, 167, 201
Redskin Rumba 203
redoble 41
Reed, Lou 295
Reeves, Diane 325
Reflejos de luna 189
Regatillo (bassist) 124
regina 50
Regina, Elis 239
regla de ocha, see santería
Reina, Félix 112, 117, 118, 211, 228
Reina Isabel 139
Reina negra 171
Reinhardt, Django 67
Reinoso, Aurelio 156
Reinoso, Celina 351
Reinoso, Nicolás 262
Reloj de pastora (El) 236, 293
Remigio (bassist) 69
Renascimento 60
Repicao 284
Repilado, Salvador 257
Repilado Muñoz, Francisco ("Compay Segundo") 153, 154
repique 41, 100, 307, 346
requinto (cordophone) 103, 189, 313
requinto (bomba drum) 99, 346
requinto (tambourine) 100

Resemblance 277
Reunion 318
Reunión With Miguelito Valdés 219
Reutilio Jr. (Domínguez, Lázaro) 14, 17, 110, 145, 152–3, 266
Revé, Elio 33, 212, 247, 250, 255–6, 258, 344
Revé Duvergel, Elio "Elito" 250, 338
Reve, Orquesta 247, 250
Revelacion, Orquesta 279, 291
Reverón, Ricardo 71
Revilla de Camargo (countess) 120
Revolving Bandstand 201
Rey, Fausto 311, 313
Rey De Reyes, Conjunto 126
Rey, Cuarteto Del 152, 213
Rey del mambo, El 21
Reyes 73, Los 251
Reyes, Chewy 96
Reyes, Eulogio "Yoyo" 231
Reyes, Ignacio 180
Reyes, Jorge 265
Reyes, Juan 106
Reyes, Orlando 129
Reyes, Oscar 335
Reyes, Pepe 156, 333
Reyes, "Pepecito" 45, 76, 117, 249
Reyes, Radamés 145
Reyes, Rodolfo 209
Reyes, Sandy 312–3
Reyes, Walfredo (de los) 4, 130, 132, 139, 180, 214, 238, 306, 323
Reyes, Walfredo (de los), Jr. 140
Reyes, Alfau, Rhadamés 306
Reynoso, "Manolo" (Manuel) 59, 68
Reynoso, Trío 311
Rezo abacuá 220
Rhapsody in Blue 259
rhumba 1, 96, 175, 330–1, 341
Rhumba Finale 195
Rhumba in Swing 193
Rhumba Rhapsody 177
Rhythm Machine 275
Ribot, Agustín 129
Ribot, Marc 328
Ricanstruction 278
Ricardito (singer) 250
Ricardo, Richie 313
Rich, Buddy 173, 204
Richards, Emil 204
Richards, Johnny 202
Richardson, Jerome 238
Rica mulata 211
Rica pulpa 203
Rico, Filiberto 331
Rico, Ricardo 310
Rico merengón 291
Rico pilón 210
Rico suave 327
Riestra, José 331, 357
Rigola, La 135, 308, 310
Rigual, Carlos 152, 332
Rigual, Elsa 66
Rigual, Mario 152, 332

Rigual, Pedro "Pituko" 66, 152, 156, 332
Rimski-Korsakov, Nicolaï 258
Rin rin lea 59
Río, Alfonso (del) 63
Ríos, Anthony 311
Ríos, Efraím 253
Ríos, Freddie 165
Ríos, José "Furito" 322
Riot 226
Risa loca 189
Riset, Panchito 56, 75, 87, 92, 106, 125, 187, 361
Rita (bassist) 66
Ritchie Family 327
Ritmo alegre 278
Ritmo bailable de película 230
Ritmo Batanga 135
Ritmo bembé 221
Ritmo Caliente 141, 184, 314
Ritmo changüí 283
Ritmo de pollos 117, 274
Ritmo Oriental, La 121, 248, 254, 294, 362
Ritmo pilón 128
Ritmos Santeros 126
Rivas, Jerry 298
River Is Deep, The 317, 364
Rivera, "Champito" 41, 169
Rivera, "Chiqui" 237
Rivera, Don 185
Rivera, Eddie "Gua Gua" 302
Rivera, Alfredo "Felito" 169
Rivera, Hector 183, 206, 223
Rivera, Ismael "Maelo" 234–6
Rivera, Iván 304
Rivera, Jerry 296
Rivera, Johnny 281, 296
Rivera, Junior 282
Rivera, Larry 186
Rivera, Margarita 234, 279
Rivera, Mario 219, 248, 316, 317–9, 338, 342
Rivera, Tomaso "Maso" 99, 182
Rivera, Rivera Castillo, Efraín "Mon" 236–7
Rivera, Niño (Andrés Echevarría) 126–7, 141, 155–6, 204, 212, 333
Rivera, Sergio 288
Rivera, Tito 138
Rivera, Yolanda 297
Rivera Alers, Ramón 176, 233
Rivera Ortiz, Juan 302
Rivero, Facundo 71, 128, 142, 149, 150–2, 156, 231
Riveros, Los 151
Rives, "El Boy" 34
Rives, Ramón "Mongo" 34
Riverside, Orquesta 126, 136, 138, 145, 152, 214, 333
Riviera, Orquesta 212
Rizo, José 324
Rizo, Marco 92
Roach, Max 193, 199, 203, 285
Roberto Roena y sus Megatones 293
Robertson, Ira Ray, see Mendoza, Chico
Robinson, Jackie 198
Robinson, Smokey 222
Robinson, Sugar Chile 98
Robles, Ralph 226
Roca de la laguna, La 101–2

Roche, Pablo "Okilapka" 48, 149
Rock It 318, 327
rock n' roll 115–7, 163, 180, 222, 224, 239
rockambo 223
Rockefeller, David 245
Rodgers and Hart 93
Roditi, Claudio 319–21, 325, 364
Rodney (Roderico Neyra) 109, 325
Rodrigues, Jair 239
Rodríguez, Adriano 258
Rodríguez, Alejandro "Mulatón" 4, 59
Rodríguez, Albita 305
Rodríguez, Alfredo 120, 271, 286, 339–40
Rodríguez, Armando 321
Rodríguez, Ignacio Loyola Rodríguez Skull "Arsenio" 6, 21, 67, 110, 115, 120–7, 131, 136, 144, 158, 168, 171, 180–1, 188, 192, 198, 217, 219, 221, 223–4, 227–9, 232, 236, 251, 261, 264, 273, 281, 284, 286, 297, 313, 328, 351, 358
Rodríguez, Bobby (bassist) 178–80, 194–5, 221–3, 228, 238, 241, 276, 316
Rodríguez, Bobby (flautist, clarinetist, saxophonist) 283, 294
Rodríguez, Camilo 129, 139
Rodríguez, Cándido 226
Rodríguez, Charles 214
Rodríguez, Charlie 281
Rodríguez, Chucho 187
Rodríguez, Felipe 217
Rodríguez, Félix, *see* Corozo
Rodríguez, Félix Manuel, *see* Capó, Bobby
Rodríguez, Florencio, *see* Carusito
Rodríguez, Frankie 279, 302–3
Rodríguez, George 226
Rodríguez, Higinio 50, 57
Rodríguez, Johnny (singer) 87, 93, 180, 315, 333
Rodríguez, Johnny (conguero) 274, 290, 316
Rodríguez, Julio 189
Rodríguez, Manuel Ubaldo "Lalo" 277, 288, 302–4
Rodríguez, Maso 94
Rodríguez, Nicolás 95
Rodríguez, Pedro "Pellín" 176, 237, 298
Rodríguez, Pete 223, 226, 294
Rodríguez, Pete (Pedro Juan) "El Conde" 229, 275, 278, 285, 288, 290, 313
Rodríguez, Rafael 106
Rodríguez, Ramón 281
Rodríguez, Raulín 314
Rodríguez, Ray 273
Rodríguez, Rick 327
Rodríguez, Roberto 282
Rodríguez, Rod 81
Rodríguez, Silvio 213, 261, 353
Rodríguez, Siro 65, 143

Rodríguez, Pablo "Tito" 174–86
Rodríguez, Víctor 237
Rodríguez, Willie 199, 284
Rodríguez de Tío, Lola 100
Rodríguez Fife, Guillermo 51
Rodríguez Juliá, Edgardo 235, 299
Rodríguez Medina, Héctor 304
Roena, Roberto (Iván Rohena Vázquez) 234, 237, 275, 287–8, 293, 298, 300
Rogers, Barry 220, 229, 236, 270, 283
Rogers, Juanito 124, 127
Rogers, Shorty 161, 202–3
Rohena Vázquez, Iván, *see* Roena, Roberto
Roig, Gonzalo 137
Rojas, Juan Carlos 263
Rojas, Martín 355
Rojas, José Antonio "Ñico" 155, 258
Rojas, "Tito" 296
"Rojitas" Rojas, Jorge Luis 252
Roland, Joe 182
Roldán, Amadeo 356
Rollins, Sonny 203, 238
Rolón, Catalino 276, 285
Román, Joseíto 164, 309
romance 32
Romance Musical 117
Romay, Pablito 116
Romero, Aldemaro 333–5
Romero, Elliott 221, 229
Romero, Hernán Ray "Little Ray" 175
Romero, Roberto, see Allen, Tito
Romeu, Antonio María 51, 58, 66, 69–71, 79, 91, 111, 117, 136, 166, 181
Romeu, Armandito 355
Romeu, Armando 72, 79, 81, 111–2, 128, 136–7, 140, 195, 198, 214–5, 255, 330, 355
Romeu, Mario 139–40, 349
Rompan el cuero 332
Rompe saragüey 9, 127
Rompiendo el hielo 286
Rompiendo la rutina 72–3, 97, 248, 286
Ron es mi medicina, El 311
Roncona (Benito González) 26
Roncos, Los 29, 54, 60, 149, 218
Roncos Chiquitos, Los 246
Rondón, César Miguel 14, 248
Rondstadt, Linda 295
Roosevelt, Theodore 84, 157
Roqué, Roberto 88
Roque, Rufino 116
Roque, Victor 313
Ros, Edmundo 38, 331, 357
Ros, Lázaro 247
Rosa, Angel 178
Rosa, Roy 204
Rosa, Orland, de la 138, 150, 152, 154, 156
Rosa, Oscar, de la 175, 185
Rosa la China 351
Rosa Rhumba 91

Rosa roja, La 54
Rosa, La Trio 152
Rosado, Josué 300
Rosales, Mario 56
Rosario, Félix (del) 311
Rosario, Ray 234
Rosario, Fernando "Willie" 268, 295–6, 299, 301, 304
Rosario Marín, Luis 298
Rosas, Edwin 297
Rosell, Electo, see Chepín
Round Midnight 200
Rouy, Gérard 161, 368
Rubalcaba, Gonzalo 22, 24, 249, 251, 262, 305, 325, 339, 342, 362, 364
Rubalcaba, Jacobo 126
Rubalcaba, William 258
Rubio, Manuel 51
Rugolo, Pete 202
Ruiz, Alberto 129
Ruiz, Frankie 296, 302–3
Ruiz, Hilton 317–8
Ruiz, Mario 68
Ruiz, Otmaro 321, 325
Ruiz, Rosendo 51, 59, 74, 117, 120, 284, 367
Ruiz, Rosendo, Jr. "Rosendito" 156
Ruiz Boza, Arístides 252
Rumba, La 25, 49, 156, 173, 182, 186, 213, 277, 303, 366
rumba abierta 173, 202
Rumba Band 331, 357
rumba brava 24–8
Rumba caliente 104, 275
Rumba en swing 25
Rumba gallega 175
Rumba Ketumba 340
Rumba matunga 156
Rumba para Monk 317
Rumba Rhapsody 87
Rumba soy yo, La 186
Rumba Symphony 25
Rumbantela, La 156
Rumbas 1, 9, 22, 25–7, 179, 195, 198, 201, 245, 247, 250, 305, 343
Rumbavana, Conjunto 129, 151, 250–1, 256, 293
Rumbera mayor 296
Rumbola 361, 195
Russell, Andy 333
Russell, Luis 85, 91, 201
Russell, George 192, 203
Russell, Ross 172, 368

Saavedra, Manolo 139, 349
Sabador 338
Sabat, Pedro Juan 87
Sabater, Jimmy 183, 224, 226, 271, 274, 277
Sabaya, Miguel 59
Sabio, El 292
Sablon, Jean 357
Sabor 4, 230, 361
Sabor 305
Sabor a mí 230
Sabor De Cuba 135
Sabor de pachanga 217
Sabor y raza 282
Sabre Marroquín, José 75, 332–3

Sabroso 46, 145, 159, 211, 223, 257, 290, 311, 314, 324
Sabrosos Del Merengue, Los 314
sabrosura, see nuevo ritmo
Sabrosura 114, 275, 283
Sabrosura, La 228
Sacando candela 218
Sacando palo del monte 232
Sacasas, Anselmo 46, 93, 98, 132, 178, 180, 232
Safora, Julio 71
Saint George Hotel 167, 272
Saint Latin's Day Massacre 226
Salamanca, "Memo" 232
Salas, Alberto 324
Salas, Brindis (de) 115
Salas, Juan Carlos 336
Salas, Kiko 32
"Saldiguera" (dancer) 29
"Saldiguera" (Estebán Lantri) 248
Saldiguera y Virulilla 155
Salgado 250
Salinas 99, 185
Salón México 110, 156, 329, 332
salsa 267–305, 338–40
Salsa (by Larry Harlow) 273
Salsa 2000 338
salsa antiyana 327
Salsa Blue 325
salsa cama 303–4, 346
Salsa con cache 303
Salsa en cinco 323
salsa dura 288
Salsa Fever 301
Salsa Mayor, La 335
Salsa Nueva 284
Salsa Picante 323
Salsa Rap 327
Salsa Refugees 317
salsa romántica 274, 280, 287–8, 296, 304, 346
Salsa y control 269
Salsamba 306
Salseros, Los (Cheo Marquetti's) 4, 76
Salseros, Los (Roland Malmin's) 338, 121
Salt Peanuts 157, 225
Saludando a los rumberos 285
salut 17–18, 27, 30, 126
Salvador, Dom 323
Salvador, Emiliano 214, 251, 259, 261, 262, 362
Salvaje 110, 151, 152, 282, 363
salve 310–11
Salve merecumbé 311
Salve sabrosona 311
Salvo Salazar, Francisco, see Pancho Majagua y Tata Villegas
Samaritana, La 289
samba 19, 25, 98, 211, 239, 266, 268, 303, 320–1, 335
Samba de una sola nota 226
Samba con salsa 268
Samba-conga 262
Sambita 317
Sampson, Edgar 167
Samuels, Dave 318
San Juan, Trío 189
San Pascual bailón 22

San Rafael, Conjunto 237
Sanabia, Augusto 330
Sanabria, Bobby 269
Sanabria, Izzy 4, 269
Sanabria, Juanito 175, 188, 204, 310
Sanabria, Nacho 234, 296
Sanborn, David 278, 324
Sánchez, Alcibíades 310
Sánchez, Ángel 286
Sánchez, Antonio "Musiquita" 72, 114, 120, 320, 325
Sánchez, Armando 3, 45, 228, 286
Sánchez, Daniel 87, 91, 106
Sánchez, David 317–8, 320–1, 324–5, 342, 364
Sánchez, Frank, see Yucateco, El
Sánchez, Frankie 183, 226
Sánchez, Louie 281
Sánchez, Luis 311
Sánchez, Maximiliano, see Bimbi
Sánchez, Narciso, see Guayabito
Sánchez, Néstor 273
Sánchez, Paquito 103
Sánchez, José "Pepe" 35, 51–2, 74–5
Sánchez, Ildefonso "Poncho" 305, 323–5, 364
Sánchez, Rafael 101
Sánchez, Ralph 87
Sánchez, Rolando 306
Sánchez, Tony 185
Sánchez de Fuentes, Eduardo 53, 368
Sánchez Ferrer, Roberto 82
Sancocho 314
Sancocho prieto, El 237, 306, 308
Sanders, Pharoah 324
Sandoval, Arturo 22, 215, 245, 251, 261–2, 287, 304–5, 318–20, 340, 368
Sandpipers, The 76
Sandunguera 247
Sanjuán, Pedro 356, 368
Sanluisea, La, see Unión Sanluisera
Sanoja, Jesús "Chucho" 355
Santa Bárbara 153, 361
Santa Cecilia 59
Santa Cecilia, La 229, 309–10
Santa Cruz, Miguel "El Pitcher" 117, 121
Santa Isabel de Las Lajas 142
¡Santa María! 103
Santa Rosa, Gilberto 300, 304, 363
Santaella, Antonio "Tato" 297
Santamaría, Ramón "Mongo" 195–9, 238–9
Santamaría, "Monguito" 223, 229, 232, 291–2
Santana, Carlos 195, 217, 241, 276, 305, 328, 364
santería 12, 14–15, 54–6, 65, 117, 128, 149, 153, 168, 177, 197, 199, 220, 223, 227, 231, 246–7, 263, 276, 279, 281, 284, 287, 289, 318, 339–40, 343, 346
Santería 11, 325, 346

Santero 142, 149
Santi, Jr., Luis 306
Santiago 93, 308
Santiago, Adalberto 273–5, 177, 281, 284, 287, 290, 293, 295–6, 301, 303
Santiago, Al 221, 315
Santiago, Charlie 284
Santiago, Doroteo 188
Santiago, Eddie 288, 296, 303–4
Santiago, Jimmy "La Vaca" 176, 183
Santiago, Joe 278, 319
Santiago, Marvin 396, 301–2, 363
Santo Domingo Serenaders 93
Santo en Nueva York, El 231
Santos, Anthony 313
Santos, Daniel 103, 127, 129, 151, 158, 188–9, 289–92, 361
Santos, Héctor 234, 237
Santos, John 305, 324
Santos, Primitivo 311
Santos, Ray 170, 176, 179, 232, 277, 282
Santurce 185
Saoco 281, 339
Sapo 328
Saquito, Ñico (Benito Antonio Fernández Ortiz) 21, 36, 45, 53, 74, 78, 121, 152–4, 255, 284, 333
Sar All Stars 252
Sarandonga 153
Sarará 128
Saratoga, Conjunto 121
Saratoga Club, Orchestra 85
Sardiñas, Israel 247
Sarria, Guido 249
Saturnino, Pernell 342
Saudades do Brasil 69
Saumell, Manuel 360
Savoy, Conjunto 182
Savoy Bearcats 85
Sax, Adolphe 79
Saxofones, Los 310
Saxofones De Santiago, Cuarteto De 265
saxophone 66, 72, 79, 86, 92, 95, 101, 136, 140–1, 166, 169, 172, 177–9, 181, 185, 215, 229, 234, 239–40, 254, 262, 264, 278, 281, 299, 310, 316, 321, 342, 352, 358
Saxofónica, La 315
Say sí sí, see Para Vigo me voy
SBOS 327
Scherazada/Sun Sun 258
Schifrin, "Lalo" (Boris) 324
Scott, Cecil 95
Scott, Rolando 70
Scritch, Edilberto 137
Scull, Isaac 54
Se escapó un león 298
Se formó el rumbón 219
Sé lo que es la rumba 303
Se mató Goyito 24
Se me cansó el corazón 287
Se me cayó el tabaco 18
Se pone bueno 301
Se que tú 290
Se soltó Ricardo Ray 226

Se te quemó la casa 221
Se va el dulcerito 51, 91
Se va el matancero, see *Chanchullo*
Se va la rumba 182
Secada, Moraima 152, 266
Seck, Pape 338
Second Afro-Cubans, The 171
Secre 32
Seeger, Pete 76
Seeley, Jim 320
Segarra, Nino 296
Seguí, Johnny 101, 183, 195, 220, 299
Seguida 328, 364
segundo (conga) 28, 30
segundo (tambourine) 100, 346
Segundo Bolona, Septeto 126
Seigneur Rochereau 334
seis 99, 103, 298, 304, 346
seis bayamonés 99
seis bombeado 99
Seis Del Solar, Los 294, 321, 364
seis fajardeño 99
seis mariandá 99
Selasié, Osario 182
Selecciones del 118
Selecta, La 296, 302, 363
Selecto, Cuarteto 70
Sensación, Orquesta 4, 110, 212, 249, 361
Sentimiento de Arsenio Rodríguez, El 125
septeto 144
Sepúlveda, Charlie 321, 364
Sepúlveda, Ray 303
Serenata rítmica 177
Serende 125
Serra, José Benito "Pepe" 55
Serrano, Joaquina "Chiquita" 331
Servando Diaz, Trio 152
Serviá, Estanislao 71, 130
Servicio obligatorio, El 52
Seven Steps to Heaven 321
Severinsen, Doc 201
Sex Cymbal 328
sexteto 169, 54–6, 60, 70, 76, 87, 121, 129–30, 333, 346
shake 210
Sharif, Omar 326
Shavers, Charlie 198
Shaw, Artie 137, 162, 165–6
Shaw, Woody 258
She's a Latin from Manhattan 283
Shearing, George 140, 165, 182, 195, 203–5, 224, 238, 240, 316, 352, 361
Sheila E (Sheila Escovedo) 321, 326–8
shekere 40, 250, 305, 346
Sheller, Marty 239, 271, 273, 366
Shepp, Archie 222
shing a ling 222–3, 226, 267, 346
Shing A Ling 226
Shishkabop 202
Shorter, Wayne 258, 325–6
Shuffle Along 85, 95

Si las nenas me dejan, qué 221
Si me comprendieras 155
Si por acaso no regreso 290
Sí sí no no 223
Si tú no, la otra 311
Si tú no sabes 296
Si tú quisieras 140
Siam, Hugo 79
Siboney 9, 19, 149, 153, 195
Siboney, Combo 215, 361
Siboney, Conjunto (Johnny López's) 180
Siboney, Cuarteto 150, 152, 185
Siboney, Orquesta (Julio Brito's) 136, 331
Siboney, Orquesta (Alberto Iznaga's) 92, 169, 186
Siboney, Orquesta (from Morón) 151
Siboney, Orquesta (Pepito Torres's) 188
Siboney, Septeto 92
Siboney, Sexteto 121
Sidewalks of Cuba 203
Siembra 279, 294, 363
Sierra Maestra 109, 135, 208, 251, 256, 264, 362
Siete Potencias, Las 281
Siete y media, Las 158
Sigan la clave 303
Sigler, Vicente 92, 95, 97
Sign and the Seal (The) 246, 325
Sigue la cosa 286
Silencio 58, 103
Silva, Angel Luis, *see* Melón
Silva, José "Chombo" 140, 144, 196, 205, 208, 221, 226, 228–9, 239, 270, 282, 286, 334, 338
Silva, Enrodo 71
Silva, Myrta 128, 300, 333
Silveira, Eliseo 56, 59, 68
Silver, Horace 198, 321
Silver Star 116, 118–19
Silvestre, Emilio 13
simalé 210
Simaní 275
Simón, Ed 321, 364
Simón, Marlon 322, 324, 364
Simon, Paul 296
Simone 321
Simonet, Manuel "Manolito" 248, 255
Simóns, Moisés 69, 80, 89–90, 134, 331, 357
Simounet, Sarah 103
Sims, Zoot 174, 238
Sin bandera 106
Sin Palabras 106
Sin sinfonía 185
Sinatra, Frank 199
Sinigual 305
Sissle, Noble 85, 167
Sitiera, La 338
Sitios llaman, Los 115, 120, 274
Skerritt, Fred 170
Sketches of a Dream 320, 364
Skins 239
Skull, René 125
Skylark 295
Sly and Robbie 318
Smith, Bessie 95

Smith, Jo-Jo 165
Smith, Marvin "Smitty" 325
Smith, Mauricio 227, 277, 293, 321, 338
Smith, Tab 162
Smith, Willie "The Lion" 89, 91, 368
Smokin' 281
"Snowboy" 339
So' caballo 122
Sobre las olas 78
Sobre una tumba una rumba 59
Socarrás, Alberto 2, 46, 67, 80, 85–6, 93–6, 167, 176, 188, 201, 203, 276, 361
Socarrás, Chepín 91
Socarrás, Dolores Eustacia 80
Socarrás, José, *see* Chepín
Socarrás, Prío, Carlos 108
Social Change 276
Social Club Antonio Maceo 115
Social Club Buena Vista 115
Sociedad, Orquesta 106
society bands 96–7, 166, 169
Sofa, El 129
Softly as in a Morning Sunrise 182
Sola y triste 88
Solamente ellos pudieron hacer este album 279
Solamente una vez 155
Solano, Jorge 313
Solano, Rafael 309
Solares, Panchito 59
Soledad 215
Soledad, La 236
Soler y Miró, Blanca Rosa 35
Solis, José 159
Solito 278
Sólo contigo basta 295
Soloff, Lew 324
Soltando chispas 180
Somavilla, Rafael 82, 138, 151, 213–15, 247
Someone to Watch Over Me 204
Somnánbulo 287
Somos diferentes 201, 364

son 31–4, 50–67, 121–30, 250–2
Son Del Barrio 339
Son Del Cauto 252, 362
Son Entero, El 252
Son Esperanza Y Tambao 253
Son Familia 314
Son igual que el cocodrilo 73
son montuno 34, 65, 117, 135, 142, 151, 179, 219, 223, 251, 268, 271, 281, 342, 344, 346
Son No. 6 250
Son Primero, Orquesta 284, 363
son reginero 50, 154
Son Reinas 340
Son Varona 264
soneo 60, 234, 248, 269, 291, 296, 342, 346
sonero 3, 32, 53, 91, 111, 115, 120, 151, 168, 232, 253, 258, 266, 268, 272, 276, 281, 289, 293, 296, 297, 301, 304, 335, 346, 366
Sonero Clasico Del Caribe 336

Soneros Del Barrio, Los 288
Sones de Ayer 126, 127
Sones De Oriente 252
Song for You 316, 317
Songo 3, 211, 244, 246–52, 253, 275, 280, 282, 287, 298, 300, 302, 303, 324, 327, 336, 337, 345, 346, 362
Songo le dio a Borondongo 248
Songo para Monk 322
Songo songo 248
Sóngoro cosongo 48, 292
Sonido Bestial 271, 302, 304
Sonido De Londres, El 339
Sonido lindo 285
Sonido Nuevo, El 241, 322
sonora 127, 346
Sonorama Seis 213, 355
sonsonete 73
Sopa de pichón 170
Sopita en botella, La 142, 290
Sorín, Rafael 138
Sorongo, ¡qué es lo que tiene el blanco de negro! 235
Sorpresa de flauta 141
Sosa, Nelo 129
Sosa, "Paquito" 178
Sotolongo, Oscar 55, 57, 68
soukous 296, 314, 334, 336
Soul Drummers, The 227
soul music 222, 224, 227, 232, 239, 269, 271, 327, 343, 347
Soul Sauce 241
Soy boricua 301, 363
Soy como soy 156
Soy la ley 290
Soy tan feliz 155
Soy tu ley 292
Space Station 317
Spanglish 170, 186, 281, 283
Spanish Fever 276
Spanish Grease 241
Spanish Songs Mama Never Taught Me 219, 223, 225, 353
Speak no Evil 288
Speck, Aurelio 32
Spice 306
Stagnaro, Oscar 318, 319
Stark, Bobby 167
Stay on It 193
Steig, Jeremy 277, 278
Stellio, Alexandre 330
Stephenson, Wilfredo 339
Stern, Bobby 325
Stern, Mike 278
Stewart, Ted 193
Sting 295
Stitt, Sonny 203
Stitt Goes Latin 203
Stockhausen, Karlheinz 321
Stollwer ("El Güero") 138
Stomping at the Savoy 167
Stop and Go Mambo 162
Stop! I'm Free Again 289
Storch, Fernando, *see* Caney
Stork Club Orchestra 94, 177
Stormy Weather 150
Story, Nat 167
Story of Love, the 201
Street Scenes 364
Stuart, Michael 296
Stubblefield, John 317, 325

Súarez, Antolín, *see* Papa Kila
Súarez, Benito 257
Súarez, Caridad 142
Súarez, Gil 226, 282
Suárez, Humberto 133, 150, 208
Suárez, Manolo 87
Suavecito 61, 335
subidor, *see* requinto
Sublime, Charanga 13, 284
Sublime, Orquesta 120, 210, 211, 249, 266
Subway Joe 226, 362
sucu-sucu 34, 48, 212, 346, 367
Sucu sucu 212
Sucu Sucu y pachanga 216
Suéltame 273
Suena el piano 298
Suena el piano Rubén 249, 298
Suena tu bongó 129
Suerte de los tontos (La) 202
Sugar, "Ricardo" (Dick) 163
Sugarhill Gang, The 327
Suite Noro Morales 226
Sullivan, Maxine 154
Sumac, Yma 149, 177
Summers, Bill 324
Summertime 238, 240
Sun of Latin Music 277
Sun Ra 238
Sunsmoke 306
Super Apollo 47:50 301
Super Cayor De Dakar 338
Super Combo 238
Super Sabador 338
Superestrellas De Gonzalo, Orquesta 284
Superimposition 291
Supertípica de Estrellas 284
Sweatman, Wilbur 85
Swing Boys 136, 138
Swing Casino 138, 256
Swinging Guaguancó 274
Sylla, Ibrahima 338
Sylvester, Jorge 321
Szabo, Gabor 241

Ta' caliente 54
Tabatié moin tombé 18
Tabito 56
Tabú 48, 82
Take Five 316
Take Six 265
Take the "A" Train 185, 238
tahona 28, 347
Tahone, Conjunto 237
Taicuba 266
Tale of an African Lobster 203
Taller Campesino 304
Tamalero, El 48
Tamalitos de Olga, Los 116, 179
Tamayo, Gustavo 112, 117–18, 135, 141, 211, 214–15, 250–1, 258
Tamayo, "Aurelio" Yeyo 159, 332
Tambambeo 186
Tambó (by Tito Puente) 276
Tambó (by Gilberto Valdés) 14, 149
tambora, of merengue 229, 307–9, 310–11, 313, 347
Tambores Afrocubanos 196

tamborito 219, 268, 293, 309, 347
"Tambú " (Héctor Hal Noble) 324
Tampeñito, El 106
Tanga 81, 171–3
Tanganito 26
tango 2, 46, 79, 85, 97–8, 128, 150, 177, 187, 268, 278, 298, 317, 322, 329, 334, 347, 357
tango congo 18–19
Taño, Antonio María "Tony" 156, 215, 247, 368
Tañón, Olga 313, 364
Tarde 326
Tarde, La 74
Tarraza, Juan Bruno 133, 332
Tarraza, Margot 133
Taylor's Dixie Serenaders 72
Terrasson, Jacky 325
Tata cuñengue 91
"Tata Güines" (Federico Arístides Soto) 16, 39, 110, 117, 138, 141, 214–15, 251, 258, 263–4, 275, 337, 340, 361–2
Taylor, Billy 165, 198–9
Te adoraré más y más 133
Te con e 190
Te fuiste 187
Te juro 308
Te picó la abeja 188
Te pones a gozar 282
Te soltó la rienda 232
Te traigo un tumbao 129
Tea for Two 174, 177
teatro bufo 21
Teclo 190
Tecolora 125
Telaraña 297
Teléfono de larga distancia, El 24
Telephone 288
Televisión pronto llegará, La 189
Tema Cuatro 247
Tema de Chaka 259
Tempo 302
Tempo Moderno 304
Tenderly 137, 175
Tenemos que echar palante 295
Tengo el ide 290
"Teofilito" (Gómez Rafael) 50
Tercinet, Alain 240, 369
Terrace, Pete 42, 175, 183, 203–4, 227
Terrero, Reutilio Domingo, *see* **Celina y Reutillo**
Terror y Kila, El 273
Terry 68
Terry, Los 264
Terry, Clark 238–40, 261
Terry, Eladio 264
Terry, Yosvany 325
Teta e, La 125, 190
Texidor, Luigi 297, 301
Thamar, Ralph 338
Theatre Marti, orchestra of 44, 80, 110, 150
There Goes The Neighborhood – Se chavó el vecindario 269
Thielemans, Toots 204, 318
Thompson, Lucky 194, 202
3-D Mambo 179
Tíbiri tábara 188, 277
Tiburón 11, 252, 269, 280

Tico All Stars, The 226, 270
Tico tico 177
Tiembla tierra 211
Tiempo de cencerro Part I 199
Tiempo pa' matar 280
Tiene calidad 278
Tiene pimienta 297, 363
Tierra 27, 53, 63, 96, 106, 211, 217, 251, 261, 328, 330, 336, 358
Tierra Caliente 251
Tiger Rag 78
Timbalaye 246, 321
timbales 39
Timbor, Angel 30
Timbre de Oro, El 60
Time 97, 100
Timidez, La 52, 35
Tin tin deo 192–3, 203, 273, 325
tingo talango 17
Tingo talango 134
Tintorera del mar 100
Tintorera ya llegó 125
"Tío Tom" (Gonzalo Asencio Hernández) 27
típica 61, 68–9, 71–2, 78–80, 88, 130, 136, 166, 179, 247, 249, 262, 274–5, 282, 284, 287, 293, 259
Típica Cubana, Charanga 249
Típica Cubana, Orchestra 249
Típica de Conciertos, Charanga 262
Típica habanera, Orquesta 249
Típica Ideal 282
Típica Juventud, Orchestra 247
Típica Novel 284, 318
Típica Palmera, Orchestra 334
Típico, Conjunto 310
Típico, Quinteto 68, 70
Típico, Septeto 4, 257
típico, style 223, 237, 257, 281–7, 310, 319, 328
Típico Cibaeno, Conjunto 93, 310
Típico Cubano, Septeto 68
Típico de Ignacio Carrillo, Sexteto 212
Típico Habanero, Sexteto 212
Típico Ladi, Conjunto 179
Típico Oriental, Grupo 68
Tirana, La 231, 301
Tiso, Wagner 326
Tito No 1 218
Tito Puente and His Concert Orchestra 276
Tito Puente in Percussion 179
Tito Puente Pa' lante 335
Tito Rodríguez en Puerto Azul 219
Tito Rodríguez Returns to the Palladium 218
Tito Rodriguez y sus Lobos del Mambo 180
Tito, Tito, Tito 219
Tizol, Juan 200
Tizol, Manuel 104

Tjader, Cal 42, 177, 182, 184, 195–6, 199, 203–4, 239, 240–1, 316, 323, 325, 364
Tjaderama 323
TNT Boys, The 226
To Be With You 224
To y van hecho 285
Todo en la vida pasará 210
Todopoderoso 291
Together 273
Tokyo Cuban Boys 334
Toledo, Junior 300
Tolentino, Juan Pablo ("Pavín") 308
TOLÚ 323
Toma jabón pa' que lave 106
Tomás, Rafael (de) 86
Tomasa (dancer) 61
Tomé, Mongo 33
Tommy 273
Tomorrow 274
Toña la Negra 127, 332
tonada 35–6
"Tongolele" (Yolanda Montes) 332
Top Percussion 179
"Topo, El " *see* Cabán Valle, Antonio 302
toque 13
Torin, "Symphony Sid " 163
Tormenta Cubana 255
Toro, Yomo (José Manuel Torres) 272–3, 282, 285, 287, 292, 344
Torre, Doris, de la 140
Torre, José María, de la 32
Torres, "Barbarito" 253
Torres, Dora, Ileana 114
Torres, Eddie 289
Torres, Fernando 82
Torres, Heriberto 88
Torres, Joe "Professor" 292, 310
Torres, José Manuel, *see* Toro, Yomo 232
Torres, Juan, *see* El Boy 196
Torres, Juan Pablo 214–5, 275
Torres, Juancito 176, 232, 276, 302
Torres, Nestor 284, 302–3
Torres, Papi 183
Torres, Pepito 185–6, 188–9
Torres, Roberto 228, 281–2, 285, 305–6
Torres, Willie 176, 183, 204, 221, 277
Torriente, Ernesto 246
Torroella, Antonio "Papaíto" 23, 69
Totico, Eugenio Arango 208, 219, 220, 239, 285, 361
Totico y sus Rumberos 246, 285, 362
Touzet, René 24, 46, 137, 161, 183–4, 202, 240, 301
Traigo bomba 232
Tras las rejas 126
Trátame como soy 340
Trato, El 337
Tremendo caché 275, 190
Tremendo coco 183
Tremendo cumbán 129, 219
Tremendo personaje 248
Tres Diamantes, Los, Trio 189

tres golpes 28, 30, 347
Tres Juanes, Los 54
Tres lindas cubanas 58, 116, 169
"Tres Patines" (Fernández, Leopoldo) *see* **Pototo y Filomeno**
Tres Reyes, Los 189
Tribute to Arsenio Rodríguez 251, 276
Tributo a Pedro Flores 277
Tricoche, Héctor 288
Trinidad, Amado 134
trio, group 153
trio, section 113
Tristeza 35, 184
Trombón criollo 141
Trombón melancólico 285
trombone 3, 20, 23–4, 79–80, 86, 96, 100, 104, 112, 130, 144, 171, 175, 215, 221–20, 227, 237, 236, 247–8, 252, 264, 268, 272, 279, 281, 284, 304, 320, 335, 337
Trombone Man 281
Trompeta querida 251
Troncoso, Bienvenido 93, 308
Tropicana, Orchestra of 135, 138
Tropicavana, Orchesta 128
Tropicube, El 231
trova 35, 74, 142, 231, 213, 250–1, 257–8, 355
trovadores 50–4
Trovador 35, 50–1, 70–1, 84, 103, 116–17, 129
Trovadores, Los Orquesta 101
Truco de Regatillo, El 124
Trujillo, Radamés 229, 308–11, 334
Truman, Harry 157
Trumbauer, Frankie 166
Trumpet Fantasy 319
Tsaba-tsaba 334
Tú has vuelto 222
Tú loco y yo tranquilo 300
Tú me acostumbraste 140, 209
Tú me quemas 304
Tú mi delirio 155, 339
Tú no eres nadie 179
Tú no sirves pa' na 103
Tu rica boca 120
Tú y mi música 258
Tú y yo 52
tumba (dance) 92, 120, 123, 135
tumba (drum) 197, 214
tumba francesa 347
Tumba la caña 19
Tumba palo cucuye 122, 125
tumbadora 28, 39, 247, 347
tumbandera 17
tumbao 19, 40–2, 65, 76, 112, 120, 123, 129, 135, 192, 197, 200, 205, 211, 214, 229, 247, 252, 265, 278, 285, 288, 316, 321, 345, 360–1
Tumbao africano 278
Tumbas, Las 18, 136
Tumbita Criolla, La 34
Tun tun neco 103
Tuna Liberal 127
Túnel, El 118
Turi 261

Turner, Tina 230
Turquino, Septeto 252
Turre, Steve 279, 319, 321, 6
Tus manos blancos 72
twist 28, 161, 201, 221, 223, 253, 338, 355
Two of Swords 321
Tyner, McCoy 259, 262, 278, 318, 325
Tyson, D. K. 318

U bla bla dú 173, 237
Ubane 11, 290, 316–17, 360, 363
Ultima copa, La 278
Ultramar, Sexteto 130
Un brujo de Guanabacoa 87
Un caramelo para Margot 228
Un cigarrillo, la lluvia y tú 219
Un cubano en Nueva York 216
Un día bonito 277
Un, dos, tres, María 294
Un meneíto suave 58
Un poco loco 200, 203, 325, 364
Un poquito de tu amor 156, 203
Una noche de amor en La Habana 134
Una rosa de Francia 49
Undercurrent Blues 202
Union, Orquesta 112
Union De Redencion, Sexteto 68, 169
Unión Dinámica 271
Union Sanluisera 249
Unique 268
Unison Riff 202
United Nations Orchestra, The 318–19
Universidad de la Salsa 298
Universo, Sexteto 68
Unknown, The 323
Uno, Dos, Tres 241
Uno, dos y tres 92–3
upa habanera 307, 347
Upa upa, El 210
Urbino, Ibrahím 142
Urcola, Diego 325
Urfe, Charanga 249
Urfé, José 24, 68, 334
Urfé, Odilio 10, 71, 247, 249, 368–9
Urfé, Orestes 249
Urfés 264, 356
Uriabón Efí 15
Urrutia, Francisco 179
Usera, Ramón "Moncho" 85–6, 106, 182, 185
Usted abusó 279, 290
Utrera, Adolfo 93
Uy que feo 100

Va la conga 93
Vacana, Combo 337
Vacuna Salk (La) 120
Vacunao 28, 29, 345, 347
Valdés, Abelardo 68, 116
Valdés, Alejandro Tomás 249
Valdés, Alfredo 61, 66, 68, 71, 76, 87, 109, 173, 178, 185, 282, 318, 332
Valdés, Jr., Alfredo 7, 285
Valdés, Amadito 256, 354
Valdés, Armando (percussionist) 68, 182

Valdés, Armando (pianist) 182
Valdés, "Bebo" (Ramón) 3, 14, 126, 129, 135, 138, 144, 149, 157, 152, 161, 179, 216, 230, 310, 318, 335, 343, 351
Valdés, Celso 116, 249
Valdés, Chino 170, 326
Valdés, "Chucho" (Jesús) 22, 140, 210, 213, 215, 247, 257, 259, 260, 261, 262, 264, 294, 325, 354, 363
Valdés, Cuco 265
Valdés, Delia 66
Valdés, Elio 117, 249
Valdés, Eliseo 144
Valdés, Felipe 24, 61
Valdés, Francisco, *see* Pozo, Chino
Valdés, Frank 87, 174
Valdés, Gilberto 10, 14, 48, 147, 149, 170, 172, 174, 175, 176, 181, 195, 229
Valdés, Guillermo 258
Valdés, Jorge Luis 261
Valdés, Joseíto 71, 120
Valdés, Joseíto (pianist and arranger) 129
Valdés, Lazarito 255
Valdés, Lázaro 144
Valdés, Manuel 56
Valdés, Marcelino 61, 67, 109, 140, 170, 219, 238, 286
Valdés, Marta 213
Valdés, Mayra Caridad 259, 261
Valdés, Merceditas 142, 149, 178, 196, 215, 239, 247, 263, 266, 360
Valdés, "Miguelito" (Juan Eugenio Lázaro) 10, 24, 68, 93, 98, 124, 125, 130, 132, 133, 139, 166, 168, 171, 178, 179, 180, 184, 187, 188, 190, 191, 192, 194, 198, 201, 219, 223, 285, 361
Valdés, Óscar (singer) 71, 259
Valdés, Óscar (percussionist) 140, 215, 259, 261, 287
Valdés, Óscar, Jr. 259
Valdés, Óscar Lázaro 255
Valdés, Patato (Carlos) 4, 37, 113, 128, 129, 136, 162, 174, 178, 190, 196, 199, 220, 228, 238, 241, 285, 293, 302, 315, 317, 319, 320, 338, 361
Valdés, Remigio 69
Valdés, Roberto 258
Valdés, Rogelio 181
Valdés, Rolando 117, 285
Valdés, Vicentico 59, 61, 71, 75, 109, 127, 133, 176, 179, 180, 187, 197, 198, 220, 227, 229, 270, 301, 361
Valdés, Zoé 209
Valdés Torres, Armando 71
Valdespí, Armando 70, 87, 88, 111, 112, 138, 154, 156
Valdespí, Raúl 71,
Vale más 274
Valentín, Bobby 212, 223, 226, 270, 276, 301, 363
Valentín, Dave 281, 284, 315, 339
Valentín, Guillermo 282

Valentino, Rudolph 82
Valenzuela, Felipe 5, 166
Valenzuela, Pablo 24, 68
Valenzuela, Raimundo 18, 23, 24
Valera, José Manuel 127
Valera Miranda, La Familja 252
Valera Miranda, Carmen 252
Valera Miranda, Félix 252
Valera Miranda, Félix Enrique 252
Valera Miranda, Félix Ernesto 252
Valero, Guadalupe 138
Valerón, Hortensia 56
Valiente, Consejo, *see* Acerina 332
Valladares, "Dioris" (Isidro) 221, 229, 363
Valle, Joe 182, 185, 188, 361
Valle, Luis 255
Valle, Moisés ("Yumurí") 255, 263
Valle, Orlando 261, 339, 362
Valle, Osvaldo 255
Valle, Pedro 255
Valle, Ramón 264
Vallejo, Orlando ("Maraca") 129
Vallenata, Charanga 289, 305
Vallenato 289, 323, 336, 347
Vallente, "Polidor" (Pedro) 170
Valoy, "Cuco" (Henry) 311, 314, 363
Valoy, Félix 258
Valvert, Félix 331
Vamos a Unirnos 224
Vamonos pa'l monte 271, 291
Vamos pa' Buenaventura 337
Vamos pa' Senegal 283
Van Merwijk, Lucas 339
Van Van, Los 245, 249, 250, 262, 303, 339, 346, 362
Vania 255
Varela, Carlos 176
Varela Martínez, Jairo 337
Variedades 187
Vargas, Domingo 68, 121, 131
Vargas, Pedro 105, 106, 133, 144, 332
Vargas, Sergio 313
Vargas, Wilfrido 312, 314, 364
Varona, Jorge 144, 251, 261
Varona, Luis 171
Varona, Orestes 116, 249
Vasarnilla 54
Vaya niña 173
Vaya pa' monte 122
Vázquez, Aníbal, see Mambo Aces
Vázquez, Avelino 308
Vázquez, Ernesto 103
Vázquez, "Frankie" (Efraín) 279
Vázquez, Javier 128, 208, 236, 268, 285, 289, 299
Vásquez, Justo 50
Vázquez, Miguel ("El Moro") 69
Vázquez, Pablo 127
Vázquez, "Papo" (Angel) 303, 321
Vázquez, Perín 106

Vázquez, Roland 323
Vázquez, Tavito 310, 314
Vega, Amado ("Mandín") 221
Vega, Joe 217
Vega, José 56
Vega, Ray 321
Vega, Tito 304
Vega, Tony 287, 296, 300, 304
Vegabajeno, Trio 240, 304
Veinte años 59, 60, 298
Velarde, "Benny" (Bayardo) 240
Velazco, Enrique, see Florecita 55, 68, 127, 154, 159, 261, 286, 332, 333, 358
Velazco Urdeliz, Germán 261, 262
Velázquez, Consuelo 332
Velázquez, Joaquín 56
Vélez, "Quito" (Rogelio) 237
Veloso, Caetano 280
Veloz, Franklin 336
Veloz, Ramón 153
Ven, anda y muévete 248
Venao, El 314
Venegas, Victor 182, 205, 228, 239
Veneros, Héctor 303
Venganza 51, 106
Venganza de Amor 29
Ventura, "Johnny" (Velázquez Gabriel, Juan de Dios) 159, 160, 185
Venus 57
Vera, Alberto, see Piloto y Vera 82
Vera, María Teresa 12, 29, 30, 33, 34, 46, 69, 79, 81, 88, 122, 184, 187
Verdad, La 89, 96, 172, 186
Vereda Tropical 70
Versalles, Orquesta 151
Vete lejos 50
Vía, Pedro 49, 73
Viana, Vicente 70
Viañez, Julio 33
Vibes Galore 141
Vibraphone 25, 92, 105, 151
Viceira, Jacomo 20
Vicentico Valdés 33, 34, 39, 41, 67, 70, 92, 93, 95, 97, 102, 103, 114, 117, 118, 139, 154, 170, 184
Vicenty, Cándido 49
"Vico C" (Luis Armando Lozada) 167
Victoria, Cuarteto 55, 68, 98
Victoria, Grupo 56, 170
Vida de mi Vida 98
Vida es un Sueño, La 66, 78, 135
Vidal, Carlos 89, 92, 96, 97, 101, 103, 105
Vieja en Camisa, La 121
Viejas Saben Mejor, Las 159
Viejo Lázaro 131, 185
Viejo verde 68
Vietnam Mambo 124
Vila, Pedro 73
Vilató, Orestes 95, 117, 141, 145, 146, 147, 166, 168
Villa, Ignacio, see Bola de Nieve 76, 77, 78
Villa Lobos, Heitor 105
Villalón, Alberto 34, 41, 46

Villalona, Fernandito 160
Villancico 8, 53
Villanueva, Gina 156
Villegas, Carlos, de see Pancho Majagua y Tata Villegas
Villegas, "Tata" (Carlos Díaz de Villegas) 29, 46
Viloria, Angel 50, 159, 185
Vincent, Fernán 76
Viola 18, 60, 177
Violin (electric) 145
Violencia, La 16
Virgen de Regla 40
Viro 10, 177
Virtuosos, Los 159
Virulilla (Alfonso Hernández) 127, 246
Visa 105
Vital, Raúl 164
Vitier, José María 136, 185
Vitier, Sergio 74, 136, 181
Viva Africa 145
Viva Kenton 85, 105
Viva la vieja 55
Viva Mambo 91
Viva Prado 105
Viva Ricardo Ray 226
Vivar, Alejandro ("El Negro") 68, 71, 73, 74, 117, 123, 141, 146, 165
Vivar, Salvador 74
Vivas, Nicolás 155
Vizcaíno, Roberto 135, 136, 187
Vizcarrondo, Leocadio 54
Vocal Sampling 136, 185
Você abusou 143
Voodoo 12, 13, 53, 143
Voodoo Dance at Midnight 142
Voodoo Suite, The 83, 84
Voy a Partir, Ingrata 41
Voz, La 149
Voz fañosa 110
Vuela la Paloma 112
Vuelve El Gigante 142
Vuelvo a mi Borinquen 46

wa wa 44, 109
Wagenaar, Bernard 104
Walker, Mark 163
Wallace, Wayne 166
Waller, Fats 51–2
Walter Winchell Rhumba 92
Walton, Cedar 162, 166
Wampo and Batanga 93
Wanted, Dead or Alive 116
Warner, Eddie 171
Washmashin 172
Watermelon Man 123, 162
Waters, Ethel 51
Watusi, El 117, 138, 177
"Watusi" (Orlando Castillo) 143, 145, 171–3
Waxer, Lise 61, 188
Webb, Art 141, 162, 166
Webb, Chick 87–8, 91
Webster, Ben 92
Weissmuller, Johnny 50
Weldon Johnson, James 45
Well You Needn't 324
wemba (clave) 12, 177
Wenders, Wim 132
Wess, Frank 123
West, Mae 52

Weston, Randy 166
What-Cha-Wa-Hoo, see Guachiguara
What Happened? 145
White, José 136
Why Not! 163
Wild Jungle 91
Wild Thing 124
White Brothers, The 104
Whiteman, Paul 46, 87, 103
Who, The 140
Whoopee Kids, see Mingo And Whoopee Kids
Wilfrido dame un consejo 312
Wilfrido (86) 312
Wilfrido Vargas 312, 314, 364
William, Al 316
Williams, Clarence 95
Williams, Esther 177
Williams, Mary-Lou 203, 241
Williams, Sandy 167
Willie Colón solo 225, 236, 367–72, 279–80, 290–1, 294
Willis, Larry 317
Wilson, Gerald 194
Wilson, Herminio "El Diablo" 33
Wilson, Lisette 295
Wilson, Shadow 203
Wilson Debriano, Alonso 321
Winters, Marilyn 165
Wladimir y La Critica 336
Wolpe, Stephan 201
Wonder, Stevie 326
woodblocks 95
Wooding, Sam 95, 167
Woodlen, Bobby 169–70
Woods, Phil 316
Woody'n You 192, 240
World Sax Quartet 320
Wright, Lammar 167

X, Groupo 339
Xavier Cugat and His Gigolos 97
Xenon, Miguel 321
Xamsa bopp 338

Y nace una estrella 114
Y sigo con mi son 286
Y tú que has hecho 53
Ya no camino más 120
Ya yo me curé 317
Yakaré 252, 362
Yambambo (by Guillén) 48
Yambambo (by Guyún) 155
Yambeque 179
yambú 28, 29–30, 218, 285, 333, 346, 347
Yambú 29, 170, 179, 180, 195, 218, 281
Yambú (by Mongo Santamaría)
Yambú (El) 29
Yare Changó 226
"Yayo El Indio" (Peguero Vega, Gabriel Eladio) 180, 221, 222, 270, 285, 295
Yeah Yeah 225
Yellowman 318
Yera, Carlos 115
Yerbero moderno 142, 212
Yesterday 231
Yesterdays 201
Yeyé olube 23

Yin, Quirino 25
Yiri yiri bon 144, 156
Yo bailo de todo 248
Yo no como candela 281
Yo no engaño a las mujeres 125
Yo no escondo mi abuela 53
Yo no puedo comer vista gacha 125
Yo pico un pan 153
Yo sé que es mentira 156
Yo sin tú 221
Yo son kanga 122
Yo soy candela 91
Yo soy la rumba 171
Yockamo All Stars 264
yoruba (music) 9, 11, 12, 14, 38, 128, 131, 148, 149, 174, 177, 195, 197, 199, 210, 211, 221, 231, 235, 247, 248, 303, 317, 318, 319, 325, 340, 344, 345, 346
Yoruba Andabo 149, 209, 247, 266
You've Lost That Lovin' Feeling 306
Young, Lester 166, 173
Young Man With a Horn 301
Yoyo, El 178
Yradier, Sebastián 329
Yuca de Catalina, La 219
"Yucateco, El" (Frank Sánchez) 226
yuka 17, 27, 31, 123
Yumbale 127
Yumbambe 222, 324
"Yumurí" (Moisés Valle) 255

Zaballa, Miguel 50, 91
Zafiros, los 212
Zalba, Javier 265
Zambele 219
Zambia 219
Zamora, Francisco ("Minini") 246
Zapatero, El 87
Zaperoko 302, 303, 363
Zarabanda 190
Zarzuela, Héctor ("Bomberita") 290
Zayas, Alberto 142
Zayas, Napoléon 309
Zayas Bazán, Rogelio 45
Zellen, Richie 322
Zequeira, Rafael 16, 52, 59
Zerquera, Pablo 24, 68, 72
Zervigón, Eddy 211, 228, 338
Zervigón, Kelvin 228, 282
Zervigón, Rudy 228
Zona franca 73
zondán 210
Zorrilla, Floro, see Floro Y Miguel
Zum Zum Ba Bae 109, 110, 149k150